Tolkien's Modern Reading: Middle-earth Beyond the Middle Ages

HOLLY ORDWAY

Published by Word on Fire Academic, an imprint of
Word on Fire, Park Ridge, IL 60068
© 2021 by Word on Fire Catholic Ministries
Printed in the United States of America
All rights reserved.

Design and layout by Rozann Lee and Cassie Pease.

Images of J.R.R. Tolkien in study, copyright © Pamela Chandler/ArenaPAL. Used with permission. All other images are in the public domain or used under fair use, or if not, all efforts have been made to contact copyright holders to secure permission.

Photo credits: Frontispiece © Pamela Chandler/ArenaPal; Fig. 1 © Blackwell's Bookshop, Holly Ordway's personal collection; Fig. 2 public domain, Project Gutenberg; Fig. 3 public domain, Google Books/Bodleian Library; Fig. 4 public domain, Wikipedia; Figs. 5–14, public domain, Holly Ordway's personal collection; Fig. 15 public domain, Wikipedia; Fig. 16 public domain, Literature Wiki; Figs. 17–20, public domain, Holly Ordway's personal collection; Fig. 21 public domain (copyright not renewed), Archive.org; Fig. 22, public domain, ISFDB; Fig. 23 fair use, Holly Ordway's personal collection; Fig. 24 © Random House, Holly Ordway's personal collection; Figs. 25–29, public domain, Holly Ordway's personal collection; Fig. 30 public domain, Wikipedia; Fig. 31a public domain, Holly Ordway's personal collection; Fig. 31b public domain, Wikipedia; Figs. 32–34 public domain, Holly Ordway's personal collection; Fig. 35–36 public domain, Wikimedia Commons; Fig. 37 fair use, Holly Ordway's personal collection; Fig. 38 © Random House, Holly Ordway's personal collection; Fig 39 public domain, Holly Ordway's personal collection; Fig. 40 © Pamela Chandler/ArenaPal.

First Edition
24 23 22 21   1 2 3 4

ISBN: 978-1-943243-72-3

Library of Congress Control Number: 2020922928

www.wordonfire.org

To Michael Ward

ACKNOWLEDGEMENTS

I should like first to thank Brandon Vogt and Word on Fire for their enthusiasm about publishing this book, and my editors, Matt Becklo and Dan Seseske, for their thoughtful and attentive work.

I gratefully acknowledge the receipt of the Clyde S. Kilby Research Grant from the Marion E. Wade Center, Wheaton College, Illinois.

Research would not be possible without the labor and assistance of archivists. I particularly wish to thank Laura Schmidt of the Wade Center, William Fliss of the Marquette University Department of Special Collections and University Archives, and Catherine McIlwaine of the Bodleian Library, University of Oxford.

I also wish to thank, within the United States, Barry Anderson for access to the Memphis C.S. Lewis Society archives, and Roger White, archivist of the Inklings collection, Azusa Pacific University; and, within the United Kingdom, Clare Broomfield of the Historic England Archive; Jonathan Bush and Mike Harkness of the Palace Green Library at Durham University; W. Graeme Clark-Hall, Archivist of the Oxford Union; Helen Drury, Photographic & Oral History Officer of the Oxfordshire History Centre; Katharine Spackman, Lead Librarian of the Oxfordshire Libraries; the staff of the British Library Manuscripts department; the Bodleian Library Scan and Deliver team; and the library staff of Merton College, Oxford.

My thanks to Owen Barfield for permission to access his grandfather's papers at the Bodleian Library, and to Michael Foster for permission to quote from "Dr. Clyde S. Kilby Recalls The Inklings."

All scholars of Tolkien owe a great debt to those who have made available previously unpublished draft material, letters, and biographical information, especially (but not limited to) Douglas A. Anderson, Michael D.C. Drout, Dimitra Fimi, Verlyn Flieger, John Garth, Diana Glyer, Wayne G. Hammond, Andrew S. Higgins, Stuart Lee, Christina Scull, John D. Rateliff, and, above all, the late Christopher Tolkien. Diana Glyer's work on the Inklings as collaborators was significant both for my conceiving of this book and the process of its writing.

My work has been strengthened by helpful feedback from readers of the draft manuscript. I particularly wish to thank Richard Jeffery for his extensive and careful comments. I also give thanks to Lisa Coutras, Ryan Grube, Jason Lepojärvi, Rebekah Valerius, and Richard C. West for their comments.

Many people gave their time and attention to answer questions and render assistance, including Simon Berry, Leonie Caldecott, Oronzo Cilli, Jeremy Edmonds, John Garth, Carl F. Hostetter, Alex Lloyd, the late Jared Lobdell, John Magoun, Marjorie Mead, Dale Nelson, Alan Reynolds, B. Daniel Speake, David Wolcott, and members of the Tolkien Society and George MacDonald Facebook groups.

I am grateful for the assistance of Fr. Guy Nicholls of the Birmingham Oratory, and the support of the parishioners of Hinksey Parish, Oxford (Holy Rood and Our Lady of the Rosary).

My thanks to Tommy Crawford, Joe Fortey, and Tim Motte for technical assistance, and to Lucas Holt for help with researching copyrights and for proofreading, and to Eleanor Parker for drawing my attention to the Feast of the Ordination of St. Dunstan. I have benefited from the encouragement of many people, including Ashley Canter, Jennifer Kulzer, and Rachel Motte.

Special thanks go to Annie Crawford for her tireless and invaluable assistance in the preparation of the Photo Gallery.

I appreciate the opportunities that I have had to give public lectures on my research as it developed. I particularly wish to express my gratitude to the Oxford C.S. Lewis Society for repeated invitations to speak, and insightful discussion, as this book was unfolding. My thanks also for opportunities to speak about my research to the Berkeley Graduate Theological Union; the C.S. Lewis Society of Madison; the Tolkien Society of Madison; the Wheaton College Tolkien Society; the Institute for Theology in the Arts at the University of St. Andrews; the Second Spring Centre for Faith and Culture, Oxford; the Canadian Roundtable in Cambridge, England; and Thorneloe University, Ontario.

Lastly, and most importantly, I joyfully acknowledge an "unpayable debt" to my friend Michael Ward for his steadfast encouragement and his invaluable feedback on the drafts of this book. Without his unfailing support over the last ten years, I might never have completed this work; and whatever its merits, they are the greater for his generous and insightful comments. With gratitude and affection, I dedicate *Tolkien's Modern Reading* to him.

La Crosse, Wisconsin
October 21, 2020
Feast of the Ordination of St. Dunstan

J.R.R. Tolkien (1892–1973)

CONTENTS

A photo gallery follows page 118.

Prelude

"That's the Inglesant house," his mother had said when she stood with him on this spot back in the summer of 1904, her last summer. "The house where *John Inglesant* was written." But Ronald hadn't then read that celebrated novel and knew nothing about it or its author. He had now remedied the omission. Five years had passed since his mother's death, exactly five years ("five summers with the length of five long winters" he whispered to himself). He had read a lot of books, an awful lot of books, since that terrible day. At the Oratory the priests said he read too much. He glanced along the road to his left, admiring for the umpteenth time the dome of Birmingham's newest church, just visible against the pre-dawn November sky. He would still make it in time to serve at Mass for Fr. Francis. But how could you read too much? he asked himself, returning his gaze to the Inglesant house. He recalled how his mother had held the handle of the garden gate on that summer's afternoon, a playful look in her eye, as if suggesting they should knock on the front door and demand to be shown round. He hadn't risen to her dare. He touched the gate now, ruminatively. The house was silent, asleep amid the gloom – yes, the encircling gloom – its inhabitants like the holy souls in purgatory, still waiting for morning. Too much for what, for whom?

John Inglesant, as it turned out, was a florid, sprawling, philosophical romance set in the English Civil War. A young man fights on the Royalist side, travels widely in Italy, struggles between loyalty to Anglicanism and the call of Rome, and finally learns to forgive the wretch who killed his brother. It was not quite like anything else Ronald had read. Take a sensational plot by Rider Haggard, fill it with gallant heroes from Herbert Hayens, mix in historical color à la William Morris, garnish with *The Hound of Heaven*'s religious fervor, and you'd still only have a rough approximation. There was nothing else even by the same author that could have prepared him for what he found in the novel, or not that was worth reading. Henry Shorthouse was in essence a one-book wonder, like Emily Brontë with *Wuthering Heights*, like Anna Sewell with *Black Beauty*. Shorthouse had written *John Inglesant* painstakingly, passionately, by the light of an old oil lamp, over the course of ten years in that front parlor just a few feet away. "There he is, still scribbling," Mrs. Warner would say to herself each night, from her door opposite, as she let the cat out. She had told young Ronald many times about her nocturnal glimpses of the great man. Just seeing the novel being written was a claim to fame.

Ronald nodded to Mrs. Warner now in the thinning gloom as she got herself through her front gate at number 19 and made a start for the Oratory. He would easily beat her to the seven o'clock Mass. She would have to stump all the way round past The Plough and Harrow and out onto the main road, whereas he could just slip in through the side door of the cellar and so up to the sacristy. He was an old hand now as an acolyte and knew precisely how long it would take to prepare the altar, and he'd be even quicker today without his little brother getting in the way. Hilary was laid up in bed, back in the top room they shared at Mrs. Faulkner's. What was it this time? Whooping cough again? Scarlet fever? Chicken pox? And today of all days. St. Hilary, pray for him!

Ronald shivered in the early air. Perhaps he had caught something himself. He looked weak and white as a ghost: tense of face, narrow-shouldered, a scrawny seventeen-year-old not yet begun to fill out. But for all his pallor he was strong enough and tough on the rugby pitch, daring, even reckless in his tackles, his body exulting in the sprints and impacts, a welcome relief from the life he lived behind his high forehead, all words and worlds, words that made worlds.

He sighed and noticed his breath. What was he going to *do* with his life? The imminent scholarship exam at Corpus Christi College reared up in his mind yet again. Oxford! He simply *must* get into Oxford! And 'Corpus Christi' – the Body of Christ: what could be better? But he had little hope; somehow something wasn't quite right about it. He shook his head deeper into his scarf.

A light suddenly showed behind the curtain of an upstairs room in the house before him. Who lived there now, he wondered? The *Inglesant* author had died the year before his mother, and all the local papers loudly lamented his demise. For if Henry Shorthouse was highly regarded on the national stage, he was virtually deified in Birmingham. But did he really deserve such attention? Ronald's mother had once pointed out a strange little man exiting St John's, Ladywood, whom he had eyed with a curiosity that was two parts admiration, three parts suspicion. A small, fabulously bewhiskered businessman with something of the renaissance count about his costume – was he a poseur or merely eccentric? He was Anglican, of course – the high church kind, despite his Quaker roots, a votary of the Oxford Movement, yet unable to bring himself to embrace the final lunacy of Romanism. How ironic that his house should have stood, should still stand, in the shadow of Newman's Oratory! So close and yet so far . . .

His novel was such a palpable hit that Shorthouse had even found himself discussing it with Prime Minister Gladstone in Downing Street, and Lord Acton had called *John Inglesant* the most thoughtful and suggestive novel since *Middlemarch*. There's glory for you! He was lionized, fêted, venerated – a nice change, no doubt, from the family firm and that dull career in chemical manufacturing he'd made do with till then. Goodbye, vitriol; hello, soft soap! Even the occasional American reader was brought to his door, earnestly voicing enthusiasm. Or so said Ronald's old maths teacher at King Edward's School, Mr. Levett. "My dear Levett, I dedicate this volume to you," Shorthouse had written, upon the novel's release in 1881, "that I may have an opportunity of calling myself your friend."

Friendship, fame, fortune, freedom . . . all flowing from *fiction*. Real things could come, somehow, from imaginings, and the Inglesant house embodied them all. Here it stood – curtains still closed, chimneys unsmoking, one lamp now showing downstairs – almost on his *own* doorstep; he could see its roof from the attic window at Mrs.

Faulkner's. A mere four hundred yards separated his cramped, decayed lodgings there in Duchess Road from this temple of fame: Number 6, Beaufort Road, where the great work first saw the light of day. So close. . . . He shook his head, bumping his fist on the gate-post. Something was not as it should be. He glanced to his left again. There, at the end of the road stood the real temple. It was time – oops, it was past time – to get to Mass. Corpus Christi beckoned.

As the tall, pale, wiry boy hastened to the Oratory, his mind began to churn. Modern literature could be so strange, exciting, debatable. For what was Shorthouse's novel really about? Its title was a nod to St. George, the Patron Saint of England (the *Ingle sant*), but its story suggested that Englishmen shunned popery if they were wise. Yet St. George had been adopted as the national saint when England was still a Catholic realm, 'Mary's Dowry,' on good terms with the rest of the Church. It didn't make sense. Where were the modern novelists who understood the old religion and the soul of the country, yet could also tell an epic tale that gripped the reader and wouldn't let go? MacDonald was too dreamy; Kipling too gung-ho; Conan Doyle too cut-and-dried. Who among them would ever be able to write a true mythology for England, for the world?

Loosening his scarf, Ronald strode across the Plough and Harrow Road, let himself carefully into the damp cellar, then hopped up the steps to the sacristy where he found Fr. Francis waiting, tapping his thumb against the thurible stand. He had done all the preparations himself.

"No Hilary?"

"Ill. Again. Plague, I think. Or cholera."

"Sorry to hear it. And what a day for it, too. Five years on . . ."

"Yes. I know. Sorry I'm late, Father."

A prayer. Ronald rings the bell, takes a dip of holy water from the stoup, pausing to wet the fingers of his guardian in turn, as the two cross themselves and process to the side altar.

"Introibo ad altare Dei," says the priest.

But Ronald's mind is on Greek, not Latin. That epigraph to *Inglesant* – how did it run? Something from the First Epistle of St. John:

Ἀγαπητοί, νῦν τέκνα Θεοῦ ἐσμεν, καὶ οὔπω ἐφανερώθη τί ἐσόμεθα . . .
"Beloved, we are God's children now: it does not yet appear what we shall be."

Tolkien the Medievalist
Turning Over a New Leaf

JOHN RONALD REUEL TOLKIEN WAS BORN A VICTORIAN, AT THE HEIGHT of British hope and glory, when the Empire covered one quarter of the globe, that Empire upon which the sun never set. He died in the reign of Victoria's great-great-granddaughter, Elizabeth, whose coronation he watched on television, the Empire now a thing of the past.

Men of his vintage saw more change than any other generation in human history: an observation so often made that it has become a commonplace. But this commonplace is true and worth restating as we assess Tolkien's modern reading and the role it played in his personal formation and creative sense. For that very word 'modern' – and its cognates, *modernity, modernist, modernize* – took on new connotations and new significance during his lifetime. At his birth, public transport went little faster than the speed of a trotting horse; by his death, supersonic flight was the modern reality. The British army still conducted cavalry charges when he was born in 1892; it possessed a nuclear arsenal when he died in 1973. He witnessed the rise of brutalism in architecture, of atonalism in music, of logical positivism in philosophy. He saw massive changes in attitudes to marriage, divorce, and the role of women. The Catholic liturgy he grew up on was transformed by the Second Vatican Council. The very coins in his pocket were different after decimalization of the pound sterling. He came into being alongside *The Adventures of Sherlock Holmes*; he passed away as Arthur C. Clarke's *Rendezvous with Rama* was released.

And during these years and decades, as young John Ronald grew into manhood and maturity, stretching his imaginative muscles . . . slowly but surely, Middle-earth was coming into existence.

J.R.R. Tolkien's legendarium – of which *The Hobbit*, *The Lord of the Rings*, and *The Silmarillion* form only a part – was the work of a lifetime. What inspired its creation? What was the soil that nourished the imagination of its author? How did Middle-earth come to be?

The most common and widely accepted answer has been that Tolkien was fundamentally rooted and grounded in the past, partaking only minimally of the modern world, and that we should therefore look to medieval literature for an understanding of his literary creations.

Many of the earliest readers thought so. Consider the words of praise on the dust-jacket of the second edition of *The Lord of the Rings*: "He has instilled elements of Norse, Teutonic and Celtic myth to make a strange but coherent world of his own"; "One takes it completely seriously: as seriously as Malory"; "If Ariosto rivalled it in invention (in fact he does not) he would still lack its heroic seriousness."[1] Early reviewers concurred. Its genre, W.H. Auden declared, was "the Heroic Quest"; one writer affirmed that in the depths of Middle-earth "we hear Snorri Sturluson and Beowulf, the sagas and the Nibelungenlied," and another described it as "perhaps the last literary masterpiece of the Middle Ages."[2]

Yet here we find something puzzling. This apparently thoroughgoing medieval work has gone on to have enduring popularity, both in its own right as a piece of literature and also as adapted into a critically and commercially successful trilogy of feature films. Not only that, both *The Lord of the Rings* and *The Hobbit* have an international reach, finding huge readerships well beyond the Anglophone world. They have been translated into several dozen languages, including Albanian, Arabic, Chinese, Czech, Greek, Hebrew, Japanese, Korean, Persian, Russian, Thai, and Turkish. The popularity of Tolkien's posthumously published tales from the legendarium is also astonishing: twelve volumes of *The History of Middle-earth*, featuring drafts and revisions of the published works, and unfinished writings in various stages of completion, were released not as academic titles for a niche audience but by a mainstream publisher. Not only are these volumes of seemingly specialist interest still in print, but the stand-alone books drawn from this body of material (such as *The Children of Húrin* and *The Fall of Gondolin*) have become best-sellers in their own right, reviewed in major newspapers. This abiding, global popularity seems to require explanation; it is not quite what one would expect of works produced in the Western European medieval tradition by an author who deliberately isolated himself from the modern world.*

Can we really suppose that Middle-earth is simply a rehash of the Middle Ages? How many people read Malory these days? Who has even heard of Ariosto? Do people take *Beowulf* to the beach? Indeed, once we press beyond immediate reactions to the work and canvass more considered responses, we find that the picture quickly becomes much more complex. Two contributors to an early critical study of *The Lord of the Rings* described the novel as "anomalous" and "genreless."[3] The label that reviewers first reached for – "medieval" – soon showed itself to be not precisely germane.

Nonetheless, the popular image of Tolkien presents him as averse to modernity, firmly (and by his own choice) stuck in the past. Didn't he think even Shakespeare was too modern? This is the point of view taken, for instance, by the BBC radio drama *Tolkien in Love* (2017), in which the Tolkien character says that "everything after 1066

---

* For instance, *The Lord of the Rings* ranked #1 in both the 1997 Waterstones Book of the Century poll and the BBC's 2007 "The Big Read" poll for "the nation's best-loved novel," was included in *The Telegraph*'s "100 novels everyone should read" in 2014, and was a finalist in the 2018 PBS "Great American Read" poll. In the first week of its release, *The Fall of Gondolin* (2018) was the #1 bestseller on the *New York Times* hardcover fiction list.

should be excised from schools." The Dome Karukoski biopic (2019) likewise implies that Tolkien's interests were thoroughly pre-modern. It is routinely assumed by cultural commentators that Tolkien was a "backward-looking person"[4]* and that he valued nothing beyond the boundaries of his professional interest in medieval literature. We need not bother, therefore, to consider his modern reading; it must have been minimal, something he dismissed as worthless, just as he rejected anything that smacked of the modern day.

After all, wasn't he an arch-conservative? Witness his curmudgeonly attitude to the twentieth century in which he regrettably found himself: he opposed the abandonment of liturgical Latin; objected to "Americo-cosmopolitanism"; described gasoline-powered chainsaws as "one of the greatest horrors of our age"; and deplored the "present design of destroying Oxford in order to accommodate motor-cars."[5] Clyde Kilby recalled, "One day while sitting in the back yard of Tolkien's house a loud motorcycle came by and totally interrupted our conversation. Tolkien said 'That is an Orc.'"[6] All these stances and statements contribute to the popular impression that he had little knowledge of or taste for anything more up-to-date than Chaucer. Although he wasn't actually responsible for the quip "Literature stops in 1100; after that there's only books," it has often been attributed to him because it is so clearly the reactionary sort of the thing he might have said. Clearly. Clearly.

The idea that Tolkien was immune to influence by his contemporaries is another part of this standard picture. His great friend C.S. Lewis famously remarked, "as for anyone influencing Tolkien, you might as well (to adapt the White King) try to influence a bandersnatch."[7] Tom Shippey remarks that "When it comes to modern writers, Tolkien was notoriously beyond influence."[8] John D. Rateliff says that Tolkien's response to suggestions of influence was to "steadfastly deny any post-medieval source."[9] (Whether he in fact *did* habitually deny post-medieval sources, as is generally taken for granted, is a question to which we will attend in the next chapter.)

Early scholarship on Tolkien's work reinforced this image of him as an isolated, medieval-focused writer. Humphrey Carpenter's account of Tolkien's creative life, as presented in his 1977 biography (the only one as yet to be authorized by the Tolkien family), along with his 1978 group study of the Inklings, seemed definitive, and has had a powerful impact for many years – tending to squelch further study of Tolkien's modern reading. We will have more to say about Carpenter's work shortly. For now let us quote his highly inaccurate statement: "the major names in twentieth-century writing meant little or nothing to [Tolkien]. He read very little modern fiction, and took no serious notice of it."[10]

According to the general consensus, then, Tolkien was clearly, notoriously, steadfastly medieval – but was he?

---

* Annika Röttinger observes that it is a "common cliché" to view Tolkien as an "anti-modern traditionalist who conservatively defends himself against any kind of industrial progress and therefore flees from reality" ("The Great War in Middle-earth," 64).

꧁ "He read very little modern fiction, and took no serious notice of it"?

It is true, as Tom Shippey argues in his magisterial *The Road to Middle-earth: How J.R.R. Tolkien Created a New Mythology*, that the power of Tolkien's writing "almost self-evidently had something to do with his job"[11] * – that job being, of course, his work as a philologist, specializing in medieval language and literature. Jane Chance notes that "Where Tolkien turned to find the stuff and fabric of this 'mythology for England' was clearly the medieval world he knew so well from his scholarly studies."[12] In making these points, Chance and Shippey, and the other critics whom they represent in this approach, are correct in what they assert but, I believe, mistaken in what, by omission, they appear to deny. As Verlyn Flieger recognizes, there is a very common tendency to conflate Tolkien's medieval scholarship with his creative work: "Because we know that Tolkien was a scholar of medieval literature and language . . . we assume that he must necessarily have written his fiction in the same mode in which he studied and taught. We are partly right."[13]

We are partly right. Flieger defines the situation nicely. Middle-earth evidently owes much to the Middle Ages, and Tolkien's deep and broad debts to medieval source material in *The Lord of the Rings*, *The Hobbit*, and *The Silmarillion* have been amply and rightly acknowledged by scholars. Yes, Tolkien was, above all things, a medievalist. That is obvious, and it cannot be gainsaid, but it does not follow that he had no interest in literature beyond the Middle Ages. Too many critics have stopped with his medieval interests, making scant attempt to trace his engagement with subsequent literature – or they have merely noted it, assuming that it must be an exception to the rule and not worth more than a passing mention.

It is the aim of this book to provide a fresh view, and to correct the critical imbalance that has affected Tolkien scholarship. His modern reading was both more far-reaching than people have realized, and more significant for his creative imagination† than has been assumed. If we recognize this, our understanding of and appreciation for Middle-earth – and of Tolkien himself – will be enriched.

Tolkien said of *The Lord of the Rings* that such a story "grows like a seed in the dark out of the leaf-mould of the mind: out of all that has been seen or thought or read, that has long ago been forgotten, descending into the deeps."[14]

Out of all that has been read. As we will discover, Tolkien read a great deal of modern literature, and in a variety of different genres, including children's stories, historical

---

* Nevertheless Shippey later noted that scholarly perspectives in this area had certain blind spots. He observed that one of the areas not adequately addressed in Tolkien criticism is "the influences on him of writers of the nineteenth and twentieth centuries, so often now deeply unfashionable, forgotten and out of print" ("Guest Editorial: An Encyclopedia of Ignorance," 3).

† 'Imagination' is often taken as synonymous with 'creativity.' However, Tolkien also used his imagination in his scholarship, literary criticism, and teaching, albeit in different modes and in different ways. By using the phrase 'creative imagination,' I am referring to his imagination as it operated in his reception and production of fictional literature and visual art.

fiction, fantastic romances, adventure, science fiction, detective stories, literary fiction, and poetry. He did so throughout his life, from childhood and youth (where he favored authors such as Edith Nesbit, Francis Thompson, and William Morris), up until right before his death (when we find him enjoying Sterling Lanier, Dylan Thomas, and Mark Twain). From the care with which he recorded his opinions it is evident that he engaged modern literature with his critical faculties in gear. This was not just holiday reading, undertaken to fill up tedious train journeys or as a distraction while recovering from illness. No, he read thoughtfully, discerningly, and receptively. To be sure, the other elements of his fertile 'leaf-mould' – principally his medieval reading, but also the study of languages, his personal friendships with the Inklings and other formative experiences, especially in the Great War – occupy a more important place in his creative imagination. My argument in this book is that they are not the *only* materials upon which he drew. Tolkien knew modern literature, and was oriented toward the modern world, to a greater degree than we have hitherto realized.* Acknowledging this aspect of his creative process will enhance our ability to interpret and enjoy his work.

Let me not be misunderstood: I shall not be arguing that his modern reading is *more* important than his medieval reading, nor even that it is *equally* important. Given his professional work as well as his personal interests, his modern reading is undoubtedly a relatively minor element in the total picture. But it is present and should not be overlooked.

As we will see in this study, the modern writers whose work was important to Tolkien included not only still-famous names such as Beatrix Potter and C.S. Lewis, but figures who will be only dimly known to many readers: Lord Dunsany, Herbert Hayens, E.H. Knatchbull-Hugessen, Wilfred Childe, Roy Campbell. Some of the authors whom Tolkien read were best-sellers at the time, but who now has heard of J.H. Shorthouse? Yet Shorthouse's novel *John Inglesant* was widely read, admired, and discussed in Tolkien's day and may have had an important influence on *The Lord of the Rings* (as we will discuss in chapter 10). Shorthouse and others are no longer household names, but they were once very much in fashion, and Tolkien knew their works well. The fact that today they have largely disappeared from the public consciousness, and even the consciousness of literary critics by and large, means that it takes strenuous mental effort to recapture his perspective.

However, before we start to make that strenuous effort, we should first ask an important preliminary question, so that we may survey the whole situation with fresh eyes. How did this oversimplification of Tolkien as nostalgic and un-influenceable become so firmly embedded in the popular and scholarly view? Four points are worth considering.

---

* By his 'modern reading' I principally mean his reading of *literature* pure and simple (see chapter 2). But I also mean, as a peripheral consideration, his 'reading' of contemporary culture more generally: what he made of visual art, of modern technology, of changes in the role of women, of the daily news, and so forth. These matters, though they are not at all my main concern, will be glanced at *en route* since they are adjacent to the path I am pursuing: his reading of modern fiction, poetry, and drama.

❧ "It's a challenge to try and tarnish": Carpenter on Tolkien

First, certain statements by Humphrey Carpenter, in his life of Tolkien and in his group biography of the Inklings, have profoundly shaped views on Tolkien's attitudes. Carpenter, as we noted above, summed up Tolkien's reading with the terse statement: "He read very little modern fiction, and took no serious notice of it."[15] Since Carpenter is to date the only biographer to have enjoyed unfettered access to the Tolkien papers, naturally his opinion carries weight. However, before we place any great trust in this verdict, we would do well to investigate Carpenter and see what claim he has to being an objective and unbiased reporter.*

Carpenter freely confessed that he brought certain very strong preconceptions to his project. In a revealing interview, he admits:

> The first biography I did in book form was the life of Tolkien, and I thought, here is this rather comic Oxford academic – the stereotype absent-minded professor – who would be lecturing on Beowulf with a parcel of fish from the fishmongers sticking out of his pocket. And the first draft of the book was written very much in that mode, treating him as slightly slapstick. At least it began that way. But as the book went on, I realized he wasn't like this at all. He had had a very strange childhood. His mother had died early (his father was already dead) and he was brought up by a Roman Catholic priest – an unlikely parent-figure. Consequently he acquired certain uptight Pauline moral values. And my caricature of the Oxford academic clashed with his [sic], and I never resolved it properly.[16]

By Carpenter's own admission, then, he began this, his first ever formal biography, in a "slapstick" mode.† He came to realize, however, that the "caricature" he was drawing had to be complexified by his discovery that Tolkien had experienced a "strange" childhood and had thereby acquired "uptight" values. Finally, he "never resolved" the two perspectives.

And it was not only the biographer himself who had mixed feelings about the work. Carpenter reveals that the first draft of his book was "deemed unacceptable by the Tolkien family."[17] Rayner Unwin, whose firm published the *Biography*, confirms that Tolkien's son, Christopher, "carefully and critically tore Humphrey's draft to pieces";

---

* Humphrey William Bouverie Carpenter was born in 1946 and grew up at Keble College, Oxford, where his father was Warden from 1939–1955 before being appointed Bishop of Oxford. Carpenter was educated at the Dragon School in Oxford and read English at Keble, after which he went into a career as a radio broadcaster and biographer. He died in 2005.

† Carpenter wrote the book in under two years, even though he was faced with a huge amount of material in a very disorganized state. Considering that Carpenter was not an experienced researcher or biographer – this was his debut – it seems a remarkably short time to devote to the whole process.

Carpenter then "retreated to his bedroom for a week or two and re-wrote the whole book which, in its revised form, Christopher approved and it was given to us to publish."[18]

It seems almost incredible that Carpenter would have been able to address such a thorough critique in a mere fortnight, and in fact he said later, "What I'd actually done was castrated the book, cut out everything which was likely to be contentious."[19] A revision that omitted the most egregious passages would indeed have been feasible to complete in just a week or two – but Carpenter didn't have the time, even if he had the inclination, to address more subtle flaws of interpretation or misrepresentation.*

Carpenter also admitted that he had convinced the Tolkien family to appoint him official biographer by "charm" and by playing on their fears: "I went to them one by one and said, 'Look, I don't know much about writing biography, but I did know your father a little, and I know Oxford, I know the milieu in which he operated, and I think if you don't get somebody who has those advantages, you'll probably find a worse biographer coming along.'"[20] Better the devil you know . . .

There is a certain roguish honesty in these disclosures, and they comport with Carpenter's own self-image as someone who knows 'the establishment' from the inside but is not part of it. Indeed, he saw himself as somewhat anti-establishment: "I am always looking for idols to demolish, because I'm that sort of person," he said. "Upsetting the loyal fans is one of my main aims. I've always explained this aggression to myself by saying that around each figure there's an absurd cult of admirers, people who want the great person to remain untarnished. And it's a challenge to try and tarnish them."[21]

Elsewhere, Carpenter reveals a dismissive attitude regarding Tolkien's academic work with the back-handed compliment: "Tolkien was probably the greatest scholar of Anglo-Saxon who ever lived; but it's a dead subject, having been replaced by structuralism."[22] In Carpenter's mind, then, Tolkien's professional career was wasted on an irrelevant and out-of-date topic, and it was his duty as an iconoclast aggressively to expose his subject's feet of clay. He came not to praise Tolkien, but to bury him, an approach that is more or less summed up in the title of his 1992 BBC radio play: "In a Hole in the Ground, There Lived a Tolkien."†

---

* For instance, Carpenter describes Tolkien's guardian, Fr. Francis Morgan, as "not a man of great intellect" and "not a clever man" (*Biography* 34, 52) but offers no evidence or explanation for this judgment. Fr. Francis had in fact been Cardinal Newman's personal secretary – hardly a role for a dullard – and José Manuel Ferrández Bru points out that his "room full of books attests to his obvious love of reading and knowledge" (*"Uncle Curro": J.R.R. Tolkien's Spanish Connection*, 57–58). Fr. Francis was also bilingual; the teenaged Tolkien attempted to teach himself Spanish with some of his books (*Letters*, 213).

† Carpenter wrote this radio play for the centenary of Tolkien's birth, and it undoubtedly added to the popular image of Tolkien as a silly, fastidious figure who was stuck in the past. Douglas A. Anderson explains that in the play, "Tolkien was portrayed with unceasing absurdity, as an irredeemably absent-minded professor who wanders around Leeds randomly shouting out strange terms like 'smakkabagms' . . . [Carpenter] had by this time forgotten virtually everything about Tolkien he had ever known, save for a few representative phrases and some facts that could be woven together into a caricature" ("Obituary," 222).

With all these facts in mind, we would be wise to approach Carpenter's judgments with caution. And I am not the first to raise such doubts about his reliability. Hammond and Scull note that the *Biography*, useful as it is, has "problems of emphasis or interpretation." Nicole M. duPlessis has carefully analyzed Carpenter's biases regarding Tolkien's marriage.[23]

The deficiencies in the *Biography* have been, until recently, difficult to detect, let alone challenge or correct. Omission of information, and interpretation in the guise of reportage, can sometimes have a stronger and more persistent distorting effect than outright error. When it comes to Tolkien's taste for and interest in contemporary literature, Carpenter's bold claim that "he read very little modern fiction, and took no serious notice of it" needs to be approached with extreme circumspection.

❧ *Letters* in the shadow of the *Biography*

Second, this mistaken 'conventional wisdom' about Tolkien was able to take a firmer hold because for years Carpenter had effectively cornered the market in Tolkien scholarship. Not only had he written the first biography (1977) and the first major study of the Inklings (1978), he was also responsible for the publication of *The Letters of J.R.R. Tolkien* (1981). Admittedly, this project was undertaken "with the assistance of Christopher Tolkien," but that very phrasing (which appears on the front cover of the book) – a most unusual way of describing editorial collaboration – suggests an uneasy relationship. The awkward phraseology indicates that something of a strain had developed between Carpenter and the Tolkien family, after his biography draft was "deemed unacceptable" and hastily revised.*

The volume of letters undoubtedly reflects something of Carpenter's unsympathetic attitude toward his subject.† Both in his selection of letters and in his editing of them we can observe an agenda at work that serves to make Tolkien seem impatient, defensive, and uninterested in anything modern.

---

* In the introduction, Carpenter says he made "the initial selection" of letters, upon which Christopher commented, and that the book in its final form "reflects my own taste and judgement rather more than his" (*Letters* 3). Interestingly, the first edition of the *Letters* has on the cover, spine, and title page, "Selected and edited by Humphrey Carpenter," while later editions have only Tolkien's name on the spine and only "Edited by Humphrey Carpenter" on the cover, leaving it to the title page to inform the reader that this is "A selection edited by Humphrey Carpenter." These small adjustments have tended to obscure Carpenter's dominant role in preparing the *Letters*.

† For instance, Carpenter's index omits the Virgin Mary, despite a number of references to her by Tolkien, including an extended passage on the Assumption, which is lumped under 'Tolkien, character and interests, Catholicism.' The index includes names of other people who are only mentioned in passing, not just recipients of letters, so this omission reflects Carpenter's lack of interest, not a standard editorial rule. The problem illustrated here is not the lack of shared belief – Tolkien studies has top-notch scholars who are not Catholics, or Christians of any kind – but rather the way that Carpenter handles material that touches on matters of central importance to his biographical subject. The revised edition of the *Letters* has an expanded index (created by Wayne Hammond and Christina Scull) that gives a full entry to the Virgin Mary.

For instance, the extract presented from a 1958 letter to Deborah Webster begins baldly with Tolkien saying, "I do not like giving facts about myself . . ." After nonetheless giving various details about himself, he concludes abruptly with "I hope that is enough to go on with."[24] Although the extract itself contains interesting details, the tone appears brusque, even irritated, as if Tolkien only reluctantly discloses personal information. A different perspective appears when we consult the full text of his remarks.[25] His reply in fact begins by thanking Webster for her letter and a book of prayers that she had sent him, and noting that he wished she had visited Oxford during the summer, when he would have been more likely to be able to meet with her in person. He then writes, "But I do not like giving 'facts' about myself other than 'dry' ones . . ."[26] The word 'But' (omitted by Carpenter without ellipsis) after the friendly opening gives his autobiographical reticence an apologetic rather than curmudgeonly flavor. He signs off "with gratitude for appreciation"[27] – again, omitted in the *Letters*. The warm tone indicates that he is not at all bothered by her inquiry, but feels complimented by her interest and is happy to respond. Carpenter's subtle nips and tucks present us with a different face: less friendly, more forbidding.

Another example of tendentious editing appears when Carpenter presents long extracts from a letter in which Tolkien criticizes a proposed cinematic treatment of *The Lord of the Rings*. Carpenter omits the passage in which Tolkien discusses a recent film version of Rider Haggard's *King Solomon's Mines* – a passage that shows Tolkien's interest in and knowledge about both cinema (still then a cutting-edge new medium) and the modern literature that could be adapted for it.[28] From the picture Carpenter provides, the reader could be forgiven for assuming that Tolkien had little or no exposure to film versions of contemporary fiction and that he had a reactionary objection to his own work being given the silver-screen treatment.

Possibly because of the conditioning effects of Carpenter's editorializing, readers of the *Letters* have tended to pay more attention to Tolkien's negative statements about his reading than his positive ones. For instance, in a review of the volume, J.I.M. Stewart comes away with the impression that Tolkien was a reader of limited sympathies:

> About other people's books he says little, and that little is commonly unfavourable. . . . [He] admits with some complacency to "not being specially well read in modern English." . . . there is a certain quirkiness in all this reiteration of a theme ("I seldom find any modern books that hold my attention" . . . "Certainly I have not been nourished by English literature") which knits with similarly persistent quirkinesses in other fields to an effect that is not exactly that of breadth of view.[29]

Stewart highlights Tolkien's negative remarks about modern authors such as Browning, Graves, and Sayers, but curiously makes no mention whatsoever of his praise for Joyce Gard, Kenneth Grahame, David Lindsay, and so on. Why such one-sidedness? It would seem that the popular idea of Tolkien as the arch-medievalist, uninterested in modern literature, had already set in sufficiently that Stewart could cherry-pick those bits from the *Letters* that supported this image without noticing his bias in doing so. An amusing side note to his derisive remarks about these supposedly narrow tastes is that Tolkien had read at least one of Stewart's own mystery novels, published under his *nom de plume* Michael Innes.[30]

We must also keep firmly in mind the fact that Tolkien wrote many more letters than are included in the volume. Carpenter noted that he had "to sift through literally thousands of letters. I mean thousands," and that Tolkien was "one of the last great letter-writers in the great English tradition of letter-writers"[31] – so we must be aware that what he presents is only a small portion of the total correspondence, not a comprehensive 'collected letters.' Out of the "thousands," Carpenter presents a mere 354, most of which are incomplete.*

✂ The mythical Tollewis

We just noted Tolkien's discussion of *King Solomon's Mines* and its recent cinematic treatment. He may well have gone to see the movie with his friend C.S. Lewis; at any rate, in giving his view of the film, Tolkien reports that he shares some of Lewis's objections to it. Tolkien and Lewis were colleagues and friends, a friendship that was especially close during the 1930s, and they had a common outlook on many things, including this particular movie. But they definitely did not see eye-to-eye about everything or live identical sorts of lives. Tolkien was Catholic, Lewis was Anglican; Tolkien was married and a father of four, Lewis was a bachelor for all but three years of his life; Tolkien played rugby and squash enthusiastically, Lewis was uninterested in sport. And we could go on. We make these observations to highlight a third distorting influence on the popular image of Tolkien's attitude toward the modern world : namely, the tendency to conflate him with his fellow Inkling, making a composite figure whom we could call 'Tollewis' along the lines of the famous description of G.K. Chesterton and Hilaire Belloc as the 'Chesterbelloc.'

For instance, Carpenter pictures Tolkien sitting at the breakfast table, where he "glances at the newspaper, but only in the most cursory fashion. He, like his friend C.S.

---

* In his introduction to the *Letters*, Carpenter claims that the "selection has been made with an eye to demonstrating the huge range of Tolkien's mind and interests" (1). However, it is notable that the volume includes not a single letter to Tolkien's brother Hilary, nor to his granddaughter Joanna, nor to his student and family friend Simonne d'Ardenne, nor to his colleague E.V. Gordon, to name just four examples of correspondence that would have shed light on Tolkien in both personal and professional contexts. We know that Tolkien did write to these people: see *The One Ring.net* (http://www.theonering.net/torwp/2010/11/16/40512-tolkien-estate-comments-on-book-cancellation/) for reference to letters quoted in a planned biography of Hilary Tolkien; see Joanna Tolkien, "Joanna Tolkien speaks at the Tolkien Society Annual Dinner," for reference to letters she received; and see TCG:C for reference to letters to d'Ardenne and Gordon. Surely some of these, or ones like them, were among the letters to which Carpenter had access.

Lewis, regards 'news' as on the whole trivial and fit to be ignored. . . . However, both men enjoy the crossword."[32] The imagined scene is extremely close to a description of Lewis that appears in the first biography of him,[33] where Lewis is described (accurately) as someone who didn't read newspapers and derided journalism as "mostly not true."[34] It seems likely that Carpenter, on seeing this account of Lewis – in which Tolkien is never mentioned – simply assumed that such a dismissive attitude to the news was equally true of his friend, and attached it to the subject of his own biography, even down to the breakfast table setting. But as we will see later in this chapter, Tolkien did read the newspapers and followed current events closely. He was attuned to the modern world in ways his friend was not.

Michael Ward cautions against this tendency toward an unreflective pairing-off of Lewis and Tolkien: it is important to recognize, he argues, that each "was a unique individual and not one half of a pair of conjoined twins. . . . The two men must be allowed to attempt different things in different ways."[35] The point applies equally well to their attitudes toward modern reading. It was Lewis, not Tolkien, who declared, "It is a good rule, after reading a new book, never to allow yourself another new one till you have read an old one in between." Now, Tolkien may in fact not have demurred much from the basic point Lewis was making – about the importance of escaping the prejudices of one's time – but, still, it was not Tolkien but Lewis who bothered to pontificate on the matter in public and lay down a rule about it. It was not Tolkien but Lewis who highlighted the need to oppose "chronological snobbery" (the unreflective assumption that the values of one's own day are superior to those of the past). It was not Tolkien but Lewis, or one side of Lewis, who was described (by their mutual friend Owen Barfield) as a "*laudator temporis acti* [praiser of times past]."[36] Lewis and Tolkien did have a great deal in common, but what can be said about one is not automatically applicable to the other. We must weigh the evidence and allow Tolkien's own preferences, interests, and habits of mind to emerge unshadowed by what we know of his friend. It is not equally true of them both that they were fighting a constant rearguard campaign against whatever smacked of the modern age.

❧ "A man loves the meat in his youth that he cannot abide in his age"

Fourth and finally, the image of Tolkien as irredeemably anti-modern has been shaped by a too-frequent disregard of context and chronology.

He certainly did have a generally negative view of industrialization, but we must remember his historical context. A man who fought in the First World War and who had two sons fighting in the Second, who experienced such air-pollution in Leeds that "chemicals in the air rotted the curtains within six months,"[37] and who was living in Oxford during the destructive imposition of the ring-road (and the obliteration of the historic neighborhood of St Ebbe's),[38] may be allowed to make the occasional biting comment about modernity as symbolized by machines, industrialization, and urbanization. For all that, his views on technology were surprisingly nuanced, as we shall see in chapter 9.*

Furthermore, Tolkien lived a long life, and some of the interviews and letters in which he speaks dismissively of modern authors come from his later years. Hammond and Scull point out that "Tolkien's thoughts sometimes changed with the years and his memories varied, so that a comment at one moment may be contradicted by another written at a different time."[39] Critics have not always been as attentive as they ought to have been to the chronology of his opinions.† Carpenter, for instance, on occasion draws general conclusions about Tolkien's preferences or attitudes (such as his alleged dislike of France) that may in actuality have reflected only a certain period in his life, or even a certain mood.‡ Moreover, Carpenter's decision to weight his selection of the *Letters* toward Tolkien's later years, when he was dealing with a steady stream of fan mail about *The Lord of the Rings*, means that his earlier years are comparatively under-represented, and we see relatively little of his imaginative formation. Such a focus is subtly conducive to a caricatured view of Tolkien as a man of narrow tastes and limited interests.

As an elderly man, Tolkien does seem to have had a reduced appreciation of different types of reading. This is, no doubt, due partly to the natural contraction of tastes and habits of mind in old age and partly to the fact that, after the success of *The Lord of the*

---

* It is interesting in this regard that Donald Swann remarked in 1968 that Tolkien "shone forth to me as the forerunner of the conservationists. . . . he foresaw the era in which we now live, when the 'age of technology' is about to be balanced by a more Franciscan attitude, and the extinction of an animal species now hurts young people as much as, earlier, the introduction of a new brand of motorbike pleased them" (foreword to *The Road Goes Ever On*, viii).

† For instance, in the *Biography* Carpenter quotes, as evidence of Tolkien's lack of interest in modern literature, a line from a letter to Edith: "I so rarely read a novel, as you know" (77). However, Carpenter gives no indication of date. The time when Tolkien was most likely to *write* to Edith was before their marriage, when he was finishing his degree at Oxford – and would have little time for leisure reading in any genre from any period, ancient, medieval, or modern. In any case, Tolkien was a man of precise vocabulary. The category of 'novel' is usually associated with literary realism, and typically excludes romances, thrillers, detective fiction, fantasy, and science fiction, all of which Tolkien did read. Even when Tolkien was still a student at Oxford, we know that he was enjoying historical romances (such as by William Morris: see chapter 5), not to mention contemporary poetry (such as by Francis Thompson: see chapter 10). Though it would be accurate to say that, in his student days, he "rarely" read works that he considered to be novels, it would not be accurate to generalize from this remark that he seldom read contemporary literature of any kind whatsoever, either then or at other periods of his life.

‡ John Garth suggests that Carpenter, in asserting Tolkien's 'Gallophobia,' "pays too much attention to mischievous hyperbole (as he does regarding Tolkien's views on Shakespeare and Wagner)." Garth points out that "Tolkien's knowledge of French extended to the niceties of dialectal Eastern Walloon pronunciation . . . [and] he felt a lingering attachment towards the region of France in which he served. In 1945 he wrote, 'I can see clearly now in my mind's eye the old trenches and the squalid houses and the long roads of Artois, and I would visit them again if I could'" (TGW, 189). See also Verlyn Flieger, "Tolkien's French Connection," in *There Would Always Be a Fairy Tale*.

Rings, Tolkien found himself subject to what we might call 'death by a thousand lit. crits.' Everyone seemed to have an idea about what gave rise to his masterpiece and often these ideas were not only inaccurate, but wildly inaccurate. As a result, Tolkien's curmudgeonly streak seems to have increased and, late in life, according to his friend George Sayer, he was "not inclined to admit to the influence on him of any other writers at all"[40] – the key word in Sayer's description being "admit." Tolkien was a bit of a contrarian to begin with, likely to disclaim the idea of being influenced simply because such a thing had been suggested. (We will return to this point in chapter 12.) Furthermore, after years of answering fan mail full of questions about Middle-earth, he seems to have begun to think of his writings as something he had discovered, rather than made. Insofar as he came to consider *The Lord of the Rings* in this way, he would naturally tend less often to recollect (and talk about) the influences on its creation, whether or not those influences happened to be modern. Thus, we cannot securely judge his attitudes as a young and middle-aged man, when he was writing the main part of his legendarium, by those he developed late in life.

❧ "I take a strong interest in what is going on"

We have seen, then, four reasons why this faulty popular image of Tolkien has taken hold, all of them traceable, in some measure, to Humphrey Carpenter.* But once we allow Tolkien to be more than a Carpenter caricature, and admit the possibility of a genuinely three-dimensional figure, we find that he confounds easy reduction to the cartoon image of a dusty bookworm in an ivory tower, out of touch with the present, and nostalgic for times before the Norman Conquest.

We must always bear in mind that Tolkien was an unusually complex man. In this connection, Clyde Kilby's perspective is of interest. Kilby, who spent a summer assisting (or attempting to assist) Tolkien with the preparation of the Silmarillion for publication, remarked: "I felt that Tolkien was like an iceberg, something to be reckoned with above water in both its brilliance and mass and yet with much more below the surface."[41] Tolkien's personality has a certain quality of elusiveness. What one observed on the surface, or at any particular moment, was true, but it was not the whole story.

His attitude toward the news, for instance, helps alert us to the unexpected dimensions of his personality. He read the newspaper every day, and to an interviewer who seemed surprised that Tolkien followed the news at all, he replied that indeed he subscribed to *three* newspapers, adding: "I take a strong interest in what is going on, both in

---

* Carpenter's work is certainly readable, but whether it is also accurate is another matter, and in this study I have relied very little on either his *Biography* or *The Inklings*. I have occasionally cited material that he quotes from Tolkien's letters or diaries, though without relying on his interpretation of it. A few times I draw on Carpenter for otherwise unsourced data; in these instances, the fact that the information relates to Tolkien's engagement with modernity and thus runs counter to Carpenter's overall presentation of him, suggests its reliability.

the university and in the country and in the world."[42] * In 1949, he co-signed a letter to the London *Times* to protest the Soviet-inspired arrest of Cardinal Mindszenty in Hungary – an instance of his very up-to-the-minute concern about violations of religious freedom.[43] His interest in international events is mentioned several times in the diary of Warren Lewis, C.S. Lewis's brother and a friend of Tolkien's. In 1946, for example, Warren recalls a group lunch with Tolkien where they "argued the morality of the Nuremburg trials," and another at which they discussed "the moral aspect of atomic bombing and total war in general." A few years later, he recalled a gathering with "Tollers very confidential and 'in the know' about the details of the Communist plot."[44] We would not expect any of this from someone stuck in the past, uninterested in the modern world.†

Tolkien strongly disliked the heedless expansion of roads and industry, but he was not against technology *per se*; he learned to drive (again, unlike Lewis) and bought a car as early as 1932.[45] Later recollections of Tolkien referred to him as someone who did not drive a car, but this was a feature of his later years, and is not uncommon among elderly people, and particularly not in Oxford and southern England, where buses, trains, and taxis are widely available.

Much has been made of the supposed narrowness of his social circle (the male-only Inklings) and of his professional world (Oxford colleges only began to go coeducational the year after his death). But Tolkien, unlike some of the other Inklings, was married for over fifty years; Lewis once irritatedly called him "the most married man I know."[46] Tolkien made a point of spending time with his wife, daughter, and granddaughters as well as with his brother, sons, and grandsons.[47] It is also worth noting his inclusion, in the 1927 'Father Christmas letter,' not only of his wife Edith (which is to be expected), but also of her cousin Jennie, and their current au pair Aslaug: they all feature among the "dear people" to whom the letter is addressed.[48] He even found time to correspond with the eleven-year-old granddaughter of his next-door neighbors in Headington, providing a thoughtful assessment of her poetry.‡ His daughter Priscilla mentioned his "many

---

* Scull and Hammond identify two of the three as *The Times* and the *Daily Telegraph*, with the third probably a local paper, which I suspect would have been *The Oxford Times*. They add, "For some period at least he took the *Sunday Times*" (TCG:RG, 1062). Commenting on the archaeological remains in the Old Forest that Frodo and company stumble upon, John Garth opines that Tolkien's "immediate spur was [Mortimer] Wheeler's Maiden Castle reports in *The Times*, small literary masterpieces filling two long columns annually from 1935 to 1938. No one interested in British antiquity would have missed them – least of all Tolkien, who had provided a learned appendix to Wheeler's report on a previous dig" (*The Worlds of J.R.R. Tolkien*, 139). He was probably also a subscriber to *The Catholic Herald*; he wrote a letter to the editor (regarding place-name origins) which was published in the 23 February 1945 issue (TCG:RG, 306). *The Herald* was in those days a weekly newspaper, now a monthly magazine.

† Lewis, however, could be astonishingly ill-informed about current events. His brother recalls a conversation about Yugoslavia, in which he says, "I thought J[ack] very stupid . . . before I found out that he was under the impression that Tito [the Yugoslavian dictator] was the King of Greece!" (BF, 236).

‡ As she recalled, "Perhaps what I take most from Tolkien's mentoring is the utter absence of condescension, the empathy of a writer for another would-be writer, however wet behind the ears:

18

years of friendship with Dorothy Everett," his colleague on the English Faculty, as being among the reasons she chose Lady Margaret Hall as her Oxford college;[49] Everett and several other women colleagues were also members of a literary and social club, "The Cave," which Tolkien co-founded in the 1930s.[50]* Another member of "The Cave" was Elaine Griffiths, whom Tolkien called "my very old friend."[51] He stayed in touch with Margaret Wiseman, the sister of his fellow T.C.B.S. member Christopher Wiseman; it was a "carefully thought out plan" that his granddaugher Joanna would attend Oulton Abbey School, as that was where Margaret (now a Benedictine nun) was headmistress.[52] He had many female students and not a few female academic collaborators in his decades as a teacher, both at Leeds and at Oxford.[53]† Moreover, he read many women writers throughout his life, and took their work seriously, as we will see later in this book. To mention just one example now (and a rather surprising example to boot), Tolkien favorably quoted Simone de Beauvoir, an existentialist and feminist writer, indicating that they shared some ideas on death, a key theme of *The Lord of the Rings*.[54] Insofar as the increase in 'mixed' settings, women's education, and professional success for women represented an effect of modernity, we see Tolkien not resisting but happily accepting and encouraging it.

As for the effects of modernity in the Church, he was emphatic about the value of one of the major changes in ecclesial practice during his lifetime: the recommendation for frequent communion.[55] With regard to the abandonment of liturgical Latin and the reconfiguring of the Mass, Tolkien remarked that he approved of the reform of the liturgy "in the abstract," although he confessed to feeling "a little dislocated and even a little sad at my age to know that the ceremonies and modes so long familiar and deeply associated with the season will never be heard again!"[56]‡ Given both the extent and the abruptness of the shift from the Tridentine Mass to the Novus Ordo, it would be startling if Tolkien had not felt disconcerted by the change; what is most notable is that he distinguishes his own emotional reaction from his approval of the reform in principle.

'I feel sympathy with [your poems], because you seem to be moved by colour, and by day's ending, twilight, evening. . . . I shall of course always be pleased (and indeed honoured) to see anything you write or publish'" (Paula Coston, "Tolkien on writing . . . and me," 14).

   * Carpenter, in his brief mention of the club, names only male members (*Inklings* 56n2) and later biographers have generally followed him (see, for instance, Philip Zaleski and Carol Zaleski, *The Fellowship*, 175–176 and Colin Duriez, *The Oxford Inklings*, 104).

   † Another instance of Tolkien's support for women in academia can be observed in the fact that he helped two of his female students from Leeds to gain employment at the Oxford English Dictionary, providing special lexicography training for one (Monica Dawn) and a recommendation for another (Stella Mills) (Peter Gilliver, *The Making of the Oxford English Dictionary*, 391, 397–398).

   ‡ George Sayer thought that Tolkien "found little or nothing wrong with the pre-Vatican II Church" ("Recollections of J.R.R. Tolkien," 13), but Tolkien's forthright observations to his son Michael about the disagreeable aspects of Mass attendance, from a "snuffling or gabbling priest" to ill-behaved laity (*Letters*, 339), refer to his pre-conciliar experience.

❧ Interpreter of tradition: Tolkien the modernizer

We must, then, give up the assumption that Tolkien was utterly backward-looking and therefore uninterested in and uninfluenced by the contemporary world. Yes, it is true that Tolkien was a man profoundly shaped by his work in medieval literature and language – but not to the exclusion of everything else. Furthermore, we should recall that Tolkien's reputation rests not only on *The Lord of the Rings* and *The Hobbit* but on something seemingly very different: his single-handed rescue of the Anglo-Saxon poem *Beowulf* from critical disdain. Today, when *Beowulf* is a standard text in many literature courses, with numerous translations, including one by Seamus Heaney, it can be difficult to realize that before Tolkien's 1936 lecture "Beowulf: The Monsters and the Critics," the poem was valued only as a source of linguistic and historical data. Tolkien changed all that and brought *Beowulf* as a work of literary art into the place of honor where it resides today. His academic victory may at first seem irrelevant to our task in this study, but we should attend to how Tolkien achieved it. Peter Milward describes Tolkien's writings on *Beowulf* in this way:

> Here was indeed the work not of a mere academic scholar, disinterring the bones of the long dead past, but of an imaginative critic, reviving those bones and breathing into them the spirit of life. . . . [Tolkien was] gifted with the ability to enter into the spirit of the old poem and to interpret it to his twentieth-century readers.[57]

Tolkien could *interpret* the medieval world for his modern readers. An interpreter must know both cultures, the old and the new. Someone who dwelt wholly in the past might well understand the poem better than anyone else, but he would not be able to share that understanding with others. Tolkien could and did communicate his insights, which suggests that he had a deeper knowledge of the modern world – even as he critiqued it – than has been recognized to date.

Tolkien greatly valued tradition, to be sure, but 'tradition' means literally 'a handing on,' passing the baton from past to present; a successful traditionalist must know both where he has come from and where he presently stands. Tolkien readily conceded that "no one of us can really invent or 'create' in a void, we can only reconstruct and perhaps impress a personal pattern on 'ancestral' material."[58] The ancestral material of medieval language and literature was of central importance to his creative process, but he also deliberately interwove the old and the new. For instance, in commenting on his interest in developing his own mythology, Tolkien remarked, "That's what I always wanted to do – mythological things like Greek or Norse myths; I tried to improve on them and modernize them – to modernize them is to make them credible."[59] This is a most extraordinary statement, for here we find Tolkien using "modernize" in a favorable way. It does not fit the popular image of him as an arch-medieval, anti-modern figure – but it *does* fit with the more well-rounded view that we find when we consider his modern reading.

❧ A superabundance of interests: Tolkien as a reader

Tolkien, throughout his life, read a great deal of modern literature, in a surprisingly wide range of genres. We know this for a fact. We know it chiefly from his letters, but also from references in his nonfiction writings, and from interviews that he gave and other conversations that were recorded by friends and acquaintances over the years. It is one of those pieces of data that has largely been overlooked while scholars focus on other aspects of the critical terrain, but in truth, it comports with what we know of his personality and his omnivorous mind.

For Tolkien was a person whose interests can be neither easily delimited nor neatly categorized. C.S. Lewis commented that "[Tolkien] is the most unmanageable man (in conversation) I've ever met. He will talk to you alright: but the subject of his remarks will be whatever happens to be interesting him at the moment, which might be anything from M.E. [Middle English] words to Oxford politics."[60] Clyde Kilby recalled that "He would go sixty miles an hour with a subject from apples to elephants. . . . He didn't mention the Beatles, but just about everything else came into Tolkien's conversation."[61] * A former student remembered walks with him in the Merton College garden, discussing subjects such as "college farms in East Anglia; pigs and their personalities; garden summerhouses; Wulfstan the Eleventh Century homilist; the birds and beasts of battle, as a set piece in Germanic verse; the influence of Hegel on *The Hobbit*, etc."[62]

With so many different interests, both professional and personal, Tolkien's reading on any one subject would very probably have seemed to himself to be somewhat limited, especially in comparison with his intense professional absorption in philological studies. As Lewis remarked, Tolkien "had been inside language"[63] and any other area of reading would probably feel shallow to him next to that. He was therefore more likely to understate, than to overstate, the extent and depth of his modern reading.

For instance, in a 1967 interview with Charlotte and Denis Plimmer, he is quoted as saying, "I don't read much now, not even fairy-stories"; on the surface, it underscores the limits of his reading. However, in a letter to the Plimmers making corrections to the draft of this interview he goes on to remark, "I read quite a lot – or more truly, try to

---

* He may not have spoken of them to Kilby, but Tolkien did, in fact, know of the Beatles, and disliked them (See TCG:C, 777). He enjoyed other forms of popular music, however. For instance, he was such a great admirer of the popular comic singing duo Flanders and Swann that he invited them to Merton College to do a mini-concert (Marco di Noia, "Best wishes from Thorin and Company! – Following Tolkien's trails in Oxford," 23). He also actively collaborated with Donald Swann in producing *The Road Goes Ever On*, a song-cycle of Tolkien's poems set to music. Swann recalled with pleasure his meetings with Tolkien and Edith, and his relief at discovering that "the piano, instead of being the last instrument you would expect to see in Middle-Earth, had some close connection with Tolkien's imagination" (foreword to *The Road Goes Ever On*, vi–vii).

read many books (notably so-called Science Fiction and Fantasy). But I seldom find any modern books that hold my attention."[64]

Here we find an amplification that, remarkably, completely reverses his meaning: from "I don't read much now" to "I read quite a lot"! His scrupulous and somewhat idiosyncratic attention to accuracy leads him to claim as properly 'read' only those books that held his attention all the way through. Far from indicating a distance from or indifference toward modern literature, Tolkien's comment reveals that he read extensively in modern fiction – but had such exactingly high standards and peculiar preferences that relatively few books suited his tastes. This is the mark of a man who is interested in and engaged with modern fiction, not one who finds it irrelevant or insignificant.

Tolkien was in fact an avid reader – a point charmingly attested to by one of his linguistic doodlings in Quenya, which translates as, "I've spent over a hundred pounds on books this year but I do not regret it at all." This was in the late 1920s; Tolkien's £100 would be the equivalent of over £6,000 ($8,000) today![65] We know that he ran up a huge tab at Blackwell's Bookshop in Oxford.* (See figure 1.) Considering that Tolkien had access to Oxford's university and college libraries for academic resources,[66] his purchases undoubtedly included titles for personal reading as well as for scholarly pursuits. In 1937, he visited the *Sunday Times* book fair in London, and wished he could have stayed longer; in 1962, he managed, despite a busy schedule, to attend the World Book Fair in London.[67]

He also used the Oxford Union Library, at least while an undergraduate. The Union is the university's student debating society; its library focuses on politics, biography, and modern history, and members are allowed to make requests for new titles in an official "Librarian's Suggestion Book." Works of fiction requested in the period of Tolkien's undergraduate career and soon after included books by authors such as M.R. James, John Buchan, Rudyard Kipling, R.H. Benson, Max Beerbohm, and E.C. Bentley.[68] Unfortunately for our purposes, Tolkien did not make any requests in the surviving Suggestion Books, but we do know that he used the library, as a year after joining the Union he had racked up a substantial fine for overdue books.[69] Later in life, he was also a patron of the Oxford City Library.[70]†

Bearing in mind his wide range of interests, as well as his regular library use and book-buying habits, it should come as less of a surprise that Tolkien read many works of modern fiction, including both genre fiction and examples of more literary or experimental styles which might otherwise seem outside of his range of interests.

---

* It was such a large tab that Basil Blackwell offered to accept Tolkien's translation of *Pearl* as partial payment (TCG:C, 272). Blackwell's Bookshop does sell academic titles but is not specifically a university bookstore; Tolkien's purchases undoubtedly included books to read for pleasure.

† His favorable view of public libraries in general can be seen in a talk that he gave at the opening of a new library, at which he remarked, "The wealth of books to be found here is food for the mind, and everyone knows that for the stomach to go without food for a long time is bad, but for the mind to go without food is even worse." Quoted in "Deddington's New Library Opened by Mrs. L. Hichens – Prof. Tolkien's Whimsical Talk," *Banbury Advertiser*, 19 Dec. 1956, 5.

Indeed, we should note the sheer diversity of Tolkien's leisure reading. He enjoyed science fiction and fantasy and kept up to date with it, reading, for instance, T.H. White's *The Sword in the Stone* soon after its publication.[71] Historical fiction, not unexpectedly, was a genre he enjoyed; for instance, he praised the works of Mary Renault.[72] (See figure 37.) Tolkien's grandson Michael recollects that "he read detective fiction for relaxation" and "went out of his way to praise Agatha Christie."[73] (See figure 35.) He enjoyed the fiction of G.K. Chesterton, but not in the ways one might predict, disliking the detective stories featuring Father Brown, the Catholic priest, but greatly enjoying antic works such as *The Flying Inn*.[74] (See figure 13.)

Perhaps more unexpectedly, Tolkien read and enjoyed a wide range of literary fiction of a distinctly modern flavor. He read "all of Sinclair Lewis,"[75] the American realistic novelist, which he presumably would not have done if he had found the novels unappealing. (See figure 32.) He so enjoyed P.H. Newby's *The Picnic at Sakkara*, a satirical comedy set in modern-day Egypt, that he lost sleep so he could go on reading it.[76]* Some of his reactions might seem typical of a crusty medievalist reading modern literature, as when he describes William Golding's *The Lord of the Flies* as "dreary stuff."[77] In 1966, Tolkien remarked to an interviewer, "I suppose I'm a reactionary. The present mainstream of contemporary literature is so boring, isn't it? I'm offering a pleasant change of diet."[78]† But even this casual remark was not one of reflexive cantankerousness. His reference to "mainstream" means he is not making a judgment of all contemporary literature, and it was precisely because he had continued to read widely in contemporary literature that he was able to assess it and find it too monotonous, seeing that a "change of diet" was called for. As we will see, his creative imagination was stimulated by influence-by-opposition, such that his familiarity with a wide and varied range of modern literature, even (perhaps especially) when it provoked him, contributed to the development of his own, alternate literary vision.

❧ "The background of my imagination": Tolkien as a writer

Not only did Tolkien read modern literature with interest, but on various occasions he openly acknowledged the ways in which it shaped his creative imagination. For instance, he recalled that George MacDonald and Andrew Lang composed "the books which most affected the background of my imagination since childhood," and specifically named MacDonald as an influence on his goblins and orcs.[79] (See figure 8.)

---

* In this he shared the view of the literati of the day, for Evelyn Waugh praised Newby's book as "subtle and very funny" and J.B. Priestley called it "brilliantly done" (endorsements on the cover of *The Picnic at Sakkara* [New York: Alfred A. Knopf, 1955]).

† Given that this was in the midst of the 'Swinging Sixties,' one can also perhaps detect a note of mischievous relish in Tolkien's self-description. The work of this 'reactionary' was at that very time being enthusiastically embraced on American college campuses by the long-haired students of the Flower Power generation, and the Beatles wanted to make a film version of *The Lord of the Rings*, starring themselves (TCG:RG, 23).

He singled out E.A. Wyke-Smith's book *The Marvellous Land of Snergs* as something of a source-book for his invention of the hobbits and recalled that the 'wargs' scene in *The Hobbit* was "in part derived" from a story by S.R. Crockett.[80] (See figures 3 and 11.) In another letter, Tolkien says that the Dead Marshes and the approaches to the Morannon in *The Lord of the Rings* owe a debt to the imagination of William Morris.[81] (See figure 18.) What precisely Tolkien meant by this comparison is a subject of some disagreement, and we will return to this issue in chapter 7, but it is plain that he is registering a debt to a modern author, William Morris – who must be distinguished, by the way, from that other William Morris (later Lord Nuffield), whom he blamed for contributing to Oxford's modern ills.*

More generally, Tolkien pointed out to the science fiction and fantasy writer Gene Wolfe that names and words in *The Lord of the Rings* could be considered either from the point of view of "their etymology within the story" or in reference to "the sources from which I, as an author, derived them."[82] Given that Wolfe was a fellow author, Tolkien may have felt free to disclose to him, more readily than to random enthusiasts who sent him fan letters, that he did draw on outside sources for material.† He doesn't specify whether those sources are ancient, medieval, or modern, but we should not be surprised if they come from all three periods.

For Tolkien was indeed shaped by his modern reading (we shall define 'modern' in chapter 2). The 'leaf-mould' of his creative imagination was supplied with material by numerous authors, some now forgotten, others still known today, including H.G. Wells, James Joyce, E.R. Eddison, W.H. Auden, and P.G. Wodehouse. Tolkien was influenced by these writers both wittingly and – which is perhaps even more significant – unwittingly, by the very fact of reading their works in the first place and belonging to the same cultural milieu in which they appeared. Even where he rejected what he found in such writings, he was still a creature of his age, since to reject something is to be influenced by it.

Just as Tolkien's experience in the First World War shaped much of what appears in *The Lord of the Rings*,[83] albeit refracted through the prism of his medievally inflected imagination, the same can be said, so I will argue, about his experience of modern literature.

Conclusion

The picture of Tolkien as fundamentally backward-looking, happily living in total rejection of the modern world, must be abandoned. Though a great medievalist, Tolkien was not merely an antiquarian, and Middle-earth is indebted to more than just the Middle Ages. Indeed, for all his love of medieval writers, Tolkien was chary of being numbered

* William Morris, 1st Viscount Nuffield, was the manufacturer of some of the earliest automobiles in Britain. The expansion of his motor-car factories in Oxford had a significant effect on the character of the city (see TCG:C, 239).

† As Bond West points out, Tolkien could be reticent: "It does seem that a lot of things influenced him that he preferred not to acknowledge" ("Wisdom and Etymology in *The Lord of the Rings*").

among their ranks and did not admire their works uncritically. Charlotte and Denis Plimmer, in their interview with Tolkien, noted that

> He dislikes being bracketed with epic-writers of the past. C. S. Lewis once declared that Ariosto could not rival Tolkien. To us Tolkien said, "I don't know Ariosto and I'd loathe him if I did." He has also been likened to Malory, Spenser, Cervantes, Dante. He rejects them all.[84]

He rejected the bracketing partly because he disliked or did not know the authors concerned and partly because of innate humility about being measured against some of the greatest names of the Middle Ages and the early modern period.

In another interview, Daphne Castell asked a question that seemed certain to provoke an explosive reaction: "I asked him what he thought of Naomi Mitchison's description of his work as 'glorified science fiction.' He said he supposed it was valid, if she means that the pleasure of 'wonder' is also produced by good science fiction, and that this pleasure must be one of the aims of the author."[85] Tolkien's mild reaction suggests that he was entirely content to have his novel described as a form of science fiction. Thus, on the one hand, Tolkien – who spent a lifetime doing painstaking work on poems such as *Pearl* and *Sir Gawain and the Green Knight* – shows no particular interest in being classed among the medieval epic-writers, yet on the other hand is unruffled about being compared to science-fiction writers: a complex and unexpected response.

And indeed Tolkien was a complex man – brilliant, playful, learned, idiosyncratic, contrarian. Rayner Unwin looked back on a long friendship and recalled the many-faceted nature of both Tolkien's conversation and his personality: "He wore his learning very lightly and could be talked to on any subject . . . the origin of some place-name, a rare flower spotted in a nearby meadow, the barbarity of French cooking, or a crux that seemed to undermine the very order of his cosmogony."[86] When asked to write a memorial essay on Tolkien, Simonne d'Ardenne, who had known him for many years, first as a student and later as a colleague and friend, said that "Tolkien's personality was so rich, so diverse, so vast and so elusive, that I was quite at a loss to choose which aspect of it to study."[87] His grandson recalled that Tolkien "had the ability to carry on several conversations at once, debating the merits of a recipe, exploding wrong theories about a place name, telling anecdotes about an eccentric character and under his breath trying to solve a linguistic matter that had arisen unnoticed by anyone else."[88]

Like the man himself, Tolkien's creative work is richly complex, as the scholarship of the last few decades has shown. As we consider the materials upon which he drew to create his imaginative world, we must not forget the vast – almost impossibly vast – scope of that project: "I had a mind to make a body of more or less connected legend, ranging from the large and cosmogonic, to the level of romantic fairy-story." The task Tolkien had set for himself was "to restore to the English an epic tradition and present them with a mythology of their own," adding that "it is a wonderful thing to be told that I have succeeded."[89]

Could such a task as composing a new mythology for England even have been envisioned with the idea of using only medieval materials? Would Tolkien's wide-ranging interests have been satisfied with reading only pre-Chaucerian works? It seems unlikely, even on the face of it and even before we turn to the evidence that will comprise the rest of this study. We ought, in fact, to *expect* a good deal of involvement with modern literature, given his omnivorous mind. His Olympian literary ambition could not have been achieved to his satisfaction by the simple recapitulation of medieval stories, however skillfully it was done. And his lively and capacious imagination, though deeply nourished by the old tales, sought out new ones as well.

Tolkien loved trees from his earliest days and loved to talk of his life's work as a 'Tree of Tales.' His fundamentally autobiographical story "Leaf by Niggle" features a painter who, inspired by a single leaf, envisions a masterpiece, a tree which becomes more complex and elaborate as he paints it, though he is never able to finish it in his lifetime – but which he discovers, after death, to be truly real and alive, and which, in his time in purgatory, he can further develop and refine. Tolkien brought into being countless leaves of his own, but he also perused innumerable leaves created by other writers, and his repeated use of the image of 'leaf-mould' as the material nourishing his creativity will be important for us to keep in mind as we make our way through the following chapters. Many and varied leaves from the woods and forests of British and American literature became part of that mulch: page after page, volume after volume, layer upon layer, eventually breaking down into the brown, fertile compost that (though unremarkable and easily overlooked in itself) provided him with the nutrients that he could draw up into new stories. It is our task in this study to look at the pages of the more modern trees that we know him to have surveyed and discern what contribution they may have made to his creative imagination.

2

The Scope of This Study
Beating the Bounds

THE FOCUS OF THIS STUDY IS TOLKIEN'S MODERN READING, BUT, AS Treebeard would caution us, we should not be hasty! Before proceeding any further, we must clarify our terms. What do we mean by 'modern' and what do we mean by 'reading'? In other words, what are the chronological and generic boundaries of our investigation? Lastly, what do we mean by 'sources' and 'influences,' and how do we justify looking for such things when Tolkien is alleged to have been impervious to influence and himself seemed to reject source-study? In this chapter, we will take each of these questions in turn.

Mapping out our journey

For those readers who wish to advance immediately to the exploration of Tolkien's reading that begins in chapter 3, I will sketch out the boundaries of our study as follows: by 'Tolkien's modern reading,' I mean works of fiction, poetry, and drama published after 1850, in English, that we know for certain Tolkien read, considering only their possible role as sources for and influences upon his Middle-earth writings, not their bearing on his other publications. For those with a more Entish approach, we will now proceed to define our terms more precisely and explain the rationale behind each of the self-imposed limitations just mentioned.

What's so special about 1850?

I take 'modern reading' to denote Tolkien's reading of works published from 1850 onwards. Modernity, of course, did not begin either in 1850 or in any other particular year, but some sort of cut-off point is necessary. In focusing on the mid-nineteenth century as the approximate starting-point of modern literature, I am following the lead of C.S. Lewis who, in his *De Descriptione Temporum*" (on the defining of ages), argues that modernity took root at some point in the decades following the deaths of Jane Austen (1817) and Sir Walter Scott (1832).[1]

1850 seems like a useful round number to settle upon. William Wordsworth, the longest-lived of the Lake Poets, died that year, in a sense closing the Romantic period.

The great novels of the 1840s (*Jane Eyre, Wuthering Heights, Vanity Fair, Dombey and Son*) had firmly established the novel as the dominant genre of the Victorian age. The publication in 1849 of Tennyson's *In Memoriam* was helping to set the somber, morally serious tone of the era, a tone that would deepen with Prince Albert's death (1861) and the Queen's subsequent decision to wear black for the rest of her life. The industrial revolution and 'railway fever' were well underway by mid-century: the 'rise of the machine,' which Tolkien would come to interrogate so fiercely, was now unstoppable. More positively, as far as Tolkien was concerned, John Henry Newman had converted in 1845, and by 1850 the Catholic hierarchy had been restored to England and Wales.

1850 is also convenient in that it marks works that were modern *for Tolkien*: books published no more than a few decades ahead of his birth in 1892. Tolkien himself used the word "modern" to refer to fairy-stories "that were written or re-written in my lifetime, or were still new enough to be books natural to give as presents when I was a child."[2] What felt recent and contemporary for Tolkien, as he grew and became a reader, would, I think, have been a somewhat wider range of material than would feel up-to-date for us in the faster-paced twenty-first century.

By choosing 1850 we will naturally just miss considering a number of authors whom we know Tolkien did read, some of them possibly quite important to his creative project. For instance, we will necessarily omit Sir Walter Scott, whom Tolkien cites as a user of the term 'Middle-earth,'[3] and Thomas Macauley, whose *Lays of Ancient Rome* (1842) Tolkien parodied as a schoolboy.[4] We must also pass over other figures whose work he knew, including Blake, Keats, Shelley, Coleridge,[5] and the aforementioned Wordsworth[6] and Austen.[7] And, of course, as we cast a wistful eye further back, we will be reminded of yet more literature that falls in between the medieval and the modern, with which Tolkien was acquainted; for instance, his grandson Michael recalled that "He always thought highly of Jonathan Swift."[8] But these periods are subjects for other studies.

Keeping things fictional (and English)

We will attend only to works of fiction, poetry, and drama, written in the English language. The decision to impose these limitations on my chosen territory is a practical one, intended to keep the material within manageable bounds, though even within these parameters, I expect there will be things I have overlooked.

An investigation of Tolkien's reading of modern nonfiction would certainly be a worthwhile task. To give just a few examples of what we will *not* be examining: he was familiar with *Birds of the British Isles* by T.A. Coward (1919), which he used for guidance when painting the Eagles' eyrie in *The Hobbit*, and with E.V. Gordon's *An Introduction to Old Norse* (1927), which influenced his illustration of Beorn's hall.[9] Aside from these examples where a clear impact on the legendarium can be traced, we could note, for instance, that he read the *Letters* of the Scottish essayist John Brown (1907), knew Christopher Dawson's book *Progress and Religion* (1929), was deeply moved by R.W. Chambers's biography of Sir Thomas More (1935, the year of More's canonization), and enjoyed Dennis Bennett's account of the Pentecostal movement in the Episcopal Church of the United States, *Nine O'Clock in the Morning* (1970). Tolkien found Bennett's book "very interesting both as a Christian and a lover of languages," no doubt because of its attention to glossolalia ("speaking in tongues").[10] And speaking of tongues, his knowledge of modern literature in languages other than English would also, of course, be a topic well worth pursuing,[11] but works in foreign tongues, no less than works of nonfiction, are beyond the scope of this study.

Books, not people

In the opening chapter, I acknowledged that 'Tolkien's modern reading' included, in a peripheral fashion, his reading of modern culture and society in general. However, I should make it clear that, when it comes to a consideration of influences upon his creation of Middle-earth, I am considering only literary and artistic works and will not be including the role of personal interactions or life experiences.* Tolkien's involvement with the T.C.B.S., the literary society he formed with friends at King Edward's School, undoubtedly had a profound influence on his creative endeavors, but I refer the reader to John Garth's *Tolkien and the Great War* for the definitive account of those interactions. Tolkien's friendship with C.S. Lewis, whose encouragement helped him to complete *The Lord of the Rings*, likewise had a crucial role in his central literary achievement, but I direct the reader to Diana Glyer's *The Company They Keep* for a finely detailed examination of the impact that Lewis and the Inklings had upon Tolkien.

Tolkien's friendships, family relationships, and literary and professional interactions all undoubtedly contributed to the genesis and shaping of his creative work, and are a fruitful and interesting area for study, but not one within the scope of this volume.

Within the bounds of Middle-earth

Lastly, I will note one more boundary: in considering the way that Tolkien's reading shaped his creative output, I am attending only to his Middle-earth writings, those works that in Tolkien scholarship are often referred to as the 'legendarium.' The legendarium comprises *The Hobbit*, *The Lord of the Rings*, and the extensive writings, unpublished in Tolkien's lifetime, which he thought of as 'the Silmarillion' and parts of which were brought out by his son, Christopher, as *The Silmarillion* (1977). Most of the rest appears in *Unfinished Tales*, the twelve volumes of *The History of Middle-earth*, and in the more accessible subsidiary volumes *The Children of Húrin*, *Beren and Lúthien*, and *The Fall of Gondolin*. In this study, we will focus mainly on *The Hobbit* and *The Lord of the Rings* as being those works of Tolkien's that were both published during his lifetime, and the source of his fame. His poetry we will consider only when it is incorporated into the

---

* I have allowed myself the leeway of occasionally referencing such material in the footnotes.

prose works of the legendarium. In the interests of keeping this study focused, we will not discuss works outside the legendarium (such as *Smith of Wootton Major*, "Leaf by Niggle," and so on), despite their great merit as stories.

⅍ Erring on the side of caution

Now that we have established our definition of 'modern,' and determined our generic boundaries, we should pause to consider other necessary parameters for this study. The most crucial of these is what we mean by 'Tolkien's reading,' as obvious as that may seem at first glance. I will be examining only those texts which we can be *certain* that Tolkien read. We will ignore the will-o'-the-wisp call of works that he *probably* read because of his professional work or interests, or *possibly* read because of apparent thematic parallels with his own work, or *conceivably might have* read given his cultural milieu and social setting. For instance, though I agree with John Garth that "given his tastes, Tolkien can hardly have missed Jules Verne's 1864 science-fiction classic *Journey to the Centre of the Earth*,"* and though I readily acknowledge that the various parallels Mark T. Hooker discerns between Verne's book and *The Hobbit*[12] are not implausible, such probabilities and apparent similarities do not constitute rock-solid evidence. I shall therefore not be expending time and effort exploring them; the risk of seeing faces in the fire is too great.†

Where, then, do we turn for evidence of Tolkien's modern reading? It comes from a range of sources: Tolkien's own writings, published and unpublished; interviews with him; accounts by family, friends, colleagues, and students; biographical studies; and finally, material in Christina Scull and Wayne G. Hammond's magisterial *J.R.R. Tolkien Companion and Guide* (revised 2017 edition). The *Companion and Guide* is accepted as the gold standard for factual information about Tolkien, with extensive direct quotes from unpublished works. I have considered even its paraphrased and summary information as very nearly equal in authority to a primary source.

Usually the evidence for Tolkien's reading consists of his own recorded comments on or references to the work in question. Sometimes a character name, phrase, or other reference by Tolkien can alert us to his knowledge of a work that he does not positively identify. However, care must be exercised when dealing with allusions. For instance, although Tolkien refers on several occasions to Jekyll and Hyde, I do not believe we can

---

* We will explore Tolkien's interest in science fiction in general, and subterranean journeys in particular, in chapter 9.

† A remarkable example of *quellenforschung* run amok appears in Susan Wendling and Woody Wendling's "A Speculative Meditation on Tolkien's Sources for the Character Gollum." They suggest that Gollum's precursors include Goliath; Golliwogs; the Jewish folklore figure of the golem; and the word Golgotha (because Gollum cries out "thief, thief" and Jesus was crucified between two thieves). They even argue that a "certain source for Gollum was the Christian Gospel, as expressed by the frequent appeals for mercy in the Catholic Mass. . . . One can even make a merciful acronym from Gollum's name: <u>GO</u>D <u>L</u>oves <u>U</u>(You) <u>M</u>ercifully!" (5). One can, yes; but one ought not.

take this as definitively establishing that he had read Stevenson's novel (though it is probable that he did so), because the Jekyll-Hyde dichotomy has become a commonplace. Here the critic must make a judgment call on each individual allusion. Other scholars may assess the probabilities differently, but I will err on the side of caution. Furthermore, I have never, at any point, taken as evidence any literary parallel, resemblance, or apparent borrowing, no matter how convincing it appears.*

Sometimes, the evidence is provided by direct statements about Tolkien's reading from those who knew him. Occasionally, it rests upon the mere fact of his ownership of a text. I readily acknowledge that owning a book is not exactly the same thing as reading a book, but it does at least indicate that Tolkien knew of its existence, had handled it, and believed it deserved space in his personal library. But these occasions are rare and very little of this study will rest on them.

I will be similarly cautious in drawing conclusions from Tolkien's professional life as an academic. For instance, his role as an external examiner (such as for the Catholic University of Ireland, the University of London, Manchester University, and others) and in developing programs of study (such as for military cadets or for prisoners of war†) does not mean that he would necessarily have read every book on the associated reading lists. In assisting with this work, he would have drawn on a general knowledge of literary history, published reviews, and the recommendations of his colleagues, not just on his personal familiarity with the texts in question.‡

Likewise, Tolkien's entries for the Oxford English Dictionary, despite containing illustrative quotations from literary works, tell us nothing about his personal reading. Peter Gilliver, himself a lexicographer at the OED, explains that, in preparing their entries, the assistants did not supply their own quotations, but rather drew upon a large supply sent in by readers, which had been written out on slips and alphabetized by keyword. Gilliver notes that the stock of quotation slips "had been accumulating for many years by the time an assistant came to work on it (over sixty years in the case of Tolkien's part of the letter W)."[13] Since all the entries were subject to revision by the Editor, who might have ended up choosing different illustrative quotations, we cannot even be certain that

---

* For instance, Mark T. Hooker observes that "There are so many parallels . . . between *Midwinter*, *The Blanket of the Dark* and *Huntingtower* on the one hand and *The Lord of the Rings* and *The Hobbit* on the other that the probability of their all occurring by pure chance is vanishingly small. It is far more likely that these three novels were among the stories of John Buchan that Tolkien liked and read" ("Reading John Buchan in Search of Tolkien," 189). I agree: it is highly likely. Indeed, titles such as these merit serious analysis. But it is not *certain* that Tolkien read them, and therefore we must handle them differently than true 'certains.'

† In 1941, Tolkien and C.S. Lewis compiled an English literature course, including examinations, for prisoners of war in Germany, through the Educational Books Section of the Prisoners of War Department (see chapter III and appendices of *Adversus Major: A Short History of the Educational Books Scheme of the Prisoners of War Department*, compiled by Robert W. Holland).

‡ Scull and Hammond note that Tolkien submitted plans for an English course for military cadets "after consultation with tutors" – tutors being the Oxford term for the instructors of the course (TCG:C, 276).

Tolkien himself selected any given sample sentence. On the other hand, Tolkien's own contributions to the general quotation fund are genuine evidence of his reading, but unfortunately only one survives: a slip from Lewis Carroll's *Sylvie and Bruno Concluded*.[14]

In the previous chapter, I noted how important it is not to merge Tolkien with his friend Lewis. The same can be said of the other Inklings and of his social circle more generally. The tastes and reading habits of his friends and acquaintances are not to be identified with his own. The fact that they can be shown to have read a particular work proves nothing about Tolkien's reading. Likewise, thematic or stylistic parallels between his writings and another work are not in themselves evidence that Tolkien knew the title in question, though, of course, they might provide corroboration or confirmation if we have other reasons to believe he was familiar with a given work.[15]

Finally, we cannot automatically assume that just because Tolkien read one book by an author, he therefore read other titles by that same author. However, there are some cases where such an assumption would be fair. For instance, if Tolkien read books from a series, it is likely that his knowledge of later titles indicates familiarity with earlier ones. As an example, since Tolkien read Olaf Stapledon's *Last Men in London*, which is the sequel to *Last and First Men*, it is reasonable to believe that Tolkien knew the first book in addition to the second. Here, I tread warily and always indicate the levels of probability involved in drawing any conclusion. 'Probables,' though often worth consideration, are not my target in this book. I am interested only in 'certains,' and in this study I have discussed only those texts that I am sure Tolkien knew. Occasionally, I have allowed myself a little speculation in the footnotes, where it is always clearly marked as such. The imaginative reconstruction featured in the prelude also involves some surmises, though it is based on careful research.* In general, my guiding principle has been to err on the side of caution.

This caution means excluding some authors who are so probable as to be *almost* certain. It is impossible to believe, for instance, that Tolkien was not acquainted with the writings of John Henry Newman, although to date, very surprisingly, we have not found direct evidence of his personal familiarity with the works of that great Victorian churchman. The indirect evidence is, however, suggestive. As a boy, Tolkien attended and served at Mass in the Birmingham Oratory, as was sketched in the prelude (see above). The Birmingham Oratory was founded by Newman and there Tolkien would have sung many of Newman's hymns, such as "Lead, Kindly Light" and "Firmly I Believe,

---

* The prelude is drawn from, among other things: biographical material on Tolkien; research in the Historic England archives; historic photographs of Beaufort Road; the findings of this study; my exploration of the Edgbaston/Ladywood area on foot; and the helpful advice of Fr. Guy Nicholls of the Birmingham Oratory. Mrs. Warner and her words are from Norman Power, "Tolkien's Walk." Details of Shorthouse's fame and habits are drawn from his obituary in *The New York Times*, *The Life and Letters of J.H. Shorthouse, edited by his wife* (1905), and other sources. The words from the liturgy of the Mass come from the Tridentine Rite. Details of the Oratory and Mass times are from *Cardinal Newman and the Church of the Birmingham Oratory: A History and a Guide* (1934). The prelude is imagined as taking place on November 14, 1909.

and Truly." No doubt he would also have heard recollections of the great man from his guardian, Fr. Francis Morgan, who had been Newman's personal secretary.[16] Norman Power points out that Tolkien must, at the very least, "have seen the manuscript of *The Dream of Gerontius* open at the page showing that fine hymn and poem, 'Praise to the Holiest in the Height.'" Simon Stacey suggests that the Old Took, Gerontius, in *The Hobbit*, is a nod to this poem. As Gerontius "is the only identifiable male hobbit name of classical origin," Stacey suggests that the echo of Newman's eponymous protagonist "is unlikely . . . to be an accident."[17]

In adulthood, Tolkien was involved both with the Newman Society in Oxford and with the national Newman Association. The latter group invited Catholic university professors to serve as Honorary Vice-Presidents, and the Annual General Meeting reports and minutes show that Tolkien accepted this invitation at least once between 1942 and 1947, and then continuously from 1949 through 1955. He was also involved to some extent in the Oxford Circle of the Newman Association, as the 1955–1956 report names Tolkien as one of three speakers in a "Brains Trust" question-and-answer event for the local group.[18]

On the basis of all this, it is what racegoers would call "a dead cert" that he read at least some of Newman's work – but, remarkably, we do not at present have solid, provable evidence of his familiarity with particular titles. And since a dead cert is not quite the same thing as a certainty, Newman escapes our net and must stand as a reminder that what we know of Tolkien's modern reading is only a fraction of the whole.

❧ "A Source gives us things to write about; an Influence prompts us to write in a certain way."

Having delimited our field of study, we turn now to considering how we will approach the material that falls within its bounds. All of Tolkien's reading contributed in some way to the formation of his creative imagination, if only as part of the fully-digested humus of his literary leaf-mould, but the contributions are not all of the same sort. Some can be considered sources, some influences.

C.S. Lewis distinguishes the two terms helpfully with the following definition: "A Source gives us things to write about; an Influence prompts us to write in a certain way."[19] Sources provide content or substance, be it a character, a plot, a theme, an image. Influences affect manner or form, the style in which an author approaches his work or the shape he gives it. There is no sharp dividing line between a source and an influence, but if we associate a source with *what* an author writes and an influence with *how* an author writes, we will not go far wrong.

As we consider the modern works that Tolkien read, we will see that some of them can properly be described as 'sources' for his own writings. We find Tolkien using this term himself when he calls E.A. Wyke-Smith's *The Marvellous Land of Snergs* "an unconscious source-book"[20] – an interesting turn of phrase, as it shows that he was aware that his imagination absorbed and used what he read on a level that was recognizable later, but not necessarily conscious at the time.* In an interview he remarked, "I've never hardly got through any fairy-stories without wanting to write one myself."[21] As we will find in the course of this study, even a single striking name or word from an otherwise unmemorable book might spark invention.

Some of Tolkien's reading served as an influence rather than a source. We will see in chapter 6 that William Morris was significant in this regard; as early as 1914 Tolkien had gotten from Morris the idea of writing a prose tale with interpolated verses. And as we will discuss in chapter 9, Tolkien undertook to write a time-travel story in part because of his wish to see more books of that sort. He enjoyed science fiction novels and they provided an impetus for him to write something of his own in like manner.

Other books provide influence-by-opposition, supplying examples of things to avoid or work against in his own writing. As Tolkien himself said, it "often happens" that a story is "the result of an irritant" – and that "the irritant will in some degree affect the presentation of the movement in the mind that it sets going"[22] – as he noted in explaining how *Smith of Wootton Major* was a reaction against George MacDonald's "The Golden Key." In more general terms, Tolkien's growing dislike of the didactic authorial voice of the Victorian fantasists shaped his revision of *The Hobbit*. Claims of influence-by-opposition are, of necessity, sometimes arguments from absence, but this does not necessarily disprove them. After all, we can gain an idea of a person's movements on a beach by the absence, as well as the presence, of footprints in the sand. We must not make over-bold assertions but, if we are careful, attending to this type of 'anti-source' can yield deeper insight into Tolkien's work.

Some authors and works are named by Tolkien as having had a particular effect on his writings. Others can be discerned to have had an effect, or can at least be argued to have had an effect, even without Tolkien specifically naming them for us. In one sense, all that Tolkien read was an influence upon him, if only in that it helped to shape his likes and dislikes, to show him what had already been done, and to suggest possibilities for new approaches.

❧ The legendary bandersnatch

If we are to consider the possibility that some of Tolkien's modern reading became source material or influences for Middle-earth, we must address a number of very reasonable objections.

First of all, wasn't he un-influenceable? It seems to be part of the conventional wisdom about Tolkien that he was so. Diana Glyer notes that as she investigated the interactions of the Inklings, "The claim I found most frequently was that no one had any

---

* Tolkien evidently had a positive view of this unconscious assimilation. He once "advised his audience that everything they read might eventually be of use to them. He had read pages which he had thought he had forgotten, and yet at the oddest times, the information which those pages had contained had proved of use to him." (Quoted in "Deddington's New Library Opened by Mrs. L. Hichens – Prof. Tolkien's Whimsical Talk," *Banbury Advertiser*, December 19, 1956, 5.)

influence on J.R.R. Tolkien." She cites a whole list of scholars who come to the same conclusion: "Carpenter, Knight, Hillegas, Carter, Rateliff, Frederick, McBride and others" all agreed that Tolkien was uninfluenceable. As Glyer concludes, and indeed as I have seen as well, the most often cited basis for this claim is Lewis's now-famous remark: "No-one ever influenced Tolkien – you might as well try to influence a bandersnatch."[23] *

So Lewis says; but is it true? Admittedly, in one interview Tolkien recalled, "After someone had criticized me I just went on my own sweet way and took no notice of it."[24] But although hostile criticism seems to have caused Tolkien to dig in his heels, he appears to have responded more flexibly to constructive criticism. In another interview, acknowledging how Lewis had considered him un-influenceable, he commented, "But that wasn't quite true. Whenever he said 'You can do better than that. Better Tolkien, please!' I used to try."[25] Lewis's label has, as it were, gone viral, while Tolkien's response of "that wasn't quite true" seems to have been largely overlooked. We have already noted the dangers of treating Lewis and Tolkien as literary twins; it seems that one such danger is that an offhand remark by Lewis has carried undue weight.

That weight was multiplied by Humphrey Carpenter, who not only quoted Lewis's remark in the *Biography*, but reinforced the idea of a Tolkien who was resistant to literary influence. For instance, Carpenter concedes that the style of "The Fall of Gondolin" "suggests that Tolkien was influenced by William Morris" but adds that any apparent similarities are "only superficial 'influences': Tolkien used no models or sources for his strange and exciting tale."[26] Even apart from the strange assumption that "style" is a "superficial" element of a tale, Carpenter gives the impression that Morris had a negligible impact – which was certainly not the case. When the *Letters* were published a few years later, we find, in the very first letter in the book, Tolkien telling Edith that he is writing "a short story somewhat on the lines of Morris' romances with chunks of poetry in between"[27] – in short, using Morris as a model. Regarding the story of the "Children of Húrin," Carpenter writes that "Again one may detect certain literary influences: the hero's fight with a great dragon inevitably suggests comparison with the deeds of Sigurd and Beowulf, while his unknowing incest with his sister and his subsequent suicide were derived quite consciously from the story of Kullervo in the *Kalevala*. But again these 'influences' are only superficial."[28]

'Again . . . again'; "superficial influences"; "no models or influences"; "only superficial." Carpenter is very definite in his statements, but it is all interpretation on his part, and indeed often counter to the evidence. In her edition of Tolkien's *Story of Kullervo*, Verlyn Flieger points out that Carpenter's judgment of the *Kalevala* connection as superficial "is quite off the mark."[29] Indeed, if Carpenter sees an element "derived quite consciously" from the *Kalevala* as a "superficial" influence, we might well ask what could possibly constitute a nonsuperficial one!

---

* George Sayer remarks that Lewis's observation was "largely true." However, in the passage that follows it is clear that Sayer is referring to personal or moral influences, not literary ones ("Recollections of J.R.R. Tolkien," 14).

Even when Carpenter quotes Tolkien directly on this topic, the frequent lack of context can have a distorting effect. Consider the famous statement by Tolkien about Wagner's Ring. Carpenter records that the "comparison of his Ring with the Nibelungenlied and Wagner always annoyed Tolkien: he once said: 'Both rings were round, and there the resemblance ceased.'"[30] This pithy statement is often used as an illustration of Tolkien's rejection of all source claims and disdain for modern culture in general. The only other reference to Wagner in the *Biography* is Carpenter's remark that Tolkien, as a schoolboy, made a "passing jibe" at Wagner, "whose interpretation of the myths he held in contempt."[31] Tolkien's tastes evidently changed as he matured, and Carpenter neglects to mention that in 1934 he met regularly with the Lewis brothers to read Wagner's Ring Cycle. A single, colorful quote shared by Carpenter has once again had an outsized effect, leading many readers (and not a few scholars) to assume that there is no point in considering any possible relationship between the works of Wagner and Tolkien.[32]

But let us return to C.S. Lewis's claim that no one ever influenced Tolkien: even if Carpenter is unreliable, surely in Lewis we have a friendly and trustworthy source? Let us examine his remark a little more closely. He is commenting on the relations of the Inklings as a whole:

> Charles Williams certainly influenced me, and I perhaps influenced him. But after that I think you would draw a blank. No one ever influenced Tolkien – you might as well try to influence a bandersnatch. We listened to his work, but could affect it only by encouragement. He has only two reactions to criticism: either he begins the whole work over again from the beginning or else takes no notice at all.[33]

Lewis is corresponding with Charles Moorman, who was at that time writing a book on connections among what he would call the "Oxford Christians."[34] Lewis is skeptical of Moorman's project; the attempt to find a common mind among the Inklings is, he thinks, "chasing after a fox that isn't there."[35] It is not surprising, then, that he deliberately downplays the idea of mutual influence: he wishes to discourage Moorman from viewing the group as a sort of hive or cabal. Even so, his statement that Tolkien was affected "only by encouragement" is quite a concession, for 'encouragement' is undoubtedly a form of influence, though admittedly of a personal rather than a strictly literary kind, and therefore outside the scope of this study.

As regards the literary influence of Lewis upon Tolkien, we will examine that below in chapter 4 and chapter 9. And there we will see that Lewis's perception of Tolkien's immunity to influence is just that: a perception, not a comprehensive statement of fact. Later critics have incorrectly taken it as an accurate and precise description of Tolkien's lack of malleability, failing to note Lewis's own caveat: "Of course it may be that, just because I was in it myself, I don't see (objectively) what was really going on."[36]

❧ From the horse's mouth?

Another objection that we have to consider is this: did not Tolkien himself disparage those who tried to search out the sources of and influences on his work? What did Tolkien himself have to say about those who claimed to have found his imaginative origins? Very little, as it happens. To be sure, he promptly corrected spurious or erroneous claims. For instance, Arne Zettersten recalls bringing to his attention an article stating "that Tolkien had been influenced by the American author James Branch Cabell. . . . Tolkien wrote back to me and denied forcefully that this was true." Later, he clarified his point to Zettersten, admitting "that he knew Cabell well, but that he had read only one of his books and that it was 'quite boring.'"[37] Responding to Richard A. Lupoff's suggestion that Edgar Rice Burroughs's adventure novels were a source for *The Lord of the Rings*, Tolkien wrote, "Spiders I had met long before Burroughs began to write and I do not think he is in any way responsible for Shelob."[38] Fair enough; and in context his remark to Lupoff that "Source hunting is a great entertainment but I do not myself think it is particularly useful,"[39] seems less a general statement about sources and more a polite discouragement of this particular writer's over-enthusiastic making of connections.

Referring to Charles Williams, Tolkien said, "I do not think we influenced one another at all! Too 'set,' and too different," and speaking of E.R. Eddison, he declared that "he was certainly not an 'influence.'"[40] But in both cases Tolkien had reason to resist being pigeonholed, in the manner of Charles Moorman, as a member of an Inklings 'circle' or 'group mind.'[41] Tolkien was already aware that his Oxford colleagues would have preferred he spend more of his time on academic writing; being labeled as part of a coterie of fantasy writers would not improve his professional relationships or wider scholarly reputation. With regard to Eddison, who attended a couple of Inklings meetings in the 1940s, Tolkien may also have wanted to squash any perceived parallels between the moral underpinnings of his and Eddison's work, for he viewed Eddison's philosophy as seriously questionable, even corrupt. He may have had similar concerns regarding Charles Williams. (We will return to these authors in chapter 9.) We should not assume that these comments tell the whole story about his reading of their work or its possible influence on him.

Tolkien's remarks on Williams and Eddison are, as it happens, the *only* explicit rejections of influence that we find in the *Letters*. Other apparent denials of influence take on a different appearance when placed in context. For example, when asked to name a book that influenced him as a teenager, Tolkien wrote "I can name no book that influenced me deeply as a book," but then immediately added, "I found certain elements in books that I liked and stored away in memory."[42]

The closest we can get to a wholesale denial of influence is in Tolkien's 1953 letter to Robert Murray: "Certainly I have not been nourished by English Literature. . . . I have never found much there in which to rest my heart (or heart and head together)." We should note the context: Murray, then studying to become a Catholic priest, had perceptively noted a resemblance between Galadriel and the Virgin Mary. Tolkien comments on this Marian connection, and says that he is grateful for his upbringing "in a Faith that has nourished me and taught me all the little that I know"; it is immediately following this observation that he makes the point about English literature. He then adds that he "was brought up in the Classics, and first discovered the sensation of literary pleasure in Homer."[43] We should note that here he is speaking of spiritual, personal nourishment, and of early influences on his aesthetic sense; his remark has nothing directly to do with the question of literary influence on his own imaginative works, let alone influence from specifically modern English literature. We tend to read such a statement as a denial of influence largely because we are conditioned to assume that denying influence is what Tolkien does.* Once the enchantment is dispelled, as it were, and we look at the evidence objectively, a less stark picture emerges. We will begin to be able to see that Tolkien was sometimes willing to concede examples of influence on his own work. For instance, he named specific, direct influences from George Dasent and Algernon Blackwood on *The Lord of the Rings* (see chapters 3 and 10). There are several other debts to his modern reading that he either openly acknowledged or implicitly indicated, as we shall discover.

Tolkien knew that hunting down the sources of his own creativity could be done heavy-handedly. This, I would suggest, is what he had in mind when he wrote in a 1972 letter, "I fear . . . that the search for the sources of *The Lord of the Rings* is going to occupy academics for a generation or two. I wish this need not be so."[44]

And it is not only Tolkien who wished that "this need not be so." Rachel Falconer, for instance, is skeptical of the value of much Tolkien criticism, objecting to the way that "stray remarks" and evidence "scraped together"[45] from his letters, writings, and interviews is used to reveal something supposedly important about the man and his works. Falconer suggests that the search for sources is "ultimately unsatisfying because, after we have sounded out the echo of Gollum's name in a Rider Haggard novel, where does it leave us? Not much closer to the mystery of origins, because in looking for signs of Tolkien in his predecessors, that is exactly what we will find."[46] There is a grain of truth to this complaint. If we assume that literary invention is mechanistic and that tracing sources is like solving a math problem, then looking at Tolkien's sources will only disappoint us and leave us nonplussed. As John Garth points out, Tolkien might have encountered the word 'hobbit' in the folklore collection *The Denham Tract*, or "he may have come across *hobbit* as an obsolete unit of measurement or an old word for howitzer; but even if he did, such things suggests little of what *hobbit* now means to us."[47] Such links would be inconsequential, illuminating nothing of substance in Tolkien's work.

---

* For instance, Paul Tankard writes, "Tolkien claimed that he . . . was subject to little by way of influence from contemporary artistic movements. But it is also true that he liked putting critics off the scent of influences." No citations are provided; evidently Tankard considers this to be common knowledge ("An Art to Depict 'the Noble and Heroic': Tolkien on Adaptation, Illustration, and the Art of Mary Fairburn," 34).

But literary criticism does not have to work this way, if we always recall the goal we have in view: that we are trying to understand a mind, not strip-search a text, let alone a particular term within a text. We are not seeking to crack riddles but to plumb the depths of imagination. We should remember how very organic Tolkien's image of his own creativity was: he pictured it as a tree, grounded in rich soil and simultaneously deepening and rising, expanding its root system while enlarging its leaf canopy, always complexifying while remaining at one with itself.

Guided by this understanding of the creative imagination, we need not fear that our study will be reductive. As Trevor Hart observes, a thoughtful study of Tolkien's sources and influences, far from undermining a sense of his originality, "simply serves to underline the remarkable contribution that his re-imagining of them made to literature."[48] And as for the smallness of some of the details that we will be assembling in this study, we should recall both Tolkien's fascination for individual leaves on his tree of tales and his observation that "My stories germinate like a snowflake around a piece of dust."[49] We will not be taking our investigation down to the level of dust particles, but we will sometimes be attending to what Falconer might consider minutiae. And we do so unembarrassedly because our *modus operandi* is not, we trust, reductive, but productive. We aim not simply to unearth origins, delving exclusively *back* into the literary past; we aim rather continually to be moving both back and forth – now backward to what Tolkien read, now forward to the effects that his reading may have had. And those effects are to be discerned not just in his legendarium, but in our own understanding of the man and the workings of his imagination.

"A perfectly legitimate procedure"

As we draw this chapter to a close, let us spend a little time examining a third objection, which relates to the question of source-hunting more generally. We have just surveyed what Tolkien had to say about readers and scholars trying to feel out the foundations of his own works, but what did he have to say about this literary-critical undertaking in principle?

In "On Fairy-stories," Tolkien favorably quotes the folklore scholar Dasent to the effect that we "must be satisfied with the soup that is set before us, and not desire to see the bones of the ox out of which it has been boiled," explaining that by 'soup' he means the tale as we find it, and by 'bones' its sources.[50] But this remark should not be taken as a definitive and universal principle. We have already seen that Tolkien's views are often more subtle and layered than isolated quotes, interpreted by the conventional wisdom about his personality and preferences, would indicate. We will be better able to understand his objections to source-hunting if we bear in mind both the context of his remarks and his habit, as Tom Shippey has noted, "of exaggerating in order to make a particular point."[51]

Tolkien did have a justifiable dislike of reductive *quellenforschung* (source-hunting); he certainly rejected the idea that identifying the sources of a tale revealed everything worth knowing about it. It is, he said, "precisely the colouring, the atmosphere, the unclassifiable individual details of a story, and above all the general purport that informs with life the undissected bones of the plot, that really count." He is willing to concede that the study of sources is a "perfectly legitimate procedure in itself," as long as the critic is not led to strange or misleading conclusions by "ignorance or forgetfulness of the nature of a story (as a thing told in its entirety)." We should also note that his "soup" remark refers to the analysis of the origins of folktales, a study that is made more difficult by the antiquity and anonymity of the tales; it is only by "rare luck," he points out, that their sources can be discovered. It is not surprising, then, that he should emphasize the value of analyzing "the soup as soup" rather than only searching for its ingredients.[52] It was this aspect of folklore studies that needed bolstering in his day.

We can see, then, that he resisted an approach to literary studies that sidelined the story as story.* The reader's experience was of pre-eminent importance for him. As Fisher has observed, Tolkien was "concerned that readers who became too absorbed with source-hunting could not possibly be enjoying his novels as self-contained *objets d'art*."[53] Simplistic source-spotting rightly annoyed him, and was, he thought, a symptom of a larger problem with how literature was taught in the modern era, an approach in which "so often it is thought and taught that enjoyment is an illiterate reaction."[54] As he observed in a 1966 interview, students were now being discouraged from enjoying stories, and taught instead merely to analyze and dissect them: "It seems to me comparable to a man who having eaten anything, from a salad to a complete and well-planned dinner, uses an emetic and sends the results for chemical analysis."[55] His objection, and a prescient one, was that an overly analytical or exclusively deconstructive approach could kill the joy of reading.

He is quite right in his objection, as a corrective to a certain narrow-minded approach to literary criticism. But as an enthusiastic reader of Agatha Christie's mystery novels, he would have admitted that the chemical analysis of a man's dinner may be very informative, if it helps to determine whether he's been poisoned by a murderer or merely been given indigestion by a careless cook. Intention matters; so does context. We cannot *only* attend to sources and influences, as that would be a limited and limiting approach to literary criticism. But it has its place if it leads to greater understanding of a work and its author.

Opining about his own critics and their search for his sources, Tolkien remarked that "the most interesting thing to consider" was "the particular use in a particular situation of any motive, whether invented, deliberately borrowed, or unconsciously

---

* For instance, he admits that the names of the dwarves in *The Hobbit* are taken from a list in the *Völuspá*, but immediately adds that this does not provide a "key" to his dwarf-mythology (*Letters*, 383). He is making a pre-emptive strike, as it were, against the use of a source-connection to make an oversimplifying, reductive reading of his work. The dwarves are not cut-and-pasted from Germanic legend, and he is right to object to any interpretation that suggests this.

remembered."[56] I agree: it is not enough simply to identify a source or influence and stop there in foolish triumph. We must go further and be attentive to context, purpose, style, effect, and above all, meaning; we must ask, 'How does Tolkien use it? What insight do we gain from having discerned this connection? What does this tell us about his writings and even about him and his own creative processes?' As long as we keep those things in mind, even Tolkien himself allows that *quellenforschung* is a "perfectly legitimate procedure."

❧ Conclusion

We have, then, set out the boundaries of our study: works of fiction, poetry, and drama, written in English and published after 1850, which we can be sure that Tolkien knew. We have restricted ourselves to considering the effect of this reading only on the works of the legendarium, not on Tolkien's other writings. We have set out a working definition of 'source' and 'influence.' Along the way, we have challenged three major assumptions about Tolkien: that he was immune to influence; that he always denied being influenced; and that he rejected the entire discipline of source study.

In fact, Tolkien himself conceded that "no one of us can really invent or 'create' in a void."[57] He recognized that he did not write in isolation and knew that he could not have done so even if he had wanted to. The uninfluenceable bandersnatch is, in short, a creature of legend; the reality is far more interesting. As we explore the full range of his modern reading and analyze its impact upon his creative imagination, we will gain new insights into the nature and value of his writings. It is a journey we are now ready to begin.

3

Victorian Children's Literature
A Professor at Play

TOLKIEN ENJOYED HIS FIRST PUBLISHING SUCCESS WITH A SPECIMEN of children's literature – namely, *The Hobbit* – and so this genre seems an appropriate point at which to start our study of his modern reading. Children's literature was important to him not only in his own childhood as an avid reader, but also throughout his adult life, as a father, grandfather, scholar, and author. As we will see, his wide and deep reading in this department of fiction provided several specific influences, as well as helping him to develop strong views about what made a good tale for a young audience. His personal likings (and dislikings) also inform and illuminate his own choices as a writer for children.

While *The Lord of the Rings* famously began life as "the new Hobbit,"* *The Hobbit* itself had its origins in the context of Tolkien's family, as he told the story to his children. Other imaginative works also emerged from his familial storytelling: we see, for instance, the elaborate Father Christmas Letters taking shape over many years, as well as *Roverandom, Mr. Bliss,* and the character of Tom Bombadil, who would eventually enter Middle-earth.† The family context is important. His second son, Michael, recalled that "he possessed the ability, rare in fathers of exceptional talent, or perhaps an ability even rare in the average, of combining fatherhood with friendship"; his nephew Julian remembered that his "kindly uncle" Tolkien "was very fond of children. . . . I have very good memories of him."[1] His granddaughter Joanna described him as "quite a family man, and it gave him great delight and pleasure to be so."[2] And George Sayer recalls seeing the elderly, widowed Tolkien playing on the floor with his great-grandchildren: "I'm Thomas the Tank Engine. Puff. Puff. Puff" (a character from the series of children's picture books about steam trains, by the Reverend W. Awdry). Sayer adds that Tolkien's "love for children . . . was yet another thing that contributed to his wholeness as a man and the success of his books."[3] Tolkien's expertise in children's literature was therefore not merely nostalgic, nor purely academic; still less was it commercially motivated. It was grounded both in his own tastes and in the interests and preferences of children he knew and loved.

---

* It was by this name that the tale was known when it was first being read aloud at meetings of the Inklings. See, for instance, CLII, 302.

† *Roverandom* began as a story to console his son Michael for the loss of a toy dog; *Mr. Bliss* was first told to the children and was inspired in part by his children's toys; and Tom Bombadil was based on a Dutch doll. See TCG:C, 143.

The Tolkiens' four offspring (John, Michael, Christopher, and Priscilla) read enthusiastically and were given every incentive to do so from an early age; Carpenter notes that they "were always provided with full nursery bookshelves."[4]* Tolkien took an active involvement in his children's (and later, his grandchildren's) reading, giving them books as gifts[5] and pointing out titles suited to their age and inclination. For instance, Joanna recalls that, when visiting her grandparents, she was "handed from his bookshelf the Narnia books . . . *The Borrowers* . . . and Andrew Lang Fairy Stories," adding that "The fact that he directed me to reading these other books before *The Lord of the Rings* is perhaps an indication of his humility."† That all four of Tolkien's children would go on to earn degrees at Oxford is testimony to a family environment that valued and encouraged bookishness from their earliest days.‡

Following upon the critical and commercial success of *The Hobbit* (1937), Tolkien was invited to give the Andrew Lang Lecture at the University of St. Andrews in 1939 – a lecture given annually in honor of Lang (1844–1912), one of the university's most famous alumni. Andrew Lang was a collector of folklore and compiler of the variously colored "Fairy Books" for children; *The Blue Fairy Book* (1889) and its eleven subsequent volumes were highly popular. Tolkien accepted the invitation and traveled up to St. Andrews in March 1939 to deliver his lecture, which he entitled "On Fairy-stories."§

Tolkien recognized a "large" field of fairy-story writers from this period: "John Ruskin, Charles Kingsley,¶ Knatchbull Hugesen [sic], Thackeray, George Macdonald,

---

* Priscilla Tolkien recalls that these included, for instance, children's books published by Raphael Tuck, such as *The Fairy Tale Book* (1934) (AH, 74).

† She also recalled "being encouraged and helped by Grandfather in my interest of different species of plants, trees, birds and animals, particularly horses. He sent me two pocket-books of British Birds, and an Encyclopaedia of horses, so that I could study them further" ("Joanna Tolkien speaks," 33).

‡ Priscilla remarks: "An important fact I would like to emphasize here was his complete belief in higher education for girls; never at any time in my early life or since did I feel that any difference was made between me and my brothers, so far as our educational needs and opportunities were concerned. . . . It was therefore, I think, a source of pride and pleasure to him that he had a daughter as well as sons at the University" ("Memories of J.R.R. Tolkien in his Centenary Year," 12).

§ Flieger and Anderson observe that "While *The Hobbit* can be seen as prologue to the lecture, the lecture must be seen as both prologue and guide to that tale's sequel, *The Lord of the Rings*, on which Tolkien was just then beginning to work. The lecture on fairy-stories came at a critical juncture in Tolkien's creative development. It marked the transition between his two best-known works, but it also functioned as a bridge connecting them, facilitating the perceptible improvement in tone and treatment from one to the other. *The Lord of the Rings* became the practical application and demonstration of the principles set forth at St. Andrews" (introduction to OFS, 15).

¶ The reference is probably to *The Water-Babies* (1863), Kingsley's only fairy-story. Tolkien's inclusion of Kingsley as a significant figure underscores his tolerance toward those whose views differed from his own: Kingsley was strongly anti-Catholic, as evidenced both by *The Water-Babies* and his historical novel *Westward Ho!* Gilliver, Weiner, and Marshall suggest that he knew *Hereward the Wake* and propose a few influences on word-choice (*Ring of Words*). In preparing

Andrew Lang – to name only a few at random of the older moderns."[6] He remarks that "If there were more time, I should like to speak more of modern fairy-stories: revealing, as they do, all the excellencies and defects possible." Familiarity with both the "excellencies" and the "defects" of the genre indicates that Tolkien read widely enough to know the field well. His characteristically self-deprecating remark that "My reading has been very chancy. . . . I am not a student but an occasional reader of literature" should be understood as a typically English manner of expression.[7]* We are, of course, intended to understand the exact opposite: Tolkien has read extensively and thoughtfully, and it is on this foundation that he is prepared publicly to examine the nature and functions of the fairy-story.

Tolkien's academic expertise in children's literature was evidenced not only in his St. Andrews lecture, but also in his examining and supervising of student work at Oxford. For instance, in 1943, Tolkien was first an examiner for Roger Lancelyn Green's thesis on Lang's fairy tales, and then (voluntarily) his supervisor for a further term, work that involved extensive discussion "about literary, or invented, fairy tales." Green recalled with gratitude that Tolkien had written detailed comments on the draft, and that his thesis was not only accepted with high praise, but later "was used as a basis for my full-scale book on Andrew Lang and his works."[8] Then in 1952, Tolkien served as an examiner for a B.Litt. thesis on "The Rise of the English Original Fairy-Story 1800–1865." Five years later, he supervised a project on English children's literature by a Japanese student, Yoko Inokuma, who would later be the translator for the Japanese edition of *Smith of Wootton Major*.[9] If we think of Tolkien's academic work solely in connection with philology, we overlook an important sideline in his professional career.

He knew J.F. Campbell's *Popular Tales of the West Highlands* (four volumes, 1860–1862), and he praised W.T. Stead's series of *Books for the Bairns* (1896–1920) – a veritable mini-library of adapted folktales and legends – as a "mine of ancient lore."[10]† He also knew the American folklorist Joel Chandler Harris's *Uncle Remus* (1881).[11] He had on his shelves a volume containing Jean Ingelow's *Mopsa the Fairy* (1869) and G.E. Farrow's *The Little Panjandrum's Dodo* (1899).‡ Although he read widely in the genre, he did not do so undiscriminatingly, describing Thackeray's *The Rose and the Ring* (1855) as "superficial, even frivolous," and remarking that "as a child I couldn't stand Hans Christian Andersen and I can't now."[12]§ (See figure 4.) Still, he liked far more than he loathed and the point,

---

for his lecture, Tolkien did consult Andrew Lang's literary-critical volume *Essays in Little* (1891), which includes a short piece on Kingsley that focuses on *Hereward the Wake* (George White, "A Piece of Bodleian History").

  * See chapter 12 for more on Tolkien's self-deprecation.

  † Stead published these short and inexpensive stories monthly from March 1896 till June 1920. In total there were 288 publications.

  ‡ These were included in an omnibus volume, published 1960, titled *To the Land of Fair Delight: Three Victorian Tales of the Imagination*, which Tolkien had in his study. (Photograph of Tolkien in his study, Pamela Chandler, ARP 1188397.) See also figure 40 (Pamela Chandler, ARP 1188396).

  § He disliked the stories' moralizing tone and what he called the "sophisticated (even bogus)

for now, is to note that he kept abreast of the works that interested him, and was willing to acknowledge the significance of authors whose work he did not personally care for.

Tolkien's knowledge of, and lifelong engagement with, children's literature is so extensive that we shall need more than one chapter to explore his reading in this area. The present chapter considers the (post-1850) Victorians that we know him to have read. George MacDonald, a Victorian writer of both children's and adult fantasy, merits his own treatment and appears in chapter 5. We turn now to four authors whose work he paid particularly careful attention to, and which had an impact upon the evolution of Middle-earth.

❧ The origins of "Moria": George Dasent's *Popular Tales from the Norse*

We begin with Sir George Webbe Dasent (1817–1896), a writer and editor for *The Times* who was also a serious amateur scholar of Norse and Icelandic literature.[13] His writings included *The Story of Burnt Njal* (1861), a translation of the Njáls Saga; *Vikings of the Baltic* (1875), a loosely novelistic version of the Jomsvikinga Saga; and *Popular Tales from the Norse* in 1859, with an illustrated edition for children following in 1862.

Tolkien knew *Popular Tales from the Norse*, mentioning it in "On Fairy-stories."[14] More significantly for our purposes, as we trace the effects of his modern reading on his creative imagination, Tolkien acknowledged that the tale entitled "Soria Moria Castle" in Dasent's work played a part in his inventing of one of the most memorable place-names in Middle-earth: Moria, known also as "Khazad-dûm," the "Dwarrowdelf," and the "Black Pit." In terms of plot-twists, Moria is one of the most important places in the whole of Tolkien's epic, given that it is where Gandalf falls in combat with the Balrog, leaving the Fellowship bereft of its leader and advisor. Its dire significance is recognized within the story itself, so that the very mention of it fills Aragorn and the others with "dismay" and "dread"; "it is a name of ill omen," according to Boromir. How did Tolkien come by this name?

In reply to a correspondent who wondered whether there was an etymological link between "the mines of Moria," the location of the wizard's self-sacrifice, and "Mount Moriah" in the Book of Genesis, where Abraham prepares to sacrifice Isaac, Tolkien declared that "there is no conceivable connexion" between the two names, calling it a "purely fortuitous similarity, more obvious in spelling than in speech, which cannot be justified from the real intended significance of my story." He goes on to explain that "Moria" first appeared in *The Hobbit*: "It was there, as I remember, a casual 'echo' of *Soria Moria Castle* in one of the Scandinavian tales translated by Dasent. . . . I liked the sound-sequence . . ."[15]

---

form" of Andersen's version of Scandinavian tales (TCG:RG, 611). Nevertheless, he seems to have considered Andersen (1805–1875) a significant author; in preparing for the lecture of "On Fairy-stories," Tolkien made the note "You must mention Hans Andersen," although in the end he did not do so (OFS, 129).

The name "Moria" may have stuck more firmly in his memory because it also appeared in Lang's *Red Fairy Book*. But whichever work first brought this appealing "sound-sequence" to Tolkien's attention, it reveals that his modern reading could and did provide source material for his own writing. "Moria" helpfully alliterated with "mines" and was linguistically useful, as it chimed in with his existing Elvish word-structure, in which the 'mor-' element meant 'dark' or 'black' (as in Mordor, Morgoth, Morannon, and so on).[16]

Tolkien's downplaying of the link with Dasent as no more than a "casual echo" means that we should not put too much weight on it, but the very fact that he makes a link at all is intriguing. He was not always entirely consistent in his linguistic rationales – for instance, over the years, he gave very different accounts of the etymology of the name "Elrond"[17] – and the protean quality of his linguistic invention offers a glimpse of the way that different influences and inspirations could be at work before he settled on a final version. He remarked elsewhere that the meaning given to words by the human mind is not arbitrary, but derives from "accidental (non-linguistic) associations" or the individual's preference for the phonetic make-up of the word. Even an apparently random utterance by an inventor of languages "has innumerable threads of connexion with other similar-sounding words in his own language"; indeed, these threads of connexion extend even to "any others that he may know."[18]

It is therefore worth spending a little time enquiring what may have made the castle in Dasent's story attract the attention of Tolkien's inventive mind. In "Soria Moria Castle," the protagonist is an idle boy named Halvor. One day he goes to sea, but the ship is blown off course and arrives at a strange land. Exploring, Halvor finds a castle where a princess is held prisoner by a murderous three-headed troll. At the princess's suggestion, Halvor takes up a massive sword hanging on the wall – after having a magically strengthening drink from the troll's flask – and kills the troll when he returns. The next day he travels to another castle where he meets a second imprisoned princess and repeats the process with a six-headed troll, and on the next, to a third castle and princess, with a nine-headed troll that he similarly dispatches. (See figure 7.) This final castle is the one called "Soria Moria Castle." Having freed the princesses and been invited to marry the youngest, Halvor is nevertheless homesick; the princesses give him a magic ring that enables him to wish himself home to see his parents, but he is forbidden from taking off the ring or mentioning their names. However, he brags about the princesses' beauty, and wishes for them to be there to be seen; they appear, but remove the magic ring while he is sleeping, and wish themselves away without him. Heartbroken, Halvor finds his way back to Soria Moria Castle with the aid of the Moon and the West Wind. He arrives just as the youngest princess is about to marry someone else, but when he makes himself known, the princess chooses to marry him instead.[19]

Soria Moria Castle has no obvious connection to Moria, the dwarves' underground kingdom, if we consider them simply as places, but when we consider what goes on in the castle and its tonal coloring, there are some interesting resonances with the mines.

Dasent's Moria is a grand building that has fallen into a dangerous, largely uninhabited condition, with someone trapped in it by a monstrous troll; and a powerful ring, first given and then lost, plays an important role in the tale. Could this tale have planted a seed in Tolkien's imagination?

It should give us pause to note that the name "Moria" appeared in a draft of *The Hobbit* as early as 1932,[20] more than thirty years before Tolkien gave his linguistic rationale for its selection. As John Rateliff points out, at this moment "a major element of Tolkien's dwarven mythology enters the legendarium. . . . [But] there is nothing in the text of *The Hobbit* to identify Moria as a *dwarrowdelf* (dwarf-delving) nor mark it as having any special significance . . . other than being the site of [Thorin's] grandfather's murder."[21] The name came first, as Tolkien says. It appealed to him as a pleasing sound-form, but we need not assume that it was therefore bereft of other significance. Having first encountered the story "Soria Moria Castle" as a child, Tolkien might well have forgotten by 1967 that it had ever had any other resonance for him. But its literary context suggests that it may also have carried non-linguistic associations of imprisonment and dangerous monsters that made it particularly suitable as the name of the place where Thorin's grandfather, Thror,[22] was killed, and which ultimately became fully developed as the former realm of the dwarves, now the deadly haunt of orcs and balrogs in *The Lord of the Rings*.

It is perhaps worth noting that although trolls are mentioned on various occasions in *The Lord of the Rings*, the first and most vivid encounter with a living and actively malicious troll is in Moria. In the room of Balin's tomb, the Fellowship is attacked by something that Gandalf suspects is an enormous "cave-troll"; two trolls also make an appearance later during the pursuit within the mines. Dasent's lengthy introduction to *Popular Tales from the Norse* includes a section on "Giants and Trolls," in which he explains that "troll" in particular means a being associated with rocks and the interior of mountains, who is "systematically malignant" and to whom direct sunlight is fatal.[23] Tolkien would eventually encounter all these characteristics of trolls elsewhere in his reading, but it is worth noting that his first exposure to the troll-tradition may well have coincided with his reading of "Soria Moria Castle" – and could help explain why he found "Moria" such a memorable sound-sequence, ultimately to become in his legendarium a "Black Chasm,"[24] a dark, abandoned, troll-haunted place. Whether or not this possible imaginative evolution is considered plausible, we cannot deny that Tolkien himself was prepared to indicate some kind of connection. He forcefully denies any link with "Moriah" from the Book of Genesis but freely volunteers a link with the work of George Dasent.

❧ Asterisk tales: E.H. Knatchbull-Hugessen's *Stories for My Children*

The formidably named Edward Hugessen Knatchbull-Hugessen, first Baron Brabourne (1829–1893), was in his day both a popular writer of children's tales – now completely forgotten – and a career politician, serving the British government first as Under-Secretary of State for the Home Department and later as Under-Secretary of State for the Colonies. He wrote more than a dozen books, including *Crackers for Christmas* (1871), *River Legends; Or, Father Thames and Father Rhine* (1875), and *The Mountain Sprite's Kingdom* (1880). He had six children, some of whom formed an early audience for his fairy-tales. Knatchbull-Hugessen was also the great-nephew of Jane Austen, and in 1884 he published an edition of her letters, with an introduction and critical commentary. As a child, Tolkien had read (or been read to from) Knatchbull-Hugessen's first book, *Puss-Cat Mew and Other Stories for My Children*; at the end of his life, he recalled having been "very fond of" the title tale from that collection.[25]

Stories for My Children is a set of various fairy tales in the late Victorian style, many of which are didactic and moralistic: "The Umbrella and Parasol; or, Pride Shall Have a Fall" gives its lesson via a boastful silk parasol and a shabby but compassionate umbrella; "The Fairy Pool" tells of two little girls playing by a tide-pool who learn that they can only see beautiful fairies (and not nasty snakes) if they have clean hearts, purified by the Holy Spirit. Others are classic fairy tales but with a modern, even surreal, flavor, such as "Ernest," in which a boy chases his ball down a well and meets a huge, cigar-smoking toad who chastises him for his intrusion. Scull and Hammond suggest that the boy's encounter with the toad (in which he flatters the toad and is complimented for his good manners) resembles Bilbo's encounter with Smaug.[26]

What is particularly notable about *Stories for My Children* – and what may have caught Tolkien's attention – is that it contains what Knatchbull-Hugessen calls "parodies of certain familiar rhymes,"[27] in which he playfully imagines that the events recorded in nursery-rhymes really happened. In "Kate's Adventures" we find the wall from which Humpty-Dumpty fell, the pie-dish in which were baked the four-and-twenty blackbirds, and the fiddle which the cat played when the cow jumped over the moon. Also in "Kate's Adventures" is the coal which Puss-cat Mew jumped over, and "in her best petticoat burnt a great hole."

This reference points us back to the first tale in the volume, "Puss-Cat Mew," a cleverly imagined 'backstory' to explain the titular nursery rhyme.* Knatchbull-Hugessen's tale begins:

> Every child knows the sweet nursery rhyme of 'Puss-cat Mew,' –
>> 'Puss-cat Mew jumped over a coal;
>> In her best petticoat burnt a great hole;
>> Puss-cat Mew shan't have any milk
>> 'Till her best petticoat's mended with silk.'
> But very few children, or big people either, know who Puss-cat Mew
> was, or what was the history upon which those lines were made.[28]

---

* The rhyme was not invented by Knatchbull-Hugessen, but is an English nursery rhyme, with variants. It is included, for instance, in *A Book of Nursery Rhyme* (1901) by Charles Welsh, and *The Little Mother Goose* (1912) by Jessie Wilcox Smith.

This history is provided by the tale. A young man named Joe Brown enters a mysterious forest where an ogre disguised as a tree attacks him (see figure 7).* He is saved by a beautiful Cat who tells him that, while he is in the forest, he has merely to call upon the name of 'Puss-cat Mew' to be helped out of any difficulty. Later, Joe carries Puss-cat Mew over the forest boundary, at which point she becomes a beautiful lady, the daughter of the Queen of the Fairies. She and Joe marry, but to retain her human shape, each year on their wedding anniversary, she must wear her embroidered petticoat, which can only be mended with fairy silk; and for three years, she must drink a cup of milk every day. On their first anniversary, despite precautions, Puss-cat Mew burns a hole in her petticoat, and she promptly turns back into a cat and disappears.

Joe then embarks on his second set of adventures to rescue his wife. A fox he meets on the way gives him three magical items, including a glove that renders him invisible. Making his way to the ogres' castle at the heart of the forest, Joe finds the ogres discussing how to capture and eat him; he uses his invisibility first to provoke the ogres into fighting amongst themselves, and later to make his way into the prison cell where his feline wife is being held.† More action ensues; the castle is blown up, friendly fairies mend the magical petticoat, Puss-cat Mew is returned to her human shape, and she and Joe live happily ever after. The ruins of the castle, the narrator coyly suggests, are now identifiable as Stonehenge.

Scull and Hammond state that the story "made a great impression on" Tolkien.[29] It is worth considering what that great impression might have been. Since the plot elements are not distinctive to Knatchbull-Hugessen, it seems much more probable that he was struck by the tale's conceit as a back-projection of a nursery rhyme's origins. Tolkien would later, as a professional philologist, do his own work of linguistic reconstruction, creating 'asterisk words' (back-projections of etymology denoting ancient words as they might have existed) and even asterisk stories, tales such as "Sellic Spell" that imagine the older tales behind a poem such as *Beowulf*. Some examples of Tolkien's nursery-rhyme asterisk-poems include "Why the Man in the Moon Came Down Too Soon" and "The Cat and the Fiddle: A Nursery Rhyme Undone and its Scandalous Secret Unlocked." Both were published in 1923, though written earlier,[30] with the latter finding its way into *The Fellowship of the Ring* as a comic song sung by Frodo at the Prancing Pony, where a hint of its backstory nature is hinted at in the narrator's remark that "Only a few words of it are now, as a rule, remembered." As we will see in chapter 5, George MacDonald probably contributed to Tolkien's choice of these particular nursery rhymes, but the idea of presenting these poems as the original versions of the later rhymes probably came from Knatchbull-Hugessen.

---

* Carpenter and Prichard suggest that the ogre who disguises himself as a tree "may have partly inspired the invention of the Ents" (*The Oxford Companion to Children's Literature*, first edition, 297–298).

† Douglas A. Anderson sees the taunting of the ogres as a parallel to *The Hobbit* (AH, 83–84). Hammond and Scull suggest that the invisibility of Joe in the prison is similar to that of Bilbo rescuing the dwarves (TCG:RG 376).

What is most notable about *Stories for My Children* in this regard is that certain tales fully flesh out their back-story world. As we read "Puss-Cat Mew," with its plot full of adventures, we forget that it has anything to do with the nursery rhyme, until we are reminded of it in the closing scene. "Kate's Adventures" is even more meta-textual: the adventures provide a frame-tale in which asterisk-stories can be embedded. We see a vestige of this approach in the first chapter of *The Hobbit* where the narrator gives a brief excursus that explains the origin of the game of Golf:

> Old Took's great-grand-uncle Bullroarer . . . charged the ranks of the goblins of Mount Gram in the Battle of the Green Fields, and knocked their king Golfimbul's head clean off with a wooden club. It sailed a hundred yards through the air and went down a rabbit-hole, and in this way the battle was won and the game of Golf invented at the same moment.[31]

In the draft of *The Hobbit*, this passage was elaborated on to provide the genesis of the game of chess as well;[32] in this form, it is even more suggestive of Knatchbull-Hugessen's approach. Tolkien pruned the joke etymology down for the final version, making the tone of *The Hobbit* more consistent, but this vestige remains. We have here a world in which we may come across surprising origins of everyday tales and pastimes – just as in the fairy-tale/modern world crossovers of *Stories for My Children*.

Professors (and dons) at play: Lewis Carroll

The mention of chess brings us neatly to Lewis Carroll (1832–1898), the pen name for Charles Dodgson, who, like Tolkien, was an Oxford don. He was a lecturer in mathematics at Christ Church, a deacon in the Church of England, and an enthusiastic amateur photographer as well as a writer of both prose and verse. Tolkien read and enjoyed Carroll's masterpieces, *Alice's Adventures in Wonderland* (1865) and *Through the Looking-glass* (1871), the latter of which, as Tolkien observed, is "based on chess."[33] He also knew his now almost forgotten works *Sylvie and Bruno* (1889) and *Sylvie and Bruno Concluded* (1893), and at least some of his poetry.[34] Having encountered Carroll's work as a child, Tolkien maintained an interest in it in adulthood; Carroll was discussed at a 1912 meeting of the Apolausticks, one of Tolkien's undergraduate societies, and references to his works can be found in his "Dragons" lecture and in his letters.[35]

Carroll's poem "The Walrus and the Carpenter," from *Through the Looking-glass*, was a particular favorite, as Tolkien wrote several versions of it in Elvish, apparently from memory.[36] In an unpublished essay, he references Lewis Carroll's parody of the "Leech-gatherer" figure from Wordsworth's poem "Resolution and Independence."* Another *Looking-glass* poem, "The Jabberwocky," is alluded to in an academic lecture where

---

* Tolkien does not give the title, but given the context, it is the song "Haddocks' Eyes," from *Through the Looking-glass*, chapter VIII (Bodleian MS Tolkien A 30/1, fol. 119).

Tolkien describes one analysis of *Beowulf* as an attempt "to take a comprehensive view, amid the tulgey wood of conjecture and the burbling of the jabberwocks. . . . It is still very well worth reading, apart from his own private theory at the end . . . which only added one more tum-tum tree to the forest."[37]

Tolkien's favorable view of Carroll comes through clearly in his reaction to the blurb on the *Hobbit* dust-jacket, which claimed that "The birth of *The Hobbit* recalls very strongly that of *Alice in Wonderland*. Here again a professor of an abstruse subject is at play."[38] Writing to his publishers, Tolkien characteristically quibbled with the terminology: though he, Tolkien, was Professor of Anglo-Saxon, Carroll was a university lecturer and not technically a professor. More positively, he was embarrassed to have his tale compared to such a classic work, saying "the compliment to *The Hobbit* is rather high": evidence that he viewed *Alice* in a glowing light. Tolkien goes on to say that if there is to be a comparison, it ought to be to *Through the Looking-glass* rather than to *Alice's Adventures in Wonderland*, for the former "is much closer in every way."[39] Tolkien's meaning is not entirely clear,* but he may have been referring to the way in which Carroll's professional expertise in mathematics is brought to bear upon *Through the Looking-glass* (which is structured around a chess problem), just as Tolkien's philological expertise informs so much of the nomenclature and linguistic background of *The Hobbit*.

Curiously, in the same letter to Unwin, Tolkien had made another (and more unexpected) connection: that *The Hobbit* "is really more comparable" to Carroll's poem "Hiawatha's Photographing"[40] (a parody of Longfellow's "Song of Hiawatha") than it is to *Alice*. Indeed, Tolkien compares *The Hobbit* not only to this poem but also to Carroll's "amateur photography" itself, thereby alluding, it would seem, to the fact that *The Hobbit* derived from his leisure activities rather than his academic pursuits. He may also have seen the comparatively light and spontaneous story of *The Hobbit* as standing over against the serious project of the Silmarillion in something of the way that Carroll's poem stands over against Longfellow's poem, and by extension the *Kalevala* itself – the great Finnish epic which meant so much to Tolkien. (We will discuss his interactions with Longfellow in chapter 11.)

Carroll's *Sylvie and Bruno* and *Sylvie and Bruno Concluded* have today faded into almost total obscurity, probably deservedly so; they shift confusingly between fairy-land and the primary world, with little by way of coherent plot. Nevertheless, Tolkien liked them and knew them well. (See figure 6.) He comments in a letter that the Professor in *Sylvie and Bruno* is "the best character (unless you prefer the mad gardener)"[41]; indeed, these two characters are enjoyably quirky, in contrast to the strained oddity of the members of the court (who lack the bracing charm of the Queens in *Alice*) and the sickly sentimentality of the children (Sylvie is bland; Bruno speaks in baby-talk that is toe-curlingly saccharine).

---

* Unfortunately, Carpenter has chosen to omit the rest of the sentence that begins with "It is much closer in every way . . . ," so we lack any explanation Tolkien might have provided for the comparison.

Peter Gilliver notes that Tolkien drew on *Sylvie and Bruno* for an illustrative quotation for the word "smirkle," which he suggested to the Oxford English Dictionary.[42] * It comes, in fact, from the sequel, *Sylvie and Bruno Concluded*, in a long poem declaimed by "the Other Professor":

> Little Birds are teaching
> Tigresses to smile,
> Innocent of guile:
> Smile, I say, not smirkle –
> Mouth a semicircle,
> That's the proper style.[43]

Tolkien was fond of chanting poetry aloud, and Christopher Tolkien recalled that verses from *Sylvie and Bruno* "formed part of his large repertoire of occasional recitation."[44] We can get a sense of what Tolkien probably enjoyed about these poems by sampling the linguistically playful songs of the "mad gardener," which appear throughout the books. These all have the same metrical pattern and nonsense-verse form. Two examples will suffice:

> He thought he saw a Rattlesnake
> That questioned him in Greek:
> He looked again, and found it was
> The Middle of Next Week.
> "The one thing I regret," he said,
> "Is that it cannot speak!"

> He thought he saw a Banker's Clerk
> Descending from the bus:
> He looked again, and found it was
> A Hippopotamus:
> "If this should stay to dine," he said,
> "There won't be much for us!"[45]

Tolkien's enjoyment of silly songs such as this may have reinforced his own preference for comic poetry; W.H. Auden, for instance, commented that "most of [Tolkien's] poems belong to the category of 'Light Verse.'"[46] A classic example appears in the opening chapter of *The Hobbit*, when the dwarves merrily sing a song of destruction while carefully (though speedily) doing the washing-up:

---

* It is the only suggested quotation by Tolkien that has survived from his work on the OED.

Dump the crocks in a boiling bowl;
Pound them up with a thumping pole;
And when you've finished, if any are whole,
Send them down the hall to roll![47]

Nor is this playful ingredient limited to *The Hobbit*. Consider, for instance, Sam's troll song in *The Fellowship of the Ring*, with verses such as the following:

"My lad," said Troll, "this bone I stole.
But what be bones that lie in a hole?
Thy nuncle was dead as a lump o' lead,
Afore I found his shinbone.
Tinbone! Thinbone!
He can spare a share for a poor old troll,
For he don't need his shinbone."[48]

Tolkien deftly uses these comic songs both to illuminate the characters' personalities and to create interludes of release from danger or suspense. His verses have the playful quality of Carroll's songs from the Sylvie and Bruno books, but with greater significance for the story.

Carroll's example as a fellow Oxford don disporting himself imaginatively in public gave Tolkien something of a professional template on which to model himself, and in that way helped provide him with permission, as it were, to publish light-hearted work that might otherwise have remained within the family. Tolkien, like Carroll, is indeed, at least some of the time, simply a "professor at play."

A multi-colored author: Andrew Lang

We end this survey of Victorian fairy-story where we came in: with the eminent name of Andrew Lang. Tolkien admired his Coloured Fairy Books, which he knew very well from his own childhood and eventually shared with his grandchildren, as well as consulting them during his research for the St. Andrews lecture.[49] * At some point, he also read Lang's original fairy tales *Prince Prigio* (1889), *Prince Ricardo of Pantouflia* (1893), and *The Gold of Fairnilee* (1888), and his collection of stories *In the Wrong Paradise* (1886).[50]

---

* Tolkien notes that "the twelve books of twelve colours . . . we owe to Andrew Lang and to his wife." (OFS, 33). Here Tolkien is correctly giving credit to Leonora Blanche Lang, who was Andrew Lang's collaborator in translating and editing the series, although in all the editions of the Coloured Fairy Books, only her husband's name appears as editor. The dozen titles comprised: *Blue* (1889), *Red* (1890), *Green* (1892), *Yellow* (1894), *Pink* (1897), *Grey* (1900), *Violet* (1901), *Crimson* (1903), *Brown* (1904), *Orange* (1906), *Olive* (1907), and *Lilac* (1910).

The Coloured Fairy Books were a distinct novelty in Tolkien's day. The growth of the new academic discipline of comparative philology in the nineteenth century led to researchers' interest in collecting folktales and gave rise, as Flieger and Anderson point out, "to the great folk and fairy tale collections that we now take for granted. Traditional though they might now seem, they had not always been there."[51] Lang mingled folktales collected by researchers (such as the brothers Grimm) with literary tales by authors such as Hans Andersen, and the series is remarkably diverse in its range of material. Although the first two volumes draw primarily on Western European sources, the *Green* and later books include a generous selection of international stories, including Chinese, Japanese, Russian, Australian, Persian, Indian, African, and Native American tales. Lang's willingness to embrace all sorts and conditions of story made the Fairy Books a rich source of interest for the young Tolkien, and perhaps helped to lay the foundation for his miscellaneous reading habits. As Ruth Berman has observed, Lang became for Tolkien "both an important example to follow – and to defy."[52]

Tolkien was born in the same year that *The Green Fairy Book* was published and described himself as "one of the children whom Andrew Lang was addressing."[53] The *Green* book is notable for its inclusion of a tale entitled "The Enchanted Ring" in which a young man named Rosimond is given a magic ring that can be used to render the wearer invisible or to take on the appearance of the King's son. He uses these powers to serve the King and bring peace to the country, before honorably ending the deception by rescuing the real Prince who had been shipwrecked far away. Rosimund's brother, however, is then granted the ring and uses it for bad ends, eventually being executed and bringing grief and shame on the family. Rosimond regains the ring, and, having realized that it is "a gift as dangerous as it is powerful," he returns it to the giver, declaring that "ill fortune seems to follow all on whom you bestow it."[54]

The *Green* book is not the only volume that features magic rings. In *The Yellow Fairy Book* we find an Estonian story, "The Dragon of the North", which features another ring of invisibility that is too dangerous to be kept. A dragon is laying waste to the land who, it is said, "can be overcome by one who possessed King Solomon's signet-ring, upon which a secret writing was engraved."[55] A young man seeks the lost ring, and steals it from a witch-maiden by trickery. A magician then reads the secret engravings upon it, and tells him how to use it to defeat the dragon. The youth is later confronted by the witch-maiden, who declares that "You stole my most precious jewel from me . . . and you must bear the punishment."[56] Scorning his plea for forgiveness, she seizes the ring, and chains him up in a cave, where he suffers for seven years. Finally the magician finds and frees him, but the ring is seen no more.

Several details in these stories are highly suggestive of Tolkien's later invention of the One Ring. In "The Enchanted Ring," the ring is found, in time, to be so powerful that it cannot be safely used. In "The Dragon of the North," we find an even stronger link: the previous keeper of the ring had only limited knowledge of the ring's uses, but calls it "precious" and is vindictive about its theft, and the ring itself is ancient, perhaps not even made by mortal hands, with secret engravings that only a magician can read, revealing its full powers. There are at least two other stories featuring rings of invisibility in the Coloured Fairy Books and Berman remarks that it is from Lang that Tolkien is likely to have made "his first acquaintance" with such rings.*

The second of the series, *The Red Fairy Book* (1890), was Tolkien's favorite. He singles out for praise in this volume the "Story of Sigurd," where Lang presents a condensed adaptation of the Old Norse saga. Sigurd slays the dragon Fáfnir and takes his treasure, despite the dragon's warning that the hoard is cursed. On the way home, Sigurd rides through a circle of flame to break an enchantment on the sleeping maiden Brynhild, to whom he gives a ring from Fáfnir's treasure as a pledge of love. Various betrayals follow, involving shape-changing and a potion of forgetfulness, such that Sigurd marries the king's daughter Gudrún instead of Brynhild, and helps to trick Brynhild into marrying Gudrún's brother Gunnar. When, eventually, Brynhild discovers the deception, she kills Sigurd and dies of a broken heart.†

Before we consider the tale itself, it is interesting to note that the illustrations of Fáfnir from this volume might have had an influence of their own.‡ Rachel Hart suggests that these images may have contributed to Tolkien's later depiction of Smaug, pointing out "clear compositional similarities in the shape and alignment of the dragon's shoulder, neck, and forearms – particularly the right claw – the skulls scattered on the floor, and the wisps of smoke arising from the head." Hart also observes that this illustration of Fáfnir matches Tolkien's explanation of the name of 'Smaug,' as coming from *smugan*, "the past tense of the primitive Germanic verb *Smugan*, 'to squeeze through a hole.' *The Red Fairy Book* has a dragon squeezing through a hole in a wall, down onto the cave floor which is littered with skulls and bone."[57] (See figure 8.)

A distinctive feature of Lang's retelling of "The Story of Sigurd" is that this tale, unlike any other in the volume, has a short editorial introduction:

> This is a very old story: the Danes who used to fight with the English in King Alfred's time know this story. They have carved on the rocks pictures of some of the things that happen in the tale, and those carvings may still be seen. Because it is so old and so beautiful the story is told here again, but it has a sad ending – indeed it is all sad, and all about fighting and killing, as might be expected from the Danes.[58]

---

* "Prince Narcissus and Princess Potentilla" (*Green*) and "The Lady of the Fountain" (*Lilac*).

† Lang adapts the tale from William Morris, whom we will discuss in chapter 7. The story is difficult to summarize, in part because it contains plot inconsistencies, which Tolkien was later to attempt to work out in his poem *Sigurd and Gudrún*. For possible influences of the Lang version of the 'Sigurd' story on *The Hobbit*, see Jane Chance, *Tolkien, Self and Other*, 56–61.

‡ We know that Tolkien drew on existing models for some of his *Hobbit* art, as with the Trolls, based on the 'Hansel and Grethel' illustration in *The Fairy Tale Book* by Jennie Harbour (AH, 74).

"This is a very old story . . ." What makes "The Story of Sigurd" exceptional in this volume is not just its plot or tone, but the fact that Lang explicitly attaches it to history, in contrast to the 'once upon a time' setting of the other tales. By placing the story in the deep past, and making an intriguing mention of the Danes, Lang opens up a small but evocative vista on a storytelling tradition. Stories come from somewhere: they come from the past, and from a larger body of stories that have left traces not just in books but on stones. Who were these people, the Danes? Why is it to be expected that their stories are full of fighting and killing? What other stories did they tell?

For a child as sensitive and imaginative as the young Tolkien, this small framing touch could well have deepened the appeal of "The Story of Sigurd," intriguing him with its glimpse of tales as yet unknown, perhaps unknowable. It is not improbable that here we find one of the earliest seeds of Tolkien's life-long fascination with the sources of old stories.

"The Story of Sigurd" was, Tolkien said, "my favourite without rival. . . . It is strong meat for nurseries."[59] Adaptation though it was, it did not fall into the error of "mollification" that the adult Tolkien saw in so many other works for children. In "On Fairy-stories," Tolkien notes that he shares the disapproval of the "tiresome"[60] modern-day fairy stories that Lang expresses in the preface to *The Lilac Fairy Book* (1910):

> They always begin with a little boy or girl who goes out and meets the fairies of polyanthuses and gardenias and apple blossoms: 'Flowers and fruits, and other winged things.' These fairies try to be funny, and fail; or they try to preach, and succeed. Real fairies never preach or talk slang. At the end, the little boy or girl wakes up and finds that he has been dreaming.
>
> Such are the new fairy stories. May we be preserved from all the sort of them![61]

Tolkien keenly appreciated the fact that children detest being infantilized; they relish a challenge and expect both that they will not understand everything and that adults will not explain everything. Children's books, like their clothes, "should allow for growth"; indeed they "should encourage it."[62] This view was the product of mature reflection coupled with personal observation. As a young man, his nascent legendarium included flower-fairies, and he once stumbled into condescension when he asked a friend's baby brother if someone lived in a garden flower. To Tolkien's chagrin, the unimpressed little boy coolly replied, "There are Stamens and a Pistil in there."[63]

The "Story of Sigurd" is bracing, even harsh, compared with what Tolkien later called the "frippery and folly/finery" of the French fairy-stories popular at the time.[64] Perhaps it was this quality that made the tale of Fáfnir so attractive to him. We can see Tolkien's appreciation of such strong flavors shaping his own work. The chapter in *The*

Hobbit in which the spiders of Mirkwood capture and web-wrap the dwarves for later consumption is potentially nightmare-inducing for younger children (or arachnophobic adults), but Tolkien does not shy away from providing vivid details. Michael Tolkien recalls that as a child, he had "a real terror" of spiders, and that his father created the spider scene in *The Hobbit* "almost entirely for my benefit to show however big a spider was, he could, in fact, be overcome."[65] Tolkien deftly balances the horrible with the heroic, and even the humorous, as Bilbo taunts the enraged spiders with his song of "Lazy Lob and Crazy Cob" while rescuing the dwarves.

"Sillinesses of manner": the *Chronicles of Pantouflia*

Tolkien's view of Lang's *Chronicles of Pantouflia* was not uncritical. Although he told Roger Lancelyn Green that he was not enthusiastic about the sub-genre of "made-up" fairy tales in general, he found Lang's first attempt along these lines to have some genuine strengths.[66] He appreciated the scene in *Prince Prigio* (1889) in which the Prince restores to life a group of brave knights who had been turned to stone. He thought it stood out as having a flavor of eucatastrophe, "a little of that strange mythical fairy-story quality, greater than the event described" which is only possible because this scene is "a piece of more serious fairy-story 'fantasy' than the main bulk of the story."* Tolkien also notes the "very neat semi-satirical semi-magical ending which is much appreciated by myself and my children."[67] However, he finds the work "unsatisfactory in many ways": it has "the half-mocking smile of the courtly, sophisticated *Conte*" and at the same time is given to "Preaching!" The sequel, *Prince Ricardo of Pantouflia* (1893), is even more unsatisfactory: Tolkien calls it a "bad failure as a story."[68] In his St. Andrews lecture, he focuses on this failure of tone: "I will not accuse Andrew Lang of sniggering, but certainly he smiled to himself, and certainly too often he had an eye on the faces of other clever people over the heads of his child-audience – to the very grave detriment of the *Chronicles of Pantouflia*."[69]

Tolkien himself did not believe he had always successfully resisted the temptation to talk down while smiling to himself. Writing in 1955 to W.H. Auden, Tolkien lamented that *The Hobbit* exhibited "some of the sillinesses of manner caught unthinkingly from the kind of stuff I had had served to me."[70] Such "sillinesses" (we may venture to suppose) include Gandalf's absurdly long eyebrows, which "stuck out further than the brim of his shady hat," and the Elves singing "tra-la-la-lally." In the latter case, a particularly arch note is struck by the narrator's comment, "and pretty fair nonsense I daresay you think

---

* "Eucatastrophe" is a key concept in Tolkien's thought. He invents the word in "On Fairy-stories," defining it as "the joy of the happy ending: or more correctly of the good catastrophe, the sudden joyous 'turn' . . . it is a sudden and miraculous grace, never to be counted on to recur . . . it denies (in the face of much evidence, if you will) universal final defeat and in so far is *evangelium*, giving a fleeting glimpse of Joy, Joy beyond the walls of the world, poignant as grief" (75). The eucatastrophic event *par excellence* in LOTR is the rescue of Frodo and Sam from Mount Doom.

it. Not that they would care; they would only laugh all the more if you told them so." A decade later, he was even more self-critical, telling an interviewer that

> 'The Hobbit' was written in what I should now regard as bad style, as if one were talking to children . . . Anything that in any way marked out 'The Hobbit' as for children instead of just for people, [my children] disliked – instinctively. I did too, now that I think about it. All this 'I won't tell you any more, you think about it' stuff . . . it's awful. Children aren't a class. They are merely human beings at different stages of maturity.[71]

The comic moments in *The Lord of the Rings* have none of this self-conscious, arch flavor. The success of its tone very probably owes something both to Tolkien's careful thought about the failings of Lang's stories and to the regret he felt about his own earlier errors of a similar kind.

Hidden paths: "East of the Sun and West of the Moon"

We close our study of Lang by turning back to the first of his many-colored volumes, *The Blue Fairy Book* (1889), which Tolkien encountered as a child and referred to many years later in his lecture "On Fairy-stories." Although he remarks that Lang's preference for French sources was "not to my taste, now or in childhood," he acknowledges that this was "a just choice in some ways at that time, as perhaps it would be still."[72] One exception to the French origin of the *Blue Fairy Book* tales deserves our notice: the Norwegian story "East of the Sun and West of the Moon." (See figure 5.) In a version of the Cupid and Psyche myth, an impoverished girl becomes betrothed to a mysterious White Bear. She disregards the Bear's warning and lights a candle to discover the identity of the man who sleeps beside her each night. He reveals that he is a Prince under his stepmother's curse, a curse which would have been lifted if she had not disobeyed; now he must go to a castle "east of the sun and west of the moon" and marry a troll-princess there. The girl resolutely follows him and, with the eventual aid of the North Wind, arrives at the castle in the nick of time; she and the Prince outwit the wicked stepmother and the hideous Princess, and are married.

Tolkien was fascinated by the phrase "east of the Sun and west of the Moon," which he probably met here for the first time.[73] The phrase provided him with the opening line of his 1915 poem "The Shores of Faëry," although he reversed Lang's order to "West of the Moon, East of the Sun." He later revised the poem, altering the celestial references so that the phrase became "East of the Moon, West of the Sun." It was this version that he copied into his *Book of Ishness* and illustrated with a striking watercolor. The poem is notable as one of the earliest texts in the legendarium, with its references to Valinor and the Two Trees.[74]

But Tolkien's engagement with this image had not ended there. He returned to it decades later in *The Return of the King*, as Frodo, on his way to the Grey Havens, murmurs to himself a new version of one of Bilbo's old walking-songs:*

> Still round the corner there may wait
> A new road or a secret gate;
> And though I oft have passed them by,
> A day will come at last when I
> Shall take the hidden paths that run
> West of the Moon, East of the Sun.

Listening to Frodo softly sing, Sam becomes aware that "the words were not quite the same" as in Bilbo's original version, which had closed with the phrase "Towards the Moon or to the Sun." Likewise, they are not quite the same as Lang's version, for Tolkien again reverses Lang's order, finishing on "Sun," but this time rhymed with "run." The fact that Tolkien revisits the phrase forty years after first writing "The Shores of Faëry" indicates what a hold it had over him and how he was prepared to adjust and re-adjust its wording to suit his artistic purposes. Frodo sings while preparing to depart into the West, yet the song ends with an image of the eastern horizon and the prospect of venturing beyond the dawn. The poignant paradox of hoping for sunrise even as the sun sets on Frodo's life in Middle-earth, the use of "run" in the context of a slow walk towards a painful parting, and the freshly minted lyrics to an old, familiar song on its last rendition, are reasons why these lines work so memorably and movingly. Lang contributed the raw material, but Tolkien's creative imagination made it richer and more emotionally powerful. He understood artistry in terms of "refraction," human sub-creators taking the white light of divine creativity as it is refracted into "many hues" and then endlessly combining these different colors "in living shapes that move from mind to mind."[75] Here we have a fine example of that very process, both in Frodo's adaptation of Bilbo's song, and in Tolkien's own adaptation of *The Blue Fairy Book*'s evocative phrase.

⚜ Conclusion

Tolkien's ideas about children's literature – what it was, and what it could and should be – were not formed in the abstract, nor solely by his recollection of what he had enjoyed as a boy; rather, he was familiar with children's books in the day-to-day life of his growing family. As a result he had a keen awareness of the needs and interests of genuine (not stereotypical) child readers. To this personal and familial acquaintance with the genre

---

* This song, beginning "Upon the hearth the fire is red," first appears when Frodo and his friends lightheartedly sing it together on the way to Crickhollow at the very start of their adventures. Its reappearance as Frodo prepares to depart Middle-earth altogether indicates how much value Tolkien attached to it. The song effectively book-ends the entire journey.

he added a keen academic interest, manifested both in his St. Andrews lecture "On Fairy-stories" and in his supervision of Oxford theses.

In this chapter, we have considered his reading of children's literature from the (post-1850) Victorian period. We have seen that one of the most important of Middle-earth place-names, Moria, came to him from Dasent's *Popular Tales from the Norse*. We have examined the lasting impression made on him by Knatchbull-Hugessen's "Puss-Cat Mew." We have caught a glimpse of Tolkien's playful side from his enjoyment of Lewis Carroll's comic poetry – Carroll in addition providing him with an example of admissible writerly behavior for an Oxford don. Finally, we have seen him interacting thoughtfully with Andrew Lang, in whose colorful *Fairy Books* he met rings of invisibility, admirably terrifying dragons, and an image of Sun and Moon that he kneaded and refined over many decades; and in whose other works he found moral and stylistic flaws that he would in turn attempt to avoid (not always entirely successfully) in his own writings.

In all these ways, we have gained insights into the nature and development of Tolkien's creative imagination. As a very literary child, as a father sharing in his family's reading, as a scholar critically examining the field, and as an author aiming to succeed in the marketplace of popular opinion, Tolkien's wide reading in modern children's literature helped shape the creation of *The Hobbit* and, by extension, *The Lord of the Rings*, which began as "the new Hobbit" before it grew darker and more suited to an adult audience.

4

Post-Victorian Children's Literature
Snergs, Rabbits, and the Problem of Narnia

Q UEEN VICTORIA DIED IN JANUARY 1901, SHORTLY AFTER TOLKIEN'S
ninth birthday. We saw in the previous chapter that many children's books
written by Victorian authors stayed in his memory far into adulthood, but it is
important to point out that his interest in the genre was not just nostalgic. He stayed up-
to-date with new authors and their latest books as the twentieth century unfolded, partly
for the sake of his own children and grandchildren, and partly because he was, simply
put, a man of letters who liked to know what was going on. A case in point is E.A. Wyke-
Smith's *The Marvellous Land of Snergs*, published in 1927 when Tolkien was thirty-five;
it became an immediate favorite of the whole family, and Tolkien later acknowledged
that it was probably a kind of "source-book" for his creation of the hobbits.[1] It is unusual
to find Tolkien making such an explicit connection between contemporary fiction and
the development of his legendarium, but it underscores the value of our present study.
By examining his modern reading we will find all sorts of links to his sub-created world,
some of them very probable, some merely arguable, and some definite, as here. Few
people have heard of Wyke-Smith these days, but his work evidently contributed, at least
at a subliminal level, to the leaf-mould from which Middle-earth arose.

We will return to the Snergs shortly. First, let us take a quick general overview of
the other post-Victorian children's literature that Tolkien knew – bearing in mind that
his reading undoubtedly extended beyond the titles and authors mentioned here, as in
this study we are considering *only* those works which we are certain he read (or at least
owned). Among the authors whose work Tolkien found most significant – and whose
influences on Middle-earth we can trace – are Beatrix Potter, Arthur Ransome, Hugh
Lofting, Edith Nesbit, Kenneth Grahame, and, of course, C.S. Lewis, whose *Narnia
Chronicles* he famously took against, though he nonetheless described them as "deservedly very popular."[2] We will discuss each of these authors in this chapter.

As we survey Tolkien's reading in this area, we begin with his familiarity with
the latest retellings and adaptations of folktales and legends: he knew Ernest Rhys's
elegantly literary rendition of English fairy tales, *Fairy Gold* (1907),[3] and he owned
copies of *The Welsh Fairy Book* (1907) by William Jenkyn Thomas, *The Irish Fairy Book*
(1909) by Alfred Perceval Graves, *Irish Fairy Tales* (1920) by James Stephens, illustrated
by Arthur Rackham, and *Stories of King Arthur* (1925) by Blanche Winder.[4] Turning

to original stories, we find on his shelves *The Silver Trumpet* (1925) by fellow Inkling Owen Barfield; he first borrowed it from C.S. Lewis but evidently thought well enough of it to acquire a copy of his own as well.[5]* He seems not to have encountered A.A. Milne's tales of Winnie-the-Pooh when they first appeared in the 1920s, or perhaps he disapproved of them. At any rate, Christopher Tolkien recalled that his father "did not read the Winnie-the-Pooh books to us; they were not in the house, and I certainly had a Pooh-less childhood."[6] Eventually, however, he made Pooh's acquaintance, but what he thought about the "Bear of Very Little Brain" is unknown.[7] About Milne's 1929 stage adaptation of *The Wind in the Willows*, "Toad of Toad Hall," Tolkien had mixed views. The play itself he described as "tolerably good fun," but he calls Milne imperceptive for having attempted to dramatize it at all.[8] He was familiar with Alison Uttley's Little Grey Rabbit series, the first of which was published in 1929, for he registers his intention to get Priscilla one of the latest books as a Christmas present.[9] He read J.B.S. Haldane's *My Friend Mr. Leakey* (1937).[10] He owned T.H. White's *The Sword in the Stone* (1938), which he read soon after its publication,[11] and knew of Ruth Winifred How's *The Friendly Farm* (1946).[12] He was sufficiently familiar with the stories of Enid Blyton (1897–1968) to have an opinion about their illustrations.† He enjoyed Joyce Gard's *Woorroo* (1961), in which a ten-year-old boy befriends a bat-person, grows his own wings, and learns to fly.[13]

He owned the first four books in Mary Norton's Borrowers series,[14] published from 1952 to 1961, which reveals that Tolkien maintained a watching brief over developments in children's literature well beyond the youth of his four children, and did so not only because of his own enduring interest in the genre, but also for his grandchildren's benefit.‡ As another example, when he was given a copy of *The Children's Treasury of Literature* (1967), edited by Bryna and Louis Untermeyer, which featured a chapter from *The Hobbit*, Tolkien perused the entire book§ and said he would pass it on to one of his grandsons.[15]

---

* Tolkien spoke of his children's response to the book, which Lewis lent to him in 1936: "They liked the sad parts because they were sad and the puzzling parts because they were puzzling, as children always do" (quoted in CLII, 198).

† Praising the work of his illustrator Pauline Baynes, Tolkien declares that she would, without doubt, "avoid the Scylla of Blyton and the Charybdis of Rackham – though to go to wreck on the latter would be the less evil fate" (*Letters*, 312).

‡ His first grandchild, Michael George Tolkien, was born in 1943.

§ We know this because he commented favorably on the illustrations in general, although he disliked those for the chapter selected from *The Hobbit*. The other modern authors in this volume include extracts from works by Rudyard Kipling (a selection from *Just So Stories*), C.S. Forester (from *Poo-Poo and the Dragons*), P.L. Travers (from *Mary Poppins*), A.A. Milne (from *Winnie-the-Pooh*), L. Frank Baum (from *The Wizard of Oz*), Hugh Lofting (from *The Story of Doctor Dolittle*), Felix Salten (from *Bambi*), Kenneth Grahame (from *The Wind in the Willows*), T.H. White (from *The Sword in the Stone*), Lewis Carroll (from the *Alice* books), and J.M. Barrie (from *The Little White Bird*), as well as the full text of John Ruskin's *The King of the Golden River*, and stories by Hans Christian Andersen, Ray Bradbury, Erskine Caldwell, Joel Chandler Harris, Lafcadio Hearn, Louis Slobodkin, Frank R. Stockton, Louis Untermeyer, Oscar Wilde, and Jay Williams.

Finding his own work anthologized a mere thirty years after its original publication must have been distinctly satisfying. *The Hobbit*, having achieved both critical and commercial success, had so thoroughly penetrated the public imagination that people knew what a hobbit was even if they hadn't read the book. Yet this fictional creature had not existed a generation earlier. Where had it come from? How did it gain such immediate and permanent acceptance among readers? The first two authors we have to consider in this chapter will help provide some answers.

"An unconscious source-book! for the Hobbits": E.A. Wyke-Smith's *The Marvellous Land of Snergs*

Edward Augustine Wyke-Smith (1871–1935) is not a well-known name today and few people have even heard of, let alone read, *The Marvellous Land of Snergs* (1927). However, Tolkien not only knew the story but was enthusiastic about it. In the draft of "On Fairy-stories," Tolkien notes "my own love and my children's love" for the book, and in particular for "the Snerg-element in that tale, and of Gorbo the gem of dunderheads, jewel of a companion in an escapade."[16]

The conceit for Wyke-Smith's story is that the kingdom of the Snergs is part of our own world, but in some way isolated from it, so that a ship attempting to sail there would find itself pushed away by contrary winds. However, a certain highly intelligent Miss Watkyns finds a mode of entrance and establishes a home for unwanted children, whom she cares for in a sort of perpetual camp, where they soon forget their origins. Miss Watkyns and her ladies are aided in their care of the children by the kind Snergs, especially the aforementioned Gorbo, a notably foolish but warm-hearted Snerg who rescues the children when they wander off.

Child-sized ("only slightly taller than the average table") and long-lived, Snergs in general are "gregarious people, loving company";[17] they have a great deal in common with hobbits as Tolkien would come to depict them a few years later. George Morrow's illustrations suggest their physical resemblance to Tolkien's under-three-foot-tall hobbits, who, as they are described in *The Lord of the Rings*, have faces that are "good-natured rather than beautiful, broad, bright-eyed, red-cheeked." It is worth observing that the Snergs are depicted with bow and arrow, for Tolkien notes particularly that the hobbits "shot well with the bow, for they were keen-eyed and sure at the mark." (See figure 3.)

Wyke-Smith suggests that Snergs "are some offshoot of the pixies who once inhabited the hills and forests of England, and who finally disappeared about the reign of Henry VIII."[18] * This description brings to mind Tolkien's remarks that the hobbits are "an unobtrusive but very ancient people, more numerous formerly than they are today." Though Snergs are small in stature, Wyke-Smith points out that they are "of great strength,"[19] just as the peace-loving hobbits are "curiously tough . . . difficult to daunt or to kill."

---

* That this disappearance occurred around the time of King Henry VIII may have appealed to Tolkien as a token (at the imaginative level) of the rupture with Rome that he considered so disastrous ecclesiologically.

The resemblances between Snergs and hobbits run deeper than appearances. Like hobbits, the Snergs live in a mixed rural setting, with one main town that has some "mills and farms a little distance away." The Snergs help out Miss Watkyns and her Society with tasks such as gardening and painting, but Wyke-Smith especially notes their skill as builders. Although they favor three- or four-story houses, they share with the hobbits a certain homebody quality: "You never know when a Snerg will finish with his house because he is always making additions to it, such as throwing out bay windows, or carrying a balcony on sticks to one of the big trees near by and then building a spare bedroom in the tree itself."[20] Tolkien notes that although hobbits are most comfortable living underground, the towns of the Shire featured many hobbit-houses built aboveground, as well as barns, sheds, and workshops; but they always built "in their own fashion," with "a preference for round windows, and even round doors." We find that hobbits even share the Snergs' tendency to extend their holes, as with Brandy Hall: built by Gorhendad Oldbuck for his family, it was expanded to keep pace with the growth of his descendants, "until Brandy Hall occupied the whole of the low hill, and had three large front-doors, many side-doors, and about a hundred windows."

Most notably, we find a strong parallel between hobbits and Snergs with regard to celebrations. Snergs are enormously fond of food and will find any excuse for having a feast. The Master of the Household's job is scheduling banquets, and he "has to hunt for a reason, such as it being somebody's birthday. Once they had a feast because it was nobody's birthday that day." Among the Snergs, "the King gives the feasts" and "presides at the head of the table,"[21] which seems to be nearly his only responsibility, but considering how often they feast, not an inconsiderable one. This innocent greediness and festivity has its echo in the hobbits' unselfconscious enjoyment of meals (having dinner twice a day if possible), and in their enthusiasm for birthday parties (though giving, rather than receiving, presents on their own birthdays): "in Hobbiton and Bywater every day in the year was somebody's birthday, so that every hobbit in those parts had a fair chance of at least one present at least once a week." And the Mayor of the Shire has as "almost his only duty to preside at banquets, given on the Shire-holidays, which occurred at frequent intervals."

We can see, then, what Tolkien may have had in mind with his remark that *The Marvellous Land of Snergs* "was probably an unconscious source-book" for his most famous invention. Admittedly, his positive response was not unqualified: "I do not think the name Snerg happily invented, and I do not like the bogus 'King Arthur' Land across the river."[22] But his generally high regard for Wyke-Smith's story is confirmed by way in which he brought it up with his publisher. Tolkien met with Stanley Unwin in October 1937, presenting him with a disorganized array of possibilities for his next book after *The Hobbit*. Unwin made a detailed memo of the conversation, noting that in addition to multiple new projects of his own, Tolkien "spoke enthusiastically of a children's book called *The Marvellous Land of Snergs*, illustrated by George Morrow. . . . He mentioned that The Hobbit took him 2 or 3 years to write because he works very slowly."[23] That

Tolkien should have spoken so positively of the Snergs in the course of a discussion about his own creative writing indicates the sort of place it occupied in his mind at that time. Perhaps his description of Gorbo as a "jewel of a companion" even finds an echo in two descriptions of his own: in a letter to Christopher he calls Sam a "jewel among the hobbits,"[24] and in *The Lord of the Rings* the elves call Frodo "a jewel among hobbits!" after he thanks them in Elvish for their hospitality.

Tolkien is careful to note that insofar as the book influenced him, it was as a source of the hobbits themselves, "not of anything else";[25] but given the importance that hobbits would gradually acquire in his imagination, not to mention in the imagination of millions of readers (and moviegoers) round the world over the succeeding decades, this one singular debt to Wyke-Smith is sufficient by itself to be of great note.

"Hobbit recalls *rabbit"*: Beatrix Potter

But it is not just to the Snergs that we should look for the imaginative prototypes of the Hobbits; the works of Beatrix Potter (1866–1943) provide intriguing antecedents too. Her twenty-three short animal tales for young children – beginning with *The Tale of Peter Rabbit* in 1902 and concluding with *The Tale of Little Pig Robinson* in 1930 – were immediately successful and have continued to be highly popular ever since.

Tolkien knew, at the least, not only *Peter Rabbit*, but also *The Tailor of Gloucester* (1903) and the tales of *Benjamin Bunny* (1904), *Mrs. Tiggy-Winkle* (1905), *Jemima Puddle-Duck* (1908), *Mr. Tod* (1912), and *Johnny Town-Mouse* (1918).[26] We catch a glimpse of his great esteem for Potter's work in a jocular remark C.S. Lewis made about how he and Tolkien "have often played with the idea of a pilgrimage to see her [at her home in the Lake District], and pictured what fun it would be to shoulder aside the mobs of people who want to show you all the Wordsworth places with the brief rejoinder 'We are looking for Miss Potter.'"[27]

The Potter tales had an important place on the bookshelves of Tolkien's children; his son Michael recalls that when his father was telling the children the stories that would become *The Hobbit*, "I was then very, still very, keen on Beatrix Potter's books," and that in his mind, "Bilbo tends to be a little like the country mouse in *Johnny Town-Mouse* . . . like so many of Beatrix Potter's people are: they're people and yet they're animals."[28]

After the success of *The Hobbit*, when Tolkien was casting about for material to satisfy his publisher's desire for a sequel, he put forward the idea of publishing an illustrated version of his 1934 poem "The Adventures of Tom Bombadil," and suggested that it be printed in the same size and shape as *Peter Rabbit*.[29] This would fulfill his aunt Jane Neave's request for "the sort of book that we old 'uns can afford to buy for Christmas presents."[30] The resulting volume, *The Adventures of Tom Bombadil*, illustrated by Pauline Baynes and published in 1962, is indeed physically similar to the Potter books.

As a keen amateur artist, Tolkien would have appreciated the skill with which Potter illustrated her own stories, but it is Potter's literary art that he explicitly admires, calling her stories "masterly."[31] Lewis notes that it was Tolkien "who first pointed out to me that her art of putting about ten words on one page so as to have a perfect rhythm and to answer just the questions a child would ask, is almost as severe as that of lyric poetry."[32] Here we can see, once again, Tolkien's appreciation of an author's attention to the genuine needs and interests of child readers. Given that Potter began publishing her stories when Tolkien was already a boy of ten, he might not have encountered them until he was himself a parent, but certainly at that point he would have seen first-hand the effectiveness of her pacing.

He also admired her handling of the fairy-tale element in her stories, noting that *Peter Rabbit* exemplified the "intense mythical value of *Prohibition* with a capital P. . . . Even Peter Rabbit was forbidden a garden, lost his blue coat, and took sick. The Locked Door stands as an eternal Temptation." Tolkien used her work as an example of the "curious wistful evanescent quality" that appears in modern fairy tales: "A thing beautiful or desirable happens – vividly 'reality' and yet farther away, without being definitely characterized as 'dream' as illustrated by Mrs. Tiggywinkle." He also includes in his praise the stories more fully in the character of beast-fables, such as *Jemima Puddle-Duck* and *The Tale of Mr. Tod*.[33]

The names of Potter's characters (Ginger and Pickles, Timmy Tiptoes, Samuel Whiskers) have much the same simplicity and rustic resonance as many of Tolkien's hobbit names (Merry and Pippin, Odo Proudfoot, Sam Gamgee). They were likewise exceedingly difficult to translate: Tolkien comments, with a touch of camaraderie, that Potter gave "translators hell." He adds, annoyed by what he has seen of the Dutch translation of *The Lord of the Rings*, "I'm not going to be treated à la Mrs Tiggywinkle = Poupette à l'épingle,"[34] a remark which deserves some unpacking, for "Mrs. Tiggy-Winkle," as the name stands, is more or less untranslatable. In English, 'tiggy-winkle' sounds perfect for the little washerwoman-hedgehog of the tale, but, like 'hobbit,' does not have any direct meaning. The French translator could have left the name alone, or used a functional version such as "Madame Hérisson" (Mrs. Hedgehog) – but instead opts for "Poupette à l'épingle," which plays on "pincushion" in French (*pelote à épingles*) and "little doll" (*poupette*) to create a name that could be translated back as "Dolly Pincushion." A cushion full of pins is visually apt for a hedgehog and "Poupette à l'épingle" trips off the tongue, but it has little to do with Potter's original name for her character. In Tolkien's comment, we can detect sympathy with the mess that has been made of Potter's original choice of name, and the subtext that he won't be treated like a pincushion or Voodoo doll: that is, won't allow himself to be needled or goaded by presumptuous translators.

He notes that another of Potter's names has fared better in translation than Mrs. Tiggy-Winkle, praising the way "Puddleduck" been rendered as "Canétang."[35] Canétang is a portmanteau word formed from the French "caneton" (duckling) and "étang" (pond): thus, literally, a pond-duckling, with the splicing of the words making it particularly witty. In principle, Tolkien would have preferred "Puddleduck" to remain untranslated, but he can grant that, in this case, it has been done well. Tolkien's appreciation of the difficult-to-translate quality of Potter's naming is echoed in his own dogged determination to see the names of *The Lord of the Rings* either left alone or, failing that, translated with some degree of sensitivity.[36]

But Beatrix Potter is best known not for hedgehogs and ducks but rabbits – most notably Peter Rabbit, of course, but also his siblings Flopsy, Mopsy, and Cotton-tail, his cousin Benjamin, his uncle Mr. Benjamin Bunny, and the ominously anonymous "Fierce Bad Rabbit." Potter's various cunicular characters may well have contributed to the overall concept of hobbits, which have a distinctly rabbity quality, especially in *The Hobbit.** We find that "in a hole in the ground there lived," not unlike a rabbit, "a hobbit." Bert the troll calls Bilbo a "nassty little rabbit." While the dwarves are trying to escape the goblins and wolves, Bilbo runs from tree to tree "like a rabbit that has lost its hole and has a dog after it." Once they have been rescued by the Eagles, Bilbo wonders whether he will be "torn up for supper like a rabbit, when his own turn came." One of the Eagles later tells him, "You need not be frightened like a rabbit, even if you look rather like one." Lastly, when Thorin discovers Bilbo's disposal of the Arkenstone, "he shook poor Bilbo like a rabbit."

Tolkien's denial to the editor of *The Observer* that Bilbo was rabbitlike[37] was very probably an instance of strategic contradiction in order to avoid spurious interpretations. Elsewhere, he states that hobbits are not "a kind of 'fairy' rabbit," which appears intended to emphasize that they should be illustrated as human-like in appearance, not anthropomorphized animals.[38] As Tom Shippey points out, "One can see why Tolkien denied the obvious connection between the two: he did not want hobbits classified as small, furry creatures, vaguely 'cute' just as fairies were vaguely 'pretty.'"[39] But he himself admitted that 'hobbits' *sounded* like 'rabbits,' and in negotiating the translation of the word for the French edition of the book, he even agreed that the suggested *hopin* was "a suitable and ingenious solution: hopin / lapin = *hobbit / rabbit*, I suppose."[40] In unpublished draft material related to the prologue to *The Lord of the Rings*, he states that the name "hobbit" is "my own invention; but not one devised at random"; he adds a note (later struck out): "I must admit that its faint suggestion of *rabbit* appealed to me. Not that hobbits at all resembled rabbits, unless it be in burrowing." He also includes a bit of philological wordplay based on the fact that the word in the Shire language for 'hobbit' resembles the Shire word for coney, "if not so clearly as *hobbit* recalls *rabbit*."[41]

Hobbits are indeed not rabbits, but they do have characteristics in common, and Tolkien repeatedly circled back to the association. We have reasonable grounds to suspect, then, that certain literary rabbits may well have formed part of the source material for their invention. The allusions to the hobbits as rabbit-like appear only in the relatively whimsical and child-oriented *Hobbit*, not in the darker and more mature *Lord of the*

---

* The rabbity tone is maintained even in peripheral remarks. For example, Golfimbul's head, knocked off by the hobbit Bullroarer Took, sailed "through the air and went down a rabbit-hole," when it might have been a fox-hole, a badger's hole, or simply 'a hole.'

Rings, and so we will do well to consider the possible influence of Potter on Tolkien's most famous creation.

For he had thought carefully about the nature of Beatrix Potter's rabbits. In his 1938 "Dragons" lecture, he suggests that the relationship between dragons and dinosaurs, although "not quite so close as the kinship of Peter Rabbit to the live lettuce-eaters of Mr McGregor's real kitchen garden," is genuine. Dragons, he says, really exist (in "Legendary History"), with two kinds, the creeping and the winged; admittedly, "Neither of these are now usually recognized by scientists." Reversing the perspective, he points out that although rabbits certainly exist,

> yet much the most interesting varieties are not recognized by zoologists. There is *lepis cuniculus braccalus* the trousered rabbit, or Potter's Rabbit, of which Peter Rabbit and Benjamin Bunny are famous specimens; there is *cuniculus sapiens Remi* or Uncle Remus' wily rabbit. These are one might say *founded on rabbit* – and are more than rabbit. Require rabbit for their explanation – but don't disprove rabbit.[42]

"Founded on rabbit," "more than rabbit," "require rabbit for their explanation" – here we see Tolkien hinting at the relationship between source material and literary creation. The "trousered rabbit" has a liminal quality, similar to hobbits in some key characteristics: human-like, but not human; quick and quiet of foot; easily overlooked by large persons; garden-loving and hole-dwelling.

Indeed, Potter's rabbits live not just in holes but in very pleasant holes – much like hobbit-holes. In *Peter Rabbit*, the four bunnies and their mother live in "a sand-bank, underneath the root of a very big fir tree," later lauded as "the neatest sandiest hole of all."[43] Here, Mrs. Rabbit makes a living by selling various goods, including "rabbit-tobacco (which is what we call lavender)."[44] The picture in *Benjamin Bunny* shows a charmingly neat and tidy entrance to the burrow, with Mrs. Rabbit's cheeses arranged for sale on a table and bunches of rabbit-tobacco strung on the back wall. (See figure 2.) Perhaps such an image helped contribute to the idea of hobbits living in comfortable holes underground, with plenty of food and a well-stocked "tobacco-jar": the very final word of *The Hobbit*.*

But probably the most obvious debt owed by Tolkien to Beatrix Potter comes neither in the size and shape of hobbits, nor in their domestic arrangements, but in their dress and accessories. A "pocket-handkerchief" plays a significant role in *Benjamin Bunny* as does one in *The Hobbit*. Bilbo's waistcoats are a consistent part of his attire, as notable for him as hoods for the dwarves: one has brass buttons, another has gold buttons, a third

---

* Although the word "tobacco" is used in *The Hobbit*, Tolkien changed it to "pipe-weed" in *The Lord of the Rings*, which further highlights that the earlier book had its origins and much of its development largely outside the legendarium, where influences from modern children's tales could have a more obvious mark on the text.

is embroidered with silk. In *Benjamin Bunny*, we meet the eponymous character's father, who is depicted as a portly, middle-aged figure wearing a fine waistcoat and smoking a pipe of rabbit-tobacco – a very hobbit-like image on all counts. (See figure 2.)

Tolkien's work at the Oxford English Dictionary included definitions and etymologies of "waistcoat." Peter Gilliver comments that he "relished the task of distinguishing the different garments denoted at different times by *waistcoat* (as he later grew to relish the garment itself)."[45] A waistcoat-wearing rabbit would have caught Tolkien's eye. More significantly, Peter Rabbit, in his first venture into Mr. MacGregor's garden, is trapped in a gooseberry net by the large brass buttons on his beautiful blue coat; he only escapes when he wiggles out of the jacket, leaving it behind him. Similarly, in *The Hobbit*, when Bilbo is escaping from the goblins under the mountain, he is for a moment caught in the crack in the door by the brass buttons on his waistcoat; he escapes, but at the cost of "his nice brass buttons" that are torn off and left behind him. The nod to Potter is unmistakable, a sign of Tolkien's deep and abiding admiration for her work.

❧ Wheat, not chaff: Arthur Ransome

One of the earliest admirers of the hobbits was Arthur Ransome (1884–1967), a journalist and foreign correspondent who achieved fame (and lasting literary success) with the twelve books of his Swallows and Amazons series, published from 1929 to 1947. They feature the four Walker children and their friends, who spend their holidays camping and sailing boats, and playing games in which they are pirates or explorers.

Arthur Ransome was a name well known in the Tolkien household. When Ransome wrote to Tolkien in 1937, referring to himself as "a humble hobbit-fancier," Tolkien wrote straight back, declaring himself "delighted" by Ransome's letter: "My reputation will go up with my children." The Swallows and Amazons stories were among their favorites, he says: "on their shelves, winnowed of the chaff left behind in the nursery, I notice that their 'Ransomes' remain."[46] He evidently thought well enough of the books to provide his children with multiple volumes in the series, and to be pleased on his own behalf as well as on theirs by the author's letter.* As late as 1966, his study shelves held a copy of the eighth installment, *Secret Water*.[47] This particular tale might have especially appealed to Tolkien, as it features the children exploring an island in order to fill in a blank map,

---

* Ransome praised *The Hobbit* but also objected to Tolkien's use of the word "men" to refer to hobbits, goblins, dwarves, and so on. Using the conceit that Tolkien was merely the transcriber, Ransome made comments such as, "may I complain that on page 27, when Gandalf calls Bilbo an excitable young hobbit, the scribe (human no doubt) has written 'man' by mistake?" Ransome's light touch succeeded. Tolkien took his advice, and replied in the same manner: "The scribe, too, is delighted to be honoured by a note in your own hand . . ." (*Signalling from Mars: The Letters of Arthur Ransome*, 249–250). Tolkien's receptiveness probably owes much to the fact that Ransome's advice concerns linguistic precision and congruity and comes from an author who was himself painstaking about correct terminology as it pertained to boats and sailing. The changes that Tolkien made at Ransome's suggestion may be small, but they do increase the internal consistency of the tale. The uninfluenceable bandersnatch is entirely missing from the scene.

with a secret semaphore code playing an important role in the story. A hand-drawn "Semaphore ABC" is included in the text of the book.

One other small matter is worth noting. Ransome did his own pen-and-ink drawings for the books; all the Swallows and Amazons volumes are copiously illustrated. His landscapes are simply and skillfully drawn, but the human figures are inelegant and lumpy, which, as Philip Pullman has observed, adds to, rather than detracts from, the charm of the pictures.* It is possible that Ransome's stylistic choice in this regard influenced Tolkien as an illustrator of *The Hobbit*. Tolkien was a talented artist, but he had weaknesses: most notably, as Hammond and Scull point out, his "limited ability to draw the human figure,"[48] evidenced by *Lake Town*, *The Hall at Bag-End*, and *Conversation with Smaug*. Assuming that Tolkien recognized these deficiencies – for he was consistently self-deprecating about his artistic competence in a way that suggests genuine self-doubt, not just English modesty – could it be that Ransome's illustrations gave him warrant for a certain deliberate awkwardness, or childishness, in the illustrations for a book that was, after all, aimed at the same age group as Swallows and Amazons?

Tolkien's art, according to critic Richard Schindler, "shares some pictorial qualities with the work of two contemporary authors and illustrators," and the two he has in mind are Arthur Ransome and the next writer we have to consider – namely, Hugh Lofting.[49]

❧ "Animal language": Hugh Lofting

Hugh Lofting (1886–1947) was a civil engineer who fought in the trenches of the Great War, where he was seriously wounded. His Doctor Dolittle tales originated in letters from the front written to his children and feature the eponymous English doctor John Dolittle, who is led by his great fondness for animals to learn both to understand and to speak different animal languages. He keeps house with a whole menagerie of friendly creatures and has various adventures on account of his interest in natural history and his chronic shortage of funds. The Dolittle series is comprised of fourteen books, of which nine were full novels published in Lofting's lifetime. The first two – the most distinctive for the freshness of the story – are *The Story of Doctor Dolittle* (1920) and *The Voyages of Doctor Dolittle* (1922), which won the Newbery Medal.

Tolkien knew and enjoyed the Dolittle books.[50] Given that Lofting was a near contemporary, his encounters with them would have come from reading them to his own

---

* Pullman opines: "Arthur Ransome was a wonderful writer, whose stories . . . have an extraordinary consistency of quality; and that quality, it seems to me, would be markedly reduced if they'd been illustrated by someone who could draw. . . . Part of the charm of Ransome's books is this very amateurish, lumpish, clumsy drawing" (*Daemon Voices*, 267f). The first two books were originally illustrated by other artists, but Ransome was dissatisfied with the results. For *Peter Duck* (the third book in the series), he did his own illustrations, and since this tale was supposed to be based on the characters' own accounts, he drew the pictures as if the children themselves had produced them. In 1938, he re-did the illustrations for the first two books, and proceeded to illustrate all subsequent volumes himself. This touch of artistic verisimilitude in *Peter Duck* would surely have pleased Tolkien.

children; his eldest son, John, would have been five years old when *The Voyages of Doctor Dolittle* appeared.

In that story we find a scene that is highly suggestive of one in *The Hobbit*. The boy narrator, Tommy Stubbins, meets the Doctor who invites him home, where they are met at the door by a most unusual housekeeper: "hopping down the stairs on one leg, came a spotless white duck. And in her right foot she carried a lighted candle!"[51] (See figure 14.) It turns out that the house is largely run by the animals, who take care of the housework. While Tommy and the Doctor are having a meal, "the door suddenly opened, and in marched the duck, Dab-Dab, and the dog, Jip, dragging sheets and pillow-cases behind them over the clean tiled floor. The Doctor, seeing how surprised [Tommy] was, explained: 'They're just going to air the bedding for me in front of the fire.'"[52]

The scene is reminiscent of the feast at Beorn's house in *The Hobbit*, where animals serve the guests. The dogs, who "could stand on their hind-legs when they wished, and carry things with their fore-feet," set up the tables. Then,

> in came some snow-white sheep led by a large coal-black ram. One bore a white cloth . . . others bore on their broad backs trays with bowls and platters and knives and wooden spoons, which the dogs took and quickly laid on the trestle-tables. . . . Beside them a pony pushed two low-seated benches with wide rush-bottoms and little short thick legs for Gandalf and Thorin . . . [Beorn] probably had them low like the tables for the convenience of the wonderful animals that waited on him.[53]

A point in favor of *Doctor Dolittle* providing some of the inspiration for this scene is that Beorn's original name, in the draft of *The Hobbit*, is "Medwed."[54] As a version of the Russian word for 'bear,' it is suitable in its meaning, but its sound is also appealing: it has the same rhyming ring to it as many of Lofting's animal characters: Dab-Dab the duck, Gub-Gub the pig, Too-Too the owl, and Chee-Chee the chimpanzee. In the final version of *The Hobbit*, Beorn speaks to his horses both in English and in "a queer language like animal noises turned into talk." The echo of *Doctor Dolittle* is even stronger if we consider the phrasing of the draft, in which Medwed/Beorn speaks to his animals in "a queer *animal language* like animal-noises turned to talk."[55]

This scene in *The Hobbit* can seem a bit out of place, even a little bit silly, when juxtaposed with the increasing seriousness of the story overall, including details such as Beorn displaying a severed head and flayed skin as evidence of how he dealt with a goblin and a warg. In no other parts of Tolkien's legendarium do we see animals acting as servants in the way that they do here. However, the scene is consistent with the story's origin if we remember that *The Hobbit* began as a tale told to, and for, Tolkien's own children — who were also the ones who read, or heard read to them, the *Doctor Dolittle* books. If the conceit of the doctor's animals serving in his house pleased the children, it is likely that Tolkien adapted the scene for his own story in order to help keep their attention and satisfy an established taste.

❧ "An author I delight in": E. Nesbit

We turn now to an author whom Tolkien discusses in the draft of "On Fairy-stories": the prolific Edith Nesbit (1858–1924). A dedicated socialist and one of the founders of the Fabian Society, Nesbit wrote dozens of books while also managing a household that included her three children and two of her husband's illegitimate offspring, whom she adopted. Her children's fiction included both fairly realistic adventures, such as *The Railway Children* (1906) and the Bastable series, and more fantastic tales, such as the Psammead series of *Five Children and It* (1902), *The Phoenix and the Carpet* (1904), and *The Story of the Amulet* (1906).

Tolkien commented that Nesbit was "an author I delight in," and his children later recalled having Nesbit books in their home,[56] so we can be confident that Tolkien knew a number of her works,* although at present we have specific reference in his available writings only to her Psammead books. In the draft of "On Fairy-stories," he describes *The Phoenix and the Carpet* and *The Story of the Amulet* as following Nesbit's "triumphant formula."[57]

These stories feature five children who discover, in an abandoned gravel pit, a "sand-fairy," or "Psammead": a furry, spider-like creature allergic to water, who has the ability to grant wishes that, at least in the first book, remain fulfilled only while the sun is up. In *Five Children and It*, the children find that their wishes often don't work out quite the way that they expect, as when a carefully thought out request to be endowed with the power of flight ends with them stranded on a roof when their wings expire at sundown, or when a careless wish that their house become a besieged castle leads to a genuinely frightening assault by armed knights.†

The Phoenix and the Carpet features the same cast, but the Psammead has only a minor role. The children discover that a replacement carpet for the nursery contains a phoenix egg, which they accidentally help to hatch; the phoenix, in turn, announces that the carpet is magical, capable of transporting them anywhere they ask. Adventures ensue.

---

* Douglas A. Anderson notes that in 1899, the popular *Strand Magazine* ran Nesbit's series *The Seven Dragons*, in which the third tale featured a dragon "lying 'on his great green scaly side'" and that it was around this time that the young Tolkien wrote a story about a "green great dragon" (*Tales Before Tolkien*, 182). Virginia Luling suggests that Tolkien's father-son approach to time-travel in *The Lost Road* may have been partly inspired by Nesbit's *The House of Arden* (1908), featuring the time-travel adventures of a brother and sister, Edred and Elfrida. Luling knows of "no other example of this particular time-travelling device: the visiting of the past in the person of an earlier person with the same name; and with it the very peculiar use of a related pair, father–son in one case, brother–sister in the other" ("Going back: time travel in Tolkien and E. Nesbit," 31).

† Tolkien included a nod to Nesbit's Psammead in his children's story *Roverandom*, which features a wizard named Psamathos Psamathides. Tolkien, aware that the Greek word for 'sand' is *ámathos*, could have come up with the name independently, but the resemblance is, I think, too strong to be coincidental. Like Nesbit's sand-fairy, Tolkien's sand-wizard "liked to lie buried in the warm sand . . . so that not more than the tip of one of his long ears stuck out; and even if both of his ears were showing, most people like you or me would have taken them for bits of stick" (*Roverandom*, 11). Both are also ancient and distinctly crotchety in their personality.

The Story of the Amulet begins with the children rescuing the Psammead from captivity in a pet shop; in gratitude, it guides them to buy an ancient amulet – or rather half of one. The whole amulet would grant their hearts' desire; the half allows them to travel in time, which they do (along with the Psammead), to find the other half. Their subsequent adventures include inadvertently bringing the Queen of Babylon to London for a brief time and visiting the island of Atlantis at the moment of its downfall. Nesbit's account of the destruction of the city by a tsunami and a volcanic eruption, as witnessed by the children until their last-minute escape via the amulet, is vivid and quite moving. (See figure 12.) It would have particularly interested Tolkien, given his recurring nightmare of a great, destructive wave, coming in over trees and fields, which he described as his "Atlantis complex," and which he bequeathed in *The Lord of the Rings* to Faramir, the character whom he said was most like himself.[58] Considering that *The Story of the Amulet* was published in 1906, when Tolkien was already fourteen, it is unlikely to have been the source of the nightmare, which he recalls having as a very young child. However, it might very well have helped reinforce the image in his memory.

What is specially of relevance, however, is Tolkien's interest in Nesbit's approach to storytelling. Tolkien identifies the second and third Psammead books as examples of the "triumphant formula" that she hit upon and that Lang "narrowly missed."[59] What was of such value to him in these two tales, and what was it that Nesbit accomplished that Lang failed to achieve?

One key feature of Nesbit's stories is the simplicity of the magical apparatus. For the most part, we encounter just one magical being at a time (the Psammead, the Phoenix), and one magical item (the amulet, the magic carpet); the story explores the effects of this particular creature or object on the lives of the children. In contrast, Tolkien objected to Lang's approach in *Prince Ricardo*, complaining that this book has "too much magic, wishing caps, seven-leagued boots, invisibility cloaks, magic spy glasses, and much else."[60] Nesbit's approach is more sparing, and therefore, in Tolkien's way of thinking, more effective.*

Another strength of Nesbit's plots is that they develop logically from her rules of magic. Much of the delight of *The Phoenix and the Carpet* and *The Story of the Amulet* comes from the unexpected but (in hindsight) entirely logical consequences of the

---

* We can also contrast Tolkien's approval of Nesbit's approach with his view of J.B.S. Haldane's *My Friend Mr. Leakey*. Tolkien remarks, "We are not in Pembroke [College] expected to descend to the level of a J.B.S. Haldane," and adds, "Not that I think that I have – except in the matter of illustrations" (letter to G.E. Selby, quoted in *J.R.R. Tolkien: The Hobbit: The Hobbit Drawings, Watercolors and Manuscripts, June 11–September 30, 1987,* 4). He is willing to share Haldane's "level" insofar as both wrote children's fantasies with illustrations, but otherwise distances himself. One reason the resemblance might have been displeasing to Tolkien is that *My Friend Mr. Leakey* is overloaded with magical items, including a top hat that produces soup and a magic purse that Leakey uses to neutralize a vicious dog by making his teeth rubber. The result is a sense of diminishing enchantment and of the absurdity of magic in general – which is perhaps Haldane's point, but not one that Tolkien would have appreciated. See also Christina Scull, "Dragons from Andrew Lang's retelling of Sigurd to Tolkien's Chrysophylax."

children's wishes. The rules are consistent. We learn that the carpet is capable of only three wished-for trips per day, it understands wishes expressed in either speech or writing, and it can exercise judgment in the interpreting of those wishes. Nesbit uses these rules to create dramatic tension, as when the children's baby brother vanishes for an afternoon, because the carpet on which he has been playing understands and obeys his gurgling baby-talk. Similarly, in order for the amulet to be used for time-travel, it must be held up toward the west, the correct words must be spoken, and the travelers must enter in sequence of age. The need to get the procedure right gives heightened drama to scenes such as their escape from Atlantis.

This systematic approach no doubt appealed to Tolkien, given his views on the value of a consistent secondary world. Moreover, Nesbit presents her magical system seriously even when the results are comic, unlike Lang in the *Chronicles of Pantouflia*. Although Lang plays with the logical possibilities of magic, as when Prince Prigio uses a fire-dragon against an ice-monster to destroy them both, he does so in a tongue-in-cheek manner. As a result, the believability of Lang's magical system (such as it is) is undermined.

Here, perhaps, we can see a subtle influence on Tolkien, as he explored the implications of the magic ring that Bilbo finds in *The Hobbit*. The idea of the One Ring (as we learn it to be in *The Lord of the Rings*) developed over time in Tolkien's imagination. The first edition of *The Hobbit* has a significantly different version of the "Riddles in the Dark" chapter.[61] The ring renders the wearer invisible, just as in the revised version, but it lacks the sinister undertones that emerge in the revised *Hobbit* and come to full fruition in *The Lord of the Rings*; it is a bog-standard magic ring, as these things go. However, Tolkien's mature and developed conception of the One Ring is much more compelling. Even its capacity to grant invisibility – now merely a side effect of its real power – has significance beyond what we see at first. The One Ring is all the more frightening because its dangers unfold consistently from its nature and powers, and because we observe its effects on the hobbits, the most ordinary and down-to-earth characters in the story.

Nesbit's approach is also notable in that her tales feature fantastical adventures happening to realistically drawn London children, and in the context of their mundane hopes, fears, and domestic problems. In contrast, Tolkien remarks, Lang "started out not from a real Family but from a Court on the model of the Contes de Fees."[62] Tolkien seems to prefer the realistic emotional dynamics of the child characters over against the stereotyped figures of the courtly tales. We might well consider whether his admiration for Nesbit's approach encouraged him to choose an ordinary figure – Bilbo Baggins – as the protagonist of his own story. The hero engages our sympathies all the more because he is an unlikely candidate for such adventures, just as normal Edwardian children going on magical jaunts through time and space hold our interest more easily than standard-issue princes from a royal court.

❧ "Deservedly very popular": C.S. Lewis's Chronicles of Narnia

We noted how, in *The Story of the Amulet*, Nesbit's children inadvertently bring the Queen of Babylon to London, an episode that very probably helped inspire C.S. Lewis to create a similar scene in one of his own works.* And this brings us to Tolkien's close friend and colleague, and to that friend's most famous work, the seven Chronicles of Narnia. The series began with *The Lion, the Witch and the Wardrobe* (1950) and concluded with *The Last Battle* (1956), which won the Carnegie Medal. These tales are often enjoyed by the very same readers who delight in Tolkien's *The Hobbit* and later grow up to enjoy *The Lord of the Rings*, which makes it all the more surprising that – according to conventional wisdom – the creator of Middle-earth despised his friend's creation of Narnia. As we have found with other aspects of conventional wisdom regarding Tolkien, however, this is not entirely accurate. Gaining a better understanding of Tolkien's views requires us to trace the evidence carefully and in some detail, but our attention will be rewarded.

Tolkien's initial exposure to *The Lion, the Witch and the Wardrobe* came when he heard a few chapters read aloud to him by Lewis in a private meeting.[63] The earliest extant reference to his reaction is in Roger Lancelyn Green's 1963 monograph, *C.S. Lewis*, where Green remarks that an early draft of *The Lion* had been "set aside owing to criticism from one of his older friends [i.e., Tolkien]." Green adds that this friend was "by then rather out of touch with children and their books, and wedded to different modes of thought where fairy-tale and fantasy were concerned."[64] Tolkien was in fact much more in touch with children and their reading than the childless Lewis.† Nevertheless, even with the touch of defensiveness detectable in Green's account (probably because *he* was the later friend who reassured Lewis that *The Lion, the Witch and the Wardrobe* was worthwhile), there is no hint of the extremely negative reaction that appears in later accounts.

Certainly, Tolkien did have different "modes of thought" about children's stories, as we see in the next account of his response, which appears in the 1974 biography of Lewis that Green co-authored with Walter Hooper:

> On 10 March 1949 Green dined with Lewis in Magdalen and thereafter followed a 'wonderful talk until midnight: he read me two chapters of a story he is writing.' . . . Lewis stopped reading with the remark that he had read the story to Tolkien, who had disliked it intensely: was it any good? Green assured him that it was more than good, and Lewis had the complete story ready to lend him (in the original manuscript) by the end

---

* Namely, *The Magician's Nephew* (1955) wherein the Queen of Charn is accidentally brought to London and wreaks havoc. The story announces a debt to Nesbit on its opening page: "This is a story about something that happened long ago when . . . the Bastables were looking for treasure in the Lewisham Road."

† Tolkien even had two grandchildren at that point (Michael, 6; Joanna, 4).

of the month. (Tolkien met Green shortly after and remarked: 'I hear you've been reading Jack's children's story. It really won't do, you know! I mean to say: *"Nymphs and their Ways, The Love-Life of a Faun."* Doesn't he know what he's talking about?')[65]

It is important, first, to bear in mind the multiple stages of transmission and interpretation involved with Green's report of Lewis's account that Tolkien had "disliked it intensely," especially as Green admired the tale as intensely as Tolkien is said to have abhorred it. Second, we should note that Tolkien's specific criticism (as relayed directly to Green) related to Lewis's handling of the faun, Mr. Tumnus; we will return to this objection later in this chapter.

Another point worth emphasizing is that Tolkien's recorded reaction comes from his hearing of the early chapters: as we saw just now, Lewis did not even have the story finished at that time. However, Tolkien does seem to have read the manuscript at some later date: Green later referred to *Lion* as a book that "he and I had read in manuscript."[66] We do not, however, have any record of his reaction to the full book.*

A third account of the conversation, again written by Green, appears in a 1974 article. Green recalls that Lewis read him the first two chapters of *The Lion, the Witch and the Wardrobe* and then "stopped suddenly and said: 'Do you think it's worth going on with?'" When Green assured him that it was, Lewis continued:

> 'I started it some time ago,' said Lewis, 'but it didn't work. There was no Aslan in it then. But just recently I saw how it ought to go, so I began again, and I can see it clearly right to the end. So I wrote these two chapters . . . But Tolkien doesn't like them . . . What do you really think?'[67]

In this account, Lewis describes Tolkien merely as not liking them – nothing stronger. Green's reply is noteworthy as well: he "pointed out how natural it was that Tolkien should not like it: for his fantasy world, the world of *The Hobbit*, was so very different – with a different greatness. As different, I think I said, as *The Princess and Curdie* from *The Wind in the Willows.*"[68] Green did not think it strange or excessive that Tolkien might not care for Lewis's new tale, and, as we will see shortly, Green's literary analogy was remarkably apt.

So far, these accounts have given us a fairly ordinary picture of two literary friends with differing tastes. But now we come to Humphrey Carpenter's dramatically different perspective; or rather we should say 'perspectives,' for Carpenter provides two versions of the matter.

---

* According to Carpenter (*Inklings*, 226), the Narnia books were not read aloud in regular meetings of the Inklings and we do not know how many Tolkien heard or read of the later Chronicles. George Sayer reported that once the subsequent volumes began to be produced, Tolkien "soon gave up trying to read them" (*Jack*, 313). That he "gave up" indicates that he made a start at any rate.

In his biography of Tolkien, Carpenter suggests that "In part the increasing coolness [in his friendship with Lewis] on Tolkien's side was probably due to his dislike of Lewis's 'Narnia' stories." No evidence is provided for this startling assertion. He goes on to describe Tolkien as "irritated" and "annoyed" by the Narnia books and giving "a snort of contempt"[69] when making his comment to Roger Lancelyn Green – though as we can see from Green's own account, this is Carpenter's interpolation into the story.

Four years later, in Carpenter's 1978 group biography *The Inklings*, the tale has grown even stronger in the telling:

> Why then did he totally reject the Narnia stories? For reject them he did. Lewis told his former pupil Roger Lancelyn Green, who sometimes drank with the Inklings at the Bird and Baby, that after listening to the opening chapters of *The Lion, the Witch and the Wardrobe* Tolkien had said he "disliked it intensely." And when Green met Tolkien shortly afterwards, Tolkien said to him, "I hear you've been reading Jack's children's story. It really won't do, you know!"[70]

Our earlier examination of the evidence provides some key corrections. Carpenter's quote of "disliked it intensely" appears to be *Tolkien's own words*, but in reality, Carpenter is attributing to Tolkien the words Green used in paraphrasing Lewis's description of Tolkien's reaction! Furthermore, Tolkien's "It really won't do" is cited without the crucial context of the following words, in which it is evident that what 'won't do' is a very specific point: "I mean to say: '*Nymphs and their Ways, The Love-Life of a Faun.*'" Carpenter knew about this comment, as he quoted it in the *Biography,* but that doesn't stop him from proceeding to the rest of his discussion as if 'it won't do' referred to not only the first Chronicle in particular but by implication the seven-volume series as a whole. Indeed, all of his supposed analysis, including his decisive summing-up that for Tolkien "It just *wouldn't* 'do,' and he turned his back on it,"[71] is Carpenter's own interpretation.

After Carpenter, the next account of Tolkien's reaction – and one that is frequently cited – is from George Sayer. In his 1988 biography of Lewis, Sayer describes Tolkien's response as being one of condemnation: "Tolkien said that he thought the book was almost worthless, that it seemed like a jumble of unrelated mythologies." Sayer goes on to say that Tolkien "detested" this mixing of mythologies and that "He also thought they were carelessly and superficially written."[72]* A decade further on, in his "Recollections of J.R.R. Tolkien," Sayer reports that Tolkien considered *The Lion* "to be 'about as bad as can be.'"[73]

---

* Sayer adds that "one suspects he envied the speed with which Jack wrote and compared it with his own laborious method of composition." This idea has been widely accepted as fact; for instance, Raymond Edwards, in his otherwise fairly measured account of the incident, says that the contrast of speeds "was surely a painful one" (*Tolkien*, 229). However, it is mere speculation, and psychologically inconsistent at that: if Tolkien thought the books were "carelessly" written, he might have criticized Lewis's approach, so different from his own painstaking process, but not envied it – particularly as *The Hobbit* was already a success.

These words are by far the harshest description of Tolkien's views on Narnia. Sayer was a friend of Tolkien's, and so his account has, not unreasonably, been taken as reliable. It seems plausible that the specific objection noted – the mixing of mythologies – is an accurate recollection of Tolkien's response. However, we should be cautious about accepting this report uncritically. Sayer's recollections are being made from a distance of several decades (forty years in the first case, fifty in the second), by which time Carpenter's misleading account of Tolkien's reaction had become the accepted view.* Indeed, in the acknowledgements of his biography, Sayer thanks Humphrey Carpenter for advice and discloses that he has made use of *The Inklings* as a resource.[74] It would not be surprising if Sayer's memory of the strength of Tolkien's reaction became somewhat simplified and condensed over time, and was influenced by Carpenter's accounts. We also lack context for the discussion: Sayer disagreed with Tolkien on the merits of the Narnia books, and Tolkien, who could delight in being contrarian, might well have chosen to play devil's advocate over against Sayer's (and earlier, Green's) lavish praise for the books.

This detailed analysis might be considered nitpicking if it were not for the profound effect that Carpenter's two biographical works have had on the general understanding of Tolkien's attitudes. With Tolkien and Lewis, we have two of the greatest writers of fantasy literature in the twentieth century, both of whom were professional literary critics; it is reasonable to wish to know, as accurately as we can, what one of them thought about the other's most famous work.

"I am glad that you have discovered Narnia"

What did Tolkien himself say about Narnia? Only one mention of it appears in the published *Letters*: in 1964, Tolkien wrote that "It is sad that 'Narnia' and all that part of C.S.L.'s work should remain outside the range of my sympathy, as much of my work was outside his."[75] This is the same snippet that Carpenter quoted in the *Biography*. It is worth observing that only a single paragraph from this letter has been printed, and therefore we lack the full context for Tolkien's comments. Even in itself, it is hardly a condemnation of the books, but rather merely a registering of his own tastes – and it is interesting to see that Tolkien found it "sad" that he did not care for Narnia; he does not take that tone with other writers whose work he disliked.

However, this was not his last word on the subject, despite Carpenter's assertion that "Tolkien could not find it in his heart to reverse his original judgement."[76] Late in his life, Tolkien remarked to a correspondent, "I am glad that you have discovered Narnia. These stories are deservedly very popular." He goes on to say quite firmly that he himself does not like them, but he calls this a "difference of taste" with Lewis.[77] This remark should

---

* A.N. Wilson's *C.S. Lewis: A Biography* contributed to the dissemination of Carpenter's view as fact. Wilson says that Tolkien "hated" *The Lion, the Witch and the Wardrobe* and lists reasons, including alleged jealousy of Lewis's speed of composition, which seem to be lifted directly from Carpenter – but no source is cited (222).

give us pause: it is not just that Tolkien notes the books' popularity (a factual statement), but that they are *deservedly* popular – suggesting that perhaps he had modified his view about their supposedly hodgepodge nature.

We also know that Tolkien provided the Narnia books to his grandchildren. Joanna Tolkien recalls: "When staying with Granny and Grandfather at 99 Holywell, and later at Sandfield Road, I was handed from his bookshelf the Narnia books,"[78] among other titles. Surely, he would not have kept on hand, much less actively recommended to his grandchildren, books that he rejected "totally" and thought were "as bad as can be." Although Tolkien personally (and somewhat regretfully) found the Chronicles outside his own range of imaginative sympathy, he could allow for the possibility that they would appeal to others.

But all that is by way of mitigation, an attempt to cancel out the background noise of the ill-founded and increasingly erroneous notion that Tolkien simply couldn't stand Narnia in any shape or form. Having cleared the decks, as it were, we can attend more judiciously to what Tolkien genuinely did object to. Now that we know he did *not* have a blind or unreasoning dislike of the Narniad as a whole, it becomes more interesting to consider these specific points of disagreement, for they have the potential to shed light on his own creative imagination.

Tolkien did disapprove of Lewis's approach to putting theology into the tales,[79] and of his mixing of mythologies. The question of theology need not be addressed here as we touch upon it later in this chapter and also at various other points in this study.* However, it will be worth considering the question of mixed mythologies. Sayer gives Tolkien's view as follows:

> Because Aslan, the fauns, the White Witch, Father Christmas, the nymphs, and Mr. and Mrs. Beaver had quite different mythological or imaginative origins, Tolkien thought it was a terrible mistake to put them together in Narnia, a single imaginative country. The effect was incongruous and, for him, painful. But Jack [C.S. Lewis] argued that they existed happily together in our minds in real life. Tolkien replied, "Not in mine, or at least not at the same time."[80]

The inclusion of Father Christmas in the list is particularly interesting, as from 1920–1943 Tolkien had created for his children the *Letters from Father Christmas*, featuring the (mis)adventures of a decidedly varied cast of characters: Father Christmas, the North Polar Bear, goblins, and even an elf named Ilbereth – a cast of characters so decidedly varied that one might consider his North Polar Bear to be not so very different, after all, from Lewis's Mr. and Mrs. Beaver. What could justify Tolkien's apparent double standard?

---

* See, for instance, our discussion of George MacDonald's theologically rich *Lilith* (chapter 5), the Christian elements in S.R. Crockett's *The Black Douglas* (chapter 6), and Charles Williams's supernatural thrillers (chapter 9).

It may be that Tolkien felt that the private family audience of his Christmas letters allowed more leeway for mixed mythologies than a book intended for publication. It may also be that Tolkien objected to Lewis's inclusion of Father Christmas not simply because it represented hodgepodge, but because he felt that this kind of hodgepodge didn't work as part of the story.* Lewis's Father Christmas apparently introduces an internal inconsistency into Narnia, for how is it that Narnians know of a person called 'Father Christmas' but show no knowledge of a character called 'Christ'? They know 'Aslan,' yes, but what it is that the Narnians understand, if anything, by 'Christmas' is left unexplained. In the *Letters from Father Christmas*, however, no attempt is made to skirt round the implications of the protagonist's name, but all sorts of explicit links with real-world Christianity are woven into the tales: there are references to the Church calendar, including mentions of St. Nicholas, St. Stephen, and All Saints,[81] and the hero's own name is repeatedly spelled "Fr. Christmas," as if referring to a priest.† In these small but significant ways, Tolkien's fantasy world is dovetailed into the primary world and the apparent Lewisian inconsistency is avoided.

We will consider another aspect of his objection – "the fauns" – in our next section, by means of a very interesting and suggestive parallel with Kenneth Grahame's *The Wind in the Willows*. But before we come onto that, we should conclude this present discussion by bringing to mind an intriguing comment that Tolkien made on his own work. In a 1937 letter, he wrote: "I don't much approve of *The Hobbit* myself, preferring my own mythology [i.e., his own background legendarium] . . . to this rabble of Eddaic-named dwarves out of Völuspá, newfangled hobbits and gollums (invented in an idle hour) and Anglo-Saxon runes."[82]

Here we find Tolkien describing his own newly published book in terms that foreshadow his critique of Narnia, calling it a "rabble." By the time Tolkien encountered *The Lion, the Witch and the Wardrobe* in the late 1940s he had spent much time and labor in producing a "Hobbit sequel" that was not at all a "rabble," but far more polished and serious and consistent. Furthermore, Lewis had been his greatest supporter through all the writing and revision of *The Lord of the Rings*. Could it be that Tolkien felt slightly

---

* In this, ironically, he shared the view of Roger Lancelyn Green, who, despite liking everything else about *The Lion, the Witch and the Wardrobe*, recalled "reacting against the presence of Father Christmas . . . and urging Lewis to omit him" (Green and Hooper, *C.S. Lewis*, 241). For more on why Lewis retained the character over Green's objections, see Michael Ward, *Planet Narnia*, 66–67.

† In the deluxe edition of *Letters from Father Christmas* (London: HarperCollins, 2019), Tolkien's "Fr. Christmas" is repeatedly expanded into "Father Christmas" in the transcriptions. The only time it is transcribed as "Fr." is on its last appearance as a signature, on page 134. (Only the 2019 edition includes images of every letter and envelope.) The published transcriptions also silently emend the frequent appearances of "X-mas," "Fr. X," and even "Xtopher" (for Christopher), thus erasing what is probably intended to be a scholarly nod to the Greek letter *chi*, which in many manuscripts of the New Testament and on many ancient icons was used as a standard abbreviation for 'Christos.' Tolkien, ever the philology professor, would have enjoyed the opportunity to remind his children that the etymology of his third son's name was 'Christ-bearer.'

disappointed that his friend would, as it were, imitate what Tolkien saw as the comparatively raw style of *The Hobbit* rather than the mature style of *The Lord of the Rings*? Or could it be that, having been self-deprecating about his own work, he expressed his views on Narnia more forcefully than they really were, trusting that his friends would interpret this as ragging or hyperbole?* Without more context for his remarks, it is difficult to judge, but we may get a little more light on the subject by turning to his thoughts on our next author, Kenneth Grahame.

"Almost perfect": Kenneth Grahame's *The Wind in the Willows*

Kenneth Grahame (1859–1932) is today justly celebrated for *The Wind in the Willows* (1908), the classic tale of the friendship between humble Mole, poetic Rat, gruff Badger, and exuberant Toad. Before its publication, he had established himself as a writer of essays, reminiscences of his own childhood, and children's stories, including *Pagan Papers* (1893), *The Golden Age* (1895), and *Dream Days* (1898).

Tolkien heartily praises *The Wind in the Willows*, describing it as an "excellent book" and a "delightful picture"; he characterizes its down-to-earth, nondream quality as a "correct tone."[83] Having enjoyed the tale, Tolkien was eager to read a follow-up work, the posthumously published *First Whisper of "The Wind in the Willows"* (1944),[84] which provided the earliest versions of the story in the form of letters Grahame wrote to his young son, along with a biographical introduction by Grahame's widow.

Tolkien humorously identified himself with Mr. Toad in a letter to Rayner Unwin, who had shown him some of the advance praise for *The Lord of the Rings*. Unwin recalled that "Tolkien yearned for such reassurances and asked to see any others that I received, promising at the same time not to be like Mr Toad."[85] It sounds as if Tolkien might have rather liked to sing a song celebrating his own brilliance:

> Those clever men at Oxford
> > Know all there is to be knowed.
> But they none of them know one half as much
> > As intelligent Mr Toad![86]

In his identification with Toad's vainglorious conceit, we find an attractive touch of self-deprecation on Tolkien's part; he is aware both of his own need for praise as an author and of the dangers of delighting in it too wholeheartedly.

"Mixed form"

What is particularly interesting about *The Wind in the Willows* is that it has marked similarities to Lewis's *The Lion, the Witch and the Wardrobe*. Both tales involve a blending

---

* See chapter 12 for Tolkien's very English habits of expression.

of different worlds and different registers, and both feature an intrusion of specifically pagan mythology in the form of a faun (*Lion*) or the faun-like god Pan (*Willows*). One would expect Tolkien's critiques of Narnia to apply here as well, but Tolkien was delighted by Grahame's tale.

As we have seen, one reason for Tolkien's dislike of *The Lion* is that it was, in his view, a mishmash of unrelated elements. In fact, the Narnia Chronicles are anything but a mishmash; they are very carefully constructed and consistent on a thematic and atmospheric level.[87] However, Tolkien's initial reaction is not surprising, given that in the first book we have Nesbit-style modern children, talking animals of the beast-fable tradition, fauns from Greco-Roman myth, Father Christmas, and more. Tolkien appears to have objected to this mixing of different elements. He certainly had a similar criticism of Andrew Lang's *Prince Ricardo* for being a muddle, jotting a note that its mix of real and wondrous material "cannot be arranged in geographical sequence, or their histories chronologically arranged."[88]

However, *The Wind in the Willows* is hardly perfectly consistent either. In the draft of "On Fairy-stories," Tolkien muses on Grahame's tale, noting that it is "unclassifiable" and describing it as made up of various elements: "beast-fable, satire, comedy, *contes des fées* (or even pantomime), wild-wood and rivers of Oxfordshire." Except for the chapter "The Piper at the Gates of Dawn," Tolkien found this mixture pleasing and describes it as "an almost perfect blend . . . of many pigments."[89] It may seem strange that Tolkien, who had an extremely high regard for consistency in a literary work, would be able to appreciate this stylistic blend; a closer examination may allow us to detect some deeper grounds for his preferences.

One reason why Grahame's mixing of elements, but not Lewis's, was pleasing to Tolkien may lie in the fact that *The Wind in the Willows* seems (at least at first) to be more fully a "blend": the different elements flow together. In contrast, Lewis's modern-day English world, fairy-tale land, and classical elements stand out distinctly in the early chapters of the first Narnia book. Grahame does have both animal and human characters, but with the exception of the Toad scenes (which are the most satiric), the animals and the humans do not mix, and the human characters are not central. As Tolkien notes, "*The Wind in the Willows* is of course a mixed form but the washerwoman and the engine driver are really only adjuncts: the story is about a Toad, a Rat and a Mole."[90] The blending is of stylistic elements (fable, satire, comedy) rather than mythological elements.

We should recall that although Nesbit's 'Psammead' stories, which Tolkien enjoyed, feature travel through time and space, they do not hop between distinct worlds: all the action (magical or mundane) takes place within the same world. Lewis's Narnia tales abound in separate but interconnected worlds (England, Narnia, Bism, Charn, Aslan's Country), with various types of portals from one world to the next (wardrobes, railway platforms, framed paintings, pools, stable doors).

In contrast, *The Wind in the Willows* has, at its heart, the River and the Wild Wood, and a small penumbra of adjacent locations, such as the dungeon where Toad is confined and the canal where he meets the Washerwoman; there are no magical portals between the animal and the human worlds or between the sub-created and the 'real' worlds. The result is that *The Wind in the Willows* feels coherent, even if its individual parts are highly varied. Tolkien may also simply have liked the components of Grahame's story (not least, the Oxfordshire landscape, lovingly and attentively described) and disliked the elements that Lewis used in his (the White Witch is very much in the style of Hans Christian Andersen's Snow Queen, and Tolkien "couldn't stand" Andersen's stories).[91] Blended colors seem to have been more to Tolkien's taste than sharp lines when it came to secondary worlds.

Pan out of place

A second point of connection between *The Wind in the Willows* and *The Lion, the Witch and the Wardrobe* is that both feature a goat-man, the kind that is called a satyr in Greek and a faun in Roman mythology. (See figure 15.) Grahame's chapter "The Piper at the Gates of Dawn" features the Greek god Pan, depicted with hooves and curling horns, while Lewis's Mr. Tumnus is specifically identified as a faun. What makes both of these characters slightly edgy for a children's story is that the figure of the satyr in particular, and the faun to a lesser extent, is associated with sexual promiscuity and violence. Tolkien finds fault with both Lewis and Grahame in this regard. As we have seen, Tolkien refers specifically to Mr. Tumnus and his home in his mocking comments, reported by Roger Lancelyn Green: "It really won't do, you know! I mean to say, *'Nymphs and their Ways, The Love-Life of a Faun'*. Doesn't he know what he's talking about?"

Tolkien's objection to Grahame's story, formed long before he encountered Lewis's tale, is similar but much gentler: "Pan has no business here," Tolkien writes, "at least not explicit and revealed." He does not object to the character of Pan in principle, or to the scene in which Pan is a character; the chapter is a tender, artfully written one, and Tolkien describes it as a "beautiful colour in itself." Rather, he dislikes the way that this element "muddies" the composition as a whole: "I personally think that in Pan we have that addition of a little colour that spoils the palate."[92] *

It is interesting that Tolkien's criticism is so mild, especially when we consider how much there is in common with *The Lion, the Witch and the Wardrobe*. In *The Wind in the Willows*, Ratty and Mole come across Pan while searching for a missing baby otter, whom they find curled up asleep, safe and sound, with Pan. In Narnia, Lucy Pevensie goes off happily with Mr. Tumnus and has a very pleasant tea in his cave. Admittedly, he intends to kidnap her and take her to the White Witch, but he soon confesses to his crime, repents, is forgiven by the tender-hearted Lucy, and helps her get back to the Wardrobe safely. In both cases – the baby otter, and Lucy Pevensie – we have a child-figure interacting with a faun-figure.

---

* "Palate" is Tolkien's spelling, perhaps a deliberate play on palate/palette.

However, there are elements in Graham's scene that give it a different tone. In *The Wind in the Willows*, we see Pan inspiring both awe (verging on terror) and love in Ratty and Mole, so that the character is in tune with the idea of 'panic' that Pan aroused in ancient myth. As Mole looks up, he

> saw the backward sweep of the curved horns. . . the stern, hooked nose between the kindly eyes that were looking down on them humorously, while the bearded mouth broke into a half-smile at the corners; saw the rippling muscles on the arm that lay across the broad chest . . . saw the splendid curves of the shaggy limbs disposed in majestic ease on the sward . . . [93]

Pan is described in a masculine but not sexual way, and he is named as "Friend" and "Helper." Furthermore, he is seen only in relation to the animal characters and does not interact with humans at all, let alone any children. Insofar as Pan displays a sort of animal magnetism, it is appropriate for the animal context.

Mr. Tumnus, on the other hand, is portrayed as thoroughly domesticated. He has a snug cave with a carpet, a shelf of books, and a painting of his father over the mantelpiece; he serves a very nice tea with boiled eggs, toast, and cake. He is presented as a perfectly safe companion for a young girl travelling abroad by herself – at any rate, perfectly safe after his repentance – in spite of the fact that fauns are traditionally and irremediably lecherous. Nevertheless, the scene includes some slightly jarring notes. One is that when Lucy is looking around Mr. Tumnus's comfortable cave, she notices a door which she "thought must lead to Mr. Tumnus's bedroom." The child reader will not think twice, but the adult reader of classics might well do so. The other is the content of Mr. Tumnus's bookshelves, which includes *Nymphs and Their Ways* and *The Life and Letters of Silenus*.

Tolkien was well aware of Lewis's command of classical literature. Nymphs are female nature-spirits who, in classical mythology, are often the target of sexual aggression by satyrs, including Silenus or Bacchus. To a classically educated adult reader, *Nymphs and Their Ways* might easily suggest pornography rather than natural history. Tolkien's reference to *The Love-Life of a Faun* – which is not in fact one of the titles on Mr. Tumnus's shelf* – seems to be his way of emphasizing the problem he has noticed. For a man with four children of his own, one of them a daughter, it may have seemed to Tolkien that Lewis's humor here was inappropriately racy, or that using a sexually charged faun-figure clashed with the setting, in a way that Grahame had largely avoided with Pan. With the benefit of hindsight, we know that Lewis handled Mr. Tumnus in an appropriate way, and that in the sequel, *Prince Caspian,* he directly addresses the seeming incongruity of

---

* It is possible that this title was in the draft version Tolkien heard, and his objection led to its removal. Since Lewis did not keep the manuscript, we cannot know for sure.

pagan sensuality appearing in a children's book.* But we must bear in mind that Tolkien, hearing only the first chapters read to him, had no idea where the story was going or what would happen to Lucy.

A third reason why Tolkien might have preferred Grahame's tale to the Narnia stories has to do with his dislike of overt religious elements in a story. Tolkien once told Walter Hooper that he found the Christian elements in Lewis's Narnia books to be too obvious.[94] Though the Narnia Chronicles are not allegory as such, Aslan is an easily recognizable Christ-figure whose sacrificial death and subsequent resurrection are central to *The Lion, the Witch and the Wardrobe*. In the Narnia books, Lewis makes the connection to Christian belief considerably more noticeable than it is, for instance, in *Out of the Silent Planet*, which Tolkien enjoyed (and which we will discuss in chapter 9). Here we should return to Tolkien's comment about *The Wind in the Willows* that "Pan has no business here: at least not explicit and revealed." Tolkien seems not to have objected in principle to the inclusion of a divine presence in the story; rather, he objects to it being made "explicit." In his view, the spiritual or Christian elements of a story should be handled with the greatest degree of indirection and subtlety. Even the very brief intrusion of direct contact with transcendence, in Grahame's work, seems to Tolkien almost to spoil the effect of the whole; but as that intrusion is limited to a single chapter, and is in any case very mild, it did not prevent him from enjoying the book overall. Tolkien put his preferences into practice: *The Hobbit*, and even more so *The Lord of the Rings*, has deeply Christian themes and echoes, but they are deliberately hidden and implicit.

Foreshadowing the Fellowship

Thus far we have compared Grahame and Lewis with the aim of tracing Tolkien's views on the proper construction of children's stories. It is worth also considering whether *The Wind in the Willows* had any influence of a more direct sort on Tolkien's writings. Here it is interesting to note that Lewis made a strong connection between Grahame's tale and *The Hobbit*. Reviewing Tolkien's book for *The Times Literary Supplement*, Lewis remarked that "Its place is with *Alice, Flatland, Phantastes, The Wind in the Willows*."[95] He expands upon this parallel in his second review of *The Hobbit*, for *The Times*:

> If you like the adventures of Ratty and Mole, you will like *The Hobbit*. . . . If, in those adventures, you prized the solidity of the social and

---

* Bacchus himself appears in the tale as part of a festive romp, prompting Susan to remark, "'I wouldn't have felt safe with Bacchus and all his wild girls if we'd met them without Aslan.' 'I should think not,' said Lucy" (chapter XI). Lewis thus acknowledges the potentially threatening sexuality of these pagan figures, while showing that the presence of Christ (in the figure of Aslan) allows the positive aspect to be enjoyed. One wonders if Tolkien's remarks on *Lion*, despite discouraging Lewis at the time, might have contributed to this element in the sequel. The fact that Tolkien eventually considered the Narnia books suitable for his granddaughter suggests that he found Lewis's final handling of these issues in *Lion* and *Prince Caspian* to be satisfactory.

geographical context in which your small friends moved, you will like *The Hobbit* even better. The hobbit himself, Mr Bilbo Baggins, is as prosaic as Mole, but fate sets him wandering among dwarfs and elves, over goblin mountains, in search of dragon-guarded gold.[96]

In this short review, Lewis's comparison of *The Hobbit* to *The Wind in the Willows* takes up nearly half of the total space; clearly, he felt it to be a significant parallel. And in so doing, he alerts us to the possibilty of further connections. For instance, Tolkien knew *The Wind in the Willows* so well, and thought so highly of it, that it is difficult to imagine that he was not making an interior nod to Grahame's "Wild Wood" when Merry and Pippin, taking one last look behind before they enter Fangorn, are compared to "elf-children in the deeps of time peering out of the Wild Wood in wonder at their first Dawn"; or that he was not glancing at Grahame's River when Faramir sits "watching the ever-moving stream; and the sad reeds were rustling"; or even that he was not recalling Toad's tasty stew, eaten on the run in a gipsy's campsite, when Sam cooks his herbs and stewed rabbit. *The Wind in the Willows* quite probably lies deep beneath these elements, and others, incorporated not in a conscious or deliberate way, but as fully digested and assimilated material in Tolkien's imagination.

We have already discussed, albeit briefly, the importance of the Oxfordshire countryside in both Grahame's and Tolkien's writings (for more on this, see the discussion of Matthew Arnold's poetry in chapter 11); we can now consider the possible influence of what we might call the 'fellowship' of Mole, Ratty, Badger, and Toad. Here we have four friends, each of a peculiar species and thus different by physique, habitat, and preferences, and each with a distinct personality. The gentle diffidence of Mole, the energetic hospitality of Rat, the bluff shyness of Badger, and the charming egotism of Toad are aspects of them as individual characters and also intrinsically related to their animal nature – they are almost archetypes. Here we see a particular approach to characterization, making use of the exterior form of each member of this animal band. As Lewis puts it,

> Does anyone believe that Kenneth Grahame made an arbitrary choice when he gave his principal character the form of a toad, or that a stag, a pigeon, a lion, would have done as well? The choice is based on the fact that the real toad's face has a grotesque resemblance to a certain kind of human face – a rather apoplectic face with a fatuous grin on it. . . . Looking at the creature we thus see, isolated and fixed, an aspect of human vanity in its funniest and most pardonable form; following that hint Grahame creates Mr Toad – an ultra-Jonsonian 'humour.'[97]

We find a very similar insight in Lewis's observation, regarding *The Lord of the Rings*, that "Much that in a realistic work would be done by 'character delineation' is here done simply by making the character an elf, a dwarf, or a hobbit. The imagined beings have their insides on the outside; they are visible souls."[98]

Can we see here an influence from Grahame upon Tolkien's approach to characterization, as well as to the diverse groupings that are so central to his tales?* In *The Hobbit*, we have a questing party comprised of dwarves, a wizard, and a hobbit, as well as a finale involving men, elves, eagles, and dwarves fighting against a common foe; in *The Lord of the Rings*, we have the Fellowship, the Nine Walkers with representatives from the races of hobbits, dwarves, elves, wizards, and men. In these modern days when we accept diversity as a virtue, it is easy to take for granted the fact that Tolkien should have assembled sundry characters for united action in this way. But in the other sources that we will examine later in this study, such diverse yet equal racial groupings are not to be found. In William Morris's fantasy tales, we might encounter a dwarf, but only as an incidental or even villainous figure; in Rider Haggard's adventure stories, native Africans may have a part to play, but the white, male protagonists unquestionably carry the story. We certainly do not see in these authors, as we do in Tolkien, characters of different races presented with equal dignity and worth, each with a vital role to fulfill. (The orcs, who might seem to be an exception, in fact are not a race of rational beings at all, but rather beasts or even tools.†) Tolkien's larger legendarium features heterogeneous kindreds interacting in significant ways, including intermarriage, but it is only in *The Hobbit* and *The Lord of the Rings* that the trope of multi-ethnic collaboration is fully developed and indeed central to the plot. Especially since *The Hobbit* was conceived originally as a story for his children, it seems at least possible that Grahame's tale of animal friends gave Tolkien an idea, or encouraged him in the execution of the idea, that a fellowship of diverse peoples was an imaginatively (and morally) good choice for his narrative.

---

* Interestingly, in *The Wind in the Willows*, Grahame occasionally uses the word "man" or "manful" when referring to Ratty, and Mr. Badger too uses the word "man" when speaking of his fellow animals. It is possible that Tolkien had this usage in the back of his mind when, in the first version of *The Hobbit*, he used the word with regard to Bilbo and the dwarves (incorrectly by Arthur Ransome's reckoning, as we saw above).

† Tolkien's ideas as to their nature changed as the legendarium developed, but maintain the basic concept that the orcs were not a race in their own right, but were created by Melkor through corruption or manipulation of other beings. In a short essay ca. 1959 called "Orcs," he writes that "The Orcs were *beasts* of humanized shape (to mock Men and Elves) . . . Melkor taught them *speech* and as they bred they inherited this; and they had just as much independence as have, say, dogs or horses of their human masters. This talking was largely echoic (cf. parrots)." He adds that "the *wills* of Orcs and Balrogs etc. are part of Melkor's power 'dispersed' . . . Sauron is just another (if greater) agent. Orcs can rebel against him without losing their own irremediable allegiance to evil (Morgoth.)" (HOME X, 410–411). We see the non-rational nature of the Orcs in their reaction when Sauron is destroyed: "As when death smites the swollen brooding thing that inhabits their crawling hill and holds them all in sway, ants will wander witless and purposeless and then feebly die, so the creatures of Sauron, orc or troll or beast spell-enslaved, ran hither and thither mindless" – while Sauron's human allies are able to make intentional choices to fight, flee, or sue for mercy.

❧ Conclusion

In this chapter, we have considered the many and various post-Victorian children's books that Tolkien knew, and have discovered that he kept abreast of children's literature for the benefit of his own immediate family and, later, his grandchildren. We have seen Tolkien himself draw a direct link between the Snergs of Wyke-Smith and his invention of the hobbits – a very great debt indeed. We have noted his high regard for the work of Beatrix Potter and the possible influence of her rabbits on his hobbits. We have observed that Tolkien admired the realistic Swallows and Amazons series, and considered how Arthur Ransome's style of illustration might well have encouraged Tolkien in his *Hobbit* art. We have traced his very probable debts to Hugh Lofting's animal servants, and seen how his appreciation for Edith Nesbit's tales sheds light on his own ideas about successful storytelling. We have unraveled the threads of his famously negative reaction to Lewis's Narnia Chronicles, and found that the issue is more complex and interesting than conventional wisdom would have it. We have discovered that his admiration for *The Wind in the Willows* provides plausible reasons for his objections to *The Lion, the Witch, and the Wardrobe.*

Tolkien's reading of modern children's literature was extensive, attentive, and characteristically opinionated. It shows us, in sum, a good deal about the workings of his creative imagination and about his preferences as a thinker and writer. Certainly, Middle-earth would have existed even if he had remained ignorant of all the books and authors mentioned in this chapter, but, equally certainly, it would not have been quite the world we know.

❧ 5 ❧

George MacDonald
The Tarnished Key

I N THE PREVIOUS TWO CHAPTERS WE CONSIDERED NUMEROUS CHILDREN'S
authors, but omitted one particularly important name: that of George MacDonald.
He deserves a separate treatment partly because he wrote in many other genres than
just children's literature and partly because Tolkien's lifelong relationship to his work was
both significant and complex.

George MacDonald (1824–1905) started his career as a Congregationalist minister
but soon turned to writing as a more remunerative way of providing for his large family.
Among his literary friends was Lewis Carroll, whom he encouraged to publish *Alice's Adventures in Wonderland*. MacDonald's fictional output was prolific and varied: two fantasy novels for adults, *Phantastes* (1858) and *Lilith* (1895); a number of children's fantasies
including *At the Back of the North Wind* (1871), *The Princess and the Goblin* (1872), and
The Princess and Curdie (1883); shorter fairy tales, including "The Golden Key" (1867);
and a large number of realistic novels, which are today largely forgotten.

MacDonald's tales played an influential role in Tolkien's reading. Tolkien himself
says that George MacDonald (along with Andrew Lang) composed "the books which
most affected the background of my imagination since childhood."[1] C.S. Lewis confirms that his friend and colleague was "soaked" in MacDonald."[2] Tolkien counted *The
Princess and the Goblin* and *The Princess and Curdie* among his early favorites and later
read them to his children.[3] He continued to read and reflect on these works as an adult,
although, as we will discuss below, in later life he drastically downgraded his opinion
of MacDonald's merits.[4] He even served as an examiner of a 1934 B.Litt thesis entitled
The Fairy Tales and Fantasies of George MacDonald.[5] Kilby's recollection that Tolkien
"thought MacDonald would have done better to retain his native dialect in some of his
writings"[6] suggests that Tolkien read at least some of his realistic fiction,* as it is these
rather than the children's or fantasy tales where he uses Scottish dialect. He certainly

---

* Dimitra Fimi suggests a possible influence from *Sir Gibbie* on one of Tolkien's most famous lines. MacDonald writes, "The one secret of life and development, is not to devise and plan,
but to fall in with the forces at work – to do every moment's duty aright – that being the part in
the process allotted to us" (chapter XLIV). Fimi suggests this resembles Gandalf's response when
Frodo remarks that he wished these events had not happened in his time: "'So do I . . . and so do
all who live to see such times. But that is not for them to decide. All we have to decide is what to do
with the time that is given us'" ("George MacDonald and one of Tolkien's most quotable lines").

read the adult fantasies, later saying that he felt "profound dislike" for *Phantastes*, but offering qualified praise for *Lilith*.[7]

Tolkien acknowledged his debts to MacDonald. In a letter discussing the origins of *The Hobbit*, he disclosed that the tale was "derived from (previously digested) epic, mythology, and fairy-story – not, however, Victorian in authorship, as a rule to which George Macdonald is the chief exception."[8] Tolkien's negative manner of phrasing slightly masks the important point he is making: namely, that MacDonald is the major (but not the only) exception to the rule that the fairy-tale sources of *The Hobbit* are generally *not* Victorian in origin. We should keep this admission in mind as we assess the vital contribution MacDonald provided to Tolkien's creative imagination.

Mining for goblins: the *Curdie* books

What influence did MacDonald have upon *The Hobbit*? Tolkien helpfully points out a specific connection, noting that his goblins and orcs "resemble"[9] MacDonald's goblins. (See figure 8.) Furthermore he says that MacDonald "has depicted what will always be to me the classic goblin. By that standard I judge all goblins, old or new."[10] Elsewhere, he explained that the goblins of *The Hobbit* and the orcs of *The Lord of the Rings* owe "a good deal to the goblin tradition . . . especially as it appears in George MacDonald, except for the soft feet which I never believed in."[11] His qualification reinforces the strength of the link; Tolkien remembered MacDonald's goblins distinctly enough, even in 1954, to make a precise exception to the comparison.

Those goblins come from *The Princess and the Goblin*, a story featuring a miner boy called Curdie and a princess called Irene, who lives in a castle atop the mountain. The goblins, hostile to humans, live in tunnels beneath the mountain, but emerge sometimes at night. Curdie rescues Irene from an attack by goblins when she is out too late; later she rescues him, in turn, with the aid of her mysterious great-great-grandmother. Curdie and the other miners keep hearing the "constant sound of the goblin hammers and pickaxes at night,"[12] and he discovers that the goblins are carving out new homes for themselves deep within the mountain. Finally, he foils a plot by the goblins to break into the castle and kidnap Irene to be the goblin prince's wife. He also learns their chief weakness: their soft, sensitive feet.

We can begin to see the goblin influence on Tolkien in 1932, when these creatures appear for the first time in one of the *Letters from Father Christmas*, very much in the MacDonald mold.[13] These *Father Christmas* goblins and later those of *The Hobbit* have an unmistakable mark of their origin in MacDonald's *Curdie* books: they are cave-dwelling, tunnel-digging, essentially subterranean creatures.

Such has been the influence of Tolkien on subsequent fantasy that for readers today, 'goblin' is strongly associated with 'underground' – but in fact MacDonald invented this detail. In Katharine Briggs's magisterial studies of fairies in English folklore, 'goblin' is a general name for a small, ugly, malignant spirit.[14] 'Hobgoblin' is another general category, of "rough, hairy spirits, which do domestic chores, work about farms, guard treasure, keep an eye on the servants, and generally act as guardian spirits of the home."[15] They are fundamentally above-ground creatures, with caves as just one option among many for dwelling places: "They will take up their abode in a farmhouse or manor but they often have a particular pool, stream, rock or cave as their permanent habitation."[16] There is no evidence in the folkloric tradition that goblins have a particular affinity for locations beneath the surface of the earth, much less mining or tunneling. The *only* allusion to such tendencies in Briggs's work is her use of an illustration from MacDonald's *The Princess and the Goblin* for the "Goblin" entry in the *Dictionary of Fairies* – notable precisely because it is MacDonald's original contribution to the goblin tradition.

With this context in mind, we can see the significance of Tolkien's goblins being so clearly subterranean: he is following MacDonald, choosing his version as the classic goblin model. Indeed, we can see a hint of this in a phrase from *The Hobbit*: the goblins drive the captured dwarves and hobbit along dark passages, "such as only goblins that have taken to living in the heart of the mountains can see through." *Taken to*: for goblins were not originally dwellers below the surface.

Not only do both MacDonald's and Tolkien's goblins live underground in a network of caves in the mountains, but they are similar in appearance, with their flat, flapping feet. Although the *feet* are not soft, Tolkien adds the curious detail that they "slipped on soft shoes" in order to pursue the fleeing dwarves in silence! We also find a similarity in behavior. MacDonald's goblins dig close to the miners' passages in preparation for a final assault. Curdie learns this when he accidentally breaks through the dividing wall and overhears the goblins conspiring with one another. Here we see a resemblance, albeit in reverse, to Tolkien's goblins of the Misty Mountains who emerge through a hidden door at the back of the cave in which Bilbo and his companions are sleeping and snatch the whole party unaware.

In MacDonald's story, Curdie follows the goblins as they gather in a "magnificent cavern":

> It rose to a tremendous height, but the roof was composed of such shining materials, and the multitude of torches carried by the goblins who crowded the floor lighted up the place so brilliantly, that Curdie could see to the top quite well. . . . At the other end of the hall, high above the heads of the multitude, was a terrace-like ledge of considerable height. . . . Upon this sat the king and his court: the king on a throne hollowed out of a huge block of green copper ore, and his court on lower seats around it.[17]

This subterranean hall prefigures the one in *The Hobbit*, where we see "a big cavern . . . lit by a great red fire in the middle, and by torches along the walls, and it was full of goblins." Bilbo and company are frog-marched to its far end where "in the shadows on a large flat stone sat a tremendous goblin with a huge head, and armed goblins were standing round him carrying the axes and the bent swords that they use."

Another connection between *The Hobbit* and the *Curdie* books has to do with song. MacDonald's goblins hate songs and, as a result, Curdie is able to deter their attacks by singing (loudly and at length) along these lines:

> Ring! dod! bang!
> Go the hammers clang!
> Hit and turn and bore!
> Whizz and puff and roar!
> Thus we rive the rocks,
> Force the goblin locks . . . [18]

In *The Hobbit*, it is the goblins themselves who sing as they haul their captives underground, with verses such as these:

> Clap! Snap! the black crack!
> Grip, grab! Pinch, nab!
> And down down to Goblin-town
>   You go, my lad!

Although the context has been reversed, the dynamic of the scene is similar, with the songs accompanying violence or the threat of violence, and the songs themselves in both cases heavily staccato, alliterative, and rhythmic.

In MacDonald's sequel, *The Princess and Curdie,* the goblins make no appearance, but an interesting narrative and thematic foreshadowing of *The Hobbit* does appear. At the end of the tale, Curdie marries Princess Irene and they rule wisely and well. However, after their death, the kingdom falls into ruin because of greed. Curdie had discovered that the mines under the mountain produced gold; indeed, "the city stood upon gold." The next king "went mining and mining in the rock under the city, and grew more and more eager after the gold, and paid less and less heed to his people." The result is catastrophic:

> . . . so greedy was the king after gold, that when at last the ore began to fail, he caused the miners to reduce the pillars . . . left standing to bear the city. And from the girth of an oak of a thousand years, they chipped them down to that of a fir tree of fifty. One day at noon, when life was at its highest, the whole city fell with a roaring crash. The cries of men and the shrieks of women went up with its dust, and then there was a great silence. Where the mighty rock once towered, crowded with homes and crowned with a palace, now rushes and raves a stone-obstructed rapid of the river. All around spreads a wilderness of wild deer, and the very name of Gwyntystorm had ceased from the lips of men. [19]

This dark, abrupt collapse into ruin is startling for a children's story; given the fairy-tale development of the plot to that point, including the rags-to-riches marriage of Curdie to Irene, one hardly expects the story to strike such a note of death and destruction.

This memorable image is one that Tolkien may have adapted for his own fictional purposes. In the opening chapter of *The Hobbit*, we hear the story of the rise and fall of the King Under the Mountain. Thorin recounts how his ancestors "mined and they tunnelled and they made huger halls and greater workshops – and in addition I believe they found a good deal of gold and a great many jewels too. Anyway they grew immensely rich and famous." This gold, of course, attracted Smaug and, as a result of his coming, the town of Dale and the land around the Mountain are laid waste, and the few surviving dwarves are dispossessed. The cycle of corruption repeats near the end of *The Hobbit* when Thorin, now reinstated as King Under the Mountain, falls under the dragon-spell, ignores the legitimate claims of the Lake-Men, and comes perilously close to outright war in order to defend his hoard.

Here we see Tolkien elaborating upon elements found in MacDonald's story, but weaving them into his own tale in a different order and with a different conclusion: the mountain, tunneled-out for gold, with the king's residence atop (or within) it; an originally prosperous and healthy society; greed for gold leading to moral decline; and a catastrophic fall of the kingdom and devastation of the surrounding landscape.

Diamond doggerel: *At the Back of the North Wind*

Turning to MacDonald's other children's fiction, another possible influence may be found in *At the Back of the North Wind*. Tolkien owned a copy of it late in his life, and even if he did not have his own copy in earlier days, he would have been familiar with it from his Oxford supervisions of student work on children's literature in general and MacDonald in particular.[20]

The protagonist is an almost incredibly good little boy, Diamond, who has adventures with the personified North Wind. At one point, Diamond meets an author who gives him a book of his own poems, one of which, "The True History of the Cat and Fiddle," Diamond sings to his baby brother. The "True History" poem purports – much like the tales of Knatchbull-Hugessen – to give the backstory of familiar nursery rhymes. It playfully blends two traditional nursery rhymes, "The Man in the Moon Came Down Too Soon" and "Hey Diddle Diddle,"[21] making the original nursery-rhyme absurdities even more comic by combining them into a single, plausible setting.

MacDonald's poem comprises four stanzas, of which the second gives an idea of his approach:

Hey, diddle, diddle!
   Went the cat and the fiddle,
Hey diddle, diddle, dee, dee!
   The dog laughed at the sport
   Till his cough cut him short,
It was hey diddle, diddle, oh me!
   And back came the cow
   With a merry, merry low
For she'd humbled the man in the moon.
   The dish got excited,
   The spoon was delighted,
And the dish waltzed away with the spoon.[22]

Tolkien would later blend the same two nursery rhymes into a comic poem of his own, "The Man in the Moon Stayed Up Too Late," which, as we noted in the chapter 3, made its way into *The Fellowship of the Ring* when Frodo sings it at The Prancing Pony. The song features "an inn, a merry old inn" where "the Man in the Moon himself came down / one night to drink his fill." Of particular note are these verses:

The landlord keeps a little dog
   that is mighty fond of jokes;
When there's good cheer among the guests,
He cocks an ear at all the jests
   and laughs until he chokes.

Here we find an intriguing detail linking Frodo's song with Diamond's: the little dog who "laughs until he chokes" in Tolkien's version, and who "laughed at the sport / Till his cough cut him short" in MacDonald's. In the original nursery rhyme, the dog simply laughs; the detail of him coughing appears to have been invented by MacDonald and then adapted by Tolkien. Furthermore, Tolkien's first version of this poem, published in 1923 in *Yorkshire Poetry*, lacks this detail, as the dog merely "laughed to see such fun"[23]; the more vivid description comes in the revision. Although Tolkien may have independently thought of mixing traditional rhymes, his choice of these two particular rhymes appears to have come from MacDonald, as signified by the tell-tale canine cough.

"Profound dislike": *Phantastes*

Of MacDonald's two adult fantasy novels, *Phantastes* (1858) is the better-known today, in large part because of C.S. Lewis's lavish praise for it.[24] In this "Faerie Romance," as it is subtitled, the protagonist Anodos takes ownership, on his twenty-first birthday, of the house and possessions bequeathed to him by his dead father. The next morning, he discovers that his bedroom has converted itself into the outdoors: a stream flows from the wash-basin over a carpet of grass. He is in Fairy Land. Adventures follow that signify growing spiritual maturity. After a chapter describing his blissful experience of death, Anodos finds himself back home, welcomed by his sisters: "I had been gone, they told me, twenty-one days. To me it seemed twenty-one years."[25]

Tolkien's opinion of *Phantastes* contrasted markedly with Lewis's extravagant fondness for it. Lewis, he says, "was evidently born loving (moral) allegory, and I was born with an instinctive distaste for it. 'Phantastes' wakened him, and afflicted me with profound dislike."[26] Here we can gain a glimpse of Tolkien's sensitivity toward being imposed upon, as it were, by an author.

Phantastes is, on the surface, an episodic and dreamlike book; MacDonald refused to spell out his meaning directly. Nevertheless, he had a moral meaning to convey. Greville MacDonald recounts that when a lady asked his father for the meaning of *Phantastes*, "His reply was to the effect that he had written the book with the sole object of giving her its meaning."[27] The protagonist's name, Anodos (Greek for "no way," or "the way upward"), gives a clue that the story is paradoxically about two things at once: a spiritual journey that is to be made both by an impassable way and a way of ascent. W.H. Auden wrote of the story that "the illusion of participating in a real dream is perfect; one never feels that it is an allegorical presentation of wakeful conscious processes."[28]* The very fact that Auden felt moved to comment that one never *feels* the allegorical presentation implies that he thought it was working, at some level, in an allegorical way – but masked. Tolkien sniffed out the mask, which was one of the reasons he took against it.

There are other reasons why Tolkien might have found it objectionable.† First, given Tolkien's preference for a consistent, well-defined secondary world, the structure of *Phantastes* would have gone against the grain. *Phantastes* has worlds within worlds, connected in a way that is psychologically resonant but not logically coherent. The novel contains various interpolated stories – something that Tolkien appreciated in authors such as Morris – but they are not presented as texts within a single story-world; rather, they are experienced as shifts in the main narrative. For instance, at a mysterious palace Anodos reads a book that draws him into participating in its stories, and at another point, he finds himself in a cottage with doors that open into four different worlds, each

---

* A.N. Wilson makes a similar point: "[MacDonald] seems to have the supreme gift . . . of writing unselfconsciously about the subconscious" (*C.S. Lewis: A Biography*, 46). The story is 'about' something else, albeit written so unselfconsciously that it doesn't feel like an allegory.

† The opening scene might also have grated on Tolkien for personal reasons. For Tolkien, himself an orphan, his twenty-first birthday was highly significant: it marked the release from his promise to his guardian to abstain from contact with Edith Bratt, and indeed he wrote to her that very day to rekindle their courtship. MacDonald's opening scene is both sentimentalized and rather clumsy in its evocation of Anodos's memories of his parents; he seems unaffected by any thoughts of his late father, and it is only when he looks into the eyes of his grandmother that "I remembered somehow that my mother died when I was a baby."

of which he enters to have adventures. Probably because of this proliferation of secondary worlds, *Phantastes* does not sustain what Tolkien would call full secondary belief. The novel's "dream realism"[29] is one of its most distinctive qualities, but it reduces the believability of Fairy Land as a secondary world.

The second point has to do with one of Tolkien's abiding obsessions: trees. In a 1956 letter, Tolkien acknowledged his creation of the Ents had "perhaps some remote influence from George MacDonald's *Phantastes* (a work which I do not actually much like)."[30]* The effect seems to have been largely that of influence-by-opposition. Clyde Kilby, in explaining Tolkien's grounds for disliking MacDonald, noted in particular that he "did not like the way in which MacDonald wrote of trees."[31] Possibly the main reason for this reaction is that, although much of the action of *Phantastes* occurs in or around forests, MacDonald's descriptions of the woods are bland. We are provided with little of the descriptive detail that the botanically-minded Tolkien would have appreciated,[32] and, more importantly, the tree characters are not far from being symbols of other things.

Three animate trees feature in Anodos's adventures, but despite being identified as distinctive tree-species, they are not convincingly drawn as such. The gentle Beech, who looks outwardly human, tells Anodos, "I long to be a woman." The Ash, who pursues and attacks Anodos, could be any sort of ogre: he is a shadowy, threatening figure, with a "Gorgon-head," "ghoul-eyes," and a "ghastly face." He closes upon Anodos with "hideous hand outstretched, like a beast of prey" – an arboreal creature, but described with a clumsy mixing of human and animal metaphors. Lastly, the evil Alder-Maid appears as a "dim white figure . . . a form of perfect loveliness"; her only distinguishing feature is a slight reddish tint to the whites of her eyes. When Anodos finally sees her clearly, she is revealed to be a crude mockery of the human shape, "hollow, as if made of decaying bark torn from a tree."[33] The Beech, Ash, and Alder do not come alive to the reader in their capacity as trees; they are too close to being moral or spiritual stand-ins.

In contrast, Tolkien's writings are full of evocative descriptions of woods and forests, and his tree characters are always depicted with close attention to their arboreal nature. Old Man Willow, who like MacDonald's Ash is hollow and black-hearted, has an appearance entirely consonant with the name: "its sprawling branches going up like reaching arms with many long-fingered hands, its knotted and twisted trunk gaping in wide fissures that creaked faintly as the boughs moved." His ash-characters are "tall straight grey Ents with many-fingered hands and long legs"; his chestnuts are "brown-skinned Ents with large splayfingered hands, and short thick legs." Quickbeam, the rowan, has "smooth shining skin on his arms and legs," with "ruddy" lips and "grey-green" hair. Tolkien thought very highly of trees, and paid attention to them as specific species and individual characters: MacDonald treats them more generally, abstractly, symbolically.

It is impossible to know for sure how much Tolkien's "profound dislike" of *Phantastes* affected his own writings, but it is important to note how the three things we have identified in his attitude to the book are so very obviously *absent* from Middle-earth.

---

* We will consider a much more direct influence upon the Ents in chapter 9.

He carefully tried to avoid allegory in *The Lord of the Rings* (a point we shall return to in our discussion of Charles Williams in chapter 9); he took Herculean pains to ensure an inner consistency of reality in his sub-created world; and he delighted in making tree characters that, though undeniably anthropomorphic, nevertheless partook more of the arboreal than the human realm. In all these ways, then, we may see the effects of influence-by-opposition, a point we shall explore further below in our discussion of "The Golden Key."

❧ "Power and beauty": *Lilith*

Although he criticized *Phantastes*, Tolkien praised MacDonald's other adult fantasy novel, *Lilith* (1895). He notes that MacDonald achieved "stories of power and beauty when he succeeded . . . and even when he partly failed, as in *Lilith*."[34] This praise is obviously qualified, but it is telling that Tolkien should still expend such warm words ("power and beauty") about a tale that he considered to be less than a complete success. Evidently, there was something about this work that caused him to adopt a forbearing attitude.

In this tale the protagonist, Mr. Vane, enters Fairyland through a magic mirror; his adventures include nursing back to health the near-dead Lilith, ruler of a nearby city. This Lilith turns out to be a fallen angel; originally created by God to be Adam's wife, she rebelled and allied herself with the Shadow, coming even to hate her own daughter.* Abandoning Adam (who was then given Eve as his human wife), she set herself up as Princess of Bulika, allied herself with the Shadow, magically stole all the water from the surface of the land, and sought to kill all the children in her territory.[35] Outside her reach, however, are the "Little Ones," a community of children who exist in a strange in-between state of growth. Most of them remain in a perpetual idyll of childhood, although some turn bad and grow up to become violent and stupid giants. But this condition is not unambiguously positive. If the children had access to water – which is denied them by Lilith's theft – they would be able to grow to full spiritual and physical maturity. Vane eventually discovers her Herod-like plans, and forms the Little Ones into an army to defeat her. These children are so innocent and good that, despite Lilith's murderous intentions, they gladly help Vane to bring about Lilith's repentance.

Throughout the novel, Lilith's hand is closed upon a talismanic egg containing the waters; at the end, faced with the necessity of surrendering this stolen treasure in order to enter into the true sleep of death, Lilith attempts to do so but finds that she is unable to unclench her hand. In the end, she asks for her hand to be cut off. Vane then buries the hand in the desert, allowing the waters to return.

Here, in Lilith's acceptance of dismemberment, when she is unable otherwise to will the release of her treasure, we hear a possible pre-echo of Frodo's providential mutilation

---

* The figure of Lilith features in Jewish folklore and the Kabbalah; she does not appear in the Bible. She is often considered a type of demon. MacDonald's innovation in his story is to feature her repentance and reconciliation with God.

when Gollum bites off the Ring-finger at the Crack of Doom. In the image of Vane carrying the severed, still-clenched hand to return the stolen waters, we might also see a parallel to the story of Beren in the Silmarillion. His hand, holding the Silmaril wrenched from Morgoth's crown, is bitten off by the wolf and carried away in its stomach, later to be recovered. The significance of the episode is very different, but the image is sufficiently striking to note as a possible contributor to Tolkien's imagining of that scene.*

Eventually Vane and the children lie down in the house of Adam and Eve, in a death-like sleep from which they will wake into real – that is, eternal – life. He stirs to find that most of the children have preceded him into wakefulness, and becomes unsure whether he is really awake or is dreaming. He resolves to be patient: "when I wake at last into that life which, as a mother her child carries, carries this life in its bosom, I shall know that I wake, and shall doubt no more."[36]

Lilith is a deeply theological novel, and in some ways it might seem more overtly so than *Phantastes*: after all, Adam and Eve are characters in the tale, and the Shadow is described using scriptural terms such as the "Prince of the Power of the Air" (Ephesians 2:2). However, for the most part MacDonald avoids giving a straightforward interpretive framework for his story, preferring instead to provide a few cryptic, allusive conversations between characters and a superabundance of images to explore the deeper themes of the tale.[37]

Tolkien wrote that "Death is the theme that most inspired George MacDonald, whether in fairy stories . . . or in what he called the 'romance' of Lilith."[38] To be "inspired" is often taken to mean "to be uplifted, to be given new life," but here the inspiration, according to Tolkien, is, paradoxically, "death." MacDonald was father to eleven children, six of whom predeceased him, several from tuberculosis. He was particularly affected by the death of his eldest child, a daughter called Lilia; the names of various female characters in this story – not only the eponymous Lilith, but also girls called Lona and Luva – suggest that there may be some sort of emotional processing going on in MacDonald as he revolved these themes of mortality and children in his imagination.

Lona is the "queen and mother and sister" of the Little Ones who, if they are good, stay as perpetual children, yet who face death with abandon. At one point, Mr. Vane tells the Little Ones that they may be hurt or killed in their attack on Lilith's city. They respond:

> "*I* don't mind being killed!" cried one of the finest of the smaller boys: he rode a beautiful little bull, which galloped and jumped like a horse.
>
> "I don't either! I don't either!" came from all sides. . . .
>
> "I would give my life," [Lona] said, "to have my mother! She might kill me if she liked! I should just kiss her and die!"[39]

---

* My thanks to Richard Jeffery for bringing this aspect of *Lilith* to my attention.

Such a scene might perhaps have put Tolkien in mind of his own not wholly dissimilar experiences in the Great War. He had witnessed many young soldiers, hardly more than boys, who never made it home to their mothers; they might have begun the war by facing death with abandon, but ended with a terrible sense of abandonment. (We will have more to say on this subject in the next chapter.) MacDonald was a man much acquainted with grief, as indeed was Tolkien, who had been bereaved of both his parents by the age of twelve, lost all but one of his close friends by 1918, and himself went through the horrors of the Somme. It is unsurprising, then, that this same theme of death should have continually troubled and fascinated him. In one of the rare instances when he said what *The Lord of the Rings* was about, he confessed, "it is about Death and the desire for deathlessness."[40] *

The theme finds expression all over the epic and in a great variety of shades and tones. We see it perhaps most memorably (and despairingly) in the Dead Marshes, and in the unheroic deaths of Denethor and Saruman. We see a kind of living death in the unnaturally long life given by the One Ring to Gollum and, to a lesser extent, to Bilbo. We see the freedom of *real* death being brought by Aragorn to the King of the Dead and his army of restless souls. We see heroic deaths or heroically chosen mortality in Boromir, Théoden, and Arwen. And we see the gradual incoming tide of death and its peaceful acceptance vividly presented in the various Ring-bearers leaving Middle-earth by ship from the Grey Havens.

In the powerful, plangent, yet not utterly hopeless depictions of dismemberment and death that fill the pages of *Lilith*, MacDonald strikes a note that resonated with Tolkien at a deep personal level. Here we can see probably the chief reason why MacDonald's work moved him to such a life-long interest and also perhaps what helped him to conceive and develop similar themes in his own writings.

❧ Shadows and key-holes: MacDonald's fairy tales

Tolkien's relationship with MacDonald's fairy tales is an intriguing topic: it illustrates the way in which his tastes could change over time, and shows the power of influence-by-opposition.

In the drafts and final version of "On Fairy-stories," Tolkien repeatedly refers to MacDonald. He remarks that the "mixture of German and Scottish flavours" in MacDonald's tales is what "makes him so inevitably attractive to myself" and mentions several specific titles, including "The Giant's Heart" and "Photogen and Nycteris," which

---

* Tolkien also explored the theme of death and deathlessness in the Silmarillion. For instance, the *Athrabeth* is a dialogue between an Elf and a human woman, Andreth, about death, immortality, and the afterlife; Andreth alludes to an event in human history that has resulted in a very different relationship between men and death than that of the Elves. Tolkien here is, of course, alluding to the Incarnation, Crucifixion, and Resurrection of Christ, but, consistent with his approach of excluding overtly Christian elements from his stories, he allows Andreth only to hint at the topic (see HOME X).

he considered "not at all for children."[41] Most notably, he gives "The Golden Key" as an example of the way in which MacDonald could achieve "stories of power and beauty" and describes it as a "nearly perfect tale (in his kind and style)."[42] As late as 1964, Tolkien remarked, "I do think well of this story of his."[43]

His views would change dramatically, as we will discuss shortly, but first it is worth exploring what positive effect "The Golden Key" might have had upon Tolkien's imagination.

In this tale, the boy, Mossy, ventures into the forest (Fairyland) where he finds a golden key at the end of a rainbow. At the same time, the girl, Tangle, thinking that she is threatened by three bears, runs into the forest and is saved from a dangerous tree by a beautiful air-fish. She is led to the house of the mysterious Grandmother, where she soon meets Mossy, who has likewise been guided by an air-fish. Together they set off to find the keyhole for the golden key. After passing through a land of shadows, they become separated, but eventually reunite inside the mountain, where Mossy opens another door with the key. The two climb up into the rainbow itself, and onward toward the land from which the shadows fall.

Considering that Tolkien possessed, as he remarked to an interviewer, "a very strong visual imagination,"[44] we can consider some possible influences from the landscape of "The Golden Key." In MacDonald's tale, the children cross a great valley that is filled with many shadows (of leaves, trees, birds, and even people) and they hope to find the land from which the shadows fall. Tolkien made a note of the "Land of Shadows" in his draft of "On Fairy-stories"[45] and, many years later, wrote that for him the most lasting image from "The Golden Key" was of "the great valley encircled by hard towering mountains, with its smooth floor on which the shadows played, the sea of shadows cast by things that could not themselves be seen."[46] As anyone who has read Tolkien's epic knows, shadows are hugely important in his imagination: they feature in the epigraph verses about the Rings of Power forged by Sauron in "the Land of Mordor where the Shadows lie." With this connection in mind, it is worth considering whether MacDonald's shadow-valley had an influence on Tolkien's depiction of Mordor.

Because MacDonald's description of the valley focuses upon the pleasing liveliness of the shadows, it is easy to miss that the physical description of this valley is surprisingly close to that of Mordor. As Mossy and Tangle proceed on their journey,

> the ground began to rise, and it got more and more steep, till the trees were all left behind, and the two were climbing a narrow path with rocks on each side. Suddenly they came upon a rude doorway, by which they entered a narrow gallery cut in the rock. It grew darker and darker, till it was pitch-dark, and they had to feel their way. At length the light began to return, and at last they came out upon a narrow path on the face of a lofty precipice. This path went winding down the rock to a wide

plain, circular in shape, and surrounded on all sides by mountains. Those opposite to them were a great way off, and towered to an awful height, shooting up sharp, blue, ice-enamelled pinnacles. An utter silence reigned where they stood. Not even the sound of water reached them.[47]

Frodo and Sam enter Mordor via the Stairs of Cirith Ungol, climbing up several sets of winding steps cut into the rock face, in complete darkness. Later, when they make their way through the rocky, waterless boundary of the Morgai, they see a vast plain guarded by encircling mountains:

Below them, at the bottom of a fall of some fifteen hundred feet, lay the inner plain stretching away into a formless gloom beyond their sight. . . . Still far away, forty miles at least, they saw Mount Doom, its feet founded in ashen ruin, its huge cone rising to a great height . . . Behind it there hung a vast shadow, ominous as a thunder-cloud, the veils of Barad-dûr that was reared far away upon a long spur of the Ashen Mountains thrust down from the North.[48]

This description – evocative of the first glimpse of the plain that the children traverse in MacDonald's tale – comes in the chapter entitled "The Land of Shadow." The resemblance does not end there. In "The Golden Key," the children take so long in crossing the plain that they grow aged; they feel "dismay," and later, when they become separated, Tangle experiences "terror" and "despair" before resolving to go onward on her own. She eventually climbs up the mountain, following a stair: "When she had ascended half-way, the stair ceased, and the path led straight into the mountain. She was afraid to enter, and turning again towards the stair, grew giddy at sight of the depth beneath her, and was forced to throw herself down in the mouth of the cave."[49] Here, the parallel ceases; Tangle is met by a fairy creature who then leads her onward to further adventures that, as Tolkien remarked, did not stick in his memory.

Bearing in mind that Tolkien made special note of the valley of shadows from "The Golden Key" in 1938 and recalled it decades later as the one image that he had retained from MacDonald's story, it is not unreasonable to ask whether it may have contributed something to Middle-earth. If the answer is yes, a likely contender is Frodo and Sam's arduous trek through the mountains, across the plain, and up the side of Mount Doom into the cave at its heart – two hobbits, where MacDonald had had two children.

Another scene worth noting in "The Golden Key" is the one in which Mossy finds the keyhole on the mountain:

He crossed the sea, and came to a great precipice of rock, up which he could discover but one path. Nor did this lead him farther than half-way up the rock, where it ended on a platform . . . He examined the face of the rock. It was smooth as glass. But as his eyes kept roving hopelessly over it, something glittered, and he caught sight of a row of small sapphires. They bordered a little hole in the rock.

"The keyhole!" he cried.

He tried the key. It fitted. It turned. A great clang and clash, as of iron bolts on huge brazen caldrons, echoed thunderously within.[50]

This scene is suggestive of *The Hobbit*, when the last rays of the sun on Durin's Day reveals the keyhole in the "smooth rock-face" of the Lonely Mountain; Thorin is then able to use his "small and curious key" to open the door, so that the dwarves and Bilbo can make their way inside. In both cases (though for different reasons) the entrance becomes closed behind the adventurers after they pass through into the mountain.

Thorin's key, "with a long barrel and intricate wards," is not golden, but made of silver. As we assess Tolkien's ongoing imaginative relationship with MacDonald, we might take this less precious metal symbolically – as a pointer to where his final verdict on "The Golden Key" would come to rest.

Devaluation: MacDonald as influence-by-opposition

Late in his life, Tolkien substantially revised and downgraded his view of MacDonald's stories, noting how "selective memory had transmuted his 'F[airy] Stories' & how much I disliked them now." Indeed, he remarked that "re-reading G.M. critically filled me with distaste." In a 1967 interview, he remarked that "I now find that I can't stand George MacDonald's books at any price at all."[51] His use of *now* indicates that Tolkien recognized that his opinion had altered over time, an alteration brought to his notice upon a recent re-reading.

As we have seen, Tolkien could become prickly, even defensive, if he thought that an interlocutor was assuming too much, whether on matters of interpretation of *The Lord of the Rings* or on questions of influence. Carpenter recalled, "I did once suggest to [Tolkien] . . . that *The Princess and the Goblin* has certain resemblances to *The Hobbit*. Beneath the mountain in both books there are goblins mining, and he was, I think, momentarily disconcerted by this suggestion and did admit that there might have been some very slight influence there, a memory from childhood, but no conscious influences." Kilby said he could "confirm" this reaction, adding that "The perfect situation for discussing this developed while I was with him, and it looked to me as if he had used MacDonald and very much didn't want to confess it,"[52] and suggesting elsewhere that "the dislike of MacDonald may have arisen partly to throw people off the scent of this deep indebtedness."[53] As late as 1954 Tolkien had been willing to name MacDonald as a source for *The Hobbit*; Tolkien's "disconcerted" reaction to Carpenter's comment suggests that he now wished to distance himself from the MacDonald connection, or at least from Carpenter's version of it.

What seems to have precipitated the reversal in his view was his undertaking, in 1964, to provide a preface to a new edition of "The Golden Key." On re-reading the story in preparation for the task, he found that it had tarnished: he now declared it "ill-written, incoherent, and bad, in spite of a few memorable passages."[54] Despite his reduced enthusiasm for the tale, Tolkien nevertheless wrote several pages of notes about MacDonald's story,[55] and began writing the preface straightforwardly enough, but – as was so characteristic of him – was thrown off course by his own inventiveness. In attempting to explain the true nature of "Faery," he began a story that would serve as an example. The preface itself was abandoned, while the illustrative story evolved into the complex, richly mythopoeic *Smith of Wootton Major*, which Tolkien himself described as "an anti-G.M. tract."[56]

As *Smith of Wootton Major* is not part of his legendarium, we will not be analyzing it here, but it is relevant to consider briefly the way in which MacDonald's tale provided a significant influence on Tolkien's work, even so late in life. Re-reading "The Golden Key" led Tolkien to describe the working of influence-by-opposition in his own creative imagination. He explained that *Smith of Wootton Major* "was (as often happens) the result of an irritant" – namely, MacDonald's work! – and that "the irritant will in some degree affect the presentation of the movement in the mind that it sets going."[57] Here we find Tolkien admitting that it "often" happens that his thoughts were set in motion by dissatisfaction with something he read – an important form of influence for a man as critical as he could be. Furthermore, we find him noting that such an influence provides more than just a push in a certain direction; it will also "affect the presentation" of the resulting story. Such a frank statement of influence shows that Tolkien himself recognized how his reading of MacDonald had repercussions upon his own work. Indeed it did, both early and late in his career, and in both positive and negative forms.

❦ Conclusion

George MacDonald stands as a significant figure among the sources and influences we have to examine in this book. As Tolkien himself said, MacDonald's writings were among those "which most affected the background of my imagination."[58] He knew his work well, and directly admitted his influence on *The Hobbit* – most notably in his identification of MacDonald's goblins as patterns for his own goblins and orcs.

This recognition of debt is (somewhat uncharacteristically) straightforward and candid on Tolkien's part. There are reasons to suppose other debts too, albeit unacknowledged. We saw how Tolkien seized upon a tiny detail in a comic song from *At the Back of the North Wind* and gave it to Frodo to sing at The Prancing Pony. We noted how Tolkien's distaste for moral allegory and imaginative inconsistency but also his love of trees combined to produce in him a "profound dislike" for *Phantastes*. We observed his deep personal resonance with the themes of dismemberment and death in *Lilith*. We also noticed how Tolkien retained a strong visual memory of certain elements from "The Golden Key" that appear to foreshadow images in *The Lord of the Rings*.

Finally, we traced the way Tolkien turned against MacDonald very strongly late in life, picking up as we did so important clues about his changing tastes and his creative process. Influence-by-opposition is an important kind of influence and all the more relevant where the opposition develops out of an earlier warmth. Tolkien had previously entertained a longstanding regard for MacDonald's work in general and for "The Golden Key" in particular (recall that years before, he had called it a "nearly perfect tale"). That Tolkien thought MacDonald worth dissenting from indicates his ongoing respect, for if he had lost all regard for MacDonald he would simply have ignored him out of existence – not written a complete story in response. But MacDonald's impression on Tolkien's imaginative and intellectual life had gone deep; indifference was not an option.

✣ 6 ✣

Boys' Own Adventure
Coming of Age

T OLKIEN CAME OF AGE DURING THE HEYDAY OF THE ADVENTURE
novelists, reading these tales in the same years that he encountered George
MacDonald and the author whom we will discuss in the next chapter,
William Morris. The genre that I have loosely called 'adventure' comprises a variety of
types, including historical fiction, stories set in exotic locations, political thrillers, and
supernatural tales, but all adventure novels are plot-driven and full of incident, though
not as fast-paced as the modern reader, accustomed to film adaptations of these tales,
might expect.

The literary legitimacy of the adventure tale has long been contested, with critics
using 'juvenile' or 'adolescent' as terms of opprobrium.[1] Admittedly, many adventure
novels were formulaic and clumsily written, compensatory fantasies with an immature
emotional register. However, other examples of the genre, such as the works of writers
like Rudyard Kipling, Robert Louis Stevenson, and John Buchan, are now generally
recognized for their literary merits, and can be found in the classics or modern fiction
sections of bookshops, their re-readability a sure sign that artistic quality knows no generic bounds.

Interestingly, we can see a parallel critical trajectory in the response to *The Lord
of the Rings*. One early reviewer dismissed it as "an allegorical adventure story for very
leisured boys" and admitted being tempted to take to the streets proclaiming "Adults of
all ages! Unite against the infantilist invasion.'"[2] Edmund Wilson declared it "juvenile
trash."[3] In 1961, Philip Toynbee called it "ill-written" and "childish" and declared, not
a little prematurely, that Tolkien's epic had "passed into a merciful oblivion."[4] Twenty
years later, another critic, hopeful that Tolkien's "cult status is diminishing," could only
account for his popularity in terms of class: "perhaps it is not so much the bookish class
which reads Tolkien as those to whom a long read does not come altogether easily."[5]
The extent to which *The Lord of the Rings* has passed through its trial by condescension is perhaps best attested by the Bodleian Library's 2018 exhibit *Tolkien: Maker of
Middle-earth*, presented in Tolkien's own University of Oxford (typically disdainful of
its dons writing anything so vulgar as best-selling fantasy novels). Though it took several
decades, the bookish seem finally to have caught up with the more discerning taste of
the boyish.

In this chapter, we will consider a number of classics and certain other works that, we can safely say, have indeed "passed into a merciful oblivion," but first let us give a quick overview of Tolkien's general reading in this area.

Tolkien enjoyed examples of various kinds of adventure stories throughout his life. As a student at King Edward's, and especially in his years as a school librarian, he had easy access to an extensive collection of popular adventure fiction. Tolkien's classmates were avid readers of these tales: in 1905, one librarian reported that "All the 80 books classed as 'Doyle,' 'Haggard,' 'Fenn' and 'School Stories' were frequently in actual circulation simultaneously."[6]* No doubt it was those boyish tastes that Tolkien had in mind when, about to leave King Edward's to begin his studies at Oxford, he donated copies of *The Lost Explorers* and *Scouting for Buller* to that very library where he had spent so many hours as a teenager[7] – two novels that we will discuss further below. He was familiar with the *Boys' Own Paper*, a weekly (and later monthly) British publication featuring wholesome adventure and sports stories aimed at the juvenile male of the species.[8] One such story that Tolkien knew was Horace Vachell's *The Hill: A Romance of Friendship* (1907), which features the idealized quotidian exploits of boys at Harrow.[9]

He read so voraciously of H. Rider Haggard that we will reserve discussion of this author for a separate chapter. He was unimpressed by Robert Louis Stevenson's *Treasure Island* (1882), although he evidently thought well enough of Stevenson's historical adventure *The Black Arrow* (1883) to give a copy to his daughter as a Christmas gift.[10]† He knew Sir Arthur Conan Doyle's historical adventure *The White Company* (1891), recommending it (along with Rudyard Kipling's *Kim* [1901], a tale of adventure and espionage set in India) to the Mexican students under his supervision on a summer tour.[11] The title of *The White Company* makes for a small but interesting possible connection with a significant group of warriors in *The Return of the King* – namely, Faramir's own guard, also called "the White Company." Faramir, we should recall, was the character in *The Lord of the Rings* with whom Tolkien specifically identified himself; perhaps here, in the name of the troop over which Faramir had personal charge, we see a nod toward a book that Tolkien had enjoyed in his youth.

He also enjoyed adventure tales that included elements of the fantastic. He "read many of Edgar Rice Burroughs' earlier works," including not only the well-known Tarzan series (1912 onward), but also the John Carter of Mars series (1917 onward), and the Pellucidar stories (1914 onward), in which outlandish adventures unfold within the

---

* "Doyle" is Sir Arthur Conan Doyle, creator of Sherlock Holmes; "Haggard" is H. Rider Haggard whom we will discuss in Chapter 8; "Fenn" is George Manwell Fenn, the now-forgotten author of works such as *Gil the Gunner: The Youngest Officer in the East* (1892), *Marcus, the Young Centurion* (1904), and *Trapped by Malays: A Tale of Bayonet and Kris* (1907).

† Tolkien seems to have imparted his enthusiasm for historical adventures to his daughter; Priscilla recalled one Christmas asking for "everything" written by Stanley J. Weyman. ("News from the North Pole," 8). Weyman was an author of historical romances such as *A Gentleman of France* (1893) and *The Castle Inn* (1898).

habitable hollow core of Planet Earth.[12]* Somewhat surprisingly, Tolkien admitted that he "rather liked"[13] Robert Howard's stories about Conan the Barbarian, suggesting he had an appreciation for American 'sword and sorcery' tales of the 1930s. His comments on the anthology *Swords & Sorcery* (1963) show he read not only a tale by Lord Dunsany (which we will discuss in chapter 10) but also stories by Poul Anderson, C.L. Moore, and Clark Ashton Smith[14] – once mighty names, some now dusty with neglect.

With our overview completed, let us now focus our attention on those authors whom we will discuss in depth in this chapter, a mix of faded and familiar figures: S.R. Crockett, Alexander Macdonald, Herbert Hayens, John Buchan, and finally – unexpectedly, but I trust explicably – J.M. Barrie.

❧ Wargs and wolves: S.R. Crockett's *The Black Douglas*

Although little-known today, S.R. Crockett (1859–1914) was extremely popular in his time, publishing over sixty novels. Many of these novels feature historical settings and events, with generous helpings of melodrama and the fantastic. *The Black Douglas* (1899) takes place in fifteenth-century Scotland, its title being the nickname of William, Earl of Douglas, a Lanarkshire nobleman who fights against the English and draws the heroes of the tale to join his cause. The historically-based plot soon gives way to a series of rather Gothic adventures featuring, among other things, the kidnapping of two girls by the villain, Gilles de Retz, and the heroes' efforts to find and rescue them.† Tolkien described the novel as "probably his best romance and anyway one that deeply impressed me in school-days, though I have never looked at it again." Its impression was such that, despite never revisiting it, Tolkien credited this novel as a source of inspiration for a memorable moment in *The Hobbit*: "the episode of the 'wargs' (I believe) is in part derived from a scene in S.R. Crockett's *The Black Douglas*."[15]

The relevant scene finds the protagonist Sholto MacKim and two of his friends pursued by wolves who hunt in the service of the evil Gilles de Retz. The three men decide to hold their ground "against the trunk of a huge pine which had been blasted by lightning" and that stands in "the centre of the open glade." One of them suggests that "It were better to find a tree that we could climb," but it is too late; "they dared not move out of the open space, and the great trunk of the blasted pine rose behind them bare of branches almost to the top." In the night, the men cannot see much, but they can hear the "devilish cries" of the wolves, and see their gleaming eyes:

---

* Roger Lancelyn Green observed that "Shelob in *The Lord of the Rings* is so like the Siths of the Barsoomian caves [from Burroughs' John Carter of Mars series] that an unconscious borrowing seems probable." (*Into Other Worlds: Space-Flight in Fiction, from Lucian to Lewis*, 130).

† Sholto is able to identify the track of the two kidnapped girls when he finds a fallen garland, "a child's chain of woodbine entwined with daisies and autumnal pheasant's eye" (chapter XLI). It is reminiscent of Aragorn, on the track of the kidnapped hobbits, finding Pippin's leaf-brooch along the way.

> Yells and howls as of triumphant fiends were borne to their ears upon the western wind. . . . Gleaming eyes glared upon them as the wolves trotted out and sat down in a wide circle to wait for the full muster of the pack before rushing their prey.[16]

As the wolves gather, we see the "blue leme [glimmer] of summer lightning" and during the subsequent fight there is "wild-fire running about the tree-tops and glinting up through the recesses of the woods as if the heavens themselves were instinct with diabolic light."[17]

Furthermore, these are no ordinary wolves, but intelligent and organized. They are led by a witch-woman, La Meffraye, in the form of a huge she-wolf. Her pack of lupine followers seems almost to have the gift of speech:

> As the soundless lightning wavered and brightened, the shadows of the wolves appeared simultaneously to start forward and then retreat, while the noise of their howling carried with it some diabolic suggestion of discordant human voices. *"La Meffraye! La Meffraye! Meffraye!"* So to the excited minds of the three Scots the wolf legions seemed to be crying with one voice as they came nearer. All the wild beasts of the wood appeared to be obeying the summons of the witch woman.[18]

A number of points in this scene correspond to the episode of the Wargs in *The Hobbit*. Here, after Bilbo is reunited with the dwarves and Gandalf following their tumultuous passage through the Misty Mountains, they are scented by a pack of wolves in league with goblins, and barely manage to climb into trees to escape them. As in Crockett's tale, the trees are mostly pines, around an open "glade in the ring of trees"; the wolves – whose threatening howls are heard before the creatures themselves are seen – gather threateningly around the company; Gandalf sets a pine-cone afire with "bright blue flame" that spreads to an "uncanny fire," setting alight some of the wolves and then the trees. Finally, the lead wolf speaks to the assembled pack "in the dreadful language of the Wargs. Gandalf understood it. Bilbo did not, but it sounded terrible to him, and as if all their talk was about cruel and wicked things, as it was."

Indeed, the scenes are sufficiently similar that it is worth noting the points on which they differ. And here we learn some interesting things about Tolkien's creative process, for he did not just imitate Crockett, but built on his work and improved it. Tolkien's scene may have been "in part derived" from *The Black Douglas*, but it was fully developed, and that in three main ways.

First, Tolkien reduces the amount of actual violence in the scene, while heightening its tension. Crockett's scene involves a detailed description of the fighting between the wolves and the men, until the wolves are called off by a mysterious voice in the distance – a rather lame ending. In *The Hobbit*, the characters don't fight the wolves but are trapped by them in the trees, only for their predicament to be doubled by the threat of fire and intensified by the goblins' mocking songs, before their unexpected rescue by the Eagles.

Second, Tolkien makes the details of the scene more significant. The howling of the wolves does not just suggest speech but is an actual wolf-language; the trees are not already "blasted" but still living, and the fact that they are living *pines* becomes a relevant factor in how their eminently combustible pine-cones, and the pitchy trees themselves, will burn; the blue fire is not mere background color, but part of Gandalf's desperate defense; the rescue by the Eagles doesn't just bring the scene to an end, but also serves to introduce a whole new cast of avian characters, who will have continuing, indeed climactic, importance both in *The Hobbit* and in *The Lord of the Rings*. In all these ways, then, we see Tolkien enriching and transforming his source material.

Third, Tolkien downplays Crockett's religiosity. In *The Black Douglas*, Sholto calls his companions to arms against the wolves when, after initially retreating, they return and encircle the group once more, but one of his men, Malise, instead "stood reverently at prayer":

> "Aid us, Thy true men," he cried in a loud and solemn voice,
> "against all the powers of evil. In the name of God – Amen!"
> The howling stopped and there fell a silence. . . .
> And far off, like an echo from another world, thin and sweet and
> silver clear, a cock crew.
> The blue leaping flame of the wild-fire abruptly ceased. The dawn
> arose red and broad in the east. The piles of dead beasts shone out black
> on the grey plain of the forest glade, and on the topmost bough of a pine
> tree a thrush began to sing.[19]

Crockett's characters seem to be saved providentially: the crowing of the cock, which is traditionally associated with Christ,* implicitly connects Malise's prayer with the coming of the dawn, which we can presume drove away the wolves. Tolkien's reticence about including explicit Christian elements in his fiction meant that he would not have featured anything so direct as an answered prayer in the dilemma of Bilbo and his friends. However, it is worth noting the nature of their rescue. It comes about thanks to the Eagles who, alerted to the situation by the baying of the wolves, come to the rescue at the very moment when Gandalf is making ready to leap down upon the goblins to his probable death; a timely intervention, indeed. Furthermore, why eagles? To be sure, eagles fit the needs of the situation, but we should bear in mind that Tolkien had a special devotion to St. John the Evangelist,[20] who is symbolized in sacred art by that very bird. In the conclusion of his version of the battle, Tolkien has inserted a providential rescue, but done so in a way fitted to his more subtle method of weaving Christian symbolism into his writing.

---

* Cock-crow is linked both to Christ's prophecy of Peter's denial (described in all four Gospels) and to his Resurrection as symbolized by sunrise.

One final point is worth mentioning. Tolkien's recollection and later adaptation of this dramatic scene from *The Black Douglas* shows the role played by the visual component of his memory. He knew this about himself. In one of the off-cuts of the BBC film interview *Tolkien in Oxford*, he remarks that "I normally preserve a very bright visual recollection of where I was, where I am and things that are associated with what I'm looking at. I shall always remember, for instance, this chap dangling the green lights"[21] – referring to a member of the film crew. Tolkien is sometimes too exclusively associated with linguistic inventiveness; his visual sense and almost eidetic memory are important features of his creativity too. His copy of *The Black Douglas* probably contained the illustrations by Frank Richards that are included in the first edition. The frontispiece depicts the battle with the wolves and is one of the most evocative pictures in the book. (See figure 11.) This nighttime tableau, with its atmospheric backdrop, ferocious-looking wolves, and foregrounded action, may well have caused the scene to stick more firmly in Tolkien's memory. But whether it was the text of the story or the illustration or both, he was inspired to adapt it for his own purposes, to the point of admitting that his version was "in part derived" from Crockett's tale.

The other element of *The Black Douglas* that Tolkien recalled was the character of "Gil de Rez as a Satanist."[22] Tolkien had forgotten the spelling (Gilles de Retz) but remembered the predominant feature of that character, for he is indeed a diabolical figure in the novel. Dale Nelson suggests that Tolkien might have drawn on de Retz when creating his own villainous protagonist, Sauron, as both "command armies of wolves or even werewolves; both torture victims in their high towers."[23] This connection is supported by the evidence of Tolkien's early writings, for in "The Lay of Leithian," Sauron is "Master of Wolves" and "lord of werewolf and of ghost."[24] In *The Lord of the Rings*, however, it is Saruman rather than Sauron who partakes more of Gilles de Retz. Saruman not only has an army of wolves and a high tower, but also resembles de Retz in attitude.

De Retz, a nobleman, "Marshal de Retz, Sieur of Machecoul," is "ambassador of the King of France"[25] – a possible connection to the silver-tongued and rather lordly Saruman whose advocacy on Sauron's behalf prompts Gandalf, unimpressed, to remark that he sounds like one of the "emissaries" of Mordor. More intriguingly, de Retz boasts of the "cost," the "vast sacrifices" that have characterized his pursuit of power:

> "I have in secret pushed my researches beyond the very confines of knowledge. The powers of the underworlds are revealing themselves to me, and to me alone. Evil and good alike shall be mine. I alone will pluck the blossom of fire, and tear from hell and hell's master their cherished mystery."[26]

De Retz's fanciful belief that he can wrest mastery from Satan represents a level of self-deception that is echoed in Saruman's attitude toward Sauron. Furthermore, his instrumentalizing of "evil and good alike" in search of power through knowledge and technical control puts one in mind of Saruman's attempted suborning of Gandalf and his degradation of Isengard into an industrialized, mechanized powerhouse.

✂ "I have the hatred of *apartheid* in my bones": Alexander Macdonald, Herbert Hayens, and influence-by-opposition

As noted above, Tolkien, in his last year at King Edward's, gave a copy of Alexander Macdonald's *The Lost Explorers* (1906) and Herbert Hayens's *Scouting for Buller* (1902) to the King Edward's school library.[27] (See figure 17.) We therefore know that he had owned and no doubt read these works, but we do not know his thoughts on them. These long-forgotten books, typical of boys' reading at the time, are worth considering for the way in which they show how Tolkien's mature views on race and empire are in some ways very different from what we might expect, given the typical assumptions and prejudices of his day.

Alexander Macdonald (1878–1939) was a Scottish explorer and Fellow of the Royal Geographical Society, whose expeditions took him all over the world (from Alaska to the Australian Outback) and provided him with materials for his tales aimed at young readers, such as *The Pearl Seekers: A Tale of the Southern Seas* (1907) and *The White Trail: A Story of the Early Days of the Klondike* (1908).

The Lost Explorers is a story of adventure in the Australian Outback, with rival gold-miners, an improbable plot involving a gold-refining invention, and a search for a mysterious mountain where the protagonists, after passing through a booby-trapped tunnel, discover a hidden valley inhabited by a 'lost race.' The teenaged heroes might have provided a point of connection for the young Tolkien. The two main characters are Bob Wentworth, eighteen years old, and Jack Armstrong, sixteen, both of whom have suffered close family bereavement. Jack's parents are dead, and he is "homeless and well-nigh penniless" when he begins work at the Clyde Engineering Works, a post "secured for him by a thoughtful friend," a situation that evokes the role of Fr. Francis Morgan, who was Tolkien's guardian after his mother died. Bob has also experienced loss:

> His father had been a sea captain, and though ten years had elapsed since he and his ship had gone to the bottom in the China seas, Bob's memory easily carried him back to their last parting; and he recalled how, child-like, he had volunteered to take care of his mother until the captain came back – and he never came back.[28]

Here is another echo of Tolkien's own life. Though Tolkien had been very small when Mabel took the boys back to England for their health, he was old enough to dictate a letter to his father, who had remained in Bloemfontein, but who died before the letter was sent.[29] Mabel and her sons never returned to South Africa.

Herbert Hayens (1861–1944) was, unlike Macdonald, a writer and editor by trade, but he shared Macdonald's taste for adventure tales in far-flung settings, aimed mainly at an audience of boys. *Scouting for Buller* is one of his many novels that have a war-time storyline; others include *Under the Lone Star: A Story of Revolution in Nicaragua* (1896),

Soldiers of the Legion: A Tale of the Carlist War (1898), and *One of the Red Shirts: A Story of Garibaldi's Men* (1901).

Scouting for Buller likewise has a young orphan as its hero, and is set in South Africa during the Boer War; given Tolkien's birth and continued interest in South Africa, the tale would have had immediate interest for him. The narrator is a young Englishman named Frank West, whose mother died when he was fourteen, and whose father is killed in circumstances that suggest he murdered his Boer neighbor, the father of Frank's friend, Barend. When war breaks out, Frank's estate is confiscated by the Boers, but Barend allows him to leave unharmed. These melodramatic events merely set the stage for wartime adventures, as Frank and another friend, Terence, are captured by Boer soldiers, escape, and eventually become scouts for the English, getting involved in various battles. The almost-forgotten murder mystery is solved at the very end of the book when Frank, recovering in the hospital, learns both that his late father is innocent of the murder charge and that he is joint heir to a box of diamonds. The story closes with Frank and Barend planning to visit England and then return to South Africa, presumably to live happily ever after.

Both *The Lost Explorers* and *Scouting for Buller*, then, are stories of orphans making good for themselves; their hearty endorsement of young men supporting and encouraging each other would likely have resonated with Tolkien and his schoolboy friends. This, and the reasons we noted above, help us see what Tolkien could have enjoyed about these tales.

But another, and problematic, element of both books is their racism and imperialism. In *The Lost Explorers*, the protagonists treat the Australian aborigines as mere obstacles in the way of their hunt for gold; the possibility of unjust exploitation is not even hinted at. More distastefully, the aborigines are described in sub-human terms: "pests," "skunks," "more ape than man," "gorilla-like." Their bodies are "repulsively scarred and painted" and "grotesquely garbed"; elsewhere a native is depicted as "a black grinning face . . . demoniacally leering."[30]

In one particularly vile episode, the group captures "a specimen" in order to extract information about where to find water. When he doesn't comply, they deliberately lace his food with salt, and allow him to suffer until he leads them to a hidden pool, in a scene that is played for laughs. The overall attitude toward the natives is summed up in a putatively positive comment that one explorer makes while studying the corpse of a member of the 'lost race': "They're bigger than an ordinary native, and their faces look almost intelligent."[31]

Scouting for Buller is slightly more readable than *The Lost Explorers*. Hayens does a reasonably good job of recognizing the humanity of the Boer enemy, and he includes a nod to the costs of war at the end, with his narrator saying, "if there are any people wicked enough to love war for its own sake, they should go into a hospital ward after an engagement, and look at the human wrecks it contains." Nevertheless, it is unabashedly colonialist in its underlying attitudes. The entire story focuses on the conflict between the Boers and the English, with the native Africans being almost completely excluded from the tale, as if they were of no importance. Insofar as they appear in the story, it is a detail of local color, as when the narrator follows a "Kaffir track." One of the few natives who makes it into the narrative at all is a boy whom they encounter on an expedition, and whom they capture and immediately threaten at gunpoint to gain information.[32]

"We are synthetic men, uprooted": Tolkien on race and empire

The issue of race in relation to Tolkien's work has been thoughtfully explored by a number of scholars.[33] The topic is complex and we must be careful not to oversimplify matters. Dimitra Fimi makes the point that "The 'races' of Middle-earth . . . come from all the different strands of Tolkien's academic knowledge and awareness: philology and linguistics, anthropology and folklore," with the result that his secondary world "reproduces some of the concepts and prejudices of the 'primary' world, while at the same time questioning, challenging and transforming others."[34] We have seen those "prejudices of the primary world" in Macdonald and Hayens; unfortunately, these elements were not uncommon in other adventure novels of the period. For instance, G.A. Henty's stories, favored by the boys at King Edward's, were "often guilty of racial and class arrogance," and Rosie Kennedy observes that "Boys' adventure stories . . . began to take on an overtly imperialist tone by the end of the nineteenth century."[35] An awareness of Tolkien's boyhood reading can help us understand his later treatment of this sensitive topic. Here it is worth calling to mind that influence can operate through negative as well as positive means, and that Tolkien was notably free of racial prejudice at a time when casual racism and anti-Semitism were, by today's standards, common.*

Early on, Tolkien rejected the colonialist attitude taken in *Scouting for Buller*. Writing to his friend Christopher Wiseman in 1914, Tolkien said that although he believed in the "duty of patriotism," he could no longer defend the Boer War and was "a more & more convinced Home Ruler."† Interestingly, he added, "I don't defend 'Deutschland über alles' but certainly do the Norwegian 'alt for Norge' which translates itself."[36] Love for country meant love and self-sacrifice for one's own native land, without trying to dominate others: patriotism, not nationalism. It is worth noting that Boromir's desire to possess the Ring for the defense of his homeland, though rooted in good intentions, betokens an unhealthily nationalist outlook derived from his father. Denethor states the priorities of his political philosophy baldly when he declares "there is no purpose higher in the world as it now stands than the good of Gondor" – as clear an example of the absolutization of national interest as one could hope to find, and it comes from a character who is shown to be self-centered, mistrustful, and oblivious to the welfare of his own family, let alone the people under his rule.

The connection to one's native land was, for Tolkien, fundamentally geographical, veritably rooted in one's home turf. C.S. Lewis recalled that "Tolkien once remarked to

---

* On Tolkien's resistance to anti-Semitic views, see, for instance, *Letters*, 37–38, and 410n.

† That is, supporting Home Rule for Ireland.

me that the feeling about home must have been quite different in the days when a family had fed on the produce of the same few miles of country for six generations. . . . there was in a sense a real (not metaphorical) connection between them and the countryside. What had been earth and air & later corn, and later still bread, really was in them." In the modern day, however, consuming foods sourced from all over the world, we "have no connection (save in sentiment) with any place on earth. We are synthetic men, uprooted. The strength of the hills is not ours."[37] For Tolkien, the rootedness of a people in a certain place had little to do with racial inheritance, and more to do with their relationship to the land and its fruits.

When we consider the attitudes so prevalent in boys' adventure novels of Tolkien's day, we can more fully appreciate how Tolkien's treatment of race in *The Lord of the Rings* pushed back *against* a backdrop of persistent, taken-for-granted racism and colonialism. Twenty-first-century readers may find certain passages regrettable, such as when the men from Far Harad, in Sauron's armies, are described as "black men like half-trolls with white eyes and red tongues," but after reading *The Lost Explorers* with its recurrent demeaning descriptions of aborigines, it is striking to see the way that Tolkien positively attempts to undercut the narrow-mindedness that breeds racism. It is inconceivable that Macdonald or Hayens could have written the scene in which Sam reflects on the slain Southron warrior whose body "came to rest" near him, after an attempted ambush on Faramir's company:

> His scarlet robes were tattered, his corslet of overlapping brazen plates was rent and hewn, his black plaits of hair braided with gold were drenched with blood. His brown hand still clutched the hilt of a broken sword. . . . [Sam] wondered what the man's name was and where he came from; and if he was really evil of heart, or what lies or threats had led him on the long march from his home; and if he would not really rather have stayed there in peace.[38]

Here, the "scarlet robes," his "black plaits of hair braided with gold," and his "brown hand" all draw our attention to the otherness of the warrior compared to the characters we have come to know, but with no negative associations in the description. Brian McFadden suggests that in his depictions of the Haradrim, Tolkien is drawing on Old English representations of the *Sigelwara* (Ethiopians), in which "they are potentially threatening at first glance, but vulnerable, human, and less fearsome on closer contact." In this scene, then, he is adapting medieval material in part to counter modern racialist views: "To Tolkien, discord and enmity result from manipulation of the perception of difference and are not inherent in difference."[39] It is worth observing that by using the hobbit's perspective, Tolkien is able to present the battle as that of "Men against Men" – emphasizing the common humanity of both sides rather than depicting the conflict in terms of Us versus Them.

Furthermore, Tolkien moves immediately to a reflection on the humanity of the fallen figure – that he had a name and a home – and to suggest that despite the evil of his cause, he might well have been misled or coerced into joining Sauron's forces. Like Sam himself, he may have preferred home and peace to travels and war. This reflection is all the more powerful if we consider that Tolkien gives it not to Frodo or Faramir, but to Sam, who embodies the common man, and who can hold a grudge (as against Gollum). If ordinary, stubborn, working-class Sam Gamgee, who has himself "brown hands,"* can intuitively recognize the shared ground between himself and this warrior from the South, physically and culturally different from himself and indeed on the other side of a deadly conflict, and respond with an impulse of compassion, then, this scene suggests, racial respect and reconciliation are at least possible.

"Wild, free, but not children": Ghân-buri-Ghân and his people

It is also particularly worth noting Tolkien's treatment of Ghân-buri-Ghân and his people, the Wild Men who, at a crucial moment, lead Théoden's forces through their woods to enable them to help break the siege of Gondor. Again, Tolkien's description highlights their strangeness: Ghân-buri-Ghân is "a strange squat shape of a man, gnarled as an old stone, and the hairs of his scanty beard straggled on his lumpy chin like dry moss. He was short-legged and fat-armed, thick and stumpy, and clad only with grass about his waist." One possible critique of the scene is that they are stereotypical aborigines, but this works to Tolkien's purposes. In appearance, they are exactly the kind of people who are cruelly exploited, ignored, dismissed with condescension, or treated with irony in so many of the adventure novels of that era. However, in *The Lord of the Rings*, the scene is presented with restraint and without disrespect.

Furthermore, Tolkien includes several nods toward the problems of race relations. In the initial discussion, when Éomer condescendingly questions how he can know the

---

* It is worth observing that Sam's hands are not brown simply from his outdoor work, but because he is brown-skinned for a hobbit. We should be alert to ways that later visual interpretations of LOTR can cause us to overlook or misread Tolkien's own descriptions. Readers' perceptions of his characters have undoubtedly been influenced by the Peter Jackson films, in which Sam is played by the pale-skinned Sean Astin (who was also given reddish-blond hair for the role) and Merry and Pippin are given blond hair. However, this is at odds with the text, where Tolkien repeatedly notes Sam's brown skin, and Merry is described as having brown hair. Furthermore, in the Preface to LOTR the Harfoot branch of the hobbits (which is the most numerous one) is noted as being "browner of skin" than the other two groups. We can reasonably conclude that Sam and indeed the average hobbit of the Shire was, in Tolkien's imagination, considerably darker of skin than is portrayed in Jackson's films. Tom Bombadil is likewise described as "brown-skinned," yet he is usually portrayed with light skin in artwork, as in *Lord of the Rings Online* or the LOTR trading cards. Conversely, the eventually villainous character of Denethor is described by Tolkien as having "skin like ivory," although in the Jackson films, the actor John Noble is not notably pale. Tolkien is perhaps somewhat more subversive of racial assumptions (or at least assumptions about pigmentation within given races, be they hobbits or humans) than he is usually given credit for.

number and location of the orcs as he claims, Ghân-buri-Ghân retorts, "Wild Men are wild, free, but not children. . . . I count many things: stars in sky, leaves on trees, men in the dark." Théoden then sides with the Wild Man, over against Éomer's doubts, saying that Ghân-buri-Ghân speaks "shrewdly," and accepting his offer of assistance. Here we see Tolkien presenting a scene in which Éomer's potentially racist assumptions about the Wild Man's intelligence – perhaps based on his imperfect command of the Common Tongue – are confronted and rebuked; and we learn shortly thereafter that Ghân-buri-Ghân's assessment of the tactical situation is indeed correct.* It is also worth recognizing that Ghân-buri-Ghân can speak more than one language and that the words he utters outside his native tongue are not mocked or treated ironically in the narrative, as for instance Hayens does with the captured African boy in *Scouting for Buller*.†

Tolkien's divergence from Hayens and Macdonald on this point is worth exploring further. We see that the Rohirrim learn to trust the Wild Men, despite their evident differences: "to no heart in all the host came any fear that the Wild Men were unfaithful, strange and unlovely though they might appear." But Tolkien does not allow the reader naively to mistake this moment of racial harmony for true reconciliation. After Théoden accepts the help of the Wild Men, Ghân-buri-Ghân makes a request in turn: rather than accepting the offered riches as a reward, he requests that the men of Rohan leave the Wild Men alone and "not hunt them like beasts any more"; Théoden replies, "So be it!" Both of these remarks are significant. First, Tolkien shows us that the warriors of Rohan, whom we have come to admire, have in the past treated the peaceable Wild Men like animals – precisely the repellent behavior of the protagonists in *The Lost Explorers*. The Rohirrim, however commendable they are in other ways, turn out to have an unjust past that they must reject. Théoden admits this: he does not argue with Ghân-buri-Ghân about the accuracy of this claim, but simply and directly agrees to change his people's ways.

Second, and significantly, Tolkien returns to this point later, reinforcing it. At the end of *The Lord of the Rings*, Aragorn proceeds with his company to the forest of Drúadan, where he has his heralds proclaim: "Behold, the King Elessar is come! The Forest of Drúadan he gives to Ghân-buri-Ghân and to his folk, to be their own for ever; and hereafter let no man enter it without their leave!" The observers hear the drums of the Wild Men acknowledging this announcement. Aragorn as High King thus both ratifies Théoden's agreement and extends it: not only will the Wild Men be left in peace, as they requested, but their sovereignty is recognized.‡

---

* Hammond and Scull point out that he or his scouts "count both accurately and in quantities that many would find difficult" as his *"score of scores counted ten times and five"* is 20 x 20 x (10 + 5) = 6,000, the 'six thousand spears to Sunlending' recorded in the poem in Book V, Chapter 3" (LOTR:RC, 557).

† Tolkien observed to an interviewer that many good writers "neglect language as an invention and a communication, the most important ingredient in human culture; and that problems of communications between alien cultures are not always carefully enough treated." Although in context he was referring to science fiction, his comment sheds light as well on his views about the depiction of cross-cultural communication such as we see here (quoted in Daphne Castell, "Talking to a Maker of Modern Myths").

‡ Virginia Luling observes that "the anthropology of Middle-earth is not evolutionary at

Embattled minorities: Tolkien on the disenfranchised

What Tolkien expressed implicitly in his stories, he was willing to express directly in his letters and public lectures. Writing in 1944 to his son Christopher, who was posted in South Africa, Tolkien notes that "The treatment of colour nearly always horrifies anyone going out from Britain, & not only in South Africa. Unfort[unately] not many retain that generous sentiment for long."[40] We should recognize that Tolkien's understated, dry English style means that his critical remark about his fellow Britons carries more bite than an American might immediately notice. Raymond Edwards remarks on Tolkien's "profound horror of apartheid and other forms of racial discrimination" and suggests that his mother's example had a significant role in shaping this attitude. Mabel, he notes, "was certainly shocked by the treatment of black servants [in South Africa] and was herself at pains to behave in a different and more humane manner."[41] John and Priscilla Tolkien write in *The Tolkien Family Album* that their grandmother "disliked the Boer attitude to the native servants"; they include a photograph with "the nurse, the maid, and the house-boy Isaak" posing alongside the family.[42]

We should not overlook the importance of Tolkien's "Valedictory Address" to the University of Oxford, in which he declared, "I have the hatred of *apartheid* in my bones."[43] Tolkien said this in 1959, when apartheid had been in effect for only ten years (and would continue until the 1990s). In his public opposition to this policy, he pre-dated the British Anti-Apartheid Movement and the international backlash against apartheid prompted by the Sharpeville massacre in 1960.* Given this context, it is note-worthy that Tolkien used his retirement speech – a significant event for the University, with the lecture-hall filled to capacity, and important enough to be reported on by the local press[44] – to repudiate a racist regime that was not yet a matter of widespread public concern in Britain. Although he immediately shifts to academic issues ("most of all I detest the segregation or separation of Language and Literature"), he reinforces his point with the barbed comment, "I do not care which of them [Lang. or Lit.] you think White."[45] Tolkien, who unlike Lewis kept up with academic politics, would have been well aware that his audience would pick up on this remark as a political statement.†

In considering reasons for Tolkien's opposition to apartheid, it is worth remem-bering that he was an English Catholic. As Virginia Luling points out, his religion was

---

all": the culture of Gondor is not an advancement on that of Rohan, and "the 'high' cultures are not about to lead on to something else even higher and better – Saruman is not an improvement except in certain aspects of technology" ("An Anthropologist in Middle-earth," 54–55).

* Tolkien delivered his address on June 5, 1959; the British Anti-Apartheid Movement was founded later that same month.

† In *The Fellowship of the Ring*, Tolkien offers a glimpse of inter-racial social harmony. In Bree, we learn, "The Big Folk and the Little Folk (as they called one another) were on friendly terms, minding their own affairs in their own ways, but both rightly regarding themselves as necessary parts of the Bree-folk. Nowhere else in the world was this peculiar (but excellent) ar-rangement to be found."

"the embattled faith of a minority with memories of persecution" and not, as in other countries, "synonymous with power and establishment"; the land he loved "was not the England that became a commercial Empire, not a conquering but a conquered nation."[46] Tolkien's own self-perception was that of someone belonging to a group that had been, and in some respects still was, disenfranchised and marginalized.* It is therefore perhaps to be expected that Tolkien also took a firm stand against anti-Semitic sentiment at a time when it was all too common. In response to a German publisher's query as to whether he was of Aryan origin, Tolkien majestically replied that "if I am to understand that you are enquiring whether I am of *Jewish* origin, I can only reply that I regret that I appear to have *no* ancestors of that gifted people . . . [but] if impertinent and irrelevant inquiries of this sort are to become the rule in matters of literature, then the time is not far distant when a German name will no longer be a source of pride."[47] In his letter to his publisher accompanying the draft responses, he described this "race-doctrine" as "wholly pernicious."[48] Nor did his attitude change with time: in 1971, he notes that his name "is not Jewish in origin, though I should consider it an honour if it were."[49]

Although Tolkien's dwarves draw their fundamental characteristics from Old Norse literature, he came over time to see certain parallels between his dwarves and the Jewish people, for instance remarking in a 1964 interview, "Wouldn't you say that in many ways [the Dwarves] remind you of the Jews? Their words are Semitic obviously, constructed to be Semitic."[50] Some critics have argued that the association is evidence of anti-Semitic stereotyping; however, as Renée Vink shows in her careful analysis of Tolkien's development of the Dwarves, there is no direct allegory or identification, but rather a loose parallel based on "language type, fighting spirit and Tolkien's qualification of his Dwarves and the Jewish people alike as 'at once native and alien in their habitations.'"[51] In fact, the growing friendship of Gimli and Legolas – dwarf and elf, respectively, two races normally at loggerheads – allows Tolkien to present a positive example of interracial harmony. Such an equal friendship, in which prejudices are faced and overcome, and in which cultural and racial difference becomes a source of mutual enrichment rather than entrenched hostility, is vastly different from anything we find in even the less overtly racist adventure novels of Tolkien's youth. His boyhood reading was indeed significant, providing material for profound influence-by-opposition.

---

* Catholic emancipation happened gradually from the mid-eighteenth century, as the penal laws were removed and restrictions eased: Catholics became able to own property and inherit land, to be employed in the civil service, and, in 1829, to take seats in Parliament. Though legally most discrimination against Catholics was over by the twentieth century, the after-effects of the Elizabethan Religious Settlement (1558–59) and the so-called "Glorious Revolution" (1688–89) could still be felt and certain barriers between Catholics and British society at large remained in place. In a number of respects, indeed, that continues to be true to this day. At Oxford, for instance, all the formerly Catholic college chapels (including those of Tolkien's three colleges, Exeter, Pembroke, and Merton) remain Anglican. Nationally, the British head of state, the monarch, is still constitutionally barred from being a Catholic. In 2013 the Succession to the Crown Act did, however, permit heirs to the British throne to marry a Catholic.

PHOTO GALLERY

THERE, in the Broad, within whose booky house
Half England's scholars nibble books or browse.
Where'er they wander blessed fortune theirs:
Books to the ceiling, other books upstairs;
Books, doubtless, in the cellar, and behind
Romantic bays, where iron ladders wind.

JOHN MASEFIELD

Whatever book you may want, wherever you may be—
ask BLACKWELL'S

❧ Figure 1 ❧

Vintage bookmark (ca. 1939) featuring Blackwell's Bookshop, Broad Street, Oxford, and a poem by the Poet Laureate, John Masefield (1878–1967). Tolkien admitted in the late 1920s, "I've spent over a hundred pounds on books this year and do not regret it at all." He corresponded with Masefield and spoke positively of his *A Letter from Pontus and Other Verse* (1936).

🌿 **Figure 2** 🌿

Illustrations by Beatrix Potter from *The Tale of Benjamin Bunny* (1904). Tolkien called her stories "masterly." Commenting on his invention of the word 'hobbit,' Tolkien remarked, "I must admit that its faint suggestion of *rabbit* appealed to me."

🌿 **Figure 3** 🌿

Children, Snergs, and a Bear: from E.A. Wyke-Smith's *The Marvellous Land of Snergs* (1927). Tolkien identified this work as "an unconscious source-book! for the Hobbits."

❧ **Figure 4** ❧

Hans Christian Andersen (1805–1875), the author of fairy tales such as "The Snow Queen" and "The Little Mermaid." Tolkien declared that "as a child I couldn't stand Hans Christian Andersen and I can't now."

122

⟡ **Figure 5** ⟡

Riding the North Wind: from "East of the Sun and West of the Moon," in Andrew Lang's *The Blue Fairy Book* (1889). Tolkien was intrigued by this fantastic celestial imagery, incorporating it into one of the earliest poems of the legendarium (1915) and later into Frodo's final walking-song in *The Lord of the Rings*.

⟡ **Figure 6** ⟡

Sylvie, Bruno, the Professor, and the Other Professor: from Lewis Carroll's *Sylvie and Bruno* (1889). Tolkien described the Professor as "the best character," and he cited a poem declaimed by the Other Professor, from *Sylvie and Bruno Concluded* (1893), in an illustrative quotation for his work on the Oxford English Dictionary. The word to be defined was "smirkle"; it is the only one of his word-slips that has survived.

Joe Brown and the Ogre.

❧ **Figure 7** ☙

Joe Brown and the Ogre: from "Puss-cat Mew" in E.H. Knatchbull-Hugessen's *Stories for My Children* (1869). In his late seventies, Tolkien recalled how, when he was a young child, he was "read to from an 'old collection' – tattered and without cover or title-page – of which all that I can now remember was . . . one story I was then very fond of called 'Puss Cat Mew.'"

❧ **Figure 8** ❧

Subterranean goblins: from George MacDonald's *The Princess and the Goblin* (1872). Tolkien said that MacDonald "has depicted what will always be to me the classic goblin." He explained that the goblins of *The Hobbit* and the orcs of *The Lord of the Rings* owe "a good deal to the goblin tradition . . . especially as it appears in George MacDonald."

❦ **Figure 9** ❧

Fáfnir the dragon: from "The Story of Sigurd" in Andrew Lang's *The Red Fairy Book* (1890). Tolkien rated the tale "my favorite without rival" and described Fáfnir as "the prince of all dragons." This illustration matches Tolkien's explanation of the name "Smaug," his dragon in *The Hobbit*, which comes from *smugan*, a Germanic verb meaning "to squeeze through a hole."

❧ **Figure 10** ❧

Tolkien identified the tale "Soria Moria Castle" as "the source of the sound-sequence
moria," which became one of the most famous place-names in Middle-earth: the Mines
of Moria, where Gandalf fell. Tolkien read the story both in George Dasent's *Popular
Tales from the Norse* (1859) and in Lang's *The Red Fairy Book* (1890), where we find this
battle with a many-headed troll.

❧ **Figure 11** ❧

Frontispiece: from S.R. Crockett's *The Black Douglas* (1889). Tolkien revealed that the narrow escape of Bilbo from the wargs in chapter 6 of *The Hobbit* "is in part derived from [this] scene in S.R. Crockett's *The Black Douglas*."

❧ **Figure 12** ❧

The Atlantis wave: from E. Nesbit's *The Story of the Amulet* (1906). Tolkien praised the "triumphant formula" of this work and called Edith Nesbit "an author I delight in." This scene would have particularly caught Tolkien's attention, as he had a recurring nightmare of a colossal, destructive wave, which he described as his "Atlantis complex," and which he bequeathed in *The Lord of the Rings* to Faramir, the character whom he said was most like himself.

129

The Song of Quoodle

They haven't got no noses,
The fallen sons of Eve;
Even the smell of roses
Is not what they supposes;
But more than mind discloses
And more than men believe.

25

❧ **Figure 13** ❧

First stanza of G.K. Chesterton's "The Song of Quoodle" from his *Wine, Water and Song* (1915). Tolkien was fond of reciting this poem, which he knew by heart.

❦ **Figure 14** ❦

The duck-housekeeper: from Hugh Lofting's *The Voyage of Doctor Dolittle* (1922). Tolkien enjoyed the Dolittle books, and they may have influenced his depiction of Beorn's animal servants in *The Hobbit*, to whom Beorn can speak, à la Doctor Dolittle, in "a queer animal language like animal-noises turned to talk."

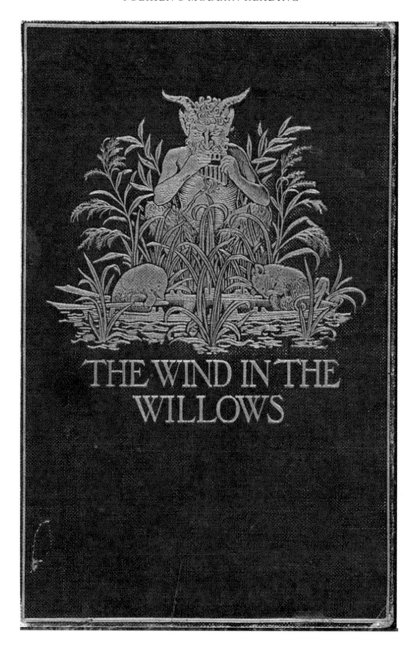

❧ Figure 15 ❧

Mole and Rat worshipping Pan: front cover of Kenneth Grahame's *The Wind in the Willows* (1908). Tolkien considered it an "excellent book," "an almost perfect blend . . . of many pigments."

❧ Figure 16 ☙

Playbill for *Peter Pan* (1907). Tolkien was deeply impressed by J.M. Barrie's play when he saw it in 1910, but later called attention to its dark aspect, noting that "children are meant to grow up and to die, and not to become Peter Pans (a dreadful fate)."

❧ **Figure 17** ☙

Alexander Macdonald's *The Lost Explorers* (1906). Tolkien gave a copy to the library of King Edward's School in his last year there before matriculating at Oxford.

A TALE OF THE HOUSE OF THE WOLFINGS AND ALL THE KINDREDS OF THE MARK WRITTEN IN PROSE AND IN VERSE BY WILLIAM MORRIS

WHILES IN THE EARLY WINTER EVE
WE PASS AMID THE GATHERING NIGHT
SOME HOMESTEAD THAT WE HAD TO LEAVE
YEARS PAST; AND SEE ITS CANDLES BRIGHT
SHINE IN THE ROOM BESIDE THE DOOR
WHERE WE WERE MERRY YEARS AGONE
BUT NOW MUST NEVER ENTER MORE,
AS STILL THE DARK ROAD DRIVES US ON.
E'EN SO THE WORLD OF MEN MAY TURN
AT EVEN OF SOME HURRIED DAY
AND SEE THE ANCIENT GLIMMER BURN
ACROSS THE WASTE THAT HATH NO WAY;
THEN WITH THAT FAINT LIGHT IN ITS EYES
A WHILE I BID IT LINGER NEAR
AND NURSE IN WAVERING MEMORIES
THE BITTER-SWEET OF DAYS THAT WERE.

POCKET EDITION

LONGMANS, GREEN AND CO.
39 PATERNOSTER ROW, LONDON
NEW YORK, BOMBAY, AND CALCUTTA
1913

❧ **Figure 18** ☙

Title page: from William Morris's *The House of the Wolfings* (1889). Tolkien wrote that "The Dead Marshes . . . owe something to Northern France after the Battle of the Somme. They owe more to William Morris and . . . *The House of the Wolfings*."

❧ Figure 19 ❧

"The death of Eric": from H. Rider Haggard's *Eric Brighteyes* (1890). Tolkien commented that "There is of course a value in heroic tales of divided allegiances and unacknowledged defeat. . . . Rider Haggard's *Eric Brighteyes* is as good (if rather longer) and as heroic as most of such things."

136

FACSIMILE OF THE SHERD OF AMENARTAS.

ONE ¹/₂ SIZE.

Greatest length of the original 10 ¹/₂ inches.
Greatest breadth   7   inches
Weight   1ᶫᵇ 5¹/₂ oz.

❧ **Figure 20** ☙

Frontispiece: from H. Rider Haggard's *She* (1887). Tolkien recalled that "as a boy *She* interested me as much as anything – like the Greek Sherd of Amenartas, which was the kind of machine by which everything got moving." Tolkien's son, Christopher, remarked "it can hardly be doubted" that the name of Kôr, the hilltop city of the Elves in his father's legendarium, was taken from Haggard's story and that "the relationship was more than purely 'phonetic.'"

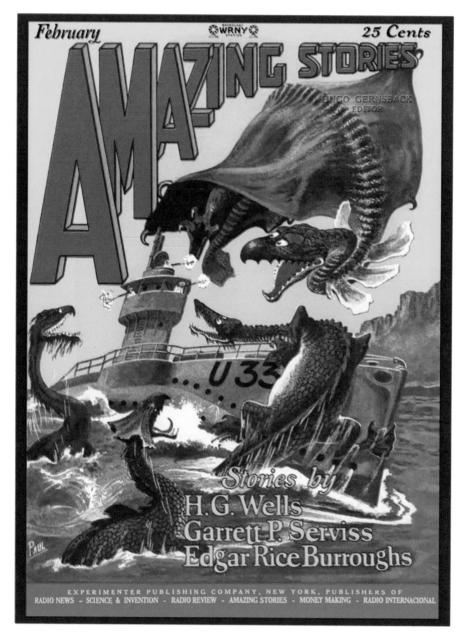

❧ **Figure 21** ❧

Tolkien stated that he "read many of Edgar Rice Burroughs' earlier works," and acknowledged H.G. Wells as one of the "Old Masters" of science fiction. Both authors appear in this issue of *Amazing Stories* (February 1927), one of the American science fiction magazines that Tolkien knew well.

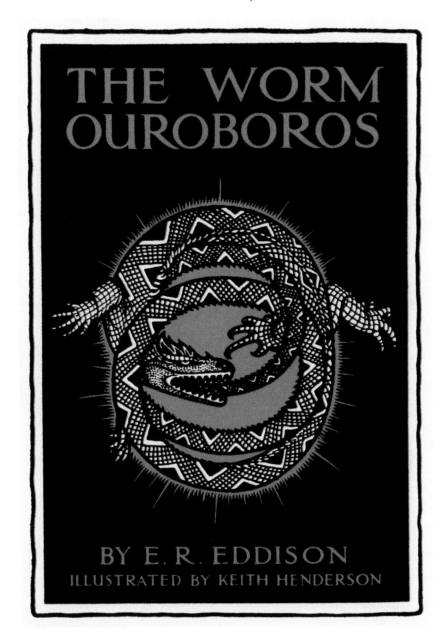

❧ **Figure 22** ❧

E.R. Eddison's *The Worm Ouroboros* (1922). Tolkien declared that he "read all that E.R. Eddison wrote" and described him as "the greatest and most convincing writer of 'invented worlds' that I have read."

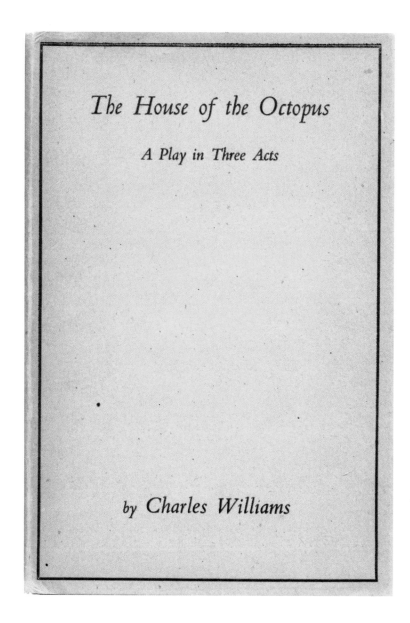

The House of the Octopus

A Play in Three Acts

by Charles Williams

❧ **Figure 23** ☙

Although Tolkien disliked the poetry of Charles Williams and called his novels "dreadful," he had a comparatively favorable view of his plays, especially *The House of the Octopus* (1945).

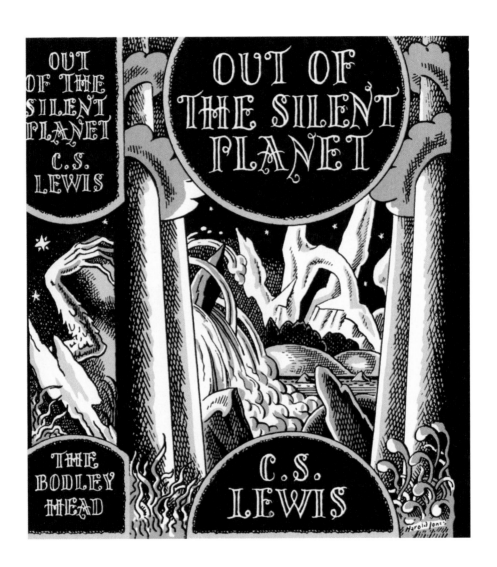

❧ **Figure 24** ❧

C.S. Lewis's *Out of the Silent Planet* (1938). Tolkien remarked, "I found the blend of *vera historia* with *mythos* irresistible." Lewis's tall, booming, angular *sorns* (see the arm and hand on the spine of the book cover) seem to have provided inspiration for Tolkien as he invented the Ents.

THE CITY OF NEVER

❧ Figure 25 ❧

Title page and illustration of "The City of Never": from Lord Dunsany's *The Book of Wonder* (1912). When Clyde Kilby came to Oxford in order to assist with *The Silmarillion*, Tolkien gave him a copy of *The Book of Wonder* "and told him to read it in preparation for his task."

THE WORKS OF
FRANCIS THOMPSON
POEMS: VOLUME II

BURNS & OATES LTD
28 Orchard Street
London W

⁂ Figure 26 ⁂

Title page and frontispiece: *The Works of Francis Thompson*, vol. II (1913). Tolkien ranked Thompson (1859–1907) "among the very greatest of all poets." It was from Thompson's poem "The Mistress of Vision" that Tolkien derived the word "Luthany," which became, in his legendarium, first a name for England and then, adapted into Elvish, the name of the elf-maiden Lúthien. Tolkien came to refer to his wife, Edith, as Lúthien: the name is inscribed on the headstone of her grave in Oxford.

aged 53.

❧ **Figure 27** ❧

J. Henry Shorthouse (1834–1903), author of *John Inglesant: A Romance*. As a boy, Tolkien passed his house in Beaumont Road, Birmingham, every day (see prelude). He later characterized Shorthouse as "a mere amateur (like myself) with no status in the literary world, [who] suddenly produced a long book. . . . I think he never wrote any more, but wasted the rest of his time trying to explain what he had and what he had not meant by *John Inglesant*. . . . I have always tried to take him as a melancholy warning, and still try to attend to . . . writing some more."

❧ **Figure 28** ❧

Title page and frontispiece: from J.H. Shorthouse's *John Inglesant* (1881). Tolkien described it as "queer, exciting and debateable – or seemed so then, few now find it possible to read. It slowly took on, and eventually became a best-seller, and the subject of public discussion from the Prime Minister downwards."

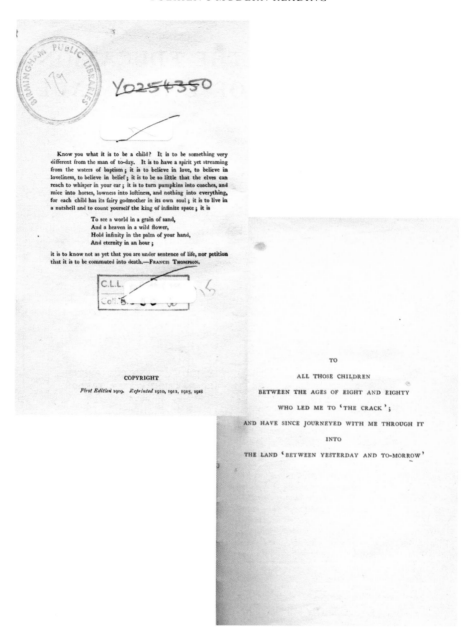

TO

ALL THOSE CHILDREN

BETWEEN THE AGES OF EIGHT AND EIGHTY

WHO LED ME TO 'THE CRACK';

AND HAVE SINCE JOURNEYED WITH ME THROUGH IT

INTO

THE LAND 'BETWEEN YESTERDAY AND TO-MORROW'

❧ Figure 29 ❧

Copyright and dedication pages: from Algernon Blackwood's *The Education of Uncle Paul* (1909). Tolkien disclosed that his own use of the word *crack* in "The Crack of Doom" was "ultimately derived from Algernon Blackwood, who . . . used it in this way in one of his books."

❧ **Figure 30** ❦

E.M. Forster (1879–1970), author of *A Room with a View* (1908), *Howards End* (1910), and four other novels. In 1954, Tolkien nominated Forster for the Nobel Prize in Literature.

❧ **Figure 31** ❧

The protagonist of Henry Wadsworth Longfellow's *The Song of Hiawatha* (1855) may have contributed to the portrayal of Bard the Bowman in *The Hobbit*. Tolkien also drew a personal parallel with the author: "if I'm remembered at all, it will be by *The Lord of the Rings*, I take it. Won't it be rather like the case of Longfellow? People remember Longfellow wrote *Hiawatha*, quite forget he was a Professor of Modern Languages!"

❦ Figure 32 ❧

Sinclair Lewis's *Babbitt* (1922). Discussing how he arrived at the word "hobbit," Tolkien admitted that it "might have been associated with Sinclair Lewis's Babbitt." He observed that "Babbitt has the same bourgeois smugness that hobbits do. His world is the same limited place."

❦ Figure 33 ❧

Sheila Kaye-Smith was a popular writer and famous Catholic convert of the 1920s. Tolkien recommended her novel *A Challenge to Sirius* (1917) to Clyde Kilby, probably because, as a Southerner, Kilby would have been interested in that part of the novel set during the US Civil War.

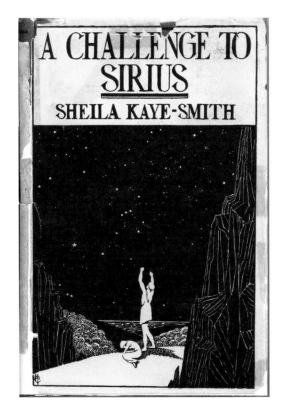

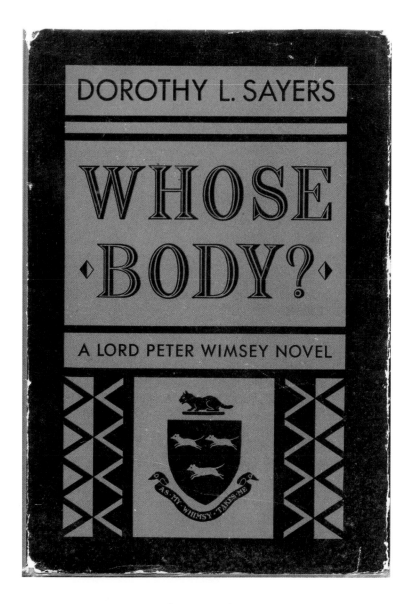

♂ **Figure 34** ☕

Tolkien read widely in the detective fiction of Dorothy L. Sayers, despite hyperbolically proclaiming a distaste for her later novels. He said that he followed Lord Peter Wimsey "from his attractive beginnings" in *Whose Body?* (1923) so far as *Gaudy Night* (1935), "by which time I conceived a loathing for him . . . not surpassed by any other character in literature known to me, unless by his Harriet. [*Busman's Honeymoon* (1937)] was worse. I was sick."

❧ **Figure 35** ☙

Agatha Christie (1890–1976), the 'Queen of Crime.' Tolkien's grandson noted that he "went out of his way to praise Agatha Christie." After reading *At Bertram's Hotel* (1965), which was inspired by Brown's hotel in London, Tolkien "stayed at Brown's, and on leaving his room to investigate footsteps heard in the corridor, found himself locked out again!"

The writings of James Joyce (1882–1941) epitomize literary Modernism, but Tolkien paid close attention to his most controversial work, *Finnegans Wake* (1939), and was sufficiently intrigued by the name Anna Livia Plurabelle to transliterate it into his invented language of Qenya.

❧ **Figure 37** ☙

Tolkien taught Mary Renault at Oxford and read a number of her novels, especially praising *The King Must Die* (1958) and *The Bull from the Sea* (1962). He remarked that a letter from Renault was "perhaps the piece of 'Fan-mail' that gives me most pleasure."

Mary Renault

THE KING MUST DIE

PANTHEON

❧ Figure 38 ❧

Musrum (1968), by Eric Thacker and Anthony Earnshaw, may well be the weirdest book that Tolkien is known to have read. Asked to write an endorsement, he replied, "I do not feel moved to say anything at all about it."

❧ **Figure 39** ☙

"The Fir-Topped Hurst" by Sir William Russell Flint: from Matthew Arnold's *The Scholar Gipsy & Thyrsis* (1910). Tolkien detached this picture from Arnold's book, framed it, and hung it on the wall of every place he lived in thereafter, including his final residence in Merton College. As Catherine McIlwaine of Oxford's Bodleian Library notes, "There is something of the Shire in these bucolic scenes."

❧ Mythopoeic adventure and moral heroism: John Buchan

Another author with a link to South Africa whom we need to consider is John Buchan. Humphrey Carpenter named Buchan as a favorite of Tolkien's for leisure reading,[52] a significant inclusion given that Carpenter otherwise minimizes the extent of Tolkien's familiarity with modern authors.

John Buchan (1875–1940), Lord Tweedsmuir, was a prolific writer as well as a distinguished civil servant, finishing his career as Governor-General of Canada. Born in Scotland and educated at Oxford, he spent part of his early diplomatic career in South Africa. Today, Buchan is best known for *The Thirty-Nine Steps* (1915), the first of a series of adventure novels whose protagonist is the daring Richard Hannay: it is followed by four others – namely, *Greenmantle* (1916), *Mr. Standfast* (1919), *The Three Hostages* (1924), and *The Island of Sheep* (1936). *Huntingtower* (1922) and its sequels, featuring the grocer-turned-romance-hero Dickson McCunn, also remain in print. Another major strand of Buchan's writing, little known today, is historical fiction, such as *Midwinter: Certain Travellers in Old England* (1923), which sometimes overlaps with what we could call mythopoeic novels, such as *Prester John* (1910) and *The Path of the King* (1921).

Although Carpenter states that Buchan was a favorite of Tolkien's, he gives no specifics, and hitherto critics have operated without knowledge of which particular titles Tolkien read. Such has been the influence of Carpenter that there are more scholarly analyses of Buchan's influence than of some authors whom Tolkien himself names as sources. Indeed, Carpenter's description of Buchan as a "favourite" has led to certain critics falling over themselves in an attempt to find connections with the legendarium, most notoriously a risible attempt by Richard Giddings and Elizabeth Holland to argue that the plot of *The Lord of the Rings* is derived, in exacting detail, from *The Thirty-Nine Steps*.[53] Other scholarly treatments have been much more valuable.[54]

By my own reckoning, there is only one title that we can identify with absolute certainty as having been read by Tolkien – namely, *Greenmantle* – and it is here that I will focus my attention.

Greenmantle

We know of his familiarity with *Greenmantle* from an unlikely source: a scholarly essay he wrote in which he assesses, among many other titles, a German academic's compilation of English vocabulary words. Tolkien observes that the compiler had been admirably comprehensive in his listing of compound-words, omitting almost nothing from Anglo-Saxon examples up to the present day, "not even John Buchan's title *Greenmantle*. This, picked up from a *Daily Telegraph* review . . . and not we think itself read, is entered as *islam. Kriegsgesch*."[55] At first glance, this reference suggests only that Tolkien recognized the title, but in fact it is a dry joke that requires knowledge of *Greenmantle*. Why would Tolkien remark that the compiler had not read the book? Because it is

155

categorized as "*islam. Kriegsgesch.*" – an abbreviation of academic German that means "Islamic military history."* We must be familiar with *Greenmantle*'s plot to appreciate Tolkien's comment.

In the novel, set (and in fact written) during the Great War, Hannay, now an officer of the British Army, is given a mission to prevent the mysterious prophetic figure known as "Greenmantle" (named thus for his ceremonial garments) from leaving Europe and making his way to the East. Greenmantle is associated with an Islamic prophecy that a new deliverer is coming out of the West,[56] and the Germans plan to manipulate him to unite the Muslim peoples against Germany's enemies in the War. Meanwhile, Hannay's friend Sandy Arbuthnot, a British officer, has infiltrated the "Companions of the Rosy Hours," a religious sect (invented by Buchan) headquartered in Constantinople. When Greenmantle dies before the German plan can come to fruition, the German mastermind, Frau Hilda von Einem, chooses his successor from among the Companions of the Rosy Hours in order to continue the dastardly plot, not knowing that the new Greenmantle is the disguised officer and spy, Sandy. Sandy plays along with von Einem, leaking information to Hannay that he then passes to the allied Russian forces about the weak place in the defenses of the Turkish city of Erzerum. Pursued by von Einem and her forces, Hannay and his company make a last stand in a rocky outcrop just outside the city. Von Einem attempts to convert them to her side, but fails; soon afterwards she is killed by a Russian shell. At the very last minute, the Russians break through, and Hannay and his company, along with Sandy, are able to join with the attacking Russian forces – and, as Sandy is still wearing his green robes, he ironically fulfills the prophecy, as the Turks are delivered from the control of Germany.

Hence we can see that Tolkien's wry observation about *Greenmantle* not being exactly Islamic military history depends on his having read the book (unlike the German academic with his list of compound-words). Not only is the military engagement fictitious rather than historical, but the Turks are hardly agents in the events described, being first manipulated by the Germans and then delivered from that manipulation by the British and their allies.

Rooted adventures

What might have appealed to him about Buchan's writings in general, and the Richard Hannay adventures in particular? One element that Tolkien would have liked was the atmosphere that Buchan created. Here we can usefully consider a conversation with Tolkien recounted by C.S. Lewis. Lewis wrote to a friend criticizing Dumas's *The Three Musketeers* for its lack of atmosphere or a sense of place: it is "an abstract world of gallantry and adventure which has no *roots*. . . . I don't think there is a single passage to show that Dumas had ever seen a cloud, a road, or a tree." Lewis goes on to say that he has been discussing this with Tolkien:

---

* My thanks to Dr. Alexandra Lloyd for translating this phrase.

> [Tolkien and I] remarked how odd it was that the word *romance* should be used to cover things so different as Morris on the one hand and Dumas . . . on the other – things not only different but so different that it is hard to imagine the same person liking both. We agreed that for what *we* meant by romance there must be at least the hint of another world – one must 'hear the horns of elfland.' For fear you shd. think I am going too much off the deep end, let me add that I have just read a real modern thriller (Buchan's *Three Hostages*) and enjoyed it thoroughly.[57]

Lewis's complaints can be reversed to give an idea of what he and Tolkien viewed as ingredients in a good romance. It must have a sense of place, a 'rootedness' in a certain setting, and an atmosphere of its own. Here, perhaps, we can see something of what Tolkien found appealing in the works of John Buchan, whose adventure stories are set in fully realized locations, both geographically and historically. This sense that the setting is organically connected to a particular, real place, rather than being a mere abstraction or amalgam of miscellaneous scenic elements, would have appealed to Tolkien's appreciation for genuine love of country, his own and others'; it helps to illuminate what he meant by referring to his own legendarium as a mythology he wished to dedicate to England, one that would "be redolent of our 'air.'"[58]

The "horns of elfland" comment has usually been taken as applying to Tolkien and Lewis's appreciation for mythopoeic literature, so it is worth noting that even Buchan's action-adventure tales contain a broad streak of the fantastic. For instance in *Greenmantle*, otherwise mostly a military-spy adventure story, we find a distinct mystical element in the Companions of the Rosy Hours. This group seems able to work a kind of magic as they dance and sing, such that Hannay has, at one point, a vision of a landscape like the African veld, but "wider and wilder and more gracious. . . . I was feeling the kind of immortal light-heartedness which only a boy knows in the dawning of his days. I had no longer any fear of these magic-makers. They were kindly wizards, who had brought me into fairyland."[59] Tom Shippey suggests that Tolkien would have valued Buchan's "readiness to see the mythical coexisting with the everyday and to sense fairyland, or in Scottish dialect *Elfhame*, as forever present on the margins of Old England."[60] The dedication to *The Thirty-Nine Steps* provides an apt description of all five Richard Hannay novels: "the romance where the incidents defy the probabilities, and march just inside the borders of the possible."

Buchan's frequent use of South Africa as a setting would also have been attractive to Tolkien, who continued to be interested in that land, even though he had spent such a short time there as a child. Richard Hannay is South African, and in *Greenmantle* and *Mr Standfast* in particular, there are numerous references to the South African landscape.* In all the books, the settings are vividly realized; they have the atmosphere in abundance that Tolkien so greatly valued in such tales.

---

* Mark T. Hooker notes that Buchan's "recurring use of untranslated Afrikaans in his narration" would have caught Tolkien's attention ("Reading John Buchan in Search of Tolkien," 163).

Another aspect of Buchan that would have appealed to Tolkien is his delineation of a heroic character with a clear moral vision. Hannay is quick-thinking and insightful, a man of action but one who never indulges in unnecessary violence. In *Greenmantle*, Hannay has several opportunities to kill an enemy whom he has rendered helpless, but – like Bilbo, like Frodo – he does not do so, even at the cost of future trouble for himself.

This point is worth emphasizing. In the medieval Norse and Germanic sagas that Tolkien knew and loved, violence, conflicting loyalties, and an existential pessimism are often on display; this sense of a man's unchangeable 'doom' or fate appears in Anglo-Saxon literature as well. The heroes of these tales regularly come to a bad end, not infrequently involving murder and suicide. Although Tolkien appreciated these tales (and in the case of *Sigurd and Gudrún*, wrote his own version of one of them), he could also be highly critical of the particular mode of the 'heroic' that they promoted. In the draft of his *Beowulf* lecture, he criticizes the modern fascination with stories of "divided allegiances and unacknowledged defeat," even calling this obsession a "superstition."[61] * Tolkien certainly acknowledged that the inevitability of death and the decay of all human works is a "theme no Christian need despise." The Northern "theory of courage," for which defeat is "no refutation,"[62] was by no means at odds with his Catholic faith. Valuing bravery and heroic deeds even in circumstances where there is no chance of success or even survival is not incompatible with the theological virtue of hope. The problem is the embrace of an obsessively despairing attitude, one that is fascinated by ruin and defeat for its own sake.

In this sense, Buchan's heroes offer a distinct contrast to the despairing Germanic model. On numerous occasions, Richard Hannay finds himself in an impossibly tight spot; this happens repeatedly in *Greenmantle*, and is seen dramatically during the siege in *The Island of Sheep*. Hannay's attitude, however, is never fatalistic: his response to an apparent dead end is to determine to do the best that he can, and to act morally, even if a positive outcome seems unlikely.

Tolkien's heroes are courageous and tough, but more than that, their conscience prompts them to protect and help others, even when it puts themselves in danger, and they have an underlying sense of hope. In this way they resemble Richard Hannay more than the protagonists of Norse sagas. For instance, Théoden, having shaken off Wormtongue's influence, rides to war knowing that it is possible, even probable, that he will die in battle. However, he is not therefore reckless: he acts prudently even while being daring. By leading his people into battle, Théoden makes it more likely that their relief of Gondor will be a success and that the armies of Sauron will be defeated. He rejoices in the possibility of a heroic death not purely for its own sake, but because it is heroism with a purpose. Tolkien is, in short, reimagining what heroism means, moving from a more superficial and adolescent vision to a more mature and nuanced one; in the process, he may well have found Buchan's Richard Hannay to be a useful model of what he could achieve.

---

* We will discuss this point further in chapter 8.

🐾 "To die will be an awfully big adventure": J.M. Barrie's *Peter Pan*

Finally, we turn to a very different sort of adventure. Sir James Matthew Barrie (1860–1937) is best known today for his character of Peter Pan, the ageless boy, who first appeared in Barrie's adult novel *The Little White Bird* (1902), then subsequently in a play (first staged in 1904) and two further novels, *Peter Pan in Kensington Gardens* (1906), illustrated by Arthur Rackham, and *Peter and Wendy* (1911).

Barrie also wrote a number of other plays, including *Dear Brutus* (1917) and *Mary Rose* (1920), in which he explores the intersection (often dangerous and traumatic) between human and fairy worlds. Tolkien had read these plays and seen *Mary Rose* performed. He discusses these in "On Fairy-stories," remarking that Barrie was successful in making his stories believable, but he did so with "characteristic shirking of his own dark issues."[63] And this shirking he found too in Barrie's development – or rather non-development – of the character of Peter Pan himself. Tolkien commented that "children are meant to grow up and to die, and not to become Peter Pans (a dreadful fate)." Arrested development is a common enough response to trauma, of course, and has been described as a kind of religious, even idolatrous, belief: "Peter Pantheism," faith in the (false) power of eternal youth.* It is an understandable mistake, but a mistake nonetheless, and Tolkien knew as much. As we saw in the previous chapter, it was the theme of death, not the avoidance thereof, that he found most striking in George MacDonald's *Lilith*, and that he himself would treat with so much care in *The Lord of the Rings*.

Tolkien himself had plenty of "dark issues" to face, including the death of both his parents by the time he was twelve years old and his military service as a Signals Officer in the Great War. The origin of the Silmarillion can be found, according to John Garth, in the writing of "The Fall of Gondolin" during Tolkien's stay in hospital in late 1916 straight after the Battle of the Somme; it is a tale whose storyline and imagery show it to be "clearly a product of Tolkien's war experience."[64]

A similar tackling of trauma through writing occurred in 1944, after a visit to Birmingham brought reminders of his friends who had died in the trenches of France: "I couldn't stand much of . . . the ghosts that rose from the pavements," Tolkien confessed in a letter to his son.[65] As Garth points out, it was a deeply distressing experience, for "Tolkien's imagination, or his perception, was sometimes indistinguishable from vision."[66]† Significantly, three weeks later, in a burst of creativity, he wrote the Dead Marshes section of *The Lord of the Rings*, and, having had this "artistic catharsis," his writer's block was broken and he was able to carry on rapidly with the tale.[67] By facing, rather than avoiding, the darkest experiences of his life, Tolkien was able to transmute

---

* The problem is not the continued enjoyment of things that children enjoy (such as fantasy stories), but rather the refusal to grow and accept the responsibilities of adulthood. As C.S. Lewis explains, "arrested development consists not in refusing to lose old things but in failing to add new things" ("On Three Ways of Writing for Children," in *On Stories*, 34).

† Tolkien certainly did have a vision a few months later, while in prayer before the Blessed Sacrament, of God's loving attention expressed as a beam of light upon a mote of dust (*Letters*, 99).

the remembered horrors of the Great War into some of the most powerful and haunting scenes in *The Lord of the Rings*.

But both of these cathartic moments were in the future when Tolkien first encountered Barrie. Tolkien saw the play *Peter Pan* in 1910, and recorded in his diary, "Indescribable but shall never forget it as long as I live. Wish E[dith] had been with me."[68] (See figure 16.) Could this encounter with Barrie's work have been the inspiration for some of Tolkien's earliest writings?

In 1915, Tolkien composed a poem titled "You & Me and the Cottage of Lost Play," later folding this idea into a prose tale, "The Cottage of Lost Play." This story, the first included in *The Book of Lost Tales*, was copied out by Edith in 1917. Here we find a traveler coming to a strange house "filled with children of every aspect, kind, and size," each with "a look of great happiness lit with a merry expectation of further mirth and joy." The host and hostess of the Cottage explain that they have built this place to care for children "who found Kôr and remained with the Eldar for ever," adding that:

> Ever and anon our children fare forth again to find the Great Lands, and
> go about among the lonely children and whisper to them at dusk in early
> bed by night-light and candle-flame, or comfort those that weep. Some
> I am told listen to the complaints of those that are punished or chidden,
> and hear their tales and feign to take their part, and this seems to me a
> quaint and merry service.[69]

The children have a special drink, *limpë*, which ensures that "our hearts keep youth and our mouths grow full of song."[70] Here we have an idealized Peter Pan environment, transposed to the nascent legendarium; not only do we have the ageless children, living happily away from their families, but we also have the detail of these children leaving their Neverland, as it were, to interact with ordinary children in the rest of the world, just as Barrie's Peter does.

The "Cottage" idea did not endure in Tolkien's mythology. Christopher Tolkien writes that "the conception of the coming of mortal children in sleep to the gardens of Valinor was soon to be abandoned in its entirety, and in the developed mythology there would be no place for it."[71] Nonetheless, Tolkien retained an interest in the Peter Pan story. Early in his life, he drew on its more nostalgic and sentimental aspects, but later he seems to have attended more fully to the dark element of the story.

The Peter Pan of Barrie's play and books is not quite the same as the Disney version that is most familiar for many modern readers. Barrie's story, in any of its forms, is unsettling; death is an underlying theme, as is a simultaneous longing for and rejection of mothers. Peter himself, the boy who never grows old, has a streak of cruelty, and is depicted as somehow outside the normal concerns of human beings. Stratford Caldecott makes a connection between Barrie's play and Tolkien's legendarium: "there is something, some note of Elvish poignancy, about Peter's doomed relationship with Wendy at the very end of that story that reminds one of the 'Athrabeth,' the background to which is the love between an old woman and an ageless elven Prince she met when she was young."[72]

But perhaps most significant is the fact that Tolkien chose ultimately not to include his early Elvish Neverland in the mature legendarium. Though deeply impressed with *Peter Pan* in his early days, Tolkien wrote "You & Me and the Cottage of Lost Play" before seeing active service on the Somme. Having faced the reality of carnage in the trenches of the Western Front, he had to revise his view of Peter's cheerful declaration, "To die will be an awfully big adventure." In the play, Peter makes this statement "as if he were a real boy at last,"[73] but he is not in fact a real boy; it is a form of play-acting. Eternally young, Peter is able to view death cavalierly precisely because it remains only an idea, not a future reality. We might ask whether Tolkien's long-lived Elves are representative of a lingering Peter Pantheism in Middle-earth. As Garth points out, "It was Peter's perpetual youth that came closest to the mark during the Great War, when so many young men would never grow old; and Tolkien's Elves, forever in the prime of adulthood, hit the bullseye."[74]

True enough; but even Elves may die, and this is perhaps Tolkien's point of departure from Barrie's vision. The Elves' perpetual life operates within the created order; they are not inherently immortal, as are the angelic Valar. And even in "the circles of the world," Elves turn out not to be utterly invulnerable: they may choose to live a mortal life, as Arwen does in her love for Aragorn.

Tolkien also explored the dark side of the desire for eternal life in one of the earliest and most significant stories of the Silmarillion: the Fall of Númenor. The Númenóreans, though they have very long lifespans, nevertheless become obsessed with cheating death entirely, even setting out to invade Valinor, the land of the immortals, an act of rebellion that leads to Númenor itself being utterly destroyed. Tolkien explained in a letter that their extended life, itself a gift, is in fact their "undoing" or at least a "temptation": it "aids their achievements in art and wisdom, but breeds a possessive attitude to these things, and desire awakes for more time for their enjoyment."[75]

Death is indeed a great adventure, and so great that it must be handled not with a boyish heartlessness or cheerful indifference, but in another way: more serious, more equivocal. As we saw in the previous chapter, MacDonald's *Lilith* modeled this kind of equivocal seriousness. With *Lilith* before him as an example to follow and *Peter Pan* before him as an example to avoid, Tolkien was well situated to tackle the themes of "death and the desire for deathlessness" that occupy so much of *The Lord of the Rings* and to do so in a mature and considered fashion, fully aware that unnatural long life, such as the Ring brings to Gollum, is a "dreadful fate," not unlike Peter's inability or refusal to grow up. In this respect we see how, in Tolkien's hands, the genre of boys' own adventure comes of age.

❧ Conclusion

In this chapter, we have seen that Tolkien read widely and with pleasure in the genre of adventure. We began with his acknowledgement that the scene involving the wargs in *The Hobbit* was in part inspired by S.R. Crockett's *The Black Douglas*. Following this lead, we saw that other elements of *The Black Douglas* have parallels in *The Lord of the Rings*, such as the villainous Gilles de Retz, a possible contributor to the figures of Sauron and Saruman.

We examined two authors of boys' own style adventures, Alexander Macdonald and Herbert Hayens, whom Tolkien read while he was a student at King Edward's School. We saw by contrast how much Tolkien's attitudes differed from the racist and colonialist ones on display in their works. Scenes such as Sam's encounter with a fallen Southron warrior and the Rohirrim's interactions with the Wild Men show the extent to which Tolkien rejected the racism that all too many of his contemporaries absorbed, a moral stance that would be taken for granted today, but which was not always the case in the 1930s and 40s when Middle-earth was taking shape.

We assessed the role of John Buchan in providing material for Tolkien's imagination, having identified, in *Greenmantle*, a specific title that we know him definitely to have read. In Buchan's heroic Richard Hannay, as well, we can trace an element contributing to Tolkien's depiction of a kind of moral agency that is not defeatist or endlessly conflicted. We have also seen how Buchan's work conveyed the qualities of atmosphere and 'rootedness' that Tolkien valued.

Lastly, we traced possible influences upon the legendarium from J.M. Barrie. Tolkien found *Peter Pan* unforgettable, and it very probably provided the inspiration for the opening story of *The Book of Lost Tales*. We saw, as well, that as Tolkien matured, he explored more fully the themes of death and deathlessness, and came to have a more critical view of Barrie's perpetually boyish protagonist.

From his reading of these modern authors, Tolkien's imagination was fed, consciously and unconsciously. Their works helped shape the mind that would produce *The Lord of the Rings*, which is among other things an adventure story. Tolkien, indeed, describes it in those terms. In a 1966 interview with Daphne Castell, when confronted with the claim that some readers found his epic to have insufficient love interest, Tolkien replied that "'There's a time and a place for everything. . . . In the time of a great war and high adventure, love and the carrying on with the race, and so on, are in the background."[76] "Great war and high *adventure*": an accurate description of at least one aspect of *The Lord of the Rings*. Tolkien's work belongs within and grew up among the company of those adventure authors whom he devoured as a boy and continued to enjoy, albeit not uncritically, when he became a man.

❧ 7 ❧

William Morris
Fellowship with the Brotherhood

P ERHAPS NO OTHER MODERN AUTHOR HAD AS MUCH IMPACT ON
Tolkien's work as William Morris.

Although today perhaps best known for his textile designs,* William Morris
(1834–1896) was a man of many talents. A socialist, a leading figure in the Arts and
Crafts Movement, and founder of the Kelmscott Press, he was also a poet, a novelist, and
a well-informed amateur scholar of mythology and medieval romance. He translated a
variety of ancient and medieval texts, including the *Odyssey*, the *Aeneid*, *Beowulf*, and a
number of northern sagas. His most widely known works today are *The Wood Beyond the
World* (1894) and *The Well at the World's End* (1896), which were reissued in 1969–70 as
part of the Ballantine Adult Fantasy series.

Tolkien "grew up on William Morris and George MacDonald," according to C.S.
Lewis. As a child, Tolkien was greatly impressed by what he called "the prince of all
dragons" in Morris's "The Story of Sigurd" (adapted by Andrew Lang in the *Red Fairy
Book*). It was, as we saw in chapter 3, his "favourite without rival."[1]

While an undergraduate at Oxford, Tolkien used the money from winning an English prize to buy several books by Morris: *The Story of the Volsungs* (1870), *The Life and
Death of Jason* (1867), and *The House of the Wolfings* (1889).[2] (See figure 18.) Other works
of his that Tolkien owned in pre-*Hobbit* years include *The Defence of Guinevere and Other
Poems* (1858), several of his translations, at least one volume of his poetic epic *The Earthly
Paradise* (1870), and the fantasy novels *The Roots of the Mountains* (1889) and *The Sun-
dering Flood* (1897).[3] He also knew, and probably owned, the utopian fantasy *News from
Nowhere* (1890).[4] Over the years he added other titles to his personal library, including a
copy of his lecture on the arts, *Some Hints on Pattern Designing* (1881),[5] so that eventually
(according to his son Christopher) he "owned nearly all of Morris's works."[6]

Tolkien's reading of Morris was sustained, extensive, and serious, and was but-
tressed by knowledge of biographical and critical studies such as J.W. Mackail's *Life of
William Morris* (1899) and A. Clutton-Brock's *William Morris: His Work and Influence*
(1914).[7] He even had a personal acquaintance with Morris's younger daughter, May, who
arranged that the Tolkiens would take on, as an *au pair*, the daughter of some Icelandic

---

* Arguably the most interesting part of the 2019 biopic *Tolkien* was its lingering display of
Morris-designed wallpaper.

friends.* So interested did he become in the man and his writings that he considered himself qualified to be an examiner of a thesis on Morris on two occasions, and to deliver a series of lectures at Oxford on "The Story of Sigurd and the Fall of the Nibelungs."[8] He mentions Morris's version of *Beowulf* in "On Translating Beowulf" and assesses it (unfavorably) in "Beowulf and the Critics."[9]

Although Tolkien may have had (predictably enough!) scholarly reservations about Morris's rendering of *Beowulf*, he otherwise nurtured a positive opinion of his output, and he shared this enthusiasm with friends and family. An admiration for Morris was one of the things Tolkien had in common with C.S. Lewis, and it no doubt featured in their conversations about how to build – or not build – a mythic world.[10] Christopher Tolkien noted "a distant but clear recollection" of having had *The House of the Wolfings* read to him by his father.[11] And significantly, Tolkien named not only that novel but also *The Roots of the Mountains* as direct influences upon *The Lord of the Rings*. We will closely analyze this intriguing connection later in the chapter.

⅏ Foreshadowing the T.C.B.S.

Another point of contact with Morris's work was visual. Morrisian designs and patterns were widely assimilated into British decorative arts of that era, and John Garth points out that Tolkien's school years in Birmingham were spent "among architecture and art heavily influenced by the Pre-Raphaelites and the Arts and Crafts Movement."[12] Hammond and Scull suggest that these designs "were a lasting inspiration to him," especially evident in the patterned, decorative borders of some of his artwork.[13]†

The Morris connection continued with the T.C.B.S., or "Tea Club, Barrovian Society," the group of like-minded pupils at King Edward's School in Birmingham who encouraged one another to make a difference in the world through their creative work. The T.C.B.S. would have known that one of Morris's Pre-Raphaelite circle, Edward Burne-Jones, had attended King Edward's himself.[14] Tolkien evidently enjoyed this connection, although he thereby annoyed his fellow T.C.B.S. member Christopher Wiseman, who criticized him for "confusing" their club "with Pre-Raphaelite brotherhoods and associations of Old Edwardians under William Morris."[15] Wiseman's remark indicates how seriously Tolkien viewed the parallels between the two groups. It may have been at this stage that Tolkien acquired the Mackail biography and possibly also the Clutton-Brock study, both of which set out Morris's ambitions for a fellowship of artists.

---

* Sigríður, the *au pair*, "retained the happiest memories of her stay [in 1929] – even though she had not enjoyed being a human gramophone for Professor Tolkien to practice [Icelandic] on!" (B.S. Benedikz, "Some Family Connections with J.R.R. Tolkien," 11).

† It is possible that Pre-Raphaelite paintings had an influence upon him as well, particularly in the way that they depicted scenes and characters from history, mythology, and literature in their own distinctive style. One example is Burne-Jones's *The Merciful Knight*, a depiction of St. John Gualbert, whose story was part of the inspiration for J.H. Shorthouse's *John Inglesant* (which we discuss in chapter 10).

The T.C.B.S.'s aim was, according to G.B. Smith, to "reestablish sanity, cleanliness, and the love of real and true beauty in everybody's breast,"[16] an ambition which, in its combination of moral, aesthetic, and social idealism, Morris would have fully endorsed. It is interesting that Tolkien should have ended up at Exeter College, Oxford, where both Morris and Burne-Jones had been undergraduates in the 1850s. Exeter, one of the oldest Oxford colleges, was also one of the most welcoming to Catholics.[17] For Tolkien, therefore, it would have had a double appeal: it was a place where he would not especially stand out because of his religion, and it strengthened his personal links to Morris and the Pre-Raphaelite Brotherhood.

✣ Making a mark: Morris's archaisms

Morris was widely known and much admired in his own day – he was in the running to succeed Tennyson as Poet Laureate – but his style raised some critical eyebrows. His biographer Fiona MacCarthy remarks that "Morris's creation of his own archaic language" was "a source of bemusement (or amusement) to his critics."[18] Tolkien, in appreciating Morris's works, was in line with popular rather than elite opinion, a position not unlike that of Tolkien scholars today.

Morris's techniques for literary archaism included syntactical inversions, the use or adaptation of words from an older vocabulary, and (paradoxically) neologisms. Many of Morris's ostensibly medieval words are in fact his own invention: examples include "amidmost," "war-fit," and a plethora of terms that he created by adding the prefix *un-* to form new but old-sounding words such as "unwrongful."[19] The result is striking, and certainly did strike the young Tolkien – with the ironic effect that a modern author influenced him toward a more archaic style.

In 1920, Tolkien read "The Fall of Gondolin" to the Exeter College Essay Club; the minutes of the meeting describe it as a treatment "in the manner of such typical Romantics as William Morris, George MacDonald, de la Motte Fouqué, etc."[20] "The Fall of Gondolin," which Tolkien later called "the first real story of this imaginary world,"[21] has a number of stylistic features that resemble Morris's romances. One of these is inverted syntax: "'Yet no blow will I strike more' [Turgon said], and he cast his crown at the roots of Glingol. Then did Galdor who stood there pick it up, but Turgon accepted it not." Another is Tolkien's use of "it is told" or "the story tells,"[22] echoing Morris's distinctive usage, as in the opening words to *The House of the Wolfings*, "The tale tells that in times long past . . . ," or the start of a chapter in *The Roots of the Mountains*, "Now tells the tale of Folk-might . . ."[23] Tolkien's story is also full of archaic vocabulary favored by Morris, such as "rede," "like to," or "nigh to," as when one character tells Tuor:

> "Therewith . . . thy lady became distraught of weariness and grief, and fared into the city wildly to my great fear – nor might I get her to sally from the burning."

> About the saying of these words were they come to the southern walls and nigh to Tuor's house, and lo! it was cast down and the wreckage was asmoke; and thereat was Tuor bitterly wroth.[24]

The quintessentially Morrisian words "therewith" and "thereat" occur frequently in this relatively short tale. As the intoxication of archaism wore off, their presence in Tolkien's writing declined precipitously: they are found in the published *Silmarillion* only three times in total, and not at all in *The Hobbit* or *The Lord of the Rings*.

In his later writings, Tolkien did adopt certain other words and phrases from Morris, but selectively and in moderation. For instance, he uses "skin-changer" in *The Hobbit* and "shield-maiden" (from "shield-may") in *The Lord of the Rings*, both words that he likely encountered in *The Roots of the Mountains*.[25] The title of that book might well have caught his eye as well: we usually talk of the 'foot' of a mountain, not its root or roots. Tom Shippey is of the opinion that "Almost certainly J.R.R. Tolkien remembered *The Roots of the Mountains* when he created Gollum,"[26] for Gollum lives in caves and passages "down at the very roots of the mountain."* "Mirkwood" is also a possible linguistic influence. It derives, as Tolkien observes, from the early German word *mirkiwidu*,[27] but no equivalent compound word appears in Old English. Morris's use of "Mirkwood" in *The House of the Wolfings* is the first version of the name in a modern English form,[28] and Tolkien considered it "too good a fortune that Mirkwood remained intelligible (with exactly the right tone) in modern English to pass over."[29] Although Tolkien certainly also encountered the source material for the name in his linguistic study, he may well have been encouraged to take "Mirkwood" for his own use, with Morris's slightly archaic spelling rather than a fully translated "Murkwood," by seeing it in *The House of the Wolfings*.

Here we can see Tolkien's literary judgment coming into play. Words like "Skin-changer" and "Mirkwood" are both linguistically sound and evocative; Tolkien could appropriate them for Middle-earth knowing that they fit perfectly. In contrast, Morris's character names are, by and large, rather unfortunate (Hall-face, Folk-might, Sun-Beam), and are often either unintentionally humorous (as in Thorkettle and Wolfkettle) or distractingly suggestive of Native American and Puritan naming traditions (as in

---

* Interestingly, Tolkien uses the very phrase "the roots of the mountains" in his 1961 translation of the Book of Jonah for the Jerusalem Bible: "The seaweed was wrapped around my head at the roots of the mountains" (chapter 2, verse 7 – or 6 in some versifications). The phrase had been rendered more prosaically in other well-established translations of the English-speaking world, such as the 1610 Douay-Rheims Version ("lowest parts of the mountains") and the 1611 King James Version ("bottoms of the mountains"). The Jerusalem Bible project was designed to render La Bible de Jérusalem (the French translation of the Vulgate) into English, but whereas the French translators had given *A la racine des montagnes* (literally "at the root [singular] of the mountains"), Tolkien pluralises it, as indeed did the Revised Standard Version of 1952. No doubt Tolkien consulted the RSV as he produced his draft and made his choice on strictly linguistic grounds, but the echo of Morris would have pleased him, and all the more so given that he had used "roots" this way in *The Hobbit*. For more on this, see Brendan Wolfe, "Tolkien's Jonah."

Face-of-god). Tolkien wisely leaves them alone – but not before toying with some dubious names himself. Early drafts of his work show that Frodo was originally Bingo, Strider was Trotter, and Gandalf was Bladorthin.[30]

Another Morrisian trace in Tolkien's early writings is the idiosyncratic term "the kindreds," used in *The House of the Wolfings* for the different clans of the Gothic tribes. In "The Fall of Gondolin," Tolkien repeatedly uses "the kindreds" in precisely the same sense, and even adopts a Morrisian style of naming them: we have a house of the "Tree," "the folk of the Swallow and the Heavenly Arch," "the people of the Fountain," "the host of the Harp," "the folk of the Hammer of Wrath."[31] These would fit side by side with Morris's kindreds: "the Elkings, the Vallings, the Alftings, the Beamings, the Galtings, and the Bearings; who bore on their banners the Elk, the Falcon, the Swan, the Tree, the Boar, and the Bear."[32] In *The Lord of the Rings*, Tolkien abandons this use; "kindred" appears only in the more modern sense, never in Morris's archaic manner to mean a tribe.*

Morris's tribes may have had one more lasting effect. Tolkien's Rohirrim refer to themselves as "the Men of the Mark," and of Rohan as "the Mark," in precisely the way Morris's Goths do in *The House of the Wolfings*. For instance, in the gathering of the warriors to resist the Romans, one of the men declaims, "Good is this which our War-duke hath spoken; say then, men of the Mark, who shall stand with Thiodolf to lead you against the aliens?" Later, Hall-Sun organizes the defense of the Hall while the men are away, anticipating "that by this road easy to wend the Romans should come into the Mark"[33] and preparing to defend it. This might help explain Tolkien's otherwise perplexing denial, in Appendix F of *The Lord of the Rings*, of a resemblance between the Rohirrim and the Anglo-Saxons, which Tom Shippey calls simply "untrue."[34] The Rohirrim obviously do owe a great deal to the Anglo-Saxons, but if Tolkien first got the idea for them from Morris, he would have plausible grounds (in a contrarian mood) to deny a direct connection.

Tolkien later defined the appropriate use of literary archaism with a precision that was perhaps shaped by the intersection of his enthusiasm for Morris with his study of genuine medieval literature. In "On Translating *Beowulf*," he acknowledges that "the diction of *Beowulf* was poetic, archaic, artificial . . . in the day that the poem was made"; many of its words had "already passed out of colloquial use" while other words "had never, in the senses given to them by the poets, been used in ordinary language at all." Nevertheless, Tolkien argues that literary diction should not use words "merely because they are 'old' or obsolete," but rather words that "remain in literary use, especially in the use of verse, among educated people."[35] Such criteria would be met by some, but by no means all, of the language and syntax that Morris used so abundantly in his novels, and indeed Tolkien's literary judgment in this respect matured over the years. After early experimentation with Morris's consistently archaic diction, Tolkien chose to apply it not liberally but carefully

---

* Tolkien does use the term "Kindreds" in this sense one additional time in the legendarium. In the later Quenta Silmarillion, he titles a section "Of the Kindreds and Houses of the Edain" (HOME XI, 218). This text is in a very high register.

and purposefully. For instance, when Faramir sees, as in a vision, the boat with his dead brother's body float by him in the river, he cries out: *"Boromir! . . . Where is thy horn? Whither goest thou? O Boromir!"* The use of "thy" and "thou," and the inversion of "whither goest thou?", give this brief scene a fittingly dreamlike, distanced effect.

Tolkien became aware that archaic language can be distancing and was willing to modernize as needed to communicate effectively. Writing to John Masefield about a planned public reading of Chaucer, he has reservations about strict fidelity to the original pronunciation, which is what Masefield seems to have suggested, and instead recommends a partially modernized pronunciation that avoids archaic usages, for the sake of the audience.[36]* In his mature style, Tolkien applied the criteria he set out in "On Translating *Beowulf*": that the language must be in continuity with literary tradition. The resulting blend of old and new in his writings can be quite subtle, as in the scene of Frodo and company arriving at The Prancing Pony in *The Fellowship of the Ring*:

> Even from the outside the inn looked a pleasant place. . . . Frodo went forward and nearly bumped into a short fat man with a bald head and a red face. He had a white apron on, and was bustling out of one door and in through another, carrying a tray laden with full mugs.
> "Can we –" began Frodo.
> "Half a minute, if you please!" shouted the man over his shoulder, and vanished into a babel of voices and a cloud of smoke.[37]

The description eschews overtly archaic diction, and yet artfully deploys words that suggest a traditional rather than a modern-day setting ('inn' and 'mugs', not 'pub' and 'glasses'). In describing the inn as full of "a babel of voices," Tolkien uses a word that is in one sense archaic, as he could have selected the more modern 'babble.' But because of its continued currency as a biblical term (the Tower of Babel) the word avoids seeming archaic while nevertheless having an ancient flavor. In these ways, he frees the scene from feeling unduly contemporary, yet without laying over it a thick patina of obviously old-fashioned terminology. It is a Morrisian effect, but done much more adroitly.

What appears to some readers as an unevenness of style in *The Lord of the Rings* reflects Tolkien's comprehensive vision for Middle-earth, covering linguistic registers from the fragmented ramblings of Gollum and the homely, rustic style of the hobbits, up to the lordly tones of Gondor and the rhapsodic language of the Elves. Morris's romances

---

* For instance, as part of his work on translating the Book of Jonah for the Jerusalem Bible, he encouraged Alexander Jones, the principal editor and translator for the project, to use 'you' rather than 'thee' and 'thou' in the translation. Jones wrote to Tolkien to thank him for his "support for the 'you' policy; without it I should have been most uneasy, having no great confidence in my own decisions." Notably, Jones adds, "like you I regret the passing of 'thou' etc." – an indication that Tolkien evidently had a personal fondness for the use of these archaic pronouns. Nevertheless, he evidently felt that effective communication to the modern reader took priority (quoted in Brendan Wolfe, "Tolkien's Jonah," 19).

remain in the highest stylistic register throughout; the result is a strong flavor, which has a certain appeal, but it is not complex or graded. In contrast, Tolkien's stylistic shifts allow him both to heighten drama with elevated diction, and to restrain it from excess via the irony or pathos of contrasting 'low' diction. We can see all this at work in the ending of the "Council of Elrond" chapter in *The Fellowship of the Ring*: as the Council discuss the matter of the Ring, the register grows gradually more lofty, until we reach the sonorous phrasing of Elrond: "Yet such is oft the course of deeds that move the wheels of the world." Such a line could be imagined as appearing in a Morris novel, but not the following, when Bilbo breaks in: "Very well, very well, Master Elrond! . . . Say no more." His chatty, matter-of-fact manner reflects his character, of course, but it also provides a refreshing change in tone, bringing the exalted language down and preparing the way for another tonal shift. As the Council reflects on the question of who will be appointed Ring-bearer, the conclusion adopts a serious middle register, expressed in the powerful simplicity of Frodo's "I will take the Ring."

✀ Prose and cons

In October 1914, Tolkien wrote to his future wife, Edith Bratt, about his plans to adapt one of the tales of the Finnish *Kalevala* "into a short story somewhat on the lines of Morris' romances with chunks of poetry in between." He was referring to *The House of the Wolfings*.[38]*

What sort of a book is *The House of the Wolfings*? The subtitle calls it a novel "written in prose and in verse." (See figure 18.) In this tale, the hardy and wholesome Goths (the "people of the Mark") fight off invasion from cruel, decadent Romans, giving rise to many opportunities for war-songs. We will consider those Romans later in the chapter; first, let us trace certain other links with *The Lord of the Rings*. Of most importance for us now is its form. The hybrid of prose and verse was not Morris's default setting; he wrote other novels in straight prose, and *The Life and Death of Jason*, which Tolkien purchased as an undergraduate, completely in verse. In *The House of the Wolfings*, Morris generously interleaves his prose narrative with speeches, songs, and even dialogue in poetry. For instance, the tribal leader Thiodolf questions newly arrived messengers in rhyming couplets:

> "What do ye sons of the War-shield? what tale is there to tell?
> Is the kindred fallen tangled in the grasp of the fallow Hell?
> Crows the red cock over the homesteads, have we met the foe too late?
> For meseems your brows are heavy with the shadowing o'er of fate."[39]

---

* Tolkien had purchased *The House of the Wolfings* that April. Of the other two books by Morris that Tolkien bought at the same time, *The Life and Death of Jason* is fully in verse, and *The Story of the Volsungs* is in prose with an appendix of songs. He would soon also read *The Roots of the Mountains*, in which Morris does not versify any of the dialogue, but does interpolate various songs into the story.

One of the messengers replies in verse; the narrative then switches to prose for some dialogue and narrative action, before Thiodolf returns to verse for a speech he gives to his men.

The blended form that Tolkien imagined in 1914 for the story of Kullervo was ultimately what he put into practice in both *The Hobbit* and *The Lord of the Rings*.[40] Examples of interpolated poetry are found throughout both works. In *The Hobbit*, we have the dwarves' teasing dish-song and their serious ballad about the Lonely Mountain; the goblins' cruel marching-chant; Bilbo's taunts of the spiders; and the Wood-elves' barrel-rolling song. In *The Lord of the Rings*, we find Tom Bombadil's ditties; Aragorn's tale of Tinúviel; Bilbo's poem about Eärendil; the songs of the Riders of Rohan; and so on. Many of these, such as the walking-song sung by Frodo, Sam, and Pippin as they trek through the Shire, evoke the embedded folk-lays of *The Roots of the Mountains*.

Morris frequently has his warriors exclaiming in verse prior to combat, or even in the very heat of battle, as when Thiodolf declares, after rejecting the safety of the enchanted hauberk:

> Now, now ye War-sons!
> Now the Wolf waketh!
> Lo how the Wood-beast
> Wendeth in onset.
> E'en as his feet fare
> Fall on and follow![41]

Tolkien made similar use of spontaneous verse spoken by his characters. When Théoden, freed from the influence of Wormtongue, has been given back his sword, he cries out:

> *Arise now, arise, Riders of Théoden!*
> *Dire deeds awake, dark is it eastward.*
> *Let horse be bridled, horn be sounded!*
> *Forth Eorlingas!* [42]

Tolkien's scene has greater dramatic effectiveness, not least because it uses a genuine Anglo-Saxon alliterative meter and holds up to being read aloud, while Morris's becomes bogged down at "Wendeth in onset" (if not before). More notable, however, is the way Tolkien weaves the interpolated poetry into the realistic fabric of his tale. In *The House of the Wolfings*, the declamations of poetry by the characters sound artificial, but then, the whole tale is told in an artificial style; we do not need really to believe that Thiodolf would versify in that manner on the spot. In contrast, Tolkien always provides a more natural, believable context for his characters to recite or speak in verse. Here, Théoden's exclamation brings his guards rushing to him, "thinking they were summoned." They are struck by "amazement" for a moment before they respond: "'Command us!' they said." In this case, we see that it is in fact unusual for someone to leap up and begin declaiming poetry; the startled reaction of the guards heightens the impact of the scene as we realize just what a decisive change this is for Théoden.

It is by no means a simple or easy feat to adapt Morris's device of verse dialogue into a tale with a very different overall tone and style, but that is precisely what Tolkien attempted. Nevertheless, many readers have balked at the verses included in *The Lord of the Rings*. In 1967, Tolkien told an interviewer that such reactions failed to recognize his intention, which was to make interpolated verse function realistically in the narrative: "A lot of the criticism of the verses shows a complete failure to understand the fact that they are all dramatic verses: they were conceived as the kind of things people would say under the circumstances."[43] Morris's works were, by that time, long out of favor with the reading public, so it may be that for many readers, Tolkien's use of mixed prose and verse was a completely new and puzzling experience, rather than (as it was for Tolkien and his first audience, the Inklings) a natural development and refinement of a Morrisian technique.

ℜ Éowyn's literary grandmothers

Not only the style but also the characters of Morris's tales prove to have intriguing connections to Tolkien's writings. In *The House of the Wolfings*, we encounter a father-daughter pair, Thiodolf and Hall-Sun, that bears a strong resemblance to the uncle-niece pair of Théoden and Éowyn. To begin with, Morris's Thiodolf, like Théoden, is a heroic war-leader who falls under a malign influence. Thiodolf loves the mysterious, not-quite-human Wood-Sun, who loves him in turn and has even borne him a child (Hall-Sun, raised as his foster-daughter). He trusts her, therefore, and accepts from her a magical mail-shirt "fashioned by the dwarfs of ancient days"[44] that she says will protect him. She is partly deceiving him; the mail-shirt keeps him safe by making him lose consciousness in the middle of the fight, shaming him in the eyes of his people. As with Théoden's decline under the maleficent attentions of Wormtongue, the magic mail-shirt gradually saps Thiodolf's will for heroism: "death seemed hateful to me, and the deeds before death vain and foolish."[45] Finally recognizing its effects, Thiodolf rejects cowardly safety, and is killed in the climactic battle against the Romans; like Théoden, he is buried with honor at the end of the novel.

Likewise, Thiodolf's daughter Hall-Sun partly resembles Éowyn. In Morris's tale, Hall-Sun is left behind when the men go to fight the Romans; after a while, she decides to take command of the remaining women, boys, and old men in order to defend the Hall of the Wolfings, telling them that "I am nothing wise in war. . . . Nevertheless ye shall do well to take me for your captain, while this House is bare of warriors." They respond "Yea, yea . . . so will we."[46] Here we may see a parallel to *The Lord of the Rings*: when Théoden rides to Helm's Deep, he names Éowyn to lead the people whom he leaves behind.

Interestingly, Tolkien heightens the importance of Éowyn's role. Unlike Hall-Sun, Éowyn is explicitly and publicly assigned the role of homestead guardian because of her courage and spirit: "She is fearless and high-hearted. All love her. Let her be as lord to the Eorlingas, while we are gone," says Hama. "It shall be so," Théoden declares, and so it is. Éowyn is affirmed not only by the non-warriors left behind but by the warriors themselves; indeed, she is named as a leader in much the same way that Thiodolf himself, in *The House of the Wolfings*, is chosen as head of the war-band by popular acclaim. In this way, Tolkien gives Éowyn a role similar to, but considerably more significant than, that of her Morrisian precursor.

The Roots of the Mountains provides another intriguing precursor to Éowyn in the form of a character called "the Bride." In this tale, the people of the Dale and its surrounding communities face hostilities from troll-like Dusky Men. The Bride is betrothed to a young man with the improbable name Face-of-god, but he jilts her for another woman. When the people of the Dale gather to fight the Dusky Men, the Bride appears, dressed for battle: "beardless, smooth-cheeked, exceeding fair of face was the warrior, but pale and somewhat haggard-eyed." She declares her intention to fight alongside the men:

> "[S]ince I have learned to be deft with mine hands in all the play of war, and that I am as strong as many a man, and as hardy-hearted as any . . . the battle-field shall be my home, and the after-grief of the fight my banquet and holiday, that I may bear the burden of my people, in the battle and out of it. . . and cast aside as a grievous and ugly thing the bed of the warrior that the maiden desires. . . . Even so have I sworn, even so will I do."[47]

The mix of pride and despair in her speech calls to mind Éowyn's frustration at being told to stay behind when the men of Rohan ride to Gondor: "All your words are but to say: you are a woman, and your part is in the house. . . . But I am of the House of Eorl and not a serving-woman. I can ride and wield blade, and I do not fear either pain or death."

The hidden sorrow of the Bride is discerned by the warrior named Folk-might, who loves her: "I saw thee hanging on the words and the looks of another man, who was light-minded toward thee, and that thou wert troubled with the anguish of doubt and fear."[48] Here we see, as it were, a rough sketch of Faramir's perceptive dealings with Éowyn, although the other man in this case, Aragorn, is not "light-minded" but the very opposite. The Bride goes to war with the men openly rather than (like Éowyn) disguised, and is seriously wounded. While she is recovering, she pledges to Folk-might that "if I live, as indeed I hope, and how glad and glad I shall be to live, then shalt thou bring me to thy house and thy bed, that I may not depart from thee while both our lives last."[49] The Bride does recover, and marries Folk-might, as Éowyn marries Faramir. Tolkien may well have been inspired by the suggestive outlines of the frustrated woman-warrior story in Morris, but in his version of the character and situation, he would deepen considerably the emotional complexity of Éowyn's relationships, both in her marriage with Faramir and in her unrequited love for Aragorn.

⚜ Navigating the route to Mordor

We turn now to one of the most important (and complicated) acknowledgements of influence that Tolkien ever made. In a memorable passage in *The Two Towers*, Gollum leads Frodo and Sam through a treacherous and noxious marsh-land, the site of many a battle in days gone by, where dead warriors now lie submerged, pale and hideous, from whom misty flames flicker up with a fatal allure. "The tricksy lights," says Gollum, "Candles of corpses, yes, yes. Don't you heed them! Don't look! Don't follow them!" About this episode and its possible relationship to either the Great War or the Second World War, Tolkien wrote:

> Personally I do not think that either war (and of course not the atomic bomb) had any influence upon either the plot or the manner of its un-folding. Perhaps in landscape. The Dead Marshes and the approaches to the Morannon owe something to Northern France after the Battle of the Somme. They owe more to William Morris and his Huns and Romans, as in *The House of the Wolfings* or *The Roots of the Mountains*.[50]

Critics have found this remark puzzling. Although the parallel between this area of Middle-earth and the devastated landscape of the Somme seems clear enough, it is not immediately apparent what the Huns and Romans have to do with it. Possibly owing to the entrenched idea that we discussed in chapter 2, that Tolkien did not read modern literature and was immune to influence, some critics seem to find it impossible to believe that Tolkien really *meant* to say that parts of *The Lord of the Rings* "owe more to William Morris" than to his wartime experiences. Rather than attempting to trace the connection, these critics ignore the Morris element and focus exclusively on the reference to the Great War.[51]

Other critics recognize that Tolkien is admitting the importance of Morris's romances, but reject the idea that Tolkien is identifying a specific point of influence upon his portrayal of "the Dead Marshes and the approaches to the Morannon," preferring to read his remark as a general observation about the plot of *The Lord of the Rings*. The sticking point appears to be what Tolkien meant by the pronoun "They" in "They owe more to William Morris and his Huns and Romans." Grammatically, "They" refers back to the subject of the previous sentence, which is "The Dead Marshes and the approaches to the Morannon." A straightforward reading of his remark is, therefore, that "The Dead Marshes and the approaches to the Morannon . . . owe more to William Morris and his Huns and Romans [than to Northern France after the Somme]."

But some critics, such as Michael Perry and John Garth, seeing no clear connection between the Dead Marshes and Morris's novels, and being perplexed by the reference to the Huns and Romans, have concluded that Tolkien shifted thoughts in mid-paragraph.[52] Garth parses the comment in the letter as follows, adding editorial square brackets to denote what he takes to be a parenthetical thought in Tolkien's mind: "'Personally I do not think that either war (and of course not the atomic bomb) had any influence upon either the plot or the manner of its unfolding. [Perhaps in landscape. The Dead Marshes and the approaches to the Morannon owe something to Northern France after the Battle of the Somme.] They owe more to William Morris and his Huns and Romans, as in *The House of the Wolfings* or *The Roots of the Mountains*.' So the *they* in the final sentence refers to the plot and its unfolding."[53] *

My own view is that the word "they" probably refers to the subject of the preceding sentence, which seems to me to be the natural way of understanding the text of the letter, especially given the parallel structure of "owe something to . . . owe more to" that links the landscape-reference with the Morris-reference. It is indeed possible that Tolkien was not precise in his phrasing or punctuation, and that he is referring to a more general influence from Morris's novels, not a specific connection to the landscape.[54] But that is precisely the crucial point: in *any* interpretation of this passage, Tolkien is pointing out a profound literary debt to Morris. However, only the portion of his remark referring to the Somme has been examined in detail. Such attention is not wasted: the exploration of his experiences in World War I, particularly in Garth's magnificent *Tolkien and the Great War*, has been fully warranted and has enlarged our understanding of Tolkien's epic most helpfully. However, the very brilliance of such scholarship has also had the inadvertent effect that Tolkien's acknowledged debt to Morris in this regard has been almost totally overlooked.

Once we recognize the full extent of Tolkien's interest in and knowledge of contemporary fiction, especially that by Morris, we will see the value in following up his observation in detail. We will explore Tolkien's acknowledgement of Morris's influence in two stages, following the order in which he remarks upon it: first "the Dead Marshes and the approaches to the Morannon" and then the "Huns and Romans."

The Dead Marshes and the approaches to the Morannon

In *The Return of the King*, Frodo and Sam are forced to make their way through the rocky barrier of the Emyn Muil before they emerge onto the land below, where they must traverse the Dead Marshes *en route* to Mordor. There are certain very suggestive similarities between this passage and what we find in the last third of *The Roots of the Mountains*, where the Dalesmen and their allies advance to retake conquered Silver-dale. Despite the pleasant name, Silver-dale has a Mordor-like feel to it. Not only is it controlled by the

---

* My thanks to John Garth for discussing the issue with me, and for his helpful comments on a 2015 blog post where I first explored some of the ideas presented in this section.

Orcish Dusky Men, it is difficult to access it swiftly or undetected. The Dalesmen decide to make their way to Silver-dale along treacherous mountain paths formed by the eruption of an ancient volcano, and come upon occupied Silver-dale secretly:

> From the height in the pass those grey slopes seemed easy to traverse; but the warriors of the Wolf knew that it was far otherwise, for they were but the molten rock-sea that in time long past had flowed forth from Shield-broad and filled up the whole valley endlong and overthwart, cooling as it flowed. . . . And that great rock-flood as it cooled split in divers fashions; and the rain and weather had been busy on it for ages, so that it was worn into a maze of narrow paths, most of which, after a little, brought the wayfarer to a dead stop, or else led him back again to the place whence he had started; so that only those who knew the passes throughly could thread that maze without immeasurable labour.[55]

As Frodo and Sam begin their journey alone to Mordor, they struggle on "the barren slopes and stones of the Emyn Muil, sometimes retracing their steps because they could find no way forward, sometimes discovering that they had wandered in a circle back to where they had been hours before." There is a suggestive similarity between the mazy journeyings through these two rocky landscapes, but it is perhaps not strong enough to indicate a very likely debt. Interestingly, though, in *The Roots of the Mountains* we find that the Dalesmen, like Frodo and Sam, move from this maze of rocks into marshes: "on the other side of the crest the heath began to be soft and boggy, and at last so soft, that if they had not been wisely led, they had been bemired oftentimes."[56] The image is suggestive of Gollum leading Frodo and Sam through the marshes, where the marshland becomes wetter, "opening into wide stagnant meres, among which it grew more and more difficult to find the firmer places where feet could tread without sinking into gurgling mud. The travellers were light, or maybe none of them would ever have found a way through." Furthermore, the Dalesmen's journey to Silver-dale has some of the same gruesome surprises as Frodo and Sam encounter in the Dead Marshes. The scouts of the Dalesmen

> found a man and a woman dead and stark naked hanging to the boughs of a great oak-tree deep in the wood. This men knew for some vengeance of the Dusky Men, for it was clear to see that these poor people had been sorely tormented before they were slain. Also the same watch had stumbled on the dead body of an old woman, clad in rags, lying amongst the rank grass about a little flow; she was exceeding lean and hunger-starved, and in her hand was a frog which she had half eaten.[57]

When, after the battle, the victorious Dalesmen enter into the recovered Hall, they find more horrors:

from the last tie-beam of the roof over the daïs dangled four shapes of men-at-arms, whom the older men of the Wolf knew at once for the embalmed bodies of their four great chieftains, who had been slain on the day of the Great Undoing; and they cried out with horror and rage as they saw them hanging there in their weapons as they had lived. . . . There they hung, dusty, befouled, with sightless eyes and grinning mouths, in the dimmed sunlight of the Hall, before the eyes of that victorious Host, stricken silent at the sight of them.[58]

In their passage through the Dead Marshes, Frodo and Sam likewise come face to face with grisly reminders of those who have fallen in battle, when beneath the bog water they see the figures of the dead: the images of proud warriors, but "all foul, all rotting, all dead. A fell light is in them." Although details differ, the overall effect in both this scene and that of the Dalesmen encountering corpses along the way to Silver-dale, is of horror and disgust. We should note as well that in *The Roots of the Mountains* the corpses of the "great chieftains" who had been killed "on the day of the Great Undoing" are "embalmed" and hung up with their weapons at their sides, not unlike Tolkien's warriors who fought "a great battle long ago . . . with long swords" and who, though "rotting," are preserved by "some devilry" so that they can still be seen, even if they cannot be touched.*

I would myself be inclined to consider this similarity merely fortuitous were it not for another connection that underscores the influence of *The Roots of the Mountains* on certain of Tolkien's landscapes. In the description of "the approaches to the Morannon" we find two words that almost certainly derive from Morris and which serve as linguistic markers of a connection. The words are "amidmost" and "ghyll." We will consider each in turn.

Although 'amidmost' sounds old-fashioned, the Oxford English Dictionary identifies it as modern, giving only two examples of its usage, both of them from William Morris in *The Earthly Paradise*.[59] Given both the rarity of the word and Morris's recurrent use of it (eight times in *The House of the Wolfings* and twelve in *The Roots of the Mountains*, for instance), we can be confident that Tolkien adopted it from Morris. Tolkien uses the word frequently in his earliest tales: for instance, it occurs a total of nineteen times in *The Book of Lost Tales*. However, he abandoned the term in his mature work; it does not appear in *The Hobbit*. Nevertheless, the word does appear in *The Lord of the Rings*, but only twice, and in both cases describing the immediate surroundings of Mordor: the mountain ranges that form the boundaries of Mordor, with "the bitter inland sea of Núrnen amidmost," and later "the great rampart of Cirith Gorgor, and the Black Gate amidmost."

---

 * It is important to keep in mind that as Tolkien drew imaginatively from many sources, tracing a particular influence does not exclude the possibility of others. For instance, John Garth suggests that the Dead Marshes "take a literary colouring from Longfellow's description of Hiawatha's night voyage towards battle, through a nightmarish waterland ruled by the evil spirit Megissogwon" (*The Worlds of J.R.R. Tolkien*, 109).

'Ghyll,' meaning "narrow ravine," is usually spelled *gill*: in that form, it is of Old Norse origin, but the spelling *ghyll* is both modern and rare.[60] It seems almost certain that Tolkien would have encountered – or at least taken note of – this distinctive spelling in Morris, who uses it repeatedly in *The Roots of the Mountains*.* We know that Tolkien did use it in 1925, in a version of the "Lay of Leithian,"[61] but it seems subsequently to have vanished from his vocabulary. It is striking, then, to see this word reappear in *The Lord of the Rings* and more striking that the only two examples of its use occur in descriptions of territory around Mordor – just as with "amidmost." The first instance is as Frodo and Sam, drawing closer to the gate of Mordor, pass through the Morgai, the inner ridge of the mountains around Mordor, which is "scored with deep ghylls." The other use of the word comes in a description from the perspective of Aragorn, Gandalf, and their army *en route* to the Black Gate, as they behold "a tumbled land of rocky ghylls and crags, behind which the long grim slopes of the Ephel Dúath clambered up."

Here we find two distinctly archaic words – 'amidmost' and 'ghyll' – that Tolkien undoubtedly met in Morris, both of which he deploys in describing the same geographical area of Middle-earth. This linguistic connection helps explain why he noted that the "approaches to the Morannon" owed a debt to Morris's novels.

These connections may seem to be slender threads, but we should recall that Tolkien himself has put us on their track. And as we have seen in earlier chapters, in instances where Tolkien himself has identified a source, he could, and often would, transmute that source material into a subtly different form as it passed through his creative imagination to serve new ends in a new context.

Huns and Romans – and Orcs

We now turn to Tolkien's specific reference of a debt to "William Morris and his Huns and Romans, as in *The House of the Wolfings* or *The Roots of the Mountains*." On the surface, the allusion is puzzling, since Tolkien did not draw exact parallels between our own history and that of Middle-earth. What might Tolkien have had in mind when he pointed out "Huns and Romans" as a specific influence?

The Huns are mentioned in *The House of the Wolfings* as "evil-eyed" past enemies of the Mark who wished to "sweep [the Goths] away from the face of the earth."[62] Although they do not appear by name in *The Roots of the Mountains*, Tolkien would have known that the Dusky Men are Huns from *William Morris: His Life and Influence*, where Clutton-Brock identifies them as such.[63] In that tale, the Dalesmen even "doubted if they were men or trolls," and declare them "worse" than "adders or evil dragons."[64]

Romans are the enemy in *The House of the Wolfings*, where Morris reverses the stereotypes of barbarian tribes and civilized Romans. Morris's Goths, who despite the name are Germanic tribes in Gaul, have a healthy and thriving culture. They must defend their

---

* Fourteen times. The word does not appear at all in *The House of the Wolfings*.

homes from invading Romans who are a decadent, corrupt enemy, far different from the common conception of imperial Rome's soldiery. These are not disciplined, exemplary heroes of order, who build straight roads and believe in the Pax Romana, but are "ugly of aspect, surly and of few words," "exceeding foul."[65]

We should observe that the Dead Marshes are the site of a historic battle between "Tall Men with long swords, and terrible Elves, and Orcses shrieking." Frodo, Sam, and Gollum must go carefully through the Marshes precisely to avoid being captured by Orcs; and the "approaches to the Morannon" are the approaches to the very gate of Mordor itself, swarming with Orcs. The landscape itself is thus readily associated with Orcs – and therefore, by at least a possible reading of Tolkien's remark, with Morris's Huns and Romans.

What if Tolkien's Orcs were, in his creative imagination, mediated through Morris's Huns and Romans? It may seem like an outlandish connection, but we should bear in mind Tolkien's creative processes; as John Garth observes, Tolkien's "instinct was to dip, mix, and layer, drawing from personal experience, reading and imagination – a touch from here, a hint from there, a flourish out of nowhere."[66]

Let us consider the evidence. Morris's Romans "are dark-skinned," "swart, crooked of body," "a grim folk, that laugheth to see others weep."[67] Tolkien's Orcs (or at least the Isengard variety) are "a grim dark band, . . . large, swart, slant-eyed." Furthermore, Morris's Romans come from "far to the south"[68] – but *far* to the south only from the perspective of the northern Germanic tribes. That they are "dark-skinned" (from the light-skinned Goths' point of view) yet from Italy, not Africa, suggests that a similar southern European home might be assigned to Tolkien's Orc – and certain points that Tolkien made about the geography of Middle-earth support a thematic association between the Roman Empire and the South of Middle-earth. In giving clues to the map of Middle-earth, Tolkien makes some surprising connections:* he notes that Minas Tirith "is about a latitude of Ravenna" (in north-east Italy), while the "City of Corsairs" is similarly near Cyprus,[69] and Gondor is matter-of-factly identified with Venice.[70] Dick Plotz recalls that after the Tolkiens' 1966 Mediterranean cruise, "Professor Tolkien is quite certain that Mordor corresponds more or less (and of course all this is more or less) to the Mediterranean volcanic basin"; only a playful comment in this context, but one that Tolkien reiterated in another letter.[71] Though neither precise nor wholly consistent, these references provide a geographical frame for Tolkien's operating assumptions. Insofar as Mordor and Gondor are 'south' in Middle-earth, they are located in the area roughly corresponding to the southern European parts of the Roman Empire, rather than to Africa and the global south.

If the dark-skinned Orcs are based at least in part on Morris's Romans and to a lesser extent his Huns (the Dusky Men), we could expect to find further connections, and indeed we do.

---

* He locates Hobbiton at the latitude of Oxford.

Morris's negative picture of the Romans is set out clearly in an early chapter when Gothic messengers report on the destruction caused by the Romans. One tribesman who has encountered them chants a vivid picture of this "most evil folk":

> "And our tree would they spoil with destruction if its fruit they may
> never possess.
> For their lust is without a limit, and nought may satiate
> Their ravening maw; and their hunger if ye check it turneth to hate,
> And the blood-fever burns in their bosoms . . ."[72]

The Romans do not merely conquer, but destroy and enslave, with "no other thought save to win the Mark and waste it, and slay the fighting men and the old carles [men], and enthrall such as they will, that is, all that be fair and young."[73] Similarly, the Orcs are brutal and savage, wantonly destructive as well as fierce in battle.

Morris's Romans are highly regimented, with abusive officers who will "smite the warriors with staves even before all men"; the servile soldiers "endure it and smite not in turn."[74] Similarly, the Orcish camp is highly organized "like some huge nest of insects, with straight dreary streets of huts and long low drab buildings," and their officers are cruel and unsparing. In Mordor, Frodo and Sam fall in for a while, disguised, with a column of Orcs, a scene that mixes military discipline ("file after file passed") with the continual threat of random violence (the officers are "slave-drivers"). Intriguingly, Tom Loback suggests the Orcs' military organization is "similar in structure to that of the Republican Roman military organization of our own world."[75]

Both Morris's Romans and Tolkien's Orcs are also associated with relatively advanced technology. The Roman warriors are "helmed with iron" and the wall around their fort is "made of clay, and burned like pots into ashlar stones hard and red, and these are laid in lime" – recognizably bricks and mortar to readers, but strange to the men of the Mark.[76] The Orcs who kidnap Merry and Pippin are "iron-shod" and wear "iron helms"; the "broad swath" trampled by their march, which "turns neither right nor left" is suggestive of the famously straight roads of the Romans. Saruman uses his Orc labor force to turn Isengard into a land of "pits and forges," and in the assault on Helm's Deep, the Orcs use advanced weaponry: "a devilry from Orthanc . . . a blasting fire."

Swart, grim, crooked of body, militarily regimented yet wantonly brutal, violent yet servile, using advanced technology and favoring iron: Morris's Romans and Tolkien's Orcs share a strong family resemblance.

The Orcs may well reflect Tolkien's attitude both toward aggressive imperialism in general, and to the Roman Empire in particular. A certain negativity on Tolkien's part toward both Italians and totalitarian rule is not unsurprising, considering that he was working on *The Lord of the Rings* during the Second World War, in which England was fighting both Nazi Germany and Fascist Italy – indeed, his son Christopher was stationed in Africa, where the Italian forces posed a major threat – and considering that

Tolkien had already displayed his disdain for Nazi obsessions with Aryan heritage.[77] But Tolkien also had a low view of the Roman Empire in particular. In a lecture, he lamented the Roman conquest, which led to "the ruin of Gaul and the submergence of its native language (or languages) arts and traditions . . . dooming to obscurity and debate the history of perhaps the most remarkable of the Cymric speaking peoples."[78] Tolkien disapproved of Hilaire Belloc's romanticizing of the Italians and the South, and went so far as to rebut it in an essay, "The Chill Barbarians of the North," which in 1928 he read to the Newman Society at Oxford. A brief report in *The Tablet* recalled that Tolkien "criticized the views associated with Mr. Belloc and maintained that the Northern culture was quite as real as the Latin, and that so far as observation of foreign lands was concerned the Romans were stupid and devoid of imagination."[79] *

This dislike of the Roman Empire is brought out explicitly in a 1944 letter to Christopher, where he wrote, "I should have hated the Roman Empire in its day (as I do), and remained a patriotic Roman citizen, while preferring a free Gaul and seeing good in Carthaginians."[80] The chronological context of this remark is interesting, coming as it does toward the end of the Second World War. He has reflected (not very optimistically) that the "Big Folk" will in all probability impose their views on post-war society, with the clear implication that he and Christopher belong to the Little Folk – one might even say, the Hobbits. It is after remarking on the state of the war in general, and on Japan and the Soviet Union, that his mind turns to Rome, because, as he says, such conflicts have "always been going on in different terms," and yet the Tolkiens "belong to the ever-defeated never altogether subdued side."[81]

For Tolkien, the Romans seem to have been symbolic (at least in part) of the totalitarian and machine culture that he so consistently opposed: the archetypal imperial power that is determined to impose its will both on nature and on other nations. This image appears very early in his writings. In *The Book of Lost Tales*, begun in 1916–1917, Tolkien included invasions from Romans ('Rúmhoth') in the history of Luthany, his imagined England, and Christopher Tolkien remarks on their "peculiar hostility" toward the Elves.[82]

We can also see this attitude reflected in a poem he wrote to Charles Williams, where Tolkien is not just bitingly critical of Williams's impenetrable writing style, but of the Byzantine Empire ("New Rome") that is the subject of Williams's poetry. As Tolkien warms to his theme, he describes the Empire as corrupt, "rotting within while outwardly alive." He is particularly severe about the military aspect of empire, with its "vast drilled armies beating neighbours down / to drag them fettered through New Order's town." To him, "New Rome" is a symbol "of Rule that strangles and of Laws that kill."[83]

The Roman Empire seems to have been associated in Tolkien's imagination with a complex mix of technological advance, decadence, and civilizational decay. Hammond

---

* The essay does not survive, but Tolkien might have been responding to Belloc's 1906 book *Esto Perpetua*, in which, among other things, Belloc praises the Roman Empire and lauds the total destruction of Carthage.

and Scull note that the exiled Númenóreans, like the ancient Romans, were great build-ers of bridges and roads, and that their history "resembles that of the late Roman Em-pire," both in the fall of the Western empire and the survival of the Eastern empire for a further thousand years.[84]* Tolkien describes Gondor in decline as "a kind of proud, venerable, but increasingly impotent Byzantium."[85]

As a historically educated man and a Catholic to boot, Tolkien would, of course, have been well aware that many important elements of civilization came from the Ro-mans – and indeed he would later thoroughly enjoy, with his daughter Priscilla, a trip to Italy. He was willing to recognize a similarity between Aragorn's coronation in Minas Tirith and "the re-establishment of an effective Holy Roman Empire with its seat in Rome"[86] – though it is worth pointing out, for the avoidance of confusion, that this comparison is to a medieval re-envisioning of the Roman Empire made "Holy" by the Christianizing of Europe, not to the ancient, pagan version that preceded the conversion of Constantine. He would thus have been able to draw on Morris's disparaging portrait of the Romans in creating his Orcs without any qualms about this portrayal being a commentary on the essential nature of Italians or a wholesale condemnation of 'the Eter-nal City' where Saints Peter and Paul were martyred.

In fact, by turning the tables, so to speak, and using the Romans as material for his Orcs, Tolkien might also have been hinting at the dangers of a corrupt and decadent civilization. He had seen first-hand, in both World Wars, that horrifically destructive wars could be instigated by nations that boasted a high degree of 'civilization.' Indeed, it is worth noting that Saruman, who seems the wisest and most learned of the wizards and is the head of their Council, is the one who is most tragically corrupted by the lust for power – and who brings together a host of Orcs to serve him.

In drawing this parallel between the Orcs and the Romans (and to a lesser extent the Huns), we can perhaps get a glimpse of what Tolkien meant when he stated that "The Dead Marshes and the approaches to the Morannon" owe "more" to William Morris and to his Huns and Romans than they do to northern France after the Battle of the Somme. Beneath the dark waters of the Marshes appear the bodies of Men and Elves and Orcs, all slain in warfare. The closer that Frodo and Sam come to Mordor, the greater is the threat of Orcish violence in the present and the more powerful the lingering place-memory of their violence in the past. As Tolkien developed these scenes, he was summoning to his imagination whole tranches of European culture from centuries past, as filtered through his reading of Morris, and giving expression to some of his deepest-held opinions about imperial might; he was also drawing on, but not simply reworking, his own present expe-rience of the Second World War and his memories of the First. And really this is what we should expect from a man with such a historical sweep to his thought, with such strong

---

* Judy Ann Ford further suggests that "Gondor represents the Roman Empire as viewed through late-ancient, early-medieval, northern European eyes." She notes the geographical loca-tion, the building in stone (unlike the Anglo-Saxons), the architecture of Denethor's hall, parallel past history, and decay. ("The White City: *The Lord of the Rings* as an Early Medieval Myth of the Restoration of the Roman Empire," 60–63)

opinions about the course of Western civilization, and who was so keen to instill a sense of diuturnity in his sub-created world.

This account of possible literary influences on the Orcs also perhaps sheds some light on the fact that the nature of the Orcs remained a vexed question for Tolkien throughout his life. Years after the completion of *The Lord of the Rings*, Tolkien wrote that "Their nature and origin require more thought. They are not easy to work into the theory and system."[87] The various attempts at explaining the Orcs, throughout the numerous component texts of *The History of Middle-earth*, over the whole of Tolkien's literary career, show that he was never entirely sure how to account for these creatures. In our own attempt to understand the Orcs, then, we will do well not to look for perfect consistency or a definitive answer, for Tolkien himself had none; but we can look to the literary sources of these creatures, in the works of William Morris, for insight into their nature and function in the tales.

❧ Conclusion

Even before the publication of *The Lord of the Rings*, the Inklings frequently compared Morris and Tolkien, as Warren Lewis noted in his diary.* To readers who knew Morris well, the connections were apparent – but they became less so for later readers, after Morris's writings fell out of popular favor and out of print. In attending to the details of the connection between the two men, we are therefore recovering a clearer view of early, and significant, influences on Tolkien's writings. He himself expressed his admiration for Morris's work on various occasions, even, as we have seen, pointing out specific debts. It was an influence that began as early as 1914, when Tolkien deliberately imitated the style of Morris's romances, and it endured for many years.

It is not surprising that Tolkien had a strong sense of fellow-feeling for Morris throughout his life: here was an author who, though not a philological specialist, appreciated, at least at an intuitive level, the power of language and its relation to a culture, a people, and a story. In the preface to *The Story of the Volsungs*, Morris wrote that the northern sagas "should be to all our race what the Tale of Troy was to the Greeks."[88] It was the sort of expansive literary vision that would strike a deep note of resonance with the young Tolkien, providing a stimulus to the vision of the legendarium of Middle-earth, which would in the coming years become comprehensive, but at that point was just beginning to develop.

---

* He writes, "it is really unfair to both to compare Tollers and Morris, as the Inklings so often do. The resemblance is quite superficial: Morris has his feet much more fully planted on the earth than Tollers: Morris's world is an agricultural and trading one, Toller's is one in which (except for a little gardening), the soil is not the source of life, it is scenery. . . . On the other hand there are whole chapters for the new Hobbit in which Morris is beaten on his own ground – especially the journeys: and indeed the whole concept of that world is far beyond Morris's powers" (BF, 206).

We have examined several of Morris's specific influences on Tolkien: his use of a blended verse/prose form, his word choices, and his application of literary archaism. Morris's influence was not stylistic only, as we saw in the parallels between Morris's women warriors and Tolkien's Éowyn. Most notable of all, though, is the specific and important influence, which Tolkien himself remarked upon, from *The House of the Wolfings* and *The Roots of the Mountains*. We have carefully followed the traces and discovered that these works contributed not only to Tolkien's construction of the landscape through which Frodo and Sam journey *en route* to Mordor, but probably helped to shape Tolkien's creation of the Orcs as he imagined Morris's Huns and Romans into his own sub-created world.

Teasing out these threads has led us to look afresh both at Morris's work and Tolkien's: we can now see more clearly, and appreciate more deeply, the way he received the Morrisian influence and made masterly creative use of it. Though William Morris may now be best known for his wallpaper designs, to Tolkien he was of far more than background interest.

❧ 8 ❧

Rider Haggard
Fresh Ore from Old Mines

RIDER HAGGARD SHARES WITH WILLIAM MORRIS THE DISTINCTION of being one of the authors whom Tolkien enjoyed in both boyhood and adulthood. Sir Henry Rider Haggard (1856–1925) was an English barrister and civil servant, knighted for his efforts in support of agriculture. As a young man, he worked in South Africa before returning to England to practice law. Haggard's career as a writer took off with the tremendous success of his third and fourth novels, *King Solomon's Mines* (1885) and *She: A History of Adventure* (1887); he wrote more than fifty novels in total, at the rate of one or two a year.

Haggard was a favorite author among the boys at King Edward's School. In 1923, for example, there were twenty-one of his titles listed in the library's fiction section, and his stories were so frequently checked out that "during the mock school strike of 1911 the sub-librarians called for a ban on 'Henty, Haggard, School Tales, etc.'"[1] *

But enjoyment of Haggard's tales was not limited to the younger set or to unsophisticated readers. We find, for instance, that his novel *Stella Fregelius* was on the shelves of the Oxford Union's 'Coffee and Smoking Room' in Tolkien's time there as an undergraduate.[2] Roger Lancelyn Green considered Haggard of equal merit with Robert Louis Stevenson, praising them both for their "literary skill" and "sheer imaginative power," and Graham Greene remarked on Haggard's gift of "enchantment," which "fixed pictures in our minds that thirty years have been unable to wear away."[3]

Tolkien's taste for Haggard was thus no idiosyncratic whimsy; he was sharing in the enjoyment of a popular and well-regarded author. He read *King Solomon's Mines* early on, and recalled that "as a boy *She* interested me as much as anything."[4] In the 1940s, Roger Lancelyn Green (who had come to know Tolkien as his thesis supervisor) discovered that Haggard was a novelist whose work Tolkien "ranked very high." Green recalled that he "was able to lend him at least one, *The Wanderer's Necklace*, which he had never read."[5] This title is among the less well known of Haggard's works, indicating that Tolkien was already familiar with many of the more famous ones. Even in his retirement, when he had become more critical of other childhood favorites (as we saw with George MacDonald), Tolkien continued to admit a liking for Haggard. In 1961, a Swedish interviewer mentioned various fantasy authors to him, and observed that "to a single name he reacts positively, that of H. Rider Haggard."[6]

---

* "Henty" refers to G.A. Henty (1832–1902), author of numerous adventure tales for boys.

Although many of the earlier critical considerations of Haggard and Tolkien attend to possible sources for plot elements,[7] I would suggest that Haggard's settings, characters, and literary devices provide the most intriguing connections. The value of source study, as John D. Rateliff points out, is "the light it casts about the way Tolkien interacted with his sources, the way he re-worked material . . . the creative alchemy by which Tolkien transformed whatever he took from his sources into something new and distinctly Tolkienesque."[8] That sort of transformation is precisely what we will explore in this chapter.

◈ Won't have "cant": *Eric Brighteyes*

We will begin with one of Haggard's lesser-known tales, the historical adventure *Eric Brighteyes* (1891), which Tolkien references in the draft manuscript of "Beowulf and the Critics." The tale is set in Iceland, where the titular Eric falls in love with the maiden Gudruda, whose evil half-sister, the sorceress Swanhild, wants him for herself. Violence and betrayal ensue; all the main characters wind up dead (and so does nearly everyone else). *Eric Brighteyes* is a rousing adventure story in the epic style, and one can see why Tolkien praised it.

His admiration, however, is qualified, as we can see in the larger context of his remark:

> There is of course a value in heroic tales of divided allegiances and unacknowledged defeat. But it is not the only mode of imagination. Almost an element of cant creeps in, as if such things had a mysterious, almost magical virtue. The musical critic Ernest Newman I remember once commented on a similar superstition that there was something inexplicable by analysis, inimitable, about old traditional music – remarking that any competent modern musician with any melodic invention could turn them out by the score to defeat the powers of discrimination of their most enthusiastic admirers. He may or may not have been right. But I feel it is true at any rate of these 'heroic-tales.' Rider Haggard's *Eric Brighteyes* is as good (if rather longer) and as heroic as most of such things.[9]

When Tolkien says that the novel "is as good . . . and as heroic as most of such things," he is pointing out that despite its merits, Haggard's novel shares the faults of its genre.

What might Tolkien have found in the novel that constituted "an element of cant" – that is, of insincerity or hypocrisy? In these tales of "divided allegiances and unacknowledged defeat" we find a fatalism that, dramatic though it might be in fiction, is disastrous in real life. *Eric Brighteyes* demonstrates this to perfection. Characters are warned repeatedly not to do certain things, do them anyway in the conviction that 'what will be will be' regardless of their choices, and suffer the consequences; fate becomes an excuse for deliberately walking into a no-win situation. Eric's troubles arise from his romantic entanglements, but they are exacerbated by his own poor judgment. As events unfold,

Eric fatalistically refuses to reconsider his response to his problems; he declares, "I am an unlucky man who always chooses the wrong road,"[10] but does not attempt to learn from his mistakes or discern how to choose rightly. For instance, at one point, having killed his host because of a misunderstanding, Eric persists on sticking with a plan of action that all his friends have advised against and that has already resulted in disaster. His companion Skallagrim attempts to reason with him, pointing out that Eric's problems stem from his stubbornness:

> "Was it not my rede that we should bide this winter through in London? Thou wouldst none of it, and what came about? Our ship is sunk, gone are our comrades, thine honour is tarnished, and dead is thy host at thine own hand. . . . if thou goest to Iceland, I am sure of this: . . . the days to come shall be even more unlucky than the days that have been."

Eric shrugs: "It may be so. . . . Methinks, indeed, it will be so. I will go back to Iceland and there play out the game."[11] (See figure 19.)

As we saw in chapter 6, in the context of discussing John Buchan's hero Richard Hannay, Tolkien presents actions as being praiseworthy when those involved are striving for a good purpose. Hope may be slender or apparently absent, but despair – no less than its opposite, presumption – is not a virtue. For instance, Éowyn's desire to die in battle because she cannot have the love of Aragorn is depicted by Tolkien with compassion but not praise. In the world of *Eric Brighteyes*, Éowyn's unfulfilled infatuation would have been glorified, she would have been killed in battle (probably causing the death of Merry as well), and it would all have been declared fated.

In contrast, Tolkien's characters acknowledge the role of providence, but they do not on that account abdicate their moral responsibility for decision-making. Furthermore, in the fabric of the tale overall, Tolkien shows that providence is working *with* the actions of his heroes (not despite them). Aragorn, like Eric, makes mistakes of judgment (after the breaking of the Fellowship, he declares himself "an ill chooser," "since we passed through the Argonath my choices have gone amiss"), but, unlike Eric, Aragorn does not lapse into depressed passivity; rather, he reviews the situation, takes counsel from his companions, and acts accordingly. Although Aragorn's decision to pursue Merry and Pippin does not result in their rescue, it does bring him into contact with Gandalf, who tells him, "You chose amid doubts the path that seemed right: the choice was just, and it has been rewarded. For so we have met in time, who otherwise might have met too late." Aragorn used his judgment rather than abandoning himself to an inexorable fate, and the result is that he is able to continue to serve the Quest, albeit in a different way. Similarly, Frodo and Sam's previous actions in sparing Gollum's life, and their dogged persistence in getting to Mount Doom, bring about the situation in which the Quest is completed despite Frodo's last-minute failure at the Crack of Doom. Here we have Tolkien's Christian understanding of providence, presented in an epic context and thereby subtly reacting against both the pagan sense of fate or doom and a certain modern tendency toward determinism.

The comparison with *Eric Brighteyes* helps underscore an important point: Tolkien's heroes are not merely imported from medieval sagas, but are subtly and consistently reworked in light of his engagement with the modern world. His heroes (Frodo, Aragorn, Théoden, and others) persist against overwhelming odds because it is the right thing to do and because there is hope, even if slight, and even if the hope is for another's good rather than their own. It may seem to the modern reader that Tolkien's heroes are old-fashioned in their certainty that they *should* do the right thing. However, Tolkien is subtly pushing back against fatalism in its modern as well as its ancient form, with the distinctly modern psychological touch that his characters sometimes disagree about what is the right thing to do, and often feel unsure of how best to do what they must do, and doubt whether they will be able to do it. This aspect of the epic particularly impressed C.S. Lewis, who declared that "the most obvious appeal of the book is perhaps also its deepest: 'there was sorrow then, too, and gathering dark, but great valour, and great deeds that were not wholly vain.' *Not wholly vain* – it is the cool middle point between illusion and disillusionment."[12]

𝕊𝕝 Giggling Gagool, quaking Quatermain: *King Solomon's Mines*

King Solomon's Mines, Haggard's third novel and first real success, introduces one of his recurring characters: the big-game hunter Allan Quatermain. In this tale, Quatermain guides Sir Henry Curtis and Captain John Good on a search for Sir Henry's missing brother. Following an ancient map, and aided by the Zulu tribesman, Umbopa, they eventually make their way into remote Kukuanaland, where they learn that Umbopa is really the long-lost heir to the Kukuana throne. Quatermain, Curtis, and Good help Umbopa reclaim his throne, and are granted passage to the fabled diamond mines of King Solomon, guided by Gagool, a supernaturally long-lived, hideous, and wicked woman who vindictively shuts them into the treasure chamber so that they will die in the dark. Eventually the three men find a way out, and the story wends to its close, including the (somewhat anticlimactic) accidental discovery of the missing brother on the way home.

Tolkien enjoyed this novel as a young man and retained his appreciation for it. In 1913, acting as a tutor for two Mexican boys on tour, he gave them *King Solomon's Mines* as one "of the best, most readable, and least palpably 'instructive' of boys books they haven't read."[13] In a 1958 letter, he quotes, approvingly, C.S. Lewis's criticism of a film version of *King Solomon's Mines* that had added a volcanic eruption and earthquake, presumably because the filmmaker felt that characters being merely trapped in an underground tomb was insufficiently exciting. Lewis objected that the changes had ruined the story by replacing Haggard's careful creation of a single, qualitatively realized danger (slow, silent suffocation) with two textureless, unatmospheric, but supposedly more dramatic dangers ("that of being burned alive and that of being crushed to bits"[14]). Tolkien called attention to Lewis's observation that "it would have been better not to have chosen in the first place a story which could be adapted to the screen only by being ruined. Ruined, at least for me," and concurred, adding that these "are my sentiments and opinions too."[15] The fact that he saw the film at all is notable, as Tolkien does not seem to have made a regular habit of going to the movie theater.*

Critics have observed that the character of Gagool has a distinct resemblance to Gollum and plays a similar role as an untrustworthy guide in the narrative.[16] She has a preternaturally extended lifespan, at one point shrieking, "I knew your fathers, and your fathers' fathers' fathers. . . . I cannot die unless I be killed by chance, for none dare slay me." Shrunken with age to the size of a child, she is grotesquely withered, like "a sun-dried corpse" with eyes "full of fire and intelligence" resembling "jewels in a charnel-house"; her wrinkled scalp is "perfectly bare, and yellow in hue."[17] Her sentences are peppered with "*ha! ha!*" at least as often as Gollum says "gollum!"

Just as Gagool seems originally to have been a human woman, so too Gollum was once a hobbit-like being, whose life has been so stretched out by the power of the Ring that he has become physically altered. At the stairs of Cirith Ungol, we get a glimpse both of Gollum's great age, and also of the horror of it, for Tolkien, unlike Haggard, has sympathy for the burden brought by unnaturally long life. Gollum is glimpsed briefly, not as a schizoid and murderous addict, but as "an old weary hobbit, shrunken by the years that had carried him far beyond his time, beyond friends and kin, and the fields and streams of youth, an old starved pitiable thing."

Although not as vividly drawn a character as Gagool, Allan Quatermain, the narrator of *King Solomon's Mines*, is worth considering as well. Quatermain is surprisingly hobbit-like for a man famous for his prowess in big-game hunting in Africa. He describes himself in *King Solomon's Mines* as "a cautious man, indeed a timid one," "a poor hunter and trader," who shrinks from a seemingly foolhardy journey.[18] † Haggard underscores Quatermain's essentially bourgeois attitude by having him lay out detailed business terms for his participation in Sir Henry's adventure:

> 1. You are to pay all expenses, and any ivory or other valuables we may get is to be divided between Captain Good and myself.
> 2. That you pay me £500 for my services on the trip before we start. . . .
> 3. That before we start you execute a deed agreeing, in the event of my death or disablement, to pay my boy Harry . . . a sum of £200 a year for five years.[19]

---

* The only other motion picture we have a record of him watching is Walt Disney's *Snow White* (TCG:C, 239). However, he evidently saw enough Disney films to draw general conclusions about their merits and demerits (see TCG:C, 652–653).

† Horace Holly, in *She*, likewise reflects on his "comfortable rooms at Cambridge. Why had I been such a fool as to leave them? This is a reflection that has several times recurred to me since, and with ever-increasing force" (chapter IV). Bilbo Baggins makes a similar remark early in the journey, and Tolkien-as-narrator adds, "It was not the last time that he wished that!"

Coming as it does hard upon the account of the fabled mines of King Solomon and Jose da Silvestra's map drawn with his own blood, this business language is incongruous. The scene has somewhat the same flavor as Bilbo's fumbling attempts to speak about his role in the dwarves' adventure ("I should like to know about risks, out-of-pocket expenses, time required and remuneration, and so forth"), and the dwarves' formal and faintly absurd contract:

> Terms: cash on delivery, up to and not exceeding one fourteenth of total profits (if any); all travelling expenses guaranteed in any event; funeral expenses to be defrayed by us or our representatives, if occasion arises and the matter is not otherwise arranged for.[20]

Haggard uses the contrast between Quatermain's mercantile attitude and the story's romantic events to create an ironic frame – the novel begins with Quatermain reflecting on the events and declaring that he is "pretty sick of adventure"[21] – but he leaves it at that, not using the opportunity to develop Quatermain's character or reflect on moral issues. For instance, Quatermain is (like Bilbo) soon knocked unconscious in the climactic battle, but notes that at least he managed to shoot a fallen enemy in the back, an action which is presented in a humorous but generally approving manner. Bilbo does no such thing, either before or after he is stunned at the Battle of the Five Armies; indeed, the contrast is sharper when we recollect that earlier he had a similarly safe opportunity to stab his enemy Gollum in the back, but declined to do so: an act of mercy that Tolkien would make into a profoundly significant part of *The Lord of the Rings*. Even within *The Hobbit* itself, Tolkien makes Bilbo's moral transformation an important and moving part of the tale. Although at the start his bourgeois attitude is used for humor, by the end, Bilbo proves to be the true hero in an unexpected way, as the 'thief in the night' Christ-figure who is willing to be despised and rejected by Thorin and company in order to become a peacemaker.[22]

A chip off the old block?

Haggard's Allan Quatermain tales evoke the landscape and atmosphere of Africa, the land of Tolkien's birth, but the most striking connection with *King Solomon's Mines* happens below-ground rather than above it, as we find an intriguing resonance between Haggard's cavernous treasure chamber and the caverns of Helm's Deep. Quatermain describes the caves they pass through *en route* to the treasure chamber as being like "the hall of the vastest cathedral he ever stood in," with rows of gigantic pillars of what looked like ice, but were, in reality, huge stalactites." He is awed by "the overpowering beauty and grandeur of these pillars of white spar, some of which were not less than twenty feet in diameter at the base, and sprang up in lofty and yet delicate beauty sheer to the distant roof":

[O]ne huge mass. . . was in the form of a pulpit, beautifully fretted over outside with what looked like lace. Others resembled strange beasts, and on the sides of the cave were fan-like ivory tracings, such as the frost leaves upon a pane. Out of the vast main aisle, there opened here and there smaller caves, exactly, Sir Henry said, as chapels open out of great cathedrals.[23]

Turning to Tolkien's caverns of Helm's Deep, we find Gimli rhapsodizing to Legolas about the "immeasurable halls" with "echoing domes" overhead, filled with "dreamlike forms . . . wings, ropes, curtains fine as frozen clouds," and branching off with "chamber after chamber . . . hall opening out of hall, dome after dome, stair beyond stair." The immediate inspiration for the caverns of Helm's Deep came from Tolkien's visits to the Cheddar Caves in Somerset,[24] but images and scenes need not have a single source.

What is most notable about Tolkien's literary cave is the reverence with which this place of underground beauty is treated, in contrast to the somewhat cavalier attitude shown in the passage from Haggard. Legolas suggests it would be best for the dwarves to leave the caves alone, lest they mar this beauty, but Gimli reassures him, "We would tend these glades of flowering stone, not quarry them. With cautious skill, tap by tap – a small chip of rock and no more, perhaps, in a whole anxious day." Why would forest-loving Legolas worry about marring such a thing? Partly we see, no doubt, Tolkien's reaction to the way that Cheddar Caves had been commercialized as a tourist attraction. Perhaps it also reflects Tolkien's response to the scene in *King Solomon's Mines* where Quatermain sees one of the stalagmites cut with

a rude likeness of a mummy, by the head of which sat what appeared to be one of the Egyptian gods, doubtless the handiwork of some old-world labourer in the mine. This work of art was executed at about the natural height at which an idle fellow, be he Phoenician workman or British cad, is in the habit of trying to immortalise himself at the expense of nature's masterpieces.[25]

Haggard's tone is amused rather than dismayed by the notion of idle cads carving immortality for themselves in a place of geological splendor. Tolkien, with his love of natural beauty and his horror at its wanton destruction, would likely have had a more negative reaction, which perhaps we see refracted in the Helm's Deep scene. Both stone and trees, caverns and forests, are part of the glory of the world; and in both cases, there is a place for proper use and artistic development, not just an appreciative gaze. The Elves live in the mallorn-trees, constructing their flets; Gimli envisions the Dwarves living in the caverns of Helm's Deep. If Haggard's characters give us a glimpse of humans as tourists (at best) or humans as careless exploiters, then Tolkien's give us a glimpse of what it might be like to be good stewards of these beautiful places. The Shire, then, is not the only place in Middle-earth that evokes Tolkien's vision of a balanced, non-utilitarian relationship of people with the land they inhabit or traverse.

Maps

The published version of *The Hobbit* has a map on its endpapers, and as such maps are not unusual in works of fantasy or adventure fiction, we perhaps take it for granted. However, Tolkien's original vision for Thror's map[26] was much more ambitious than we see in its final form – and this ambition may well have been inspired by an intriguing map in *King Solomon's Mines*.

When Curtis and Good explain their plans for a rescue mission, Quatermain reveals that he has the necessary map, given to him by a dying Portuguese man, who in turn got it from his ancestor, Jose da Silvestra. The map, drawn on a scrap of linen with da Silvestra's own blood for ink, is labeled in Portuguese; Haggard adds a touch of verisimilitude by noting that the map has been rendered in English for the book, and giving the Portuguese in a footnote. The map is printed at the relevant passage in *King Solomon's Mines*: a rough sketch showing a couple of rivers, the mountain range and the pass between "Sheba's Breasts," the road to the treasure cave, and the path through the desert.[27]

Just as Quatermain produces the map for Curtis, so Gandalf produces his map for the dwarves, which was hitherto unknown to them but (as it happens) turns out to be essential for their mission. Gandalf, like Quatermain, received it from its dying previous owner, and is able to give its provenance.

Here it is worth observing that the 1905 edition of *King Solomon's Mines*, with illustrations by Russell Flint, supplemented the black-and-white sketch with a full-color, fold-out map. The 'linen' of this map is shown to be dirty brown and tan, and the blood-writing (in Portuguese) is of course reproduced in red; it is done realistically, even depicting the creases in the fabric and the frayed edges of the cloth. It seems not unlikely that Tolkien would have known of this edition; indeed, it may have been this work that first introduced him to the art of Russell Flint, whose watercolors he would later hang in his rooms at Exeter College. (See chapter 11.)

Like both versions of Haggard's map, Thror's Map is intended as a *facsimile* (not as a modern rendering of the map or a decorative item); it even has a yellowed 'manuscript-page' appearance, complete with faint marks of wear.* It was an important part of *The Hobbit* from the beginning – Tolkien recalled later, in a letter to W.H. Auden, that he had produced it very early in the process of composition[28] – and he put a great deal of effort into its creation. For instance, he intended the 'moon-runes' (text readable only by moonlight) to be printed on the reverse side of the page, so that they would only be visible when the map page was held up to the light. A version of the map sent to Allen

---

* See the 75th Anniversary edition. Some editions, such as the 1997 one illustrated by Alan Lee, replace the facsimile map with a re-drawn version featuring sharp black lettering on a pure white background.

& Unwin in 1936 includes a box in the lower-left corner with the text: "Thror's Map. Copied by B. Baggins. For moon-runes hold up to a light."[29] By indicating that the map is Bilbo's copy and not the original, Tolkien neatly makes imitation moon-lettering into a feature of textual authenticity, for of course Bilbo would not have been able to reproduce the functioning moon-runes.

Given that Tolkien intended the reader to be able to hold up the map and look through it to see the (imitation) moon-runes, it seems highly probable that he had in mind a fold-out sheet like that of the Russell Flint map; otherwise it would have been awkward to manipulate in this way. In the end, however, the publisher made the decision to print it on the end-paper rather than a fold-out sheet, with the moon-runes in outline to indicate that they are different from the other runes.[30] It is a reasonable solution, but unfortunately the final version also omits the attribution of Bilbo as copyist, such that both parts of Tolkien's attention to verisimilitude are missed in this case. As Tolkien originally envisioned it, Thror's map would have served both for the instruction of the reader and as an artifact within the story, strikingly similar in conception and execution to the map of Jose da Silvestra in *King Solomon's Mines*.

She-which-must-be-remade

Haggard's second major success, *She*, combines the 'Englishmen adventuring in Africa' element with a substantial dose of the supernatural. In this tale, a young man named Leo Vincey discovers that he is the lineal descendant of an ancient Egyptian priest of Isis, named Kallikrates, who had the misfortune to be desired by the fearsome queen Ayesha ("She-who-must-be-obeyed"). Angered by Kallikrates's refusal to abandon his wife Amenartas, Ayesha murdered him and awaited his reincarnation. Meanwhile Amenartas fled, bore Kallikrates's son, and swore his descendants to revenge, recording the story on a vase, a fragment of which – the "Sherd of Amenartas" – was in time passed down to Leo Vincey. Traveling to Africa to determine whether the story is true, Leo and his guardian Horace Holly arrive at Ayesha's hidden kingdom, where she and her retinue live in catacombs near the deserted city of Kôr. Having fascinated both Leo and Holly with her beauty and power, Ayesha intends to induct Leo, whom she declares to be the spitting image of Kallikrates, into her condition of quasi-immortality. However, when she steps for a second time into the secret fount of energy at the volcano's heart it unexpectedly revokes her agelessness, and she withers and dies. Leo and Holly return to England, determined to seek her in her reincarnated form.

She had made its mark in Tolkien's imagination as early as 1915, when he wrote a sonnet entitled "Kôr: In a City Lost and Dead," using the image of the abandoned, ancient city that he derived from the pages of Haggard's novel. In Tolkien's legendarium, Kôr would later become the hilltop city of the Elves in Eldamar. Christopher Tolkien says that "it can hardly be doubted" that the name itself comes from Haggard's book, and that "the relationship was more than purely 'phonetic.'"[31] Haggard's vast, ruined, and silent Kôr is an impressive but also depressing sight. Tolkien's Kôr shares much of the same imagery, but as John Garth perceptively notes, Tolkien evokes a "fine balance" of both grandeur and desolation: "Even empty, his city stands as an enduring tribute to its unnamed inhabitants – a mood that anticipates Moria in *The Lord of the Rings*."[32] Tolkien had already explored the image of a strange city on a hill in his painting *Tanaqui*, so it is notable that he chose "Kôr" rather than "Tanaqui" as the name of his literary city; Garth suggests that this renaming "may be seen as a direct challenge to Haggard's despairing view of mortality, memory, and meaning."[33] The young Tolkien was already transmuting Haggard's imagery for his own imaginative ends.

We find a further echo in Tolkien's mature work. Haggard describes the ruined temple in the city as "Court upon dim court, row upon row of mighty pillars . . . space upon space of empty chambers. . . . And overall, the dead silence of the dead, the sense of utter loneliness, and the brooding spirit of the Past!"[34] These ruins are suggestive of Minas Tirith, seen from Pippin's point of view as he enters the city with Gandalf. Vast and splendid as it is, Minas Tirith is decaying and half-empty, with many ancient houses that are "silent, and no footstep rang on their wide pavements, nor voice was heard in their halls, nor any face looked out from door or empty window."

In this regard, the larger imaginative context of Haggard's city is significant for being associated with the dead and with ancient Egypt. Ayesha and her people live in the burial chambers of the ancient people of Kôr, wear cloth taken from the bodies of mummies, and use the embalmed corpses to make bonfires. Ayesha says that those few who escaped the plague-ridden city in its last days "sailed North [and] may have been the fathers of the first Egyptians."[35] Tolkien's Númenóreans are likewise fascinated by the preservation of the dead, a backward-looking tendency that helped bring about the fall of their city, and that plays a part in Denethor's madness. Furthermore, Tolkien points out that in "many ways" the Númenóreans of Gondor "resembled 'Egyptians' – the love of, and power to construct, the gigantic and massive. And in their great interest in ancestry and in tombs."[36]* The rich combination of images of the ancient, abandoned city of Kôr itself, its connection with the dead, and its association with ancient Egyptians, seems to have had a lasting effect on Tolkien's imagination.

Haggard and heavenly queens

Turning from the city to its inhabitants, we now consider the eponymous She, the ancient yet seemingly ageless queen Ayesha. Having bathed once in the Fire at the heart of the

---

* Along these lines, it is worth noting, from *She*, the "Head of the Ethiopian," a mountain peak carved into a massive head, which the travelers see as their ship approaches its African destination: "the top of the peak, which was about eighty feet high by one hundred and fifty thick at its base . . . was stamped [with] a most fiendish and terrifying expression." It is a monument made by a "forgotten people . . . perhaps as an emblem of warning and defiance to any enemies who approached the harbour" (chapter 5). This image is suggestive of the Pillars of the Kings that the Fellowship see as they pass down the river Anduin: "two great kings of stone. . . . the silent wardens of a long-vanished kingdom." However, the Kings prompt a reaction of "awe and fear" in Frodo rather than mere surprise mixed with curiosity and horror, as in *She*.

mountain, Ayesha is functionally immortal. Long-lived beings are not uncommon in folklore and fantasy, but the idea of conditional immortality – life until one is killed – is, according to John Rateliff, "one of Tolkien's signature contributions to the fantasy genre," a "stunning conceptual break"[37] between the categories of human mortality and true immortality. Rateliff suggests that in this sense Ayesha was an inspiration for Tolkien's Elves, who are naturally immortal within the created order, but not invulnerable. A point in support of this connection is that Ayesha also reincarnates: her last words to Leo and Holly are "I shall come again,"[38] and the novel's sequel is *Ayesha: The Return of She*. Similarly, Tolkien allows for his Elves to be reincarnated; as a Catholic, he certainly did not believe that reincarnation was possible for humans,* but as Elves are an invented race, he had a free hand. The commingling of conditional immortality with reincarnation is more distinctive than mere longevity, so it is striking that both of these elements were present in Haggard's tale.

Given this suggestive connection between Ayesha and the Elves, it is not surprising that many critics have also seen a resemblance between Ayesha and one of Tolkien's most significant Elf-women, Galadriel.[39] Both Ayesha and Galadriel are extremely old (two thousand years in Ayesha's case, longer for Galadriel) and yet remain strikingly beautiful, and both are dressed in white. Both women disclaim having magical powers, but each has a basin filled with water, which they use for some kind of divination or viewing of memories.† More significantly, both Ayesha and Galadriel are powerful women, rulers of their respective domains, and have an immediate effect on the men who see them; their beauty and presence are overwhelmingly impressive.

What can we make of this parallel? It is worth noting that Tolkien explicitly identifies Galadriel as a figure possessing certain similarities to the Virgin Mary,‡ and his Catholic piety had a strongly Marian element. He described "Our Lady" as the one upon whom "all my own small perception of beauty both in majesty and simplicity is founded" and had a fondness for St. Bernadette, the visionary of Lourdes.[40] Tolkien regarded Mary, the Mother of God, as "blessed among women" (Luke 1:42), the model Christian disciple, paragon of humility yet also the one honored as Queen of Heaven (Revelation 12:1–3) and therefore Queen of All the Saints; a frequent image in medieval art is the coronation of Mary by Christ. In Mary, then, who is a model both of meekness and majesty, Tolkien had a sophisticated counterexample to all images of power expressed in terms of domination and exploitation.

---

* The basis for rejecting reincarnation is scriptural: "It is appointed unto men once to die, and after this the judgment" (Hebrews 9:27, Douay-Rheims translation).

† Some of these may be fortuitous correspondences. The white dress may reflect the influence of a particular style of representing women in illustrations in the nineteenth century (see Nancy Martsch, "The 'Lady with the Simple Gown and White Arms' or Possible Influences of 19th and Early 20th Century Book Illustrations on Tolkien's Work"). The mirror connection is somewhat weakened by the fact that in Tolkien's first imaginings of the scene, the mirror is that of "King Galdaran," who is later written out of the story (HOME VII, 249-50).

‡ "I owe much of this character to Christian and Catholic teaching and imagination about Mary" (*Letters*, 407).

"My empire," Ayesha declares, "is of the imagination."[41] However, what she expresses in this intriguing phrase is her policy of rule by terror; for instance, she coldly tortures
some of her people to death to ensure their fear and obedience. Ayesha is a literal *femme
fatale*: she freely admits having murdered her beloved Kallikrates, and later murders a rival for Leo's affections in front of his very eyes, yet Leo is still drawn to Ayesha's embrace
with hardly a backward glance. Some of this heady mix of fear and fascination is echoed
in Galadriel, but with a crucial difference. Boromir finds her unsettling, but he dislikes
her awareness of his thoughts precisely because he has something to hide. Galadriel may
indeed be "perilously fair," as Faramir suggests, but Tolkien is careful to delineate exactly
how it is that she is dangerous: neither in her nor Lothlórien is there any evil, Aragorn
says, "unless a man bring it hither himself." Sam makes the same point in more homely
language: "you could dash yourself to pieces on her, like a ship on a rock; or drownd
yourself, like a hobbit in a river. But neither rock nor river would be to blame."

As the wearer of the ring Nenya, Galadriel has power in her domain, like Ayesha,
but hers is sustaining and protective rather than deadly and terrorizing. Even so, Tolkien
shows that she has the potential to turn to evil. When Frodo freely offers her the One
Ring, she is at least momentarily tempted. Galadriel envisions herself in control of the
Ring, with a self-description that combines traditionally Marian descriptions (the Morning Star, the Star of the Sea, Our Lady of the Snows) with images of domination that
would do Ayesha proud. She will be a Queen, "beautiful and terrible as the Morning and
the Night! Fair as the Sea and the Sun and the Snow upon the Mountain! Dreadful as the
Storm and the Lightning! . . . All shall love me and despair!" But she chooses to refuse the
ring and to accept the loss of power: "I will diminish, and go into the West, and remain
Galadriel." Tolkien does not make Galadriel a perfect Marian figure, nor does he simply
transpose the dangerous attraction of Ayesha into Middle-earth, but rather creates a
powerful female character who believably chooses the path of humility.

She is the very model of a modern meta-textual

For an otherwise straightforward adventure tale, *She* starts off in a curiously delayed
manner. The novel begins with an introduction giving the history of the book now in
the reader's hands: the narrator, Horace Holly, sent Haggard-as-editor a manuscript and
supporting artifacts with the request that it be published if he judged it right to do so.
Holly's letter is included in the text, providing invented extra-textual references before
we even get into the main story. We soon learn that a dying friend had entrusted his
son Leo to Holly's care, along with a locked box and a letter to be given to Leo on his
twenty-fifth birthday. When in chapter III that birthday comes, Holly and Leo open
the chest and find further documentary evidence therein. Thus the tale begins with an
elaborate chain of provenance: the reader receives the story from Haggard-as-editor, who
had it from Holly, who in turn had the story from Vincey senior, who had it from ancient
documents that we are now about to examine.

Tolkien takes a similar approach in *The Lord of the Rings*, as he creates the appearance of an editor at work, via the prologue, appendices, and notes.* He takes a further page from Haggard's book, as it were, by connecting his fictional story to previously published writings in the reader's own world. In *She*, we are told that the editor was chosen by Holly because he had read "a book of yours describing a Central African adventure"[42] – namely, Haggard's earlier novel *King Solomon's Mines*. Likewise, in the opening paragraph of the prologue, Tolkien tells the reader that *The Lord of the Rings* itself will supply some information about hobbits, and that "Further information will also be found in the selection from the Red Book of Westmarch that has already been published, under the title of *The Hobbit.*"

Like Haggard, Tolkien is leveraging the existence of a previous novel for the verisimilitude of the sequel; since *The Hobbit* exists, perhaps the rest of the Red Book exists as well. This suggestion is rendered more plausible by Tolkien's retroactive assimilation of *The Hobbit*'s revision history into the world of *The Lord of the Rings*. In the first edition of *The Hobbit*, written with no sequel in mind, Gollum *gives* Bilbo the ring (not yet identified as the One Ring in Tolkien's imagination). Later realizing that this action was incompatible with the addictive quality of the Ring as it had subsequently developed, Tolkien re-wrote the "Riddles in the Dark" chapter of *The Hobbit* – but rather than simply ignoring the first version, he made the revision itself a fact to be recognized in the sequel, on the grounds that Bilbo had at first lied about how he acquired the Ring.[43] This sly move develops the effects of the Ring on Bilbo's character while also creating greater verisimilitude than either version would have done by itself. These editorial touches are both self-consciously literary, inviting the reader to enjoy the meta-textual joke, and disarmingly serious in their invitation to treat the book as authentic history. The effect is distinctly modern, indeed somewhat proleptic of the postmodern.†

Perhaps the most significant instance of Tolkien's skillful use of the editorial conceit, and one that has garnered well-deserved critical attention, is the conversation between Sam and Frodo in Cirith Ungol.[44] Sam wonders if they will ever be in a tale: "We're in one, of course; but I mean: put into words, you know, told by the fireside, or read out of a great big book with red and black letters, years and years afterwards." For a moment, the reader is made simultaneously aware of the story from both the inside (sharing Frodo

---

* The publication history of *The Lord of the Rings* shows Tolkien actively working to polish the editorial frame. The first-edition foreword had both the imagined editor's voice and Tolkien's own authorial voice. In the second edition, he moved his authorial voice to a new foreword and gave over the prologue to the 'editor.'

† Another instance of Tolkien's meta-textual sophistication appears in the unfinished *Notion Club Papers*, written around 1945. The conceit for the story is that a bundle of papers, consisting of notes from the meetings of this Inklings-style club, was discovered in 2012 and subsequently edited and published by a "Howard Green"; in addition to writing a foreword and a note to the second edition, Tolkien created a faux title page for the 2014 edition of *Leaves from the Notion Club Papers*. He also created facsimiles of the manuscript pages in Quenya and Adunaic, allegedly produced by the character Lowdham (HOME IX, 154; 319–321)

and Sam's experiences) and the outside (realizing that we are reading the book to which Sam refers). What's more, the characters experience the same doubling: Sam reflects on himself, Frodo, and even Gollum as literary characters. Narrative self-consciousness is frequently used in modern and postmodern literature, but more usually to disrupt the reader's expectations and create ironic distance from the story-as-story. Tolkien's use of the technique is perhaps all the more notable because he uses it for non-ironic ends, evoking an awareness of the story-as-literary-text *within* the context of 'secondary belief' in the story-as-story. The effect goes beyond the creation of Haggard-style verisimilitude, to draw the reader into a sense of participation within a story so capacious that it has room for characters who themselves perceive that they are in a tale larger than their own immediate concerns.

"They are coming": The Sherd's Tolkienian descendants

The most ingenious part of the editorial frame in *She* is a meta-textual artifact: the Sherd of Amenartas. It was this item in particular that Tolkien noted years later in an interview: "I suppose that as a boy *She* interested me as much as anything – like the Greek Sherd of Amenartas, which was the kind of machine by which everything got moving."[45]

When Holly and Leo unpack the chest that Leo has inherited, they find, among other things, the all-important potsherd, which is described at length in the text; briefly, it is "densely covered on the convex side . . . with writing in the later uncial Greek character. . . . Also there were numerous inscriptions on the inner side, but these were of the most erratic character, and had clearly been made by different hands and in many different ages."[46] Taking verisimilitude one step further, between the serial version of *She* and its book publication, Haggard had the Sherd manufactured as a physical object. He even went so far as to have its authenticity assessed by the antiquary Sir John Evans, who, having viewed it, commented, "All I can say is that it might *possibly* have been forged." And indeed it was very realistically done.[47]* The book version of *She* includes an image, captioned in serious museum style: "Facsimile of the Sherd of Amenartas. One ½ size. Greatest length of the original 10 ½ inches. Greatest breadth 7 inches. Weight 1 lb 5 ½ oz." Early editions even print the facsimile in color. (See figure 20.)

The Sherd was a device by means of which a spell of (apparent) deep history could be cast: the multilingual inscriptions, the attention to the smallest details, and the combination of the literary and visual elements serve to create a link between true and feigned history.† Though no linguist himself, Haggard evidently took pains to create credible-seeming inscriptions, asking his scholarly friends to supply texts in Greek, medieval Latin, and medieval English.[48] These multiple layers of language also contribute to

---

* The Sherd is now on display at the Norwich Castle Museum and Art Gallery in Norfolk. Were it not labeled as a "fake ancient pot," non-expert viewers could easily mistake it for a real one. See http://norfolkmuseumscollections.org/collections/objects/object-4062191913.html/.

† Haggard also provides a line drawing of the scarab and a proliferation of transcriptions, transliterations, and translations of the Sherd, from both the parchment rolls and the Sherd itself.

a sense of authenticity in the story. At least some of Haggard's schoolboy audience would have been able to read the Greek and Latin passages – including the young Tolkien, talented classicist that he was* – and thus delight more fully in the sense of veraciousness.

That Haggard's example did, in fact, fire Tolkien's imagination is, I would suggest, evident in *The Lord of the Rings*, most notably in the Book of Mazarbul.

In their passage through the Mines of Moria, the Fellowship discover a slab "deeply graven" with runes that reveal it to be the tomb of Balin, last lord of Moria; Tolkien includes these runes as a small black-and-white drawing in the text. Near it they find a tattered book that Gandalf identifies as the "Book of Mazarbul"; it "had been slashed and stabbed and partly burned, and it was so stained with black and other dark marks like old blood that little of it could be read." The final page is enough to show that the dwarves came to a terrible end in Moria: "The last thing written is in a trailing scrawl of elf-letters: *they are coming.* There is nothing more."

That Tolkien had the Sherd in mind is strongly suggested by a comment he later made about the language of the Book of Mazarbul. The writing on the facsimiles is in Elvish script, but once transliterated, the words are in English. Tolkien admits that this was "erroneous": "It is one thing to represent all the dialogue of the story in varying forms of English: this must be supposed to be done by 'translation'. . . . But it is quite another thing to provide *visible* facsimiles or representations of writings or carvings supposed to be of the date of the events in the narrative."[49] He footnotes this statement with the remark, "The sherd of Amenartas was in Greek (provided by Andrew Lang) of the period from which it was supposed to have survived, not in English spelt as well as might be in Greek letters."[50] Haggard had, on this point, out-done Tolkien in verisimilitude.

However, Tolkien certainly matched Haggard in the attention to detail he lavished on his artifact. He first drew, in ink and colored pencil, detailed sketches that indicate where he planned to burn or tear the finished versions.[51] Then, as the Bodleian curators explain, he "went to meticulous lengths to produce facsimiles of the damaged pages, tearing and setting fire to the paper, and even creating a line of binding holes . . . where the purported 'Book' would have been sewn."[52] Tolkien considered these facsimiles to be more than mere ornament. He created them sometime before March 1947,[53] but only (and reluctantly) dropped the idea of including images of them in the text in 1953. He felt the facsimiles were needed to accompany the chapter, and laments that "Without them the opening of Book Two, ch. 5 (which was meant to have the facsimiles and a transcript alongside) is defective."[54] When he accepted that color facsimiles would raise production costs too much, he rejected Unwin's suggestion of line-blocks (black and white images, embedded in the text); this would make them "too illegible to be interesting

---

* Tolkien's studies of Latin and Greek at King Edward's enabled him to read, write, and speak these languages. For instance, he took part in a 1911 performance of a play by Aristophanes in ancient Greek, and the King Edward's boys "conducted debates in Latin" (TGW, 17–18). See also Giampolo Canzonieri, "Tolkien at King Edward's School," 148.

(or too unveracious to be worth inclusion)."[55] The word "unveracious" is significant; Tolkien was keeping the function of these images firmly in mind. They were not intended as illustrations, and if they could not produce the desired effect of verisimilitude, it was better to omit them entirely.

It is worth considering whether Haggard's curious bit of literary pottery might have had a thematic as well as a visual influence. As we saw earlier, Tolkien described the Sherd as "the kind of machine by which everything got moving" in the novel. At one level, he surely meant simply 'narrative device,' a literary equivalent of Alfred Hitchcock's 'MacGuffin,' an invention to move the story along.[56] However, "machine" is such a significant word for Tolkien, deeply related to the themes of power in *The Lord of the Rings*, that it is worth at least briefly considering whether the term has additional ramifications.

Christopher Tolkien took pains to explain that his father was not anti-technology as such: "He wasn't an unreasonable man, he wasn't an eccentric. . . . he recognized that one must live, in the world, to an extent, as it is. So he had a telephone, he even had a tape recorder, when they were quite new-fangled." But Christopher recalled that for Tolkien, a great evil of the modern age was the "coercion of other minds and other wills." The use of machines for tyranny "is really why he hated machines": they provided modern tyrants with a terribly effective form of manipulation and domination. We see this view embodied in the mechanized horrors of Saruman's Isengard and Sauron's Mordor, but it is most subtly and powerfully expressed in the One Ring which, as Christopher goes on to say, is "the supreme machine, in mythological terms. . . . The Ring is the ultimate machine because it was made for coercion, made by Sauron to coerce."[57] *

The Sherd in *She* has certain intriguing similarities with the Ring in this regard. The Sherd is inherited by Leo Vincey, who learns that it has been passed on from father to son through the generations; likewise, Frodo inherits the Ring as Bilbo's heir, and we eventually learn how it passed from Sauron's hand all the way to Bilbo's. The Sherd is engraved with a message revealing its origins, just as the Ring has its identifying script, made visible in fire. The Sherd is also connected to evil: on it, Amenartas records the murder of her husband Kallikrates and enjoins vengeance on her son and all of his line. Here, too, we have parallel themes of power and control. The long-dead Amenartas seeks to exert control over her descendants through the Sherd; but ironically, in seeking to learn if this tale is true, Leo Vincey ends up falling completely under the power of Ayesha, and accepting his ancestor's murderer as his own lover – thereby both compromising his own ethical sense, and achieving the very opposite of the charge given him by Amenartas. The Sherd, then, gets the story moving, but ultimately turns against those who use it, betraying both Amenartas and Leo Vincey in different ways. Tolkien's recollection of it after many years, coupled with his reference to it as a "machine," suggests that the Sherd made a strong imprint on his imagination; it seems possible that it contributed something to the eventual formation of the One Ring.

---

* We will discuss Tolkien's views on technology in more detail in chapter 9.

❧ Conclusion

Having encountered Rider Haggard's adventure tales as a boy, Tolkien appreciated them throughout his life, and as we have seen, certain key elements of Haggard's tales provided him with rich material for later creative adaptation and transformation. He noted in *Eric Brighteyes* both the strength of the tale and the weakness of its fatalistic ethos; *The Lord of the Rings* would embody a re-visioning of this approach to heroic character.

We traced, in *King Solomon's Mines*, possible links to Tolkien's work both in character and locale, and saw how Haggard's use of the map in this tale, as both an element in the story and as an artifact for the reader, may have helped inspire the creation of Thror's map in *The Hobbit*. Turning to *She*, we observed a number of connections with Tolkien's writings, including the city of Kôr, and the character of Ayesha, "She-who-must-be-obeyed," who has certain resemblances to Galadriel. Of greatest interest, however, is Haggard's extensive use of meta-textual devices to create verisimilitude, most notably the facsimile of the Sherd of Amenartas. This element in *She* seems certainly to have influenced Tolkien's facsimile pages of the Book of Mazarbul.

As a medievalist, Tolkien was thoroughly immersed in the world of manuscripts and their editing; he knew intimately the real-world work of which the frame of *The Lord of the Rings* is an analogue. The history of the writing of the legendarium also shows that, early on, he experimented with creating various scribal traditions and complex relationships of authors and editors for the tales. Other modern influences contributed as well, but Haggard is especially notable as a source because Tolkien encountered both *She* and *King Solomon's Mines* early in his youth, furnishing his retentive memory and vivid imagination with possibilities for narrative options before the first of the tales of the legendarium, let alone *The Hobbit* or *The Lord of the Rings*, was penned. Haggard's approach, implemented with perfectionist precision, was well suited to appeal to Tolkien, a scholar with a playful streak and a predilection for near-obsessive attention to detail. It seems likely that Haggard's tales encouraged him to explore this literary territory.

Rider Haggard had a gift for lively storytelling and for creating memorable images of people and places, but he was far from being a truly great writer. C.S. Lewis, in analyzing Haggard's "mythopoeic gift," comments that, in reading *King Solomon's Mines* and *She*, the words "if only" come to mind: "If only we could have had this very same story told by a Stevenson, a Tolkien, or a William Golding."[58] Tolkien has not retold these stories, but he has done something better: he has drawn on the best ideas and images in Haggard's work, transmuting and refining them, freshening them up, and so making them an integral part of the world of Middle-earth.

⚜ 9 ⚜

Science Fiction
From Asimov to Zimiamvia

WE TURN NOW FROM THE MYTHOPOEIC TO THE SCIENTIFIC. GIVEN that science fiction was born out of the scientific revolution and came of age in the industrial era,* this genre might be supposed to have little to attract the attention of Tolkien. With its steaming test tubes and surging space rockets, with its mistrust of tradition and belief in progress, what could science fiction conceivably offer that might appeal to a technology-averse philology professor?

But these questions crassly stereotype both the genre – which often challenges the boundary-pushing nature of scientific developments (as in Mary Shelley's *Frankenstein*) – and Tolkien himself, whose attitude to the modern products of scientific progress was more nuanced than the popular notion of him would allow. His attitude to the literary genre in which these technological gizmos appear was in fact surprisingly warm and welcoming. Tolkien was of the opinion that science fiction "performs the same operation as fantasy – it provides Recovery and Escape . . . and wonder."[1] This is no small matter. The two genres may be widely separated in superficial appearance (there are typically no rockets or computers in fantasy), and may also be differentiated in chronological setting (for as Tolkien noted, "science fiction deals with the future or even contemporary times, while fantasy fiction often takes place in the past"[2]). Nevertheless, both science fiction and fantasy can perform "the *same* operation," imaginatively speaking: to enable the reader to recover a fresh view of reality, escape from the limitations of ordinary life, and awaken wonder.

Not only was Tolkien prepared to equate the two genres in terms of their potential imaginative effect, he even recognized that, in a certain respect, science fiction had the edge. The contemporaneity of science fiction, with its patina of "scientific knowledge," meant that its authors "are more easily able to produce suspension of disbelief. The legendary laboratory 'professor' has replaced the wizard."[3]

Though known for his wizards, Tolkien was not immune to the charms of the laboratory professor. He was, as one interviewer described him, "fascinated by both science

---

* The genre's roots arguably go as far back as ancient literature. Brian Aldiss and David Wingrove make a case for its genesis around the time of the Industrial Revolution in *Trillion Year Spree: The History of Science Fiction*. See also Robert Scholes and Eric S. Rabkin, *Science Fiction: History, Science, Vision*.

fiction and fantasy fiction," an interest that was deep and lasting. He was flattered by early notices of *The Lord of the Rings* that compared it to "super Science Fiction." Clyde Kilby remarked that Tolkien "told me more than once of his pride in being chosen a member of a science-fiction writers' association in the United States."[4]

Tolkien's best-known link with science fiction comes from his 'wager' with C.S. Lewis, who had observed that "there is too little of what we really like in stories" and that, therefore, "we shall have to write some ourselves."[5]* Lewis took on a space-travel story, which became *Out of the Silent Planet*, and Tolkien took on a time-travel story, which became the unfinished *The Lost Road*. We will return to *Out of the Silent Planet* later in this chapter, but for the moment it is worth noting what the venture reveals about Tolkien's reading: only if he knew the science-fiction field well could he have agreed that there was "too little" of what he liked currently being written. In a 1966 interview, he shows himself to be confidently up-to-date with the genre, remarking that "The relationship between science fiction and fantasy is difficult and topically important. At present, there's a good deal of serious dissention among [science fiction] writers, especially in the Science Fiction Writers' Association of America."[6]

Tolkien enjoyed a diverse array of sub-genres in science fiction, from classics, to more fantastic tales, to what is often called 'hard' science fiction. He read Samuel Butler's *Erewhon* (1872); admired John Christopher's dystopian tale *The Death of Grass* (1956), which explores the catastrophic consequences of a worldwide extinction of grasses; named Isaac Asimov as an author he enjoyed; and knew the stories of Ray Bradbury.[7] Late in life, he was sent a copy of Frank Herbert's *Dune* (1965) by its editor, most likely in hopes that he would endorse it, but Tolkien disliked it.[8] He read the work of Arthur C. Clarke[9] and indeed met Clarke on two occasions: at a luncheon in 1957 when *The Lord of the Rings* received the International Fantasy Award from the World Science Fiction Convention,[10] and, more convivially, in Oxford, when Tolkien and Lewis together met Clarke and his friend Val Cleaver for a lengthy lunch at the Eastgate Hotel. They discussed science-fictional (and scientific) issues and "a fine time was had by all," according to Clarke, who recalled that "neither side converted the other, and we refused to abandon our diabolical schemes of interplanetary conquest."[11]

A further glimpse of the extent to which Tolkien kept abreast of the field can be seen in a small but significant reference to the "Robot Age" in "On Fairy-stories."[12] The word 'robot' would have been a relative neologism in 1939, when Tolkien prepared his lecture. 'Robot' derives from the Czech play *R.U.R.* (*Rossum's Universal Robots*) by Karel Čapek, translated into English in 1923, and was made more familiar to science-fiction readers by Isaac Asimov, but Tolkien's use of the word pre-dates by more than a decade the publication of Asimov's robot stories. He probably encountered the term in American science-fiction magazines such as *Astounding Science-Fiction*, *Amazing Stories*, or *Wonder*

---

* Although it is usually referred to a 'wager,' none of Tolkien's or Lewis's remarks on it suggest any element of competition or challenge; Tolkien once says that they "tossed up" for their respective topics (*Letters*, 347), which suggests a simple coin flip.

Stories (the first edited by John W. Campbell, the latter two by Hugo Gernsback). All these published robot stories in the 1930s.[13] Tolkien's familiarity with these magazines is demonstrated in *The Notion Club Papers*, where he has his characters use the term 'scientifiction' for what we would now call 'science fiction': this portmanteau word was coined by *Amazing Stories* editor Hugo Gernsback in 1923, but did not last long.[14] (See figure 21.) As late as 1967, Tolkien was still keeping up with the genre, as we know from his reference to a Gene Wolfe story published in *Orbit 2: The Best New Science Fiction of the Year*.[15] In short, Tolkien knew the field of science fiction very well, such that he could declare with confidence that "It's a very good medium for the imagination to work with" – though not an easy one, for as he remarks, "it's been much misused by lesser writers."[16]

Lesser writers may fail in their handling of the medium, but what about the greater exponents of the genre? In this chapter, we will examine a selection of authors whom Tolkien considered worthy of his attention, beginning with the 'Old Master' H.G. Wells, and proceeding to several less-familiar names, such as Joseph O'Neill, whose *Land Under England* may have contributed to the scene of Frodo's mental struggle against Sauron on Tol Brandir. We then turn to several authors who had very different ethical and philosophical views from Tolkien: Olaf Stapledon, whose telepathic space-travel concept Tolkien found intriguing; David Lindsay, whose *A Voyage to Arcturus* Tolkien praised for its power; and E.R. Eddison, whose work he read in its entirety. We will close the chapter by turning to two of his fellow Inklings: namely, Charles Williams, whose effect on Tolkien provides an example of influence-by-opposition, and C.S. Lewis, whose *Out of the Silent Planet* he admired, and which had a key role to play in his creation of the Ents.

ꙮ Technophobe – or (moderate) technophile?

Before we turn to our literary analysis, however, it is worth considering the apparent contradiction involved in tracing influences from science fiction, with its emphasis on avant-garde technology and the future, to Tolkien's tales of Middle-earth, a setting which is resolutely pre-modern and low-tech. A short survey of Tolkien's attitude toward technology will help us gain a more informed view of his creative engagement with this genre.

As we saw in chapter 1, the popular stereotype of Tolkien is of a man stuck in the past, who would reflexively and wholeheartedly reject "the white heat of the scientific revolution"[17] that science fiction appears to embrace.* This image is on display, for

---

* The stereotype appears in scholarly studies as well. For instance, Christopher Butynskyi alleges that "J.R.R. Tolkien's well-known technophobia led him to see despair, not hope, in the fast-paced age of technology" (*The Inklings, the Victorians, and the Moderns*, 109), citing remarks in two of Tolkien's wartime letters to his son Christopher, who was an RAF pilot at the time. Concern about death-dealing war machinery and the use of atomic bombs hardly constitutes an irrational fear of technology (i.e., a "phobia"). Curiously, Lewis's views, expressed "in language similar to Tolkien's," are presented not as "technophobia" but as a critique of "a corrupt and excessive use of technology" (110). As with Tolkien's alleged ignorance of modern literature, so too

instance, in the BBC radio drama *Tolkien in Love*, in which Edith labels the young John Ronald as a "Luddite,"[18] a description that is evidently intended to be taken as accurate. It is not.

To begin with, Tolkien was a willing, even enthusiastic adopter of modern technology. He used that newfangled device, the typewriter, not only for mundane administrative tasks such as letter-writing, but also for preparing manuscripts both as an academic and as a creative writer.* He was up-to-date on typewriter designs and their innovative features; he owned at least two such machines, one of which had a special keyboard with philological symbols, and he dedicates several paragraphs to the subject in a letter to his grandson Michael. He was also an early adopter of the ballpoint pen, both for his writing and for his visual art. Not only were ballpoints brand-new at that point (post-World War II), they were also foreign (imported from America). Tolkien knew them well enough to consider Bics the best of the bunch.[19]

Tolkien was also intrigued by the potential of audio recordings and the radio, two technologies that, again, were brand new in his day. As early as 1930, he recorded a lesson for the *Linguaphone Conversational Course* in English, and would later read various poems onto tape recorders, once even doing his own sound effects. In a letter to his grandson, Tolkien commented knowledgeably on the merits of different models of audio recorders.[20] He made a number of radio presentations on Anglo-Saxon and Middle English verse for the BBC, becoming in the process something of a 'media don.'[21] † His consistent interest in using up-to-the-minute technology is the mark of a man eager to see his work available in new media, exploiting the developments of modernity for his own ends.‡

Today, typewriters, ballpoint pens, and tape recorders seem old fashioned and hardly worth describing as 'technology' at all, but we should bear in mind that in Tolkien's lifetime they were indeed at the cutting-edge of progress in personal communication; the equivalent today would be if he had a desktop computer and smartphone, both equipped with voice-recognition software.

---

his supposed hostility to modern technology has acquired the status of an accepted fact and one that is apparently "well-known." The reality of the situation, as this chapter attempts to show, is somewhat different.

   * He often revised his imaginative work on the typewriter, resulting in typescripts that show significant changes from earlier handwritten versions. See, for instance, "The Tale of Tinúviel," in HOME II.

   † Hoping to be allowed to read *Sir Gawain* himself, he practiced his delivery with a rented tape-recorder: "I go to London tomorrow for an audition. . . . I made some three voice experiments and recordings of the temptation scenes. An enormous improvement" (quoted in Sayer, "Recollections of J.R.R. Tolkien," 12). Although he was not in the end chosen, he did write an introduction to it, published in *Radio Times* (Dec. 4, 1953, pg. 9). See also Dimitra Fimi, "Tolkien on 1930s BBC Radio via historical issues of Radio Times."

   ‡ Tolkien's often-noted disapproval of C.S. Lewis's BBC broadcasts on Christianity is better understood not as an objection to the medium, the technology, or the subject, but rather as an objection to Lewis working outside of his own discipline: Lewis was a literary critic, not a theologian.

If Tolkien accepted technology insofar as it helped his writing, what about the automobile, which he is often assumed to have despised? Once again, we find that his views were more complex than we might expect. He was an automobile owner in the 1930s; that he later did not keep a car is readily understandable when we consider the combined factors of wartime petrol rationing, the expenses of a family with four children, a reliable bus service, and the fact that he could easily bicycle from his home on Northmoor Road to the center of Oxford.* When he did own a car, he used it to take the family on outings; later, he bought a car for one of his children.[22] In an interview with the BBC Tolkien even declared that he loved automobiles: "Love riding them, like driving them." When pressed for more details, he explains that the problem is not the automobile *per se*, but the excessive number of them: "Anything that's good in one and two is nearly always bad at 5,000." He adds that the proliferation of cars has resulted in destructive road-building, such that a driver "is no longer able to do the things for which motor cars were made. . . . nowadays, before you can get to the brooks [for a picnic], the state road-makers have smashed the brook and cut the trees down so that you can get there. I should have thought it's the road-makers more than the motor car which I dislike, they really are ruthless and foolish."[23] Similarly, he disapproved of the destruction often brought about by the expansion of railroads, yet he encouraged his sons' fascination with model railways.†

We can see, then, that Tolkien objected strenuously to the abuses of technology, but did not find technology to be evil in and of itself. As he reminds the reader in "On Fairy-stories," when discussing the genre of fantasy, *abusus non tollit usum* (abuse does not preclude proper use). His opposition to the machine age was qualified, more so than is often supposed. For example, in the BBC interview referenced above, Tolkien offered surprising responses to questions about industry ("I've no objection to that as such") and factories ("They might be better than they are. It depends on what you mean by a factory, I mean a factory may be a very big or a very large, or very small thing"[24] ‡). Given the opportunity to criticize industry and technology as extravagantly as he liked, he chose a sober response.

Nor was he blindly nostalgic about premodern conditions. Although he objected to the noise of automobiles in Oxford,§ he pointed out to the interviewer that medieval

---

* Desmond Albrow recalls that his father-in-law had "bought the professor's old car when petrol rationing brought normal motoring to an end in the war" ("A brush with greatness").

† See, for instance, his dry remark that the dinosaurs that once lived in Oxfordshire "must have been almost as devastating to the district as the G.W.R. [Great Western Railway]" (Dragons, 41). Nonetheless, Tolkien bought the children model trains for Christmas (see *Letters from Father Christmas*), and Michael Tolkien recalled his father encouraging his interest in steam engines ("The Wizard Father"). In 1933, Tolkien gave Michael the book *A Register of All the Locomotives Now in Use on the London & North-Western Railway* (Oronzo Cilli, "Tolkien, trains and two discoveries: Meccano and Hornby").

‡ We should remember that even in *The Lord of the Rings*, the Shire has a mill for grinding grain.

§ As did many other people at the time; an "Oxford Noise Abatement Society" was founded

Oxford "was an 'extraordinarily deafeningly noisy place' due to the 'enormous wains' with steel wheels on the setts of the High Street." Especially notable is a portion toward the end of this interview. Stuart Lee explains that the interviewer is "pressing Tolkien further on his views on modernisation and 'progress, building roads, pylons and so on,'" and notes the "balanced" quality of Tolkien's reply. Having lamented being "born into a country which has developed and changed very quickly" such that "I practically can't go back to any site which is even visibly similar," Tolkien adds:

> I'm sensible enough to realise that a lot of this is essential at any rate; it's not peculiar to our time. . . . Dash it, nobody in ancient England thought anything about oaks, trees, I mean they'd devastated the whole of the south-eastern country for smelting, for building ships and so on; no, it's not a new thing.[25]

This is not generic nostalgia for a rural past: Tolkien laments the rapid industrialization of his childhood landscape, while recognizing that this type of loss is not peculiar to modernity.

Part of the reason that Tolkien has been saddled with the Luddite image is that he is often lumped together with C.S. Lewis in this regard – and Lewis could much more fairly be described as being a technophobe. Lewis never learned to drive a car and disapproved of modern transport in principle.* He exclusively used a dip pen all his life, relying on his brother to type letters where necessary. Indeed, Lewis objected to the very idea of using a typewriter, remarking that he could "no more drive [a typewriter] than a locomotive (I'd sooner drive the locomotive too)"; he advised an aspiring writer, "Don't use a typewriter. The noise will destroy your sense of rhythm."[26] We must not conflate the two just because they were friends and both scholars of medieval literature.

We should also bear in mind Tolkien's lifelong interest in science. He remarked that the books he most enjoyed as a teenaged boy "were mostly scientific in reference, especially botany and astronomy."[27] A good deal of specific astronomical detail is worked into the *Letters from Father Christmas*, and his daughter Priscilla recalled that "my brother Christopher and I were encouraged to learn about the stars and planets and eclipses of the sun and moon."[28] Tolkien's interest in science and nature is apparent in the details of his literary creation. Kristine Larsen points out that "he utilizes a tremendous amount of the scientific understanding of his day in fleshing out the details of Middle-earth," and that he clearly distinguishes between "the study of the natural world without intent to master or control it . . . and the ever-increasing battle between technology and the environment."[29]

---

in 1931. (John Garth, *The Worlds of J.R.R. Tolkien*, 180).

* In his autobiography, Lewis asserted that "The truest and most horrible claim made for modern transport is that it 'annihilates space.' . . . a modern boy travels a hundred miles with less sense of liberation and pilgrimage and adventure than his grandfather got from travelling ten. Of course if a man hates space and wants it to be annihilated, that is another matter. Why not creep into his coffin at once? There is little enough space there" (*Surprised by Joy*, chapter X).

With this more complete view of Tolkien's attitude toward science and technology, it becomes less strange that he should have been so interested in science fiction. We are now prepared to consider his reading in this genre.

❧ An Old Master: H.G. Wells

The first author to consider is that giant of the genre Herbert George Wells (1866–1946), whose best-known works include *The Time Machine* (1895), *The Invisible Man* (1897), and *The War of the Worlds* (1898). (See figure 21.) Although his fame now rests on his science-fictional tales, Wells was prolific in other literary genres, and wrote on political, social, and historical topics in his nonfiction works. Most notably, his massive *The Outline of History* (1920) presented a distinctly materialist, secular view of history that, for instance, flatly rejected the divinity of Christ and the continuity of the Church's teachings. G.K. Chesterton directly challenged Wells's view of history in *The Everlasting Man*, a book that (as we will see in chapter 11) Tolkien greatly appreciated.

Despite his sharply differing views on matters theological, Tolkien held Wells's science fiction in high regard. In *The Notion Club Papers*, Tolkien has a character describe H.G. Wells as one of "the forgotten Old Masters"[30] of science fiction, indicating both Tolkien's positive view of the author and his deep knowledge of the genre, past and present. This section of *The Notion Club Papers* includes a thoughtful commentary on the gravity-repelling "cavorite" invented by the fictional Dr. Cavor in *The First Men in the Moon* (1901). Elsewhere, Tolkien speaks highly of the "enchantment of distance" created in *The Time Machine*, despite the fact that the Machine itself is "preposterous and incredible."[31] He also knew Wells's short story "The Man Who Could Work Miracles," in which he found an inaccurate use of the word "miracles."[32] A note about "Mr Snooks" in Tolkien's linguistic doodling suggests that he may also have been acquainted with the satiric tale "Miss Winchelsea's Heart."[33]*

Tolkien brought his knowledge of Wells to bear on his academic work. In "On Fairy-stories," Tolkien draws on an aspect of *The Time Machine* that intrigued him (its description of future humanity having evolved into two sub-species: the surface-dwelling, child-like Eloi, and the subterranean Morlocks who cannibalistically exploit them as livestock) to highlight the dangers of condescending to children in their reading: "Let us not divide the human race into Eloi and Morlocks: pretty children . . . with their fairytales (carefully pruned), and dark Morlocks tending their machines."[34] He also

---

* In Wells's tale, the snobbish Miss Winchelsea objects to the vulgar-sounding name of her suitor, Snooks. A less etymologically finicky friend marries him instead and convinces him to change his name to Sevenoaks, from which Snooks derives. Wells's ironic intersection of the social and the etymological is suggestive of Tolkien's snobbish Sackville-Bagginses, whose name, Tom Shippey observes, reflects their reaction against the resolutely middle-class name of Bilbo's Bag End (*The Road to Middle-earth*, 82). This story appears in the same 1927 anthology as "The Man Who Could Work Miracles."

uses Wells's tale to explain a point of comparative mythology in another lecture. Tolkien observes that, unlike the Norse gods who battle against monsters alongside men, the Greek gods are allied with, even akin to, such monsters: "Their race is rather like that far off vision of men in Wells's *Time Machine* divided into two, the fair who live in the sun, and the dark cannibals beneath the earth, beautiful and hideous yet of one origin."[35] Tolkien's use of these references shows how his academic expertise and his awareness of popular culture were not kept in hermetically sealed compartments, any more than were his creative writing and his modern reading. His scholarly work, like his imaginative enterprises, engaged with the contemporary world.

✿ "With some pleasure": Joseph O'Neill's *Land Under England*

The Irish author Joseph O'Neill (1886–1953) enjoyed moderate popularity in his day, with five novels to his credit; *Land Under England* (1935) is the only one to remain in print. Tolkien read it soon after its publication, remarking that he considered it a good example of 'feigned history,' a science-fiction sub-genre of which he said he was "extremely fond." He read it "with some pleasure," although he also called it "weak" and "distasteful to me in many points."[36] Although hardly fulsome praise, it demonstrates again the breadth of his reading and confirms how ready and able he was, at least earlier in his life, to enjoy even flawed examples of the genre.

The title of *Land Under England* sums up its premise: a young man, searching for his vanished explorer father, discovers an entrance into an extensive world below ground. Here he encounters a totalitarian civilization created by the descendants of ancient Romans. As we saw in chapter 7, Tolkien had a strong dislike of the Roman Empire and indeed of all totalitarian rule, imperial or otherwise; the fact that this 'lost world' story casts imperial Romans as villains would have made it more to his taste.

The members of this subterranean State use telepathic communication and are dominated by a few "Masters of Knowledge" and "Masters of Will"; most people have their individuality submerged into the communal mind, and function as automata. The narrator's first encounter with the State results in his capture by sailors and subsequent mental interrogation. Looking into the eyes of the ship's commander, the narrator finds them "vacuous . . . yet penetrative like searchlights . . . turned on me in a fixed, paralysing stare. . . . They seemed to hold and dominate me with an almost sickening effect." Suddenly he realizes with horror that he is being mentally "invaded": "It would be impossible for anyone who has not experienced it to understand the sense of violation that I felt when I found another mind in possession of mine, overpowering it, seizing my will, laying hands on my personality."[37]

Here we see a mind-to-mind struggle between a practiced dominating force and a seemingly weak prisoner. In a later scene the narrator, having resisted the first blast of attack, is attacked again:

> I don't know how long our eyes were locked in that struggle, but to me
> then it seemed an eternity. Time had ceased. Everything had ceased, ex-
> cept those eyes that tore at me. I could feel waves of some strange power
> pouring over me. I was giving way. . . . I would rather die than give way.
> Straightaway my mind sprang up. Some force seemed to rush to its aid
> from the depths of my personality. It was as if my soul had come into
> action and flung into the contest powers greater than my own.[38]

The imagery of mental assault is suggestive both of the attack by Sauron on Pippin
through the *palantír*, and of the struggle that Frodo experiences when he puts on the
Ring at the summit of Tol Brandir and senses the "fierce eager will" of the Eye of Sauron
seeking him out:

> He heard himself crying out: *Never, never!* Or was it: *Verily I come, I come
> to you?* He could not tell. Then as a flash from some other point of power
> there came to his mind another thought: *Take it off! Take it off! Fool, take
> it off! Take off the Ring!* The two powers strove in him. For a moment,
> perfectly balanced between their piercing points, he writhed, tormented.
> Suddenly he was aware of himself again, Frodo, neither the Voice nor the
> Eye: free to choose, and with one remaining instant in which to do so. He
> took the Ring off his finger.[39]

O'Neill's scene of mental invasion and resistance offers several points of resemblance to
this passage in *The Fellowship of the Ring*. We see, for instance, the narrator is divided in
his own inner self: "I was giving way. . . . I would rather die than give way," just as Frodo
finds himself unsure of whether his cry is rejection or acceptance of Sauron's will. It is
particularly notable that in both cases a "power" apart from the narrator's conscious self
comes to his aid at the moment of need. Rescue for both O'Neill's narrator and Frodo
comes suddenly and unexpectedly – with a "rush," in a "flash," respectively. Most intriguingly, in both cases, this rescuing power is unidentifiable, but is perceived as simultaneously outside and inside the character's own self. For O'Neill's narrator, it is "some
force" from within his own "personality" or "soul," yet it cannot be totally identified with
his own inner self, because it brings to the struggle "powers greater than [his] own." For
Frodo, the Voice comes "from some other point of power," yet it manifests itself in him as
a "thought," and in his moment of clarity, he describes the two forces in terms of his own
identity: "Suddenly he was aware of himself again, Frodo, neither the Voice nor the Eye."

The idea of mind control is an important element in the plot of *Land Under
England*. Although much of the story is unremarkable, these depictions of mental attack
and resistance, especially combined with the images of the totalitarian underground
State, may well have provided Tolkien with material that he would draw on in his imagining of Sauron's control of Mordor and his assault on the hobbits and their homeland.[40]

❧ Influence-by-opposition on a cosmic scale: Olaf Stapledon

We now turn to science fiction of a more philosophical bent, beginning with the work of the British philosopher Olaf Stapledon (1886–1950). Although little known today, he was once a prominent cultural figure, who used fiction to present his ideas on ethics to a popular audience. Tolkien's mention of Stapledon in *The Notion Club Papers* (in which he loosely dramatizes the Inklings' discussions) undoubtedly reflects his work having been brought up in the group's conversations. Indeed, C.S. Lewis named Stapledon as a direct influence on his writing of *Out of the Silent Planet*, and Roger Lancelyn Green includes him in his literary study *Into Other Worlds* (1958).

Tolkien knew *Last Men in London* (1932), and thus probably had read *Last and First Men* (1930), the book to which it is a sequel.[41] Both novels use the conceit of having been dictated by a Neptunian from the far future, a member of the eighteenth and last species of humanity, who can project his thoughts across space and time into a human's mind, experience life through it, and manipulate the attitudes and actions of that person. *Last and First Men* follows the whole future history of the human race, from the present day to two billion years hence; the more satiric *Last Men in London* focuses on the Neptunian's telepathic habitation of a single man in present-day London.

Stapledon's "telepathic notion" that allowed the Neptunian to narrate the books interested Tolkien; in *The Notion Club Papers*, he has the character Ramer comment that it "worked pretty well" but was "too vague. . . . *how* does the mind travel through Space or Time, while the body is static?"[42]* Although Tolkien took up the issue in both *The Notion Club Papers* and *The Lost Road*, he never arrived at a satisfactory resolution to the problem of telepathic travel.

Tolkien's eye would also have been caught by the manner in which Stapledon advanced philosophical and ethical ideas through science fiction. Stapledon even uses the terms "true myth" and "false myth" to describe the operations of fantastic tales like his *Last and First Men*. However, his definition of these terms is radically different than Tolkien's. A true myth, for Stapledon, merely conveys "the highest admirations possible within that culture";[43] he is not interested in questions of supernatural reality. Furthermore, the 'myth' of both novels is secular-humanist with a strong progressive bent. *Last Men in London* consistently attacks Christian sexual morality and presents a point of view completely at odds both with what Tolkien believed about marriage as a Catholic and about the importance of marriage in civil society.

Tolkien's interest in Stapledon's work demonstrates his willingness to pay attention to authors whose views differed in very significant ways from his own. It may also provide an example of influence-by-opposition, for if Stapledon could promote anti-Catholic

---

* Kristine Larsen notes a number of similarities in "the space and time travel mechanisms of Tolkien's and Stapledon's works" ("Lessons of Myth, Mortality, & the Machine in the Dream State Space-Time Travel Tales of J.R.R. Tolkien and Olaf Stapledon," 183). See also Larsen, "From Dunne to Desmond: disembodied time travel in Tolkien, Stapledon, and *Lost*."

ideas through popular fiction, could not Tolkien promote Catholic ideas in the same manner? Moreover, the success of Stapledon's tales suggested a willingness on the part of readers to embrace fictional worlds that ventured outside typical narrative parameters. Readers willing to follow the development of no fewer than eighteen human species over two billion years, with no appreciable plot, would surely be capable of following the stories that formed the Silmarillion.

✣ "Powerful" and "mythical": David Lindsay's *A Voyage to Arcturus*

Another author who addressed philosophical themes in his fiction, and like Wells and Stapledon did so from a non- or even anti-Christian perspective, was David Lindsay (1876–1945). Tolkien notes in 1938 that he read Lindsay's novel *A Voyage to Arcturus* "with avidity" and favorably compares it to C.S. Lewis's recently written *Out of the Silent Planet*, saying that Lindsay's novel is "both more powerful and more mythical" – but he goes on to say that it is also "less rational, and also less of a story."[44] What sort of book was this?

A Voyage to Arcturus (1920) was the only one of Lindsay's five novels that established any sort of readership for him, though even this sold poorly.* In order to reference it in his letter of 1938, Tolkien must have seen the first, 1920 Methuen edition. Quite possibly, he had been lent the book by Lewis, who had read it around 1935.[45] Significantly, Tolkien later acquired a copy of his own, as one of the books from his personal library sold after his death was the 1946 Gollancz reprint.[46]

A Voyage to Arcturus is a deeply weird book; Roger Lancelyn Green calls it "vividly real but frighteningly incomprehensible," and critic E.H. Visiak describes the experience of reading as "violently disturbing. The reader's very intellect is assailed; his imagination is appalled."[47] Simply the fact that Tolkien liked it – and liked it well enough to get his own copy – shows that his tastes in reading were more adventurous and more complex than we tend to assume.

The story follows Maskull, a man eager for adventure. Along with his friend Nightspore, he attends a séance, during which a stranger, Krag, bursts in and kills the protoplasmic body that the medium had summoned. Subsequently, Maskull accepts Krag's offer to travel to Tormance, a planet of the star Arcturus. After a journey via crystal torpedo, Maskull awakens to find himself strangely transformed: a third eye (of sorts) has appeared on his forehead, knob-like protrusions project from his neck, and a tentacle has emerged from his chest. A kindly woman, who gives him a blood transfusion to help him adjust to the tremendous gravity of Tormance, tells him about Crystalman, the god of their planet, whom she believes to be good. As Maskull journeys throughout Tormance, each area produces physiological changes in his organs, and nearly everywhere that he goes he murders someone or causes someone's death. Later, reuniting

---

* The 1920 edition was "a plain flop. . . . 596 copies were sold and 834 'remaindered.'" Victor Gollancz, "Publisher's Note," *A Voyage to Arcturus* (London: Victor Gollancz Ltd., 1946), 5.

with Krag, Maskull learns that Crystalman is evil, and is defeating the true divine force called Muspel. The confusion and suffering experienced by Maskull (not to mention the reader) has been part of his enlightenment. Maskull dies, and then mysteriously is, or becomes, Nightspore (who had seemingly been left behind on Earth); he is then sent back to Earth, where he experiences a vision of Crystalman feeding on Muspel-energy. Maskull/Nightspore perceives that Muspel, far from being all-powerful, is fighting for survival against "sin masquerading as eternal beauty, against baseness masquerading as nature, against the Devil masquerading as God." He determines that he must participate in this "grim death-struggle,"[48] and returns to the planet of Tormance to continue the fight against Crystalman.

What on Earth (so to speak) does it all mean? Even those critics who have ventured to discuss the book are not entirely sure. Visiak points out "the resemblance of the Arcturan to the Buddhistic teleology" in the way that "beauty and pleasure are opposed to sublimity."[49] Galad Elflandsson writes that Lindsay was a mystic who held that "life as we live it is an illusion, a battleground between *real* reality and the snaring, evil deceit of beauty that masquerades as goodness."[50]*

As an imagined secondary world, the planet Tormance feels genuinely alien. Tolkien would naturally have been interested in Lindsay's world-creation, which included making Arcturus into a double-star system, containing one blue and one yellow sun.[51] With his keen interest in astronomy, as we have already noted, it would not have escaped Tolkien's attention that the color of a star is more than a merely aesthetic feature. The jotted phrase "Blue Sun" in an early draft of his lecture "On Fairy-stories" may well owe its presence to Lindsay.[52] Indeed, Lindsay makes it a significant element in the construction of his imagined world, in which the blue sun Alppain has two additional primary colors, ulfire and jale, which have philosophical significance in the tale.

Tolkien's praise for *A Voyage to Arcturus* addresses its overall tone and engagement with philosophical issues: that it is "mythical" and that "no one could read it merely as a thriller and without interest in philosophy, religion and morals."[53] He was attentive to these topics being explored in the medium of fiction, and Lindsay's novel would have been especially interesting in that its philosophy is mostly enacted rather than didactic. Comparing it with Lewis's *Out of the Silent Planet*, Tolkien calls it more "powerful," in the sense of presenting a strong and distinctive literary flavor, and "mythical," in the sense of having a dreamlike quality. But it is also "less of a story": its primary interest resides in the ideas and atmosphere, not in the plot (a string of unconnected incidents) or the characters (most of whom are unpleasant, and all of whom are undeveloped).

Tolkien's interest in *A Voyage to Arcturus* also illustrates his abiding concern with the inner consistency of reality in secondary worlds. In *The Notion Club Papers*, the character Guildford (who loosely represents Tolkien himself†) dislikes spaceships be-

---

* Elflandsson points out that by the end of his life, Lindsay's own "fatalism was grown so great that he actually died from blood poisoning caused by neglect of his rotting teeth." (8)

† In his notes, Tolkien connects the NCP characters with specific Inklings: Tolkien is

cause he finds them implausible (this is long before Neil Armstrong had landed on the Moon, of course). But, he adds, authors "like Lindsay, or Lewis" offer "a way of escape: into inconsistency, discord. . . . You *can* land on another world in a space-ship and then drop that nonsense, if you've got something better to do there than most of the earlier writers had." Guildford goes on to argue that the crystal torpedo and back rays by which Maskull arrives on Tormance are "unnecessary"; a better method would have been "the séance connexion; or the suggestion of the dark tower at the end."[54] Here we find Tolkien exploring one of his abiding concerns: the creation of a world so convincing and integrated that the reader's belief in it can be easily maintained. It was so important to him to avoid any kind of unevenness that he revised an entire chapter of *The Lord of the Rings* to correct an inconsistency in the phases of the moon, and agonized over whether to revise the cosmology of the legendarium to include a scientifically accurate round world rather than the initial flat world of the mythology.[55] He was, at least in some ways, more forgiving as a reader than as a writer.

🦋 Almost an Inkling: E.R. Eddison

We move now into the borderlands between the philosophical and the mythopoeic in science fiction with a figure who was personally known to Tolkien. Eric Rücker Eddison (1882–1945) was a British civil servant best known today for *The Worm Ouroboros* (1922), a tale of heroic adventure on the planet Mercury. His writing also included the Zimiamvian trilogy of *Mistress of Mistresses* (1935), *A Fish Dinner in Memison* (1941), and the posthumously published *The Mezentian Gate* (1958). These peculiar novels, set in the fantasy world of Zimiamvia, involve science-fictional elements such as multiple universes and psychic travel. Although not regarded formally as a member of the Inklings, Eddison attended two of its meetings in the mid 1940s, with Tolkien in attendance on both occasions. On his first visit, he read from his recently published *A Fish Dinner in Memison*; on his second, from the manuscript of *The Mezentian Gate*, with Tolkien noting its "power and felicity of expression."[56]

Tolkien proclaimed himself familiar with "all that E.R. Eddison wrote," and praised him as "the greatest and most convincing writer of 'invented worlds' that I have read," whose works he consumed "with great enjoyment for their sheer literary merit."[57] These plaudits are particularly interesting in view of his equally strong opposition to what he called Eddison's "peculiarly bad" views; he believed that Eddison "was coming to admire . . . arrogance and cruelty" under the influence of "an evil and indeed silly 'philosophy.'"[58] The disagreement was mutual: Tolkien says that "Eddison thought what I admire 'soft' (his word: one of complete condemnation, I gathered)."[59] The two men may well have locked horns at the first Inklings gathering that Eddison attended, which was evidently

---

Latimer, later called Guildford. Lewis is Franks/Frankley (HOME IX, 150). In a touch of self-deprecation, Tolkien gives Guildford a dislike for both heroic warriors and "hideous" science-fiction magazines (164).

rather lively. A few days after this meeting, Eddison wrote to Lewis to express his appreciation for the experience and also to offer an oblique apology for apparently excessive zeal
in argument. In the mock-Elizabethan style that he and Lewis employed in their correspondence, he wrote: "I tasted wisdome as wel as good ale at your fireside, all be it, I am
much afeared, pouring you out on my parte some provokements in exchange, & talking
sometimes indeed as a man will write at a first drafting, or with purpose but to flush a
quarry & see whose falcon . . . will mount swiftliest highe enow to strike it downe."[60]

What ideas of Eddison's might Tolkien have found objectionable? His philosophy,
especially embodied in the Zimiamvian stories, is consciously pagan or pantheistic: he
explains that "God is protean. . . . In which of his manifestations we worship him – or
them – is to be determined by our idiosyncrasies, upbringing, & personal preference."[61]
Eddison conceived of the universe as engaged in a constant and eternal struggle between
the opposing principles of 'Zeus' and 'Aphrodite,' noting that Zimiamvia "had to contain
an element of evil" because it is "a heaven of *action*."[62] Goodness is equated with stagna-
tion and boredom. Both the pantheism and the dualism of this view (which holds to the
necessity of evil) would have run contrary to Tolkien's Catholic faith, which maintains
that God and creation are distinct, and that God's perfect goodness has no ontologically
equivalent opposite. Tolkien also held that suffering is morally serious, as evinced to an
infinite extent by the sacrifice of Christ on the cross, and would therefore have rejected
Eddison's treatment of the problem of evil. In an introductory note explaining his views,
Eddison says that suffering can be seen as "amusing" if we truly believe in immortality.
Traumatic experiences, he suggests, can be held lightly, as if they were "episodes invented
perhaps, and then laid aside, as we ourselves might conceive and in a few minutes later
reject again some theory of the universe, in conversation after supper."[63] With regard to
their respective handling of the problem of pain, it is perhaps worth noting that Tolkien
saw front-line service in the Great War whereas Eddison worked for the Board of Trade
throughout the war years.

Despite their philosophical differences, Tolkien was able to appreciate Eddison's
literary creations, of which *The Worm Ouroboros* is the best known, a story of high adventure on the planet Mercury, where mighty lords participate in an eternally repeating
cycle of war against their enemies. (See figure 22.) Proper names are one of the most
distinctive aspects of the novel: the Lord Gro, the Lord Brandoch Daha, Gorice the
King, the mountains of Koshtra Pivarcha and Koshtra Belorn, Melikaphkhaz, and (in-
congruously) Demonland as a home for the protagonists. Tolkien was not impressed. He
declared that even those few people who take name creation seriously "have no notion
how to set about making a group of names or supposed alien words that belong to (and
feel and look like belonging to) a real language with a definite character of its own." The
results are often "childish" or "absolutely appalling. . . . E.R. Eddison is a notable example, all the more because he was a great writer."[64]

Tolkien's declaration that Eddison "was certainly not an 'influence,'" which we discussed in chapter 2, seems to be accurate in the sense of a direct positive influence.

Eddison could not have had any formative effect on the creation of the legendarium, since Tolkien points out that he read the books "long after they appeared."[65] But he had read them at least by the 1940s, which allows for some influence in other ways. Perhaps seeing the failure of tone in names like "Demonland," "Witchland," and "Impland" helped him let go of "Bingo," "Trotter," and "Bladorthin." Eddison's choice to call his world "Mercury" also prompted a clarification as to the nature of Middle-earth. Tolkien is very firm that his own Middle-earth is another name for a region of the real world; his tales are set "in a period of the actual Old World of this planet." He draws a specific contrast, saying that Middle-earth "is not a name of a never-never land without relation to the world we live in (like the Mercury of Eddison)."[66]

On a constructive note, Tolkien would likely have been interested by the writing of a heroic epic for the modern day, as well as by the fact that Eddison's imagined Mercury has a well-developed history and culture. *The Worm Ouroboros* even includes a lengthy appendix, an "Argument: with Dates" that presents key points of Mercurial history. Appendices were not common features of novels at that time, and perhaps Eddison's example encouraged Tolkien in his own inclusion of no fewer than six at the end of *The Return of the King*.[67]

Sacramental theology and spiritual thrillers: Charles Williams

Thus far in this chapter we have seen that disagreement with an author on philosophical or moral grounds did not, in Tolkien's mind, necessarily entail disapprobation on literary grounds. This context helps us to approach the work of Charles Williams (1886–1945), who is, after Lewis and Tolkien, the best-known of the Inklings. Tolkien once described Williams as "a comet that appeared out of the blue, passed through the little 'provincial' Oxford solar system, and went out again into the unknown."[68] Williams had become friends with C.S. Lewis in 1936; three years later, when Williams's employer, the Oxford University Press, moved its London staff to Oxford for safety during the war, Lewis and Tolkien arranged for him to be able to lecture at the university, despite his not having a degree. Though a relative latecomer to the Inklings, he swiftly became an integral part of it, until his sudden and unexpected death just after V.E. Day.

Williams considered himself primarily a poet; on his gravestone in Holywell Cemetery in Oxford is inscribed "Poet" and the words "Under the Mercy," his oft-used prayer-like valediction in letters and conversations. He also produced literary biographies, studies on Dante, works of theology, and plays, some of which were commissioned for literary festivals such as the Canterbury Festival. However, Williams is mostly remembered today for his novels. Although they are difficult to place in any genre, the novels' frequent use of the occult and what we might consider supernatural gadgetry (Tarot cards, the Grail, and so on) align them with the more fantastical side of science fiction (or at least sufficiently for our purposes in this chapter).

Tolkien said he had read "a good many" of these seven novels, including *The Place of the Lion* (1931).[69] He recognized some merit to Williams's writings, but did not enjoy them, remarking that "in spite of things in them which seemed to me memorable, I neither liked nor understood his novels and poetry."[70] At Inklings meetings, Tolkien listened to Williams reading aloud drafts of his works in progress: they included *All Hallows' Eve* (1945) and extracts from a long sequence of Arthurian poems, which left him profoundly unimpressed.[71] It is quite a common reaction to these poems, which are extremely ornate, full of obscure allusions, and colored by his strange brand of mysticism. Tolkien's assessment was not based solely on hearing it read aloud, for he also owned a copy of *The Region of the Summer Stars* (1944), a collection of Arthurian poems dealing mainly with Arthur in Britain and with the Grail quest. Along with this volume, Tolkien owned *Arthurian Torso* (1948),[72] which comprises Williams's unfinished prose work *The Figure of Arthur* and a commentary by C.S. Lewis attempting to explicate his approach to the Arthuriad. It seems not to have convinced Tolkien, who said forthrightly: "I disliked [Williams's] whole Arthurian business with great intensity and considered it rather nonsense."[73]

However, Tolkien's expressions of dislike specifically refer to Williams's "novels and poetry," which constituted only a portion of his prolific output. Tolkien also heard or read a number of Williams's plays, including *Terror of Light*,[74] set at the first Pentecost and featuring the ghost of Judas Iscariot, and *The House of the Octopus*, in which the demonic Marshal of P'o L'u attempts to invade a Pacific island and destroy the Christian faith of its people, and is opposed by the Flame, the "Lingua Coeli." (See figure 23.) Tolkien seems to have had a more favorable view of the latter play than of any other of Williams's works. In *The Notion Club Papers* (1945), Tolkien includes a wry commentary on how the Inklings' writings will be largely forgotten in the future. When it comes to Williams, Guildford remarks that "few even of the Twentieth Century experts could have named any work of Williams, except perhaps *The Octopus*. That was still occasionally played, because of the great revival of missionary interest after the Far-eastern martyrdoms in the sixties."[75]

His personal relationship with Williams was complex. He got on well with him in the company of the Inklings, and expressed a liking for him. Nonetheless, a certain feeling of tension often comes across in his comments.[76] In this connection, Tolkien's poem addressed to Williams is of interest. It begins and ends with genuine warmth, in praise of "Our dear Charles Williams," and acknowledges the value of much that he wrote: "play, preface, life, short verse, review or note."[77] However, the poem is sharply critical of his Arthurian poetry. Tolkien is particularly acerbic with regard to his positioning of a picture of a woman's naked body over the map of Europe, which appears in the endpapers of his *Taliessin Through Logres*.[78] The poem is an oddly conflicted one, in which Tolkien takes himself to task for squandering thirty lines on fault-finding in a poem intended to praise. He even asks the self-reflective question, "What's biting you? Dog in the Manger's fleas?"[79] This fretful back-and-forth is very different from the wholeheartedly appreciative poem Tolkien wrote for another of his literary friends, W.H. Auden, despite the fact that their relationship also had moments of friction.[80]

Given Tolkien's slightly strained attitude toward Williams, it is not surprising that he should have declared, "Williams had no conceivable influence on me."[81] Here, Tolkien is undoubtedly referring to direct, positive literary effects, and in that sense his disavowal of influence is accurate.* However, influence can also take the form of resistance. Recognizing that another writer's work is not to one's liking can provide both motivation to do things differently and clarity on how to do it.

What was Tolkien's objection to Williams's novels, which he calls "dreadful"?[82] We can be reasonably sure it was not on the grounds of their being 'spiritual thrillers.' As we saw in chapter 6, Tolkien enjoyed the works of John Buchan, whose stories often include strange or supernatural characters or events intruding into the ordinary world. He approved of the genre in principle and was sufficiently interested to survey Williams's efforts in the field, even if he did not like the final product.

One possible reason for Tolkien's dislike of these novels is the overt presence of theological elements within them. The key word here is *overt*. As discussed in chapters 4 and 5, he did not enjoy Christian allegory that he considered too obvious, as with the Narnia books, but could appreciate stories that handled religion more subtly. Indeed, we will see shortly that he admired Lewis's *Out of the Silent Planet* and *Perelandra* and had no objection to the appearance of angels and Christian theology in those tales, where they are carefully smuggled in and not easily identified as such.

Williams's approach would perhaps have grated, not so much because his theology was at times questionable in its orthodoxy, but because he takes such an odd, angular, even shocking approach to presenting the supernatural. Verlyn Flieger points out a "striking disparity between his avowed Christian impulse and his focus on the occult and the demonic."[83] The plot of *War in Heaven* centers upon attempts to control the Holy Grail (the chalice used by Jesus at the Last Supper), and includes a detailed account of a Satanic rite. *Descent into Hell* gives a psychologically realistic internal portrait of a man choosing and experiencing damnation. *All Hallows' Eve* features a dead woman who is not quite sure that she is dead, and a disturbingly effective false preacher. In *The Place of the Lion*, Platonic archetypes erupt into our world, wreaking havoc. A common thread through all of these thrillers is that the experience of the supernatural in ordinary life (whether for good or for bad) is disturbing, unsettling, even alienating.

Such an emphasis would have run contrary to Tolkien's sense of the importance of natural theology, in which God is present in and through the natural order, as well as in the supernatural order. It would also have offended against the Catholic principle that 'grace perfects nature,' the belief that the supernatural doesn't descend into nature like a

---

* Kathryne Hall suggests that Saruman may have been influenced by Simon the Magus in *All Hallows Eve*, but the similarities are best accounted for by their similar roles in the story. See "Beings of Magic: A Comparison of Saruman the White in Tolkien's *The Lord of the Rings* and Simon the Clerk in Williams' *All Hallows' Eve*."

pikestaff thrust into a bowl of petals, shattering and disrupting that which it touches, but rather brings nature up to completion in ways that may require conversion, even conversion at great cost, but which are fundamentally harmonious and fulfilling.

Tolkien would also have been temperamentally out of sympathy with Williams's characteristic take on the interface between the natural and supernatural worlds, in which material objects have quasi-divine properties, as in *Many Dimensions* where the Stone of Suleimon is inscribed with the Tetragrammaton and depicted as if it *is* God in some way, or in *The Greater Trumps*, where a set of tarot cards give the user power not just to read the future but to shape it. Tolkien's description of Williams as a "witch-doctor"[84] is telling in this regard. Doctors, like witches and wizards, have their own proper realm of activity, but a witch-doctor confuses these categories, attempting to use natural powers as a tool to manipulate and control divine powers: a kind of mechanization of the supernatural, rather than a sacramentalizing of the natural.

Tolkien knew that skepticism and anti-Christian ideas were becoming more frequently and effectively expressed in popular literature, for he read works by many of these authors – including Wells, Stapledon, and Eddison, whom we have discussed in this chapter, and Matthew Arnold, whom we will encounter in chapter 11. Tolkien would have been aware of the need for Christians to be attentive to how they expressed their faith in works of imaginative literature. In this regard it is useful to bear in mind his seemingly paradoxical statement that *The Lord of the Rings* is "a fundamentally religious and Catholic work; unconsciously so at first, but consciously in the revision. That is why I have not put in, or have cut out, practically all references to anything like 'religion.'"[85] It is an odd statement at face value – he has deliberately made the story "fundamentally religious and Catholic" by *omitting* any references to religious practices or worship by his characters?

Here the contrast with Williams is particularly instructive. The spiritual elements in Williams's thrillers are vividly presented, but they are arguably so fantastically depicted, even lurid, that it becomes difficult to believe that such things really happen outside of a story. The idea of God, or at least of a supernatural dimension to reality, does come through – indeed, Williams is deadly serious on this point – but it is all too easy to take the violent interface between the natural and supernatural as entirely fictional, or as representative of a magical or preternatural realm accessible only to initiates.

Tolkien's approach in *The Lord of the Rings* is quite different. Religion, he says, "is absorbed into the story and the symbolism."[86] In this way, the story's natural theology and its Christian resonances can be expressed without any Williams-style jagged edges between the realms of nature and grace. Tolkien offers rich theological connections below the surface, such as the resemblance of Galadriel to the Virgin Mary (see chapter 8), the Eucharistic quality of the *lembas* bread, the parallel between Frodo's failure at Mount Doom and the petition "lead us not into temptation" in the Lord's Prayer,[87] and the coincidence of certain dates in the history of Middle-earth with those from the liturgical calendar.* All of these elements are so deeply embedded in the story that they

---

* The Fellowship sets out from Rivendell on December 25 (the date of the Nativity of

do not obtrude. The tale, he said, is consciously "built on or out of certain 'religious' ideas, but . . . does not mention them overtly, still less preach them."[88] Built on – but not preached about. Readers with knowledge of these things can notice them and catch the echoes – or not, as they prefer. As he put it, the story "is mainly concerned with [the] Fall, Mortality, and the Machine": the theological foundation of these themes, even when presented implicitly, makes them richly suited for what he called "applicability," which rests in the "freedom of the reader" to make connections.[89]

This profound imaginative paradox – omitting religious elements to make the book more thoroughly Christian – is a deliberate literary and even, we may dare to say, evangelistic strategy, and one that may well have been shaped by friction against Williams's theological thrillers in the key years when Tolkien was writing *The Lord of the Rings*.

❧ "Out of the Talkative Planet": C.S. Lewis

Having discussed C.S. Lewis's Narnia Chronicles in chapter 4, we now turn to examine this author as a writer of science fiction. Lewis is the best-known of Tolkien's friends and colleagues, and his personal impact was incalculable; *The Lord of the Rings* would never have been completed without his encouragement.* However, our concern here is not Lewis's personal influence on Tolkien as his friend and fellow Inkling, but the way that Tolkien responded to Lewis's fiction. He heard *The Screwtape Letters* read aloud at Inklings meetings, and seems to have found the conceit amusing or at least memorable, alluding to the interference of a "minor imp of Slubgob's brood" with regard to plumbing problems in his house.[90] He owned a copy of *Till We Have Faces*,† but unfortunately we have no record of his thoughts on the book.

Of greatest interest to us is Tolkien's view of Lewis's science-fictional Ransom Trilogy, comprised of *Out of the Silent Planet* (1938), *Perelandra* (1943), and *That Hideous Strength* (1945). Tolkien heard the first two of these read aloud at Inklings meetings, and owned copies of all three.[91] He also gave a playful nod to both Lewis and the Ransom books in his unfinished *Notion Club Papers*, titling the manuscript at one stage as "Beyond Lewis, or Out of the Talkative Planet."[92] ‡

David Downing points out that the Ransom Trilogy is difficult to categorize, with some critics preferring "labels such as 'interstellar fantasies'. . . 'cosmic romances' . . . or

---

Christ); the Ring is destroyed on March 25 (the traditional date of the Crucifixion, as well as the date of the Annunciation). Tolkien writes that "Dec. 25 (setting out) and March 25 (accomplishment of quest) were intentionally chosen by me" (LOTR:RC, 264).

  * As Tolkien wrote in 1965, the "unpayable debt" that he owed to Lewis was "sheer encouragement. . . . But for his interest and unceasing eagerness for more I should never have brought The L. of the R. to a conclusion" (*Letters*, 362).

  † It appears on his shelves in a 1966 photograph, along with *Out of the Silent Planet*, *Perelandra*, and *That Hideous Strength*. He owned two copies of *Out of the Silent Planet*, one of which is the edition in figure 24. See also figure 40.

  ‡ Lewis was notoriously talkative. For examples, see Michael Ward, *Planet Narnia*, 285n1.

'space fables.'" This genre-blending characteristic underscores what Downing argues is Lewis's greatest gift as a writer of science fiction: "his ability to recast the motifs of the cosmic voyage into those of spiritual pilgrimage."[93] This mythic style, in which Christian ideas are central to the narrative but generally subsumed within it, was very much to Tolkien's taste. He considered the trilogy "good . . . in itself," although he felt that the Charles Williams flavor of the third book, *That Hideous Strength*, weakened the story.[94] *

Tolkien evidently considered the second book, *Perelandra*, an advance on the earlier volume, for he applauded his daughter Priscilla's "good taste"[95] in preferring it to the first book. Here we may trace an interesting connection to his legendarium. In a 1964 interview, Tolkien compared the Valar, the 'gods' of his legendarium, to the angels of Lewis's Ransom Trilogy, drawing attention to the fact that Lewis and he are both working with the idea of a divine prohibition.[96] Just as the Númenóreans are free to sail anywhere other than westward toward Eressëa and the lands of the Valar, so too the inhabitants of Perelandra may visit the Fixed Land, the only land mass in the oceanic world, as long as they do not stay there overnight. Tolkien and Lewis take the idea in different directions: the Númenóreans rebel and their land is destroyed, while the Queen of Perelandra is able to reach full, unfallen spiritual maturity, thanks to Ransom's defeat of her tempter. But the underlying concept is the same: a reimagining of the fall of man, its circumstances and consequences. Given that Tolkien continued to develop his legendarium long after he read the Ransom Trilogy, it would not be at all surprising if his concept of the Ban of the Valar and the fall of Númenor was shaped in part by his admiration for *Perelandra*. The very fact that, unprompted, he draws a parallel between his work and Lewis's suggests that the Fixed Land had become a fixed point of reference in his imagination.

Even if *Perelandra* eventually became his favorite, Tolkien's highest praise was for the first volume of the trilogy, *Out of the Silent Planet*, which he had read in manuscript. In a letter to Stanley Unwin, whom Tolkien hoped would publish the story, he wrote that he "was so enthralled that I could do nothing else until I had finished it." He goes on to say that the story has "a great number of philosophical and mythical implications that enormously enhanced without detracting from the surface 'adventure,'" and calls this combination "irresistible."[97] † (See figure 24.)

Tolkien declared to Unwin that *Out of the Silent Planet* had "very successfully" passed the "test" of plausibility as a story of a voyage to a strange land.[98] He was of course trying to help his friend get his novel published, and so is likely to have expressed himself with especial warmth; nevertheless, his quibbling about science-fictional transportation methods in *The Notion Club Papers* shows that Tolkien truly did see credibility as a

---

* Clyde Kilby recalled that he found "the ending of *That Hideous Strength* weak and embarrassing" ("Woodland Prisoner," 55).

† Although he says, in a letter to Unwin, that some of Lewis's "items of linguistic invention . . . do not appeal to me," he admits that that is "a matter of taste" and reports that certain details in philology have been "corrected to my satisfaction." He adds that "the theme of three distinct rational species (*hnau*) requires more attention to the third species, Pfifltriggi" (*Letters*, 33). The implication is that he found the portrayal of the other two species acceptable.

necessary test. In that story, Guildford and Frankley (the Lewis stand-in) agree that the plot mechanism of having Ransom kidnapped by Weston and Devine is "not bad," which translated into American usage means 'very good.'[99] *

Out of the Silent Planet was Lewis's share of the agreement or 'wager' with Tolkien to write the sort of science-fiction tale they enjoyed. Although, as we mentioned above, Tolkien never completed his side of the bargain, it was not without effect: he later pointed out that the "Númenórean-Atlantis theme" from *The Lost Road* made its way into *The Lord of the Rings*.[100] Lewis's tale served, at the least, as an instance of influence-by-example, encouraging Tolkien to have a go at a new genre and showing how plausibility could be successfully blended with mythic resonance.

Enter the Ents

Out of the Silent Planet was a book that Tolkien thought well of and that stimulated his creative energies, but did it have any specific influence on his legendarium? Perhaps surprisingly, the answer is 'yes.'

The Ents are among the most intriguing and mysterious beings in Middle-earth. They appear for the first time in the fourth chapter of *The Two Towers*, which Tolkien recalled that he wrote without planning ahead. The Tree-folk, he said, "presented themselves to my sight, without premeditation or any previous conscious knowledge."[101] Tolkien did not at first know what to make of these new creatures, of whom Treebeard is the prime example. In the supporting materials for *The Lord of the Rings* appears a page of notes which sheds some light on the question. Under a heading "Notes for *Treebeard*," he asks, "Are the Tree-folk ('Lone-walkers') *hnau* that might have gone tree-like, or trees that have become *hnau*?"[102] †

The word "*hnau*" is crucially important here. It is Lewis's invention, and appears in *Out of the Silent Planet*. Ransom, having landed on Malacandra (that is, Mars) and been befriended by the alien hrossa (creatures roughly like a six-foot tall otter), learns that their word *hnau* means 'rational, incarnate being,' of which there are three races: the hrossa, the sorns, and the pfifltriggi. Humans are also *hnau* – at least potentially, for as the story goes on, we realize that *hnau* also includes a moral dimension: *hnau* do not kill or mistreat other *hnau*. Ransom is recognized as *hnau*, but Weston and Devine, the

---

* In *Out of the Silent Planet*, Weston tells Ransom that it is no good trying to explain how the space-ship works: "Unless you were one of the four or five real physicists now living you couldn't understand. . . . If it makes you happy to repeat words that don't mean anything – which is, in fact, what unscientific people want when they ask for an explanation – you may say we work by exploiting the less observed properties of solar radiation." Lewis thus provides a sop to the reader, while also indulging in a touch of satire on the use of techno-babble in science-fiction stories.

† Tolkien confessed that he had "no recollection of inventing Ents" (*Letters*, 231), but he also says that they "grew rather out of their name" (*Letters*, 208), the name 'Ent' being an Anglo-Saxon word for 'giant.' The apparent incompatibility of these two accounts reminds us that the process of creativity can be obscure, even to the author himself, and certainly leaves room for the influence of Lewis's sorns.

scientists who have come to Malacandra intending to dominate and exploit the planet, are only half-*hnau*; they murder Ransom's hrossa friend and are willing to exterminate whole races to gain their ends. Tolkien's use of this word to muse over his Ents reveals the nature of what he was debating: the Ents are rational and can use language, but to what extent are they also morally responsible beings?

The Ents certainly prove to be *hnau* in their treatment of Merry and Pippin and their response to Saruman's villainy. Exploring the question with this concept in mind very probably also helped Tolkien to develop the idea of the huorns. If the Ents are "trees that have become *hnau*," having been first woken up by the Elves and taught to speak, the Huorns are Ents who are losing their *hnau* character, retaining the ability to speak but with a diminished or unstable moral sense. As Merry describes them, "They still have voices . . . but they have become queer and wild. Dangerous. I should be terrified of meeting them, if there were no true Ents about to look after them."

The connection runs even deeper. Having come to know the hrossa, Ransom is later sent to a member of the second race on Malacandra, the sorn named Augray, who will help him on his journey. Here, for the first time, we see a sorn up close, and in Ransom's interactions with Augray, we find a striking note of resemblance between the sorns and the Ents.

The sorns, or *séroni* as they as called in the hrossa language, are generally solitary, living in caves on the highlands of Malacandra. They are giant creatures, humanoid but angular: when seated, Augray's "knees rose high above its shoulders on each side of its head." Its mode of walking is equally distinctive: "It lifted its feet very high and set them down very gently. Ransom was reminded alternately of a cat stalking, a strutting barn-door fowl, and a high-stepping carriage horse." It moves quickly, "between six and seven miles an hour." Its face is "solemn," its hands "fan-shaped, seven-fingered, mere skin over bone like a bird's leg and quite cold." Its voice "boomed" at Ransom, and other sorns "exchange a horn-like greeting" as they pass.[103]

Turning back to Treebeard, we find that, like Augray, he is "at least fourteen foot high" and his feet "had seven toes each." Like the sorns, he has a strange gait: he "stalked" with "long deliberate strides." He resembles the sorn in angularity, but, as befits a tree-herd, he is stiffer and more vertical in posture. Just like a sorn, he has a "booming" voice and makes a "horn-call" to the other Ents.

We find, too, intriguing parallels between hobbit-Ent and human-sorn interactions. The first conversation between Ransom and Augray has to do with names: where Ransom came from, and what he and his species are called. Augray then carries Ransom to meet Oyarsa at what turns out to be a great gathering, with Ransom riding on the sorn's shoulder. Disconcerting as this mode of travel is, he soon finds that it is "surprisingly comfortable"; in fact, "ludicrous and even tender associations came crowding into his mind. It was like riding an elephant at the zoo in boyhood – like riding on his father's back at a still earlier age."[104] Treebeard's dealings with Merry and Pippin follow very much the same pattern: they first discuss names; then he takes them on a journey to a gathering of Ents, the Entmoot, stopping along the way to allow them to eat and rest. Merry and Pippin travel with him first by riding in his arms, and later on his shoulders. In so doing, they "felt, oddly enough, safe and comfortable."

In short, Treebeard in particular, and the Ents in general, are curiously like the sorns of Lewis's imagined Mars – in appearance, voice, manner, and even initial interactions with a new species. The fact that Tolkien drew directly on Lewis's idea of the *hnau* to shape the concept of the Ents as sentient, morally responsible beings makes it not just possible but probable that these additional resemblances are no mere accident, but rather emerged from his unconscious assimilation of a striking element in a tale he had greatly enjoyed a few years earlier. It is worth noting in this context that, according to Nevill Coghill, Tolkien "modelled Treebeard's way of speaking, '*Hrum, Hroom*', on the boom- ing voice of C.S. Lewis."[105] Both *Out of the Silent Planet* and its author appear to have been a factor in the creation of one of Middle-earth's most memorable characters.

ꙮ Conclusion

In this chapter, our exploration of Tolkien's reading of science fiction began with uncover- ing his surprisingly relaxed views on technology. This biographical detail contributes to the overall picture of a man whose tastes and attitudes were not nearly as narrow as the popular image would have us believe. For Tolkien to have had a hearty and life-long relish for science fiction was no great departure from character.

We have examined Tolkien's views on H.G. Wells as one of the "Old Masters" of the genre, and considered his reading of authors with very different philosophical views from his own, notably Olaf Stapledon and E.R. Eddison. We have seen that Joseph O'Neill's novel of an underground civilization, *Land Under England*, may have provided Tolkien with material for the powerful scene of Sauron's mental assault on Frodo. We have considered how David Lindsay's strange, surreal novel *A Voyage to Arc- turus* sheds light on Tolkien's approach to presenting ideas in fiction. We have noted how the spiritual thrillers of Charles Williams served as an influence-by-opposition and have suggested that this influence helps to explain a seeming paradox in Tolkien's expressed views about the Christian element in *The Lord of the Rings*. And we have re- turned to C.S. Lewis, whose science-fiction trilogy Tolkien admired, despite his mixed views about Narnia, and have found that the first of these novels probably contributed to his creation of the Ents.

The breadth of Tolkien's science-fictional reading and the variety of influences that we have examined in this chapter tell us something valuable about his creativity. Middle-earth is a prescientific, preindustrial world; we do not usually think of it as a science-fictional place. Nevertheless, Tolkien was content to have *The Lord of the Rings* categorized as "science fiction," observing that this was a "valid" description, in that "the pleasure of 'wonder' is also produced by good science fiction, and that this pleasure must be one of the aims of the author."[106]

With an awareness of his fairly neutral views about technology in itself – over against the abuse thereof, which roused him to a passion – it is worth considering that Tolkien's premodern Middle-earth does not represent an avoidance of modern technology, but rather an idiosyncratic manner of engaging with the issues raised by it.

Tolkien's willingness to validate the classifying of *The Lord of the Rings* as a kind of science fiction reminds us of how he viewed the relations between science fiction and the genre within which his epic work is normally placed – namely, fantasy. Tolkien observed that science fiction "performs the same operation as fantasy – it provides Recovery and Escape . . . and wonder." But why put it that way round? Could the resemblance not work in the other direction? Seen from the other end, one might equally well claim – as he seems to allow – that fantasy performs the same operation as science fiction, by providing wonder, escape, and recovery. Writers of science fiction, he said, had "replaced the wizard" with the "legendary laboratory professor."[107] What if the author of Middle-earth, like the contrarian he was, simply reversed that process?

✥ 10 ✥

Fine Fabling
Beyond the Walls of the World

I N EARLIER CHAPTERS, WE HAVE ENCOUNTERED MYTHOPOEIC AND
fantastic tales in the context of children's stories, historical romances, thrillers and
adventures, and science fiction. Yet some tales do not fit comfortably within even these
capacious categories. Stories that blur the boundaries between spirit and matter, that mix
(or seem to mix) the supernatural and the natural, have become less common – perhaps
less respectable – in the modern age. One way of viewing this shift is to understand it
as part of a conflict between 'disenchantment' and 'enchantment.' 'Enchantment' offers
a view of reality in which actions and objects are imbued with objective meaning and
spiritual value; 'disenchantment' rejects this, holding that there is no deeper significance
to our experiences. John Garth observes that the canonized literature of the First World
War fully embraced the disenchanted view of what had transpired in 1914-1918: no
heroism, no meaning, only passive suffering, despair, disillusion, and skepticism.[1]

However, the divide has much deeper roots: first the Protestant Reformation and
then, more decisively, the scientific revolution and the Enlightenment struck blows
against the enchanted model of the cosmos. The Real Presence vanished from the
Mass; the planetary influences disappeared from the heavens; and eventually art and
literature became steadily more 'realistic,' more preoccupied with the empirical and the
immediately sensible. Stories that presented the intermingling of the natural and the preternatural, let alone the supernatural, were increasingly associated with mindsets deemed
medieval, Catholic, prescientific, superstitious. As the eighteenth-century Anglican divine Richard Hurd famously lamented, "what we have gotten by this revolution, you will
say, is a great deal of good sense. What we have lost, is a world of fine fabling."[2]

Fine fabling: stories that present the marvelous, the uncanny, the preternatural; high
romance and Gothic tales; literature that embraces the mystical and numinous, that
finds room for a sacramental view of reality. Here we find writers who, in many cases,
do not fit comfortably into other categories, or who no longer suit our modern tastes as
readers – but who were important to their original readers.

Under the heading of 'fine fabling,' we will encounter a number of authors whom
Tolkien read with interest – and in some cases deeply admired – who are otherwise
all too easily lost to sight. Tolkien read stories of supernatural fiction, including the
Ghost Stories of an Antiquary (1904) by M.R. James,[3] and knew of the work of Sabine

Baring-Gould[4] (1834–1924), an Anglican priest, who is best known for the hymn "Onward, Christian Soldiers," but who was also a novelist and prolific short story writer, with an interest in folklore especially as it related to ghosts and werewolves. He knew the poetry of Wilfred Childe, a friend and colleague at Leeds, who was also the author of *Dream English: A Fantastical Romance* (1917). Writing to Allen and Unwin about Childe as a possible endorser of *The Hobbit*, Tolkien noted that he was at one time well known as a poet "and is still a good one," adding that he is "specially interested in elves and related creatures."[5] On the more horror-tinged side of the fabulous, he had read H.P. Lovecraft's tale "The Doom That Came to Sarnath" (1920) and Clark Ashton Smith's "The Testament of Athammaus" (1932).[6] He once met Walter de la Mare, and had read at least one collection of his stories, *Broomsticks & Other Tales* (1925); he found de la Mare's tales disturbingly indicative of "a much darker and more hopeless" view of the world than his own.[7] He was acquainted with Owen Barfield's poetic drama *Orpheus*,[8] and in 1944 heard Barfield's unpublished play *Medea* read at an Inklings meeting.[9] He read, in manuscript, Roger Lancelyn Green's children's fantasy *The Wonderful Stranger* (1950), in which a magician from ancient Rome is transported to modern-day Liverpool,[10] and appreciated another tale for younger readers, Sterling Lanier's *The War for the Lot: A Tale of Fantasy and Terror* (1969).[11] Tolkien's publisher sent him Joy Chant's young adult fantasy tale *Red Moon and Black Mountain* (1970) for an endorsement, presumably with a reasonable expectation that he might enjoy it, but we do not have a record of his response.[12]

In this chapter, we will consider four 'fine fabulists' who stand out as particularly significant for Tolkien. He was familiar with the ironic, exotic tales of Lord Dunsany, who may well have provided Tolkien with an example for the Silmarillion. He was a great enthusiast for the dreamlike, mystical poetry of Francis Thompson, and we will see that Thompson contributed to certain elements of the legendarium. He read Algernon Blackwood, the prolific author of supernatural fiction, whose idiosyncratic vocabulary helped him devise one of the most important place-names in his entire body of work: "The Crack of Doom." And he had a long-lasting, personal interest in J.H. Shorthouse, whose strange tale *John Inglesant: A Romance* very probably influenced his development of an all-important theme in Middle-earth – namely, pity.

❧ Prolegomena to the Silmarillion: Lord Dunsany's *Book of Wonder*

Although Edward John Moreton Drax Plunkett (1878–1957), the eighteenth Baron of Dunsany, Ireland, is read now only by a niche audience, his work was genuinely popular through the 1920s and 1930s, Tolkien's young adult years. He published more than 150 tales of travel, adventure, fantasy, and the supernatural in the Jorkens series, as well as essays, poetry, and autobiography. His prose fantasy includes the novels *Don Rodríguez: Chronicles of Shadow Valley* (1922) and *The King of Elfland's Daughter* (1924), as well as the collections *The Gods of Pegāna* (1905), and *The Book of Wonder* (1912). A number of his out-of-print titles were revived in the early 1970s as part of Ballantine Books' attempt to capitalize on the popularity of *The Lord of the Rings*. The reprinting of Dunsany's prose fantasy obscures the fact that, in his own time, he was much better known as a playwright: W.B. Yeats thought highly enough of Dunsany's plays to produce several of them, and the BBC commissioned Dunsany to write radio drama.[13]

Tolkien himself drew a clear connection between Dunsany's fiction and his own writings. In 1966, when Clyde Kilby came to Oxford in order to assist with assembling *The Silmarillion*, Tolkien gave him a copy of *The Book of Wonder* "and told him to read it in preparation for his task."[14] (See figure 25.) If in Tolkien's mind Dunsany's tales were essential preparatory reading for Kilby as he got to work on the mythic underpinnings of Middle-earth, it is worth considering what influence they might have had.

Dunsany's approach to conveying the depth of his secondary world may well have made an impression on Tolkien. A recurring feature of Dunsany's fantasy tales is the use, as Raymond Edwards points out, "of unexplained and resonant allusion to names, places, things otherwise unknown or glimpsed at the margins of another picture." He observes that this became "one of the mature Tolkien's favourite narrative techniques, and he probably learnt it first from Dunsany." We see this in many small details in *The Lord of the Rings*, whether mythological, archaeological, or historical: the constellation called "the Swordsman of the Sky, Menelvagor with his shining belt"; the ancient standing-stones known as the Púkel-men that line the road to Dunharrow; the reference to the Battle of Bywater in "The Scouring of the Shire" as "the only battle since the Greenfields, 1147, away up in the Northfarthing." The effectiveness of this allusive technique may have been increased by the fact that Dunsany's early collections, including *The Book of Wonder*, were illustrated by the gifted artist Sidney Sime. (See figure 25.) Tolkien had a very visual imagination, and Sime's delicate, fantastical scenes may have provided a model for some of Tolkien's early efforts in drawing and painting.[15]

Dunsany was, like Tolkien, a war writer. In the preface to *Tales of Wonder*, written while recovering from a war wound, he remarks that "writing in a day when life is cheap, dreams seem to me all the dearer, the only things that survive. Just now the civilization of Europe seems almost to have ceased, and nothing seems to grow in her torn fields but death, yet this is only for a while and dreams will come back again and bloom as of old."[16] Although this attitude echoes that of Tolkien and his friends in the T.C.B.S., determined to continue writing even in the midst of the horrors of the trenches, Dunsany's acid, tongue-in-cheek approach – which Tolkien describes as treating "horror as a grim jest, amusing for itself"[17] – is very different from Tolkien's fundamentally serious attitude toward war, suffering, and death. Nonetheless, the fact of a fellow writer responding to the shared trauma of the Great War with tales of imagined worlds, may well have encouraged him to carry on with his own stories, and, by opposition, to imbue his own stories with the moral seriousness that he felt Dunsany's lacked.

Tolkien took particular note of some stories from *The Book of Wonder* (1912).[18] One of these is "Chu-Bu and Sheemish," in which Dunsany's sardonic style has a relatively gentle touch. In this tale, two carved idols, each jealous of the attention given to the other, attempt to assert their superiority by causing a miracle, only to see their efforts result in the collapse of the temple in which they both stand. The narrator retrieves Chu-bu from the rubble and keeps him on his mantelpiece. The tale ends with the dry comment, "Chu-bu cannot do much, though once I am sure that at a game of bridge he sent me the ace of trumps after I had not held a card worth having for the whole of the evening. And chance alone could have done as much as that for me. But I do not tell this to Chu-bu." This story evidently stuck in Tolkien's mind; in a 1972 letter about his status as a cult figure, he humorously likens himself to Dunsany's ineffective idols, noting that his fame makes him feel "extremely small and inadequate" but admitting that his nose can still be tickled by "the sweet smell of incense," even though he is "a very modest idol (younger than Chu-Bu and not much older than Sheemish)."[19]

The stories in *The Book of Wonder* offer a generous sampling of memorable names: Zretazoola in the city of Sombelenë, Slith the thief, Bombasharna, Ammuz, the Gnoles, and so on. It would not be surprising if some of these names sparked invention for him, especially as Tolkien classes Dunsany alongside Jonathan Swift in the category of notable (if not always successful) "name-inventors."[20] We know that one name in particular caught Tolkien's eye: the title character in "The Distressing Tale of Thangobrind the Jeweller." A thief who specializes in stealing precious jewels, Thangobrind is commissioned by a merchant prince to steal a diamond from the gods (with his daughter's soul as payment). Tolkien remarked that this name is "singularly inapt for [its] purpose";[21] the heavy, orotund syllables of "Thangobrind" perhaps seemed out of place in a tale about a sneaking jewel thief. Here we catch a glimpse of Tolkien's ideas about the need for fittingness between sound and sense, especially in his proper names. It is possible, however, that Tolkien repurposed "Thangobrind" for his own "Thangorodrim,"[22] but if so, he gave it a suitably weighty referent, in the form of the mountains above Morgoth's stronghold in the north.

Dunsany's tales frequently include an intersection between the present-day world and a fantastic one that is accessible only intermittently or by chance. Tolkien seems to have enjoyed the comic use of such contrasts, as in "Chu-Bu and Sheemish," with its idol who, at best, can deliver the narrator a decent card at bridge. However, Dunsany often used this literary device to create a more caustic tone, as with the conclusion of "The Distressing Tale of Thangobrind the Jeweller." The thief comes to an unpleasant end, and so the daughter of his erstwhile employer escapes having her soul bartered for the gem. However,

> the only daughter of the Merchant Prince felt so little gratitude for this great deliverance that she took to respectability of a militant kind, and became aggressively dull, and called her home the English Riviera, and had platitudes worked in worsted upon her tea-cosy, and in the end never died, but passed away at her residence.[23]

Tolkien said this story was in "Dunsany's worst style," singling out this "ghastly final paragraph!" for critique; he objected to the way that "Dunsany, for the sake of a joke, pricked his own illusion."[24] The problem is not the change in tone or the introduction of anachronism, both of which Tolkien makes use of in his own work; rather, it is more that he faults Dunsany for destroying the spell of the story as story. Tolkien's own tonal shifts are not cynical or bathetic; they have a freshening or lightening effect, even in a serious or tragic tale, and serve to heighten and enlarge, rather than undercut or undersell the sub-created world. The fact that Tolkien regretted the way Dunsany here "pricked his own illusion" suggests that he generally considered him to have been successful in evoking a credible secondary reality, and that, on the whole, he rated *The Book of Wonder* as a book of wonder.

Dunsany's most lasting influence on Tolkien, however, may well derive from his overall body of work and its popularity in his day.

Tolkien's awareness of Dunsany as a significant cultural figure is evidenced in a letter to his publisher, Stanley Unwin. Here, Tolkien deals with a remark from the test-reader of his *Silmarillion* sample, concerning its "eye-splitting" names. These names, Tolkien contends, are "a large part of the effect," and he goes on to explain that their consistency and linguistic foundation enable them to "achieve a reality not fully achieved to my feeling by other name-inventors (say Swift or Dunsany!)"[25] Tolkien knew that his publisher would recognize the Dunsany reference, not least because the test-reader's report described the "mad, bright-eyed beauty" of Tolkien's tale as the sort that readers "can only stand in very small doses, like . . . a very few chapters of Lord Dunsany."[26] It is an apt comparison, and not a negative one; in fact, it helps to explain Tolkien's positive reception of a report that includes serious criticism.

Both the test-reader in his report and Tolkien in his response to Unwin, treat Dunsany as a well-known and appropriate point of reference, because Dunsany's works were given serious consideration by reviewers, as notices in *The Observer*, *The Times*, *The Manchester Guardian*, and even *The New York Times* attest. A 1919 review essay on Dunsany includes praise of *The Gods of Pegāna* that is worth quoting at length:

> [It] was an attempt to create an Olympus of his own and people it with an assemblage of deities, each with a personality and a power over human life acutely conceived and visualized. . . . As an achievement of the imagination, this bible of the gods of Pegana is simply amazing. Except in being polytheistic, its conception of the godhead has no trace of the influence of the Greeks, or of any other people. It lives in an unknown region, weirdly remote and spacious – surrounded by clouds of dusky splendor and illumined with the light that never was on sea or land. The very names of the deities are uncannily beautiful . . . Kib . . . Limpang-Tung . . . Yobarneth-Lahai . . . Hobith . . . Mana-Tood-Sushai.[27]

The reviewer goes on to note that "The thought of Dunsany the theologian is occupied mainly with the immensities of time and of space, the visual glories of mountain and sea, the ceaseless panorama of change, and the ultimate annihilation of all things."[28] In short, we have a complete secondary world, from its names to its theological underpinnings, which the reviewer treats with respect.

We should recall that Tolkien followed the news and so saw many reviews that would have escaped his newspaper-averse friend C.S. Lewis. Since Dunsany's fantastic cosmology was taken seriously by readers and reviewers, how much more – Tolkien perhaps thought to himself – would readers appreciate a world with a far richer linguistic and literary foundation, such as Middle-earth? It would not have been an unreasonable conclusion for him to draw.

The fact that Tolkien's method of creation results in more authentic-sounding names constitutes, he evidently believes, a legitimate selling-point for *The Silmarillion* – and Tolkien's reference to Dunsany may be especially strategic. His *Plays of Gods and Men* (1917) and *Tales of Three Hemispheres* (1920) were published by Stanley Unwin's uncle, in whose publishing house Stanley had begun his career; and Dunsany's *The Sword of Welleran* (1908) and *A Dreamer's Tales* (1910) were published by George Allen & Sons, the publishing house that Stanley purchased to create George Allen & Unwin. Tolkien could therefore drop Dunsany's name into his letter knowing full well it would be recognized and acknowledged as belonging to someone who, if not a bestseller, was at least a reliable mid-list author. The reference shows, in fact, that Tolkien's dealings with his publisher were more canny than is sometimes supposed, given the occasional major misstep in their relations, and his belief in the suitability of *The Silmarillion* for publication was based on empirical evidence pertaining to comparable works.

✒ "Among the very greatest of all poets": Francis Thompson

The English Catholic poet Francis Thompson (1859–1907) was a favorite of Tolkien's. (See figure 26.) Trained in medicine but never practicing as a doctor, Thompson struggled to make a living as a writer, ending up destitute, homeless, depressed, and opium-addicted.* He was discovered by Wilfred and Alice Meynell, who as literary critics and publishers were in a position to support his work; they also rescued him from the streets of London and ensured that he was nursed back to health. After a few productive years, Thompson died, age forty-seven, of tuberculosis.

Insofar as Thompson is remembered today, it is for a single poem, "The Hound of Heaven," an account of the pursuit of a lost soul by Christ, who is imagined as the Hound from which the narrator tries to flee. Thompson's highly sentimental† and ornate

---

* Most likely from pain medication. Opium-laced painkillers and sleep aids were legal and common at the time.

† As in the opening lines of "Ex Ore Infantium": "Little Jesus, wast Thou shy / Once, and just so small as I? / And what did it feel like to be / Out of Heaven, and just like me?"

style has not aged well, and he is now out of print and out of fashion. But Thompson was both popular and well regarded by his contemporaries, and we should be careful not to judge his writing only by the canons of twenty-first century taste. Admittedly, as Raymond Edwards observes, his language can be "saccharine and awkwardly verbose," but he also rises to moments of real power, and his "phantasmagoric"[29] imagery can be captivating if one allows for its elaborate style of presentation. In an interesting congruence of influences, Algernon Blackwood, whom we shall discuss in a moment, used a quote from Thompson's poetry as an epigraph in *The Education of Uncle Paul*. (See figure 29.)

Tolkien knew Thompson's work in depth and encountered it early; he owned a copy of the three-volume *Works of Francis Thompson* by 1914, and gave a lecture to the Exeter College Essay Club while an undergraduate in which he described him as "among the very greatest of all poets." The talk was so profoundly in earnest that the Club secretary minuted: "One was conscious that [the speaker] has felt himself to be in perfect harmony with the poet."[30] Years later, in his lecture on the *Kalevala*, he quoted from Thompson's essay "Paganism Old and New," and alluded to "The Hound of Heaven" in a letter to his son Michael, in which Tolkien shared some of his own experience of faith.[31] *

Edwards states, fairly enough, that while Thompson's poetry about children may seem overly sentimental to readers today, it would have had a different effect on Tolkien, for whom "early childhood was a precious time of lost happiness and unstained promise; he was obviously predisposed to find Thompson's presentation of it attractive." Another reason for Tolkien's admiration was Thompson's skill with language; Edwards notes his "unusually exact" botanical descriptions, the "deft control of complex metres," and the "force of language and metaphor" in his verse, along with his ability to introduce "theological themes and reflexions into quite disparate subjects."[32]

This was an exciting combination. In his Exeter College talk, Tolkien argues that Thompson's rich vocabulary, drawing on both "an extraordinary knowledge of the Elizabethan" and "a large acquaintance with the technicalities of modern science," allowed the poet to serve as a "re-uniter" of disparate elements in modern English literature. He spoke of Thompson's capacity to integrate the mystical and the rational, highlighting (as the Club secretary recorded) "the images drawn from astronomy and geology, and especially those that could be described as Catholic ritual writ large across the universe."[33] Commenting on this report, John Garth remarks, "It sounds like a foretaste of Middle-earth."[34] The attraction was evidently deep and strong.

But Thompson may have encouraged Tolkien as a creative artist in even more ways than this. Tolkien's lecture begins with a biographical overview, in which he notes the "remarkable fact" that "through the most complete misery, squalor, and degraded

---

* Although Tolkien could be extremely self-critical about his own failings in devotional practice, he recognized the constancy of his love for Christ in the Blessed Sacrament: "Not for me the Hound of Heaven, but the never-ceasing silent appeal of Tabernacle." A tabernacle is a lockable metal box, often highly ornate, fixed in place either against a wall or on a pedestal in a church, where the Blessed Sacrament (the consecrated bread) is kept or 'reserved' between Masses, providing a focus for prayer and devotion.

company [Thompson] preserved not only a saintly attitude of charity towards mankind, but a burning enthusiasm for the ethereally fair," in sharp contrast to "many others who never were plunged in the same darkness and yet lost their clear vision."[35] Considering that only months later, Europe would be plunged into a war that tested to destruction many a writer's clear vision, Tolkien's comment seems strangely prophetic. Thompson's ability to focus on beauty even in the midst of deprivation and darkness is strongly suggestive of Tolkien himself and his work on the legendarium during the war years; it may well be that Thompson became something of a role model for the young signals officer on the Western Front.

A figure of such importance to Tolkien as a burgeoning writer would surely have had an influence on his work, and indeed we can trace some intriguing connections.* We find the first of these in the creation-story of the Two Trees of Valinor, Telperion and Laurelin. Waxing and waning, they bring day and night to Middle-earth. Their light has a physical quality, such that it can be gathered up like dew and stored in pools; Tolkien describes it as "the dews of Telperion and the spilth of Laurelin."[36] The word *spilth* is a direct link to Francis Thompson, for Tolkien writes in a note on the typescript that 'spilth' is "meant to indicate that Laurelin is 'founded' on the laburnum. [From] 'jocund spilth of yellow fire' [by] Francis Thompson."[37]

The image comes from the opening "Proem" of Thompson's *Sister Songs*; it is worth quoting more than the two lines that Christopher Tolkien includes in *The History of Middle-earth*. The poet, yearning for the spring, muses that the dreaming earth "stirs and murmurs" at the summons of the "voice of light."

> [Spring] came, nor knew we that it came,
>   In the sun's eclipse.
>   Yet the birds have plighted vows,
> And from the branches pipe each other's name;
>   Yet the season all the boughs
>   Has kindled to the finger-tips, –
> Mark yonder, how the long laburnum drips
> Its jocund spilth of fire, its honey of wild flame!
> Yea, and myself put on swift quickening,
> And answer to the presence of a sudden Spring.[38]

Thompson's birds that "have plighted vows" would surely have reminded the young Tolkien of Edith, his fiancée at last after the "eclipse" of their years apart. The golden-flowered laburnum, an image of the awakening of life and love, is fitting for its association with the Two Trees that would bring light to Middle-earth.

---

* Raymond Edwards also notes an allusion to "Daisy," a sentimental poem about childhood, in Tolkien's "You & Me and the Cottage of Lost Play" (*Tolkien*, 43). For a discussion of Thompson's probable influence on Tolkien's poetry and literary criticism, see Megan Fontenot, "'No pagan ever loved his god': Tolkien, Thompson, and the Beautification of the Gods."

The second connection to the legendarium – to which Tolkien himself has drawn our attention – is the name "Luthany" in Thompson's poem "The Mistress of Vision." Christopher Tolkien records that, in his father's copy of the *Collected Poems*, "he made a marginal note against one of the verses that contains the name *Luthany*."[39] Something about the word caught Tolkien's eye.

In the early stages of the legendarium, "Luthany" is a name for England, a notable use, considering that Tolkien envisioned his tales as providing the English people with "a mythology of their own."[40] Adapting the word to his Elvish tongues, Tolkien makes it "Lúthien" and gives it the meaning "friend."[41] It later becomes the name of the elf-maiden whose romance with Beren forms one of the most powerful and moving tales in the legendarium – a connection that may have a thematic as well as a phonetic aspect.

The title character of "The Mistress of Vision" is a beautiful lady who sits in a secret garden, "a mazeful wonder." There, this "Lady of fair weeping"

> Sang a song of sweet and sore
> And the after-sleeping;
> In the land of Luthany, and the tracts of Elenore.

Singing "through a dream-night's day," she captivates the listener, who is caught in

> That garden of enchanting
> In visionary May;
> Swayless for my spirit's haunting,
> Thrice-threefold walled with emerald from our mortal mornings grey.[42] *

The poem ends on a note of lament, and indeed Edwards notes that "The Mistress of Vision" has as its theme "the rootedness of inspiration in suffering,"[43] which Tolkien would have found most relevant, given the long and painful courtship preceding his marriage with Edith. He would also have observed the way that Thompson weaves his faith into the poem, with the garden's fruitful vine taking on an association with Christ's crown of thorns.

In *The Silmarillion*, Tolkien's Lúthien lives in the land of Doriath, which is sheltered from the outer world by enchanted "mazes"[44] – echoing Thompson's "mazeful" garden. The singing and dancing of Lúthien, who will in time be a 'lady of fair weeping' herself, likewise captivate Beren, who is entranced into silence. After they embrace, he falls "upon the ground in a swoon, as one slain at once by bliss and grief,"[45] echoing both the "after-sleeping" and the air of enchantment associated with the Mistress's song. In the end the lovers leave the protective shelter of Doriath, with Lúthien choosing to share Beren's mortality, the pair no longer walled off safe from what the Mistress would call "mortal mornings grey."

---

* It is also worth noting the sound-resemblance between "Elenore" and Tolkien's flower *elanor*, which becomes the name of Sam's daughter at the end of *The Lord of the Rings*.

In Thompson's poem we have the interweaving of love, longing, sorrow, and pain, which we see throughout the tale "Of Beren and Lúthien." Since we know that Tolkien not only admired Thompson's work fervently, but also that he derived the name Lúthien from "Luthany," it is reasonable to suggest that the images and theme of "The Mistress of Vision" contributed some of the source material for this, one of his very greatest tales. We can therefore fairly claim that Thompson's influence on Middle-earth was profound, for this tale was richly meaningful for Tolkien at the most personal level; he identified himself with Beren and Edith with Lúthien, and those names are inscribed on the headstone above their shared grave in Wolvercote Cemetery, Oxford.

🦊 Tracking down the Crack of Doom: Algernon Blackwood's *The Education of Uncle Paul*

Our next author for this chapter is also one of the most intriguing. Algernon Blackwood (1869–1951) is best known for his short stories, which explore the preternatural and supernatural, but he also wrote eleven novels, largely forgotten today, that explore the strange and numinous aspects of the world. Although Tolkien would not have shared or approved of Blackwood's implicit pantheism, he would have appreciated his deep connection with nature. Whether presented as threatening or welcoming to man, Blackwood's trees are always described attentively and evocatively.* More significantly, Tolkien himself pointed out a direct influence from Blackwood on *The Lord of the Rings*: the name "the Crack of Doom."

In 1967, faced with the problem of how to translate the names in his epic for foreign editions while retaining their original meanings, Tolkien wrote for his publisher a document on "The Nomenclature of *The Lord of the Rings*." In the entry for the "Crack of Doom," Tolkien explains that his use of "crack" is in the sense of "volcanic fissure." He goes on to say that "this use is ultimately derived from Algernon Blackwood, who as my memory seems to recall used it in this way in one of his books read very many years ago."[46]

But which book? Hitherto, the source, as Douglas A. Anderson puts it, has "eluded researchers."[47] However, I believe that we can now identify the book in question with certainty. A word-search of the full text of all eleven of Blackwood's novels reveals that the only book in which Blackwood uses "crack" in a sense corresponding to Tolkien's usage is *The Education of Uncle Paul* (1909).† (See figure 29.) As we will see, its appearance in that novel is richly meaningful and sheds light on Tolkien's decision to adopt the word.

It is important to note, at this juncture, that Tolkien's use of 'crack' in this way is more distinctive than it may appear to many readers. At the time he was writing, 'crack'

---

* Jared Lobdell argues that Blackwood and Tolkien share "a sense of man (or hobbit) as interloper in the woods, of the trees as sentient entities," and suggests that "The Willows" may have influenced Tolkien's character of Old Man Willow (*The World of the Rings*, 9).

† I have also done a full-text search of his short stories, of which there are more than a hundred; none of them use "crack" in the sense of "fissure."

was more commonly associated with *sound* than with *space*. In his "Nomenclature" entry, Tolkien begins by recording that the modern usage of the term 'crack of doom' comes from "'the announcement of the Last Day,' by a crack/peal of thunder" and thus *"crack* could be applied to the sudden sound of horns or trumpets."[48] In the Oxford English Dictionary, this auditory meaning remains the first definition. However, Tolkien is using 'crack' in the geological sense, and specifically as "volcanic fissure" – at that time, not a common usage.[49] The OED's earliest example for 'crack' as used to mean a fissure in mountaineering is from 1923, more than a decade later than its appearance in *The Education of Uncle Paul*. Blackwood's use of the term would, therefore, have caught Tolkien's linguistically attentive eye much more than it catches ours today.

It is worth noting that 'crack' in this mountaineering sense was not a common usage for Tolkien; it seems to be entirely absent from his early writings and appears for the first time in *The Hobbit*.* This point underscores the significance of his comment in the *Nomenclature*. Wherever and whenever else Tolkien might have seen it, it was Blackwood's usage, in a particular book, that caught his eye, and that he identified as the source for the 'Crack' of Doom in Middle-earth. It behooves us, then, to consider what significance there is to Blackwood's use of it, such that it would prompt Tolkien to adopt the word.

The title character of *The Education of Uncle Paul* is a middle-aged man who, after twenty years working in the American wilderness, returns to his native England to visit his recently widowed sister. Paul is skeptical of the merits of civilization and finds himself unable to express his deep feelings about nature to his practical-minded sister. Her children, however, soon get past Paul's defenses, revealing that they share his mystical perceptions. They draw him into participation in their imaginative world, and at a key point in the story introduce him to the "crack between Yesterday and To-morrow." As one of the children explains, "the world is old and worn. . . . [Yesterday and To-morrow] don't join as they once did, and, if we're *very* quick, we can find the crack and slip through. . . . And, once inside there, there's no time, of course. . . . *Anything* may happen, and *everything* come true." It is still a place of moral responsibility. As the girl Nixie explains, "All broken things and all lost things come here and are happy again. . . . And once you've found it, nothing can break it or lose it again." However, she adds, "all my broken things come here and live happily – if I broke them by accident; but if I broke them in a temper, they are still angry and frighten me, and sometimes even chase me out again."[50]

The remainder of the story focuses on Paul's imaginative and spiritual growth, as he becomes a writer of children's tales; the "crack" is identified with daydreams, children's play, or even "creative imagination."[51] These themes, though not particularly effective in the novel, would nevertheless have been of interest to Tolkien. Even though Blackwood makes relatively little use of the "crack between Yesterday and To-morrow" in the

---

* A full-text search of all the pre-*Lord of the Rings* material in *The History of Middle-earth* shows that the word is only used in the auditory sense. 'Crack' as a thin fissure in rock appears once in *The Fall of Gondolin,* but only in the last version of the tale, ca. 1951 (FG, 161).

narrative, it remains a rich and suggestive image, all the more so because we know Tolkien to have been interested in time-travel. Here we have a fissure that is both chronological and physical, mathematically thin and yet "very stretchy," enough for people to squeeze through. The children intuit that it is their youth (and Paul's childlikeness, often referenced in the story) that allows them to pass, for one of them notes that "Every year it's harder to get through."[52]

The fissure in time leads to a state of timelessness, another dimension of sorts, one associated with broken things and their healing. Here, perhaps, we can see why the term, and the images surrounding it, resonated with Tolkien, and why this "crack" may have seemed an appropriate word to describe the fissure into which the Ring of Power must be cast for its destruction and the healing of Middle-earth.* Blackwood's "crack" opens to a place beyond the time-laden circles of the world, a place "where *anything* may happen, and *everything* come true."[53] Is it too fanciful to think, in this connection, of Sam's delighted exclamation when he wakes to find that, the Ring having entered the Crack of Doom, he has escaped death and been reunited with his friends: "Is everything sad going to come untrue?"

It is worth noting that in the early drafts of *The Lord of the Rings*, this fissure is not called the Cracks of *Doom* but the Cracks of *Earth*. At one point Gandalf says, "you would have to find one of the Cracks of Earth in the depth of the Fiery Mountain, and drop it in there, if you really did wish to destroy it – or to place it out of all reach until the End."[54] We see, then, that the 'Crack' or 'Cracks' part of the name came first, in the earliest conception of the unmaking of the Ring, and at a stage in the storytelling process when the Ring might even have been placed "out of all reach until the End" rather than actually destroyed. Only later did "Doom" replace "Earth" as more fitting for this apocalyptic fissure, connoting ultimate judgment and the achievement of true release from the temptation to wield coercive power. For the Ring must be cast away not with anger or carelessness or even heroism, but through seeming accident: Gollum's fatal misstep, providentially enabled by the hobbits' earlier ministrations of pity. Blackwood's "Crack between Yesterday and To-morrow," with its more than merely natural associations, is thus brought to maturity in the molten furnace of Tolkien's imagination.

🐿 "A mere amateur (like myself)": J.H. Shorthouse and *John Inglesant*

We turn now to one of the most intriguing and least well known influences on Tolkien's writings. Joseph Henry Shorthouse (1834–1903) was raised as a Quaker but in adulthood became a devout member of the Church of England. (See figure 27.) Although

---

* The word may also have carried a personal association for Tolkien. After his friend Rob Gilson was killed in action in 1916, Tolkien wrote to G.B. Smith, saying that he felt "something had gone crack" (*Letters*, 10) For a man as sensitive to word choice as Tolkien, his choice of 'crack' for his feeling about the fracturing by death of the T.C.B.S. is significant; at some level, it may have helped him find that same word particularly memorable when he encountered it in Blackwood, in the literary context of loss, brokenness, and healing.

he had weak health throughout his life, and suffered from epilepsy, Shorthouse was a prosperous businessman who was able to devote his leisure time to writing.[55] *John Inglesant: A Romance* (1881) was his debut novel; at first privately printed, it was later picked up by a publisher and became a great success, as none of Shorthouse's later works would be.

Although *John Inglesant* and its author are long forgotten today, in Tolkien's time the novel was widely read, "a best-seller, and the subject of public discussion from the Prime Minister downwards,"[56] as Tolkien remarks in a letter. The National Portrait Gallery in London still has a photographic portrait of Shorthouse from the 1880s listed among its holdings. His book continued to be commented on and referred to in the public press for a very long time, especially in *The Guardian* (the weekly Anglican newspaper), with references to it as late as 1926. Upon the settlement of a lawsuit between Anglicans and Catholics over ownership of the Priory Church of St. Giles, Malvern (a church that is mentioned in the novel), the newspaper emphasized the literary connection: "One may trust that the village immortalised in 'John Inglesant' will now return to its normal Arcadian repose."[57] Even in 1951, Ronald Knox could use the character of John Inglesant as a reference to explain an obscure saint, counting on readers of the *Sunday Times* knowing the tale.[58] Nor was its readership limited to Christians: Thomas Hardy and Philip Larkin read it as well.*

Tolkien had an abiding interest in J.H. Shorthouse and *John Inglesant*. In a 1964 letter, he recalls it having been a significant book – "queer, exciting and debatable"[59] – in his youth. Interestingly, the context of his extended paragraph on Shorthouse is a discussion of the various ingredients of his own writing; evidently, the book came readily to mind when reflecting on early sources and influences. And though the encounter with *Inglesant* occurred early in life, Tolkien's interest in it persisted to the end. In the last year of his life, Tolkien sent to Norman Power† a volume of essays which, he says, "contains an interesting account . . . of J.H. Shorthouse and John Inglesant, his book."[60] Tolkien specifies that this is an *extra* copy[61] – so he had his own copy to keep, and was not simply passing along a volume he no longer wanted.

Shorthouse's own home, named Inglesant after his claim to fame, was located in that part of Birmingham where Tolkien spent many of his formative years; he would have walked past the house on his way to and from daily Mass at the Oratory. Later, when the orphaned Tolkien brothers were moved to Duchess Road, he could even see

---

* Hardy copied a sentence from *John Inglesant* into one of his notebooks, and in 1945, Larkin wrote: "I am still reading *John Inglesant*, very slowly. An unusual book, not exactly my meat." See Alan Jenkins, "Glittering loneliness: Alan Jenkins on Philip Larkin and his parents," *The Times Literary Supplement*, August 20, 2019, https://www.the-tls.co.uk/articles/public/philip-larkin-letters-home-jenkins/.

† Norman Power (1916–1993) studied at Worcester College, Oxford, and was from 1952 till his retirement in 1988 Anglican vicar of St John's, Ladywood, close to the Birmingham Oratory. He first met Tolkien when the latter gave a talk at Worcester College in 1938.

it from his home.[62]* The mere geographical proximity of the house of the author might seem irrelevant, but Tolkien thought it worth noting on two occasions a decade apart: in his letter to Norman Power, he remarks on "JHS being a resident at No 6 Beaufort Road," and in his letter to Christopher Bretherton, he notes that "in Beaufort [R]oad was a house, occupied in its palmier days, by Mr Shorthouse."[63]

To a boy already interested in word formation, 'Inglesant' would have been read immediately as "English saint,"† and thus would have carried an appealing charge, given his deep-rooted interest both in his faith and in one day creating a mythology for the English people. This name would have stayed all the more firmly in his memory as being attached to a place he knew.‡ And if the name of Shorthouse's home appealed, so would his protagonist's Christian name, John, which Tolkien shared and which was a family name. Tolkien, as we noted in chapter 6, also had a particular devotion to St. John the Evangelist.[64] §

The coincidence of location may have been the impetus for Tolkien to reflect on other biographical parallels between himself and Shorthouse. He remarks that Shorthouse was "a mere amateur (like myself) with no status in the literary world, [who] suddenly produced a long book."[65] That he saw a similarity between their authorial careers may account for his interest in the essay on *John Inglesant*, which traces the novel from its genesis and early rejections, to being printed at Shorthouse's own expense, then reissued by Macmillan, and eventually becoming a smash hit, "selling some 80,000 copies in the nineteenth century, and then reprinting annually until well into the 1920's."[66]

But if the novel was an encouraging example, it was also a cautionary tale. Tolkien notes that this long book, though hugely popular in its day, had lost its appeal: "few now find it possible to read."[67] The fate of the novelist, too, was something of a warning. Tolkien points out that in later years, Shorthouse became rather odd in his personal behavior, and "wasted the rest of his time trying to explain what he had and what he had not

---

* My research with the Historic England Archives has located the site of the now-demolished 'Inglesant' house, and confirms that Tolkien would have passed it on the way to the Oratory both from Oliver Road, where he lived while his mother was still alive, and from his later lodgings at Duchess Road. In Tolkien's time, Beaufort Road continued past its current terminus to connect with Ladywood Road, making it the direct route to the Oratory from Oliver Road.

† 'Ingle' = Angle (English); 'sant' is a variant of Old/Middle English 'saint.' Tolkien himself used the invented name "Ingilnórë," Ingle's land, for the first version of the Lonely Isle, which John Garth observes is "an obvious pun on *England*" (*The Worlds of J.R.R. Tolkien*, 49).

‡ English houses are frequently identified by names rather than, or in addition to, street numbers (as with Thomas Hardy's Max Gate and G.K. Chesterton's Top Meadow). Sadly, I have not been able to discover any street-level image of the Inglesant house. However, an aerial photograph from the RAF shows that the house was similar to its neighbors, and an extant photograph of Beaufort Road just past the Inglesant house at the time Tolkien lived in the area, shows that these are large and handsome houses.

§ His interest in Shorthouse's tale might well have been augmented by the fact that *Inglesant* takes a key part of its plot from the story of St. John Gualbert, known as "The Merciful Knight" and depicted in a painting of that name by the Pre-Raphaelite Edward Burne-Jones (who was an alumnus of both King Edward's School and Exeter College).

meant in *John Inglesant*." Tolkien adds, "I have always tried to take him as a melancholy warning, and still try to attend to my technical carboys [Shorthouse's business was in chemical manufacture], and to writing some more."[68] Tolkien's own "technical carboys" were, of course, his responsibilities as a university professor, to which he attended with diligence,[69] even if he failed to finish some of the academic projects he started.

Norman Power argues that *John Inglesant* was "a strong influence" on Tolkien, "an influence unnoticed by the critics, but of which the great man was himself aware."[70] Power does little to substantiate this claim, but I agree with his basic thrust, for it seems improbable that Tolkien would have been so interested in a man whose writings were of no particular account with him. I will now try to show that *John Inglesant* was indeed significant in Tolkien's eyes, and this is where we turn to the principal link between Tolkien and Shorthouse – namely, the literary content of their most famous works.

A "debatable" English saint

John Inglesant is an unwieldy tale and difficult to summarize. Set in the seventeenth century, it follows the title character, a boy raised in the Church of England, but guided by a rather sinister Jesuit mentor who intends to use him as a means for bringing England back into the Roman fold. The novel purports to be drawn from old family documents, and it concludes with excerpts from letters to account for the last years of Inglesant's life in England. It even has an "Introduction" by the supposed compiler of the story, one "Geoffrey Monk," a meta-fictional touch that would surely have pleased Tolkien. Although a few other references in the body of the book maintain this historiographical conceit, for the most part it is a straightforward narrative.

Inglesant lives a "life of romance and excitement, combined with a certain spiritual Quixotism."[71] In his travels he encounters a range of Christian environments, from Nicholas Ferrar's quiet community at Little Gidding, to the network of persecuted Jesuits in England, to the decadent Catholicism of Rome. Each of these settings gives rise to much theological and spiritual introspection. Parallel to this spiritual narrative is a more conventionally melodramatic storyline. Inglesant is caught up in the events of the English Civil War, fighting in battle and at one point being imprisoned and sentenced to death for treason. His twin brother, having become entangled in intrigue on the Continent, is murdered by an Italian named (significantly) Malvolti.* Inglesant's search for his brother's murderer leads him into an extended and varied series of adventures in Italy.

Tolkien used four adjectives in describing the book: "long," "queer," "exciting," and "debatable." The first three are obviously apt word choices. The fourth – "debatable" – is less immediately obvious, but its usage suggests something of why Tolkien should have been both unimpressed by the novel and deeply intrigued by it, for the novel not only had debatable literary qualities (taking purple prose to the level of purple fever) but also invited serious doctrinal debate on the rival claims of the Church of England and the

---

* 'Malvolti' translates approximately as "ill will."

Catholic Church. It is worth expanding on this latter point, as it helps us appreciate Tolkien's interest in the book and what that shows about his reading.

The hero's surname reflects and reinforces his English loyalties, and the author takes pains to ensure we do not miss the significance. Inglesant, in the course of his adventures, actually acquires the title "Cavaliere di San Giorgio" and his benefactor declares that "he well represented the patron saint of his nation, St George of England." (See figure 28.) Shorthouse reiterates in the authorial voice that he closely resembles "a splendid renaissance St. George," and at a pivotal moment in the narrative, he is even mistaken for the saint by a humble country priest. But is England essentially Anglican or Catholic or neither?

On the one hand, *John Inglesant* appears to be celebrating the *via media* of the Anglican Church over against the supposed absolutism of the Church of Rome. In the concluding chapter, Inglesant is questioned as to the authority of the Catholic Church. His interlocutor suggests that "The Church of England . . . speaks with bated assurance, while the Church of Rome never falters in its utterance, and I confess seems to me to have a logical position. If there be absolute truth revealed, there must be an inspired exponent of it, else from age to age it could not get itself revealed to mankind." In reply, Inglesant declares, "This is the Papist argument. . . . there is only one answer to it – Absolute truth is not revealed."[72]

On the other hand, Shorthouse seems at various points to be presenting the Catholic view favorably and there is even an indication that Inglesant has apparently converted.[73] The narrator recounts that "about this time he must have been formally received into the Romish Church, for he confessed and received the sacrament at low mass; but no mention of the ceremony occurs." Inglesant is later shown receiving the sacrament at a Catholic Mass. Furthermore, we should not miss the irony that his patriotic English title – "Cavaliere di San Giorgio" – is bestowed by the Italian, Catholic, Duke of Umbria.[74]*

So is Inglesant Anglican, Catholic, or neither? The third possibility is not completely to be discounted for Shorthouse also includes details that subvert the identification of Inglesant with England's saint altogether. His armor is covered with "arabesques not of the most Christian type, and the perfect sword-blade was engraved with hieroglyphics not of the most saintly kind."

Shorthouse keeps the reader guessing as to where this Englishman's true allegiances lie. He paints a highly admiring portrait of the saintly Benedictine monk Father de Cressy, who challenges Inglesant to compromise no longer: "You wish this life's wisdom, and to walk with Christ as well. . . . The two cannot walk together, as you have found." Inglesant "came away very sorrowful from Serenus de Cressy," like the rich young man who "went away sorrowful" (Matt. 19:22) after rejecting Christ's command to forsake

---

* Umbria is a region of central Italy. Its name comes from the Umbrian people, whose name is derived, at least according to Pliny the Elder, from the Greek word denoting rain-clouds or thunder-storms. One wonders whether Shorthouse is not complicating the ecclesiological purport of his story even further here with a sly glance at Newman's motto, *Ex umbris et imaginibus in veritatem* (Out of shadows and images into truth).

worldly wealth. The implication seems plain, but Shorthouse immediately refuses clarity by adding, "Whether [Inglesant] also, at the same, was turning away from Jesus Christ, who can tell?" But if this throws too much shade on Inglesant's Anglicanism, Shorthouse balances the scales by depicting a Catholic church that is "swept and garnished,"[75] a deliberate allusion to the words of Christ about a soul cleansed but only so as to be possessed by seven devils worse than before (Luke 11:25). The message of Shorthouse's story, if one can identify a particular 'message,' is that religious matters are not easily settled.

Inglesant, then, was a book that gave rise to serious discussion about theological and ecclesiological issues, and indeed it was personally significant to a number of Catholic converts, including the historian Christopher Dawson and the philosopher and pacifist E.I. Watkin. Ronald Knox, recording in his memoir *A Spiritual Aeneid* that he had "learned to admire" Shorthouse's novel so much that it became an "old friend," remarks that "it has a strong cultus among Anglicans as a religious romance. . . . Readers of Mgr. Benson's *Confessions of a Convert* will remember that he, after leaving Eton, conceived an 'absolute passion' for *John Inglesant*."[76]

Given that Tolkien was a Catholic from early childhood, not an adult convert from Anglicanism as were Knox and Benson, it is interesting that he took such note of the novel; Tolkien, it seems, was keeping up with the fashion in his reading! Far from being interested only in Catholic matters, he was also interested in books that imaginatively presented, or appeared to present, an Anglican point of view and provoked theological debate.

"Full of pity"

John Inglesant, then, was a book that stayed in Tolkien's memory throughout his life; and we have seen that the story addressed significant theological themes in a complex manner. Various points of influence could be traced;* here, we will consider just one – but one that bears on the very heart of Tolkien's work: the theme of pity.

In *John Inglesant*, the note of pity is repeatedly struck, and comes to its fullness in the climax of the tale. The theme is hinted at early on when Inglesant's Jesuit mentor encourages him to feel "pity for mankind," connecting this with the divine nature: "Nothing but the Infinite pity is sufficient for the infinite pathos of human life." Later, when debating with his ducal patron the difficulties of the spiritual life, Inglesant's eyes are "full of pity, not only for the old Duke, but for himself and all mankind." Another character, a mysteriously prophetic Italian, speaks about feeling "a strange emotion of pity" upon observing a skilled craftsman who is unable to work because of failing sight, begging for alms to support his children, and adds, "I think the man was no bad emblem of the life of each of us."[77]

---

* For instance, Inglesant receives a "message from beyond the grave" in the form of a boat-man whose "boat seemed to move of its own accord, like the magic bark in some romance of chivalry" (ch. XXXIII); this is suggestive of Faramir's vision of the dead Boromir in the elven-boat. Dale Nelson also finds a parallel between a scene involving a crystal ball and that of the *palantír* ("'Queer, Exciting, and Debatable': Tolkien and Shorthouse's *John Inglesant*," 5).

Tolkien, too, brings up pity repeatedly in *The Lord of the Rings*, consistently portraying it as a characteristic of the most admirable characters. We see, for instance, that Théoden has pity on Wormtongue, giving him an opportunity to prove his loyalty; Aragorn pities Sam and Frodo as he searches for them through the *palantír*; Faramir feels love and pity when he sees the vision of his dead brother in the boat; Gandalf pities Sauron's slaves, while the armies of Mordor that besiege Gondor are "pitiless"; Merry is motivated by pity to help Éowyn in her fight with the Nazgûl. Sam feels pity for Frodo's suffering on the way to Mount Doom, and offers to carry the Ring; but his failure to feel pity for Gollum when, in a moment of vulnerability, Gollum reaches out to touch the sleeping Frodo, closes off the last chance of Gollum's repentance. Interestingly, Sam, no less than Gollum, is described at one point as "miserable": a significant word, for it is derived from a Latin root meaning "deserving of pity, mercy" – hence the petitionary prayer *miserere nobis* ("have mercy on us") that Tolkien would have often said in the course of the Catholic liturgy. Upon meeting Saruman during the Scouring of the Shire, Frodo says, "I pity you," and after Saruman is killed by Wormtongue, he looks at the wizard's corpse with "pity and horror." In fact, Tolkien told a correspondent that *The Lord of the Rings* is "founded on Pity; on the triumph and the defeat of Pity."[78]

But it is not just in a general concern with the theme of pity that we can see a very significant connection between *John Inglesant* and *The Lord of the Rings*; it is a key element in the way each story unfolds.

Shorthouse and Tolkien build up to their climax with preliminary encounters that develop and foreshadow the motif of pity and its spiritual significance. About two-thirds of the way through Shorthouse's tale, Inglesant saves a stranger from being beaten by the mob for showing disrespect toward the Blessed Sacrament. Shorthouse signals that this is a significant moment in his protagonist's religious development. Inglesant reflects, "it came into his mind more powerfully than ever, that the moment foretold to him by Serenus de Cressy was at last indeed come. Surely it behoved him to look well to his steps, lest he should be found at last absolutely and unequivocally fighting against his conscience and his God." Later, the poor stranger says to Inglesant,

> "[D]o you think that last night, when beaten, crushed, and almost breathless . . . and looking up I saw you . . . in your courtier's dress of lace and silver, calm, beneficent, powerful for good, you did not seem to my weak human nature . . . beautiful as an angel of light? Truly, you did; yet I tell you . . . that to the divine vision, of us two at that moment you were the one to be pitied."[79]

Here, Inglesant is implicitly likened to the devil, who can appear as "an angel of light" (2 Cor. 11:14). It is an equivocal description, given that he has just saved the man's life, but it will turn out to be a resonant bit of foreshadowing, suggesting that Inglesant's very salvation is mysteriously bound in some way to the experience of pity.

We see a surprisingly similar encounter near the end of Frodo and Sam's journey to Mount Doom. At the foot of the mountain, Gollum attacks Frodo in order to seize the Ring. Frodo rebukes him – and at that moment, Sam has a quasi-mystical vision of the two figures. Gollum is "a crouching shape . . . a creature now wholly ruined and defeated," while Frodo stands before him, "stern, untouchable now by pity, a figure robed in white, but at its breast it held a wheel of fire." Like Inglesant in the vision of the poor stranger, Frodo is a figure of purity ("robed in white") yet strangely ambiguous: "untouchable now by pity" for Gollum, but become, in fact, pitiable himself. The "wheel of fire," held at the breast, is soon to break Frodo's will at the crux of the story. Here we have something of the same reversal of perspective that Shorthouse gives the reader when the poor stranger sees the powerful Inglesant as a beautiful, rescuing "angel of light," yet someone to be pitied more than himself.

Significantly, at this moment of mystical insight, Sam himself is given a moral test: like Frodo before him, he has the opportunity to kill Gollum.

> It would be just to slay this treacherous, murderous creature, just and many times deserved; and also it seemed the only safe thing to do. But deep in his heart there was something that restrained him: he could not strike this thing lying in the dust, forlorn, ruinous, utterly wretched.[80]

We can see, then, that the theme of pity is deeply woven into the fabric of both tales, even without considering its significance at the climax of the two works. Before we do consider that matter, it may be worth observing that pity is not widely recognized as a virtue; it is too often associated with condescension. Mercy – that more theological term – is virtuous, but pity tends to be tinged with superiority, even smugness. It is even more uncommon as a virtue in, of all things, an adventure story. With that in mind, let us turn to consider in detail the climatic renunciation scene in *John Inglesant* and its possible connection to *The Lord of the Rings*.

"It was Pity that stayed his hand"

Throughout the novel, Inglesant seeks to avenge his brother's death, and when the opportunity arises, it is "the crisis of his life." Purely by accident, or so it seems, he comes across the murderer, Malvolti:

> Alone and weary, his clothes worn and threadbare, [Malvolti] came toiling up the pass. Inglesant reined in his horse suddenly, a strange and fierce light in his eyes and face. The Italian started back like some wild creature of the forest brought suddenly to bay, a terrified cry broke from him, and he looked wildly round as if intending flight. The nature of the ground caught him as in a trap; on the one hand the sloping hillside steep

and open, on the other tangled rugged ground, slightly rising between the road and the precipice, cut off all hope of sudden flight.[81]

Trapped, and observing that Inglesant is reaching for his gun, Malvolti "with a terrible cry . . . threw himself on his knees before the horse's head, and begged for pity – pity, and life." Inglesant considers killing him, declaring him "a murderer and a villain . . . a cruel secret midnight cut-throat and assassin; a lurker in secret corners to murder the innocent," and asks his companions, "what say you, gentlemen? what is his due?" They declare that Malvolti deserves death, but Inglesant instead chooses pity, and brings him as a prisoner to the village church, where he hands him over to the priest, explaining, "as I came across the mountains this morning on the way to Rome, I met my mortal foe, the murderer of my brother, a wretch whose life is forfeit by every law. . . . I give him over to the Lord. I give up my sword into the Lord's hands, that He may work my vengeance upon him as it seems to Him good."[82]

Only later in the novel does this encounter have its true significance. While searching for his wife's missing brother, Inglesant re-encounters Malvolti, now a blind, holy friar who has taken the name "Father Grazia" and serves among plague victims. Inglesant looks at his former enemy, "pitying the look in the blind man's face"; then, hearing how Malvolti was brought to this new life, "no feeling but pity was in his heart."[83] Vengeance, in "the Lord's hands," has been accomplished not through violence but by *grazia*, grace, conversion of soul.

Significantly, it is only through his old enemy's aid that Inglesant is able to bring his quest to a resolution. Malvolti agrees to help in the search for Inglesant's brother-in-law, who also happens to be Malvolti's nemesis, "the ravisher of my sister – the destroyer of my own sight." Days later, apparently by chance, they discover the very man, so ravaged by leprosy that none can bear to look at him, much less offer him comfort. The blind Malvolti, who "lived only to meet and bless his enemy," goes to him and offers him consolation and peace in his last moments.[84] In this way, life-preserving pity given freely to an undeserving "wretch" triumphs over death and judgment, and results in unforeseen consequences of transformation, not just for one character but for many.

The relationship enacted here between Shorthouse's characters strongly prefigures the interactions between Gollum and the hobbits, Bilbo, Frodo, and Sam. In the introduction to *The Fellowship of the Ring*, when Tolkien reminds readers of how the Ring was discovered, he emphasizes the role of pity in that encounter: "Bilbo was tempted to slay him with his sword. But pity stayed him, and though he kept the ring . . . he would not use it to help him kill the wretched creature at a disadvantage." The significance of pity toward Gollum is further emphasized in an early exchange between Frodo and Gandalf. Frodo declares that it was "a pity that Bilbo did not stab that vile creature, when he had a chance!" To this, Gandalf replies, "It was Pity that stayed his hand. Pity, and Mercy: not to strike without need. . . . Be sure that he took so little hurt from the evil, and escaped in the end, because he began his ownership of the Ring so. With Pity." Gandalf goes on to caution Frodo not to rush to judgment, even if Gollum does "deserve" death: "Many that live deserve death. And some that die deserve life. Can you give it to them? Then do not be too eager to deal out death in judgement." Frodo will later vividly recollect this moment when he and Sam discover that Gollum has been following them. Faced with the task of judging the captive Gollum, "It seemed to Frodo then that he heard, quite plainly but far off, voices out of the past" calling to mind the words of his conversation with Gandalf. As a result, he decides on mercy: "'Very well,' he answered aloud, lowering his sword. 'But still I am afraid. And yet, as you see, I will not touch the creature. For now that I see him, I do pity him.'"

Like the undeserving Malvolti at the hands of Inglesant, Gollum escapes death because first Bilbo, and then Frodo and Sam take pity on him; later, it is Gollum who leads the Ring-bearer into Mordor, and ultimately becomes the means by which the Quest is completed. It is not through force of arms that the mighty men of Middle-earth (Aragorn and his armies) win victory; nor even is it through the long-suffering heroism of Frodo and Sam that the Ring is destroyed. As Verlyn Flieger notes, Frodo "fails in his quest," a fact that "many readers (to Tolkien's great concern) . . . miss."[85] In a 1963 letter, Tolkien notes that many readers forget "that strange element in the World that we call Pity or Mercy, which is also an absolute requirement in moral judgement (since it is present in the Divine nature)." He is explicit that although Frodo has indeed failed, "his exercise of patience and mercy towards Gollum gained him Mercy."[86] His framing of the scene is reminiscent of Shorthouse's authorial commentary in *Inglesant*, that "The supreme effort of Divine mercy surely is that which shapes the faltering and unconscious actions of man into a beneficent and everlasting work."[87] It is worth noting, as a small but suggestive detail, that the climactic moment of *Inglesant* takes place in the mountains – as does the climax of Frodo and Gollum's interactions on Mount Doom. The moral highpoint of each tale is given an objective correlative.

Ever since his days in the trenches, Tolkien knew firsthand that "some that die deserve life." His close friend, G.B. Smith, prayed that if he were killed in the war, Tolkien would express what the T.C.B.S. had hoped to say: "May God bless you my dear John Ronald and may you say the things I have tried to say long after I am not there to say them, if such be my lot."[88] He was killed not long afterwards. The mystery of death and suffering, and the equally deep mystery of "the pity of war, the pity war distilled" – in Wilfred Owen's famous phrase – was something that Tolkien would reflect on deeply and unfold richly as he told his story of the War of the Ring.

We can perhaps discern a final sign of the importance *John Inglesant* had for Tolkien in what is presented as an interpolated letter at the conclusion of Shorthouse's tale, when a Mr. Valentine reports on encountering Inglesant in later days. At a gathering, Inglesant plays a piece of music upon his violin, which greatly moves the writer:

> It seemed to me as though thoughts, which I had long sought and seemed
> ever and anon on the point of realizing, were at last given me, as I listened

to chords of plaintive sweetness broken now and again by cruel and bitter discords – a theme into which were wrought street and tavern music and people's songs, which lively airs and catches, upon the mere pressure of the string, trembled into pathetic and melancholy cadences. In these dying falls and closes all the several parts were gathered up and brought together, yet so that what before was joy was now translated into sorrow, and the sorrowful transfigured into peace, as indeed the many shifting scenes of life vary upon the stage of men's affairs.[89]

We would not be far off the mark, I believe, if we caught an echo of this poignant sentiment near the end of *The Lord of the Rings* in the chapter entitled "The Field of Cormallen." Frodo and Sam have been rescued; they are brought before Aragorn the King and the assembled company, and a minstrel of Gondor sings the lay of "Frodo of the Nine Fingers and the Ring of Doom":

And all the host laughed and wept, and in the midst of their merriment and tears the clear voice of the minstrel rose like silver and gold, and all men were hushed. And he sang to them, now in the elven-tongue, now in the speech of the West, until their hearts, wounded with sweet words, overflowed, and their joy was like swords, and they passed in thought out to regions where pain and delight flow together and tears are the very wine of blessedness.[90]

𝔖 Conclusion

In this chapter, we have explored selected works of 'fine fabling,' beginning with Lord Dunsany's mannered and ironic fantasies. Although Dunsany's striking nomenclature is perhaps the element most superficially similar to Tolkien's, we saw that his influence more probably lies in the example that he provided of commercially and critically successful literary fiction in a sub-created world. The international success of Dunsany's stories of Pegāna – and the connection to Tolkien's own publisher – help to explain Tolkien's otherwise seemingly groundless confidence in the viability of *The Silmarillion*.

Turning to Tolkien's favorite poet, Francis Thompson, we have discovered Thompson's role in providing names and imagery for portions of the Silmarillion, including the development of the tale of Beren and Lúthien, that was emotionally so important for Tolkien as a suitor and husband.

Next, we found an important influence in the writings of Algernon Blackwood. Tolkien himself noted that a story by Blackwood was the source of the name "Crack of Doom," the volcanic chasm where the Ring of Power was forged and destroyed. We have now identified that story as *The Education of Uncle Paul*, allowing us to explore its rich implications as raw material for a place-name that is crucial to the world of Middle-earth.

Lastly, we explored J.H. Shorthouse's remarkable novel *John Inglesant*. In this strange, long-forgotten work – one that was personally significant to Tolkien throughout his life – we found a story of moral conflict and competing loyalties, a story that issues in a providentially freeing climax consequent upon the exercise of pity. In these respects, we discerned powerful resonances with what is not just a key theme, but perhaps the key theme, of *The Lord of the Rings*.

❧ 11 ❧

Tolkien's Catholic Taste
Here Comes Everybody

OUR ENQUIRIES UP TO THIS POINT HAVE FOCUSED, NATURALLY enough, on Tolkien's modern reading insofar as it overlaps in some way with Tolkien's own writing – in *The Hobbit, The Lord of the Rings*, and *The Silmarillion*. We have examined his familiarity with children's literature, fantasy, adventure, romance, science fiction, and 'fine fabling.' These genres and forms are the most probable places to find sources – or at least traces – of modern influence on his work. However, we must not stop there. To complete our picture, we need to conduct a *tour d'horizon* of his acquaintance with post-1850 literature. In this chapter, therefore, we will adopt a comprehensive approach and consider whatsoever we know Tolkien to have read of modern prose, poetry, and drama composed in English, not yet collected in other chapters, in order to fill out our canvas to the maximum extent.

We will find that Tolkien was a man of almost catholic taste – 'catholic' here meaning, of course, "all-inclusive, all-encompassing." Though there was a lot he didn't like, there was not much he wouldn't sample. He was, after all, a man of letters, an academic in the field of English literature; he would have felt something approaching a professional responsibility to know what was being written in his day (and not just in British English, but in American English too, as we shall see), quite apart from the fact that he was naturally a man with an abiding curiosity and interest in the world around him. By catholic, I don't mean undiscriminating: clearly, he made choices. But who would have thought he would choose to read the surreal, hallucinogenic *Musrum* by Eric Thacker and Anthony Earnshaw? It was sent to him by the publisher for a possible blurb, and did not in the end earn his endorsement – he sent the carefully polite reply that it was "outside the range of my interests and I do not feel moved to say anything at all about it" – but he read it nonetheless.[1]* (See figure 38.) He was prepared to take risks. He not only chanted verses from G.K. Chesterton's *The Flying Inn* (as might have been expected), he also spent time getting to know writers whose work one might have assumed would be altogether beyond

---

* *Musrum* is a truly weird book, in which the title character struggles with the Weedking over control of the Great Mushroom. Much of the book is made up of odd drawings (including 38 variations of a skull-and-crossbones, pp. 59-68) and cryptic statements such as "Musrum is terribly afraid of sponge-cats. / Keep your sponge-cat under control" (7), "The eyes of wolves are flowers fertilized in evil brains" (82), and "Starshades; seedkings; sharp moonlight; gnarled ropehole; fungoid music weeping remotely" (135). One suspects that the authors knew firsthand how "the Giant Mushroom . . . gained mastery" (157–8) (London: Jonathan Cape, 1968).

the scope of his imaginative sympathy. A case in point is James Joyce's *Finnegans Wake*, which represents the high-water mark of experimental, impenetrable modernism. Yet Tolkien was intrigued by a name that he found there, as we shall discuss further below.

Joyce's protagonist in *Finnegans Wake* is one Humphrey Chimpden Earwicker, whose initials are taken to stand for 'Here Comes Everybody' and who is somehow the sign of a "truly catholic assemblage."[2] With only slight hyperbole, one might use this phrase – 'Here Comes Everybody' – to denote the modern authors whom Tolkien read. So far in this book we have already named more than seventy authors; in this chapter we shall survey those who remain, 'filling up the corners,' as a hobbit would say. (For a full list of the authors and works discussed in this book, see the appendix.) The remnant includes Dylan Thomas, whose poetry Tolkien praised; E.M. Forster, whom he nominated for the Nobel Prize; Agatha Christie, of whom he was an aficionado, and Dorothy L. Sayers, of whom he was not. Tolkien's wide-ranging, 'come-one-come-all' approach happily explodes the stereotype of a tweedy, nostalgic medievalist who read little or nothing of modern literature. Here, indeed, comes everybody.

❧ The Americans are coming

Tolkien never visited America, but Americans sent him books to read – an example being Wendell Berry's *The Hidden Wound* (1970)[3] * – and not a few visited him in person. Probably the best-known such visitor is Clyde Kilby, who helped him organize materials pertaining to *The Silmarillion*, and went on to found the Wade Center at Wheaton College, Illinois, now the major center for Inklings study in the United States.

Tolkien surprised Clyde Kilby with his "broad knowledge of American literature," and "especially that of Mark Twain"; one specific title by Twain that he knew was *A Connecticut Yankee in King Arthur's Court* (1889).[4] He knew (and disliked) at least one of the novels of James Branch Cabell, an American fantasist whose style ran to the satiric, and saw John Balderston's time-travel play *Berkeley Square* (1926).[5] Poets whose work he knew included Henry Wadsworth Longfellow and T.S. Eliot; we shall examine his views on them slightly out of sequence, here in our survey of Americana, rather than in the poetry section at the end of this chapter. One novelist he knew well was Sinclair Lewis, the first American writer to receive the Nobel Prize for Literature. Tolkien said that he had read *all* of Lewis's books,[6] which, if true, is impressive given that he published no fewer than twenty-four novels between 1912 and 1951. These included *Main Street*, *Elmer Gantry*, and *Arrowsmith*, all dealing with aspects of American culture, especially as it is embodied in small-town life. But it was his novel *Babbitt* (1922) that won him greatest notice, both with the public at large and with Tolkien.

---

* The book is Berry's attempt to probe and heal the "hidden wound" created by slavery and its legacy of racism, recognizing his own unwitting complicity in the system as a white man raised in the American South. Tolkien, through his secretary, acknowledged receipt of the book with thanks.

In a hole in the ground there lived a . . . Babbitt?

At the presentation of the Nobel award, special attention was given to *Babbitt*, a satire upon American middle-class culture and social conformism. (See figure 32.) Tolkien's familiarity with this novel is apparent in his 1947 paper for the Oxford Dante Society, in which he uses an anecdote from *Babbitt* as part of his opening – an example of the way that he was willing to draw on modern fiction in order to make medieval literature accessible to his audience.[7] It is this work that Tolkien cites as a possible source for what is probably his most famous invention, the hobbit. He explained to an interviewer that the word *hobbit* "might have been associated with Sinclair Lewis's Babbitt."[8]

The similarity in sound between *hobbit* and *Babbitt* is not the only reason Tolkien refers to the work of the man from Minnesota. He goes on, "Babbitt has the same bourgeois smugness that hobbits do. His world is the same limited place."[9] This is no small admission. Here Tolkien has conceded three things: a linguistic debt, a parallel with his protagonist's personality, and a parallel with the constrained home life of Hobbiton.

George F. Babbitt certainly has something in common with Bilbo at the start of *The Hobbit*. A well-fed member of the bourgeoisie, he has a hidden romantic streak, dreaming "of the fairy child, a dream more romantic than scarlet pagodas by a silver sea."[10] However, this underdeveloped aspect of Babbitt's personality emerges in a way that one cannot imagine occurring in the Shire: his discontent with his life of small-town social-climbing leads him to have an extramarital affair. Although he eventually gives up his fling and returns to his wife, it is at the cost of accepting a stultifying routine that leaves him feeling defeated and disappointed.

Bilbo's character development in *The Hobbit* shows, like Babbitt, a reaction against "smugness" that allows him to embrace his Tookish, romantic side and to go off on adventures. Unlike Babbitt, however, Bilbo's motivation for leaving home is more morally sound, and he returns happily enough to his roots. Of course, this combination of similarity and difference is entirely to be expected. No author worth his salt, let alone an author as exacting and careful as Tolkien, ever takes over a source or an influence lock, stock, and barrel. There is always a transforming alchemy at work in the process of digestion, assimilation, and reconstruction. Nevertheless, we have here a striking example of Tolkien freely admitting a connection between his work and that of a contemporary American writer. In earlier chapters we noted how the hobbits were influenced by the Snergs of Wyke-Smith and the rabbits of Beatrix Potter. Here, we can see that the very name 'hobbit,' as well as something of hobbit character and environment, finds a parallel in a Sinclair Lewis novel. Who would have thought that this most English of fictional kindreds should have been influenced by such an unlikely transatlantic source? Of Tolkien's reading habits it might be said, as he himself has Gandalf say of hobbits: "You can learn all there is to know about their ways in a month, and yet after a hundred years they can still surprise you."

Longfellow, long admired

The poet Henry Wadsworth Longfellow (1807–1882) was one of the most popular writers of his day. The author of narrative and lyric poems such as *The Song of Hiawatha*, "A Psalm of Life," and "Paul Revere's Ride," he received the rare honor, for an American, of a memorial in Poets' Corner, Westminster Abbey.

Tolkien was sufficiently interested in Longfellow to read at least some critical or biographical material about the poet; he also knew of his poem *Evangeline*, which, with its tragic story of separated young lovers, and its setting in the "forest primeval" of Acadia, has much that would have resonated with him.[11] However, it is *The Song of Hiawatha* (1855) that chiefly caught his attention: a long narrative poem recounting the life, heroic deeds, and eventual apotheosis of its eponymous Native American hero.

Tolkien encountered this poem as a young man when, in 1912, he attended a performance of choral settings of *Hiawatha* at the Exeter College Music Society's summer concert. By 1914 he knew both the poem and the poet well enough to reference them in his talk on the *Kalevala* at Corpus Christi College, repeated a few months later at Exeter. He also mentions *Hiawatha* in the draft of his "Valedictory Address," the lecture he delivered before the University of Oxford in 1959.[12] We see, then, that his admiration for, or at any rate interest in, Longfellow was long-lasting, from his student days right through to the end of his academic career.

Hiawatha is written in the same meter, unrhymed trochaic tetrameter, as that used in the original Finnish verse of the *Kalevala*. Tolkien remarks that Longfellow "pirated" this meter and the idea of the poem, but with "none of its spirit at all." As we might expect by now, Tolkien also took note of his characters' names, observing that they "are often too good to be inventions."[13]

John Garth points out a number of intriguing connections between the writings of the two men. The name of Tolkien's Wanōna in "The Story of Kullervo" echoes that of Longfellow's Wenonah, the mother of Hiawatha; moreover, "each woman is wayward, and dies in anguish after being seduced among the flowers by the wrong suitor." In Tolkien's tale of Túrin, which brings the story of Kullervo into the legendarium of Middle-earth, Túrin's sister Lalaith, who dies of a fever, is named for the brook Nen Lalaith – Elvish for "water of laughter" – and in Longfellow's poem, after Hiawatha's wife Minnehaha falls ill and dies, her spirit "is summoned back to the waterfall after which she was named, Laughing Water." In *The Hobbit*, Bard the Bowman is told by a thrush to fire his one remaining arrow at the uncovered spot on Smaug's breast, rather as Hiawatha defeats Megissogwon, the spirit of wealth, after a woodpecker flies to his shoulder and tells him to shoot at the spirit's only weakness, a tuft of hair on his head.[14] (See figure 31.) Furthermore, just as Smaug's underbelly is encrusted with gems, Megissogwon is also clothed in wealth, for he is clad in wampum, the shells used as Native American currency.[15]

Hiawatha may seem quaint to modern readers, but in its day it represented an up-to-date approach to preserving oral literature through literary reimaginings. Longfellow consulted an Ojibway chieftain and used as sources the work of John Heckewelder, a missionary, and Henry Rowe Schoolcraft, a geographer-anthropologist. The result was "an effect that held few traces of scholarly procedure – it was that of a thorough-going re-creation."[16] Longfellow's reworking of an indigenous mythology for his own nation, as Elias Lönnrot had done for the Finnish people, would have been a project deeply appealing to Tolkien who wished to provide a mythology for England. He was not, however, particularly impressed by the results, remarking that *Hiawatha* "is not a genuine storehouse of Indian folklore, but a mild and gentle bowdlerising of the Kalevala coloured I imagine with disconnected bits of Indian lore and perhaps a few genuine names."[17] Tolkien's standards for such things were high.

But even if he did not find *Hiawatha* entirely up to par, he would have seen in Longfellow something of a professional model. Though not a lifelong academic like Tolkien, Longfellow knew multiple languages, and became the Smith Professor of Belles Lettres of Modern Languages at Harvard, where he helped found the comparative literature program. He was also a translator, most notably of Dante's *Divine Comedy*. Furthermore, his poetry made him both popular and wealthy; for instance, his narrative poem *The Courtship of Miles Standish* sold ten thousand copies in London on its day of publication.[18]

Tolkien himself drew a personal parallel with Longfellow. When asked whether he preferred to be remembered for his philological or his fictional writings, he replied, "if I'm remembered at all, it will be by *The Lord of the Rings*, I take it. Won't it be rather like the case of Longfellow? People remember Longfellow wrote *Hiawatha*, quite forget he was a Professor of Modern Languages!"[19] Tolkien evidently saw humor in the fact that an author, however great his achievements, cannot dictate how (or whether) posterity will recall him. Nonetheless, it was surely an encouragement to him, on some level, that Longfellow had achieved success in both high-brow academic and popular literary pursuits, even if such 'crossover' or interdisciplinary fame was more easily gained and more generously regarded in America than in England.

"A mumbled descant": T.S. Eliot

One American who came to Oxford was Thomas Stearns Eliot (1888–1965). He won a scholarship to Merton College in 1914 and arrived in time to help defeat a motion proposed by the Junior Common Room that "this society abhors the Americanization of Oxford." The abhorrence seems to have been mutual; Eliot so disliked the place that he spent most of his time in London, and there is no evidence that his paths crossed with Tolkien while they were both in Oxford.

However, Tolkien did come across Eliot's work. He certainly knew *Four Quartets* sufficiently well to discuss it with others. Paul Johnson recalls taking part, as a freshman, in a discussion of the poems in 1946: "Lewis played the exegete on 'Little Gidding,' with a mumbled descant from Professor Tolkien and expostulations from Hugo Dyson . . . who repeated at intervals, 'It means anything or nothing, probably the latter.'" Lewis, and evidently Dyson as well, apparently disliked the poem, but what was Tolkien's view? Johnson does not say, but he describes the discussion as "puzzled and inconclusive,"[20] which at least suggests that the three dons did not take exactly the same line on the poem.

In fact, Tolkien seems to have had at least a cautiously positive view of Eliot. In a 1965 letter, he remarks that "T.S. Eliot has gone," in the context of the "melancholy subject" of the deaths of old friends and colleagues. Eliot had died only the previous week, so Tolkien was current with his information. Furthermore, Tolkien adds that the poetic epitaph that John Masefield wrote for the occasion, published in *The Times*, was "a perfect specimen of bad verse."[21] This elegy seems not to have been reprinted in any of Masefield's collections of poetry, which, judging from the four lines quoted in a *Church Times* retrospective piece, is just as well:

> May many an English flower and little bird
> (Primrose and robin redbreast unafraid)
> Gladden this garden where his rest is made
> And Christmas song respond, and Easter song.[22]

It is not so much that the verse is saccharine, trite, and metrically uneven, but that – as Tolkien aptly put it – it is "ludicrous" as a tribute to Eliot, that most unsentimental and wrenching of Modernist poets. Had Tolkien disapproved of Eliot, he might have been amused; the fact that he seems almost angered by it suggests that he had some sort of regard for Eliot's writings, or at any rate knew them well enough to see the mismatch of style and subject in Masefield's elegy.

Language games: the Modernists

Having touched on Eliot we have touched upon Modernism, a literary (and indeed artistic)* movement for which Tolkien is generally assumed to have had little patience. Yet, as we have seen in earlier chapters, he read and often appreciated the work of authors

---

* It is worth noting Tolkien's favorable view of the very modern, even experimental, paintings of Cor Blok (1934–) as an indication of the range of his tastes in the visual arts. Blok's works – including two that Tolkien purchased for himself – depict scenes from *The Lord of the Rings* with squarish figures, drab colors, and near-abstract designs; without Tolkien's explicit expression of approval, one would expect the opposite reaction. Tolkien bought *The Battle of the Hornburg* and *Dead Marshes III*; these, along with *Dunharrow*, which was gifted to him by Blok, "were framed and displayed in the Tolkien home for many years" (Pieter Collier, foreword to *A Tolkien Tapestry*, 8. See also Tolkien's 1962 letter to Blok, in *A Tolkien Tapestry*, 6). Collier notes that, when asked about who should illustrate a deluxe edition of *The Lord of the Rings*, Tolkien "suggested Cor Blok or Pauline Baynes as the possible artist" (8). Some images appear in Pieter Collier, "Interview with Cor Blok."

whose personal philosophy and approach to aesthetics differed greatly from his own (Eddison, for instance, who espoused a form of pantheism, and Haggard, whose interest in spiritualism and reincarnation made its way into some of his novels). We find that he had a similar breadth of mind when it came to Modernist writers; he read their works with an intrigued and not wholly antipathetic attitude.

In the early 1930s, Tolkien, along with Lewis, was invited to join a new literary club, founded by the Oxford undergraduate Edward Tangye Lean. This club has mostly been noted as the source of the name 'Inklings,' but it is worth attending to its nature in a bit more detail. Lean wrote regularly for the student magazine, *Isis*, and there (according to Peter Gilliver) showed himself to be "a self-consciously 'modern' writer . . . and as a reviewer, he enthusiastically tackled trendy and even avant-garde authors, such as Roy Campbell, James Joyce, Osbert Sitwell, and Stephen Spender."[23] Gilliver observes that Lean "stands out strongly and colourfully among his contemporaries – in ways which might seem to make him the unlikeliest person to have persuaded J.R.R. Tolkien and C.S. Lewis to join him in establishing a forum for the discussion of their literary activities."[24] Not only did Tolkien accept the invitation to join Lean's society, he even became the "scribe and keeper" of the club's Record Book, and read his poem "Errantry" to the group.[25] Tolkien was not Lean's tutor, so his participation had no sense of obligation about it. He might merely have wished to encourage literary activity (of any kind) among the undergraduates, but it is more reasonable to conclude that he had an interest, however qualified, in the Modernist authors whom Lean championed.

One Modernist author whose work Tolkien knew was the American novelist, poet, and playwright Gertrude Stein (1874–1946). His interest in her literary experiments is indicated by his inclusion of her name, and a few comments about sound and meaning, in his notes related to his 1931 lecture "A Secret Vice." Furthermore, both Stein and James Joyce figured in the post-lecture discussion.[26] Dimitra Fimi and Andrew Higgins, remarking upon how the 1920s and '30s were a time of change in linguistic theory and literary experimentation, observe that "A Secret Vice" and its accompanying notes "seem to engage with, and respond to, these contemporary trends and contexts."[27]

From Anna Livia Plurabelle to Eärendil?

The writings of James Joyce (1882–1941) represent the apogee of Modernist incomprehensibility and, again surprisingly, Tolkien knew of Joyce's work and responded to it with a fair degree of tolerance and thoughtfulness. (See figure 36.) He was sufficiently intrigued by Joyce's literary experiments to transliterate the name Anna Livia Plurabelle into his invented language of Qenya, and also to write several pages of notes about Joyce's work.[28] The name is significant both because Anna Livia Plurabelle herself is a major character, and because her name was given as the title of the first standalone publication of that work which eventually became *Finnegans Wake*, but which took Joyce seventeen years to complete, and only appeared in its finished form in 1939.[29] Beginning in 1924, extracts from what was then called the "Work in Progress" were published in various literary journals, and the section called *Anna Livia Plurabelle* was published in the US in 1928, and in the UK in 1930. This volume is almost certainly what Tolkien had read and was responding to, both in his linguistic doodle and the other notes he wrote about it, around the time that he was developing his lecture "A Secret Vice" and his "Essay on Phonetic Symbolism." The date of these notes (1930–1931) is significant, as it indicates that Tolkien was aware of Joyce's work while it was still incomplete.*

In her analysis of these notes, Margaret Hiley rightly draws attention to the way that Tolkien shares Joyce's interest in the *sound* of language.[30] Tolkien observes that most of the time our awareness of the meaning of language makes it difficult to appreciate "the independent contribution of the *sound part*"; we attend to what the words mean rather than to their purely sonic effects, their sheer musicality: "It needs an ear and training to appreciate it."[31] He seems to be recognizing some merit in Joyce's experiment, remarking that there is a slender sort of "meaning" to the text – he puts the word in inverted commas – which might better be called "atmosphere," but that this "is so clearly subordinate to *sound*, that one necessarily pays chief attention to the latter."[32] Nor does this emphasis on sound appear to be a bad thing: he adds that it is "unfair to call it a mere 'metrical' experiment. One might call music a mere 'accompaniment'."[33]† Indeed, it could be said that Tolkien's use of untranslated Elvish poetry in *The Lord of the Rings* has a Joycean flavor: Hiley suggests that his "sprinklings of invented languages . . . enable readers momentarily to give themselves up to pure sound."[34]

Hiley also draws attention to the section "On Translation" in Appendix F of *The Lord of the Rings*, where we learn that the name Merry, for instance, is really only a translation into English from the hobbits' Westron language in which he was known as "Kalimac," or "Kali" for short; Sam's name, likewise, is really "Ban"; and so on. This linguistic reversal has a "dislocating" effect on the reader, Hiley argues: "The secondary reality constructed in *The Lord of the Rings* is suddenly defamiliarized and the reader's response to it alienated." The technique, she suggests, is similar to Joyce's use of "dislocutions" in *Finnegans Wake*, serving "to shock readers into realizing that the reality they have let themselves be drawn into is constructed out of a medium that shifts and changes . . . we are forced to admit that there *is* no world other than the language, or rather layers of languages ('lashons of languages,' to quote the *Wake*), used to construct it."[35]

---

   * If Tolkien read other sections of *Finnegans Wake*, the countless different names given by Joyce to his protagonist Humphrey Chimpden Earwicker (including "Haromphreyld," "Finn MacCool," and "Mr Makeall Gone") might have also stuck in his mind, given the huge variety of names and titles that he gives to, for instance, Gandalf and Aragorn. Gandalf is known as Stormcrow, Mithrandir, Incánus, Tharkûn, Olórin, Láthspell, among other names; Aragorn as Strider, Wingfoot, Thorongil, Elessar, Envinyatar, Estel, and so on.

   † In this regard, Tolkien is certainly far more favorably disposed to Joyce's work than was C.S. Lewis, who dismissed the so-called "stream of consciousness" method as "steam of consciousness" (see Walter Hooper, Preface to *The Dark Tower and Other Stories*, ed. Walter Hooper [San Diego: Harcourt Brace & Co., 1977], 11.)

In fact, Hiley goes so far as to claim that Tolkien criticizes Joyce for being insufficiently radical, suggesting that "*Finnegans Wake* only goes part of the way towards the ideal of 'pure sound' that Tolkien, in these notes at least, appears to view as the ideal . . . a completely new language (or languages) that makes no reference in its sound patterns to any meanings attached to them in existing languages."[36] However, Tolkien does not in fact articulate such an ideal. He makes it clear that although he is interested in pure sound, the three elements of a word (letters, sound, and meaning) should "cohere and be in a coherent relationship one to another," even if the sound or form might, in a given context, be more important than the meaning. If this coherence is lacking, the resulting randomness is, he says, "satanic and anarchic"; a pattern that is merely "visualized (without interpretation)" would be "disjointed or artificial or 'monstrous.'" His notes conclude with the observation that the "best results are achieved . . . by making a 'language' in which the sounds do 'mean' something (though only perhaps to the author)."[37]

A careful consideration of the appendix "On Translation" shows that although it certainly does disrupt readers' perceptions, Tolkien is not here "on the brink of passing into a world of 'pure sound'"[38] as Hiley suggests. For one thing, Tolkien, in his editorial voice, observes that he has "translated all Westron names according to their senses" – such that we can know that "Kali" as the hobbits heard it would have had the same cheerful associations as "Merry" does for the English-language reader. Tolkien goes on to explain that he has used a mixture of translation and transcription, rather than rendering all names in the original language, because he wished to preserve the hobbits' perception of the contrast between familiar, ordinary names, and those that evoked a long-distant past: "All names if merely transcribed would seem to modern readers equally remote . . . to refer to Rivendell as Imladris was as if one now was to speak of Winchester as Camelot." Tolkien's move in the Appendix reminds readers of the fact that languages change over time: something that as a philologist he knew intimately, but that is not in most readers' conscious awareness. It is disconcerting in the sense that it opens up new vistas into linguistic reality, not in the sense that it altogether dissolves linguistic security.

A further point of interest comes in Tolkien's mention of "Merry Messenger" in his notes on Joyce. This refers to his poem "Errantry," the earliest extant version of which begins with "There was a merry passenger, / a messenger, a mariner." "Errantry" went through many different revisions before becoming "Eärendil Was a Mariner," which Bilbo recites at Rivendell in *The Fellowship of the Ring*.[39] The commonality among all the versions of the "Merry Messenger" is the exceptionally complex rhyme-scheme and meter. In *The Lord of the Rings* it is a serious piece, but in its original form it was, as Tolkien commented, "a piece of verbal acrobatics and metrical high-jinks . . . intended for recitation with great variations of speed."[40] The first published version of "Errantry" was in the *Oxford Magazine* in 1933, but it was read before that (sometime between 1931 and 1933) at the undergraduate 'Inklings' group founded by Edward Tangye Lean, who, as we saw above, was distinctly interested in Modernist authors. In fact, Lean published a review of *Anna Livia Plurabelle* in the October 29, 1930, issue of the student magazine *Isis*, which may have been the occasion of Tolkien's becoming aware of the book in the first place.[41] Given the overlap of dates between Tolkien's reading of "Errantry" to this Modernist-favoring student group, and the reference to the poem in his notes on Joyce, it seems fairly evident that Tolkien saw some connection between what he was doing in his metrically complex and playful poem, and what Joyce was attempting in his own metrical experiment. We can see in the work of both men an attention to sound as the predominant element, and also a certain playful circularity: as Tolkien explained, the reciter of "Errantry," upon coming to the end of the poem, "was supposed at once to begin repeating (at even higher speed) the beginning, unless somebody cried 'Once is enough.'"[42] The completed *Finnegans Wake* is structurally circular: it begins in the middle of a sentence, and ends with a sentence that leaves off at precisely the point where it would join the opening sentence, so that the book literally takes the reader back to where the book begins.

The consideration Tolkien gives to Joyce's work is less surprising when we bear in mind that both men were fascinated by language and in pushing the boundaries of genre. Tom Shippey points out that "both *Ulysses* and *The Lord of the Rings* are evidently works of the twentieth century, neither of them readily describable as novels, which are engaged in deep negotiation with the ancient genres of epic and romance."[43]* Tolkien would not have appreciated Joyce's irreverence toward Homer's *Odyssey*, but he himself occasionally sought more realism in epic and romance than is found in many a traditional tale. He once said that he disapproved of "those old romances where a knight in full armour sets off on a journey without even a cake in his hand,"[44] and he may be making a similarly practical point in *The Hobbit* when he has his eponymous hero lament that he has started his adventure without so much as a pocket handkerchief. Perhaps there is even a certain affinity at some level between Bilbo Baggins and Leopold Bloom. At any rate, Stephen Fry sees a degree of overlap, declaring "What I . . . admire about Tolkien is that, like Joyce, his protagonists are reluctant heroes, grounded in a reality, no matter how fantastical the world they inhabit."[45]

❧ Realistic fiction and satire

Tolkien's name will forever be associated with fantasy, but he had a taste for realistic fiction too. His appreciation of this department of literature is underscored by his knowledge of that keen-eyed observer of contemporaneous political and ecclesiastical culture, Anthony Trollope.[46]

He also evidently thought well of another realist, E.M. Forster, even going so far as to nominate him (albeit unsuccessfully, as it turned out) for the Nobel Prize in

---

* Margaret Hiley observes that Tolkien's mythic structures indicate that his work is "perhaps closer to modernists such as Eliot, Yeats, and Pound than has hitherto been assumed" ("Stolen Language, Cosmic Models: Myth and Mythology in Tolkien," 843).

Literature.[47] * (See figure 30.) Forster, the author of several novels, including *A Room with a View* (1908), *Howards End* (1910), and *A Passage to India* (1924), shows an interest in critiquing social class and conventions, particularly with regard to the effects of colonialism, which would have resonated with Tolkien.† It is not known for certain which of Forster's novels he read, and so I make no comment myself upon their possible influence on Middle-earth (in keeping with the parameters of this study laid out in chapter 2). However, I stretch my own principle just a little in order to note here in the main text what that insightful scholar Verlyn Flieger has to say about *Howards End*. She points to the scene where Margaret Schlegel muses on a topic that was very much on Tolkien's mind: "Why has not England a great mythology? Our folklore has never advanced beyond daintiness. . . . England still waits for the supreme moment of her literature – for the great poet who shall voice her, or, better still, for the thousand little poets whose voices shall pass into our common talk." Flieger suggests that this passage could have made an impression on the young Tolkien.[48] If she is right, it is something of a paradoxical situation, that Forster, the realist agnostic humanist, should perhaps have helped inspire the life's work of Tolkien, the devout Catholic fantasist.

A different sort of realism appears in the novels of Mary Renault, the pen name of Eileen Mary Challan, who had been one of Tolkien's students at Oxford in the 1920s. Renault is probably best known today for her fictional treatment of ancient Greek heroes, which are retold to be historically plausible, without supernatural events, but she also wrote a number of novels set in contemporary times. A common element in all her work is attention to psychological realism, particularly with regard to emotional bonds between men, and an interest in exploring homosexual themes. Renault herself lived openly with her female partner, Julie Mullard, in South Africa, where they emigrated in 1948 and became part of the gay expatriate community. Tolkien read a number of her books, naming in particular *The King Must Die* (1958) and *The Bull from the Sea* (1962) as ones that he found engrossing; he also remarked that an appreciative letter from Renault was "perhaps the piece of 'Fan-mail' that gives me most pleasure."[49] (See figure 37.) His respect for her as an author is suggested as well by his comment, in a letter, that he is curious as to how she would answer the sort of questions about unfinished work that

---

* Dennis Wilson Wise points out the role of "normal academic politicking" in the nomination: at that time, Tolkien was attempting to help create the Chair in Medieval and Renaissance English at Cambridge University for C.S. Lewis. Forster was a Cambridge man, and his nomination by Tolkien, Lord David Cecil, and F.P. Wilson may have been intended to "mollify any potential resistance in Cambridge to adding Lewis to its professorial ranks" ("J.R.R. Tolkien and the 1954 Nomination of E.M. Forster for the Nobel Prize in Literature," 144). Be that as it may, Tolkien need not (and in my opinion would not) have put his name to the letter if he did not have a genuine admiration for Forster's work; Cecil and Wilson could have made the nomination by themselves.

† Dennis Wilson Wise, confirming what we saw of Tolkien's views on Roman and British imperialism (see chapters 6 and 7 above), remarks that, like Forster, Tolkien recognized how "colonialism has a detrimental effect on the colonizer (to say nothing of the colonized)" ("J.R.R. Tolkien and the 1954 Nomination of E.M. Forster for the Nobel Prize in Literature," 149–50).

he is faced with.[50] We can see from his admiration of Renault and indeed Forster[51] that Tolkien's disagreement with them on matters of sexual ethics did not at all impede his appreciation of their literary work.

Tolkien appreciated social critique by other authors too. He was familiar with the writings of Saki (H.H. Munro), referring to the malign aunts and other female relatives who feature in stories such as "Sredni Vashtar." He heard read some of the work of Edith Somerville (better known by her pseudonym Martin Ross).[52] He was unenthusiastic about Naomi Mitchison's Arthurian novel *To the Chapel Perilous* (1955), perhaps because its satiric tone seemed to him to undercut the story.[53] Other satirists he apparently thought better of include A. Neil Lyons, whose novel *Arthur's: The Romance of a Coffee Stall* (1908)[54] is a mix of social critique and gentle humor; H.G. Wells in his social-satiric mode with *The History of Mr Polly* (1910);* and P.H. Newby, whose *Picnic at Sakkara* (1954), a satiric tale of a hapless English professor getting caught up in student protests in Egypt, Tolkien liked well enough to stay up late reading it.[55]

Other works did not keep him up late, or at least not for reasons that the author concerned would have welcomed. The novels of Amanda McKittrick Ros – *Irene Iddesleigh*, for example – were so exceptionally badly written that they were read aloud, as a humorous activity, at Inklings meetings.[56] The game was to see who could deliver her overwrought and strangulated prose the longest without bursting into laughter.

More seriously, Tolkien evidently read, or was at least acquainted with, the work of Iris Murdoch, whose novels often include philosophical and psychological themes; he was pleased to receive a fan letter from her, and they continued to correspond.[57] He also knew the writing of Henry Seton Merriman, whose carefully researched novels set in various foreign countries were highly regarded at the time.[58] He owned a copy of Gwyn Jones's collection *The Buttercup Field and Other Stories* (1945), and thought well enough of the author to bring him to an Inklings meeting in 1947, where Jones read one of his stories.[59] He was familiar with the work of Jacobine Hichens, including her novel *Noughts and Crosses* (1952),[60] which presents an Anglican perspective on the question of 'mixed marriages,' with its protagonist struggling to decide whether she can in conscience marry the Catholic man she loves.† He was willing to read William Ready's *The Poor Hater* (1958), with its critical take on Irish and Irish-American political issues.[61] He strongly disliked what he read by Ford Madox Ford, although we do not know what it was.[62] He received copies of David Grant's historical novel *Waes* (1967) and Andrea Giovene's sprawling Italian novel *The Book of Sansevero* (1970); if he had views on either of these titles, no records of them seem to have survived.[63] He called William Golding's

---

* According to his grandson Michael, Tolkien "was fascinated by the miraculous capacity of small and insignificant people (like H.G. Wells's Mr Polly) to achieve the unexpected in face of apparently insuperable odds" ("Autobiographical essay").

† *Noughts and Crosses* was Hichens's first novel: it received a brief notice in *The Catholic Herald* (June 20, 1952, p. 3) and was published in the U.S. the following year as *The Marriage of Elizabeth Whitacker*. She wrote only two other novels: *Touch and Go* (1953) and *Profit and Loss* (1955). Tolkien's reference to her work in a 1956 letter shows how he kept up with new releases in fiction.

Lord of the Flies "dreary stuff."[64] Yet it was this "dreary stuff" which in large part would win for Golding (in 1983) the Nobel Prize for Literature* that eluded E.M. Forster in 1954 and indeed that later eluded Tolkien himself, for he was nominated for the award in 1961 but did not receive it. That *The Lord of the Flies* came out just two months after the first part of *The Lord of the Rings* and had such a similar title presumably didn't help Tolkien to look upon it with favor.

✣ From Poirot to Psmith: light fiction

Not all of Tolkien's reading was of weighty and serious literary material; he also found time for some light reading.

Mystery stories were a particular favorite. Clyde Kilby recalled that Tolkien did "a good deal of reading of detective stories," and his grandson noted that he "went out of his way to praise Agatha Christie." (See figure 35.) He seems in one instance to have attempted a little detection of his own: his children recalled that, after reading Christie's *At Bertram's Hotel* (1965), which was inspired by the hotel Brown's in London, "he stayed at Brown's, and on leaving his room to investigate footsteps heard in the corridor, found himself locked out again!" Walter Hooper recalls visiting Tolkien in the hospital, late in his life, and finding him reading a Christie novel.[65]

Nor was she the only mystery writer he enjoyed. He read at least one novel by Michael Innes (the pen name of his Oxford colleague J.I.M. Stewart), noting that the etymological puzzle in it was more interesting than the murder plot. He does not provide the title, and hitherto scholars have not publicly recognized it by name, but having examined the letter in which he refers to it, I have been able to identify it as *The Bloody Wood*.[66]

Tolkien read all of Dorothy L. Sayers's Lord Peter Wimsey mysteries, but seems to have undergone a sea change in his opinion of them. He said that he "followed P. Wimsey from his attractive beginnings" in *Whose Body?* (1923) as far as *Gaudy Night* (1935), by which point, he said, he detested both Lord Peter and his love interest, Harriet Vane. Nonetheless, he persisted and read the final installment of the series, *Busman's Honeymoon* (1937), disliking it even more intensely than *Gaudy Night*.[67] (See figure 34.) Sayers's detective fiction steadily evolved from the classic crime puzzle to something not far removed from the psychological novel. Tolkien's initial favorable reaction, and his gradual lowering of esteem as he read each book in turn, suggests that he preferred detective fiction to focus on the mystery and its solution. This would be in line with his liking for

---

* In the citation accompanying the award, the Nobel Committee praised "the perspicuity" with which Golding's works "illuminate the human condition in the world today." Tolkien evidently found little in *Lord of the Flies* that he considered illuminating of the human condition. For more on the perspicuity, or lack thereof, in Golding's novel, see Rutger Bregman, *Humankind: A Hopeful History* (London: Bloomsbury, 2020), 21–40. Bregman relates what he calls "the real *Lord of the Flies*," an account of six teenaged Catholic schoolboys who were castaway on a remote Pacific island in June 1965 and who, unlike Golding's characters, did not descend into savagery, but maintained order and cared for one another until they were rescued over a year later.

Agatha Christie, his remark about Innes's *The Bloody Wood* (which is more psychological than puzzle-oriented), and his dislike of Chesterton's Father Brown stories, which depend on spiritual and moral insight rather than on clever plotting for their effects. Kilby recalls that Tolkien declared Sayers to be "a 'fair' writer of detective stories but believed he found some 'vulgarity' both in them and in her *Man Born to be King* [radio plays dramatizing the life of Jesus]." His views on *The Man Born to be King* (1943) seem also to have worsened over time, as Carpenter records that Tolkien once "greatly admired" the work, and Tolkien gave a copy to his son Michael.[68]

Tolkien also knew the writings of the comic novelist P.G. Wodehouse (1881–1975), best known for his stories of Jeeves and Wooster. He remarked in a letter that the title of his own *Smith of Wootton Major* is intentionally suggestive of the title of an early Wodehouse novel.[69]* Connections such as this one underscore the remarkable variety of influences affecting Tolkien's creative imagination; it is a tributary that would be far too fanciful to infer, were it not that Tolkien himself had certified it.

Literary brothers and sisters: Catholic writers

We now turn to a category of writers whom we would naturally expect Tolkien to have read and favored, for as well as being catholic in his literary taste, Tolkien was Catholic in his religious faith, and given the seriousness with which he practiced his Christianity, it is no surprise to find that he was interested in the work of other literary-minded Catholics of his day. We have already seen that he deeply admired the writings of Francis Thompson and appreciated those of Wilfred Childe (see chapter 10). There were many other co-religionists whose work he read and enjoyed.

He had in his library Coventry Patmore's *The Wedding Sermon* (1862),[70] which, though written before Patmore's reception into the Church, shares the emphasis on the theological mystery of love and marriage expressed in the poetry that he wrote after becoming a Catholic. He knew the work of the Jesuit poet-priest Gerard Manley Hopkins, being sufficiently taken by his writings to read and remark upon a volume of his private correspondence.† He was well-acquainted with the work of Hilaire Belloc, the

---

* This is surely one of the Psmith novels, which include *Psmith in the City* (1910) and *Psmith, Journalist* (1915). The joke is that the "P" is silent: "'I am Psmith,' said the old Etonian reverently. 'There is a preliminary P before the name. This, however, is silent. Like the tomb. Compare such words as ptarmigan, psalm, and phthisis'" (*Psmith, Journalist*, chapter XXVIII). The reasoning behind Tolkien's allusion is obscure. Perhaps the linguistic playfulness of the name "Psmith" simply provided an amusing contrast in Tolkien's mind with his own serious linguistic purposes in *Smith*. As Tom Shippey has pointed out, *Smith* has an element of linguistic allegory; it may be that Tolkien, in true English fashion, wanted to counterbalance that serious element with a light-hearted linkage to a comic novel. The more serious an Englishman is underneath, the more frivolous he tends to become on the surface (see chapter 12 for more on this point).

† The book in question is *The Correspondence of Gerard Manley Hopkins and Richard Watson Dixon*, ed. Claude Colleer Abbott (OUP, 1935). It contains a good deal on Hopkins's poetic theory of sprung rhythm, which may shed light on Tolkien's interest in metrical schemes for his own

pugnacious controversialist and prolific author whose writings include novels, poetry, history, biography, and works on politics and economics;[71]* as we noted in chapter 7, Tolkien read to the Oxford Newman Society an essay called "The Chill Barbarians of the North," in which he criticized Belloc's views about the superiority of Latin over Northern culture.[72]† He also read the work of Sheila Kaye-Smith, a popular writer and famous Catholic convert of the 1920s, who was considered a successor to Thomas Hardy in chronicling the life of the English rural poor.[73] Tolkien recommended her novel *A Challenge to Sirius* (1917) to Clyde Kilby, probably because, as a Southerner, Kilby would have been interested in that part of the novel set during the US Civil War.‡ (See figure 33.) Later in life, he became acquainted with the work of Elizabeth Jennings, a friend of his daughter Priscilla, and commented extensively on her volume *A Way of Looking* (1955), with special attention to the Atlantis poem, "New Worlds."[74]

At Newman Society events, Tolkien had occasion to meet and mingle with various Catholic authors. We know that he was present at a lecture given by Belloc in 1931, and attended a 1939 dinner at which the novelist Evelyn Waugh was among the guests.[75] Humphrey Carpenter, with his unfriendly, or at least uninterested, attitude toward Tolkien's Catholicism, is likely to have underplayed the importance of these interactions, but we can still manage to discern some of the principal figures in question.§ These

---

poetry. Tolkien discusses a point from it in some detail in a letter to C.S. Lewis (see *Letters*, 128). Tolkien might also have appreciated Hopkins's very precise use of botanical imagery in his poetry.

* We do not know what fictional titles he may have read, but in 1945, Tolkien gave two volumes of Belloc's nonfiction to his son Michael: *Characters of the Reformation* (1936) and *The Crisis of Civilization* (1937) (TCG:C, 313). In the latter book, Belloc argues that Catholics should write fiction, and do so with a light touch: "fiction which is composed with the object of direct argument in favor of the Faith is far less effective than fiction naturally inspired by a knowledge of what the Faith is and its effects upon Society" (*The Crisis of Civilization* [New York: Fordham University Press, 1937], 240). As we saw in chapter 9, Tolkien disliked overt theological elements in fiction. It may well be that Belloc's championing of the indirect and implicit method of infusing one's works with one's faith strengthened his determination to keep the theological element in Middle-earth understated and wholly integrated with the warp and woof of the text.

† Considering Belloc's voluminous output, it is uncertain which book Tolkien was critiquing, but possible candidates include *The Path to Rome* (1902) and *Esto Perpetua* (1906). These highly personal and vividly written travelogues, although not fiction, can be described as 'literary nonfiction.'

‡ *A Challenge to Sirius* follows an Englishman, Frank Rainger, through his whole life, from childhood, to adventures in America, and back to England. Tolkien's own interest in it may have stemmed from the novel's lament for the loss of an older, deeply rooted way of life at the hands of a 'machine' culture. At one point, Frank reflects: "What better battle can a man fight than the battle of freedom and open spaces, of agriculture and the soil, of warmth and growth and sunshine and romance, the battle of the South against the North?"

§ The fact that we have relatively little indication in the *Letters* or Carpenter's biography of Tolkien's engagement with modern Catholic writers (most notably Newman) is, I suspect, due at least in part to Carpenter's selection criteria. As an atheist who had rejected an Anglican upbringing (see Anderson, "Obituary," 221) and who described Tolkien's Christian values as "uptight," Carpenter was unlikely to find references to Catholic writers either interesting or relevant. If we include G.K. Chesterton and Ronald Knox, two of the most important Catholic literary figures of the twentieth century, whom we will now consider in more detail, taking them in reverse order.

"Torn in pieces": Ronald Knox

Ronald Knox (1888–1957), the Eton-educated son of an Evangelical Anglican bishop, was one of the most famous Catholic converts of Tolkien's day. Just four years older than Tolkien, Knox had enjoyed a celebrated undergraduate career at Oxford and later, after his conversion, became Catholic chaplain to the University between 1926 (the same year that Tolkien moved back to Oxford to take up his professorship at Pembroke College) and 1939, so the two men overlapped in Oxford for thirteen years. Walter Hooper reports that Tolkien came to know Knox during this time, the acquaintance being close enough that Tolkien attended the farewell dinner given to Knox upon his retirement as chaplain.[76]

Knox wrote numerous apologetics and devotional works, including *The Belief of Catholics* (1927) and *The Mass in Slow Motion* (1948). He was known for his wit, an early example being a lampoon on theological partisanship, entitled *Absolute and Abitofhell* (a pastiche of Dryden's *Absalom and Achitophel*). He also wrote several detective novels and was a member of the Detection Club, whose first president (as we will see below) was G.K Chesterton.

We have evidence of Tolkien's familiarity with the writings of Ronald Knox from a report by Warren Lewis of an unofficial Inklings gathering in which they discussed translation in general and Knox's recent Bible translation in particular. Warren notes that "Ronnie Knox's bible . . . was torn in pieces by Tollers," who said that Knox "had written so much parody and pastiche that he had lost what little ear for prose he ever had."[77] Tolkien must have been thinking not only of *Absolute and Abitofhell*, but also works such as the satirical "Studies in the Literature of Sherlock Holmes" (1912), a mock-scholarly essay assuming the real existence of Holmes and Watson; *Barchester Pilgrimage* (1935), a sequel to Anthony Trollope's *Barchester Chronicles* written in faux-Trollopian style; and his *tour de force* of pastiche, *Let Dons Delight* (1939), in which a conversation among dons in an Oxford Senior Common Room is revisited every half century from 1588 to 1938, each section being written in the linguistic register of that era, and gradually evolving into modern diction by the time we return to the frame story.

We do not know which of these particular works Tolkien had in mind when he criticized Knox's "parody and pastiche," but he evidently knew some or all of them well enough to come down hard on his translation of Scripture, a view which, as it happens, was not shared by C.S. Lewis, who was prepared to describe it in public as "particularly

look at interviews with Tolkien himself and with those who knew him, as well as materials such as his translation of Catholic prayers into Elvish, it is apparent that his faith was more important to him, and more integrated into his life, than the *Biography* and *Letters* show.

good."[78] Tolkien's catholic taste, including his taste for work by fellow Catholics, was voracious, but not partisan.

"Brilliant smash and glitter": G.K. Chesterton

We conclude this discussion of Catholic authors with a figure who will conveniently take us from prose to poetry, for Tolkien loved the work of G.K. Chesterton (1874–1936) in both modes. A prolific journalist, novelist, poet, and public speaker, Chesterton's notable early works include the anarchic *The Man Who Was Thursday* (1908); the Christian apologetics work *Orthodoxy* (1908), with its famous chapter "The Ethics of Elfland"; and the long historical poem *The Ballad of the White Horse* (1911). In addition to hundreds of essays in his characteristically playful and paradoxical style, he also wrote studies of various great thinkers and writers that were a mix of biography, literary criticism, and moral analysis: they include works on Robert Browning, Charles Dickens, and George Bernard Shaw.[79] He is nevertheless most widely known as the author of the Father Brown detective stories, in which a Catholic priest solves mysteries by means of his deep knowledge of human nature.[80] Chesterton was the first president of the Detection Club, formed in 1930 and having among its members Agatha Christie, Dorothy L. Sayers, and other stars of the Golden Age of mystery writing.

Chesterton and Tolkien were near-contemporaries. They were born only eighteen years apart, and Chesterton died, relatively young, at sixty-two, when Tolkien was forty-four. It is possible that Tolkien even heard Chesterton speak in person, for he gave an evening lecture on the topic of "Romance" at the Oxford Examination Schools in the Trinity term of 1914, when Tolkien was in residence.[81] Both men were also amateur artists of considerable talent and enthusiasm; Priscilla recalled that art supplies gave her father "particular pleasure, and they continued to do so right through his life."[82]* Although he only saw a few examples of Chesterton's art, in the illustrated anthology *The Coloured Lands*, it is interesting to note that Tolkien's early *Ishness* paintings show intriguing resemblances to his landscapes, in their use of color and abstract form.[83] The two men were responding to similar artistic and cultural influences.

Tolkien read widely in Chesterton's work from a fairly early age, though much of it was nonfiction and therefore does not concern us.†

---

* She and her brother John also recalled that their father "demonstrated how white could be an addition to a painting, rather than an absence of colour" (TFA, 58) – a view that Chesterton took in his essay "A Piece of Chalk," which appears in *Tremendous Trifles* (1909).

† While still at King Edward's School, he donated to the library copies of the apologetics works *Heretics* and its follow-up, *Orthodoxy* (TCG:C, 16). George Sayer recalls that Tolkien had "a great liking and appreciation for *The Everlasting Man*" (1925); Tolkien said that he felt its arguments to be "absolutely valid" (in Carpenter et al., "A Dialogue," 21). And Tolkien thought well also of Chesterton's ideas about storytelling, as we see in his discussion of some key ideas from *The Coloured Lands* in his lecture "On Fairy-stories" (OFS, 57, 68, 153, 192–3). He seems also to have been familiar with Chesterton's literary criticism (BC MS B, 91).

He knew *The Man Who Was Thursday* and *The Napoleon of Notting Hill*,[84] but did not enjoy the Father Brown stories (as we saw above), despite having a long-standing interest in detective fiction.[85] He certainly delighted in Chesterton's comic poetry. George Sayer recalls him knowing "by heart" a number of poems: "The Song of Quoodle," "The Song against Grocers," and "The Rolling English Road."[86] These are all featured in *The Flying Inn* (1914), a satiric tale of a near-future England in which the personal freedom of ordinary people, in particular the poor, is under attack from a paternalistic government intent on improving public health by abolishing alcohol. However, it is possible that Tolkien knew the poems not from the novel, but from a collection entitled *Wine, Water and Song: Poems by G.K. Chesterton* (1915), which reproduced the poems from *The Flying Inn*. (See figure 13.) Either way, we may perhaps see a Chestertonian influence upon one telling detail in *The Return of the King*, where we learn that Lotho Sackville-Baggins, after taking over the Shire as 'Chief,' "didn't hold with beer, save for his Men, and closed all the inns." In its way, this amounts to a capsule summary of *The Flying Inn*, with its exposé of the way that Prohibition is used in order to gain social control of the working classes for the benefit of a bureaucratic elite.*

Chesterton's comic verses are well-suited for chanting aloud, especially in a pub or while on a walking-tour, as with "The Rolling English Road":

> Before the Roman came to Rye or out to Severn strode,
> The rolling English drunkard made the rolling English road.
> A reeling road, a rolling road, that rambles round the shire,
> And after him the parson ran, the sexton and the squire;
> A merry road, a mazy road, and such as we did tread
> The night we went to Birmingham by way of Beachy Head.[87]

This is more jaunty than Tolkien's own "The Road goes ever on and on," but there is perhaps a small debt to Chesterton here; at any rate, the mention of "the shire" catches the eye.

Of Chesterton's other poetry, Tolkien had once upon a time enjoyed *The Ballad of the White Horse*. When he revisited the ballad to help Priscilla understand it, he found the poem unsatisfactory on the ground of its historical inaccuracy, but even on a second, less enthusiastic reading, he still approved the "brilliant smash and glitter of the words and phrases."[88] It is worth noting that the last book of the poem is titled "The Scouring of the Horse," referring to the way that the White Horse, carved through the turf into the chalk of a hilltop near Uffington, must be periodically cleansed of weeds. Malcolm Guite observes that in this section, Chesterton addresses the problem of the victorious warriors

---

* One of the books in Tolkien's personal library was the intriguingly titled *The Infidel Grape: An Anthology in Miniature in Praise of Wine* (1960), a booklet of extracts from oenophile literature by various authors, including modern translations of ancient verse by E. Powys Mathers (1892–1939), an extract from George Meredith's 1879 novel *The Egoist*, and poetry from Thomas Love Peacock (1785–1866). Wade Center, JRRT Lib. PN6071.D7 I53 1960.

who "find corruption at home and have to confront evil in another form and in their own native place." In the image of weeds obscuring the White Horse, Chesterton "calls England to an eternal vigilance." Here, Guite suggests, Tolkien may well have found the title, and perhaps even influence for the content, of "The Scouring of the Shire."[89]

Tolkien also admired the poem *Lepanto* without, as far as we know, any second thoughts; Priscilla recalled that her father enjoyed reciting it.[90] It is shorter and more restrained in style than *The Ballad of the White Horse* and hews more closely to the historical narrative. At 143 lines, the poem is long enough that if Tolkien indeed recited the entire poem from memory, rather than reading it aloud or recalling selected passages, it highlights the retentive quality of his memory, a fact worth bearing in mind more generally as we consider how his reading influenced his creativity.

Lepanto was immediately popular, and gained added resonance for readers during the Great War; John Buchan wrote to Chesterton in 1915 to say that "The other day in the trenches we shouted your Lepanto."[91] The poem's subject is the Christian defense of the West against an invasion of the Ottoman Turks in 1571, when the Holy League, assembled by Pope Pius V, achieved an unlikely victory at Lepanto in the Gulf of Patras. The outcome was attributed to the Virgin's intercession, and the day of the battle, October 7, became dedicated to Mary as Our Lady of Victory (soon thereafter renamed the Feast of Our Lady of the Holy Rosary). This aspect of *Lepanto* was likely part of its attraction for Tolkien, who had an unabashed devotion to the Blessed Virgin, and whose character of Galadriel, we should remember, has Marian resonances.*

Chesterton's poem has some intriguing points of similarity with the final battle of the West against the forces of Sauron. Like the Holy League, the forces led by Aragorn in *The Lord of the Rings* are a diverse coalition who, despite being badly outnumbered in their assault upon Mordor, are ultimately victorious (though the details of the battles are of course significantly different). Furthermore, the leader of the Holy League is Don John of Austria, whom Chesterton describes as "a crownless prince" upon a "nameless throne."[92] Aragorn keeps his true identity hidden for much of Tolkien's story, making him effectively "nameless," while nevertheless being the subject of the poetic prophecy that "The crownless again shall be king."

❧ Acknowledging the unacknowledged legislators: Poetry

Having examined Chesterton's poetry, as earlier in this chapter we examined that of Longfellow and Eliot, we have anticipated the final area of literary exploration in our summary survey of Tolkien's catholic taste. In his "Defence of Poetry" (1821), Percy Bysshe Shelley described poets as "the unacknowledged legislators of the world." It would be consistent with Shelley's description for Tolkien to refrain from acknowledging his debts to the modern poetry he read. However, he does admit an interest in certain

---

* He says that it is upon Our Lady that "all my own small perception of beauty both in majesty and simplicity is founded" (*Letters*, 172).

figures, and we can question what it was about them that led to his notice. Some of Tolkien's reading of poetry has already been treated in the context of other genres and forms (see the discussion of Carroll and Thompson in Chapters 3 and 10 respectively), but more remains to be considered. In this section we will attempt to trace those poets whom we have not already named, quickly surveying everyone we know him to have read, from Tennyson to John Wain, before spending a little more time on his contemporary, Roy Campbell, and then returning to the nineteenth century with a discussion of Matthew Arnold, whom we will consider alongside Russell Flint, the artist who illustrated one of his volumes of poetry that was of long-standing significance to Tolkien.

From Tennyson to John Wain

Tolkien was sufficiently interested in the poetry of Alfred, Lord Tennyson to translate into Elvish some lines from his poem "Break, Break, Break." He was moved by "Charge of the Light Brigade" because of the "heroism of obedience and love" displayed in the events recounted (the cavalry charge of British forces against the Russians during the Battle of Balaclava in 1854), but was not impressed by the quality of the verse.[93] He also knew Tennyson's folkloric ballad "The Voyage of Maeldune."[94] Here, an Irish chieftain and his crew, on a mission of vengeance, encounter various strange islands, including the Silent Isle, the Isle of Shouting, and the Isle of Fruits. Finally they come to the deadly Isle of the Double Towers, where two towers, one "of smooth-cut stone, one carved all over with flowers," clash against each other in a perpetual earthquake; there, the crew take sides with one or the other tower, and kill each other. Hallam Tennyson noted that the scene was "symbolical of the contest between Catholics and Protestants."[95] Finally the remnant of the crew pass on to "the Isle of a Saint who had sail'd with St. Brendan of yore," who counsels them to return home and "suffer the Past to be Past," which they indeed do.

At King Edward's School, Tolkien read the poetry of Rudyard Kipling and Walter de la Mare, with what opinion we do not know, and encountered the work of Robert Browning.[96]* He praised Dylan Thomas.[97]† He was acquainted at least with the 'fairy poetry' of W.B. Yeats.[98] He knew the melancholic work of H. Rex Freston, having bought a copy of *The Quest of Beauty* (1915) when it was published, and had enough of an interest in Freston to speak about him to a student literary society.[99] He wrote an introductory note for his T.C.B.S. friend Geoffrey Bache Smith's posthumously published collection *A Spring Harvest* (1918), which he co-edited. He corresponded with John Masefield, whose *A Letter from Pontus* (1936) he appreciated. He discussed the work

---

* Tolkien later registered a dislike of Browning's *The Pied Piper* (1842), which falls just outside the range of our study (see *Letters*, 311). We do not know what view he had of Browning's other works.

† Thomas's most famous poem, "Fern Hill," a meditation on a rather Shire-like rural childhood, includes a reference to "the house high hay," which, although probably nothing more than a verbal coincidence, does suggest the "High Hay" at Buckland in *FOTR*. Maureen F. Mann remarks on the way both Tolkien and Thomas took pleasure in the sound (not just the meaning) of language, in "'Certainly not our sense': Tolkien and Nonsense," 14–15.

of A.E. Housman with the Inklings. He had a friendly acquaintance with W.H. Auden and read several volumes of his poetry, such as *Shield of Achilles* (1952) and *About the House* (1965), finding the latter engrossing.[100]

He knew Alan Rook and was pleased to receive a copy of his *These Are My Comrades* (1943), a free-verse collection focused on wartime experiences.[101] He singles out for praise the poem "Aeroplane" as "an almost flawless example" of Rook's "poignant 'snap' technique."[102] To be sure, he doesn't say that he enjoys it, but he could easily have avoided making any comment at all, since he also laments being overworked. Here we see another example of how Tolkien could appreciate a poet's technique even when the style was very different from his own.

He owned a copy of C.S. Lewis's narrative poem *Dymer* (1926), appreciated his collection *Poems* enough to give it as a gift, and thought well of Lewis's poem "The Dragon Speaks" from *The Pilgrim's Regress* (1933), which he quotes in its entirety in his *Beowulf* lectures.[103] * He supported fellow Inkling Adam Fox as Oxford Professor of Poetry, and commended him as a "practising poet," citing the long historical poem *Old King Coel* (1937) as a notable example of Fox's work.[104] Tolkien subscribed to a volume of poetry by a junior member of the group, John Wain, who would make a name for himself as one of the 'Angry Young Men' of post-war British literature.[105] The title of this volume, *Mixed Feelings* (1951), quite probably summarizes Tolkien's own attitude to Wain's work.

"A powerful poet": Roy Campbell

Another 'angry young man,' though of an earlier vintage, is Roy Campbell (1901–1957), a Catholic convert whose tumultuous career included living in Spain at the outbreak of the Spanish Civil War. Campbell supported Franco against the Republicans, which led to his being labeled as a Fascist by his literary detractors, but he was also strongly anti-Communist and, later, anti-Nazi. In 1944, Campbell turned up unexpectedly at an Inklings gathering at The Eagle and Child; Tolkien was gratified to learn that Campbell had come to Oxford at least in part to see him. Two days later, Campbell joined Lewis and Tolkien at an evening gathering in Lewis's Magdalen rooms.†

---

* Lewis's poem evokes something of both *Beowulf* and "The Lay of Fáfnir," while expressing the narrator's draconian personality in a distinctly modern presentation. The dragon is highly intelligent, with an advanced vocabulary; he reflects on his own past life, regrets that he ate his wife, and broods over the possibility of a thief plotting to steal his hoard. Any attempt to deprive him of his wealth he regards as "merciless," given that he has no joys in life except gold, while men have "ale upon the benches, / Warm wives in bed, and song, and sleep the whole night." Here we see a psychologically complex portrayal of a dragon, one who is capable of intellectual deceit and moral manipulation. Is this, perhaps, a foreshadowing of the insidious Smaug? The dating of BC MS A (1932–1933) indicates that Tolkien read *The Pilgrim's Regress* during his prime *Hobbit*-writing years. Tolkien's dragon is much more than a *Beowulf*- or Fáfnir-style scaly monster that is skilled at gold-gathering and death-dealing; he has "rather an overwhelming personality," which may very well have been colored by Lewis's dragon-poem that Tolkien held in such high regard.

† In a letter to Christopher, Tolkien noted that he hoped to meet with Campbell again. In

Tolkien called Campbell a "powerful poet," referencing his books *The Flaming Terrapin* (1924) and *Flowering Rifle: A Poem from the Battlefield of Spain* (1936), and would later record his shock upon hearing of Campbell's death. He was also interested in the widely traveled Campbell's perspective on current events, remarking in a letter to Christopher about the Magdalen evening that Campbell "had most interesting things to say about the situation at Gib[raltar], since the war (in Spain)."[106] Tolkien praised Campbell in letters and conversations with others as well, including his grandson Michael and his student J.S. Ryan.[107]

That Campbell's very contemporary poetry should attract Tolkien's notice underscores his engagement with world events. *Flowering Rifle* is highly political; Campbell portrays the horrors of the Spanish Civil War with blunt and brutal phrases. For instance, the narrator, threatened by soldiers, has to "take with gratitude their rifle-butts – / My face a pulp, that it might save my guts."[108] Campbell's vivid portrayal of these horrors perhaps touched a personal note for Tolkien: Priscilla recalled that the "whole period of the Spanish Civil War cast a great shadow over my father's life" and that he had said "how terrible it would have been" if Fr. Francis Morgan, his guardian, who was partly of Spanish extraction, had been alive at the onset of the war.[109]

The Flaming Terrapin is a biting critique of contemporary culture through the lens of a surrealistic retelling of the story of Noah. After the Flood, Satan "comes prowling on the ravaged earth" and sires "Monsters perverse, and fosters feeble minds." Here the poem shifts to the present day, in which "Foul Mediocrity" reigns:

> All day, all night God stares across the curled
> Rim of the vast abyss upon the world:
> All night, all day, the world with eyes as dim
> Gazes as fatuously back at him. . . .
> Each Nation's banner, like a stinking clout,
> Infecting Earth's four winds, flaunts redly out,
> Dyed with the bloody issues of a war,
> For hordes of cheering victims to adore.

Campbell goes on to castigate "Plutocracy" and "Patriotism" and also "priests and churchmen" who are so "muddled and perplexed" that they are "heedless of the strife."[110]

Tolkien's praise for Campbell's poetry – very different from the commonsensical quatrains of Fox's *Old King Coel* or the flowery verses of Francis Thompson – shows the wide range of his taste as well as his ability to appreciate poetry being used overtly for political and social critique.

1946, Campbell attended a full Inklings meeting, where he read from his translations of Spanish poetry, a meeting at which Tolkien was probably present (TCG:C, 331).

Matthew Arnold and William Russell Flint

The final author in this section stands at the opposite pole from G.K. Chesterton, who provided the segue into it. Chesterton was confidently, even bombastically, Christian in his writings, whereas Matthew Arnold (1822–1888), a poet, essayist, and literary critic, was well known as a religious skeptic. Though he valued the moral and social aspects of Christianity, one of his best known poems today is "Dover Beach," a melancholic lament for the loss of faith. He was twice elected Professor of Poetry at Oxford, and it is to his poem "Thyrsis" that we owe the now-famous description of Oxford as the city of "dreaming spires."

Tolkien encountered Arnold's writings at King Edward's School; in 1910 a paper on his poetry was read at the Literary Society of which Tolkien was a member.[111] We can trace a more specific, and intriguing, connection with Arnold after Tolkien arrived in Oxford. He furnished his college rooms with four prints[112] taken from the 1910 edition of *The Scholar Gipsy & Thyrsis*.[113] These prints, all of them watercolor landscapes illustrated by William Russell Flint, were evidently much valued by Tolkien: he displayed them in his room in every place that he lived, including his final residence in Merton College.[114] We will return to these illustrations below.

What might Tolkien have appreciated in Arnold's poems? "The Scholar Gipsy" has a certain resonance with Tolkien's own life and hopes. In the poem, the narrator recalls the tale of "that Oxford scholar poor" who, despite his "quick inventive brain" is unsuccessful in academia, and instead sets off to roam with the gipsies. Years later, meeting some of his erstwhile colleagues in a country lane, he reports that the gipsies have "arts to rule . . . the workings of men's brains." He intends to learn this art and share it with the world, though he must await "heaven-sent moments for this skill," which, it seems, never come.

The scholar-gipsy is subsequently glimpsed in various places around Oxford, and the narrator suggests that his single-minded focus would keep him perpetually fresh and young, "in unclouded joy." The poem closes with the narrator's melancholy reflection that the scholar-gipsy ought to stay away from him and his companions, for if he came close he would be infected by their timorousness and "then thy glad perennial youth would fade, / Fade, and grow old at last and die like ours."[115]

For Tolkien in his young manhood, when success in academia was far from certain, as well as in his old age, when his powers were fading, this poem would have offered a subtle and moving commentary on the learned life and the passing of time. And perhaps the scholar-gipsy came to contribute something to Tolkien's most famous scholar-wizard, for he wears a "hat of antique shape, and cloak of grey," and has a habit of appearing and disappearing unexpectedly – being glimpsed at an ale-house, a ferry, the meadows near Godstow bridge, at a homestead in the hills, and even "Wrapt in [his] cloak and battling with the snow" as he climbed the "wintry ridge" and "gain'd the white brow of the Cumner range,"[116] not wholly unlike Gandalf on Caradhras.

The second poem in the volume, "Thyrsis," was written to commemorate the death of Arnold's friend, the poet Arthur Hugh Clough. It would have appealed immediately to Tolkien because its recurring image is the "tree-topped hill" where the narrator recalls spending time with his now-dead friend. Not only does this "Signal-Elm, that looks on Ilsley Downs" remind him of one departed friend, it serves as an image of hope that another friend, the Gandalf-like scholar-gipsy, is not dead. Interestingly, the narrator's perspective is frequently turned westward: he describes a "single elm-tree bright / Against the west," a "lonely Tree against the western sky," and calls on us to see "Backed by the sunset . . . Bare on its lonely ridge, the Tree! the Tree!" We should recall that the West is a significant direction in Tolkien's mythology, associated with the Elves and with deathlessness. Arnold's Tree becomes a longed-for point of reunion: ""Thyrsis, let me give my grief its hour / In the old haunt, and find our tree-topped hill! / Who, if not I, for questing here hath power?" At the end, the narrator finds comfort in the imagined whisper of his dead friend:

> *Why faintest thou? I wandered till I died.*
> *Roam on! the light we sought is shining still.*
> *Dost thou ask proof? Our Tree yet crowns the hill,*
> *Our Scholar travels yet the loved hillside.*[117]

Tolkien encountered Arnold's poem in this illustrated edition when he was nineteen, beginning his time at Oxford. Over the years, as he experienced the Great War, and later moved back to Oxford with his family, both "Thyrsis" and "The Scholar Gipsy" would have become increasingly entwined with his own experiences. The Oxford and Oxfordshire context, the repeated tree imagery, and the theme of loss of male friends, all would have made the poems and their accompanying artwork ever more poignantly meaningful. In the Shire, the most important single tree is the Party Tree, which is strongly associated with the love between Bilbo and Frodo; finding it wantonly felled upon their return home is one of the hardest blows that the hobbits endure. However, the seed given to Sam by Galadriel, once planted, grows to a tree that is both a new living thing and a reminder of the Quest and its losses. Sam's Mallorn, with its potent associations of friendship, community, and loss, may find some of its roots in Arnold.

"The Fir-Topped Hurst"

We know of Tolkien's reading of Matthew Arnold via his ownership of four prints from *The Scholar Gipsy & Thyrsis*, landscapes that were so important to Tolkien that he had them on display all of his adult life. It is therefore worth pausing to consider the influence of these illustrations in their own right. We have seen repeatedly in our study that Tolkien, in addition to being an accomplished visual artist, had a very strong visual memory. We know that he drew on visual sources for inspiration in his own work, both artistic and written.*

---

* For instance, Priscilla Tolkien recalls that his painting of the Eagles' eyrie in *The Hobbit*,

It is also worth noting that in his own work, both literary and visual, Tolkien was "fascinated by symbols," as his daughter-in-law Baillie explained: "From the very beginning he explored the interrelationship of words, pictures, and symbols." Perceptively, she notes a "deceptive combination of naturalism and formality" in his visual art and suggests that these varied elements need "to be interpreted for an understanding of his imagination, many-faceted and extraordinarily unified."[118]

With this in mind, let us turn to the four Russell Flint watercolors that Tolkien had on his walls throughout his life. As Catherine McIlwaine notes, there is "something of the Shire in these bucolic scenes."[119] In particular, I am struck by the scene entitled *The Fir-Topped Hurst*. Here we see an Oxfordshire landscape, which we can identify as cultivated land from the farming implements in the corner of the image. (See figure 39). It rises into a hill, topped with a small cluster of trees, showing dark against a blue sky touched with white wisps of clouds. The image would have been evocative for him, not only because it would bring to mind his own life in Oxford as a young man, and then a husband and father, but also because the tree on a hill would, for someone of his devout faith, have naturally suggested the hill of Calvary – the "green hill far away," as the words of the popular English hymn have it.[120] The cross of Christ is referred to as a "tree" in the Bible (for example, Galatians 3:13; 1 Peter 2:24) and often symbolized as such in medieval Christian imagery, most strikingly in *The Dream of the Rood*.

In several respects, there is a strong visual echo of *The Fir-Topped Hurst* in one of Tolkien's most famous paintings: *The Hill: Hobbiton-across-the Water*. Here again we have the mixture of cultivated land and trees, with the same color palette in golds, greens, and blues as the Russell Flint painting, though brighter and sharper. The foreground of Tolkien's painting is of the town of Hobbiton itself, but as the eye travels farther back, we find the Hill, rising up from the land around it with the same gentle swell as in Russell Flint's picture. And at the top of the Hill is a single tree, of the same rounded shape as the tight cluster of trees on the hurst, silhouetted against a blue sky with white clouds.*

And so we find in the poetry of Matthew Arnold and the art of Russell Flint a depiction of the English countryside that would be taken up by Tolkien's prehensile mind and remade for a new role in Middle-earth. As the significance of that tree atop 'The Hill'

"Bilbo Woke Up With Early Sun in His Eyes," was based on the picture of the Golden Eagle from the children's Wayside and Woodland books ("My Father the Artist," 6). The specific volume was T.A. Coward's *Birds of the British Isles and Their Eggs, First Series: Families Corvidae to Sulidae* (1920), illustrated by Archibald Thorburn, plate 132. His drawing of the trolls in *The Hobbit* seems to be directly modeled on the illustration by Jennie Harbour of "Hansel and Grethel" that appeared in *The Fairy Tale Book* (1934) (AH, 74). His idea "of someone being caught in a closing crack of a great willow probably came to him in part from Arthur Rackham's drawings of gnarled trees" (Scull and Hammond, *The Art of* The Lord of the Rings, 43).

* It is also worth observing the placement of the hedge circling the top of the hill, which, with its distinctly shaped bushes, has the appearance of a draped string of beads, culminating in a larger bush like a pendant bead next to Bilbo's door. The image is strikingly evocative of a rosary – at least for those viewers who are accustomed to handling rosaries. It is subtle, but very much in line with Tolkien's approach to embedding Christian imagery in his work.

draws on literature and painting and England and faith, so the legendarium more generally draws on the many layers of material provided by all that he had read and seen and known and believed, the 'leaf-mould' of his creative imagination. His modern reading, visual no less than verbal, was a crucial part of it.

⚜ Conclusion

We have now considered *all* the modern literature (within the parameters defined in chapter 2) that we are certain Tolkien read. In chapters 3 through 10, we examined specific authors and texts in some detail. In this present chapter, we have 'filled up the corners' by surveying the remaining authors that we know Tolkien was familiar with (Americans, Modernists, realists, satirists, genre fictionists, humorists, Papists, poets), and finished with a consideration of the link between written word and visual image, as seen in Russell Flint's watercolors.

Exploring Tolkien's remarkably catholic taste, as expressed in what he read and what he thought about it, helps us better understand his overall literary approach, and perhaps serves to explain something of the sheer *scale* of his legendarium. Whereas Jane Austen famously worked on a little piece of ivory, two inches wide,[121] Tolkien, by complete contrast, painted a canvas so large that he never even finished it in his lifetime and it was left to his son, Christopher, to bring major portions of it before the public in the decades following his death. His omnivorous tastes in modern reading reveal something characteristic about his sub-created world: nothing was too small or too grand, too weird or too ordinary, too silly or too dark, to be left out. Hugh Benson, who so loved *John Inglesant*, once remarked: "The Catholic who aspires to count all men as his brethren employs every vehicle that his romantic brain can suggest."[122] Tolkien's catholic taste in literature is, we might fairly say, but a manifestation of his Catholic faith: extensive, expansive, inclusive. Taste and faith alike are formative for Middle-earth.

What, then, shall we conclude? What has our journey through Tolkien's reading revealed to us about his writing and its critical assessments hitherto? What have we learned about his creative processes and the fruits of his labors? We will consider these questions in our final chapter.

✣ 12 ✣

Tolkien's Modern Reading

TOLKIEN'S INTENSELY CREATIVE AND ORIGINAL MIND WAS NOURISHED by many sources; as he said of *The Lord of the Rings*, a story such as this "grows like a seed in the dark out of the leaf-mould of the mind: out of all that has been seen or thought or read, that has long ago been forgotten, descending into the deeps."[1] Indeed, in 1968, he told an interviewer that creative works express "all the things you think you've forgotten. You have got to have known something to be able to forget it; it's not a negative."[2] He was well aware that his creative imagination did not always and only depend on his conscious memory; all that he had experienced, studied, read, and reflected on, even if forgotten, formed a positive contribution to the development and working of his artistic sensibility. He assimilated his reading so thoroughly that he once remarked, "the books that have remained in my mind remain as those things which I acquired and don't really seem much like the book itself." His reading was "digested," as he himself put it, and made available for use by his imagination in ways that went well beyond the conscious or the deliberate.[3]

It is because creativity works in such mysterious ways that we have considered it proper to suggest sources for and influences upon the legendarium even where Tolkien himself has not explicitly acknowledged them. Having carefully determined that he was familiar with a given work, it has been a fair undertaking to propose various possible contributions that his modern reading made to Middle-earth. And that is why it has been so essential to focus upon the works that we are *certain* he knew. Though some of the links that we have argued for in the preceding pages seem to us strong enough to be evaluated as being beyond reasonable doubt, there is inevitably a degree of doubt attendant upon other more tenuous links. We frankly admit that, but at least we can be sure that Tolkien knew the works we have been surveying. Where we have been hypothesizing, our hypothesis rests on a firm footing.

In this study, then, we have carefully considered all that we *know* Tolkien to have read, of post-1850 English-language literature in poetry and prose. In the process, we have traced a number of connections between his modern reading and the creation of his legendarium, discovering sources and influences of various kinds. We have noted the occasions when Tolkien himself granted that his modern reading influenced his fiction, including how George Dasent and Algernon Blackwood helped him arrive at the names "Moria" and "Crack of Doom"; how George MacDonald helped him depict goblins; how

William Morris helped him find the mixed prose-and-verse form of one of his earliest tales. These are Tolkien's own admissions of indebtedness, and there are others.

But beyond these indisputable debts, our survey has, I trust, provided a larger perspective on his creative imagination. We have seen how sheer example works as an influence: Tolkien sees that a thing can be done, then imitates it (as with the meta-textual artifact, the Sherd, that Rider Haggard made for *She*). We have seen how a kind of emulous rivalry works as an influence: Tolkien sees something done, then decides to do it better (as with the improvements he made to Crockett's wargs scene in *The Hobbit*). We have seen how disagreement or opposition works as an influence (as with J.M. Barrie, whose superficial treatment of maturation and mortality provoked Tolkien to articulate a more developed theme of death and the desire for deathlessness). And on top of all this we have gained insight into his views on genre, form, style, and language, and have observed his willingness to expose himself, imaginatively, to authors whose views he may have found unappealing or even downright rebarbative.

Perhaps most important of all, we have seen the huge numbers of different modern writers and works that he engaged with: by my tally it is 148 authors and more than 200 works. Whether or not my arguments *apropos* specific sources and influences have been convincing, this exploration of Tolkien's reading has, I believe, established beyond reasonable doubt that he read far more extensively in modern literature, and thought much more highly of it, than we would expect from Humphrey Carpenter's dismissive comments that "He read very little modern fiction, and took no serious notice of it," and that "for him English literature ended with Chaucer."[4] The picture Carpenter bequeathed to scholarship has been seriously misleading; the popular view of Tolkien as stuck in the past and interested only in medieval literature is simply incorrect.

Even with the evidence before us, however, such a reversal of perspective is startling.* In chapter 1, we examined four reasons for the development of the popular idea of Tolkien as uninfluenceable and backward-looking: Carpenter's tendentious biography; his misleading editorializing of the letters; the mistaken assumption that Tolkien was similar in every respect to Lewis; and an unbalanced focus on the opinions expressed by Tolkien in his later years. But we should dig more deeply. Why has the idea of an anti-modern Tolkien been so persistent – in the teeth of the evidence, as we have seen? Why has Tolkien's attitude been so consistently misread?

---

* I readily admit, however, that the reversal is not complete. The evidence that I have collected remains only a partial representation of what he read. We do not yet have a complete Collected Letters; we do not have a complete listing of his personal library, which, alas, was dispersed after his death; and even if we had both of those things, we could never have a full record of works that he read but neither owned nor had occasion to mention in his letters or writings. To give a more specific example, as we saw in chapter 2, Tolkien would certainly have known the writings of John Henry Newman, but remarkably there is no record of which works he knew or what he thought of them. Newman, then, serves as an ideal representative of the "cloud of witnesses": those authors whom Tolkien surely read, but whose names do not appear in his body of work. Their influences, if any, are invisible and untraceable – at least as yet. I hope this study will prompt other scholars to research these matters further.

We will consider four further points in this regard: the influence of his biographers before and after Carpenter; an undue extrapolation from Tolkien's views on the Oxford English Syllabus; and two notable but under-acknowledged aspects of Tolkien's personality – namely, his tendency toward hyperbole and his innate English habit of self-deprecation.

"Rogue" biographers

Humphrey Carpenter was not the first biographer to misrepresent Tolkien; that dubious honor goes to William Ready, whose *The Tolkien Relation* (1968) certainly contributed to the idea of Tolkien as stuck in the past. Ready is contemptuous of the Birmingham Oratory (pervaded with "the dusty feeling of defeat") and of the men's colleges at Oxford (the male companionship of the dons is "not [part of] growing up, but a defense against it"); he describes Tolkien as "conservative, traditional, and rigid," a man who "loves England for what it used to be for him."[5] When he read the published book, Tolkien declared that Ready was "a rogue" who had spoken with him on a short visit under false pretenses, and had "embroidered [his recollections of the conversation] with wholly illegitimate deductions of his own and the addition of baseless fictions."[6] *

After Ready in the late '60s came Daniel Grotta in the mid '70s. Though less spectacularly bad than its predecessor, Grotta's *J.R.R. Tolkien: Architect of Middle Earth* (1976) is both unauthorized and unreliable. The Tolkien family attempted to hinder it, denying Grotta access to documents, asking friends and family members not to speak to him, and refusing permission to publish some of the information he did find.[7]

Tolkien's publisher, Rayner Unwin, felt strongly that an authorized biography was needed; meanwhile, the "stop-gap solution" was the photographic record that would eventually become *The Tolkien Family Album*. Unwin felt that for this small project, "it did not seem necessary to have a very experienced author. . . . I didn't think a mixture of photographs and extended captions needed any great qualifications." And so they hired the young Humphrey Carpenter, then working for Radio Oxford. However, as Unwin recalled, "It soon became apparent that Humphrey had dug himself so enthusiastically into the project that a full-scale biography was in the making."[8] In 1978, Carpenter told an interviewer, "People ask me, how did you come to be 'chosen' to be the authorized biographer. The answer is, there was no choosing; I rather forced myself upon the Tolkien family!"[9]

Carpenter, then, gained authorized status partly fortuitously and partly because of his own maneuvering; he was not the carefully chosen and qualified researcher that might reasonably be expected by his readers. However, to the wider reading public, and

---

* The most striking of these fictions is the claim that Tolkien's mother, had, prior to her marriage, "worked with her sisters as a missionary among the women of the Sultan of Zanzibar" (Ready, 6). This utterly unfounded claim has, as Hammond and Scull remark, "cast a long shadow over later biographies and biographical sketches" (TCG:RG, 161).

to scholars unaware of Christopher Tolkien's dissatisfaction with the draft of the *Biography* (see chapter 1), Carpenter's presentation would have seemed objective and balanced in comparison to Ready's breathless and lurid claims. Carpenter's judgments went on to have an outsize effect, partly because of the book's early date, its authorized status, and his unrepeated access to family papers, and partly because it stood over against both Ready's 'rogue' book and Grotta's contested one. Without evidence to the contrary, it was reasonable to accept Carpenter's assessment about Tolkien's modern reading at face value. However, that is precisely what we can no longer do.

As we have seen, despite having compiled the *Letters* and written biographies both of Tolkien himself and of the Inklings as a group, Carpenter seems neither to have well understood, nor particularly to have liked, Tolkien – or, for that matter, any of the other Inklings.

A 1984 article about his interactions with Tolkien is characteristic. The account is one of repeated failures to "get him to broadcast or do things" (Carpenter acknowledges here that a straightforward approach would have been better than the convoluted tactics he pursued) and a general inability to get on the elderly, widowed Tolkien's wavelength. Carpenter's last communication with him, regarding a canceled appointment, was a "rather cross letter," saying, "You're obviously bored at the prospect of having to put up with my company, so I shan't bother you any more." Tolkien wrote back what Carpenter admitted was a "charming" note, saying, "I'm certainly not bored, I'd like to see you" – but they never did meet again.[10]

With regard to the Inklings as a whole, in a 1979 interview, Carpenter was asked, "Who of the Inklings do you think you'd have had the strongest rapport with?" His reply is telling: "I don't think I would with any. One looks about at other groups that *do* exist still in Oxford and says, 'Oh, there's that little clique in the corner again chatting away and reading their own poems. No, I'm not the sort of person who goes in for that sort of thing.' I suspect I would have been extremely rude about it at the time." He goes on to disparage "Lewis and his cronies" as "a mutual congratulations society" – something that more extensive recent research has demonstrated it certainly was not.[11]

All biography necessarily reflects the attitudes and preconceptions of its writer, but the extent to which the biographer's own personality shapes, interprets, and potentially distorts the material can vary a great deal. Carpenter seems to have been relatively uninterested in striving for objectivity, remarking that "having finished writing a biography, one could go back to the source material and write several completely different lives of the same person, which would be just as long, and which used different material to tell a very different story."[12] * There was a mischievous and irresponsible streak in Carpenter, and Tolkien was not the only figure to have suffered from it: Robert Runcie† and Joseph

---

* He also commented that, in a biography, "the principal agenda is always the personality of the biographer. . . . we're all really writing about ourselves. That's the hidden agenda" ("Learning about Ourselves," 273)

† Robert Runcie was Archbishop of Canterbury from 1980–1991. Upon his retirement, he commissioned Carpenter to write his biography, intending that it should be published after his

Lyne* were among his other victims. But there seems to have been a particular reason for his animus toward Tolkien. Carpenter admitted: "With Tolkien, the personal agenda was my own childhood. I'd lived in the same culture as him, in an Oxford academic family. I wanted to portray that milieu, about which I had very mixed feelings."[13] †

Carpenter's inaccurate assessment of Tolkien's reading habits has shaped subsequent approaches to the topic, both at the popular and at the scholarly level. At the popular level, the BBC radio drama *Tolkien in Love* depicted Tolkien as ignorant of contemporary fiction and of the opinion that "Everything after 1066 should be excised from schools." And at the scholarly level, even such a leading authority as Michael Ward admits he was misled. In his magisterial *Planet Narnia: The Seven Heavens in the Imagination of C.S. Lewis*, Ward wrote, "It must be emphasised that Tolkien's literary tastes were quite extraordinarily narrow (he read little in English literature after Chaucer)"; he went on to state that Tolkien disliked "most modern literature." Having read a draft of this book, Ward has revised those judgments. "I repent in dust and ashes," he confessed to me in an email. "Though I know Lewis like the back of my hand, I'm no specialist on Tolkien, and I trusted that Carpenter knew what he was talking about. Clearly, he didn't!"[14]

To regain a more reliable perspective, it is helpful to look at what literary critics had to say on this subject in the period before Carpenter muddied the waters. Writing in 1974, three years before Carpenter's *Biography*, Colin Wilson makes a direct comparison with Proust and T.S. Eliot, noting that "*The Lord of the Rings* is a significant work of twentieth century literature, as significant as *Remembrance of Things Past* or *The Waste Land*. . . . its symbols constitute a kind of *exploration* of the real world."[15] Wilson knew almost nothing about the man himself (he is even unsure whether Tolkien is a Catholic), but on the basis of Tolkien's writings alone, placed him firmly in the wider literary context of the twentieth century. Another pre-Carpenter-era critic, Richard C. West, began his analysis of the medieval interlace structure of *The Lord of the Rings* by noting that "the book is addressed to the modern world," and goes on to say, "Lover of the past though he certainly is, J.R.R. Tolkien was nonetheless our contemporary."[16] In 1972, Donald Davie devoted a chapter of *Thomas Hardy and British Poetry* to a thoughtful comparative analysis of how Kingsley Amis and J.R.R. Tolkien explore the problems of authority and power.[17]

---

death. The result was a deliberately provocative and headline-seeking work that came out while Runcie was still alive, but during his final illness, and much to his distress. See Rachel Donnelly, "Runcie calls new biography of him 'highly misleading'" (*Irish Times*, 9 Sept. 1996, https://www. irishtimes.com/news/runcie-calls-new-biography-of-him-highly-misleading-1.84330).

* Joseph Lyne (1837–1908) was an Anglican Benedictine who tried to reintroduce monasticism into the Church of England and whose religious name was Fr. Ignatius of Jesus. Carpenter's very first biographical foray was a play about him, which has never been published. The Father Ignatius Memorial Trust remarked that "we must admit to not having felt very happy about it" (The Father Ignatius Memorial Trust newsletter, Spring 1975, 2).

† Though from a devout Anglo-Catholic home (he was the only son of the Bishop of Oxford), Carpenter was a self-described atheist by age 21.

After Carpenter's biographies of Tolkien and of the Inklings, in 1977 and 1978 respectively, commentators became less interested in, or at any rate less confident about, placing Tolkien amongst his modern literary contemporaries. Carpenter had effectively muffled the topic. Only in recent years has scholarship begun to shift toward a more nuanced view.

✂ A syllabus of errors

"Literature stops in 1100; after that there's only books." This remark is frequently (mis)attributed to Tolkien. A.N. Wilson repeats the line in his biography of C.S. Lewis, correctly noting that it was not said by Tolkien, but claiming that it was said by a colleague "under Tolkien's influence" and "echoed Tolkien's own position."[18]* In fact, Tolkien never said this, but the idea that he did (or that he believed it) seems to have come from a fundamental misunderstanding of his work in reforming the Oxford English Syllabus, distorted and exaggerated further over time, as with the game called 'telephone.' The extent to which this idea has wormed its way into the popular understanding of Tolkien is illustrated by a remark from Andrew Marr, one of Britain's leading broadcasters and journalists. Marr declares that Lewis and Tolkien "both thought the English syllabus should stop with Geoffrey Chaucer. . . . it meant leaving out some half-decent writers like William Shakespeare, but for them this was a price worth paying in order to marinate themselves in everything from the early sagas to the magical romances, the old stories which gave them the tools for their own fiction."[19] Marr assumes (as many have done) that what Tolkien thought was best to teach in his field was identical to what he enjoyed reading and to what he used as source material for his own writing.

But such a view is really rather peculiar. As a general rule, we do not automatically assume that academics' reading interests are restricted to their field of study. Classicists are not expected to disparage all literature after Homer and Virgil; scholars of foreign languages are not barred from reading books in their native tongue; experts in poetry do not shock us if they read the occasional novel. Why, then, do readers so persistently assume that Tolkien's tastes were rigidly circumscribed by his attitude toward the Oxford English Syllabus?

The source of the problem can very probably be traced to Carpenter's simplified and dramatized treatment of Tolkien's involvement with the reform of the Syllabus – an issue that is considerably knottier and more complex than most people realize. Because this issue has had such a significant knock-on effect upon views of Tolkien, it is worth unpacking it in some detail.

---

* Scull and Hammond clarify that the actual originator of the phrase, Alistair Campbell, was "a friend to Tolkien but not 'under his influence', and the remark was made only in jest, as part of the continuing feud in the Oxford English School between Literature and Language" (TCG:RG, 1055). The remark is sometimes quoted as "There's no literature after 1830, only books," a reference to the fact that the syllabus for the Honour School of English Language and Literature ended in those days at 1830 (Cockshut, "Lewis in Post-War Oxford," 74).

Long before Tolkien arrived on the scene, Oxford's English School had faced a difficulty with the Syllabus.* The basic problem was that, since English literature includes texts in earlier forms of the language (Old and Middle English), which cannot be read at all without special training, any attempt to cover English as a whole is faced with the problem of reconciling 'Language' and 'Literature' elements.

Tolkien valued both the linguistic and the literary sides, but, as he argued in his 1930 article "The Oxford English School," the division of material at Oxford was incoherent and pedagogically ineffective. As Helen Gardner, one of Tolkien's colleagues in the English Faculty, explained, he had the "conviction that a proper study of modern literature required the linguistic training that the study of earlier literature gave" as well as a "sense of the continuity of English literature." There were necessarily tradeoffs: Gardner adds that "In order to make time for a more extended study of earlier literature and to preserve the principle of continuity, the study of English Literature ended at 1830 and a paper on the Victorian Age remained as an optional extra paper which almost nobody offered."[20]

By 1933, a new English Syllabus was in place, in line with Tolkien's ideas of reform. There were now three different options for students in the Oxford English School: Course I (medieval philology and literature up to Chaucer); Course II (philology and literature up to Shakespeare and Milton); and Course III (literature up to 1830, with an optional paper that could include later texts).[21] Tolkien was by no means opposed to the study of modern literature in principle. In 1931, he indicated that he "would agree to the modification" of making the Victorian paper required rather than optional, but considered that the issue was best decided by the tutors in charge of modern literature.[22]

However, Carpenter gives no hint of these complexities, nor even mentions that there were three distinct options available to students. He sets out the issue in broad strokes:

> One faction believed that [the Syllabus] ought to be based on ancient and medieval texts and their language, with at most only a brief excursion into 'modern' literature – by 'modern' they meant anything later than Chaucer. . . . On the other side were those who thought the most

---

* The term 'Syllabus' may also be misleading to American readers, for whom 'syllabus' usually refers to a detailed document for a college course that covers every last detail of lectures, discussions, readings, writing assignments, tests, and grading. The Oxford English Syllabus is more what Americans would call a 'curriculum' or 'degree plan.' It indicates the available 'courses' (i.e., areas of specialization) and the 'papers' (i.e., what Americans would call 'courses' or 'classes') included in them, and indicates the core, 'set texts' that students are expected to know for their eventual examinations, but it does not specify further. Individual tutors (instructors) assign essays and additional reading, and recommend which lectures their students should attend. Tolkien's involvement with the Oxford English Syllabus should be understood, then, as being at a fairly high conceptual level, not as micromanagement. See further, the present-day Oxford English Faculty course summary and structure, https://www.english.ox.ac.uk/course-summary and https://www.english.ox.ac.uk/course-structure.

important thing was to study the whole range of English literature up to the present day.[23]

Carpenter correctly presents Tolkien as squarely in the former camp. Very naturally, Tolkien was in favor of teaching medieval language and literature, for he was at that time the Rawlinson and Bosworth Professor of Anglo-Saxon; it was his responsibility to ensure that the subject was taught, and taught well, and to convince his colleagues on the English Faculty, who were responsible for teaching the other subjects, of the merits of giving a substantial place to medieval literature in the Syllabus.

Carpenter does present some of the grounds for Tolkien's views: for instance, that the Syllabus ought to encourage a literary approach to early and medieval writings and not treat them merely as a quarry for students studying the history of the language. However, he gives equal or even more attention to what are not academic reasons at all, suggesting that Tolkien rejects the wider literary focus in part because he simply doesn't know modern literature well enough (despite the fact that no English faculty member would have lectured on every subject on the Syllabus anyway). He hints that there was some mischief-making afoot too, for Tolkien "took an impish delight in challenging established values" (which is an odd rationale to suggest for what is presented as an ultra-conservative position). Most significantly for our purposes, Carpenter argues that the "deeper and more important reason" for Tolkien's stance on the Syllabus "was that his own mind and imagination had been captivated since schooldays by early English poems such as *Beowulf, Sir Gawain and the Green Knight*, and *Pearl*, and by the old Icelandic *Völsungasaga* and *Elder Edda*. These were all the literature that he needed."[24]

But as this book has demonstrated, he "needed" a great deal of modern reading too. Even if we grant that medieval works were what Tolkien privately *preferred*, it is not true that his personal tastes were what decisively shaped his professional views on the Syllabus, nor that the Syllabus dictated his leisure reading. The whole issue of Syllabus Reform was a pedagogical one: as an Oxford professor he was fully aware that students have only a limited time for their studies and therefore that breadth in coverage must come at the expense of depth of study, and vice versa. It is a dilemma well known to any teacher; one must make choices and prioritize. This is precisely what Tolkien and the other members of the English Faculty were attempting to do, each very naturally fighting for his or her own corner.

Questions of syllabus content are not necessarily the same as questions of relative merit. An Oxford student could be expected to have the ability to read and analyze a text written in modern English without special training (even if such training can enable them to do so at a higher level). However, that same student could not be expected to be able to read an Old English text without special training, let alone to understand its nuances. Tolkien, very properly (from the point of view provided by his professorial Chair), wished to equip students with the tools necessary for tackling literature that would not otherwise be accessible to them.

It was therefore neither backward-looking, still less "radically reactionary" (as A.N. Wilson would have it), for Tolkien to favor an English education centered on pre-1830s literature. His professional opinion on the Syllabus tells us nothing, in and of itself, about the extent or the nature of his modern reading.

Faculty meetings and curriculum development are prosaic matters that don't make for dramatic reading in a biography. Carpenter notched up the warfare element in order to keep the attention of his readers, but his approach lent itself to oversimplifications and misunderstandings. When Tolkien did explicitly address the subject, his manifesto on syllabus reform, "The Oxford English School," was an irenic proposal, with no disparagement of modern literature.[25] But such a cool-headed approach did not comport with the figure that Carpenter wished to paint. He preferred to tag Tolkien as part of a die-hard anti-modern tribe, and certainly his professional expertise in medieval writers and *relative* unfamiliarity with more contemporary works made it a plausible picture to offer the public, one that generations of readers have now accepted as accurate and balanced. In reality, though, the truth is quite different and much more mundane. Tolkien knew very well that English literature continued after 1100, and his own modern reading was extensive; he just didn't think there was room for it in the Syllabus.

We cannot, however, look only to biographical issues for the reasons why Tolkien's attitude toward modern literature (and about literary influence) has been so often misunderstood. We should also consider certain aspects of Tolkien's personality that have made it more difficult to interpret his own stated views, the first aspect being his predilection for hyperbole.

❧ "An element of acting": Tolkien's hyperbole

"I can't stand George MacDonald's books at any price at all"; "as a child I couldn't stand Hans Christian Andersen and I can't now"; "I conceived a loathing for [Peter Wimsey] (and his creatrix) not surpassed by any other character in literature known to me."[26] These are emphatic reactions – but can they be taken at face value?

C.S. Lewis once remarked that "Tolkien's lively mind sometimes leads him (with perfectly innocent intentions) to overstate things." Christopher Tolkien noted that his father had a tendency toward the "rhetorical superlative." John Garth has identified it as a habit of "mischievous hyperbole."[27]

The most famous exhibition of this is in Tolkien's reaction to the early chapters of *The Lion, the Witch and the Wardrobe*: "It really won't do, you know! . . . Doesn't he know what he's talking about?"[28] Such a comment is not exactly measured, but it could easily have been delivered in a chaffing or mock-ferocious manner, characteristic of the way the Inklings interacted at their gatherings. Carpenter heightened his reaction into irritation, annoyance, and contempt;[29] unfortunately, later biographers have often intensified it even further. For instance, in their otherwise generally solid volume *The Fellowship*, Philip and Carol Zaleski describe Tolkien's reaction to the first

Narnia Chronicle as "apoplectic,"[30] for which, as we have seen, there is no evidence. Roger Lancelyn Green, to whom the remark was made, merely recalled, years later, that Tolkien's general disfavoring of invented fairy-tales "tallies with his later outburst to me about C.S. Lewis's first Narnian story"[31] – the word "outburst" being a word that conveys Tolkien's characteristically lively mode of delivery without any especially negative connotations.

Tolkien's expressions of "mischievous hyperbole" are often considerably softened and clarified when we see them in their original context – if it is available. In chapter 4 we saw, for example, that Tolkien later showed appreciation of the Narnia books, calling them "deservedly very popular." We find another instance in the context of Tolkien's scathing put-down of Dorothy L. Sayers's novels. Bear in mind that if he had, as he said, followed Lord Peter "from his attractive beginnings so far [as *Gaudy Night*]," then he had read as many as *nine* Wimsey novels up to that point, and despite his dislike of *Gaudy Night* he still bothered to read its sequel, *Busman's Honeymoon*, which he declared made him "sick."[32] An act of literary masochism? Or an indication that, despite his ostentatious dispraise, he still found something worthwhile in them? Most probably, he kept reading for the mystery-puzzle plots, despite finding the character development uncongenial. And he seems to have been more measured in his conversation years later with Clyde Kilby, who recalled that Tolkien "found Dorothy Sayers a 'fair' writer of detective stories" despite a touch of "vulgarity."[33] The later assessment is less deliciously quotable, but it is probably more representative of his overall opinion.

Tolkien's habit of overstatement also seems to have been an expression of his personality more generally, and not just of his approach to literary criticism. For instance, his secretary Joy Hill recalls how, over a meal, "he suddenly brought up something about a jacket design, which irritated him, and suddenly in a flash, and this was typical, he got rather cross. . . . I said 'Well, I'm not responsible for that jacket design, so don't take it out on me.' And then, it was like – and this happened every time he was cross – thunder moving away and the sun coming out. With a charming smile, and he was always terribly courteous, he said, 'my dear, I'm so very sorry. I've been so unfair.'"[34] It seems to have been in his nature often to react forcefully, and to follow this either by nuancing of his point, or apologetic backtracking.

Owen Barfield recalled his first meeting with Tolkien in the 1920s, at which Tolkien was "in a ridiculously combative mood and seemed to me to contradict nearly everything I said." Nonetheless, their conversation was "entirely good humoured and enjoyable; and his random belligerence had only made me laugh."[35] In a similar vein many years later, George Sayer observed Tolkien's remarkable range of expressions in conversation with the Lewis brothers: one moment smiling and genial, he might "burst into savage scathing criticism, looking fierce and menacing. Then he might soon become genial again." Perceptively, Sayer felt there was "an element of acting about this gesturing" even though "much that he said was extremely serious."[36] Tolkien had a flair for the dramatic, even the slightly histrionic, in his self-expression.

Having this pattern in mind helps us better understand some of the opinions Tolkien expressed regarding his reading. For instance, Clyde Kilby recalls that Tolkien "said he did not like Russian writers and could not read them."[37] Such a definitive statement would tend to make us think that he did *not* read any Russian literature, but with his habits of speech in mind, we can see that "could not read them" may merely indicate that he disliked some or much, though presumably not all (or else why would he have kept reading?) of what he *had* read – and so, although phrased negatively, this remark discloses a positive fact: that he knew enough Russian literature to come to this conclusion.

Likewise, Tolkien's extravagantly negative comments about George MacDonald, Hans Christian Andersen, Dorothy L. Sayers, and others should be read with the awareness of his predilection for "rhetorical superlatives." With his eminently quotable declarations and not-so-quotable backtracking or nuancing, Tolkien has himself helped contribute to the confusion readers have about his real views.

The importance of being English

Fourth – and in sharp contrast to the preceding section – we must consider the characteristic English propensity for irony and self-deprecation. Having just examined Tolkien's taste for hyperbole, we need to recognize an equally strong, and equally misleading, tendency he had toward *under*statement. The relevance of Tolkien's English habit of downplaying his real views or gently mocking himself as he expresses those views has perhaps not received as much attention as it merits, especially considering that so many of his readers and critics are Americans, a people famously separated from the English by a shared language. The many similarities between English and American culture can obscure the very real, and significant, differences.*

Tolkien's self-deprecating approach can be observed in "On Fairy-stories," which he begins with the disclaimer that although he loves fairy-stories, he has "not studied them professionally," and notes that his examples will be drawn from "the few" instances of the genre that he knows. Later, he prefaces a discussion of terminology with the remark that "Ridiculous though it may be for one so ill-instructed to have an opinion in this critical matter, I venture to think the verbal distinction philologically inappropriate, and the analysis inaccurate."[38] The unwary American reader might take "ill-instructed" at face value, and interpret "venture to think" as genuinely tentative, but in fact the ironic understatement of his expertise conveys what Tolkien would *never*, as an Englishman, say directly: "I am a world-class authority on this subject!"

---

* In this connection, it is worth noting that C.S. Lewis was *Irish*, while Tolkien was English; a subtle but significant distinction that helps to explain why Lewis's nonfiction writing tends to be more accessible to the average American than Tolkien's. The Irish tend to be more forthright and temperamentally unguarded than the understated, litotic, reserved English. (Of course this is a vast generalization with any number of particular exceptions.) Americans, partly because of the large Irish immigrant population, and partly because the English settlers were, by definition, untypically English, tend on the whole to be more like the Irish than the English in this regard.

Here we can turn to anthropologist Kate Fox's very helpful work, *Watching the English: The Hidden Rules of English Behaviour*. She observes that the English are "more acutely sensitive than any other nation to the distinction between 'serious' and 'solemn,' between 'sincerity' and 'earnestness.'. . . if you are not able to grasp these subtle but vital differences, you will never understand the English."[39] For the English, the problem with being solemn or earnest is that both of these violate the unspoken norm of reserve and restraint. Being 'solemn' implies a lack of self-awareness, leading to pomposity, while being 'earnest' suggests a lack of emotional self-restraint, leading to embarrassing gushiness. The English often go to great lengths to avoid such displays. As Bertrand Russell remarked, "The highest praise that many English people ever use is 'not bad.'"[40]

We catch a glimpse of this tendency in Tolkien's interviews. In one of them, he accepts the label of "lazy" – "God help us, *yes*. I'm fighting the natural inertia of the lazy human being" – yet also declares that he is "working like Hell! A pen is to me as a beak is to a hen."[41] Only his self-deprecation about laziness allows him to go on and reveal that he is actually making diligent and laudable efforts (for such a revelation on its own would be too self-congratulatory). In another, after the interviewer praises the poetry in *The Lord of the Rings*, Tolkien "admits that he prefers writing verse to almost anything else. (Parenthetically, he adds, 'Almost impossible to sell verse, though.')"[42] Lest his sincerity about his poetry be mistaken for earnestness, he immediately deflates it with a touch of Eeyore-ishness.

Tolkien's reaction to favorable reviews of *The Lord of the Rings* provides another illustration of his being sensitive, even allergic, to solemnity and fervor in regard to his own writings. For instance, in a 1968 interview, he was quizzed about having his work compared to that of Dante. Tolkien fired back to say that Dante "doesn't attract me. He's full of spite and malice. I don't care for his petty relations with petty people in petty cities." Yet Tolkien was a member of the Oxford Dante Society from 1945 to 1955 and read a paper to the Society in 1947. Not surprisingly, then, we find him backtracking later, explaining that his remark about Dante was "outrageous" and adding, "I do not seriously dream of being measured against Dante, a supreme poet."[43] Here we see that Tolkien reacted hyperbolically – as we have discussed above – to something that perhaps only an Englishman would find a severe irritant. It was so irritating because it was the direct opposite of the proper English strategy of *understating* one's credentials; it failed to recognize the importance of *not* being earnest.

Kate Fox points out that English self-deprecation requires saying "the opposite of what we intend people to understand." Strange as it may sound, this approach is perfectly comprehensible to the English: "everyone understands that the customary self-deprecation probably means roughly the opposite of what is said, and is duly impressed, both by one's achievements and by one's reluctance to trumpet them." All is well, as long as the English are interacting with those who "understand the rules" of this mode of speech.[44]

However, self-deprecation and mirror-talk as linguistic strategies do not come naturally to Americans. Even critics who are aware of this aspect of English communication may find it difficult to recognize in practice – and as a great many Tolkien scholars are American, this barely visible linguistic barrier can have more of a distorting or confusing effect than we may have realized. Clyde Kilby puzzled over an aspect of Tolkien's personality that he could identify, but not understand: "a kind of consistent inconsistency that was both native . . . and developed, almost deliberate, even enjoyed."[45] Native, indeed: it is very English. Significantly, Kilby observed that Tolkien "could say almost opposite things without the least bit of trouble"[46] – an apt description of the ease with which the English can shift between deadpan mirror-talk and straightforward non-ironic delivery. Kilby was evidently somewhat bewildered by this aspect of Tolkien's personality, noting that he "was a very complex character. I can describe C.S. Lewis, but I can't describe Tolkien."[47] However, what seemed inconsistent and contradictory to Kilby – an American who spent only a summer in Oxford with Tolkien – was very probably rooted in Tolkien's thoroughgoing Englishness.

It is helpful, in interpreting Tolkien's various statements about his sources, influences, reading preferences, and creative process, to realize that he is often hyperbolic in what he denies or rejects, but modest and ironic in what he affirms or claims. We also should keep in mind that he was so deeply read in his professional specialty of philology that he would have been predisposed to view his reading in other areas as genuinely limited by comparison. There was some honest humility in his disclaimers at the start of "On Fairy-stories": though undoubtedly very English things to say, they would not have struck him as merely a rhetorical pose.

Nevertheless, we only need to read "On Fairy-stories" with a clear head to see that, even if Tolkien has not, in his own view, studied the genre professionally, he has certainly studied it widely, deeply, and thoughtfully. The huge range of sources (mostly modern) on which he draws – Andersen, Barrie, Carroll, Chesterton, Dasent, Dunsany, Grahame, Kingsley, Knatchbull-Hugessen, Lang, Milne, Morris, Nesbit, Potter, Stevenson, Wells, and Wyke-Smith – demonstrates this resoundingly. And it should not surprise us. Of course he would deploy all his considerable learning in composing this lecture, because it wasn't a casual talk at a student club in the next-door Oxford college, but a full-dress academic lecture at the University of St. Andrews. The breadth and depth of expertise about modern literature on display in "On Fairy-stories" prompts us to ask the question: if this isn't professional study, what is? Tolkien follows the exceedingly English pattern of downplaying the range of his knowledge. And as with his scholarly knowledge, so with his imaginative inspirations, for, as his interviewer John Ezard perceptively noted, "he is a canny man who knows how to hide and husband his creative resources."[48] John Garth observes that Tolkien was a "master synthesist" who was nevertheless "rightly wary" of revealing too much about his use of sources, and calls him "a poker player; he holds his cards close to his chest."[49] Tolkien habitually undersells both his familiarity with and his indebtedness to modern literature – but we needn't, and shouldn't, and mustn't believe him.

❧ One 'rule' to bind them all?

The rogueries of biographers, the battles over the Oxford English Syllabus, and Tolkien's habits of hyperbole and understatement have all conspired to obscure our view of his real relation to the modern world. "It is certainly one of the worst mistakes to make about my father to think of him merely as a dreamy, absent-minded scholar wrapped up in learned pursuits," Priscilla said in 1977.[50] His outward-looking perspective persisted even after his retirement. Charlie Carr, the university 'scout' who looked after Tolkien at Merton after Edith died, recalled his daily conversations with Tolkien: "Local news. National news. Anything, it was good. Most interesting man."[51] When Pope John XXIII convoked the Second Vatican Council in 1961, he urged Catholics to "read the signs of the times" (quoting Matthew 16:3),[52] but Tolkien would have needed little urging, for he had been doing so throughout his life.

Of course, even a more nuanced view can be overstated, and in avoiding the Scylla of Humphrey Carpenter, we must not disappear into the Charybdis of regarding Tolkien as some kind of modernist-in-disguise. But our consideration of his wide reading has demonstrated that his interest in and engagement with the modern world was part of his basic habit of mind; it was characteristic of him.

For many years, readers and critics have assumed quite the opposite: that *of course* Tolkien didn't read modern literature, and that therefore any evidence to the contrary must be an exception to the rule. Scholars have gradually noted ever more numerous and ever larger exceptions to this rule, but few people have recognized that perhaps the 'rule' was no rule at all.

I myself did not expect, when I began this study, to come to these conclusions. It was in the process of tracking down the various references to Tolkien's modern reading, and then in reading those works for myself, that I discovered, little by little, that he was far more widely read than I had ever imagined. The findings I have presented in this book are, indeed, mostly little – at least when each finding is considered in itself. Each fragment of information may appear, on its own, to be unimportant, easily disregarded, but when dozens, scores, hundreds of such pieces are put together, we begin to see a new image. And this new image enables us to consign that so-called rule – that Tolkien was seriously interested in nothing later than Chaucer – to the critical junk-heap where it belongs. Once we have done so, our approach to his work will be liberated. We will be able to roam freely back and forth across the centuries, as he did, in order to consult all the leaves of all the trees that dropped down into the mulch of his creativity. Many, probably most, of those leaves are ancient or medieval, but not a few, as we have seen, are modern.*

---

* We should bear in mind that Tolkien also knew a great deal of the literature from the period between the end of the Middle Ages and the post-1850 writings that I have been examining in this book. For instance, he enjoyed the writings of the eighteenth-century satirist Jonathan Swift; his grandson Michael recalls that "when I opted to specialise in 17th and 18th century literature for my second degree at Oxford he showed equal interest and was full of amusing anec-dotes about the authors I chose to read" ("Autobiographical essay on my grandfather"). In 1933,

❦ A new leaf

What, then, have we gained from our study of Tolkien's modern reading?

First, we have gained a deeper understanding of Tolkien himself, and of his complex, subtle, often contrarian personality. His reading was, as we have seen, very catholic, in the sense of being wide-ranging. Tolkien's interest in contemporary authors, many of whom had sharply contrasting philosophies of life, and some of whom chose to write in genres and styles very different from his own preferences, shows that, for all his apparent curmudgeonliness, he could be remarkably broad-minded, patient, and tolerant. And we have learned, *en route*, a great deal more about his attitudes toward women, race, technology, the news, ancient Romans, and many other things besides. In addition, we have had to recognize his changing tastes and perspectives over the course of his long life, his divergences from as well as his similarities to C.S. Lewis, the (sometimes malign) influence of his biographers, the context of his work on the Oxford English Syllabus, his tendency toward hyperbole, and his deep-seated Englishness. All these findings serve to refine and expand our portrait of Tolkien as a man.

Second, we have gained a more accurate picture of Tolkien as a writer, adding his post-1850 reading as one piece in the larger mosaic. His willingness to draw on modern authors for source material, and to be influenced by them – subtly or overtly, by assimilation or by opposition – shows that he was actively engaged with contemporary literary culture. To be sure, his modern reading is not a large piece, let alone the central piece in this mosaic. His debts to medieval literature are profound; his love of language is at the heart of Middle-earth; his formative life experiences, not least in the Great War, but also his enduring love for Edith (his "Lúthien") and their children, and his decades-long interaction with the Inklings – these, too, are essential to understanding his work as a writer. To highlight the importance of Tolkien's reading of modern literature is not in any way to downplay or diminish the significance of these other influences that shaped and nourished his output. Rather, it is to correct an oversight with the aim of heightening the resolution of the overall portrait.

Third, this richer view of Tolkien as a man and as a writer gives us a deeper understanding of the workings of his imagination. By considering the ways in which he used, transformed, and responded to the modern literature that he read, we have gained new lights on his creative process. We have seen, for instance, how he brought Rider Haggard's technique of using framing devices to a greater pitch of dramatic intensity; how he used archaisms far more adroitly than Morris; and how he felt at liberty to borrow certain names and terms (Luthany, Kôr, and so on), even while maintaining the most exacting standards of linguistic inventiveness. Our examination of his modern reading not

---

Tolkien was a guest of honor at the annual dinner of the Oxford University Mermaid Club, an undergraduate society dedicated to the reading of sixteenth- and seventeenth-century English drama; he was also a guest at their annual dinner in 1938 (Bodleian Library MS. Eng. e. 2311, fols. 59–62, 86–89). These leaves from the Tree of Tales merit consideration as well.

only shows him to be a more interesting man and a more informed writer, but also a better writer, a more canny writer: we have obtained insights into his world-building skills.

One particular thing that I hope has been made evident in this study is that the process of inspiration is complex: multiple influences often contribute to the same aspect of creativity. We have seen, for instance, how Tolkien himself named both Wyke-Smith's Snergs and Sinclair Lewis's *Babbitt* as ingredients in the shaping of the hobbits, and in addition to those two sources we have shown, by way of his own acknowledgement of the hobbit-rabbit connection, that there is a link to Beatrix Potter's work as well. Three ingredients (and there are no doubt others) converged and combined to help generate his creation of the hobbits. This is how digested mulch operates, and often it is impossible to separate out individual elements. At least with regard to hobbitry, though, this analysis of his modern reading has enlarged our understanding of his creative process. We have seen that Middle-earth does not emerge onto the page *ex nihilo*, but from an astonishingly wide array of texts, assimilated and transformed into something uniquely inclusive, detailed, varied, and integrated.

Finally, this richer view of Tolkien and his creative imagination enables a more nuanced analysis of the themes and ideas in his work. This will better enable us to answer the puzzling question of how it is that his work resonates so strongly with readers of his day and age. For, after all, why should an epic fantasy about a quest to dispose of a magic ring, featuring elves and dwarves, wizards and warriors, speak so profoundly to the twentieth century and now to the twenty-first? Why does Tolkien's work have such staying power, with its appeal widening and increasing over time?

I would venture to suggest that it is because his work contains a timeless quality – and that this quality is not a negative one (arising out of total detachment from modern-day concerns), but rather a positive one, deriving from an engagement with the present that is united with a discerning valuation of the past. According to Eugene Vinaver, Tolkien once said that "his typical response upon reading a medieval work was to desire not so much to make a philological or critical study of it as to write a modern work in the same tradition."[53] His scholarly interests were not those of an antiquarian whose eye is forever fixed on his rear-view mirror, but of the translator who looks both ahead and behind, aiming to preserve the best that history had to offer by making it accessible to contemporary readers. And to achieve that translation, he had to know both languages, as it were – tongues ancient and modern. John Garth remarks on the way that *The Book of Lost Tales* is in fact a fusion of *three* literary genres that Tolkien admired: it is not only "a foundational myth for England, like the one that Virgil's *Aeneid* had furnished for Rome," but also "a collection of stories within a story, like Geoffrey Chaucer's fourteenth-century Canterbury Tales" *and* "a lost-world story, like Henry Rider Haggard's *She*."[54]* Classical, medieval, and modern: all interwoven in the earliest tales

---

* I suspect that Tolkien would have been amused and not displeased to see Stephen Colbert finding a connection between his work and that of Chance the Rapper. Colbert argues that the latter uses the same very rare metrical and rhyming pattern as Tolkien's "The Song of Eärendil"

of Middle-earth. Like a tree whose roots go deep into soil and deeper into rock while its leaves yet take in sunlight high aboveground, Tolkien participated in the recent past, the distant past, *and* his own day – and thus could do more than merely reject or react to the problems of his time: he could challenge and reorient the contemporary status quo in unexpected ways.

This multi-layered quality of his legendarium is one reason for its success. As Verlyn Flieger observes, "His work could not have spoken so powerfully to his own century if he had completely succeeded in escaping it."[55] And spoken powerfully not only to his own century, but now to the twenty-first century too; his voice continues to be heard. William Fliss observes that Tolkien is "transgenerational," having the "rare ability to attract a popular audience in each new generation."[56] Because his artistry is diachronic it naturally, almost inevitably, extends its reach over time. Indeed, in some ways, its reach is not merely continuing, but intensifying, showing its value more tellingly as the years go by.

For example, take the theme that is at the heart of *The Lord of the Rings* and foreshadowed in *The Hobbit*: that of renunciation, of relinquishing the will to power. Although *The Hobbit* ostensibly centers upon a quest *for* something – to recover the dwarves' gold – the turning-point of the story occurs as Bilbo gives up the Arkenstone, and by extension his entire share in the treasure and his place in the dwarves' company, in order to forestall the terrible conflict between the dwarves and the men of Dale and their Elvish allies. This theme, deepened and enriched, becomes also the centerpiece of *The Lord of the Rings*. As Malcolm Guite points out, "Tolkien had the complete range of Icelandic myths at his disposal. . . . But he made a radical reversal, which was entirely right for his century and for ours."[57] The magic ring has a long lineage in ancient and medieval literature, but Tolkien gives us something new in the Fellowship's mission to destroy it, to renounce utterly the *libido dominandi* that it signifies. This radical re-visioning is in principle remarkably similar to James Joyce's reworking of ancient Greek epic, with Homer's *Odyssey* re-imagined as unfolding over the course of a single day in the streets of twentieth-century Dublin.*

I do not mean to imply that Joyce gave Tolkien the idea of reimagining ancient myths for the modern day, but I am suggesting that it should no longer surprise us to speak of Joyce and Tolkien in the same breath. Tolkien engages the attention of modern readers in part because he addresses quintessentially modern concerns.[58] Tom Shippey situates Tolkien alongside writers such as Orwell, Golding, and Vonnegut, who addressed "the most pressing and most immediately relevant issues of the whole monstrous twentieth century – questions of industrialised warfare, the origin of evil, the nature of humanity."[59] His objection to scientism – science taken as an end in itself,

---

(Ryan Reed, "See Stephen Colbert Break Down Chance the Rapper's 'Favorite Song' [feat. Childish Gambino]").

   *   Readers of Joyce even celebrate 'Bloomsday' on June 16, the day that the events of *Ulysses* take place, in a similar way that Tolkien enthusiasts celebrate 'Tolkien Reading Day' on March 25, the date of the destruction of the Ring.

unconstrained by a moral code – put him in good company, for, as Dominic Sandbrook observes, many of Tolkien's contemporaries, even the quondam science-promoter H.G. Wells, came to see science "as a force for death and destruction," the source of "mustard gas, the machine gun, the submarine, the tank and the bomber." Sandbrook notes, as well, how "in his lament that an old world was falling victim to the factory and the bulldozer, Tolkien was far from alone. . . . In the recollections of writers such as E. Nesbit, E.M. Forster, Graham Greene and Evelyn Waugh, the theme of a ruined paradise recurs again and again."[60]

In choosing fantasy as his preferred literary form to address these concerns, Tolkien was not rejecting realism as a literary mode, but rather finding his own voice. In doing so, he appeared to some to be turning his back on the twentieth century, but in fact he was engaging with it all the more profoundly. As he recalled in a letter to Christopher, he had attempted diary-keeping, but found it unsatisfactory: "So I took to 'escapism': or really *transforming experience into another form and symbol* . . . and it has stood me in good stead in many hard years since."[61] What could be more up to date than keeping a daily diary? Yet that very journalistic impulse is what motivated Tolkien to turn to the transformative genre of fantasy. In "On Fairy-stories," he remarked that fantasy "is founded upon the hard recognition that things are so in the world as it appears under the sun; on a recognition of fact, but not a slavery to it."[62] Part of what Tolkien brought to the workings of his fantastic imagination was a clear-eyed acknowledgment of, but not a weak-willed acquiescence in, the facts of the modern world. And this was informed in no small part by his modern reading, which, allied with his medieval reading, opened up new possibilities for his writing.

In crafting his heroes, Tolkien turned to warrior-figures like Beowulf, but also drew on Longfellow's protagonist from *The Song of Hiawatha*; he adapted his dwarves from Germanic legend, but also developed his Ents from Lewis's sorns; he made use of the bleak tragedy of Kullervo from the *Kalevala,* but also re-purposed Shorthouse's meditation on pity in *John Inglesant*. This dense blend of sources and influences helps explain the nature of readers' responses to *The Lord of the Rings*. When it originally appeared, many critics found it baffling: it was something unprecedented, for which they had no adequate classification. Given that Tolkien was not the first to write secondary-world fantasies for adult readers, nor the first to popularize traditional stories for modern audiences, we should ask what it was that made *The Lord of the Rings* so startling. Part of the answer, at least, is that Tolkien, like a scribe of the kingdom, brought out from his storehouse treasures both old and new.

Coda

In this book, we have seen that Tolkien's modern reading was both more extensive, and more significant in its influence on the legendarium, than has hitherto been recognized. In making this case, we have not rejected, displaced, or dismissed other elements that contributed to his creative imagination. Far from it. Tolkien was fundamentally a medievalist, and his deep knowledge of and love for the literature of the Middle Ages is at the heart of his work. His lifelong fascination with language provides another stream feeding into his creativity. Crucial early experiences, such as the death of his mother, friendships with the T.C.B.S., and involvement in the Battle of the Somme likewise contributed to the shaping of his imagination. All these elements are vitally important to our understanding of Tolkien and his work. What we have attempted to do in this study is to show that modern literature has a place in the picture as well. We readily concede that it is a relatively minor role, all things considered, but it matters. If Tolkien's portrayal of the hobbits teaches us anything, it is that the small and apparently negligible can be surprisingly important elements in the overall scheme of things.

At the unveiling of the beautiful Aubusson tapestries of his father's *Hobbit* art, Christopher Tolkien shared a touching recollection from his childhood.[63] When he was a very young and highly strung little boy, upstairs in bed at night, knowing that his father was still working in his study, Christopher would sometimes become fearful that he would work so hard and so late that something terrible would happen, that perhaps his father might even collapse and die. On one occasion, unable to hear any noise from downstairs, he became so overwrought that he made his way down to his father's study to check nothing was wrong. Tolkien was working on a watercolor, the picture of Rivendell. Relieved to find his father alive and well, Christopher began to weep, and, he recalls, a single tear – "but a substantial one" – dropped onto the painting. His father, however, did not chastise him or discard the work in progress. Rather, he picked up his brush and re-painted the tree where the tear had fallen, gently incorporating the little splash into his design: "he had to change the leaves." Though the image of Rivendell had been growing in his mind's eye since at least 1911 when he visited Lauterbrunnen on a family hiking trip, it was not immune to continuing influence: Tolkien was able to adapt it in response to new circumstances, even late in the day. He folded into his work something fresh and unexpected, something vital and important: a tear-drop from his own flesh and blood. From one perspective, the change was minor, almost negligible, but from another, it made a world of difference.

❦ Figure 40 ❦

Tolkien, aged 74, in his study at 76 Sandfield Road, Headington, Oxford. On his shelves can be seen books such as Arthur Ransome's *Secret Water* (1939), Mary Norton's Borrowers series (1952–1961), and Joyce Gard's *Woorroo* (1961).

Appendix
A Comprehensive List of Tolkien's Modern Reading

The following chart lists all of the post-1850 English literature (fiction, poetry, or drama) or authors thereof that we know Tolkien to have interacted with: a total of 148 authors and more than 200 titles.

The five columns indicate how we know of his familiarity with the authors and titles listed:

1) From his writings, both published versions and drafts, including lectures [**Writings**]
2) From his correspondence, both in the published *Letters* (1981) and other sources [**Letters**]
3) From his interviews [**Interviews**]
4) From the fact that he:
   a. Supervised a thesis on the author/work listed [**Taught**]
   b. Heard the author/work read aloud, discussed in a gathering (e.g. the Inklings), or attended a performance [**Heard**]
   c. Owned a copy of the work [**Owned**]
   d. Owned an anthology containing the work (or a portion of the work) [**Owned***]
   e. Gave a copy as a gift [**Gave**]
5 From reports by other people [**Reported**]

The table is comprehensive in the sense that it shows all the authors and all the particular works that we know Tolkien to have interacted with. By 'particular' we mean those that are specifically named or identified either by Tolkien himself or by the other sources of information. We do not list the entire oeuvre of, for example, Sinclair Lewis, even though Tolkien said that he read "all of Sinclair Lewis"; we assume that "all" is not to be taken absolutely literally, and since there is therefore no *terminus ad quem* we list only *Babbitt*, because that is the title Tolkien singled out for comment. With the Lord Peter Wimsey novels of Dorothy L. Sayers, however, there is a knowable range to Tolkien's reading, for he states that he followed Wimsey from his "beginnings" (which indicates the first book, *Whose Body?*, even though Tolkien doesn't explicitly name it) "as far as" *Gaudy Night*, and thence to its sequel, *Busman's Honeymoon*. We can legitimately deduce from this evidence that he read all eleven books in the Wimsey series.

This appendix thus reflects the parameters outlined in chapter 2: it covers only those works we are certain that he knew, even though we know he read a great deal more than these. It distills the findings presented in *Tolkien's Modern Reading*; the evidence upon which this chart is based is cited in the relevant places in the text.

Author/title	From his writings	From his letters	From his interviews	From five other facts	From reports
Hans Christian Andersen – fairy tales	Writings	Letters	Interviews	Owned*, Gave	Reported
Poul Anderson – "The Valor of Cappen Varra"	Writings			Owned*	
Matthew Arnold – *The Scholar Gipsy & Thyrsis*				Heard, Owned	
Isaac Asimov		Letters			
W.H. Auden – *About the House*; *The Shield of Achilles*		Letters			
Reverend W. Awdry – Railway Stories series					Reported
John Balderston – *Berkeley Square*				Heard	
Owen Barfield – *The Silver Trumpet*				Owned	Reported
– *Medea*; *Orpheus*	Writings			Heard	
Sabine Baring-Gould		Letters			
J.M. Barrie – *Peter Pan*	Writings	Letters		Heard	
– *The Little White Bird*				Owned*, Gave	
– *Dear Brutus*; *Mary Rose*	Writings			Heard	
L. Frank Baum – *The Wizard of Oz*				Owned*, Gave	
Hilaire Belloc	Writings				Reported
Wendell Berry – *The Hidden Wound*				Owned	
Algernon Blackwood – *The Education of Uncle Paul*	Writings				
Enid Blyton		Letters			
Ray Bradbury – "Switch on the Night"			Interviews	Owned*, Gave	
Robert Browning	Writings	Letters			
John Buchan – *Greenmantle*	Writings				Reported

Author/title	From his writings	From his letters	From his interviews	From five other facts	From reports
Edgar Rice Burroughs – John Carter of Mars series; Pellucidar series; Tarzan series	Writings	Letters			
Samuel Butler – *Erewhon*	Writings				
James Branch Cabell					Reported
Erskine Caldwell – "Molly Cottontail"				Owned*, Gave	
J.F. Campbell – *Popular Tales of the West Highlands*	Writings				
Roy Campbell – *The Flaming Terrapin*; *Flowering Rifle*		Letters			Reported
Lewis Carroll – *Alice's Adventures in Wonderland*; *Through the Looking-glass*	Writings	Letters		Owned*, Gave	
– *Sylvie and Bruno*; *Sylvie and Bruno Concluded*	Writings	Letters			Reported
– "Hiawatha's Photographing"		Letters			
Joy Chant – *Red Moon and Black Mountain*				Owned	
G.K. Chesterton – *Ballad of the White Horse*		Letters			
– The Father Brown stories; *The Flying Inn*; *Lepanto*					Reported
– *The Coloured Lands*; *The Napoleon of Notting Hill*	Writings				
– *The Man Who Was Thursday*	Writings				Reported
Wilfred Childe – poetry		Letters			
Agatha Christie – *At Bertram's Hotel*					Reported
John Christopher – *The Death of Grass*		Letters			
Arthur C. Clarke			Interviews		
Sir Arthur Conan Doyle – *The White Company*		Letters			

Author/title	From his writings	From his letters	From his interviews	From five other facts	From reports
S.R. Crockett – *The Black Douglas*		Letters			
George Dasent – *Popular Tales from the Norse*	Writings	Letters			
Lord Dunsany – *The Book of Wonder*	Writings	Letters		Owned*, Gave	
E.R. Eddison – *The Worm Ouroboros; Mistress of Mistresses; A Fish Dinner in Memison; The Mezentian Gate*		Letters	Interviews	Heard	
T.S. Eliot – *The Four Quartets*		Letters			Reported
G.E. Farrow – *The Little Panjandrum's Dodo*				Owned*	
Ford Madox Ford		Letters			
C.S. Forester – *Poo-Poo and the Dragons*				Owned*, Gave	
E.M. Forster					Reported
Adam Fox – *Babylon: A Sacred Satire; Old King Coel*		Letters		Owned	
H.R. Freston – *The Quest of Beauty and Other Poems*	Writings			Owned	
Joyce Gard – *Woorroo*		Letters		Owned	
Andrea Giovene – *The Book of Sansevero*				Owned	
William Golding – *The Lord of the Flies*			Interviews		
Kenneth Grahame – *The Wind in the Willows; First Whisper of "The Wind in the Willows"*	Writings	Letters		Owned*, Gave	
David Grant – *Waes*				Owned	
Alfred Perceval Graves – *The Irish Fairy Book*				Owned	
Roger Lancelyn Green – *The Wonderful Stranger*					Reported
H. Rider Haggard – *Eric Brighteyes*	Writings				

Author/title	From his writings	From his letters	From his interviews	From five other facts	From reports
H. Rider Haggard – *King Solomon's Mines*		Letters		Gave	
– *She*			Interviews		Reported
– *The Wanderer's Necklace*					Reported
J.B.S. Haldane – *My Friend Mr. Leakey*	Writings	Letters			
Joel Chandler Harris – *Uncle Remus*	Writings			Owned*, Gave	
Herbert Hayens – *Scouting for Buller*				Gave	
Lafcadio Hearn – "The Boy Who Drew Cats"				Owned*	
Frank Herbert – *Dune*		Letters			
Jacobine Hichens – *Noughts and Crosses*		Letters			
Gerard Manley Hopkins		Letters			
A.E. Housman				Heard	
Ruth Winifred How – *The Friendly Farm*				Gave	
Robert E. Howard – Conan the Barbarian stories				Owned*	Reported
Jean Ingelow – *Mopsa the Fairy*				Owned*	
Michael Innes – *The Bloody Wood*		Letters			
M.R. James – *Ghost Stories of an Antiquary*	Writings				
Elizabeth Jennings – *A Way of Looking*		Letters			
Gwyn Jones – *The Buttercup Field and Other Stories*				Heard, Owned	
James Joyce – *Finnegans Wake*	Writings			Heard	
Sheila Kaye-Smith – *A Challenge to Sirius*					Reported
Charles Kingsley	Writings				

Author/title	From his writings	From his letters	From his interviews	From five other facts	From reports
Rudyard Kipling – *The Jungle Book*; *Just So Stories*				Owned*, Gave	
– *Kim*		Letters		Gave	
– poetry				Heard	
E.H. Knatchbull-Hugessen – *Puss-Cat Mew and Other Stories for My Children*	Writings	Letters			
Ronald Knox					Reported
Henry Kuttner – "The Citadel of Darkness"				Owned*	
Andrew Lang – *Blue, Red, Green, Yellow, Pink, Grey, Violet, Crimson, Brown, Orange, Olive*, and *Lilac Fairy Books*	Writings			Taught, Owned	Reported
– *Prince Prigio*; *Prince Ricardo of Pantouflia*; *In the Wrong Paradise*	Writings				
– *The Gold of Fairnilee*					Reported
– *The Book of Dreams and Ghosts*; *The Magic Ring and Other Stories from the Yellow and Crimson Fairy Books*					Reported
Sterling Lanier – *The War for the Lot*		Letters			
Fritz Leiber – "When the Sea-King's Away"				Owned*	
C.S. Lewis – *The Lion, the Witch and the Wardrobe*				Owned, Heard	Reported
– *The Chronicles of Narnia*		Letters		Owned	Reported
– *Dymer*; *Till We Have Faces*				Owned	
– *The Great Divorce*; *The Screwtape Letters*		Letters		Heard	
– *Out of the Silent Planet*; *Perelandra*	Writings	Letters	Interviews	Heard, Owned	
– *The Pilgrim's Regress*	Writings				
– *Poems*				Gave	

Author/title	From his writings	From his letters	From his interviews	From five other facts	From reports
– *That Hideous Strength*		Letters		Owned	Reported
Sinclair Lewis – *Babbitt*	Writings	Letters	Interviews		
David Lindsay – *A Voyage to Arcturus*		Letters		Owned	
Hugh Lofting – Doctor Dolittle series				Owned*, Gave	Reported
Henry Wadsworth Longfellow – *Evangeline*	Writings				
– *The Song of Hiawatha*	Writings		Interviews	Heard	
H.P. Lovecraft – "The Doom that Came to Sarnath"				Owned*	
A. Neil Lyons – *Arthur's: The Romance of a Coffee Stall*	Writings				
Alexander Macdonald – *The Lost Explorers*				Gave	
George MacDonald – *At the Back of the North Wind*				Owned*	
– Fairy tales (including "The Golden Key")	Writings	Letters		Taught	Reported
– *Lilith*	Writings				
– *Phantastes*		Letters			
– *The Princess and the Goblin; The Princess and Curdie*	Writings	Letters			Reported
Walter de la Mare – *Broomsticks*		Letters		Owned	
– poetry				Heard	
John Masefield – *A Letter from Pontus*		Letters			
E. Powys Mathers – poetry				Owned*	
Amanda McKittrick Ros – *Irene Iddesleigh*				Heard	
George Meredith – *The Egoist*				Owned*	
Henry Seton Merriman					Reported
A.A. Milne – *Toad of Toad Hall*	Writings				

Author/title	From his writings	From his letters	From his interviews	From five other facts	From reports
A.A. Milne – *Winnie-the-Pooh*				Owned*, Gave	
Naomi Mitchison – *To the Chapel Perilous*		Letters			
C.L. Moore – "Hellsgarde"	Writings			Owned*	
William Morris – *The Earthly Paradise*; *The Life and Death of Jason*; *The Story of the Volsungs*; *The Sundering Flood*				Owned	
– *The Defence of Guinevere and Other Poems*	Writings			Owned	
– *The House of the Wolfings*		Letters		Owned	Reported
– *News from Nowhere*	Writings				
– *The Roots of the Mountains*		Letters		Owned	
Iris Murdoch		Letters			
E. Nesbit – *The Phoenix and the Carpet*; *The Story of the Amulet*	Writings	Letters		Owned	
P.H. Newby – *Picnic at Sakkara*		Letters			
Mary Norton – *The Borrowers*; *The Borrowers Afield*; *The Borrowers Afloat*; *The Borrowers Aloft*				Owned	Reported
Joseph O'Neill – *Land Under England*		Letters			
Coventry Patmore – *The Wedding Sermon*				Owned	
Thomas Love Peacock – poetry				Owned*	
Beatrix Potter – *The Tale of Peter Rabbit*; *Benjamin Bunny*; *Mrs. Tiggy-Winkle*; *Jemima Puddle-Duck*; *Mr. Tod*; *Johnny Town-Mouse*; *The Tailor of Gloucester*	Writings	Letters			Reported

Author/title	From his writings	From his letters	From his interviews	From five other facts	From reports
Arthur Ransome – Swallows and Amazons series		Letters			
– *Secret Water*				Owned	
William Ready – *The Poor Hater*		Letters		Owned	
Mary Renault – *The Bull from the Sea*; *The King Must Die*		Letters			
Ernest Rhys – *Fairy Gold: A Book of Old English Fairy Tales*					Reported
Alan Rook – *These Are My Comrades*		Letters		Owned	
Martin Ross				Heard	
John Ruskin – *The King of the Golden River*	Writings			Owned*, Gave	
Saki (H.H. Munro)		Letters			
Felix Salten – *Bambi*				Owned*, Gave	
Dorothy L. Sayers – *Whose Body?*; *Clouds of Witness*; *Unnatural Death*; *The Unpleasantness at the Bellona Club*; *Strong Poison*; *Five Red Herrings*; *Have His Carcase*; *Murder Must Advertise*; *The Nine Tailors*; *Gaudy Night*; *Busman's Honeymoon*		Letters			Reported
– *The Man Born to Be King*				Gave	Reported
G.B. Shaw – *Arms and the Man*				Heard	
J.H. Shorthouse – *John Inglesant: A Romance*		Letters			
Louis Slobodkin – "The Amiable Giant"				Owned*, Gave	
Clark Ashton Smith – "The Testament of Athammaus"	Writings			Owned*	

Author/title	From his writings	From his letters	From his interviews	From five other facts	From reports
G.B. Smith – *A Spring Harvest*	Writings				
Olaf Stapledon – *Last Men in London*	Writings				
W.T. Stead – Books for the Bairns series	Writings				
Gertrude Stein	Writings			Heard	
James Stephens – *Irish Fairy Tales*				Owned	
Robert Louis Stevenson – *The Black Arrow*				Gave	
– *Treasure Island*	Writings				Reported
Frank R. Stockton – *Ting-a-Ling Tales*				Owned*, Gave	
Alfred, Lord Tennyson – poetry	Writings			Owned*	
Eric Thacker and Anthony Earnshaw – *Musrum*		Letters		Owned	
William Makepeace Thackeray – *The Rose and the Ring*	Writings				
Dylan Thomas					Reported
William Jenkyn Thomas – *The Welsh Fairy Book*				Owned	
Francis Thompson – *Complete Works*	Writings	Letters		Owned	
P.L. Travers – *Mary Poppins*				Owned*, Gave	
Anthony Trollope		Letters		Heard	
Mark Twain – *A Connecticut Yankee in King Arthur's Court*		Letters			Reported
Louis Untermeyer – "The Kitten Who Barked"				Owned*, Gave	
Alison Uttley – Little Grey Rabbit series	Writings				

Author/title	From his writings	From his letters	From his interviews	From five other facts	From reports
Horace Annesley Vachell – *The Hill: A Romance of Friendship*	Writings				
John Wain – *Mixed Feelings*				Owned	
H.G. Wells – *The First Men in the Moon*; *The Time Machine*; short stories	Writings				
– *The History of Mr Polly*					Reported
T.H. White – *The Sword in the Stone*				Owned, Owned*, Gave	Reported
Oscar Wilde – "The Selfish Giant"				Owned*, Gave	
Charles Williams – *All Hallows' Eve*		Letters		Heard	
– *The House of the Octopus*	Writings				
– *The Place of the Lion*		Letters	Interviews		Reported
– *The Region of the Summer Stars*	Writings	Letters		Heard, Owned	
– *Terror of Light*				Heard	
Jay Williams – "Raoul the Owl"				Owned*, Gave	
Blanche Winder – *Stories of King Arthur*				Owned	
P.G. Wodehouse – Psmith books		Letters			
Gene Wolfe – "Trip, Trap"		Letters			
E.A. Wyke-Smith – *The Marvellous Land of Snergs*	Writings	Letters			Reported
W.B. Yeats – poetry				Owned*	

LIST OF BIBLIOGRAPHICAL ABBREVIATIONS

AH: *The Annotated Hobbit*, by J.R.R. Tolkien, revised and expanded edition, ed. Douglas A. Anderson

ASV: *A Secret Vice*, by J.R.R. Tolkien, ed. Dimitra Fimi and Andrew Higgins

BC: *Beowulf and the Critics*, by J.R.R. Tolkien, ed. Michael D.C. Drout

Biography: *J.R.R. Tolkien: A Biography*, by Humphrey Carpenter

BF: *Brothers and Friends* by Warren Lewis, ed. Clyde S. Kilby and Marjorie Lamp Mead

CLI: *Collected Letters of C.S. Lewis, Vol. 1*, ed. Walter Hooper

CLII: *Collected Letters of C.S. Lewis, Vol. 2*, ed. Walter Hooper

CLIII: *Collected Letters of C.S. Lewis, Vol. 3*, ed. Walter Hooper

Dragons: "Dragons" lecture, by J.R.R. Tolkien, in *J.R.R. Tolkien: The Hobbit 1937–2017* by Christina Scull and Wayne G. Hammond

FG: *The Fall of Gondolin*, by J.R.R. Tolkien, ed. Christopher Tolkien

HH: John D. Rateliff, *The History of The Hobbit*, revised and expanded one-volume edition

Hobbit: *The Hobbit*, 75th Anniversary Edition, by J.R.R. Tolkien

HOME: *The History of Middle-earth*, by J.R.R. Tolkien, ed. Christopher Tolkien

Inklings: *The Inklings: C.S. Lewis, J.R.R. Tolkien, Charles Williams, and their friends* by Humphrey Carpenter

Kullervo: *The Story of Kullervo*, by J.R.R. Tolkien, ed. Verlyn Flieger

Letters: *The Letters of J.R.R. Tolkien*, by J.R.R. Tolkien, ed. Humphrey Carpenter

LOTR: *The Lord of the Rings: 50th Anniversary One-Volume Edition,* by J.R.R. Tolkien

LOTR:RC: *The Lord of the Rings: A Reader's Companion*, 60th anniversary edition by Wayne G. Hammond and Christina Scull

MC: *The Monsters and the Critics*, by J.R.R. Tolkien, ed. Christopher Tolkien

MME: *Tolkien: Maker of Middle-earth*, ed. Catherine McIlwaine

OFS: *Tolkien On Fairy-stories*, by J.R.R. Tolkien, expanded edition, ed. Verlyn Flieger and Douglas A. Anderson

Silmarillion: *The Silmarillion*, by J.R.R. Tolkien, second edition*

SWM: *Smith of Wootton Major*, by J.R.R. Tolkien, extended edition, ed. Verlyn Flieger

TCG:C: *The Tolkien Companion and Guide: Chronology* 2nd edition, by Christina Scull and Wayne G. Hammond

TCG:RG: *The Tolkien Companion and Guide: Reader's Guide,* 2nd edition, by Christina Scull and Wayne G. Hammond

TFA: *The Tolkien Family Album*, ed. John and Priscilla Tolkien

TGW: *Tolkien and the Great War*, by John Garth

TS: *Tolkien and the Silmarillion*, by Clyde S. Kilby

---

* In the main text, 'the Silmarillion' (not italicized) refers to the larger body of writings that Tolkien called by that name, from which *The Silmarillion* was selected, first by Tolkien in his initial attempt to publish it, and then by Christopher Tolkien in the posthumously published volume.

NOTES

Chapter 1

1. Dust-jacket for *The Lord of the Rings*, 2nd ed. (London: George Allen & Unwin, 1980).
2. W.H. Auden, "The Hero Is a Hobbit"; Donald Barr, "Shadowy World of Men and Hobbits"; William Blisset, "Despots of the Rings," 449.
3. R.J. Reilly, "Tolkien and the Fairy Story," 128; Charles Moorman, "The Shire, Mordor, and Minas Tirith," 202.
4. Dominic Sandbrook, *The Great British Dream Factory*, 351.
5. Simon Tolkien, "My Grandfather J.R.R. Tolkien"; *Letters*, 65; George Sayer, "Recollections of J.R.R. Tolkien," 6; Letters, 235.
6. Clyde S. Kilby, "Dr. Clyde S. Kilby Recalls J.R.R. Tolkien and C.S. Lewis, 1980," 11.
7. CLIII, 824.
8. CLIII, 397.
9. John D. Rateliff, "*She* and Tolkien," 6. This piece appeared shortly before the *Letters* came out; he cites Lin Carter (an imperfect source), Kilby's *Tolkien and the Silmarillion*, Carpenter's *Inklings*, and the Resnik interview.
10. *Inklings*, 158.
11. Tom Shippey, *The Road to Middle-earth*, 6.
12. Jane Chance, *Tolkien the Medievalist*, 3.
13. Verlyn Flieger, *Green Suns and Faërie*, 254.
14. Quoted in *Biography*, 131.
15. *Inklings*, 158.
16. Humphrey Carpenter, "Learning about Ourselves: Biography as Autobiography," 270.
17. Carpenter, "Learning about Ourselves," 270.
18. Rayner Unwin, *George Allen & Unwin: A Remembrancer*, 249.
19. Carpenter, "Learning about Ourselves," 270.
20. Carpenter, "Learning about Ourselves," 271.
21. Carpenter, "Learning about Ourselves," 273, 275.
22. Quoted in Charles Noad, "'Tolkien Reconsidered': A Talk by Humphrey Carpenter," 14.
23. Wayne G. Hammond and Christina Scull, "Truth or Consequences: A Cautionary Tale of Tolkien Studies"; Nicole M. duPlessis, "On the Shoulders of Humphrey Carpenter: Reconsidering Biographical Representation and Scholarly Perception of Edith Tolkien."
24 *Letters*, 288–289.
25. The letter is printed in full in Deborah Webster Rogers and Ivor A. Rogers, *J.R.R. Tolkien*.
26. Quoted in Deborah Webster Rogers and Ivor A. Rogers, *J.R.R. Tolkien* 125.
27. Deborah Webster Rogers and Ivor A. Rogers, *J.R.R. Tolkien*, 126.
28. See TCG:C, 557.
29. J.I.M. Stewart, "Favourite Subjects" (final ellipsis in original).
30. TCG:C, 715.
31. Priscilla Tolkien and Humphrey Carpenter, "Table Talk: A Transcript of the After-dinner speeches at the 1976 Annual General Meeting of the Tolkien Society," 41.
32. *Biography*, 121.
33. That account features a scene of Lewis at breakfast in the Common Room of Magdalen College, and we are told that he "never read the paper at all: he would skim the headlines of *The Times* and sometimes do the crossword" (Green and Hooper, *C.S. Lewis*, 149).

34. CLIII, 778.
35. Michael Ward, *Planet Narnia*, 10.
36. See C.S. Lewis, "On the Reading of Old Books" (Introduction to St. Athanasius, *On the Incarnation*); *Surprised by Joy*, chapter 13; Owen Barfield, *Light on C.S. Lewis*, ed. Jocelyn Gibb (London: Geoffrey Bles, 1965), xv. See also Lewis's letter to Don Giovanni Calabria, 15 September 1953, in CLIII, 364.
37. TFA, 45.
38. See James Stevens Curl, *The Erosion of Oxford*, Oxford: Oxford Illustrated Press, 1977.
39. LOTR:RC, xiii.
40. George Sayer, in Humphrey Carpenter et al., "A Dialogue," 21.
41. TS, 6.
42. Henry Resnik, "An Interview with Tolkien," 39.
43. Douglas A. Anderson, "Tolkien and the Newman Association." See chapter 2 for more on Tolkien's involvement with the Newman Association.
44. BF, 189, 195, 235.
45. TFA, 63.
46. George Sayer, "Recollections of J.R.R. Tolkien," 14.
47. See, for example, the account of his 1955 holiday in Italy with Priscilla (TCG:C, 488–99).
48. The full salutation is "My dear people – John, Michael, Christopher, also Aslaug, also Mummy, also Auntie Jennie, also Daddy, there seem to get more and more of you every year." However, this can only be seen in the reproduction of the letter: the transcription has only "My dear people: there seem to get more and more of you every year" without ellipses. Furthermore, only the edited transcript appears in pre-2012 editions. Editorial omissions like this add up to distort the overall picture.
49. Priscilla Tolkien, "Memories of J.R.R. Tolkien in his Centenary Year," 12.
50. TCG:RG, 1232–33.
51. Inscription on a volume of *The Lord of the Rings*. Pieter Collins, "The most expensive Tolkien book in the world," *Tolkien Library*, Dec. 18, 2008, http://www.tolkienlibrary.com/press/856-most-expensive-Tolkien-book-in-the-world.php.
52. Joanna Tolkien, "Joanna Tolkien Speaks," 34. Joanna recalled that she was "a remarkable woman who had a formative influence on my life."
53. See John D. Rateliff, "The Missing Women: J.R.R. Tolkien's Lifelong Support for Women's Higher Education," in *Perilous and Fair*, eds. Janet Brennan Croft and Leslie A. Donovan; and Raymond Edwards, *Tolkien*.
54. Stuart Lee, "Tolkien in Oxford," 156.
55. *Letters*, 339. The editorial note says that this is "possibly" a reference to frequent communion, but it seems certain, given that Tolkien has just recommended to Michael that he make his communion daily if possible.
56. TCG:C, 514.
57. Peter Milward, "Perchance to Touch: Tolkien as Scholar," 31.
58. Quoted in *Sotheby's English Literature, History, Fine Bindings, Private Press Books, Children's Books, Illustrated Books and Drawings 10 July 2003*, 297.
59. Henry Resnik, "An Interview with Tolkien," 40.
60. CLIII, 1329.
61. Clyde S. Kilby, "Dr Clyde S. Kilby Recalls The Inklings," 4.
62. John S. Ryan, "J.R.R. Tolkien, C.S. Lewis, and Roy Campbell," 28.
63. Quoted in *Biography*, 143.
64. Charlotte and Denis Plimmer, "The Man Who Understands Hobbits," 35; *Letters*, 377.
65. J.R.R. Tolkien, *Tengwesta Qenderinwa and Pre-Fëanorian Alphabets Part 2*, 143; UK inflation rate, officialdata.org.

66. The Bodleian does not keep records of books requested, but a fortunate accident preserved some of the request slips that Tolkien filled out for titles he consulted while preparing "On Fairy-stories" (see George White, "A piece of Bodleian History: Clues from the Stacks"). In addition to using the Bodleian Library *in situ*, he borrowed books from his college libraries. These included various academic works from the Exeter College library in 1911–1920. Merton College records show a few borrowings of scholarly titles in 1949, 1956, and 1957. Pembroke College's records have not survived.
67. TCG:C, 219, 652.
68. Oxfordshire History Centre archives, O22/11/A2/21 and O22/11/A2/22. I consulted records for the years 1911–1920.
69. Oxford Union Library archive for May 18, 1912 (Wade Center Archives JRRT MS-6). Tolkien's fine of £1-7-6 would be more than £100 today. The other fines on the page are roughly the same. The Suggestion Book contains a protest, ca. 1912–1913, about the "excessive" fines, to which the Committee responded: that the fine is one shilling for a late book, increasing if not paid. (Oxfordshire History Centre archives, O22/11/A2/22). At twenty shillings in the (pre-decimal) pound, this suggests that Tolkien may have had more than two dozen late books over the course of the year.
70. Clara Finley, "The Morrisian Interview Series, #2: John J. Walsdorf."
71. TCG:RG, 1058.
72. *Letters*, 377.
73. Michael Tolkien, "Autobiographical essay on my grandfather."
74. TS, 26; Mike Foster, "'That most unselfish man.'"
75. John D. Rateliff, "Tolkien and Sinclair Lewis."
76. TCG:C, 481.
77. Henry Resnik, "An Interview with Tolkien," 38.
78. Atticus, "Tolkien Talking," 9.
79. OFS MS B, 207; *Letters*, 31.
80. *Letters*, 215n; 391n.
81. *Letters*, 303.
82. Quoted in Gene Wolfe, "The Tolkien Toll-free Fifties Freeway to Mordor & Points beyond Hurray!" 9.
83. See TGW.
84. Charlotte and Denis Plimmer, "The Man Who Understands Hobbits," 35.
85. Quoted in Daphne Castell, "The Realms of Tolkien," 148.
86. Rayner Unwin, "Tributes to J.R.R. Tolkien," 32.
87. S.T.R.O. [Simonne] d'Ardenne, "The Man and the Scholar," 33.
88. Michael Tolkien, "Autobiographical essay on my grandfather."
89. *Letters*, 144; *Letters*, 230–31.

Chapter 2

1. C.S. Lewis, *Selected Literary Essays*, 7.
2. OFS MS B, 249.
3. Stuart Lee, "Tolkien in Oxford," 146. He also gave at least one of Scott's novels, *The Abbot*, as a Christmas gift to Priscilla (Azusa Pacific University Inklings Collection).
4. TGW, 19, 290.
5. LOTR:RC, 24; *Kullervo*, 101, 115; HH, 899; BC MS A, 38.

6. In the unpublished essay "Some thoughts on the translation of poetry – especially Old English," Tolkien compares the Old English poem "The Wanderer" to Wordsworth's "Resolution and Independence" (1807) (Bodleian MS Tolkien A 30/1, fol. 119). Tolkien also knew Wordsworth's infamous 'stuffed owl' sonnet (*Letters*, 353).

7. *Letters*, 72.

8. Michael Tolkien, "Autobiographical essay on my grandfather." See also Tolkien's undergraduate lecture notes, Bodleian Library, MS. Tolkien A 21/4, Notebook 3.

9. AH, 160; Priscilla Tolkien, "My Father the Artist," 8; J.S. Ryan, "Two Oxford Scholars' Perceptions of the Traditional Germanic Hall."

10. BF, 184; OFS, 44n1, 72n1; TCG:C, 191; Naomi Collyer, "Recollections of Professor J.R.R. Tolkien," 2.

11. For a consideration of possible German influences, see Julian Eilmann, *J.R.R. Tolkien: Romanticist and Poet*; for Tolkien's reading of Greek and Latin texts, see *Tolkien and the Classics*, ed. Roberto Arduini et al.

12. John Garth, *The Worlds of J.R.R. Tolkien*, 93; Mark T. Hooker, "Journey to the Center of Middle-Earth."

13. Peter Gilliver, Jeremy Marshall, and Edmund Weiner, *Ring of Words: Tolkien and the Oxford English Dictionary*, 11.

14. Peter Gilliver, "At the Wordface: J.R.R. Tolkien's Work on the *Oxford English Dictionary*," 175. Rachel A. Fletcher examined a set of OED slips now in the possession of the University of Toronto, identifying sixty-six in Tolkien's handwriting, two of which (for *styan* and *wade*) were not previously known. This collection does not include any quotation slips originated by Tolkien, so although it provides insight into his lexicography work, it contributes no further data for his modern reading. ("Tolkien's Work on the Oxford English Dictionary: Some New Evidence from Quotation Slips," 3–4).

15. For instance, Verlyn Flieger suggests an influence from George Du Maurier's 1891 novel *Peter Ibbetson* (*A Question of Time*, 29–36); this is plausible as the novel was widely known, and dealt with themes of dreams and temporality of interest to Tolkien, but we do not have independent evidence that he had read it. Therefore I will not be considering the connection sufficient in its own right to indicate his familiarity with the work in question.

16. For more on Tolkien's relationship with his guardian, see José Manuel Ferrández Bru, *"Uncle Curro": J.R.R. Tolkien's Spanish Connection*.

17. Norman Power, "Ring of doom"; Simon Stacey, "Tolkien's Tone and the Frequent Failure to Hear It," 79.

18. Archives of the Newman Association, Palace Green Library, Durham UK. Newman Association Governing Committees' papers, Annual Reports D1/J/1/1/1; Annual General Meetings, Minutes 1947–1957 D1/C/1/2; Annual Report for 1955–56 D1/J/1/1/5. It was as an Honorary VP that, in 1949, he co-signed a letter to the London *Times* on an issue of religious freedom (see chapter 1, note 43).

19. C.S. Lewis, "The Literary Impact of the Authorised Version," in *Selected Literary Essays*, 133.

20. *Letters*, 215n.

21. Denis Gueroult, interview with Tolkien for BBC radio, "Now Read On."

22. TCG:RG, 1217.

23. Diana Pavlac Glyer, *The Company They Keep*, xvi-xvii; CLIII, 1049.

24. Henry Resnik, "An Interview with Tolkien," 40.

25. Charlotte and Denis Plimmer, "The Man Who Understands Hobbits," 32.

26. *Biography*, 100.

27. *Letters*, 7.

28. *Biography*, 104.

29. Verlyn Flieger, "Tolkien, *Kalevala*, and 'The Story of Kullervo,'" in *Kullervo*, 133.

30. *Biography*, 206.
31. *Biography*, 54.
32. CLII, 137n. Owing to other commitments, Tolkien could not attend the full set of operas in the Ring cycle in London, as planned, but Priscilla Tolkien recalls that her father did attend at least one (TCG:C, 185). See further Renée Vink, *Wagner and Tolkien: Mythmakers*, 4–14.
33. CLIII, 1049.
34. Charles Moorman, *The Precincts of Felicity: The Augustinian City of the Oxford Christians*.
35. CLIII, 1049.
36. CLIII, 1049.
37. Arne Zettersten, *J.R.R. Tolkien's Double Worlds and Creative Process*, 199.
38. Quoted in Richard A. Lupoff, *Edgar Rice Burroughs: Master of Adventure*, 276–277.
39. Quoted in Lupoff, 276–277.
40. *Letters*, 209; *Letters*, 258.
41. See Diana Pavlac Glyer, *The Company They Keep*, 28–30.
42. Evelyn B. Byrne and Otto M. Penzler, eds., *Attacks of Taste*, 43.
43. *Letters*, 172.
44. *Letters*, 418.
45. Rachel Falconer, "Earlier Fantasy Fiction: Morris, Dunsany, and Lindsay," 304.
46. Falconer, 304.
47. John Garth, *The Worlds of J.R.R. Tolkien*, 192–193n5.
48. Trevor Hart, Review of *There and Back Again: J. R. R. Tolkien and the Origins of* The Hobbit by Mark Atherton, 154.
49. Quoted in Kay Holmes, "The Master Hobbit at 80," 45.
50. OFS, 39–40.
51. Tom Shippey, "Why Source Criticism?", 8.
52. OFS, 38–40.
53. Jason Fisher, "Tolkien and Source Criticism," 30.
54. Quoted in Daphne Castell, "Talking to a Maker of Modern Myths."
55. Quoted in Daphne Castell, "The Realms of Tolkien," 146.
56. *Letters*, 418.
57. Quoted in *Sotheby's English Literature, History, Fine Bindings, Private Press Books, Children's Books, Illustrated Books and Drawings, 10 July 2003*, 297.

Chapter 3

1. Michael Tolkien, "The Wizard Father"; Julian Tolkien, "Related to Tolkien."
2. Joanna Tolkien, "Joanna Tolkien speaks at the Tolkien Society Annual Dinner," 32.
3. George Sayer, "Recollections of J.R.R. Tolkien," 25.
4. *Biography*, 167.
5. For instance, see TCG:C, 375.
6. OFS MS B, 249
7. OFS MS B, 249
8. Roger Lancelyn Green, "Recollections," 7.
9. TCG:C, 422, 536.
10. OFS, 37n1; *Kullervo*, 68.
11. Dragons, 40; BC MS B, 103.
12. OFS, 76n1; Kay Holmes, "The Master Hobbit at 80," 46.
13. A successful and popular author, Dasent also wrote several novels of contemporary fiction: *The Annals of an Eventful Life* (1870), *Three to One* (1872), and *Half a Life* (1874).

14. OFS, 37n1.
15. *Letters*, 383–384.
16. *Letters*, 382–383.
17. LOTR:RC, 43–44.
18. *Letters*, 375.
19. "Soria Moria Castle," in George Dasent, *Popular Tales from the Norse*.
20. HH, 73; for dating, see HH, xxii–xxiii.
21. HH, 80.
22. In *The Hobbit*, Thorin's grandfather's name is given as "Thror" (no accent mark); in *The Lord of the Rings* Tolkien revised it to "Thrór." I have used the *Hobbit* spelling here and in the discussion of Thror's map in chapter 8, as that is the text being discussed.
23. George Dasent, introduction to *Popular Tales from the Norse* (second edition), cxxviii, cxxx.
24. *Letters*, 382.
25. *Letters*, 407. Oronzo Cilli gives Edward Bulwer-Lytton's *The Pilgrims of the Rhine* as the book in question (*Tolkien's Library*, 35), but this is in error. Tolkien had forgotten the author's name, and tentatively suggested Bulwer-Lytton as the author, but he was mistaken (as the footnote in *Letters* indicates).
26. TCG:RG, 376. They also see a connection between the picture of Ernest with the toad and Tolkien's illustration "Conversations with Smaug."
27. E.H. Knatchbull-Hugessen, preface to *Puss-Cat Mew and Other Stories for My Children*.
28. E.H. Knatchbull-Hugessen, *Puss-Cat Mew and Other Stories for My Children*.
29. TCG:RG, 1053.
30. See further AH, 85–86.
31. *Hobbit*, 18.
32. HH, 8.
33. Quoted in Atticus, "Tolkien Talking," 9.
34. OFS, 36, 55, 60; *Letters*, 22, HOME, x–xi.
35. TCG:C, 209; Dragons, 40; *Letters*, 94.
36. J.R.R. Tolkien, *The Qenya Alphabet*, Q5, Q6, Q39c, Q39d, and Q40.
37. BC MS B, 103.
38. *The Hobbit* facsimile first edition, dust jacket flap.
39. *Letters*, 22.
40. *Letters*, 22.
41. *Letters*, 22.
42. Peter Gilliver, "At the Wordface," 175.
43. Lewis Carroll, *Sylvie and Bruno Concluded*, chapter XXIII.
44. HOME IX, x.
45. Lewis Carroll, *Sylvie and Bruno*, chapter VI; chapter VII.
46. Quoted in Joe R. Christopher, "Tolkien's Lyric Poetry," 144.
47. *Hobbit*, 13.
48. LOTR, 207.
49. Joanna Tolkien, quoted in Josh Long, "Disparaging Narnia," 39; in OFS, he mentions the *Blue, Green, Lilac* (36), and *Pink* volumes (pp. 30, 54, 36, 210). Bodleian Library records show that he also consulted the Orange, Brown, Crimson, Violet, and Yellow Fairy Books, as well as Lang's *The Book of Dreams and Ghosts* (1897) and *The Magic Ring and Other Stories from the Yellow and Crimson Fairy Books* (1906), (George White, "A piece of Bodleian History"). For more on Tolkien's engagement with Lang in this lecture, see Sharin Schroeder, "Genre Problems: Andrew Lang and J.R.R. Tolkien on (Fairy) Stories and (Literary) Belief."
50. OFS, 76, OFS MS B, 249; Roger Lancelyn Green, "Recollections," 7; Tolkien alludes to a 'fable' from *In the Wrong Paradise* in his "Valedictory Address."

51. Introduction to OFS, 20.
52. Ruth Berman, "Tolkien as a Child of *The Green Fairy Book*," 127.
53. OFS, 54.
54. Andrew Lang, "The Enchanted Ring," in *The Green Fairy Book*, 142, 144.
55. Andrew Lang, "The Dragon of the North," in *The Yellow Fairy Book*, 11.
56. Andrew Lang, "The Dragon of the North," in *The Yellow Fairy Book*, 21.
57. Rachel Hart, "Tolkien, St. Andrews, and Dragons," 11. *The Red Fairy Book* edition that Tolkien would have seen was illustrated by H.J. Ford and Lancelot Speed.
58. Andrew Lang, prefatory note to "The Story of Sigurd," *The Red Fairy Book*.
59. OFS MS A, 188–189.
60. OFS, 30.
61. Andrew Lang, introduction to *The Lilac Fairy Book*.
62. OFS, 58.
63. OFS MS B, 248. For more on this incident, which seems to have had a strong effect on Tolkien, see John Garth, "J.R.R. Tolkien and the Boy Who Didn't Believe in Fairies."
64. OFS MS A, 188.
65. Michael Tolkien, "An Interview with Michael Hilary Reuel Tolkien," 8.
66. Quoted in Roger Lancelyn Green, "Recollections," 7.
67. OFS 76; OFS MS B, 250.
68. OFS, 76; OFS MS B, 250; OFS MS B, 249.
69. OFS, 56–57.
70. *Letters*, 215.
71. Quoted in Philip Norman, "The Prevalence of Hobbits."
72. OFS, 33.
73. A version of the tale also appears in the 1903 expanded edition of George Dasent's *Popular Tales from the Norse*, but Lang's Fairy Books were more directly aimed at child readers.
74. *Biography*, 84; HOME II, 'Readings of the earliest version' 271-272; Hammond and Scull, *J.R.R. Tolkien: Artist and Illustrator*, 47–48.
75. J.R.R. Tolkien, "Mythopoeia," in *Tree and Leaf*, 87.

CHAPTER 4

1. *Letters*, 215n.
2. Quoted in Josh Long, "Disparaging Narnia," 39
3. He consulted it while preparing his lecture "On Fairy-stories" (George White, "A Piece of Bodleian History"). Despite being subtitled "a book of old English fairy tales," it also includes a few more recent works by authors such as Robert Browning, Wordsworth, and Keats.
4. All four of these books appear in a photograph of his study in 1966. The copy of *The Irish Fairy Book* appears to be the 1938 edition. (Photograph of Tolkien in his study, Pamela Chandler, ARP 1188397.)
5. CLII 198; *The Silver Trumpet* appears on his shelves in 1966. (Photograph of Tolkien in his study, Pamela Chandler, ARP 1188397.)
6. Quoted in Jared C. Lobdell, "Mr. Bliss: Notes on the Manuscript and Story," 5.
7. An extract from *Winnie-the-Pooh* was included in *The Children's Treasury of Literature* (1967), which Tolkien was given. See page 62 note 4 below.
8. OFS, 79.

9. J.R.R. Tolkien, *The Father Christmas Letters*, 1941 letter. These are animal tales in the Beatrix Potter mode, illustrated by Margaret Tempest. The first book was published in 1929, with a new volume nearly every year until 1975.

10. Dragons, 59.

11. *The Sword in the Stone* appears on his shelves in 1966 (Photograph of Tolkien in his study, Pamela Chandler, ARP 1188397); TCG:RG, 1058.

12. TCG:C, 375.

13. *Letters*, 309.

14. Joanna Tolkien, quoted in Josh Long, "Disparaging Narnia," 39. A photograph of Tolkien in his study (figure 40) shows the four books on his shelves: *The Borrowers* (1952), *The Borrowers Afield* (1955), *The Borrowers Afloat* (1959), and *The Borrowers Aloft* (1961). This was the complete series at that time (the final volume was not published until 1982).

15. J.R.R. Tolkien, letter to Joy Hill, http://tolkiengateway.net/wiki/Letter_to_Joy_Hill_(5_January_1967).

16. OFS MS B, 249–250.

17. E.A. Wyke-Smith, *The Marvellous Land of Snergs*, chapter 4; chapter 14 (Gorbo is "fairly young" at age 250); chapter 4.

18. Wyke-Smith, *Snergs*, chapter 4.

19. Wyke-Smith, *Snergs*, chapter 4.

20. Wyke-Smith, *Snergs*, chapter 4.

21. Wyke-Smith, *Snergs*, chapter 4.

22. OFS MS B, 250n.

23. Rayner Unwin, *George Allen & Unwin: A Remembrancer*, 81.

24. *Letters*, 88.

25. *Letters*, 215n.

26. OFS MS B, 229; OFS, 36n2; Dragons, 40; *Letters*, 251; OFS MS B, 217; OFS MS B, 217; Michael Tolkien, "An Interview with Michael Hilary Reuel Tolkien," 5.

27. CLII, 538.

28. Michael Tolkien, "An Interview with Michael Hilary Reuel Tolkien," 5.

29. Christina Scull and Wayne G. Hammond, introduction to *The Adventures of Tom Bombadil*, 12.

30. Quoted in *Biography*, 245.

31. OFS MS B, 217.

32. CLII, 537–8.

33. OFS MS B, 229, 281, 217.

34. *Letters*, 251.

35. *Letters*, 251n.

36. For details on Tolkien's interactions with the Dutch translator, and the details of the translation, see Renée Vink, "Tolkien and (the) Dutch."

37. J.R.R. Tolkien, letter to the editor, *The Observer*, February 20, 1938, p. 9. See also *Letters*, 30.

38. *Letters*, 35.

39. Tom Shippey, *The Road to Middle-earth*, 79.

40. TCG:RG, 1332.

41. HOME XII, 49.

42. Dragons, 43, 40.

43. Beatrix Potter, *The Tale of Peter Rabbit; The Tale of Benjamin Bunny*.

44. Beatrix Potter, *The Tale of Benjamin Bunny*.

45. Peter Gilliver, "J.R.R. Tolkien and the OED."

46. Quoted in Arthur Ransome and J.R.R. Tolkien, *Signalling from Mars: The Letters of Arthur Ransome*, 249.

47. Photograph of Tolkien in his study, Pamela Chandler, ARP 1188397. See also figure 40 (Pamela Chandler, ARP 1188396).
48. TCG:RG, 65.
49. Richard Schindler, "The Expectant Landscape: J.R.R. Tolkien's Illustrations for *The Hobbit*," 27n19.
50. TCG:RG, 1061.
51. Hugh Lofting, *The Voyages of Doctor Dolittle*, chapter 3.
52. Lofting, *The Voyages of Doctor Dolittle*, chapter 4.
53. *Hobbit*, 117.
54. HH, 229ff. Douglas A. Anderson notes that Tolkien could have encountered the Russian name "Medvedko" in his friend R.W. Chambers's *Beowulf: An Introduction* (1921, 1932), where Chambers explains that the name means "John Honey-eater," i.e. John Bear. Anderson suggests that Tolkien adopted it for Beorn in the anglicized form of "Medwed." If this is the case, it need not displace the likely debt to *Dolittle*; Tolkien could, and often did, have multiple sources for any particular name, image, or idea (see Anderson, "R.W. Chambers and *The Hobbit*," 143).
55. HH, 237 (emphasis added).
56. TCG:RG, 845-846.
57. OFS MS B, 251.
58. *Letters*, 213, 232, 233n.
59. OFS MS B, 249, 251.
60. OFS MS B, 250.
61. See AH.
62. OFS MS B, 251.
63. George Sayer, *Jack: A Life of C.S. Lewis*, 312.
64. Roger Lancelyn Green, *C.S. Lewis*, 36–37.
65. Roger Lancelyn Green and Walter Hooper, *C.S. Lewis*, 240–241.
66. Roger Lancelyn Green, "Recollections," 7.
67. Roger Lancelyn Green, "C.S. Lewis," 104 (ellipses in original).
68. Green, "C.S. Lewis," 104.
69. *Biography*, 204.
70. *Inklings*, 223.
71. *Inklings*, 224 (emphasis in original).
72. George Sayer, *Jack*, 312–313.
73. George Sayer, "Recollections of J.R.R. Tolkien," 14.
74. George Sayer, *Jack*, xiv–xv.
75. *Letters*, 352.
76. *Inklings*, 204.
77. Quoted in Josh Long, "Disparaging Narnia," 39.
78. Joanna Tolkien, "Joanna Tolkien speaks," 34.
79. Nan C.L. Scott, "A Visit with Tolkien," 12.
80. George Sayer, *Jack*, 312–313.
81. J.R.R. Tolkien, *Letters from Father Christmas*, 74; 84, 142, 179; 117. "Rye St Anthony" (141) is, however, a joke about Priscilla's school of that name, which has a distinctive red uniform.
82. HOME VI, 7.
83. OFS, 79, OFS MS B, 247, OFS, 79.
84. *Letters*, 90.
85. Rayner Unwin, *The Making of* The Lord of the Rings, 7.
86. Kenneth Grahame, *The Wind in the Willows*, chapter X.
87. See Michael Ward, *Planet Narnia: The Seven Heavens in the Imagination of C.S. Lewis*.

88. OFS MS B, 251.
89. OFS MS B, 247, 249.
90. OFS MS B, 217.
91. TCG:RG, 1053.
92. OFS MS B, 249, 247.
93. Kenneth Grahame, *The Wind in the Willows*, chapter VII.
94. Walter Hooper, "Narnia: The Author, the Critics, and the Tale," 110.
95. C.S. Lewis, "A world for children," in *Image and Imagination*, 95.
96. C.S. Lewis, "Professor Tolkien's hobbit," in *Image and Imagination*, 97.
97. C.S. Lewis, "On Stories," in *On Stories and Other Essays on Literature*, 13.
98. C.S. Lewis, "The dethronement of power," in *Image and Imagination*, 108.

CHAPTER 5

1. OFS MS B, 207.
2. CLIII, 1458; see also CLII, 103.
3. TCG:C, 6, *Biography*, 167.
4. It is probable that Tolkien also read MacDonald's seminal essays "The Fantastic Imagination" and "The Imagination: Its Function and its Culture," and drew upon these ideas for OFS. See Verlyn Flieger and Douglas A. Anderson, Editors' Commentary, OFS 98; Paul Michelson, "George MacDonald and J.R.R. Tolkien on Faërie and Fairy Stories" and Frank Bergmann, "The Roots of Tolkien's Tree: The Influence of George MacDonald and German Romanticism on Tolkien's Essay 'On Fairy-stories.'"
5. TCG:C, 186. The thesis was by Mary M. McEldowney.
6. TS, 31.
7. J.R.R. Tolkien, Note to Kilby in SWM, 86; OFS, 44.
8. *Letters*, 31.
9. *Letters*, 185.
10. OFS MS B, 250.
11. *Letters*, 178.
12. George MacDonald, *The Princess and the Goblin*, chapter 8.
13. As Jason Fisher points out: see "Reluctantly Inspired," 115.
14. Katharine Briggs, "Goblins," in *A Dictionary of Fairies: Hobgoblins, Brownies, Bogies and Other Supernatural Creatures* (London: Allen Lane, 1976), 194.
15. Katharine Briggs, *The Anatomy of Puck: An Examination of Fairy Beliefs among Shakespeare's Contemporaries and Successors* (London: Routledge and Kegan Paul, 1959), 15.
16. Katharine Briggs, *Fairies in English Tradition and Literature* (London: Bellew Publishing, 1989), 38.
17. George MacDonald, *The Princess and the Goblin*, chapter 9.
18. MacDonald, *The Princess and the Goblin*, chapter 6.
19. George MacDonald, *The Princess and Curdie*, chapter 35.
20. It is included in *To the Land of Fair Delight: Three Victorian Tales of the Imagination*, which appears on Tolkien's shelves. (Photograph of Tolkien in his study, Pamela Chandler, ARP 1188397; see also figure 40. [Pamela Chandler, ARP 1188396]) TCG:C, 422, 536, 186.
21. See also Christina Scull and Wayne G. Hammond, introduction to *The Adventures of Tom Bombadil*, 177ff.
22. George MacDonald, *At the Back of the North Wind*, chapter XXIV.

23. J.R.R. Tolkien, "The Cat and the Fiddle: A Nursery-Rhyme Undone and Its Scandalous Secret Unlocked," 2–3.

24. See C.S. Lewis, *Surprised by Joy*, chapter XI.

25. George MacDonald, *Phantastes*, chapter XXV.

26. J.R.R. Tolkien, Note to Clyde Kilby, SWM, 86.

27. Quoted in W.H. Auden, introduction to *The Visionary Novels of George MacDonald*, viii.

28. Auden, introduction to *The Visionary Novels of George MacDonald*, vii.

29. Auden, introduction to *The Visionary Novels of George MacDonald*, vii.

30. J.R.R. Tolkien, letter to L.M. Cutts, quoted in *Sotheby's English Literature, History, Fine Bindings, Private Press Books, Children's Books, Illustrated Books and Drawings 10 July 2003*, 297.

31. TS, 31.

32. Tolkien's botanical descriptions in his own tales provide sufficient material for entire books about them: *The Plants of Middle-earth* by Dinah Hazell (2006) and *Flora of Middle-earth* by Walter S. Judd and Graham A. Judd (2017).

33. George MacDonald, *Phantastes*, chapter IV; VI ; IV; IV; VI.

34. OFS, 44. In MS B he phrases it the other way round, saying that MacDonald "only partly succeeded" (226).

35. See George MacDonald, *Lilith*, chapter XXIX and chapter XV.

36. MacDonald, *Lilith*, chapter XLVII.

37. See further, Courtney Salvey, "Riddled with Evil: Fantasy as Theodicy in George MacDonald's *Phantastes* and *Lilith*," *North Wind* 27 (2008): 16–34.

38. OFS MS B, 242.

39. MacDonald, *Lilith*, chapter XXXIV.

40. *Letters*, 262.

41. OFS MS B, 250; OFS, 37; OFS MS B, 250. Tolkien probably knew the edition called *Fairy Tales by George MacDonald*, illustrated by Arthur Hughes (1867; reissued by George Allen & Unwin in 1920), which contains all the stories that Tolkien references; furthermore, it includes the story Tolkien calls "Photogen and Nycteris" by exactly that title, although it sometimes appears under different titles elsewhere.

42. OFS, 44, OFS MS B, 250.

43. *Letters*, 351.

44. Quoted in Philip Norman, "The Hobbit Man," 36.

45. OFS MS B, 250.

46. J.R.R. Tolkien, Note to Clyde Kilby, SWM, 91.

47. George MacDonald, "The Golden Key."

48. LOTR, 922–923.

49. MacDonald, "The Golden Key."

50. MacDonald, "The Golden Key."

51. TCG:RG, 1215; Tolkien, Note to Clyde Kilby, in SWM, 85; Henry Resnik, "An Interview with Tolkien," 40.

52. Humphrey Carpenter, George Sayer, and Clyde S. Kilby, "A Dialogue," 20–24.

53. TS, 31.

54. Quoted in *Biography*, 244.

55. These are preserved in the Bodleian archives, among other materials related to *Smith of Wootton Major*, ca. January 1965. Unfortunately, these are in light pencil in Tolkien's fast handwriting and are very difficult to decipher (Bodleian MS Tolkien 9, fol. 5–6).

56. J.R.R. Tolkien, "Genesis of the story," in SWM, 86.

57. TCG:RG, 1217.

58. OFS MS B, 207.

CHAPTER 6

1. For more on this genre, see Sharin Schroeder, "She-who-must-not-be-ignored: Gender and Genre in *The Lord of the Rings* and the Victorian Boys' Book."
2. Maurice Richardson, review of *The Two Towers*, *The New Statesman*, 735.
3. Edmund Wilson, "Oo, Those Awful Orcs," 314.
4. Philip Toynbee, "Dissension Among the Judges," 19.
5. Fred Inglis, *The Promise of Happiness: Value and Meaning in Children's Fiction*, 192, 200.
6. *The King Edward's School Chronicle*, quoted in Burns, "The Desire of a Tale-Teller," 20.
7. TGW, 79; TCG:C, 31.
8. J.R.R. Tolkien, letter to Michael George Tolkien, Oct. 28, 1966 (British Library Add MS 71657).
9. J.R.R. Tolkien, "Philology: General Works [1923]," 29.
10. TCG:C, 51; OFS, 55; Inscription on *The Black Arrow* by Robert Louis Stevenson, Azusa Pacific University Inklings Collection.
11. TCG:C, 51. Oronzo Cilli suggests that Tolkien had read Conan Doyle's *The Sign of Four* (*Tolkien's Library*, 60). However, the reference in *Beowulf and the Critics* is simply to "Andaman islanders." It is Michael Drout in his notes who observes, as an example of its usage, that the villain in *The Sign of Four* is an Andaman Islander. It is indeed probable that Tolkien, who enjoyed detective stories (see chapter 11), had read this novel, but not, I think, certain. I therefore err on the side of caution and will not be considering it.
12. J.R.R. Tolkien, letter to Richard A. Lupoff, quoted in *Edgar Rice Burroughs: Master of Adventure*, 276–277; J.R.R. Tolkien, "Smith of Wootton Major essay," in SWM, 116. With regard to *Mars*, Tolkien remarked, "I retain no memory of the Siths or the Apt" (another type of monster from the *Mars* books); his phrasing indicates that he had read at least some of these tales, despite not finding them memorable (quoted in Lupoff, 277).
13. L. Sprague de Camp, letter to *Mythlore*, 41.
14. TCG:RG 1058. L. Sprague de Camp had sent him a copy of the volume; it also included tales by Fritz Leiber and Henry Kuttner.
15. *Letters*, 391n.
16. S.R. Crockett, *The Black Douglas*, chapter XLIX.
17. Crockett, *The Black Douglas*, chapter XLIX.
18. Crockett, *The Black Douglas*, chapter XLIX.
19. Crockett, *The Black Douglas*, chapter XLIX.
20. *Inklings*, 51–52.
21. Quoted in Stuart Lee, "Tolkien in Oxford," 159.
22. *Letters*, 391n.
23. Dale Nelson, "Literary Influences, Nineteenth and Twentieth Century," 367. See also Jared Lobdell in *England and Always: Tolkien's World of the Rings*.
24. HOME III, 228, 337.
25. Crockett, *The Black Douglas*, chapter XLI.
26. Crockett, *The Black Douglas*, chapter XLI.
27. TCG:C, 31. For a discussion of these novels in terms of Tolkien's attitude toward 'true or feigned history,' see Maggie Burns, "The Desire of a Tale-Teller."
28. Alexander Macdonald, *The Lost Explorers*, chapter I.
29. MME, 122–123.
30. Alexander Macdonald, *The Lost Explorers*, chapter XII; X, XII, X.

31. Macdonald, *The Lost Explorers*, chapter XII; XIV.

32. Herbert Hayens, *Scouting for Buller*, chapter XXIX; XVIII; XXII.

33. For an overview of scholarship on Tolkien and race, see Robin Anne Reid, "Race in Tolkien Studies: A Bibliographic Essay."

34. Dimitra Fimi, *Tolkien, Race and Cultural History*, 159.

35. Daniel Hahn, *The Oxford Companion to Children's Literature*, 2nd ed. (Oxford: OUP, 2015), 6; Rosie Kennedy, *The Children's War: Britain, 1914–1918* (Basingstoke: Palgrave Macmillan, 2014), 15. See also Robert Dixon, *Writing the Colonial Adventure: Race, Gender and Nation in Anglo-Australian Popular Fiction, 1875–1914* (Cambridge: Cambridge University Press, 1995).

36. TCG:C, 7; TCG:RG, 1399.

37. CLI, 909.

38. LOTR, 660–661.

39. Brian McFadden, "Fear of Difference, Fear of Death: The *Sigelwara*, Tolkien's Swertings, and Racial Difference," 156.

40. *Letters*, 73.

41. Raymond Edwards, *Tolkien*, 21.

42. TFA, 16–17.

43. MC, 238.

44. TCG:RG, 1374.

45. MC, 238.

46. Virginia Luling, "An Anthropologist in Middle-earth," 53. See further, Jane Chance's excellent analysis "*Apartheid* in Tolkien," in *Tolkien, Self and Other: "This Queer Creature."*

47. *Letters*, 37–38.

48. *Letters*, 37.

49. *Letters*, 410n.

50. Denis Gueroult, interview with Tolkien for BBC radio, "Now Read On."

51. Renée Vink, "'Jewish' Dwarves: Tolkien and Anti-Semitic Stereotyping," 141.

52. *Biography*, 168.

53. Richard Giddings and Elizabeth Holland, *J.R.R. Tolkien: The Shores of Middle-earth* (London: Junction, 1981). Tom Shippey remarks that their book "is as misguided about Tolkien and Buchan as about pretty well everything else" ("Guest Editorial," 3).

54. See, for instance, Marjorie Burns, "Three Stories Holding Hands: *The Wind in the Willows, Huntingtower,* and *The Hobbit*" in *A Wilderness of Dragons*; Tom Shippey, "Buchan, John"; Douglas A. Anderson, Introduction to "The Far Islands" by John Buchan, in *Tales Before Tolkien*; and Mark T. Hooker, "Reading John Buchan in Search of Tolkien."

55. Tolkien, "Philology. General Works [1925]," 63.

56. John Buchan, *Greenmantle*, chapters I, XII.

57. CLII, 103.

58. *Letters*, 144.

59. John Buchan, *Greenmantle*, chapter XI.

60. Tom Shippey, "Buchan, John," 78.

61. BC MS A, 90.

62. MC, 23; 20–21.

63. OFS, 82; OFS MS B, 273.

64. John Garth, "'As under a green sea': visions of war in the Dead Marshes," I:20.

65. *Letters*, 70.

66. John Garth, "As under a green sea," I:11.

67. Garth, "As under a green sea," I:20.

68. Quoted in *Biography*, 55.

69. HOME I, 15, 20.
70. HOME I, 17.
71. HOME I, 31–32. The idea may have re-emerged years later in *Roverandom*, where the Moon has a place for children to play while they are asleep. See also Dimitra Fimi, "'Come sing ye light fairy things tripping so gay': Victorian Fairies and the Early Work of J.R.R. Tolkien."
72. Stratford Caldecott, "Tolkien's Search for England," 45.
73. J.M. Barrie, *Peter Pan*, Act III.
74. TGW, 298.
75. *Letters*, 154.
76. Quoted in Daphne Castell, "The Realms of Tolkien," 150.

CHAPTER 7

1. CLII, 103; OFS, 55; OFS MS A, 188.
2. John Garth, *Tolkien at Exeter College*, 26.
3. TCG:RG, 799; TCG:C, 96; TCG:RG, 799. Tolkien also mentions *The Defence of Guinevere* in his essay "Chaucer as Philologist: the Reeve's Tale," 139.
4. HOME IX, 172.
5. TCG:RG, 798. Tolkien's own pattern designing is well illustrated in *Tolkien: Maker of Middle-earth*.
6. Richard Mathews, *Fantasy: The Liberation of Imagination*, 87.
7. Mathews, *Fantasy: The Liberation of Imagination*, 87.
8. In 1935 and 1952. TCG:C, 190, 407; TCG:C, 266. See also BC MS A, 34.
9. MC, 56; BC MS B, 97.
10. See C.S. Lewis's 1937 essay "William Morris" (now published in *Selected Literary Essays*). For Lewis's self-confessed "keen enthusiasm" for Morris, see his address "Fern-Seed and Elephants."
11. Richard Mathews, *Fantasy: The Liberation of Imagination*, 87.
12. John Garth, *Tolkien at Exeter College*, 4.
13. Wayne G. Hammond and Christina Scull, *J.R.R. Tolkien: Artist and Illustrator*, 10.
14. TGW, 14.
15. Quoted in TGW, 185.
16. TCG:RG, 1285.
17. See John Garth, *Tolkien at Exeter College*, and also "Exeter College History," Exeter College, Oxford. https://www.exeter.ox.ac.uk/wp-content/uploads/2017/04/college_history.pdf, 7ff.
18. Fiona MacCarthy, *William Morris: A Life for Our Time*, 199, 259.
19. Peter Gilliver, Jeremy Marshall, and Edmund Weiner, *The Ring of Words*, 71, 206.
20. TCG:RG, 799. For details on the various versions of this tale, see Christopher Tolkien's commentary in FG.
21. FG, 22.
22. FG, 93; 42, 89.
23. William Morris, *The House of the Wolfings*, chapter I; *The Roots of the Mountains*, chapter L.
24. FG, 98.
25. Gilliver et al., *The Ring of Words*, 96, 71.
26. Tom Shippey, introduction to *The Wood Beyond the World*, xvii.
27. *Letters*, 369.
28. Gilliver et al., *The Ring of Words*, 165.
29. *Letters*, 370.

30. See HOME VI.
31. FG, 61, 74–75.
32. William Morris, *The House of the Wolfings*, chapter I.
33. Morris, *House of the Wolfings*, chapter VIII; chapter XIV.
34. Tom Shippey, *The Road to Middle-earth*, 133. For more on this topic, see Deborah A. Higgens, *Anglo-Saxon Community in J.R.R. Tolkien's* The Lord of the Rings.
35. MC, 54–55. For instance, Tolkien criticized Morris's use of "leeds" (from Old English "leode") for "people."
36. *Letters*, 40. This comment is in reference to Tolkien's recitation of the "Nun's Priest's Tale" at the 1939 Oxford Summer Diversions. It remains unclear whether or not Tolkien convinced Masefield of the merits of using "modern pronunciation," as no text seems to have survived. See further, John Bowes, *Tolkien's Lost Chaucer*, chapter 6.
37. LOTR, 152–153.
38. *Letters*, 7.
39. Morris, *The House of the Wolfings*, chapter XIX.
40. See Carl Phelpstead, "'With chunks of poetry in between': *The Lord of the Rings* and Saga Poetics," for more on "the seminal influence of William Morris' prosimetric romances" (23) on Tolkien's writing.
41. Morris, *The House of the Wolfings*, chapter XXVIII.
42. LOTR, 517.
43. Quoted in Philip Norman, "The Prevalence of Hobbits."
44. Morris, *The House of the Wolfings*, chapter III. For a brief discussion of Morris's dwarf in *The Wood Beyond the World* in relation to Tolkien's dwarves, see Gerard Hynes, "From Nauglath to Durin's Folk," 26.
45. Morris, *The House of the Wolfings*, chapter XXVI.
46. Morris, *The House of the Wolfings*, chapter XIV.
47. William Morris, *The Roots of the Mountains*, chapter XXVI.
48. Morris, *The Roots of the Mountains*, chapter XXXVI.
49. Morris, *The Roots of the Mountains*, chapter L.
50. *Letters*, 303.
51. See, for instance, Michael Livingston's essay in *Baptism of Fire: The Birth of the Modern British Fantastic in World War I*, ed. Janet Brennan Croft, which quotes only the first half of Tolkien's remark (9), and Tom Shippey's *The Road to Middle-earth*, where he makes no mention of the Dead Marshes connection and names Morris only in passing, in an appendix. As another example, in Margaret Sinex's essay "'Tricksy Lights': Literary and Folkloric Elements in Tolkien's Passage of the Dead Marshes," she omits the final sentence of the quote in the main text and makes no mention of Morris (94). Sinex does remark in a footnote that "Intriguingly, Tolkien goes on to suggest that the Dead Marshes and the devastation before the Morannon "owe more to William Morris and his Huns and Romans, as in *The House of the Wolfings* or *The Roots of the Mountains*'." (109n1). This is, however, the sole reference to Morris in the entire essay.
52. See Michael W. Perry, "Morris, William," *J.R.R. Tolkien Encyclopedia*, 440. Tom Shippey's view has varied. In a 2019 essay, he finds Garth's interpretation convincing (Shippey and John Bourne, "A Steep Learning Curve: Tolkien and the British Army on the Somme," 18). Writing elsewhere the same year, he says, in reference to this passage, that "Tolkien's Dead Marshes reflect memories of the Somme, but Thiepval and Ypres also stirred memories of William Morris" ("William Morris and Tolkien: Some Unexpected Connections," 232–33).
53. John Garth, *The Worlds of J.R.R. Tolkien*, 188.
54. Unfortunately, Carpenter excerpted only a single paragraph from this letter in the *Letters*, so it is impossible to say whether Tolkien provided more explanation or context for his remark.

55. William Morris, *The Roots of the Mountains*, chapter XLI.

56. Morris, *The Roots of the Mountains*, chapter XLII.

57. Morris, *The Roots of the Mountains*, chapter XLIII.

58. Morris, *The Roots of the Mountains*, chapter XLVII.

59. "Amidmost," *The Oxford English Dictionary*, Compact Edition, 45.

60. "Gill, sb2," *The Oxford English Dictionary*, Compact Edition, 671. According to the OED, "The spelling *ghyll*, often used in guide-books to the Lake district, seems to have been introduced by Wordsworth."

61. HOME III, 169, line 326n.

62. Morris, *The House of the Wolfings*, chapters III, VIII. Tom Shippey also suggests that the Battle of the Pelennor Fields and the death of Théoden resemble the historical Battle of the Catalaunian Plains against the Huns (*The Road to Middle-earth*, 18).

63. Clutton-Brock writes that *The Roots of the Mountains* "is a tale of the same people [as *The House of the Wolfings*] but later in date; for now they are fighting with the Huns, not the Romans; at least we may guess the Dusky Men, whom they overcome, to be the Huns" (A. Clutton-Brock, *William Morris: His Life and Influence* [London: Williams and Norgate, 1914], 179).

64. Morris, *The Roots of the Mountains*, chapters XXIX, XXV.

65. Morris, *The House of the Wolfings*, chapters VIII, XXIV.

66. John Garth, *The Worlds of J.R.R. Tolkien*, 15.

67. Morris, *The House of the Wolfings*, chapters VIII, XXIV.

68. Morris, *The House of the Wolfings*, chapter VIII.

69. J.R.R. Tolkien, annotations on a map by Pauline Baynes, *Tolkien: Voyage en Terre du Milieu*, ed. Christian Bourgois, 72–73. See also Daniel Helen, "Tolkien's annotated map of Middle-earth transcribed."

70. *Letters*, 223.

71. Dick Plotz, "Many Meetings with Tolkien," 40; J.R.R. Tolkien, letter to Mr. Galbraith, 8 March 1956. In "Tolkien, J.R.R. Two autograph letters signed to William Galbraith," Oxford, 8 March 1965; 12 April 1956. (Marquette University Department of Special Collections and University Archives, Lot 306.).

72. Morris, *The House of the Wolfings*, chapter VIII.

73. Morris, *The House of the Wolfings*, chapter VIII.

74. Morris, *The House of the Wolfings*, chapter VIII.

75. Tom Loback, "Hoth, Hothri, Hothron: Orc Military Organization and Language," 17.

76. Morris, *The House of the Wolfings*, chapter VIII.

77. See *Letters*, 37-38.

78. TCG:RG, 741. See also Tom Shippey, "Goths and Romans in Tolkien's Imagination." For Tolkien's favorable view of the Goths, see Robert Murray, "A Tribute to Tolkien," 879–80; Murray recalls Tolkien arguing that if the Goths had not tragically become followers of the heresiarch Arius, their vernacular Bible and liturgy "would have served as a model for all the Germanic peoples and would have given them a native Catholicism which would never break apart."

79. "University Notes – Oxford," *The Tablet*, April 7, 1928, 467.

80. *Letters*, 89. For more on Tolkien's dislike of imperialism, see James Obertino, "Barbarians and Imperialism in Tacitus and *The Lord of the Rings*."

81. *Letters*, 89.

82. HOME I, 8; HOME II, 330.

83. Quoted in *Inklings*, 125.

84. TCG: RG, 493–494.

85. *Letters*, 157.

86. *Letters*, 376.
87. HOME X, 409.
88. William Morris and Eiríkr Magnússon, translator's preface to *The Story of the Volsungs*.

Chapter 8

1. Maggie Burns, "The Desire of a Tale-Teller" 20; TGW 78.
2. Oxfordshire History Centre archives, O22/11/A2/22.
3. Roger Lancelyn Green, introduction to *The Prisoner of Zenda and Rupert of Hentzau* by Anthony Hope, Everyman's Library edition (London: Dent, 1966), vii; Graham Greene, "Rider Haggard's Secret," in *Collected Essays* (London: Penguin Books, 1970), 209.
4. TCG:C, 51; Henry Resnik, "An Interview with Tolkien," 40.
5. Roger Lancelyn Green, "Recollections," 7. Green notes that "probably Tolkien did not like Haggard's treatment of the Viking background in the earlier parts of the story."
6. Jan Broberg, "In the Company of Tolkien," 158–159.
7. See, for instance, Clive Tolley, "Tolkien and the Unfinished"; Dale Nelson, "Tolkien's further indebtedness to Haggard"; and John D. Rateliff, "*She* and Tolkien."
8. John D. Rateliff, "*She* and Tolkien, Revisited," 157.
9. BC MS A, 90.
10. Rider Haggard, *Eric Brighteyes*, chapter XXV.
11. Haggard, *Eric Brighteyes*, chapter XXI.
12. C.S. Lewis, "The gods return to earth," in *Image and Imagination*, 103.
13. TCG:C, 51.
14. C.S. Lewis, "On Stories," in *On Stories and Other Essays on Literature*, 5.
15. TCG:C, 557.
16. See further, William N. Rogers II and Michael R. Underwood, "Gagool and Gollum: Exemplars of Degeneration in *King Solomon's Mines* and *The Hobbit*."
17. Rider Haggard, *King Solomon's Mines*, chapter XV; chapter IX.
18. Haggard, *King Solomon's Mines*, chapter II. See also Mark T. Hooker, "Frodo Quatermain," in *A Tolkienian Mathomium*.
19. Haggard, *King Solomon's Mines*, chapter III.
20. *Hobbit*, 28. See further, William H. Green, "King Thorin's Mines: *The Hobbit* as Victorian Adventure Novel." Green suggests a number of parallels between the novels, many of which are likely coincidental, however.
21. Haggard, *King Solomon's Mines*, chapter I.
22. See Michael Ward, "A Thief in the Night: The Christian Ethic at the Heart of *The Hobbit*."
23. Haggard, *King Solomon's Mines*, chapter XVI.
24. *Letters*, 407.
25. Haggard, *King Solomon's Mines*, chapter XVI.
26. Regarding the spelling of 'Thror,' see chapter 3, note 22.
27. Haggard, *King Solomon's Mines*, chapter II.
28. *Letters*, 215. See also HH for a full account of Thror's Map in *The Hobbit*'s complex composition history.
29. Wayne G. Hammond and Christina Scull, *J.R.R. Tolkien: Artist & Illustrator*, plate 85.
30. HH, 118n16.
31. HOME II, 329n.
32. TGW, 80.
33. The painting is reproduced in MME, 206; TGW, 80.

34. Haggard, *She*, chapter XXIII.
35. Haggard, *She*, chapter XVI.
36. *Letters*, 281.
37. John D. Rateliff, "*She* and Tolkien: Revisited," 153. See also Mark T. Hooker, "Tolkien and Haggard: Immortality," in *A Tolkienian Mathomium*.
38. Haggard, *She*, chapter XXVI.
39. See John D. Rateliff, "*She* and Tolkien"; Stephen Linley, "Tolkien and Haggard: Some Thoughts on Galadriel"; Clive Tolley, "Tolkien and the Unfinished."
40. *Letters*, 172; BF, 203. The Marian apparitions at Lourdes, France, took place in 1858, and were declared worthy of belief by the Church in 1862. Bernadette Soubirous, the girl who saw the apparitions, was declared a saint in 1933.
41. Haggard, *She*, chapter XV.
42. Haggard, introduction to *She*.
43. See AH, 128–131.
44. See, for instance, Verlyn Flieger, "A Post-modern Medievalist," in *Green Suns and Faërie*.
45. Henry Resnik, "An Interview with Tolkien," 40, spelling corrected. The interview was done by telephone and Resnik wrote "shard of Amynatas" for "Sherd of Amenartas." Tolkien spells it correctly in his own writings.
46. Haggard, *She*, chapter III.
47. Quoted in *She* (Oxford: Oxford University Press, 1991), 32n.
48. Daniel Karlin, explanatory notes to *She* (Oxford: Oxford University Press, 1991), 278.
49. HOME XII, 299.
50. HOME XII, 320n14.
51. Marquette University, *The Invented Worlds of J.R.R Tolkien*, 6.
52. Bodleian Library, J.R.R. Tolkien: *The Lord of the Rings. A display of original manuscripts and artwork*, item 8. See also Hammond and Scull, *J.R.R. Tolkien: Artist & Illustrator*, images 155 and 156.
53. Wayne G. Hammond and Christina Scull, *J.R.R. Tolkien: Artist & Illustrator*, 163.
54. *Letters*, 247–248.
55. *Letters*, 168.
56. See J.R.R. Tolkien, letter to Colin Bailey, May 13, 1964, Wade Center, JRRT L-Bailey W.
57. Christopher Tolkien, *J.R.R.T: A Film Portrait of J.R.R. Tolkien*, dir. Derek Bailey.
58. C.S. Lewis, "The Mythopoeic Gift of Rider Haggard," in *On Stories and Other Essays on Literature*, 97.

CHAPTER 9

1. Quoted in Daphne Castell, "The Realms of Tolkien," 148.
2. Quoted in Jan Broberg, "In the Company of Tolkien," 158.
3. Quoted in Daphne Castell, "The Realms of Tolkien," 148.
4. Jan Broberg, "In the Company of Tolkien," 158; *Letters*, 181; Clyde S. Kilby, *A Well of Wonder*, 193.
5. Quoted in *Inklings*, 65–66. See also *Letters*, 29 and Tom Shippey, "The Ransom Trilogy," in *The Cambridge Companion to C.S. Lewis*.
6. Quoted in Daphne Castell, "The Realms of Tolkien," 148.
7. HOME IX, 172; *Letters*, 377n; *Letters*, 377n; Jan Broberg, "In the Company of Tolkien," 158.

8. J.R.R. Tolkien, letter to John Bush, 12 March 1966, quoted in Oronzo Cilli, *Tolkien's Library*, 118. See also TCG:C Addenda & Corrigenda for pp. 672 and 677, http://www.hammondandscull.com/addenda/chronology2.html.

9. Jan Broberg, "In the Company of Tolkien," 158.

10. TCG:C, 539.

11. Arthur C. Clarke, *Voices in the Sky*, 150–151.

12. OFS, 70.

13. See *The Encyclopedia of Science Fiction*, ed. John Clute and Peter Nicholls (New York: St Martin's Griffin, 1995), 1018.

14. See Robert Scholes and Eric S. Rabkin, *Science Fiction*, 36–37, and Brian Aldiss and David Wingrove, *Trillion Year Spree*, 219.

15. *Letters*, 381n. The volume also includes tales by Kate Wilhelm, Joanna Russ, R.A. Lafferty, and Brian W. Aldiss – some of them rather edgy.

16. Quoted in Daphne Castell, "The Realms of Tolkien," 148.

17. From the influential 1963 speech by Harold Wilson, leader of the Labour Party who would be elected Prime Minister the following year. See "Harold Wilson's 'white heat of technology' speech 50 years on," *The Guardian*, September 19, 2013, https://www.theguardian.com/science/political-science/2013/sep/19/harold-wilson-white-heat-technology-speech.

18. *Tolkien in Love*, BBC radio drama, written by Sean Grundy, BBC Radio 4, August 19, 2017.

19. *Letters*, 344; J.R.R. Tolkien, letter to Michael George Tolkien, July 29th, 1966. British Library Add MS 71657; MME 186; J.R.R. Tolkien, letter to Michael George Tolkien, September 16th, 1965. British Library Add MS 71657.

20. TCG:RG, 1063. See also Priscilla Tolkien et al., "Facets of Tolkien" part 2; J.R.R. Tolkien, letter to Michael George Tolkien, March 6th. 1968, British Library Add MS 71657.

21. TCG:RG 891–92, 1197–98.

22. TFA; *Biography*, 245.

23. Quoted in Stuart Lee, "'Tolkien in Oxford' (BBC, 1968): A Reconstruction," 150. Only a small portion of the extensive interviews with Tolkien appeared in the final BBC film. Lee discovered and transcribed all the surviving 'lost' footage.

24. Stuart Lee, "Tolkien in Oxford," 150.

25. John Garth, *The Worlds of J.R.R. Tolkien*, 151, 161.

26. CLIII, 939; CLIII, 1109.

27. Quoted in Evelyn B. Byrne and Otto M. Penzler, *Attacks of Taste*, 43.

28. Priscilla Tolkien, "News from the North Pole," 9. The 1938 Father Christmas letter mentions the gift of an astronomy book. See also Kristine Larsen, "'A Little Earth of His Own': Tolkien's Lunar Creation Myths," and Jorge Quiñonez and Ned Raggett, "Nólë i Meneldilo: Lore of the Astronomer."

29. Kristine Larsen, "Lessons of Myth, Mortality, & the Machine in the Dream State Space-Time Travel Tales of J.R.R. Tolkien and Olaf Stapledon."

30. HOME IX, 165.

31. OFS, 34.

32. OFS MS B, 253n. Flieger and Anderson suggest that his reference to the "green sun" indicates knowledge of Wells's "The Plattner Story" (OFS, 111).

33. J.R.R. Tolkien, *Tengwesta Qenderinwa and Pre-Fëanorian Alphabets Part 2*, 142–143.

34. OFS, 58. See also OFS MS A, 178.

35. BC MS A, 65.

36. *Letters*, 33.

37. Joseph O'Neill, *Land Under England*, chapter 6.

38. O'Neill, *Land Under England*, chapter 6.

39. LOTR, 401.

40. There are other suggestive points about *Land Under England*. John Garth notes a resemblance between the narrator's early encounter with a giant, subterranean spider-like creature, and Tolkien's Shelob in her lair (*The Worlds of J.R.R. Tolkien*, 98).

41. HOME IX, 175; Flieger and Anderson also suggest that an allusion in the manuscript of "On Fairy-stories" refers to *Last and First Men* (OFS, 197).

42. HOME IX, 175.

43. Olaf Stapledon, preface to the English edition of *Last and First Men*, in *Last and First Men & Star Maker* (New York: Dover, 1968), 9.

44. *Letters*, 34.

45. Walter Hooper, *C.S. Lewis: A Companion and Guide*, 205.

46. Auction listing, quoted in Wayne G. Hammond and Christina Scull, "From Tolkien's Library."

47. Roger Lancelyn Green, *Into Other Worlds*, 181; E.H. Visiak, "The Arcturan Shadow," 7.

48. David Lindsay, *A Voyage to Arcturus*, chapter XXI.

49. E.H. Visiak, "The Arcturan Shadow," 10.

50. Galad Elflandsson, "David Lindsay and the Quest for Muspel-fire," 9.

51. Lindsay, *A Voyage to Arcturus*, chapter II.

52. OFS, 111. Tolkien had read *A Voyage to Arcturus* by March 1938; he began working on the OFS lecture around December, 1938.

53. *Letters*, 34.

54. HOME IX, 163–164.

55. *Letters*, 80; HOME X, 5–6. He discussed this with Katherine Farrer.

56. CLII, 560; *Letters*, 84.

57. *Letters*, 377n2; *Letters*, 258. If Tolkien meant "all" literally, this would include Eddison's *Styrbiorn the Strong* (1926), a modern novelistic retelling of a Norse saga, as well as Eddison's nonfiction. However, I have taken Tolkien's praise for Eddison as a writer of "invented worlds" to mean that he was, at any rate, most familiar with Eddison's science-fictional works.

58. *Letters*, 377n2; *Letters*, 258.

59. *Letters*, 258.

60. Quoted in CLII, 554.

61. Quoted in Paul E. Thomas, introduction to *Zimiamvia: A Trilogy* (New York: Dell, 1992), xliii.

62. Paul E. Thomas, introduction to *Zimiamvia: A Trilogy*, xxxvii.

63. E.R. Eddison, "A Letter of Introduction," in *Zimiamvia: A Trilogy*, 321. For a detailed examination of Eddison's philosophical-theological views, see Joseph Young, "'On This I Stake My Salvation': E.R. Eddison's Easter Manifesto," and *Extrapolation: A Journal of Science Fiction and Fantasy*, vol. 54, no. 1 (2013), 73–93; and "Aphrodite on the Home Front: E.R. Eddison and World War II," *Mythlore* 117/118, vol. 30, no. 3/4 (Spring/Summer 2012): 71–88, and Anna Vaninskya, *Fantasies of Time and Death*, chapter 3.

64. Quoted in Daphne Castell, "The Realms of Tolkien," 150.

65. *Letters*, 258.

66. J.R.R. Tolkien, "Tolkien on Tolkien," 39.

67. Appendices are still relatively rare in literary fiction, but, probably due at least in part to Tolkien's influence, it is now not uncommon to find appendices in science fiction and linguistic glossaries in fantasy. See, for instance, Frank Herbert's *Dune* (1965), Peter F. Hamilton's *The Reality Dysfunction* (1996), Stephen R. Donaldson's *Lord Foul's Bane* (1977) and Robert Jordan's *Eye of the World* (1990).

68. TS, 71.

69. Quoted in Henry Resnik, "An Interview with Tolkien," 40; TCG:C 196.

70. Quoted in Resnik, "An Interview with Tolkien," 40.
71. J.R.R. Tolkien, letter to Caroline Whitman Everett, 24 June 1957, quoted in John D. Rateliff, "'And Something Yet Remains to Be Said': Tolkien and Williams," 53; *Letters*, 349.
72. Both books appear on his study shelves in a 1966 photograph. (Photograph of Tolkien in his study, Pamela Chandler, ARP 1188397.)
73. Quoted in Resnik, "An Interview with Tolkien," 40.
74. TCG:C, 255.
75. HOME IX, 219n52.
76. See, for instance, *Letters*, 349, 361–2, and Tolkien's letter to Mother Mary Anthony, April 12, 1966, Wade Center JRRT-Lanthony W. John D. Rateliff has observed that Tolkien's earlier comments about Williams tend to be more positive than those written in later years ("'And Something Yet Remains to Be Said': Tolkien and Williams").
77. Quoted in *Inklings*, 123.
78. A reproduction of this bizarre image appears in Grevel Lindop's biography *Charles Williams: The Third Inkling*, plate 24 (Oxford: Oxford University Press, 2015.)
79. Quoted in *Inklings*, 125.
80. The poem appeared in *Shenandoah: The Washington and Lee Review*, vol. 18, no. 2 (Winter 1967): 96–97. See also Carl Phelpstead, "'For W.H.A.': Tolkien's Poem in Praise of Auden."
81. Quoted in Henry Resnik, "An Interview with Tolkien," 40.
82. Quoted in Nan C.L. Scott, "A Visit with Tolkien," 12.
83. Verlyn Flieger, "Time in the Stone of Suleiman," in *The Rhetoric of Vision: Essays on Charles Williams*, ed. Charles A. Huttar and Peter J. Schakel (Cranbury, NJ: Associated University Presses, 1996), 75.
84. *Inklings*, 121.
85. *Letters*, 172.
86. *Letters*, 172.
87. *Letters*, 251–252.
88. *Letters*, 283–84.
89. *Letters*, 145; *Letters*, 262, 298; LOTR, foreword to the second edition, xxiv.
90. Diana Pavlac Glyer, *The Company They Keep*, 17, 30, 76; *Letters*, 108. Elsewhere he remarks on Lewis's dedication of the book to him, but it is not clear what he thinks of the book itself (*Letters*, 342); photograph of Tolkien in his study, Pamela Chandler, ARP 1188397.
91. Glyer, *The Company They Keep*, 1, 17, 127; photograph of Tolkien in his study, Pamela Chandler, ARP 1188397.
92. HOME IX, 148.
93. David Downing, "Science Fiction," 299, 310.
94. *Letters*, 342.
95. *Letters*, 89.
96. Denis Gueroult, interview with Tolkien for BBC radio, "Now Read On."
97. *Letters*, 33. See *Letters*, 29, for praise of the book as "an exciting serial."
98. *Letters*, 33.
99. HOME IX, 164.
100. *Letters*, 342.
101. *Letters*, 334; see also 231. See further, Luke J. Chambers, "*Enta Geweorc* and the Work of Ents."
102. HOME VII, 411.
103. C.S. Lewis, *Out of the Silent Planet*, chapters 15–16.
104. Lewis, *Out of the Silent Planet*, chapter 15, chapter 16.
105. *Biography*, 198.
106. Quoted in Daphne Castell, "The Realms of Tolkien," 148.

107. Quoted in Castell, "The Realms of Tolkien," 148.

Chapter 10

1. TGW, 301–306.
2. Richard Hurd, *Letters on Chivalry and Romance* (1762), Letter XII. See further Kevin L. Morris, *The Image of the Middle Ages in Romantic and Victorian Literature* (Abingdon, UK: Routledge, 2019).
3. OFS MS B, 261.
4. He mentions Baring-Gould's work in a letter to his grandson Michael, April 24th, 1957, although it is not clear what, if anything, he had read of it (British Library Add MS 71657).
5. TCG:RG, 229. Aurelia, the protagonist of *Dream English*, has suggestive parallels to Tolkien's Goldberry.
6. These are included in the collection *Swords and Sorcery*, given to him by L. Sprague de Camp. Tolkien was distinctly unimpressed, declaring the stories badly written in general and uniformly poor in their nomenclature. He is particularly scathing with regard to Smith's tale; Lovecraft's escaped specific comment (TCG:C, 1058; see Tolkien, *Critique of "The Distressing Tale of Thangobrind the Jeweler"*).
7. *Letters*, 253. He owned a copy of *Broomsticks* (Cilli, *Tolkien's Library*, 68).
8. Tolkien mentions *Orpheus* in his 'College of Cretaceous Perambulators' mock exam (1938) (Papers of Owen Barfield. Dep. c. 1104, folio 5 recto). See also MME, 245. *Orpheus* was written in the 1930s, although not published until 1983.
9. TCG:C, 302.
10. Roger Lancelyn Green, "Recollections," 7. Tolkien may also have read Green's unpublished novel *The Wood That Time Forgot*; C.S. Lewis read the manuscript in 1945, critiqued it, and asked if he might show it to Tolkien (CLII, 672).
11. J.R.R. Tolkien, letter to Sterling Lanier, 24th January 1973 (Marquette University Department of Special Collections and University Archives MSS-4, Box 2, Folder 44). See also TCG:C, Addenda & Corrigenda for pg. 803, http://www.hammondandscull.com/addenda/chronology2.html.
12. TCG:C, 787.
13. Clara Kuck, "Dunsany and mythology in modern drama," 91; "Wireless Notes – New Radio Play by Lord Dunsany," *The Manchester Guardian*, April 16, 1934, 10. See also Darrell Schweitzer, introduction to *The Ginger Cat and Other Lost Plays* by Lord Dunsany (Cabin John, MD: Wildside Press, 2005). His obituary in the *Manchester Guardian* was titled "Playwright of fantasy" (October 28, 1957, 4).
14. HH, 64n28.
15. Raymond Edwards, *Tolkien*, 44.
16. Lord Dunsany, preface to *Tales of Wonder*.
17. OFS MS B, 247.
18. *Letters*, 375n; see also OFS MS B, 247.
19. *Letters*, 418.
20. *Letters*, 26.
21. Quoted in L. Sprague de Camp, letter to *Mythlore*, Mythlore 50, vol. 13, no. 4 (Summer 1987): 41.
22. Cecila Dart-Thornton, introduction to *The Book of Wonder and The Last Book of Wonder*, xvii.
23. Lord Dunsany, *The Book of Wonder*.

24. Quoted in L. Sprague de Camp, *Literary Swordsmen and Sorcerers*, 243; quoted in letter from L. Sprague de Camp, *Mythlore* 50, vol. 13, no. 4 (Summer 1987): 41; quoted in L. Sprague de Camp, *Literary Swordsmen and Sorcerers*, 243.

25. *Letters*, 26.

26. Quoted in MME, 219. This is a newly published section, not included in the *Letters*.

27. John Corbin, "The Gods of Dunsany," *The New York Times*, Sunday, January 26, 1919, 42.

28. Corbin, "The Gods of Dunsany," 42.

29. Raymond Edwards, *Tolkien*, 42.

30. HOME I 29n; L.L.H. Thompson, "Report on J.R.R. Tolkien's paper on Catholic poet Francis Thompson (4 March 1914)," 288–289. The original text of this lecture has not survived, but an attendee, L.L.H. Thompson, took detailed notes for the club minutes, which are preserved in the Exeter College Library. The transcript of these notes appears in Appendix 5 of Andrew S. Higgins, *The Genesis of Tolkien's Mythology*. A few pages of Tolkien's notes or drafts for the lecture are preserved in the Bodleian archives. Unfortunately, these are written in pencil and in some of his least legible handwriting (Bodleian MS Tolkien A 21/13 Box 1).

31. *Kullervo*, 114; *Letters*, 340.

32. Raymond Edwards, *Tolkien*, 43, 41.

33. L.L.H. Thompson, "Report," 289.

34. Garth, *Tolkien at Exeter College*, 30.

35. L.L.H. Thompson, "Report," 288.

36. HOME X, 155.

37. HOME X, 157.

38. Francis Thompson, *The Works of Francis Thompson. Poems: Volume I*.

39. HOME II, 329. Christopher limits himself to noting that this connection supplies only "the origin of the name as a series of sounds," but since it does provide that origin, it may also have further significance.

40. HOME II, 301; *Letters*, 231. Stratford Caldecott notes the connection to Thompson's 'Luthany' in this regard. ("Tolkien's Search for England.")

41. HOME II, 301, 304. At an early stage of the tale, Tolkien has his traveller Ælfwine receive the name, in the form Lúthien, from the Elves as a marker that he is a friend of Luthany. Later he drops the use of 'Lúthien' for Ælfwine, making it available for his elf-maiden.

42. Francis Thompson, *The Works of Francis Thompson. Poems: Volume II*.

43. Edwards, *Tolkien*, 44.

44. *Silmarillion*, 30; 164.

45. *Silmarillion*, 165.

46. LOTR:RC, 768.

47. AH, 106.

48. LOTR:RC, 767.

49. LOTR:RC, 768; "Crack," OED Compact Edition, 1096–7. The use of "crack" (noun) to mean a fissure of any kind only appears in definition 7, and there, its reference to a crack in a *mountain* appears only in 7a and 7e.

50. Algernon Blackwood, *The Education of Uncle Paul*, chapter XIV; chapter XV.

51. Blackwood, *The Education of Uncle Paul*, chapter XXVII.

52. Blackwood, *The Education of Uncle Paul*, chapter XIV.

53. Blackwood, *The Education of Uncle Paul*, chapter XIV.

54. HOME VI, 265.

55. Morchard Bishop, "*John Inglesant* and Its Author," 71. Shorthouse is sometimes incorrectly identified as "John" rather than "Joseph," probably through association with his famous character.

56. *Letters*, 348.

57. "Church and Mansion Described in 'John Inglesant' the Subject of a Lawsuit," *The Guardian*, Friday, February 6, 1914, 7; "The Little Malvern Church," *The Guardian*, Thursday, May 14, 1914, 8.

58. Ronald Knox, *Stimuli* (London: Sheed and Ward, 1951), 83.

59. *Letters*, 348.

60. Quoted in Norman Power, "Ring of doom," 1247.

61. J.R.R. Tolkien, letter to Canon [Norman] Power, July 8, 1973, Wade Center, JRRT L-Power 1, X.

62. Norman Power, "Ring of doom." See also Lucy Matthews, "The Unveiling of a plaque commemorating J.R.R. Tolkien in Birmingham, March 17th 1977."

63. Quoted in Norman Power, "Ring of doom," 1247; *Letters*, 348.

64. MME, 10; *Inklings*, 51.

65. *Letters*, 348.

66. Morchard Bishop, "*John Inglesant* and Its Author," 74.

67. *Letters*, 348.

68. *Letters*, 348.

69. Thomas Honegger observes that in addition to Tolkien's published academic essays and lectures, the Bodleian Library holds "thousands of pages of Tolkien's lecture and research notes and drafts," which represent "the product of a long and busy academic life. . . . The relatively few essays that Tolkien saw into print during his lifetime constitute thus the proverbial tip of the iceberg and are witnesses to a time when the demands of the recurrent research assessment exercise had not yet forced academics to publish as much as possible in whatever form" ("Academic Writings," 28).

70. Norman Power, "Ring of doom," 1249. See also J.S. Ryan, "Those Birmingham Quietists: J.R.R. Tolkien and J.H. Shorthouse."

71. J.H. Shorthouse, *John Inglesant: A Romance*, chapter IX.

72. Shorthouse, *Inglesant*, chapter XXXII; chapter XXXIX.

73. Shorthouse, *Inglesant*, chapter XVIII.

74. Shorthouse, *Inglesant*, chapter XXXII.

75. Shorthouse, *Inglesant*, chapter XIX; chapter XXXIII.

76. See Joseph Pearce, *Literary Converts*, 20–40; Ronald Knox, *A Spiritual Aeneid* (London: Longmans Green, 1918), 32, 156.

77. Shorthouse, *Inglesant*, chapter VI; chapter XXVI; chapter XXVII.

78. J.R.R. Tolkien, letter to Miss [Joyce] Biddell, 24 October 1955, quoted in *Sotheby's English Literature, History, Children's Books and Illustrations, London, 12 July 2016*, 148.

79. Shorthouse, *Inglesant*, chapter VI; chapter VII.

80. LOTR, 944.

81. Shorthouse, *Inglesant*, chapter XXXII.

82. Shorthouse, *Inglesant*, chapter XXXII.

83. Shorthouse, *Inglesant*, chapter XXXIV; chapter XXXV.

84. Shorthouse, *Inglesant*, chapter XXXVI.

85. Verlyn Flieger, *A Question of Time*, 6.

86. *Letters*, 326.

87. Shorthouse, *Inglesant*, chapter XXXVI.

88. Quoted in MME, 157.

89. Shorthouse, *Inglesant*, chapter XXXIX.

90. LOTR, 954.

Chapter 11

1. Quoted in TCG:C, 769.
2. James Joyce, *Finnegans Wake*, book I, chapter 2.
3. Oronzo Cilli, *Tolkien's Library*, 18.
4. Clyde Kilby, "Tolkien as Scholar and Artist," 9; TS 31; J.R.R. Tolkien, letter to Naomi Mitchison, 8 December 1955, quoted in Seth Kaller, "J.R.R. Tolkien Writes his Proofreader."
5. Arne Zettersten, *J.R.R. Tolkien's Double Worlds and Creative Process*, 199; Verlyn Flieger, *A Question of Time*, 58.
6. John D. Rateliff, "Tolkien and Sinclair Lewis." See also J.R.R. Tolkien, letter to Harry Bauer, November 1966, http://tolkiengateway.net/wiki/Letter_to_Harry_C._Bauer. Even Carpenter concedes that Tolkien enjoyed Sinclair Lewis's books.
7. Bodleian MS Tolkien A 13/1 box 2, fol. 170.
8. Quoted in Charlotte and Denis Plimmer, "The Man Who Understands Hobbits," 32.
9. Quoted in Plimmer, "The Man Who Understands Hobbits," 32.
10. Sinclair Lewis, *Babbitt* (New York: Collier, 1922), chapter 1.
11. In his "Kalevala" lecture, he mentions "Evangeline" and quotes an American critic who had written an "appreciation" of Longfellow (*Kullervo*, 78).
12. John Garth, "The road from adaptation to invention," 19; for dating of the ms, see Verlyn Flieger, "Introduction to the Essays," *Kullervo*, 63–64; Bodleian MS Tolkien 23, fol. 72.
13. *Kullervo*, 78.
14. John Garth, "Tolkien's death of Smaug: American inspiration revealed."
15. John Garth, "Inspiration in Unlikely (and Likely) Places."
16. Horace Gregory, introduction to *Evangeline and Selected Tales and Poems* by Henry Wadsworth Longfellow (New York: Signet Classics, 1964), xxviii.
17. *Kullervo*, 78.
18. Edward M. Cifelli, preface to *Evangeline and Selected Tales and Poems* by Henry Wadsworth Longfellow (New York: Signet Classics, 1964), xi.
19. Denis Gueroult, interview with Tolkien for BBC radio, "Now Read On."
20. Carole Seymour-Jones, *Painted Shadow: The Life of Vivienne Eliot* (New York: Doubleday, 2002), 7–8; Paul Johnson, *Creators: From Chaucer and Dürer to Picasso and Disney* (New York: HarperCollins, 2006), 223.
21. *Letters*, 353.
22. Quoted in Martyn Halsall, "Poet who crossed frontiers," *Church Times* 27 February 2015, https://www.churchtimes.co.uk/articles/2015/27-february/features/features/poet-who-crossed-frontiers.
23. Peter Gilliver, "The First Inkling: Edward Tangye Lean," 70.
24. Gilliver, "The First Inkling," 77.
25. *Letters*, 388; HOME VII, 85.
26. ASV, 100–101; ASV, xxxiii.
27. Dimitra Fimi and Andrew S. Higgins, introduction to ASV, xlii. See also Dimitra Fimi, "Language as Communication vs. Language as Art: J.R.R. Tolkien and early 20th-century radical linguistic experimentation."
28. J.R.R. Tolkien, item Q17 in *Parma Eldamberon* 20, 87–88; ASV, 91–92.
29. See Robbert-Jan Henkes, Erik Bindervoet, and Finn Fordham, "Note on the Text" and "Chronology," *Finnegans Wake* (Oxford: Oxford University Press, 2012).
30. Given that "Anna Livia Plurabelle" was the title of the newly published Faber and Faber volume, his use of this name in his notes very probably refers not just to the character, but to the whole extract; this is the way in which Hiley, who studied the manuscript of the notes for her analysis, treats it. The manner in which Tolkien's notes were reproduced in print in

A Secret Vice somewhat obscures this point, as several words that are pencilled in the upper right corner of the manuscript are reproduced in print above the name Anna Livia Plurabelle and in the same font and size (ASV, 91). In the manuscript, the name is written carefully in Tolkien's most legible handwriting, in black ink, and appears to be positioned as a header for the notes that follow (see Bodleian MS Tolkien 4, fol. 44).

31. ASV, 91–92.
32. ASV, 92.
33. ASV, 92.
34. Margaret Hiley, "'Bizarre or dream like': J.R.R. Tolkien on *Finnegans Wake*," 117.
35. Hiley, "'Bizarre or dream like': J.R.R. Tolkien on *Finnegans Wake*," 121–122.
36. Hiley, "'Bizarre or dream like': J.R.R. Tolkien on *Finnegans Wake*," 118.
37. ASV, 91–92.
38. Hiley, "'Bizarre or dream like': J.R.R. Tolkien on *Finnegans Wake*," 121.
39. See HOME VII, 84–105, for Christopher Tolkien's detailed explanation of the extremely complex composition history of this part of *The Lord of the Rings*.
40. Quoted in HOME VII, 85.
41. Gilliver, "The First Inkling: Edward Tangye Lean," 70n12.
42. HOME VII, 85.
43. Tom Shippey, *J.R.R. Tolkien: Author of the Century*, 311.
44. Quoted in William Cater, "The filial duty of Christopher Tolkien," 62.
45. Stephen Fry, "The Hobbit & The Lord of the Rings: Stephen Fry's Planet Word," June 13, 2015, https://www.youtube.com/watch?v=kGfVBl4GTW4.
46. BF, 96; *Letters*, 61.
47. TCG:C, 443.
48. Verlyn Flieger, *Green Suns and Faërie*, 179–180.
49. *Letters*, 377n.
50. TCG:C, 741.
51. Forster's novel about homosexual relationships, *Maurice*, was published posthumously in 1971. It is possible that Tolkien was simply not aware of Forster's – and even Renault's – views on sexual ethics, but I think this unlikely.
52. *Letters* 308; unpublished diary of Warren Lewis, Wade Center, Vol. XVII, folder 3 of 4, 19 July 1934.
53. J.R.R. Tolkien, letter to Naomi Mitchison, December 8, 1955, quoted in Seth Kaller, "J.R.R. Tolkien Writes his Proofreader"; TCG:C, 487. In his eventual letter to Mitchison, he shares his thoughts on her book with diplomacy and charity.
54. J.R.R. Tolkien, "Philology. General Works [1923]," 28.
55. TCG:C, 481.
56. TCG:C, 249, 331.
57. *Letters*, 353; A.N. Wilson, *Iris Murdoch As I Knew Her* (London: Hutchinson, 2003), 224. Tolkien also sold one of his writing desks to Murdoch (Wilson, *Iris Murdoch As I Knew Her*, 33).
58. Unpublished diary of Warren Lewis, Wade Center, Vol. XXI, folder 1 of 4, 19 December 1950.
59. TCG:C, 314; BF, 200.
60. J.R.R. Tolkien, letter to Miss Stanley-Smith, 22 November 1956, quoted in Oronzo Cilli, *Tolkien's Library*, item 983. See also http://tolkiengateway.net/wiki/Letter_to_Miss_Stanley-Smith_(22_November_1956).
61. TCG:C, 568.
62. J.R.R. Tolkien, letter to Nancy Smith, reproduced in full in *Christie's Fine Printed Books and Manuscripts 24 May 2002*; see also http://tolkiengateway.net/wiki/Letter_to_Nancy_Smith_(30_May_1966).

63. TCG:C, 764; Oronzo Cilli, *Tolkien's Library*, 96.

64. Henry Resnik, "An Interview with Tolkien," 38.

65. TS 26; Michael Tolkien, "Autobiographical essay on my grandfather"; Stuart and Rosie Clark, eds. "Oxonmoot '74 Report" 9; Walter Hooper, personal communication to the author, June 13, 2016.

66. TCG:RG, 1058; J.R.R. Tolkien, letter to Donald Swann, November 18, 1966 (Wade Center JRRT L-Swann 9 X).

67. *Letters*, 82.

68. TS, 26; *Inklings*, 189; Oronzo Cilli, *Tolkien's Library*, 250.

69. Letter to Michael George Tolkien, October 28, 1966, British Library Add MS 71657, item 47. Oronzo Cilli gives Wodehouse's *The Man with Two Left Feet* as a title that Tolkien knew (*Tolkien's Library*, 315) but this is in error. The source he cites is actually an illustrative example given by Scull and Hammond in their explanatory notes to *Farmer Giles of Ham* (p. 200).

70. Auction listing, quoted in Wayne G. Hammond and Christina Scull, "From Tolkien's Library." This would be the twenty-four-page *The Wedding Sermon* (Burns and Oates, 1911). It first appeared in Patmore's collection *The Victories of Love* (1862) and was later anthologized alongside his Catholic poetry in *Mystical Poems of Nuptial Love*, ed. Rev. Terence L. Connolly, SJ, 1938.

71. Priscilla recalled that her father was "steeped in the works of Chesterton and Belloc" (letter to David Cofield, quoted in *Beyond Bree* [September 1992]: 8).

72. Unfortunately, the text of the lecture has not survived. "University Notes – Oxford," *The Tablet*, April 7, 1928, 467.

73. John D. Rateliff, editorial notes to "Woodland Prisoner" by Clyde S. Kilby, 58n3. Kaye-Smith wrote dozens of books, including the proto-feminist *Joanna Godden* (1921) and *Superstition Corner* (1934), a tale of Catholics during the Penal Times.

74. TCG:C, 508. For more on Jennings's lifelong friendship with Priscilla Tolkien, see Dana Greene, *Elizabeth Jennings: "The Inward War"* (Oxford: OUP, 2018).

75. Martin D'Arcy, *Laughter and the Love of Friends: Reminiscences of the Distinguished Priest and Philosopher Martin Cyril D'Arcy, S.J.*, ed. William S. Abell (Westminster, MD: Christian Classics, 1991), 112–113. D'Arcy says that Knox invited Belloc to speak at the occasion "when the chaplaincy at Oxford was enlarged"; this would have been 1931. See "A History of the Chaplaincy," at Oxford University Catholic Chaplaincy: https://www.catholic-chaplaincy.org.uk/home/student-chaplaincy/about-us/our-history/; TCG:C, 243.

76. CLII, 769n35; TCG:C, 243.

77. BF, 242. Tolkien, the Lewis brothers, and Humphrey Havard met sociably that evening at the latter's house.

78. C.S. Lewis, "Modern Translations of the Bible," an essay that was originally published as an introduction to J.B. Phillips's *Letters to Young Churches: A Translation of the New Testament Epistles* (London: Macmillan, 1947).

79. Tolkien read the study of Shaw, which suggests an interest in the playwright's work, and indeed we know him to have seen *Arms and the Man* (TCG:C, 296). In "Dragons," Tolkien writes, "Mr Bernard Shaw might say as he did of the calculations of the astronomers that 'the magnitude of the lie seemed inartistic'" (43), a remark that appears in Chesterton's *George Bernard Shaw* (1909), where he notes that Shaw said this "somewhere" (chapter 4). I have been unable to trace it to any published book by Shaw; it must have had its origins in Chesterton's recollection of something Shaw said in person.

80. Father Brown made his first appearance in the story "The Blue Cross." Eventually, five volumes of tales were published, the first being *The Innocence of Father Brown* (1911) and the last *The Scandal of Father Brown* (1935).

81. "Mr. G.K. Chesterton on Romance," *The Guardian*, May 18, 1914, 9.

82. Priscilla Tolkien, "My Father the Artist," 6.

83. Chesterton's art is mostly unpublished. However, an impressive collection of it, including a number of his landscapes, is held by the G.K. Chesterton Library at the University of Notre Dame's London Gateway.

84. TCG:RG, 226; BF, 412; OFS MS A, 192. *The Man Who Was Thursday* is also mentioned in the Cretaceous Perambulators notes (Papers of Owen Barfield. Dep. c. 1104, folio 5 recto. See also MME, 245). See also Edmund Weiner, "A possibly unnoticed instance of echoes of G.K. Chesterton in the works of J.R.R. Tolkien."

85. TS, 26. Tolkien had a number of Chesterton books in his personal library as well (TCG:RG, 226).

86. Mike Foster, "'That most unselfish man,'" 23.

87. G.K. Chesterton, *Wine, Water and Song*, 22.

88. *Letters*, 92. See further Christopher Clausen, "*The Lord of the Rings* and *The Ballad of the White Horse*," and Thomas Egan, "Chesterton and Tolkien."

89. Malcolm Guite, "The Ballad of the White Horse."

90. Mike Foster, "'That most unselfish man,'" 23.

91. Maisie Ward, *Gilbert Keith Chesterton* (New York: Sheed and Ward, 1943), 371.

92. G.K. Chesterton, *Lepanto*, line 16.

93. J.R.R. Tolkien, *Tengwesta Qenderinwa and Pre-Fëanorian Alphabets Part 2* 132-133; J.R.R. Tolkien, "The Homecoming of Beorhtnoth Beorhthelm's Son," in *Tree and Leaf* 148.

94. It is included in *The Irish Fairy Book*, by Alfred Perceval Graves and illustrated by George Denham, which appears on Tolkien's shelves in a 1966 photograph. (Photograph of Tolkien in his study, Pamela Chandler, ARP 1188397.)

95. Quoted in Matthew Reynolds, *The Realms of Verse 1830–1870: English Poetry in a Time of Nation-Building* (Oxford: Oxford University Press, 2001), 264.

96. Raymond Edwards, *Tolkien*, 33; TCG:C, 22.

97. George Sayer, "Memories of J.R.R. Tolkien."

98. Two poems by Yeats, "A Faery Song" and "The Stolen Child," appear in *The Irish Fairy Book* by Alfred Perceval Graves, which Tolkien owned. (Photograph of Tolkien in his study, Pamela Chandler, ARP 1188397.)

99. TCG:RG, 449–50, 1059.

100. TCG:RG, 449–50; see Janet Brennan Croft, "Doors into Elf-mounds: J.R.R. Tolkien's Introductions, Prefaces, and Forewords"; TCG:C, 234; TCG:C, 347; TCG:C, 506, Letters, 368. Only two letters to Auden are included in the *Letters*, but it is clear from context that others exist.

101. TCG:C, 277.

102. Alan Rook, *These are My Comrades*, 11; J.R.R. Tolkien, postcard to [Alan] Rook, 21 April 1943, quoted in *Christie's Valuable Books and Manuscripts, Sale 12141, 1 December 2016*, https://www.christies.com/lotfinder/Lot/tolkien-j-r-r-1892-1973-autograph-postcard-6041053-details.aspx.

103. In 1967, he gave a copy of *Poems* to Fr. Louis Bouvier. *Dymer* appears on his shelves in a 1966 photograph. Hammond and Scull, Addenda to TCG:C for Aug. 29, 1967; photograph of Tolkien in his study, Pamela Chandler, ARP 1188397; BC MS A, 57–58.

104. *Letters*, 28, 36. Fox sent him a copy of *Babylon: A Sacred Satire* (1929) (Cilli, *Tolkien's Library* 90, where the series name ["English poem on a sacred subject"] is incorrectly listed as the title of the book). For more on the rather notorious campaign to get Fox elected Professor of Poetry, see *C.S. Lewis at the Breakfast Table and Other Reminiscences*, ed. James T. Como (London: Collins, 1980), 89–95.

105. TCG:C, 393.

106. *Letters*, 95. See also John S. Ryan, "J.R.R. Tolkien, C.S. Lewis, and Roy Campbell"; TCG:C, 532, 536; *Letters*, 96.

107. Tolkien, letter to Michael George Tolkien, April 24th, 1957 (British Library Add MS 71657); John S. Ryan, "J.R.R. Tolkien, C.S. Lewis, and Roy Campbell," 29.

108. Roy Campbell, *Flowering Rifle: A Poem from the Battlefield of Spain* (London: Longmans Green, 1939), 88.

109. Quoted in José Manuel Ferrández Bru, *"Uncle Curro": J.R.R. Tolkien's Spanish Connection*, 121.

110. Roy Campbell, *The Flaming Terrapin* (London: Jonathan Cape, 1924), 47–49.

111. TCG:C, 25.

112. MME, 284.

113. In later editions of *The Scholar Gipsy & Thyrsis*, the Russell Flint images are printed on the book's pages, but this is not the case with the edition available at the time Tolkien acquired these images. The 1910 edition features Russell Flint's images as separate leaves, each lightly attached along the top edge to a blank supporting page and protected by its own tissue paper. Evidently, they are intended for detaching and framing, and this, no doubt, is where Tolkien got his copies. The 'Medici' mark on the framed prints indicates that he had them framed by the Medici Society, a company founded in 1908 which "has not only framed its own reproductions and those by outside publishers but has also framed original paintings for sale and original artworks brought in for framing by members of the public." (http://www.medici.co.uk/c/73/Vintage-Reproductions---FAQ)

114. MME, 284.

115. Matthew Arnold, "The Scholar Gipsy."

116. Matthew Arnold, "The Scholar Gipsy."

117. Matthew Arnold, "Thyrsis."

118. Baillie Tolkien, introduction to *Catalogue of an Exhibition of Drawings by J.R.R. Tolkien*, 7.

119. MME, 284.

120. By Cecil Frances Alexander (1818–1895).

121. As she put it, "the little bit (two Inches wide) of Ivory on which I work with so fine a Brush." *Jane Austen's Letters to Her Sister Cassandra and Others*, ed. R.W. Chapman, 2nd ed. (London: Oxford University Press, 1959), 469.

122. Robert Hugh Benson, *Papers of a Pariah* (London: Smith, Elder & Co., 1907), 125. In making this remark, Benson was referring to the celebration of the Mass, but it is surely applicable to Tolkien's comprehensive approach to sub-creation too.

CHAPTER 12

1. Quoted in *Biography* 126.

2. Quoted in Stuart Lee, "Tolkien in Oxford," 159.

3. Quoted in Henry Resnik, "An Interview with Tolkien," 40; *Letters*, 31.

4. *Inklings*, 158; *Biography*, 77.

5. William Ready, *The Tolkien Relation*, 10, 19, 167, 182.

6. TCG:RG, 161.

7. TCG:RG, 161.

8. Rayner Unwin, *George Allen & Unwin: A Remembrancer*, 249.

9. Quoted in Melinda Gipson, "The Kodon Interview with Humphrey Carpenter," 4.

10. Humphrey Carpenter, "One expected," 16.

11. Quoted in Melinda Gipson, "The Kodon Interview with Humphrey Carpenter," 8–9; see Diana Pavlac Glyer, *The Company They Keep*.

12. Humphrey Carpenter, "Learning about Ourselves," 274.

13. Humphrey Carpenter, "Learning about Ourselves" 278.
14. *Tolkien in Love*, BBC radio drama, written by Sean Grundy, BBC Radio 4, August 19, 2017; *Planet Narnia*, 9; Michael Ward, personal communication to the author, December 24, 2018.
15. Colin Wilson, *Tree by Tolkien*, 27.
16. Richard C. West, "The Interlace Structure of *The Lord of the Rings*," 75.
17. Donald Davie, "Lucky Jim and the Hobbits."
18. A.N. Wilson, *C.S. Lewis: A Biography* (New York: W.W. Norton, 1990), 103.
19. Andrew Marr, "Fantasy," episode 2 of his documentary series *Sleuths, Spies and Sorcerers: Andrew Marr's Paperback Heroes*, BBC1, 2016.
20. Helen Gardner, "British Academy obituary" for C.S. Lewis, in *Critical Thought Series 1: Critical Essays on C.S. Lewis*, ed. George Watson (Cambridge: Scolar Press, 1992), 16.
21. See TCG:RG, 954–955.
22. TCG:C, 169.
23. *Inklings*, 24.
24. *Inklings*, 25.
25. See J.R.R. Tolkien, "The Oxford English School."
26. Henry Resnik, "An Interview with Tolkien," 40; Kay Holmes, "The Master Hobbit at 80," 46; *Letters*, 82.
27. CLIII, 476; LOTR:RC, 45; TGW, 189.
28. Roger Lancelyn Green and Walter Hooper, *C.S. Lewis*, 240–241.
29. *Biography*, 204.
30. Philip Zaleski and Carol Zaleski, *The Fellowship*, 384.
31. Roger Lancelyn Green, "Recollections," 7.
32. *Letters*, 82.
33. TS, 26.
34. Joy Hill, in Oxfordshire History Centre Archives, "The Ringmaker in Oxford," part 4.
35. Owen Barfield, "Foreword," 9.
36. George Sayer, "Recollections of J.R.R. Tolkien," 7.
37. Clyde S. Kilby, *A Well of Wonder*, 198.
38. OFS, 27.
39. Kate Fox, *Watching the English: The Hidden Rules of English Behaviour*, rev. ed. (London: Hodder & Stoughton, 2014), 79.
40. Bertrand Russell, "Can Americans and Britons Be Friends?" in Bertrand Russell's *America: His Transatlantic Travels and Writings, Volume One 1896–1945*, ed. Barry Feinberg and Ronald Kasrils, (Abingdon, UK: Routledge, 2014), 331.
41. Quoted in Philip Norman, "From London: Lord of the Flicks," 29.
42. Daphne Castell, "The Realms of Tolkien," 150.
43. Charlotte and Denis Plimmer, "The Man Who Understands Hobbits," 35; TCG:RG, 1235, 1236; *Letters*, 377.
44. Kate Fox, *Watching the English*, 94–96.
45. TS, 6.
46. Clyde S. Kilby, in Carpenter, Sayer, and Kilby, "A Dialogue," 21.
47. Clyde S. Kilby, "I'd like to have you come," 18.
48. John Ezard, "Light going," 9. Ezard, who first interviewed Tolkien in 1966, became a personal friend (John Ezard, "Tolkien's Shire," 4).
49. John Garth, "Inspiration in Unlikely (and Likely) Places."
50. Priscilla Tolkien, "Talk Given at the Church House Westminster on 16.9.77," 5.
51. Charlie Carr, in Oxfordshire History Centre Archives, "The Ringmaker in Oxford," part 4.

52. Pope John XXIII, Apostolic Constitution *Humanae Salutis*, December 25, 1961. See also the *Catechism of the Catholic Church*, no. 1788. As regards the Catholic Church's teaching on modernism, see the 1907 encyclical of Pope Pius X, *Pascendi Dominici Gregis*.

53. Richard C. West, "The Interlace Structure of *The Lord of the Rings*," 78.

54. John Garth, *The Worlds of J.R.R. Tolkien*, 52.

55. Verlyn Flieger, *A Question of Time*, 6. To this we might add his perspective as a Catholic with a belief in what Newman called "the development of doctrine."

56. William Fliss, Tolkien archivist, Marquette University Department of Special Collections and University Archives. Email to the author, November 6, 2019.

57. Malcolm Guite, "Once and Future: The Inklings, Arthur, and Prophetic Insight," 497. See further, Randel Holmes, *Tolkien's World*, 45–48.

58. Recognition of Tolkien's post-medieval connections opens up exciting new vistas for scholarship, as indeed we have begun to see. Diana Pavlac Glyer has shown that the interactions of the Inklings were a crucial part of Tolkien's creative process. Scholars such as Verlyn Flieger, Jason Fisher, and others have explored broader territory with regard to Tolkien's sources of inspiration, and the meticulous research of Christina Scull and Wayne Hammond has yielded vastly more material for scholars to assess. Commentators have acknowledged the applicability of *The Lord of the Rings* to the atomic era and how it yields insights for economic and political analysis, and even gender relations. See, for instance, Tom Shippey, *J.R.R. Tolkien, Author of the Century*; Patrick Curry, *Defending Middle-Earth: Tolkien: Myth and Modernity*; Joshua Hren, *Middle-earth and the Return of the Common Good: J. R. R. Tolkien and Political Philosophy*; Jonathan Witt and Jay Richards, *The Hobbit Party: The Vision of Freedom that Tolkien Got, and the West Forgot*; and Margaret Thum, "Hidden in Plain View: Strategizing Unconventionality in Shakespeare's and Tolkien's Portraits of Women."

59. Tom Shippey, *The Road to Middle-earth*, xix. See also Patchen Mortimer, "Tolkien and Modernism," and E.L. Risden, "Middle-earth and the Waste Land: Greenwood, Apocalypse, and Post-War Resolution."

60. Dominic Sandbrook, *The Great British Dream Factory*, 359; 364.

61. *Letters*, 85 (emphasis added).

62. OFS, 65.

63. Christopher Tolkien, "Christopher Tolkien and the 'Aubusson weaves Tolkien' project."

BIBLIOGRAPHY

Agøy, Nils Ivar. "The Christian Tolkien: A Response to Ronald Hutton." In *The Ring and the Cross*, ed. Paul E. Kerry, 71–105.

Aldiss, Brian, and David Wingrove. *Trillion Year Spree: The History of Science Fiction*. Thirsk, UK: House of Stratus, 2001.

Anderson, Douglas A. "Obituary: Humphrey Carpenter (1946–2005)." *Tolkien Studies*, vol. 2 (2005): 217–224.

———. "R.W. Chambers and *The Hobbit*." Notes and Documents. *Tolkien Studies*, vol. 3 (2006): 137–147.

———. "Tolkien and the Newman Association." *Tolkien and Fantasy* (blog). November 22, 2011. http://tolkienandfantasy.blogspot.com/2011/11/tolkien-and-newman-association.html.

———. .ed *The Annotated Hobbit*. J.R.R. Tolkien. Revised and Expanded Edition. Boston: Houghton Mifflin, 2002.

———. .ed *Tales Before Tolkien: The Roots of Modern Fantasy*. New York: Del Rey, 2003.

Arduini, Roberto, Giampaolo Canzoniere, and Claudio A. Testi, eds. *Tolkien and the Classics*. Zurich: Walking Tree, 2019.

Arduini, Roberto, and Claudio A. Testi, eds. *Tolkien and Philosophy*. Zurich: Walking Tree, 2014.

'Atticus.' "Tolkien Talking." *Sunday Times*. November 27, 1966, 9.

Auden, W.H. "The Hero Is a Hobbit." Review of *The Fellowship of the Ring. The New York Times*. October 31, 1954.

———. Introduction to *The Visionary Novels of George MacDonald*, ed. Anne Fremantle. New York: The Noonday Press, 1956.

Bailey, Derek (director). *J.R.R.T: A Film Portrait of J.R.R. Tolkien*. [also called *J.R.R. Tolkien: A Portrait* or *J.R.R. Tolkien: An Authorized Film Portrait*]. Narrated by Judi Dench. Landseer, 1996. https://www.youtube.com/watch?v=rNqVqzIxi3A.

Barfield, Owen. Foreword. *VII (Seven): An Anglo-American Literary Review*, vol. 1 (1980), 9.

Barella, Cecilia. "Tolkien and Grahame." In *Tolkien and the Classics*, ed. Roberto Arduini et al., 155–165.

Barr, Donald. "Shadowy World of Men and Hobbits." Review of *The Two Towers. The New York Times*. May 1, 1955.

Basso, Ann McCauley. "Fair Lady Goldberry, Daughter of the River." *Mythlore* 103/104, vol. 27, no. 1/2 (Fall/Winter 2008): 137–146.

Benedikz, B.S. "Some Family Connections with J.R.R. Tolkien." *Amon Hen* 209 (2008): 11–13.

Bergmann, Frank. "The Roots of Tolkien's Tree: The Influence of George MacDonald and German Romanticism on Tolkien's Essay 'On Fairy-stories.'" *Mosaic* X, no. 2 (Winter 1977): 5–14.

Berman, Ruth. "Tolkien as a Child of *The Green Fairy Book*." *Mythlore* 99/100, vol. 26, no. 1/2 (Fall/Winter 2007): 127–135.

Berry, Simon. "Finrod, Job, and 'estel': the Roots of Hope in Tolkien." Lecture delivered to the Oxford C.S. Lewis Society, Oxford, England. January 26, 2016.

Biemer, Marie-Noëlle. "Disenchanted with their Age: Keats's, Morris's, and Tolkien's Great Escape." *Hither Shore 7* (2010): 60–75.

Birzer, Bradley J. "Two Tolkiens, One Better World." Review of *The Fall of Gondolin* by J.R.R. Tolkien. *The American Conservative*. April 3, 2019. https://www.theamericanconservative.com/articles/two-tolkiens-one-better-world.

Bishop, Morchard. "*John Inglesant* and Its Author." In *Essays by Divers Hands: Being the Transactions of the Royal Society of Literature*, Vol. XXIX, ed. E.V. Rieu, 73–86. London: Oxford University Press, 1958.

Blisset, William. "Despots of the Rings," *South Atlantic Quarterly* 58 (Summer 1959): 448–456.

Blok, Cor. *A Tolkien Tapestry: Pictures to Accompany The Lord of the Rings*. Edited by Pieter Collier. London: HarperCollins, 2011.

Bodleian Library. *J.R.R. Tolkien: Life and Legend. An Exhibition to Commemorate the Centenary of the Birth of J.R.R. Tolkien (1892–1973)*. Oxford: Bodleian Library, 1992.

———. *J.R.R. Tolkien:* The Lord of the Rings. *A display of original manuscripts and artwork by J.R.R. Tolkien to celebrate the fiftieth anniversary of publication*. Bodleian Exhibition Room. July 26, 2004–September 18, 2004.

Bonechi, Simone. "Tolkien and the War Poets." In *Tolkien and the Classics*, ed. Roberto Arduini et al., 205–215.

Bowers, John M. "Tolkien's Goldberry and The Maid of the Moor." *Tolkien Studies*, vol. 8 (2011): 23–36.

———. *Tolkien's Lost Chaucer*. Oxford: Oxford University Press, 2019.

Brace, Keith. "In the Footsteps of the Hobbits." *Birmingham Post. Midland Magazine* (May 25, 1968).

Breit, Harvey. "Oxford Calling." In and Out of Books. *The New York Times*. June 5, 1955.

Brewer, Derek. "The Tutor: A Portrait." In *Remembering C.S. Lewis*, ed. James. T. Como, 115–151.

Broberg, Jan. "In the Company of Tolkien," part of "Two Swedish Interviews with Tolkien," by Morgan Thomsen and Shaun Gunner. *Hither Shore* 9 (2012): 150–161.

Buck, Claire. "Literary Context, Twentieth Century." In *J.R.R. Tolkien Encyclopedia*, edited by Michael D.C. Drout.

Bülles, Marcel. "Tolkien criticism – reloaded." *Hither Shore 1* (2004): 15–23.

Bunting, Nancy. "Inspiration: Tolkien and *The Black Douglas*." Part I. *Minas Tirith Evening-Star*, vol. 41, no. 1 (Autumn 2013): 25–36.

———. "Inspiration: Tolkien and *The Black Douglas*." Part II. *Minas Tirith Evening-Star*, vol. 41, no. 2 (Summer 2014): 22–32.

———. "Tolkien's Homecoming." *VII (Seven): An Anglo-American Literary Review*, vol. 34 (2017): 31–46.

Burchfield, Robert. "My Hero: Robert Burchfield on J.R.R. Tolkien." *The Independent Magazine*, March 4, 1989, 42.

Burns, Maggie. "The Desire of a Tale-Teller." *Mallorn* 48 (Autumn 2009): 19–24.

———. ". . . a local habitation and a name. . ." *Mallorn* 50 (Autumn 2010): 26–31.

Burns, Marjorie. *Perilous Realms: Celtic and Norse in Tolkien's Middle-earth*. Toronto: Toronto University Press, 2005.

———. "Three Stories Holding Hands: *The Wind in the Willows, Huntingtower*, and *The Hobbit*." In *A Wilderness of Dragons*, ed. John D. Rateliff, 42–71.

———. "Tracking the Elusive Hobbit (In Its Pre-Shire Den)." *Tolkien Studies*, vol. 4 (2007): 200–211.

Butts, Dennis. "Exploiting a Formula: The Adventure Stories of G.A. Henty (1832–1902)". In *Popular Children's Literature in Britain*, eds. Julia Briggs, Dennis Butts, and M.O. Grenby, 149–163. Aldershot, Hampshire: Ashgate, 2008.

Butynskyi, Christopher. *The Inklings, the Victorians, and the Moderns: Reconciling Tradition in the Modern Age*. Lanham, MD: Fairleigh Dickinson University Press, 2020.

Byrne, Evelyn B. and Otto M. Penzler. *Attacks of Taste*. New York: Gotham Book Mart, 1971.

Caine, William Coy. "A Comparison of the Major Works of J.R.R. Tolkien and E.R. Eddison." Master of Arts thesis, Lamar State College of Technology, 1969.

Caldecott, Stratford. *The Power of the Ring: The Spiritual Vision Behind* The Lord of the Rings *and* The Hobbit. 2nd ed. New York: Crossroad, 2012.

———. "Tolkien's Search for England." In *Inklings of Truth*, ed. Paul Shrimpton, 41–55.

Caldecott, Stratford, and Thomas Honegger, eds. *Tolkien's* The Lord of the Rings: *Sources of Inspiration*. Zurich: Walking Tree, 2008.

Canzonieri, Giampolo. "Tolkien at King Edward's School." In *Tolkien and Philosophy*, eds. Roberto Arduini and Claudio A. Testi, 145–150.

Carpenter, Humphrey. *The Inklings: C.S. Lewis, J.R.R. Tolkien, Charles Williams, and Their Friends*. London: HarperCollins, 1997. First published 1978.

———. *J.R.R. Tolkien: A Biography*. Boston: Houghton Mifflin, 2000. First published by George Allen & Unwin, 1977.

———. "Learning about Ourselves: Biography as Autobiography." In *The Art of Literary Biography*, ed. John Bachelor, 267–279. Oxford: Clarendon, 1995.

———. ". . . one expected him to go on a lot longer." *Minas Tirith Evening-Star*, vol. 9, no. 2 (January 1980): 13–16.

———. "'Tolkien Reconsidered': A Talk by Humphrey Carpenter given at the Cheltenham Festival of Literature. Monday 12th Oct. 1987." Reported by Charles E. Noad. *Amon Hen* 91 (May 1988): 12–14.

Carpenter, Humphrey, George Sayer, and Clyde S. Kilby, "A Dialogue." *Minas Tirith Evening-Star*, vol. 13, no. 1 (Jan-Feb. 1984): 20–24.

Carter, Lin. *Tolkien: A Look Behind "The Lord of the Rings."* New York: Ballantine Books, 1969.

Castell, Daphne. "The Realms of Tolkien." *New Worlds SF* 50, no. 168 (November 1966): 143–154.

———. "Talking to a Maker of Modern Myths." *The Glasgow Herald*, August 6, 1966.

Cater, William. "The filial duty of Christopher Tolkien." *Sunday Times*, September 25, 1977, 61–62.

Caughey, Anna. "'A Curious and Inexplicable Object': *The Lord of the Rings* and the Critical Tradition." Talk delivered at the Oxford C.S. Lewis Society, November 25, 2014.

Chambers, Luke J. "*Enta Geweorc* and the Work of Ents." *Tolkien Studies* 16 (2019): 9–20.

Chance, Jane. *Tolkien, Self and Other: "This Queer Creature."* New York: Palgrave Macmillan, 2016.

———. ed. *Tolkien and the Invention of Myth: A Reader*. Lexington, Kentucky: The University Press of Kentucky, 2004.

———. ed. *Tolkien the Medievalist*. New York: Routledge, 2003.

Chance, Jane, and Alfred K. Siewers, eds. *Tolkien's Modern Middle Ages*. Basingstoke, Hampshire: Palgrave Macmillan, 2005.

Chapman, Vera. "Belladonna Goes to a Party." *Mallorn* 6 (1972). 34-36.

Christopher, Joe R. "C.S. Lewis's Two Satyrs." *Mythlore* 128, vol. 34, no. 2 (Spring/Summer 2016): 83–93.

———. "J.R.R. Tolkien and the Clerihew." *Mythlore* 80, vol. 21, no. 2 (Winter 1996): 263–271.

———. "J.R.R. Tolkien, Narnian Exile." *Mythlore* 55, vol. 15, no.1 (Autumn 1988): 37–45.

———. "J.R.R. Tolkien, Narnian Exile: Part II." *Mythlore* 56, vol. 15, no. 2 (Winter 1988): 17–23.

Cilli, Oronzo. "Tolkien, trains and two discoveries: Meccano and Hornby." *Tolkieniano* (blog). November 25, 2017. https://tolkieniano.blogspot.it/2017/11/tolkien-i-treni-e-due-scoperte-meccano.html.

———. *Tolkien's Library: An Annotated Checklist*. Edinburgh: Luna Press, 2019.

Clark, George, and Daniel Timmons, eds. *J.R.R. Tolkien and his literary resonances: views of Middle-earth*. Westport, CT: Greenwood Press, 2000.

Clark, Stuart, and Rosie Clark. "Oxonmoot '74 Report." *Amon Hen* 13 (October 1974): 6–11. Some (but not all) of the anecdotes are repeated in "From the Past" in *Amon Hen* 50 (May 2, 1981).

Clarke, Arthur C. "Memoirs of an Armchair Astronaut." *Holiday*, May 1963. In *Voices from the Sky: Previews of the Coming Space Age*. New York: Pyramid, 1967.

Clausen, Christopher. "*The Lord of the Rings* and *The Ballad of the White Horse*," *South Atlantic Bulletin* 39, no. 2 (May 1974): 10–16.

Clutton-Brock, A. *William Morris: His Life and Influence*. London: Williams and Norgate, 1914.

Cockshut, A.O.J. "Lewis in Post-War Oxford." *Journal of Inklings Studies*, vol. 6 no. 1 (April 2016): 61–85.

Collier, Peter. "Interview with Cor Blok about the Tolkien Calendar 2011." *Tolkien Library* (blog). March 9, 2010. http://www.tolkienlibrary.com/press/937-Interview-Cor-Blok-Tolkien-Calendar-2011.php.

Collyer, Naomi. "Recollections of Professor J.R.R. Tolkien." *Arda*, vol. 5 (1985): 1–3.

Conrad-O'Briain, Helen, and Gerard Hynes, eds. *Tolkien: The Forest and the City*. Dublin: Four Courts Press, 2013.

Corbin, John. "The Gods of Dunsany." *The New York Times*. Sunday, January 26, 1919.

Coston, Paula. "Tolkien on writing . . . and me." *Writing Magazine*, August 2014, 12–14.

Coutras, Lisa. *Tolkien's Theology of Beauty: Majesty, Splendor, and Transcendence in Middle-earth*. New York: Palgrave Macmillan, 2016.

Cramer, Zak. "Jewish influences in Middle-earth." *Mallorn* 44 (August 2006): 9–16.

Croft, Janet Brennan, "Doors into Elf-mounds: J.R.R. Tolkien's Introductions, Prefaces, and Forewords." *Tolkien Studies*, vol. 15 (2018): 177–195.

———. Introduction to *Perilous and Fair,* ed. Janet Brennan Croft and Leslie A. Donovan, 1–7.

———. ed. *Baptism of Fire: The Birth of the Modern British Fantastic in World War I*. Altadena, CA: Mythopoeic Press, 2015.

———. ed. *Tolkien and Shakespeare: Essays on Shared Themes and Language*. Jefferson, NC: McFarland, 2007.

Croft, Janet Brennan, and Leslie A. Donovan, eds. *Perilous and Fair: Women in the Works and Life of J.R.R. Tolkien*. Altadena, CA: Mythopoeic Press, 2015.

Croft, Janet Brennan and Annika Röttinger. eds. *"Something Has Gone Crack": New Perspectives on J.R.R. Tolkien in the Great War*. Zurich, Switzerland: Walking Tree Press, 2019.

Curry, Patrick. *Defending Middle-Earth: Tolkien: Myth and Modernity*. London: Harper Collins, 1997.

Curtis, Anthony. "Remembering Tolkien and Lewis." *British Book News* (June 1977): 429–430.

d'Ardenne, S.T.R.O. "The Man and the Scholar." In *J.R.R. Tolkien: Scholar and Storyteller*, ed. Mary Salu and Robert T. Farrell, 33–37.

Dart-Thornton, Cecila. Introduction to *The Book of Wonder and The Last Book of Wonder* by Lord Dunsany, xiii-xix. Victoria, Australia: Leaves of Gold Press, 2013.

Davie, Donald. "Lucky Jim and the Hobbits." In *Thomas Hardy and British Poetry*, 83–104. New York: Oxford University Press, 1972.

de Camp, L. Sprague. Letter to *Anduril*. *Anduril* 1 (The Bulletin of the Tolkien Society). April 1972.

———. Letter to *Mythlore*. *Mythlore* 50, vol. 13, no. 4 (Summer 1987): 41.

———. *Literary Swordsmen and Sorcerers: The Makers of Heroic Fantasy*. Sauk City, WI: Arkham House, 1976. Ebook: London: Gollancz, 2014.

Doughan, David. "Commentary: Women, Oxford and Tolkien." *Mallorn* 45 (2008): 15–20.

Downing, David. "Science Fiction." In *Reading the Classics with C.S. Lewis*, ed. Thomas L. Martin, 297–312. Grand Rapids, MI: Baker, 2000.

Drayton, Paul, and Humphrey Carpenter. "A preparatory school approach." In *Music Drama in Schools*, ed. Malcolm John, 1–19. Cambridge: Cambridge University Press, 1971.

Drout, Michael D.C., ed. *Beowulf and the Critics*, by J.R.R. Tolkien. Tempe, AZ: ACMRS, 2002; revised second edition, 2011.

———. ed. *J.R.R. Tolkien Encyclopedia: Scholarship and Critical Assessment*. New York: Routledge, 2007.

Duriez, Colin. *The Oxford Inklings: Lewis, Tolkien and Their Circle*. Oxford: Lion Hudson, 2014.

———. *Tolkien: The Making of a Legend*. Oxford: Lion Hudson, 2012.

Echo-Hawk, Roger. *Tolkien in Pawneeland: The Secret Sources of Middle-earth*. Self-published, CreateSpace, 2013.

Eden, Bradford Lee, "Sub-creation by any Other Name: The Artist and God in the Early Twentieth Century." In *Sub-creating Arda,* ed. Dimitra Fimi and Thomas Honegger, 359–370.

———. ed. The Hobbit *and Tolkien's Mythology: Essays on Revisions and Influences*. Jefferson, NC: McFarland & Company, 2014.

Edwards, Raymond. *Tolkien*. London: Robert Hale, 2014.

Egan, Thomas. "Chesterton and Tolkien." *The Chesterton Review*, vol. VI, no. 1 (Fall-Winter 1979–80): 159–161.

———. "Chesterton and Tolkien: The Road to Middle-Earth." *VII (Seven): An Anglo-American Literary Review*, vol. 4 (1983): 45–53.

Eilmann, Julian. *J.R.R. Tolkien: Romanticist and Poet*. Zurich: Walking Tree Press, 2017.

Eilmann, Julian, and Alan Turner, eds. *Tolkien's Poetry*. Zurich: Walking Tree Press, 2013.

Elflandsson, Galad. "David Lindsay and the Quest for Muspel-fire." In David Lindsay, *A Voyage to Arcturus*, 7–14. Secaucus, NJ: Citadel Press, 1946.

Etkin, Anne. *Eglerio! In Praise of Tolkien*. Greencastle, PA: Quest Communications, 1978.

Ezard, John. "Tolkien in Oxford." Presenter, BBC archive. First broadcast March 30, 1968. http://www.bbc.co.uk/archive/writers/12237.shtml.

———. "Hobbit and Lord of the Rings author J.R.R. Tolkien dies." *The Guardian*, September 3, 1973.

———. "Light going: John Ezard celebrates J.R. Tolkien's [sic] 80th birthday." *The Guardian*, January 8, 1972, 9.

———. "Tolkien's Shire." *The Guardian*, December 28–29, 1991, 4–6.

———. "Writers Talking–1: The Hobbit Man." *Oxford Mail*, August 3, 1966, 4.

Falconer, Rachel. "Earlier Fantasy Fiction: Morris, Dunsany, and Lindsay." In *A Companion to J.R.R. Tolkien*, ed. Stuart D. Lee, 303–316.

Ferrández Bru, José Manuel."*Uncle Curro*": *J.R.R. Tolkien's Spanish Connection*. Edinburgh: Luna Press Publishing, 2018.

Fimi, Dimitra. "Come sing ye light fairy things tripping so gay": Victorian Fairies and the Early Work of J. R. R. Tolkien." *Working With English: Medieval and Modern Language, Literature and Drama* 2 (2005–2006): 10–26

———. "George MacDonald and one of Tolkien's most quotable lines." Dimitra Fimi (website). July 9, 2017. http://dimitrafimi.com/george-macdonald-and-one-of-tolkiens-most-quotable-lines/.

———. "Language as Communication vs. Language as Art: J.R.R. Tolkien and early 20th-century radical linguistic experimentation." *Journal of Tolkien Research*, vol. 5, no. 1 (2018).

———. "Tolkien and the Art of Book Reviewing: A Circuitous Road to Middle-earth." Lecture for Oxonmoot, Oxford, England, September 2016. Dimitra Fimi (website). http://dimitrafimi.com/2017/05/17/tolkien-and-the-art-of-book-reviewing-a-circuitous-road-to-middle-earth/.

———. "Tolkien on 1930s BBC Radio via historical issues of Radio Times." January 3, 2019. Dimitra Fimi (website). http://dimitrafimi.com/tolkien-on-1930s-bbc-radio-via-historical-issues-of-radio-times/.

———. *Tolkien, Race and Cultural History: From Fairies to Hobbits*. New York: Palgrave Macmillan, 2009.

———. "'Twas the Night Before Christmas' and J.R.R. Tolkien's Tinfang Warble." Dimitra Fimi (website). December 31, 2016. http://dimitrafimi.com/twas-the-night-before-christmas-and-j-r-r-tolkiens-tinfang-warble/.

———. "Was Tolkien really racist?" The Conversation, December 6, 2018. https://theconversation.com/was-tolkien-really-racist-108227.

Fimi, Dimitra, and Thomas Honegger, eds. *Sub-creating Arda: Worldbuilding in J.R.R. Tolkien's Work, Its Precursors, and Its Legacies*. Zurich: Walking Tree, 2019.

Finley, Clara. "The Morrisian Interview Series, #2: John J. Walsdorf." *The Morrisian* (blog), April 12, 2013. http://themorrisian.blogspot.com/2013/04/the-morrisian-interview-series-2-john-j.html#more.

Fisher, Jason. "More on Tolkien and the Nobel Prize." *Lingwe: Musings of a Fish* (blog), April 8, 2015. http://lingwe.blogspot.co.uk/2015/04/more-on-tolkien-and-nobel-prize.html.

———. "Reluctantly Inspired: George MacDonald and J.R.R. Tolkien." *North Wind: A Journal of George MacDonald Studies*, vol. 25, article 8.

———. ed. *Tolkien and the Study of His Sources: Critical Essays*. Jefferson, NC: McFarland, 2011.

Fletcher, Rachel A. "Tolkien's Work on the Oxford English Dictionary: Some New Evidence From Quotation Slips." *Journal of Tolkien Research*, vol. 10, issue 2, article 10 (2020).

Flieger, Verlyn. *Green Suns and Faërie: Essays on J.R.R. Tolkien*. Kent, OH: Kent State University Press, 2012.

———. Introduction to *The Story of Kullervo* by J.R.R. Tolkien. Edited by Verlyn Flieger, ix-xxiii.

———. *A Question of Time: J.R.R. Tolkien's Road to Faerie*. Kent, OH: Kent State University Press, 1997.

———. *Splintered Light: Logos and Language in Tolkien's World*. Revised edition. Kent, OH: Kent State University Press, 2002.

———. *There Would Always Be a Fairy Tale: More Essays on Tolkien*. Kent, OH: Kent State University Press, 2017.

Flieger, Verlyn, and Douglas A. Anderson. Introduction, commentary, and notes to *Tolkien On Fairy-stories* by J.R.R. Tolkien. Edited by Verlyn Flieger and Douglas A. Anderson. London: HarperCollins, 2014.

Flieger, Verlyn, and Carl F. Hostetter. eds. *Tolkien's Legendarium: Essays on The History of Middle-earth*. Westport, CT: Greenwood, 2000.

Fontenot, Megan N. "'No pagan ever loved his god': Tolkien, Thompson, and the Beautification of the Gods." *Mythlore* 133, vol. 37, no. 1 (Fall/Winter 2018): 45–62.

Ford, Judy Ann. "The White City: *The Lord of the Rings* as an Early Medieval Myth of the Restoration of the Roman Empire." *Tolkien Studies*, vol. 2 (2005), 53–73.

Forest-Hill, Lynn, ed. *The Mirror Crack'd: Fear and Horror in JRR Tolkien's Major Works*. Newcastle upon Tyne, UK: Cambridge Scholars Publishing, 2008.

Foster, Mike. "'That most unselfish man': George Sayer, 1914–2005: pupil, biographer, and friend of Inklings." *Mythlore* 101/102, vol. 26, no. 3/4 (Spring/Summer 2008): 5–26.

Friedman, Barton. "Tolkien and David Jones: The Great War and the War of the Ring." *Clio* XI (Winter 1982), 115–136.

Garth, John. "'As under a green sea': visions of war in the Dead Marshes." In *The Ring Goes Ever On,* ed. Sarah Wells, I:9–21.

———. "Atlantis and Mars: New Light on Tolkien, Lewis, and their Science-Fiction Pact." Lecture at the Oxford C.S. Lewis Society, January, 17 2017.

———. "'Francis Thompson': Article for Exeter College Essay Club." In *J.R.R. Tolkien Encyclopedia*, ed. Michael Drout, 220–221.

———. "Ilu's Music: The Creation of Tolkien's Creation Myth." In *Sub-creating Arda: Worldbuilding in J.R.R. Tolkien's Work, its Precursors, and its Legacies*, ed. Dimitra Fimi and Thomas Honegger, 117–152. Zurich: Walking Tree, 2019.

———. "Inspiration in Unlikely (and Likely) Places." *The Prancing Pony Podcast*, Alan Sisto and Shawn E. Marchese, hosts. Episode 166, May 10, 2020. https://theprancingponypodcast.com/2020/05/10/166-inspiration-in-unlikely-and-likely-places-an-interview-with-john-garth/.

Garth, John. "J.R.R. Tolkien and the Boy Who Didn't Believe in Fairies." *Tolkien Studies*, vol. 7 (2010): 279–290.

———. "'The road from adaptation to invention': How Tolkien Came to the Brink of Middle-earth in 1914." *Tolkien Studies* 11 (2014): 1–44.

———. *Tolkien at Exeter College: How an Oxford Undergraduate Created Middle-earth.* Oxford: Exeter College, 2014.

———. *Tolkien and the Great War: The Threshold of Middle-earth.* Boston: Houghton Mifflin, 2003.

———. "Tolkien's death of Smaug: American inspiration revealed." *The Guardian*, December 9, 2014.

———. "When J.R.R. Tolkien bet C.S. Lewis: the wager that gave birth to *The Lord of the Rings.*" *The Telegraph,* December 8, 2016. http://www.telegraph.co.uk/books/what-to-read/jrr-tolkien-bet-cs-lewis-wager-gave-birth-lord-rings/.

———. "When Tolkien reinvented Atlantis and Lewis went to Mars." John Garth (website). March 31, 2017. https://johngarth.wordpress.com/2017/03/31/when-tolkien-reinvented-atlantis-and-lewis-went-to-mars/.

———. *The Worlds of J.R.R. Tolkien: The Places that Inspired Middle-earth.* Princeton: Princeton University Press, 2020.

Giddings, Robert and Elizabeth Holland: *J.R.R. Tolkien: The Shores of Middle-earth.* London: Junction, 1981.

Gilbert, Sir Martin. "Tolkien in the First World War." In *Penultimate Adventures with Britannia: Personalities, Politics and Culture in Britain*, ed. Roger Louis, 67–70. London: I.B. Tauris, 2007.

———. "What Tolkien taught me about the Battle of the Somme." *FT Magazine* 29/30 (July 2006). http://www.martingilbert.com/tolkein-read-more/.

Gilder, Joseph B. "G.K. Chesterton as an Artist." *The Bookman* (June 1913): 468–471. http://www.unz.org/Pub/Bookman-1913jun-00468.

Gilliver, Peter M. "The First Inkling: Edward Tangye Lean." *Journal of Inklings Studies*, vol. 6, no. 2 (October 2016): 63–77.

———. "J.R.R. Tolkien and the OED." Blog of the *Oxford English Dictionary*. August 14, 2012. https://public.oed.com/blog/jrr-tolkien-and-the-oed/.

———. *The Making of the Oxford English Dictionary.* Oxford: Oxford University Press, 2016.

———. "At the Wordface: J.R.R. Tolkien's Work on the *Oxford English Dictionary.*" *Mythlore* 80, vol. 21, no. 2 (Winter 1996). In *The J.R.R. Tolkien Centenary Conference*, ed. Patricia Reynolds and Glen H. GoodKnight, 173–186.

Gilliver, Peter, Jeremy Marshall, and Edmund Weiner. "The Word as Leaf: Perspectives on Tolkien as Lexicographer and Philologist." In *Tolkien's The Lord of the Rings: Sources of Inspiration*, ed. Stratford Caldecott and Thomas Honegger, 57–83.

———. *Ring of Words: Tolkien and the Oxford English Dictionary.* Oxford: Oxford University Press, 2006.

Gilson, Christopher. "His Breath Was Taken Away: Tolkien, Barfield and Elvish Diction." *Tolkien Studies*, vol. 14 (2017): 33–51.

Gipson, Melinda. "The Kodon Interview with Humphrey Carpenter, Biographer of Tolkien, Inklings." *Kodon* (1979): 3–9. Published by Wheaton College, Wheaton, IL.

Glyer, Diana Pavlac. *The Company They Keep: C.S. Lewis and J.R.R. Tolkien as Writers in Community*. Kent, Ohio: Kent State University Press, 2007.

GoodKnight, Glen. "C.S. Kilby in Southern California." *Mythlore* 1, vol. 1, no. 1 (January 1969): 27–29.

———. "Death and the Desire for Deathlessness." *Mythlore* 10, vol. 3, no. 2 (1975): 19.

Graff, Eric S. "The Three Faces of Faërie in Tolkien's Shorter Fiction: Niggle, Smith, and Giles." *Mythlore* 69, vol. 18, no. 3 (Summer 1992): 15–19.

Green, Roger Lancelyn. *C.S. Lewis*. London: The Bodley Head, 1963.

———. "C.S. Lewis." In *Puffin Annual* 1, ed. Kaye Webb. London: Puffin Books, 1974.

———. *Into Other Worlds: Space-Flight in Fiction, from Lucian to Lewis*. London: Abelard-Schuman, 1957.

———. "Recollections." *Amon Hen* 44 (May 1980): 6–8.

Green, Roger Lanceyln, and Walter Hooper. *C.S. Lewis: A Biography*. Revised edition. San Diego: Harcourt, Brace, and Co., 1994. First published 1974.

Green, William H. "King Thorin's Mines: The Hobbit as Victorian Adventure Novel." *Extrapolation*, vol. 42, no. 1 (Spring 2001): 53–64.

Grotta, Daniel. *The Biography of J.R.R. Tolkien: Architect of Middle-earth*. Philadelphia: Running Press, 1978.

Gueroult, Denis. Interview with Tolkien for BBC radio, "Now Read On" (full recording, not aired). The Randolph Hotel, Oxford, January 20, 1964 [1965]. *On Basil Bunting and J.R.R. Tolkien (Author Speaks)*. Cassette tape. Audio-Forum. Guilford, Connecticut: 1980. [Portions of this interview, transcribed, appear in *Minas Tirith Evening-Star*, vol. 13, no. 1 (Jan-Feb. 1984); previously printed in *News from Bree* 13 (Nov. 1974) and *Minas Tirith Evening-Star*, vol. 4, no. 3 (June 1975): 3-7; in these, the interviewer's name is incorrectly given as David Gerrolt.]

Guite, Malcolm. "The Ballad of the White Horse: a complete reading in 9 podcasts." *Malcolm Guite* (website). Oct. 10, 2011. https://malcolmguite.wordpress.com/2011/10/10/the-ballad-of-the-white-horse-a-complete-reading-in-9-podcasts/.

———. "Once and Future: The Inklings, Arthur, and Prophetic Insight." In *The Inklings and King Arthur*, ed. Sørina Higgins, 493–506.

Gustafsson, Lars. "Tolkien, the Peculiar Professor." Part of "Two Swedish Interviews with Tolkien," Morgan Thomsen and Shaun Gunner. *Hither Shore 9* (2012): 150–161.

Hall, Alaric, and Samuli Kaislaniemi. "'You tempt me grievously to a mythological essay': J.R.R. Tolkien's correspondence with Arthur Ransome." In *Ex Philologia Lux: Essays in Honour of Leena Kahlas-Tarkka*, ed. Jukka Tyrkkö, Olga Timofeeva, and Maria Salenius, 261–280. Helsinki: Société Néophilologique, 2013. http://eprints.whiterose.ac.uk/78192/.

Hall, Kathryne. "Beings of Magic: A Comparison of Saruman the White in Tolkien's *The Lord of the Rings* and Simon the Clerk in Williams' *All Hallows' Eve*." In *Inklings Forever Volume X,* ed. Joe Ricke and Rick Hill, 388–395. Hamden, CT: Winged Lion Press, 2017.

Hammond, Wayne G., and Christina Scull. *The Art of* The Hobbit. Boston: Houghton Mifflin Harcourt, 2012.

——. *The Art of* The Lord of the Rings *by J.R.R. Tolkien*. Boston: Houghton Mifflin Harcourt, 2015.

——. *J.R.R. Tolkien: Artist & Illustrator*. Boston: Houghton Mifflin, 1995.

——. "From Tolkien's Library." *Too Many Books and Never Enough* (blog). May 5, 2018. https://wayneandchristina.wordpress.com/2018/05/05/from-tolkiens-library/.

——. "Tolkien's Library: An Annotated Checklist (2019) by Oronzo Cilli" [review]. *Journal of Tolkien Research*, vol. 7, issue 1, article 10 (2019).

——. "Truth or Consequences: A Cautionary Tale of Tolkien Studies." *Too Many Books and Never Enough* (blog). January 31, 2010. https://www.hammondandscull.com/papers/Hammond_Scull_Scholars_Forum.html.

——. ed. *Lord of the Rings, 1954–2004: Scholarship in Honor of Richard E. Blackwelder*. Milwaukee, WI: Marquette University Press, 2006.

Hart, Rachel. "Tolkien, St. Andrews, and Dragons." In *Tree of Tales*, ed. Trevor Hart and Ivan Khovacs, 1–11.

Hart, Trevor. Review of *There and Back Again: J. R. R. Tolkien and the Origins of The Hobbit* by Mark Atherton. *Journal of Inklings Studies*, vol. 5, no. 1 (April 2015): 152–154.

Hart, Trevor, and Ivan Khovacs, eds. *Tree of Tales: Tolkien, Literature, and Theology*. Waco, TX: Baylor University Press, 2007.

Havard, R.E. "Professor J.R.R. Tolkien: A Personal Memoir." *Mythlore* 64, vol. 17, no. 2 (Winter 1990): 61.

Helen, Daniel. "Tolkien's annotated map of Middle-earth transcribed." *The Tolkien Society* website. November 10, 2015. https://www.tolkiensociety.org/2015/11/tolkiens-annotated-map-of-middle-earth-transcribed/.

Helen, Daniel and Morgan Thomsen. "A recollection of Tolkien: Canon Gerard Hanlon." *Mallorn* 54 (Spring 2013): 40–42.

Helms, Philip W. "Life, Death and Motherhood: J.R.R. Tolkien and Robert E. Howard." *Minas Tirith Evening-Star*, vol. 17, no. 1 (Spring 1988): 3–5, 14.

Helms, Randel. *Tolkien's World*. London: Thames and Hudson, 1974.

Higgens, Deborah A. *Anglo-Saxon Community in J.R.R. Tolkien's* The Lord of the Rings. Toronto: Oloris Publishing, 2014.

Higgins, Andrew S. *The Genesis of J.R.R. Tolkien's Mythology*. PhD thesis, School of Education, Cardiff Metropolitan University, 2015.

Higgins, Sørina, ed. *The Inklings and King Arthur: J.R.R. Tolkien, Charles Williams, C.S. Lewis, and Owen Barfield on the Matter of Britain*. Berkley, CA: Apocryphile Press, 2017.

Hiley, Margaret. "'Bizarre or dream like': J.R.R. Tolkien on *Finnegans Wake*." In *Joycean Legacies*, ed. M.C. Carpentier, 112–126. London: Palgrave Macmillan, 2015.

———. *The Loss and the Silence: Aspects of Modernism in the Works of C.S. Lewis, J.R.R. Tolkien & Charles Williams*. Zurich: Walking Tree, 2011.

———. "Stolen Language, Cosmic Models: Myth and Mythology in Tolkien." *MFS Modern Fiction Studies*, vol. 50, no. 4 (Winter 2004): 838–860.

Hindle, Alan. "Memories of Tolkien." *Amon Hen* 32 (May 1978): 4–6.

Hix, Melanie Renee. *Mythologies of Power: H. Rider Haggard's Influence on J.R.R. Tolkien's* The Lord of the Rings. Master of liberal arts thesis, Oklahoma City University, 2004.

Hogan, Tom. "Tolkien's time in Erin." *The Irish Times*. March 17, 2012. http://www.irishtimes.com/opinion/letters/tolkien-s-time-in-erin-1.483679.

Holland, Robert W., ed. *Adversus Major: A Short History of the Educational Books Scheme of the Prisoners of War Department*. London: Staples Press, 1949.

Holmes, Kay, "The Master Hobbit at 80." *The Sunday News Magazine*, February 13, 1972, 44–46.

Honegger, Thomas. "Academic Writings." In *A Companion to J.R.R. Tolkien*, ed. Stuart Lee, 27–40.

———. "The Rohirrim: Anglo-Saxons on Horseback? An Inquiry into Tolkien's Use of Sources." In *Tolkien and the Study of His Sources*, ed. Jason Fisher, 116–132.

———. ed. *Reconsidering Tolkien*. Zollikofen, Switzerland: Walking Tree, 2005.

Honegger, Thomas, and Maureen F. Mann, eds. *Laughter in Middle-earth: Humour in and around the Works of J.R.R. Tolkien*. Zurich: Walking Tree, 2016.

Honegger, Thomas, and Frank Weinreich, eds. *Tolkien and Modernity 2*. Zurich: Walking Tree, 2006.

Hooker, Mark T. "Journey to the Center of Middle-earth." In *The Tolkienaeum*, 1–12. Expanded version of "Journey to the Center of Middle Earth." *Beyond Bree* (May 2013): 3–5.

———. "Reading John Buchan in Search of Tolkien." In *Tolkien and the Study of His Sources*, ed. Jason Fisher, 162–192.

———. *The Tolkienaeum: Essays on J.R.R. Tolkien and His Legendarium*. Llyfrawr, 2014.

———. *A Tolkienian Mathomium: A Collection of Articles about J.R.R. Tolkien and His Legendarium*. Llyfrawr, 2006.

Hooper, Walter. *C.S. Lewis: A Companion and Guide*. London: HarperCollins, 2005.

———. "Narnia: The Author, the Critics, and the Tale." In *The Longing for a Form: Essays on the Fiction of C. S. Lewis*, ed. Peter J. Schakel, 105–118. Kent, OH: The Kent University Press, 1977.

Houghton, John Wm., Janet Brennan Croft, Nancy Martsch, John D. Rateliff, and Robin Anne Reid, eds. *Tolkien in the New Century: Essays in Honor of Tom Shippey*. McFarland: Jefferson, NC, 2014.

Hren, Joshua. *Middle-earth and the Return of the Common Good: J. R. R. Tolkien and Political Philosophy*. Eugene, OR: Cascade Books, 2018.

Hunt, Peter, ed. *J.R.R. Tolkien: The Hobbit and the Lord of the Rings*. Basingstoke: Palgrave Macmillan, 2013.

Hunter, John. "The Reanimation of Antiquity and the Resistance to History: Macpherson-Scott-Tolkien." In *Tolkien's Modern Middle Ages*, ed. Jane Chance and Alfred K. Siewers, 61–75.

Hynes, Gerard. "From Nauglath to Durin's Folk: *The Hobbit* and Tolkien's Dwarves." In The Hobbit *and Tolkien's Mythology*, ed. Bradford Lee Eden, 20–37.

Inglis, Fred. *The Promise of Happiness: Value and Meaning in Children's Fiction*. Cambridge: Cambridge University Press, 1981.

Isaacs, Neil D., and Rose Zimbardo, eds. *Tolkien and the Critics: Essays on J.R.R. Tolkien's* The Lord of the Rings. Notre Dame: University of Notre Dame Press, 1968.

———. *Understanding* The Lord of the Rings: *The Best of Tolkien Criticism*, eds. New York: Houghton Mifflin, 2004.

Jacobs, Alan. *The Narnian: The Life and Imagination of C.S. Lewis*. New York: HarperCollins, 2005.

Kaller, Seth. "J.R.R. Tolkien Writes his Proofreader with a Lengthy Discussion of the *Lord of the Rings*, Including Criticism of Radio Broadcasts of his Work." *Seth Kaller, Inc: Historic Documents and Legacy Collections*. https://www.sethkaller.com/view-item.php?id=1195.

Kerry, Paul E., ed. *The Ring and the Cross: Christianity and The Lord of the Rings*. Madison, WI: Fairleigh Dickinson University Press, 2011.

Kilby, Clyde S. "Dr. Clyde S. Kilby Recalls The Inklings." Notes from an interview with Michael Foster, October 10, 1980. Marquette University Department of Special Collections and University Archives.

———. "Dr. Clyde S. Kilby Recalls J.R.R. Tolkien and C.S. Lewis, 1980." Interview notes collected by Annette Brown, Michael Foster, and Sue Storts, Wheaton College, October 10, 1980. Wade Center Oral History Archive.

———. "I'd like to have you come." [Recollections of Tolkien.] *Minas Tirith Evening-Star*, vol. 9, no. 2 (January 1980): 17–19.

———. "Many Meetings with Tolkien (transcripts of talks by Dr. C. S. Kilby and Dick Plotz)." *Niekas* 18 (December 1968): 39–40.

———. "Meeting Professor Tolkien." *Christian History*, issue 78 (2003).

———. "Tolkien and Coleridge." *Tolkien Journal*, vol. 4, no. 1, article 4 (January 15, 1970): 16–19. https://dc.swosu.edu/tolkien_journal/vol4/iss1/4.

———. "Tolkien as Scholar and Artist." *Tolkien Journal*, vol. 3, no. 1 (1967): 9–11.

———. *Tolkien and the Silmarillion*. Berkhamstead, Herts.: Lion Publishing, 1976.

Kilby, Clyde S. *A Well of Wonder: Essays on C.S. Lewis, J.R.R. Tolkien, and the Inklings*, ed. Loren Wilkinson and Keith Call. Brewster, MA: Mount Tabor Books, 2016.

———. "Woodland Prisoner." *VII (Seven): An Anglo-American Literary Review*, vol. 27 (2010): 48–60.

Kroeber, Karl. *Romantic Fantasy and Science Fiction*. New Haven, CT: Yale University Press, 1988.

Kuck, Clara. "Dunsany and mythology in modern drama." Master of Arts thesis, Boston University, 1932.

Larsen, Kristine. "From Dunne to Desmond: disembodied time travel in Tolkien, Stapledon, and *Lost*." *Mallorn* 53 (Spring 2012): 26–30.

———. "'It passes our skill in these days': Primary World Influences on the Evolution of Durin's Day." In The Hobbit *and Tolkien's Mythology*, ed. Bradford Lee Eden, 40–58.

———. "Lessons of Myth, Mortality, & the Machine in the Dream State Space-Time Travel Tales of J.R.R. Tolkien and Olaf Stapledon." In *A Wilderness of Dragons*, ed. John D. Rateliff, 176–195.

———. "'A Little Earth of His Own': Tolkien's Lunar Creation Myths." In *The Ring Goes Ever On*, Tolkien Proceedings 2005, vol. II, 394–403.

Lazo, Andrew. "A kind of mid-wife: J.R.R. Tolkien and C.S. Lewis – sharing influence." In *Tolkien the Medievalist*, ed. Jane Chance, 36–49.

Lee, Stuart, "'Tolkien in Oxford' (BBC, 1968): A Reconstruction." *Tolkien Studies*, vol. 15 (2018): 115–176.

———. ed. *A Companion to J.R.R. Tolkien*, ed. Stuart Lee. John Wiley and Sons, Chichester, West Sussex, UK, 2014.

Lewis, C.S. *The Collected Letters of C.S. Lewis, Volume I*. Edited by Walter Hooper. New York: HarperCollins, 2000.

———. *The Collected Letters of C.S. Lewis, Volume II*. Edited by Walter Hooper. New York: HarperCollins, 2004.

———. *The Collected Letters of C.S. Lewis, Volume III*. Edited by Walter Hooper. New York: HarperCollins, 2007.

———. ed., *George MacDonald: An Anthology*. New York: HarperCollins, 2001. First published 1946.

———. *Image and Imagination*. Edited by Walter Hooper. Cambridge: Cambridge University Press, 2013.

———. *On Stories and Other Essays on Literature*. Edited by Walter Hooper. Orlando, FL: Harcourt, 1982. First published in *Essays Presented to Charles Williams*, 1947.

———. *Selected Literary Essays*. Cambridge: Cambridge University Press, 1969.

Lewis, Warren. *Brothers and Friends: The Diaries of Major Warren Hamilton Lewis*, ed. Clyde S. Kilby and Marjorie Lamp Mead. San Francisco: Harper & Row, 1982.

Linley, Stephen. "Tolkien and Haggard: Some Thoughts on Galadriel." *Anor* (The Cambridge Tolkien Society bulletin) 23 (1991): 11–16.

Loback, Tom. "Hoth, Hothri, Hothron: Orc Military Organization and Language." *Parma Eldalameron* [*The Book of Elven Tongues*] 8 (1990): 17–19, ed. Christopher Gilson, vol. 2, no. 4. 1989, 17–19.

Lobdell, Jared C. "C.S. Lewis's Ransom Stories and Their Eighteenth-Century Ancestry." In *Word and Story in C.S. Lewis*, ed. Peter J. Schakel and Charles A. Huttar, 213–231. Columbia, Missouri: University of Missouri Press, 1991.

———. *England and Always: Tolkien's World of the Rings*. Grand Rapids, MI: Eerdmans, 1981.

———. "Mr. Bliss: Notes on the Manuscript and Story." In *Selections from the Marquette J.R.R. Tolkien Collection*, ed. Charles B. Elston. Milwaukee, 5–9. Wisconsin: Marquette University Library, 1987.

———. *The World of the Rings: Language, Religion, and Adventure in Tolkien*. Chicago: Open Court, 2004.

———. ed. *A Tolkien Compass*. 2nd ed. Peru, IL: Open Court, 2003. First published 1975.

Long, Josh. "Disparaging Narnia." *Mythlore* 121/122, vol. 31, no. 3/4 (Spring/Summer 2013).

Lowe, Shirley. "Priscilla Tolkien talks to Shirley Lowe about Life with Father, Professor J.R.R. Tolkien." *Over* 21 (December 1976): 32.

Luling, Virginia. "An Anthropologist in Middle-earth." Proceedings of the 1992 Tolkien Centenary Conference. *Mythlore* 80, vol. 21, no. 2 (Winter 1996): 53–57.

———. "Going back: time travel in Tolkien and E. Nesbit." *Mallorn* 53 (Spring 2012): 30–31.

Lupoff, Richard A. *Edgar Rice Burroughs: Master of Adventure*. New York: Ace, 1965.

Macarthur, Chris. "Frankenstein, The Monster, Melkor, Sauron and Gollum." *Amon Hen* 275 (January 2019): 10–13.

MacCarthy, Fiona. *William Morris: A Life for Our Time*. London: Faber and Faber, 1994.

MacLeod, Jeffrey J., and Anna Smol. "Visualizing the Word: Tolkien as Artist and Writer." *Tolkien Studies* 14 (2017): 115–131.

MacSwain, Robert, and Michael Ward, eds. *The Cambridge Companion to C.S. Lewis*. Cambridge: Cambridge University Press, 2010.

Makins, Marian W. "Memories of (Ancient Roman) War in Tolkien's Dead Marshes." In "War of the Senses – The Senses in War. Interactions and Tensions Between Representations of War in Classical and Modern Culture," ed. Annemarie Ambühl, special issue, *thersites: Journal for Transcultural Presences & Diachronic Identities from Antiquity to Date* 4 (2016): 199–240.

Manlove, Colin. "MacDonald's Counter-literature." In *Inklings Forever* 5 (2006), article 35. https://pillars.taylor.edu/inklings_forever/vol5/iss1/35.

———. "MacDonald's Theology and his Fantasy Fiction." In *Inklings Forever* 5 (2006), article 34. https://pillars.taylor.edu/inklings_forever/vol5/iss1/34.

———. "Parent or Associate? George MacDonald and the Inklings." In *George MacDonald: Literary Heritage and Heirs*, ed. Roderick McGillis, 227–238.

Mann, Maureen F. "Artefacts and Immersion in the Worldbuilding of Tolkien and the Brontës." In *Sub-creating Arda*, ed. Dimitra Fimi and Thomas Honegger, 335–358.

———. "'Certainly not our sense': Tolkien and Nonsense." In *Laughter in Middle-earth*, ed. Thomas Honegger and Maureen F. Mann, 9–36.

Marquette University. *The Invented Worlds of JRR Tolkien: Drawings and Original Manuscripts from the Marquette University Collection*. Milwaukee, WI: Marquette University, 2004. Catalogues and Gallery Guides, 48. https://epublications.marquette.edu/haggerty_catalogs/48.

——. *J.R.R. Tolkien: The Hobbit: The Hobbit Drawings, Watercolors and Manuscripts, June 11–September 30, 1987*. Exhibition catalogue. Patrick & Beatrice Haggerty Museum of Art. Milwaukee, WI: Marquette University, 1987.

Martsch, Nancy. "The 'Lady with the Simple Gown and White Arms' *or* Possible Influences of 19th and Early 20th Century Book Illustrations on Tolkien's Work." In *Tolkien in the New Century*, ed. John Wm. Houghton et al., 29–40.

——. "Tolkien's Reading," *Beyond Bree* (April 1997): 4–6.

——. "Tolkien's Reading: 'On Fairy-Stories,'" *Beyond Bree* (August 1997): 1–4.

Massouras, Alexander. "Tolkien's tennis shoes." *The Times Literary Supplement*, April 3, 2017.

Mathison, Phil. *Tolkien in East Yorkshire 1917–1918: An Illustrated Tour*. Newport, East Yorkshire: Dead Good Productions, 2012.

Matthews, Lucy. "The Unveiling of a plaque commemorating J.R.R. Tolkien in Birmingham March 17th 1977." *Amon Hen* 26 (May 1977): 4–5.

McIlwaine, Catherine. "J.R.R. Tolkien: A Biographical Sketch.," in *Tolkien: Maker of Middle-earth*, ed. Catherine McIlwaine, 10–19.

——. ed. *Tolkien: Maker of Middle-earth*. Oxford: Bodleian Library, 2018.

McFadden, Brian. "Fear of Difference, Fear of Death: The *Sigelwara,* Tolkien's Swertings, and Racial Difference." In *Tolkien's Modern Middle Ages*, ed. Jane Chance and Alfred K. Siewers, 155–169.

McGillis, Roderick, ed. *George MacDonald: Literary Heritage and Heirs*. Wayne, PA: Zossima Press, 2008.

Medcalf, Stephen. "'The Language Learned of Elves': Owen Barfield, *The Hobbit* and *The Lord of the Rings*." *VII (Seven): An Anglo-American Literary Review*, vol. 16 (1999): 31–53.

Michelson, Paul E. "The Development of J.R.R. Tolkien's Ideas on Fairy-stories." In *Inklings Forever* 8 (2012), article 13. https://pillars.taylor.edu/inklings_forever/vol8/iss1/13.

——. "George MacDonald and J.R.R. Tolkien on Faërie and Fairy Stories." In *Inklings Forever* 9 (2014), article 11. https://pillars.taylor.edu/inklings_forever/vol9/iss1/11.

Milbank, Alison. *Chesterton and Tolkien as Theologians: The Fantasy of the Real*. London: T&T Clark, 2009.

——. "Tolkien, Chesterton, and Thomism." In *Tolkien's* The Lord of the Rings: *Sources of Inspiration*, ed. Stratford Caldecott and Thomas Honegger, 187–198.

Milward, Peter. "Perchance to Touch: Tolkien as Scholar," *Mythlore* 22, vol. 6, no. 4 (Fall 1979): 31-32.

——. "Tolkien, the Ring, and I." *The Chesterton Review*, Volume 28, no. 1/2 (February/May 2002): 119–123.

Moorman, Charles. "The Shire, Mordor, and Minas Tirith." In *Tolkien and the Critics*, ed. Neil D. Isaacs and Rose A. Zimbardo, 201–217.

Mortimer, Patchen. "Tolkien and Modernism." *Tolkien Studies*, vol. 2 (2005): 113–129.

Murray, Robert. "A Tribute to Tolkien." *The Tablet*, Sept 15, 1973, 879–80.

Nejrotti, Chiara. "From Neverland to Middle-earth." In *Tolkien and the Classics*, ed. Roberto Arduini et al., 185–195.

Nelson, Dale. "Haggard's *Heu-Heu* and *The Hobbit*." *Beyond Bree* (December 2005).

———. "Haggard's *The Treasure of the Lake* and Tolkien's 'Tower of Cirith Ungol' Episode." *Beyond Bree* (January 2006).

———. "Literary Influences, Nineteenth and Twentieth Century." In *J.R.R. Tolkien Encyclopedia*, ed. Michael D.C. Drout, 366–378.

———. "*The Lord of the Rings* and a Late-Victorian Thriller: The Companions Against Dracula Compared to the Fellowship of the Ring." *Beyond Bree* (May 2013).

———. "Possible Echoes of Blackwood and Dunsany in Tolkien's Fantasy." *Tolkien Studies*, vol. 1 (2004): 177–181.

———. "Tolkien's further indebtedness to Haggard." *Mallorn* 47 (Spring 2009): 38–40.

———. "'Queer, Exciting, and Debatable': Tolkien and Shorthouse's *John Inglesant*." *Beyond Bree* (January 2006): 4–5.

Nicolay, Theresa Freda. *Tolkien and the Modernists: Literary Responses to the Dark New Days of the 20th Century*. Jefferson, NC: McFarland & Company, 2014.

di Noia, Marco. "Best wishes from Thorin and Company! – Following Tolkien's trails in Oxford." *Amon Hen* 212 (2008): 18–23.

Noetzel, Justin T., and Matthew R. Bardowell, "The Inklings Remembered: An Interview with Colin Havard." *Mythlore* 119/120, vol. 31, no. 3/4 (Fall/Winter 2012).

Norman, Philip. "From London: Lord of the Flicks." *Show: The Magazine of Film and the Arts* I, no. 1 (January 1970): 29.

———. "The Hobbit Man." *The Sunday Times Magazine*, January 15, 1967, 34–36.

———. "The Prevalence of Hobbits." *The New York Times Magazine*, January 15, 1967, 30–31, 97, 100–102.

Obertino, James. "Barbarians and Imperialism in Tacitus and *The Lord of the Rings*." *Tolkien Studies*, vol. 3 (2006): 117–131.

TheOneRing.net, "Tolkien Estate comments on book cancellation." November 16, 2010. http://www.theonering.net/torwp/2010/11/16/40512-tolkien-estate-comments-on-book-cancellation/#more-40512.

Oxfordshire History Centre Archives. "The Ringmaker in Oxford." Sound recording. OXOHA/MT/677.

Partridge, Michael, and Kirstin Jeffrey Johnson, eds. *Informing the Inklings: George MacDonald and the Victorian Roots of Modern Fantasy*. Hamden, CT: Winged Lion Press, 2018.

Pask, Kevin. *The Fairy Way of Writing: Shakespeare to Tolkien*. Baltimore, MD: Johns Hopkins University Press, 2013.

Pearce, Joseph. *Literary Converts: Spiritual Inspiration in an Age of Unbelief.* London: HarperCollins, 1999.

———. ed. *Tolkien: A Celebration: Collected writings on a literary legacy.* San Francisco: Ignatius Press, 1999.

Pełczyński, Zbigniew. "My J.R.R. Tolkien Memories." *Simbelmynë* #2 (31). http://www.elendilion.pl/wp-content/uploads/2019/01/Sn_31_English.pdf.

Perry, Michael W. "Morris, William." In *J.R.R. Tolkien Encyclopedia*, ed. Michael D.C. Drout, 439–441.

Pezzini, Giuseppe. "The Authors of Middle Earth: Tolkien and the Mystery of Literary Creation." *Journal of Inklings Studies*, vol. 8, no. 1 (2018): 30–64.

Phelpstead, Carl. "'For W.H.A.' – Tolkien's Poem in Praise of Auden." In *Tolkien's Poetry*, ed. Julian Eilmann and Alan Turner, 45–58.

———. "'With chunks of poetry in between': *The Lord of the Rings* and Saga Poetics." *Tolkien Studies*, vol. 5 (2008): 23–38.

duPlessis, Nicole M. "On the Shoulders of Humphrey Carpenter: Reconsidering Biographical Representation and Scholarly Perception of Edith Tolkien." *Mythlore* 134, vol. 37, no. 2 (Spring 2019): 39–74.

Plimmer, Charlotte and Denis. "The Man Who Understands Hobbits." London *Daily Telegraph Magazine*, March 22, 1968, 31–32, 35.

Plotz, Dick. "Face to Face With R.D. Plotz." *Seventeen*, April 1966, 153.

———. "J.R.R. Tolkien Talks about the Discovery of Middle-Earth, the Origins of Elvish." *Seventeen*, January 26, 1967, 92–93, 118.

———. "Many Meetings with Tolkien (transcripts of talks by Dr. C. S. Kilby and Dick Plotz)." *Niekas* 18, December 1968, 39–40.

Podles, Mary. "Tolkien and the New Art: Visual Sources for *The Lord of the Rings*." *Touchstone*, (Jan/Feb. 2002): 41–47.

Power, Canon N. (Norman) S. "Ring of Doom." *The Tablet*, December 20/27, 1975, 1247–38.

———. "Tolkien's Walk (An Unexpected Personal Link with Tolkien)". *Mallorn* 9 (1975): 16–19.

Price, Meredith. "'All Shall Love Me and Despair': The Figure of Lilith in Tolkien, Lewis, Williams, & Sayers." *Mythlore* 31, vol. 9, no. 1 (Spring 1982): 3–7.

Pullman, Philip. *Daemon Voices: Essays on Storytelling.* Oxford: David Fickling Books, 2017.

Quiñonez, Jorge, and Ned Raggett. "Nólë i Meneldilo: Lore of the Astronomer." *Vinyar Tengwar* 12 (July 1990): 5.

Ransome, Arthur. *Signalling from Mars: The Letters of Arthur Ransome*, ed. Hugh Brogan London: Pimlico, 1998.

Rateliff, John D. "'And Something Yet Remains to Be Said': Tolkien and Williams." *Mythlore* 45, vol. 12, no. 3 (Spring 1986).

———. "Grima the Wormtongue: Tolkien and His Sources." *Mallorn* 25 (September 1988): 15–17.

————. *The History of The Hobbit*, revised and expanded one-volume edition. London: HarperCollins, 2013.

————. Letter to *Beyond Bree* (March 2006): 4.

————. "Introduction to 'Woodland Prisoner': Clyde S. Kilby Speaks on Tolkien." *VII (Seven): An Anglo-American Literary Review*, vol. 27 (2010): 45–47.

————. "The Lost Explorers." *Sacnoth's Scriptorium* (blog), July 30, 2010. http://sacnoths.blogspot.co.uk/2010/07/lost-explorers.html.

————. "The Missing Women: J.R.R. Tolkien's Lifelong Support for Women's Higher Education." In *Perilous and Fair*, ed. Janet Brennan Croft and Leslie A. Donovan, 41–69.

————. "*She* and Tolkien." *Mythlore* 28, vol. 8, no. 2. (Summer 1981): 6–8.

————. "Tolkien and Sinclair Lewis." *Sacnoth's Scriptorium* (blog), April 15, 2013. http://sacnoths.blogspot.co.uk/2013/08/tolkien-and-sinclair-lewis.html.

————. ed. *A Wilderness of Dragons: Essays in Honor of Verlyn Flieger*. Wayzata, MN: Gabbro Head Press, 2018.

Ready, William. *The Tolkien Relation: A Personal Inquiry*. [Also published as *Understanding Tolkien and* The Lord of the Rings.] New York: Henry Regnery, 1968.

Reed, Ryan. "See Stephen Colbert Break Down Chance the Rapper's 'Favorite Song' (feat. Childish Gambino)," *Rolling Stone*, August 29, 2018. https://www.rollingstone.com/music/music-news/stephen-colbert-breakdown-chance-the-rapper-childish-gambino-favorite-song-716865/.

Reid, Robin Anne. "Race in Tolkien Studies: A Bibliographic Essay." In *Tolkien and Alterity*, ed. Christopher Vaccaro and Yvette Kisor, 33–76.

Reilly, R.J. "Tolkien and the Fairy Story." In *Tolkien and the Critics*, ed. Neil D. Isaacs and Rose A. Zimbardo, 128–150.

Reis, R. H. "George MacDonald: Founder of the Feast." *Tolkien Journal* 2, no. 1 (1966): 3–5.

Resnik, Henry. "The Hobbit-Forming World of J.R.R. Tolkien." *The Saturday Evening Post*, July 2, 1966, 90–94.

————. "An Interview with Tolkien," March 2, 1966. *Niekas* 18 (Spring 1967): 37–43.

Richardson, Maurice. Review of "The Two Towers," *The New Statesman and Nation*, December 18, 1954, 735–736.

Risden, E.L. "Middle-earth and the Waste Land: Greenwood, Apocalypse, and Post-War Resolution." In *Tolkien in the New Century*, ed. John Wm. Houghton et al., 57–64.

Rissik, Andrew. "Middle Earth, middlebrow." Review of *J.R.R. Tolkien: Author of the Century* by Tom Shippey. *The Guardian*, September 1, 2000.

Rogers, Deborah Webster, and Ivor A. Rogers, *J.R.R. Tolkien*. Boston: Twayne Publishers, 1980.

Rogers, William N. II, and Michael R. Underwood. "Gagool and Gollum: Exemplars of Degeneration in *King Solomon's Mines* and *The Hobbit*." In *J.R.R. Tolkien and His Literary Resonances*, ed. George Clark and Daniel Timmons, 121–132.

Ryan, John S. *In the Nameless Wood: Explorations in the Philological Hinterland of Tolkien's Literary Creations.* Zurich: Walking Tree Publishers, 2013.

———. "J.R.R. Tolkien, C.S. Lewis, and Roy Campbell." In J.S. Ryan, *The Shaping of Middle-earth's Maker: Influences on the Life and Literature of J.R.R. Tolkien*, 25–29. Highland, Michigan: American Tolkien Society, 1992.

———. "Perilous Roads to the East, from Weathertop and through the Borgo Pass." *Minas Tirith Evening-Star*, vol. 17, no. 1 (Spring 1988): 12-14.

———. "Those Birmingham Quietists: J.R.R. Tolkien and J.H. Shorthouse (1834–1903)." In J.S. Ryan, *Tolkien's View: Windows into his World*, 3–15. Zurich: Walking Tree Publishers, 2009.

———. "Two Oxford Scholars' Perceptions of the Traditional Germanic Hall." *Minas Tirith Evening-Star*, vol. 19, no. 1 (Spring 1990): 8–11.

Salu, Mary, and Robert T. Farrell, eds. *J.R.R. Tolkien: Scholar and Storyteller. Essays in Memoriam.* Ithaca, NY: Cornell University Press, 1979.

Sandbrook, Dominic. *The Great British Dream Factory: The Strange History of Our National Imagination.* London: Penguin Books, 2016.

Sandner, David. "Mr. Bliss and Mr. Toad: Hazardous Driving in J.R.R. Tolkien's *Mr. Bliss* & Kenneth Grahame's *The Wind in the Willows*." *Mythlore* 82, vol. 21, no. 4 (Winter 1997).

Sayer, George. *Jack: A Life of C.S. Lewis.* Second edition. Wheaton, IL: Crossway Books, 1994.

———. "Memories of J.R.R. Tolkien." Talk delivered to the Oxford C.S. Lewis Society, November 25, 1986.

———. "Recollections of J.R.R. Tolkien." In *Tolkien: A Celebration*, ed. Joseph Pearce, 1–16.

St. Clair, Gloria Ann Strange Slaughter. *Studies in the Sources of J.R.R. Tolkien's* The Lord of the Rings. PhD thesis, University of Oklahoma, 1969.

Schindler, Richard. "The Expectant Landscape: J.R.R. Tolkien's Illustrations for *The Hobbit*." In *J.R.R. Tolkien: The Hobbit: Drawings, Watercolors and Manuscripts*, 14–27. Milwaukee, WI: Marquette University, 2004.

Scholes, Robert, and Eric S. Rabkin, *Science Fiction: History, Science, Vision.* Oxford: Oxford University Press, 1977.

Schroeder, Sharin. "Genre Problems: Andrew Lang and J.R.R. Tolkien on (Fairy) Stories and (Literary) Belief." In *Informing the Inklings: George MacDonald and the Victorian Roots of Modern Fantasy*, ed. Michael Partridge and Kirstin Jeffrey Johnson, 149–179.

———. "She-who-must-not-be-ignored: Gender and Genre in *The Lord of the Rings* and the Victorian Boys' Book." In *Perilous and Fair*, ed. Janet Brennan Croft and Leslie A. Donovan, 70–96.

Scott, Nan C.L., "A Visit with Tolkien." *The Living Church*, February 5, 1978, 11–12.

Scoville, Chester N. "Pastoralia and Perfectibility in William Morris and J.R.R. Tolkien," in *Tolkien's Modern Middle Ages*, ed. Jane Chance and Alfred K. Siewers, 93–104.

Scull, Christina. "Dragons from Andrew Lang's retelling of Sigurd to Tolkien's Chrysophylax." In *Leaves from the Tree: JRR Tolkien's Shorter Fiction*, 49–62. London: The Tolkien Society, 1991.

———. "What Did He Know and When Did He Know It? Planning, Inspiration, and *The Lord of the Rings*." In *Lord of the Rings, 1954–2004: Scholarship in Honor of Richard E. Blackwelder*, ed. Wayne G. Hammond and Christina Scull, 101–112. Milwaukee, WI: Marquette University Press, 2006.

Scull, Christina, and Wayne G. Hammond. Introduction to *The Adventures of Tom Bombadil,* ed. Christina Scull and Wayne Hammond, 7–26. London: HarperCollins, 2014.

———. Introduction to *Roverandom* by J.R.R. Tolkien, ed. Christina Scull and Wayne G. Hammond, ix–xxii. Boston: Houghton Mifflin, 1998.

———. Addenda to *Roverandom* by J.R.R. Tolkien, ed. Christina Scull and Wayne G. Hammond. Boston: Houghton Mifflin, 1998. http://www.hammondandscull.com/addenda/roverandom.html.

———. Addenda & Corrigenda for *The Tolkien Companion and Guide*, Revised and expanded edition. http://www.hammondandscull.com/addenda/chronology2.html.

———. *The J.R.R. Tolkien Companion and Guide: Chronology.* Revised and expanded edition. Boston: Houghton Mifflin, 2017.

———. *The J.R.R. Tolkien Companion and Guide: Reader's Guide.* Revised and expanded edition. Boston: Houghton Mifflin, 2017.

———. "Lecture on Dragons." In *J.R.R. Tolkien: The Hobbit 1937-2017: A commemorative booklet celebrating the 80th anniversary*, 37–38. London: HarperCollins, 2018.

———. *The Lord of the Rings: A Reader's Companion.* Revised edition. London: HarperCollins, 2014.

Seddon, Eric. "*Letters to Malcolm* and the Trouble with Narnia: C.S. Lewis, J.R.R. Tolkien, and Their 1949 Crisis." *Mythlore* 99/100, vol. 26, no. 1 (Fall/Winter 2007): 61–82.

Segura, Eduardo, and Thomas Honegger, eds. *Myth and Magic: Art according to the Inklings*. Zurich: Walking Tree, 2007.

Seland, John. "The Friendship Between C.S. Lewis and J.R.R. Tolkien." In *Inklings Forever* 1 (1997), article 6. 29-36. https://pillars.taylor.edu/inklings_forever/vol1/iss1/6.

Shippey, Tom. "Buchan, John." In *J.R.R. Tolkien Encyclopedia*, ed. Michael D.C. Drout, 77–78.

———. "Goths and Romans in Tolkien's imagination." In *Tolkien: The Forest and the City*, ed. Helen Conrad-O'Briain and Gerard Hynes, 19–33.

———. "Guest Editorial: An Encyclopedia of Ignorance." *Mallorn* 45 (Spring 2008): 3–5.

———. Introduction to *The Wood Beyond the World* by William Morris, v–xix. Oxford: Oxford University Press, 1980.

———. *J.R.R. Tolkien: Author of the Century*. Boston: Houghton Mifflin, 2000.

———. "The Lewis Diaries: C.S. Lewis and the English Faculty in the 1920s." In *C.S. Lewis and His Circle: Essays and Memoirs from the Oxford C.S. Lewis Society*, ed. Roger White, Judith Wolfe, and Brennan Wolfe. Oxford University Press, 2015.

———. "The Ransom Trilogy." In *The Cambridge Companion to C.S. Lewis*, ed. Robert MacSwain and Michael Ward, 237–250.

———. *The Road to Middle-earth*. Revised edition. London: HarperCollins, 2005.

———. *Roots and Branches: Selected Papers on Tolkien*. Zollikofen, Switzerland: Walking Tree Publishers, 2007.

———. "Why Source Criticism?" Introduction to *Tolkien and the Study of His Sources*, ed. Jason Fisher, 7–16.

———. "William Morris and Tolkien: Some Unexpected Connections." In *Tolkien and the Classics*, ed. Roberto Arduini et al., 229–245.

Shippey, Tom and John Bourne, "A Steep Learning Curve: Tolkien and the British Army on the Somme." In *"Something Has Gone Crack,"* ed. Janet Brennan Croft and Annika Röttinger, 3–25.

Shrimpton, Paul, ed. *Inklings of Truth: Essays to Mark the Anniversaries of C.S. Lewis and J.R.R. Tolkien*. Oxford: Grandpont House, 2018.

Simonson, Martin. "*The Lord of the Rings* in the Wake of the Great War: War, Poetry, Modernism, and Ironic Myth." In *Reconsidering Tolkien*, ed. Thomas Honegger, 153–170.

———. "Recovering the 'Utterly Alien Land': Tolkien and Transcendentalism." In *Myth and Magic*, ed. Eduardo Segura and Thomas Honegger, 1–20.

Sinex, Margaret. "'Tricksy Lights': Literary and Folkloric Elements in Tolkien's Passage of the Dead Marshes." *Tolkien Studies*, vol. 2 (2005): 93–112.

Sisto, Alan, and Shawn E. Marchese, hosts. *The Prancing Pony Podcast*. theprancingponypodcast.com.

Smith, Laura Lee. "'This of course is the way to talk to dragons': Etiquette-based Humour in *The Hobbit*." In *Laughter in Middle-earth*, ed. Thomas Honegger and Maureen F. Mann, 107–132.

Spooner, Kaleigh Jean. "'History Real or Feigned': Tolkien, Scott, and Poetry's Place in Fashioning History." Master of Arts thesis, Department of English, Brigham Young University, 2017.

Stacey, Simon. "Tolkien's Tone and the Frequent Failure to Hear It." In *Inklings of Truth*, ed. Paul Shrimpton, 75–97.

Steiner, George. "Tolkien, Oxford's Eccentric Don." *Tolkien Studies* 5 (2008): 186–188. Originally published in *Le Monde*, September 6, 1973.

Stewart, J.I.M. "Favourite Subjects." Review of *The Letters of J.R.R. Tolkien. London Review of Books*, vol. 3, no. 17 (September 17, 1981). https://www.lrb.co.uk/v03/n17/jim-stewart/favourite-subjects.

Swann, Donald. Foreword to the Second Edition, *The Road Goes Ever On: A Song Cycle*. 2nd ed. Music by Donald Swann, poems by J.R.R. Tolkien, v–ix. London: George Allen & Unwin, 1978.

Tankard, Paul. "An Art to Depict 'the Noble and Heroic': Tolkien on Adaptation, Illustration, and the Art of Mary Fairburn." *Journal of Inklings Studies*, vol. 9, no. 1 (April 2019): 19–42.

Tayar, Graham. "Tolkien's Mordor." Letter to *The Listener*, July 14, 1977.

Testi, Claudio A., "André Breton and J.R.R. Tolkien: Surrealism, Subcreation and Frodo's Dreams." *Journal of Tolkien Research*, vol. 6, no. 2 (2018).

———. "Tolkien and Aquinas." In *Tolkien and the Classics*, ed. Roberto Arduini et al., 57–71. Zurich: Walking Tree, 2019.

Thompson, L.L.H. "Report on J.R.R. Tolkien's paper on Catholic poet Francis Thompson (4 March 1914)." In Andrew S. Higgins, *The Genesis of J.R.R. Tolkien's Mythology*, appendix 5, 288–290.

Thum, Maureen. "Hidden in Plain View: Strategizing Unconventionality in Shakespeare's and Tolkien's Portraits of Women." In *Perilous and Fair*, ed. Janet Brennan Croft and Leslie A. Donovan, 281–305.

Tolkien, Baillie. "Introduction" to *Catalogue of an Exhibition of Drawings by J.R.R. Tolkien: at the Ashmolean Museum Oxford 14th December – 27th February 1976–1977 and at the National Book League 7 Albemarle Street London W1 2nd March – 7th April 1977*, 6–7. Oxford: The Ashmolean Museum, 1976.

Tolkien, Christopher. "Christopher Tolkien and the 'Aubusson weaves Tolkien' project." Cité internationale de la tapisserie Aubusson, February 7, 2019. https://youtu.be/rQmh_Sfq88Y.

———. *The Silmarillion – J.R.R. Tolkien. A brief account of the book and its making.* Boston: Houghton Mifflin, 1977.

Tolkien, Hilary. *Black & White Ogre Country: The Lost Tales of Hilary Tolkien*, ed. Angela Gardner. Moreton-in-Marsh, Great Britain: ADC Publications, 2009.

Tolkien, Joan. "Origins of a Tolkien tale." Letter to *The Sunday Times*, October 10, 1982, 25.

Tolkien, Joanna. "Joanna Tolkien speaks at the Tolkien Society Annual Dinner, Shrewsbury, April 16, 1994." In *Digging Potatoes, Growing Trees*, vol. 2, ed. Helen Armstrong, 31–36. Telford, The Tolkien Society, 1998.

Tolkien, J.R.R. *Beowulf and the Critics*, ed. Michael D.C. Drout. Tempe, AZ: Arizona Center for Medieval and Renaissance Studies, 2002.

———. *Beowulf: A Translation and Commentary, together with Sellic Spell.* Edited by Christopher Tolkien. Boston: Houghton Mifflin, 2014.

———. "The Book of Jonah" (translation). *Journal of Inklings Studies*, vol. 4, no. 2 (October 2014): 5–9.

———. "The Cat and the Fiddle: A Nursery-Rhyme Undone and Its Scandalous Secret Unlocked." *Yorkshire Poetry*, vol. 11, no. 19 (October/November 1923): 1–3.

———. "Chaucer as a Philologist: *The Reeve's Tale*." Reprinted in *Tolkien Studies*, vol. 5 (2008): 109–170.

———. *Critique of "The Distressing Tale of Thangobrind the Jeweler,"* available: http://tolkiengateway.net/wiki/Critique_of_%22Distressing_Tale_of_Thangobrind_the_Jeweler%22.

————. "Dragons." In *J.R.R. Tolkien: The Hobbit 1937–2017: A commemorative book-let celebrating the 80th anniversary*, by Christina Scull and Wayne G. Hammond, 39–62. London: HarperCollins, 2018.

————. *The Fall of Gondolin*. Edited by Christopher Tolkien. Boston: Houghton Mifflin Harcourt, 2018.

————. "'Genesis of the story': Tolkien's Note to Clyde Kilby." In *Smith of Wootton Major*, ed. Verlyn Flieger, 85–87.

————. *The History of Middle-earth*. Three-volume edition. Edited by Christopher Tolkien. London: HarperCollins, 2017.

————. *Letters from Father Christmas*. Deluxe edition. Edited by Baillie Tolkien. London: HarperCollins, 2019.

————. *The Letters of J.R.R. Tolkien*. Edited by Humphrey Carpenter. London: George Allen and Unwin, 1981.

————. *The Lord of the Rings*. 50th Anniversary one-volume edition. Boston: Houghton Mifflin, 2004.

————. *The Monsters and the Critics and Other Essays*. Edited by Christopher Tolkien. London: HarperCollins, 2006.

————. "On 'The Kalevala' or Land of Heroes." In *The Story of Kullervo* by J.R.R. Tolkien, 67–89.

————. "On Translating Beowulf." In *The Monsters and the Critics and Other Essays* by J.R.R. Tolkien, 49–71.

————. "The Oxford English School." *The Oxford Magazine*, vol. XLVIII, no. 21 (May 29, 1930): 778–780, 782.

————. "Philology: General Works [1923]." *The Year's Work in English Studies*, vol. IV (for 1923), ed. Sir Sidney Lee and F.S. Boas. London: Oxford University Press, 1924, 20–37.

————. "Philology: General Works [1924]." *The Year's Work in English Studies*, vol. V (for 1924), ed. F.S. Boas and C.H. Herford, London: Oxford University Press, 1926, 26–65.

————. "Philology: General Works [1925]." In *The Year's Work in English Studies*, vol. VI (for 1925), ed. F.S. Boas and C.H. Herford. London: Oxford University Press, 1927, 32–66.

————. *The Qenya Alphabet*. Edited with introduction and commentary by Arden R. Smith. In *Parma Eldalameron* 20, ed. Christopher Gilson. Mountain View, CA: The Tolkien Trust, 2012.

————. *A Secret Vice: Tolkien on Invented Languages*. Edited by Dimitra Fimi and Andrew Higgins. London: HarperCollins, 2016.

————. *The Silmarillion*. 2nd ed. Edited by Christopher Tolkien. Boston: Houghton Mifflin, 2001.

————. *Smith of Wootton Major*. Extended edition. Edited by Verlyn Flieger. London: HarperCollins, 2005.

———. *The Story of Kullervo.* Edited by Verlyn Flieger. London: HarperCollins, 2015.

———. *Tengwesta Qenderinwa* and *Pre-Fëanorian Alphabets Part 2*, ed. Christopher Gilson, Patrick H. Wynne, and Arden R. Smith. In *Parma Eldalameron* 18, ed. Christopher Gilson. Mountain View, CA: The Tolkien Trust, 2009.

———. *Tolkien On Fairy-stories*, ed. Verlyn Flieger and Douglas A. Anderson. London: HarperCollins, 2014. "On Fairy-stories" first published 1947 in *Essays Presented to Charles Williams*, ed. C.S. Lewis.

———. *Tree and Leaf.* London: HarperCollins, 1964.

Tolkien, J.R.R., with Donald Swann. *The Road Goes Ever On: A Song Cycle.* Second edition. Music by Donald Swann, poems by J.R.R. Tolkien. London: George Allen & Unwin, 1978 (first edition 1968).

Tolkien, John. "Reminscences of Lewis and Tolkien." Talk given at the Oxford C.S. Lewis Society, February 23, 1988.

Tolkien, John and Priscilla Tolkien. *The Tolkien Family Album.* London: HarperCollins, 1992.

Tolkien, Julian. "Related to Tolkien." Interview by Sandra Carter. *This Is Local London*, December 14, 2001. https://www.thisislocallondon.co.uk/news/307760.related-to-tolkien/.

Tolkien, Michael. "Autobiographical essay on my grandfather, J.R.R. Tolkien, based on a public talk requested by The Leicester Writers' Club at College of Adult Education, Wellington Street, October 19th, 1995." http://www.michaeltolkien.com/page73.html.

———. "An Interview with Michael Hilary Reuel Tolkien." Transcribed by Gary Hunnewell with help from Sylvia Hunnewell from a radio program, "Radio Blackburn." Interviewer Derek Mills. *Minas Tirith Evening-Star*, vol. 18, no. 1 (Spring, 1989): 5–9. Joint issue with *Ravenhill*.

———. "Lecture on J.R.R. Tolkien Given to the University of St Andrews Science Fiction and Fantasy Society, 2nd May, 1989." http://www.michaeltolkien.com/page74.html.

———. "The Wizard Father," *Sunday Telegraph*, September 7, 1973.

Tolkien, Priscilla. "The *Letters* of J.R.R. Tolkien." Talk given at the Oxford C.S. Lewis Society, April 30, 1991.

———. "Memories of J.R.R. Tolkien in his Centenary Year." *The Brown Book*, Lady Margaret Hall, Oxford, December 1992, 12–14.

———. "My Father the Artist." *Amon Hen* 23 (December 23,1976): 6–7. Reprinted in *Minas Tirith Evening-Star*, vol. 13, no. 1 (Jan-Feb. 1984), 8–9.

Tolkien, Michael. "Morality [in the work of J.R.R. Tolkien]." Talk given at the Oxford C.S. Lewis Society, May 20, 1986.

———. "News from the North Pole." *Oxford Today*, vol. 5, no. 1, Michaelmas, 1992, 8–9.

———. "Talk Given at the Church House Westminster on 16.9.77." *Amon Hen* 29 (1977): 4–7.

Tolkien, Priscilla, and Humphrey Carpenter, "Table Talk: A Transcript of the After-dinner speeches at the 1976 Annual General Meeting of the Tolkien Society." *Mallorn* 10 (1976): 34–43.

Tolkien, Priscilla, Humphrey Carpenter, and Raynor [sic] Unwin. "Facets of Tolkien." Sound recording, 1977. Marion E. Wade Center Archives, JRRT-Y/SR-51.

Tolkien, Simon. "My Grandfather J.R.R. Tolkien." First published by *The Mail On Sunday* 2003. http://simontolkien.com/mygrandfather.

———. "Tolkien's grandson on how WW1 inspired *The Lord of the Rings*." *BBC Britain*, January 3, 2017. http://www.bbc.com/culture/story/20161223-tolkiens-grandson-on-how-ww1-inspired-the-lord-of-the-rings.

Tolley, Clive. "Tolkien and the Unfinished." In *Scholarship & Fantasy:* Proceedings of *The Tolkien Phenomenon*, Turku, May 1992, ed. K. J. Battarbee. *Anglicana Turkuensia*, no. 12 (1993): 151–164.

Tomko, Michael. *Beyond the Willing Suspension of Disbelief: Poetic Faith from Coleridge to Tolkien*. London: Bloomsbury, 2016.

Toynbee, Philip. "Dissension Among the Judges." *The Observer*, August 6, 1961, 19.

Unwin, Rayner. *George Allen & Unwin: A Remembrancer*. Privately printed for the Author by Merlin Unwin Books. Ludlow: Merlin Unwin Books, 1999.

———. *The Making of The Lord of the Rings*. Oxford: Willem A. Meeuws, 1992.

———. "Tributes to J.R.R. Tolkien." Special J.R.R. Tolkien Centenary Issue. *Mythlore* 69, vol. 18, no. 3 (Summer 1992): 32.

Vaccaro, Christopher and Yvette Kisor, eds. *Tolkien and Alterity*. Cham, Switzerland: Palgrave Macmillan, 2017.

Vaninskaya, Anna. *Fantasies of Time and Death: Dunsany, Eddison, Tolkien*. London: Palgrave Macmillan, 2020.

———. "Modernity: Tolkien and His Contemporaries." In *A Companion to JRR Tolkien*, ed. Stuart Lee, 350–366.

Vernon, Matthew, ed. *Tolkien: Influenced and Influencing*. Proceedings of the 17th Tolkien Society Seminar, St. Martin's College, Carlisle, July 17, 2004. Cambridge: The Tolkien Society, 2005.

Vincent, Adele. "Tolkien, Master of Fantasy." *Courier-Journal & Times* (Louisville, KY), Sunday September 9, 1973, E6.

Vink, Renée. "'Jewish' Dwarves: Tolkien and Anti-Semitic Stereotyping." *Tolkien Studies* 10 (2013): 123–145.

———. "Tolkien and (the) Dutch." In *Tolkien and the Netherlands,* ed. Renée Vink and René van Rossenberg. Drukkerij Hodack, n.p., 2016. 5–38.

———. *Wagner and Tolkien: Mythmakers*. Zurich: Walking Tree Publishers, 2012.

Visiak, E.H. "The Arcturan Shadow." In *A Voyage to Arcturus* by David Lindsay, 7–11. London: Victor Gollancz, 1946.

Ward, Michael. *Planet Narnia: The Seven Heavens in the Imagination of C.S. Lewis*. Oxford: Oxford University Press, 2008.

———. "A Thief in the Night: The Christian Ethic at the Heart of *The Hobbit.*" *Christian Research Journal*, vol. 35. no. 6 (2012): 26–36.

———. "A woefully unconvincing Tolkien biopic." *Catholic Herald*, May 3, 2019, 28–29.

Weiner, Edmund. "A possibly unnoticed instance of echoes of G. K. Chesterton in the works of J. R. R. Tolkien." *Philoloblog*, March 27, 2016. http://philoloblog.blogspot.com/2016/03/a-possibly-unnoticed-instance-of-echoes.html.

———. "Wan, dim, and pale: the OED and Tolkien." Talk given at the Tolkien Symposium at Merton College, November 18, 2014. *Philoloblog*. http://philoloblog.blogspot.com/2016/03/wan-dim-and-pale-oed-and-tolkien.html.

Weingrad, Michael. "Harold Bloom: Anti-Inkling?" *Jewish Review of Books* 37 (Spring 2019). https://jewishreviewofbooks.com/articles/5203/harold-bloom-anti-inkling/.

Weinreich, Frank, and Thomas Honegger, eds. *Tolkien and Modernity 1.* Zurich: Walking Tree: 2006.

Wells, Sarah, ed. *The Ring Goes Ever On: Proceedings of the Tolkien 2005 Conference: 50 Years of* The Lord of the Rings. In two volumes. Coventry, England: The Tolkien Society, 2008.

Wendling, Susan, and Woody Wendling. "A Speculative Meditation on Tolkien's Sources for the Character Gollum." In *Inklings Forever* 8 (2012), article 28. https://pillars.taylor.edu/inklings_forever/vol8/iss1/28.

West, Richard C. "The Interlace Structure of *The Lord of the Rings.*" In *A Tolkien Compass*, ed. Jared Lobdell, 75–91.

———. *Tolkien Criticism: An Annotated Checklist.* Revised Edition. Kent, OH: Kent State University Press, 1981.

White, George. "A piece of Bodleian History: Clues from the Stacks." Oxford Libraries Graduate Trainees: A Bodleian Libraries weblog. December 21, 2017. http://blogs.bodleian.ox.ac.uk/oxfordtrainees/2017/12/21/a-piece-of-bodleian-history-clues-from-the-stacks/.

Wilson, A.N. *C.S. Lewis: A Biography.* London: Collins, 1990.

Wilson, Colin. *Tree by Tolkien.* Santa Barbara, CA: Capra Press, 1974.

Wilson, Edmund. "Oo, Those Awful Orcs." *The Nation*, vol. 82, April 14, 1956, 312–314.

Winst, Silke. "Modern Tales in a Medieval Tradition: Formation of Meaning and Narrative Strategies in Tolkien's *The Children of Hurin.*" *Hither Shore* 8 (2011): 40–54.

Wise, Dennis Wilson. "J.R.R. Tolkien and the 1954 Nomination of E.M. Forster for the Nobel Prize in Literature." *Mythlore* 131, vol. 36, no. 1 (Fall/Winter 2017): 143–165.

Wolfe, Brendan. "Tolkien's Jonah." *Journal of Inklings Studies*, vol. 4, no. 2 (October 2014): 11–26.

Wolfe, Gene. "The Tolkien Toll-free Fifties Freeway to Mordor & Points beyond Hurray!" *Vector*, 67/68 (Spring 1974): 7–11.

Young, Joseph. "Aphrodite on the Home Front: E.R. Eddison and World War II," *Mythlore* 117/118, vol. 30, no. 3/4 (Spring/Summer 2012): 71–88.

————. "'On This I Stake My Salvation': E.R. Eddison's Easter Manifesto," *Extrapolation: A Journal of Science Fiction and Fantasy*, vol. 54, no. 1 (2013), 73–93.

Zaleski, Philip, and Carol Zaleski, *The Fellowship: The Literary Lives of the Inklings: J.R.R. Tolkien, C.S. Lewis, Owen Barfield, Charles Williams.* New York: Farrar, Straus and Giroux, 2015.

Zettersten, Arne. *J.R.R. Tolkien's Double Worlds and Creative Process: Language and Life.* New York: Palgrave Macmillan, 2011.

INDEX

Numbers in **bold** indicate the main treatment of an author or text.
Footnote symbols *, †, ‡, §, and ¶ are numbered as 1, 2, 3, 4, and 5, respectively.